# JSP: The Complete Reference

## About the Author...

Phil Hanna has more than 20 years experience as a programmer, systems architect, analyst, and project manager. He has developed network-based software at IBM, and served as a consultant to Chase Manhattan Bank. He is the author of *Instant Java Servlets,* and works as a software developer for SAS Institute.

# JSP: The Complete Reference

**Phil Hanna**

Osborne/**McGraw-Hill**
New York Chicago San Francisco
Lisbon London Madrid Mexico City
Milan New Delhi San Juan
Seoul Singapore Sydney Toronto

Osborne/**McGraw-Hill**
2600 Tenth Street
Berkeley, California 94710
U.S.A.

To arrange bulk purchase discounts for sales promotions, premiums, or fund-raisers, please contact Osborne/**McGraw-Hill** at the above address. For information on translations or book distributors outside the U.S.A., please see the International Contact Information page immediately following the index of this book.

**JSP: The Complete Reference**



1234567890 CUS CUS 01987654321

ISBN 0-07-212768-6

**Publisher**
Brandon A. Nordin

**Vice President & Associate Publisher**
Scott Rogers

**Acquisitions Editor**
Rebekah Young

**Project Editor**
Mark Karmendy

**Acquisitions Coordinator**
Paulina Pobocha

**Technical Editor**
Karl Moss

**Copy Editor**
Marcia Baker

**Proofreader**
Sossity Smith

**Indexer**
Rebecca Plunkett

**Computer Designers**
Melinda Moore Lytle
Kelly Stanton-Scott

**Illustrator**
Michael Mueller

**Series Design**
Peter F. Hancik

This book was composed with Corel VENTURA™ Publisher.

**To Mary**

# Contents at a Glance

## Part III JSP in Action



## Part IV JSP and Other Web Components



## Part V Appendixes

# Contents

# Part V
## Appendixes

# Preface

The first wave of a new technology is often outpaced by the expectations it generates. Those riding the second wave benefit from the experience of their predecessors and the real value emerges. This has been the case with Java. Client-side browser applications (applets) have encountered limitations in three areas:

- Browser incompatibilities
- Security overkill
- Performance problems due to long download times

The emergence of server-side Java has changed all this. Java Servlets and JavaServer Pages (JSP) provide a secure, robust, and platform independent technology for bringing the power of Java to e-commerce and enterprise Web computing. This being the case, interest in JSP is flourishing and the demand for JSP skills is running high. Nearly all the Fortune 500 companies now have or will soon deploy server-side Java applications.

The purpose of this book is to provide a complete reference to JSP technology, starting with the Web programming environment and elements of JSP, then a deeper examination of advanced topics.

## How this Book Is Organized

This book consists of five parts, starting with high-level overviews and proceeding to deeper examination of topics.

### Part I, "The Web Programming Environment"

The opening section of the book provides an introduction to the Web as a programming environment and introduces servlets, JSP, and the Web network protocol.

- **Chapter 1, "The Web Marketplace"**
  The first chapter explores the Web as a marketplace for ideas, products, services, and applications—how we got where we are today, and what will drive future directions. It introduces Java and explains its significance in the network computing model.
- **Chapter 2, "Evolution of the Web Application"**
  Chapter 2 is a description of how the application programming model has evolved as the Web has matured, and how experience with each phase has driven requirements for the next.
- **Chapter 3, "Overview of the Hypertext Transfer Protocol (HTTP)"**
  This chapter introduces the underlying language of the Web client/server model, Hypertext Transfer Protocol (HTTP). It develops the basic concepts critical to understanding the Web programming environment.
- **Chapter 4, "Introduction to Servlets"**
  The intimate connection between JSP and servlets is explained in this overview chapter. The essential features that they share are outlined and demonstrated.
- **Chapter 5, "JSP Overview"**
  Chapter 5 provides an overview of JavaServer Pages (JSP) as a server-side scripting environment, a description of the servlet engine, and several tutorial examples. Only the basics are covered here—Part II considers the topic in depth.

### Part II, "Elements of JSP"

This part deals with the syntax and semantics of JSP, equipping the reader with the skills necessary to create working code. Topics include basic syntax, scriptlets, expressions, declarations, including files, forwarding requests, and specifying page behavior. Developing custom tags is examined at length.

- **Chapter 6, "JSP Syntax and Semantics"**
  This chapter covers the basic syntax of JavaServer Pages, describing how they merge HTML templates and Java code.

- **Chapter 7, "Expressions and Scriptlets"**
  This chapter describes the basic model of incorporating Java code fragments into a JavaServer Page. It covers legal and illegal uses and describes how the code fragments are composed by the translator into a working servlet.
- **Chapter 8, "Declarations"**
  This chapter considers declarations and advanced usage of Java code within a JSP. It covers the three most common uses for declarations, providing examples for all three.
- **Chapter 9, "Request Dispatching"**
  This chapter discusses how HTTP requests can be handled by more than one server-side component. It describes two methods for including other files, and explains why one method may be preferable to the other. It covers how to use the `<jsp:forward>` action to pass a request on to another JSP for processing.
- **Chapter 10, "The Page Directive"**
  Chapter 10 describes in detail how the page directive is used to specify the attributes and behavior of a JavaServer Page. Complete examples are given for each attribute.
- **Chapter 11, "JSP Tag Extensions"**
  Extensions to the JSP architecture are considered in this chapter, in particular the ability to define custom tags.

## Part III, "JSP in Action"

This part looks at how JSP works with JDBC, JavaBeans, and other major components of the Java environment. Includes detailed coverage of debugging and deployment.

- **Chapter 12, "HTML Forms"**
  Chapter 12 describes HTML Forms, the most common client for servlets and JavaServer Pages.
- **Chapter 13, "Database Access"**
  Most JSP pages of any consequence need to access a database. This chapter includes a comprehensive look at Java database connectivity and how it can be used in Web-based applications.
- **Chapter 14, "Session and Thread Management"**
  HTTP is a stateless protocol, but JavaServer Pages can use HTTP sessions to overcome this limitation. This chapter explores the issues involved and describes techniques available to the developer.
- **Chapter 15, "JSP and JavaBeans"**
  This chapter describes JavaBeans and shows how they can be used in conjunction with JavaServer Pages to isolate business logic into reusable components.

- **Chapter 16, "JSP and XML"**
  XML is emerging as the universal language for structured data storage and interchange. This chapter examines how JSP can use XML both for input and output.
- **Chapter 17, "JSP Testing and Debugging"**
  Debugging techniques are frequently ignored in programming tutorials but are indispensable knowledge. JavaServer Pages present their own challenges. This chapter outlines a basic methodology that can be applied and the tools that are available.
- **Chapter 18, "Deploying Web Applications"**
  Chapter 18 describes how to move JSP pages out of the development environment into the production Web environment.
- **Chapter 19, "Case Study: A Product Support Center"**
  This chapter brings together elements discussed throughout the book in a Web-based system for managing a technical support center.

### Part IV, "JSP and Other Web Components"

Part IV deals with the larger context in which JavaServer Pages are used—how they can communicate with servlets, applets, Perl scripts, FTP, CGI, ASP, and other server-side agents.

- **Chapter 20, "Communicating with Other Clients"**
  Although HTML forms in Web browsers are the most common client environment, JSP pages can be used to support any client that can understand the HTTP protocol. Chapter 20 shows how this can be done.
- **Chapter 21, "Communicating with Other Servers"**
  Further developing the ideas of the previous chapter, this chapter describes how JSP components can access other protocols. The JavaMail API is discussed.

### Part V, "Appendixes"

The book concludes with three appendixes, covering the Servlet API, JSP API, and HTTP reference.

## The Lyric Note

Most of the examples in this book are set in the context of a hypothetical company—The Lyric Note. This is an Internet-based music company that sells books, gifts, sheet music, music software, and musical instruments. I have populated it with fifty employees working in eleven departments, and a large product catalog.

## Servlet and JSP API Levels

As this book is written, the predominant levels of the Servlet and JSP APIs are 2.2 and 1.1, respectively. There are public drafts of the 2.3 and 1.2 levels, but these are not officially the standards, and are subject to change. This presents a problem for an author trying to present timely material. Which is more important, discussing what is actually implemented in the servlet engines people use today, or examining new levels that no one can actually run yet? I have attempted to do a little of both. The main body of the book is devoted to Servlet 2.2 and JSP 1.1, while the appendixes list the API from the latest public drafts of the 2.3 and 1.2 specifications.

## Updates

Errata, examples, and updates can be found on my Web site: http:// www.philhanna.com.

# Acknowledgments

It would not have been possible to write this book without the collaboration and support of a number of people.

I would first like to thank my acquisitions editor at Osborne/McGraw-Hill, Rebekah Young, who conceived this project and worked with me to shape the scope and coverage. Thanks also to Mark Karmendy, who applied his considerable skills to ensure that everything came together, and to Marcia Baker for her careful copy editing. Thanks also to Osborne's Production staff for the great job laying out pages. Karl Moss, my technical editor, provided invaluable assistance and useful suggestions.

I am indebted to Brian Flagg for his advice and technical assistance with the Product Support Center case study, and to Tina Armstrong for feedback on its Model-View-Controller approach. My appreciation to Pierre R. Schwob, CEO of Classical Archives, LLC, for permission to include composer reference material in the Lyric Note product catalog. Angela Allen and David Biesack provided helpful comments on the custom tags material. Many thanks to Jack Keller for his skill in reinforcing structural integrity, and to Chris Bailey, a singularly creative thinker and a great source of ideas.

I am very grateful for the support of Alan Eaton and Keith Collins of SAS Institute, who made it possible for me to undertake this project.

Most of all, I would like to thank my wife, Mary, my children, Eleanor and John, and my mother-in-law, Ann Jordan, for their support, encouragement, kindness, and patience.

# Part I

## The Web Programming Environment

Part I provides an introduction to the Web as a programming environment, focusing on both business and technical aspects. After examining the evolution of the Web application, it touches on the underlying client/server architecture and the protocol used to support it. Part I concludes with an introduction to JavaServer Pages (JSP).

# Chapter 1

## The Web Marketplace

In the heart of Rome near the river Tiber lies the Roman Forum. Two thousand years ago, the *Forum Romanum* was the center of power in the Roman world. It was the place where triumphal marches took place, where ordinary goods and services were exchanged, and where news and opinions were freely shared (from which we get the common meaning of the word "forum"). Though partly built of stone, bricks, and mortar, its expansion was made possible by a new technology: concrete.

Today, the Internet is the global electronic marketplace. The Internet is becoming the dominant center for the exchange of goods, services, and information, both for business enterprises and individual consumers. Like the Roman Forum, the growth of the Internet is made possible by advances in technology—new computer languages, wide acceptance of networking standards, and inexpensive hardware.

This book is about JavaServer Pages, an enabling technology that brings together Web browsers, Web servers, and database systems to make applications that are easy to develop, access, and deploy. Java technology has proven to be unsurpassed in connectivity, reliability, scalability, and security. This technology, more than any other, promises to drive the network computing model, and with it, the global electronic marketplace.

No one can predict future trends with certainty. Even the *Forum Romanum* was eventually covered with grass and became *il Campo Vaccino* —the field of cows. But it is safe to say that the degree to which an enterprise can successfully exchange products, services, information, and ideas will continue to depend on the degree to which it has access to the marketplace.

The Complete Reference

# Chapter 2

## Evolution of the Web Application

One of the most remarkable things about the World Wide Web is it wasn't originally conceived as an application environment. Yet today, Web applications are the mainstay of most Internet use—in particular, of e-commerce use. This chapter briefly traces the origins of the World Wide Web, Web applications, and associated technologies, setting the context for more detailed technical exploration in the remainder of the book.

## Birth of the Web

The World Wide Web and its associated *Hypertext Transfer Protocol (HTTP)* grew out of work done at the European Laboratory for Particle Physics (CERN) in 1990. Tim Berners-Lee developed HTTP as a networking protocol for distributing documents and wrote the first Web browser. The system was used at CERN and other high-energy physics laboratories and universities in 1991 and 1992, and grew steadily in popularity. In 1993, the advent of the Mosaic browser led to the explosion of commercial Web use. In five years, more than 650,000 Web servers were in use worldwide, with uncounted millions of users.

## Growth of the Web Programming Model

The idea of using the Web as an application environment developed over time, with each stage of technology serving as a springboard for new ideas. The first operational model had the Web server simply serving up documents on request. In this environment, the content doesn't change unless a human author supplies a new version of a document. The client/server interaction is illustrated in Figure 2-1.

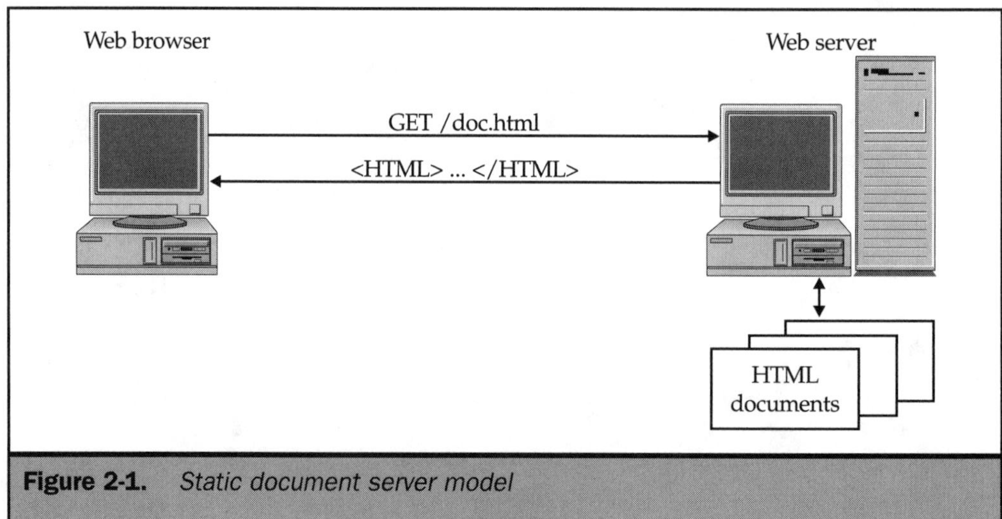


**Figure 2-1.** *Static document server model*

HTTP is a simple request/response protocol in which a Web browser asks for a document (typically using a GET command), and the Web server returns the document in the form of an HTML data stream preceded by a few descriptive headers. Chapter 3 examines HTTP in greater detail.

What quickly became apparent is if humans could revise the documents handled by the Web server, so could a text-processing program like a Perl script. The Web browser is unaware of the difference because the result of an HTTP request is still an HTML data stream. What's more, the browser can send more than just a request—it can send parameters, either by embedding them in the URL or by sending a data stream with the request. This suggests an HTTP request can be interpreted as a database query and the query results can be used to build an HTML document dynamically. With the development of the NCSA HTTPd Web Server came a new specification designated the *Common Gateway Interface (CGI)*.

A CGI program is invoked by the Web server in response to certain types of requests, usually requests for documents in a particular directory or filenames having a particular extension, such as `.cgi`. The request parameters are passed as key/value pairs, and the request headers as environment variables. The program reads these parameters and headers, performs the application task at hand (typically accessing a database to do so), and then generates an HTTP response. The response is sent back to the requesting Web browser as if it were an ordinary static document. Figure 2-2 illustrates the process flow.

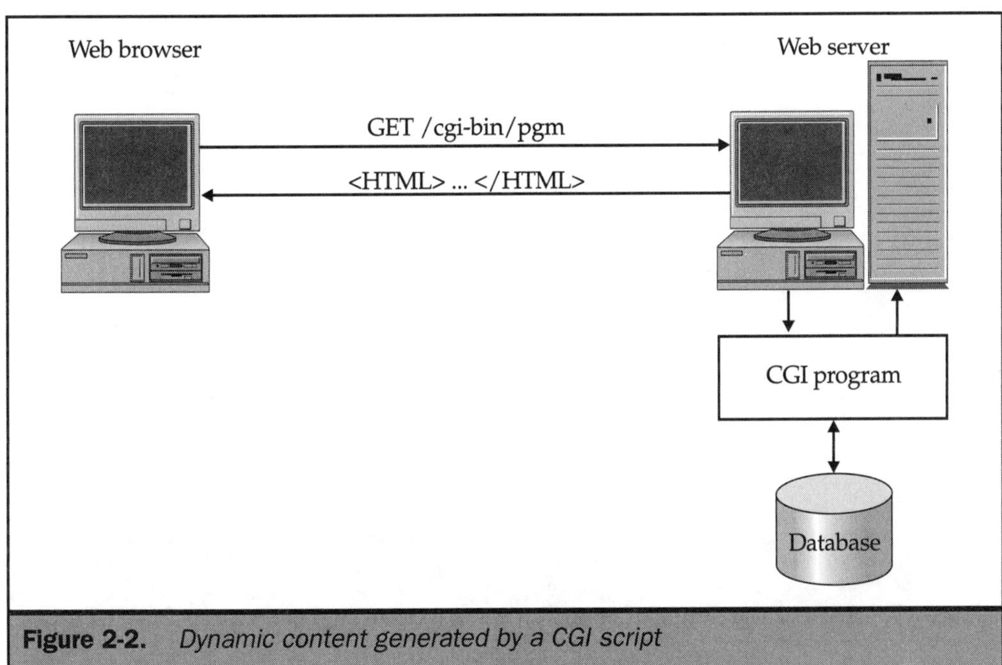


**Figure 2-2.** *Dynamic content generated by a CGI script*

CGI is convenient, but it has one big drawback. Ordinarily, CGI spawns a new process for each HTTP request[1]. This isn't a problem when traffic is low, but it creates a great deal of overhead when the traffic level increases. This being the case, CGI in general doesn't scale well.

A significant improvement came with the release in 1997 of the Java Servlet API, followed quickly by the *JavaServer Pages (JSP)* API. These related technologies bring the full power of Java to the Web server, with database connectivity, network access, and multithreaded operations, and, notably, a different process model. Servlets and

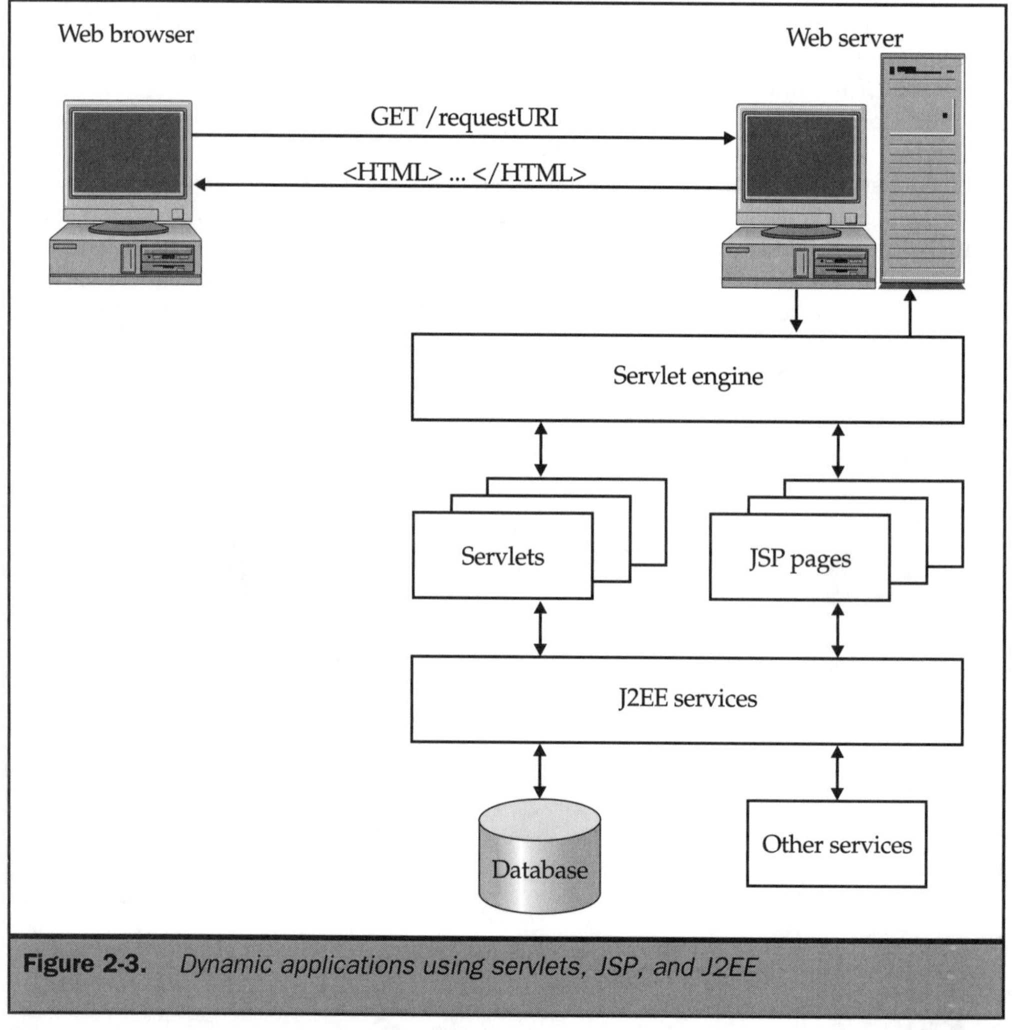


**Figure 2-3.** *Dynamic applications using servlets, JSP, and J2EE*

1 Improvements on this exist, such as FastCGI, which handles all requests from a single persistent process.

JSP pages operate from a single instance that remains in memory and uses multiple threads to service requests simultaneously. As Figure 2-3 shows, servlets and JSP pages can make use of the full *Java 2 Enterprise Edition (J2EE)* environment for sophisticated, robust applications.

## The Shift from Client-Side to Server-Side Solutions

The Web application model has evolved as the Web has matured, and experience with each phase has driven requirements for the next. The initial wave of client-side Java in the form of applets was phenomenally popular, but led to some disappointment as reality intruded. Considerable incompatibilities occurred between browsers, lengthy downloads over slow modems, and security restrictions that limited applet usefulness. Because of this, applet development slowed[2], and server-side Java has been the biggest growth area.

Server-side Java has none of the restrictions of the applet environment. No browser inconsistencies occur because the browser isn't required to host a Java virtual machine. The browser only has to render HTML, which even the oldest browsers do reasonably well. Also, no client-side setup is involved and no download of large class files. Likewise, security considerations are limited to those already handled by the Web server, which is typically in a closed environment with controls in place.

JSP has proved to be a successful server-side technology and an excellent base for developing Web applications. The remainder of this book explores JSP in-depth to demonstrate why this is so.

2 Many observers believe client-side Java is poised for a comeback. The Java plug-in eliminates browser inconsistencies and allows Swing components to be used. Moreover, high-speed Internet connections are making download considerations increasingly unimportant.

# Chapter 3

# Overview of the Hypertext Transfer Protocol (HTTP)

This chapter introduces the underlying language used by the Web client/server model. In doing so, it develops the basic concepts critical to understanding the Web programming environment. The chapter presents several examples of Web browsers and servers using this language to communicate. Additional details about the protocol can be found in Appendix C.

# What Is HTTP?

Whereas *Hypertext Markup Language* (*HTML*) is the language used to describe the insides of Web documents, *Hypertext Transfer Protocol* (*HTTP*) is the language used to describe how these documents are sent over the Internet. The key to understanding Web programming is understanding this protocol and the environment in which it operates.

## A Language for Requesting Documents over the Internet

HTTP prescribes the rules by which browsers make requests and servers supply responses. This set of rules, or *protocol*, includes ways to

- Ask for a document by name
- Agree on the data format
- Determine who the user is
- Decide how to handle outdated resources
- Indicate the results of a request

and other useful functions.

HTTP consists of a set of commands written as lines of ordinary ASCII text. When you use a Web browser, you don't enter the HTTP commands directly. Instead, when you type a URL or click a hyperlink, the browser translates your action into HTTP commands that request the document from the server specified in the URL. The Web server finds the document and sends it back to the browser, where it's displayed, along with its associated graphics and other hyperlinks.

## The HTTP Specification

Internet standards are usually specified in a *Request for Comments* (*RFC*) published by the *Internet Engineering Task Force* (*IETF*). These RFCs are widely accepted by the Internet research and development community. Because they're standards documents, they tend to be written in formal language, like that of a legal document. This makes them unsuitable as tutorials, but invaluable for reference.

RFCs are numbered and never change when issued. If a standard is updated, a new RFC is issued. Being standards, RFCs are widely available on the Internet. A good, readable online source is Brent Baccala's *Connected: An Internet Encyclopedia* (http://www.freesoft.org/CIE), which maintains HTML versions of most RFCs and provides a full-text search engine.

Several RFCs deal with HTTP:

| | |
|---|---|
| RFC 1945 | A description of HTTP version 1.0 |
| RFC 2068 | The initial description of version 1.1 |
| RFC 2616 | An updated version of the 1.1 specification |

Unless otherwise specified, this book uses the HTTP 1.1 standard as documented in RFC 2616.

## HTTP Request Model

The specification describes HTTP as a stateless request/response protocol whose basic operation is as follows:

1. A client application, such as a Web browser, opens a socket to the Web server's HTTP port (80, by default).
2. Through the connection, the client writes an ASCII text request line, followed by zero or more HTTP headers, an empty line, and any data that accompanies the request.
3. The Web server parses the request and locates the specified resource.
4. The server writes a copy of the resource to the socket, where it's read by the client.
5. The server closes the connection.

Figure 3-1 illustrates this basic operation.

A key consideration is this model is *stateless*. This means in handling a request, the Web server doesn't remember anything about previous requests from the same client. The protocol is simply a request ("please give me this document") and a response ("OK, here it is"). Obviously, this imposes limitations on application programming, which

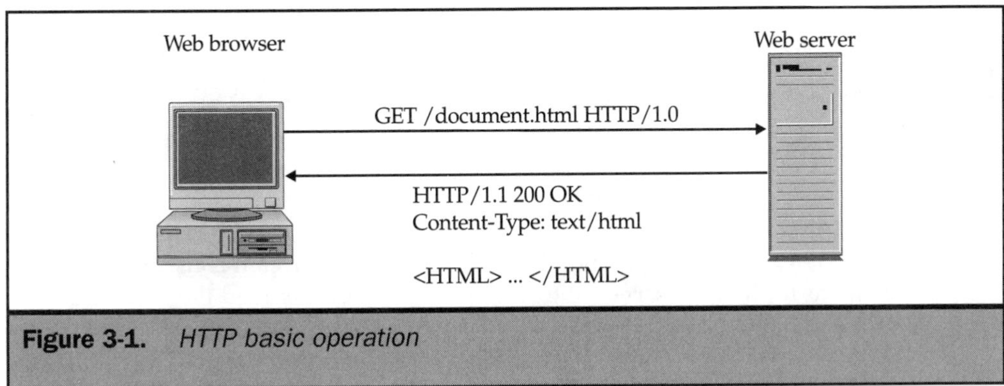


**Figure 3-1.** *HTTP basic operation*

typically requires a great deal of back-and-forth conversation, as well as complex objects that must be initialized and have their state maintained.

The way around this is to have the server assign an identifier to the session represented by a set of client requests, and to have the client remember the identifier and supply it to the server with each request. This technique is explored in depth in Chapter 14.

Let's examine each of these steps in greater detail.

## Connecting to the Web Server

A Web server operates by listening for requests on a particular well-known port number, usually port 80, although any available port can be used. If a Web server listens on a different port, URLs that refer to this server must include a colon and the port number immediately after the server name. For example,

```
http://www.mycompany.com/mypath.html
```

refers to an HTML document known to a Web server running on the www.mycompany.com host on the default port 80. If the server is running on port 4311 instead, the URL looks like this:

```
http://www.mycompany.com:4311/mypath.html
```

Why bother with alternate port numbers, especially because they introduce that ugly URL syntax? Because this allows more than one server to be running on a single host. An experimental Web server with different capabilities may need to coexist with the main server. The Tomcat and JRun servlet engines, for example, can run a mini HTTP server for testing servlets and JSP pages. Most Web servers provide some means of hiding this alternate syntax by mapping the URLs to a different namespace.

A client, such as a Web browser, initiates an HTTP request by opening a TCP/IP socket to the Web server port, and then opening input and output stream over the socket. In Java terms, this would amount to a few lines of code:

```
Socket socket = new Socket("www.mycompany.com", 80);
InputStream istream = socket.getInputStream();
OutputStream ostream = socket.getOutputStream();
```

The parameters required to open the socket are the Web server host name and the port number. The server host name is extracted from the URL, while the port number is either implied or also extracted from the URL. The output stream is used to send HTTP commands to the Web server; the input stream is used to read the response.

## Sending the HTTP Request

Once the socket connection is made, the Web browser writes an HTTP command to request the document. A request has up to four parts.

The first part is the *request line*. This consists of three tokens, separated by spaces: the request method, the request URI, and the HTTP version. The following shows a typical request line:

```
GET /mypath.html HTTP/1.0
```

In this example, the request method is `GET`, the URI is `/mypath.html`, and the HTTP version is `HTTP/1.0`.

The HTTP specification defines eight possible methods, shown in Table 3-1. Of all these methods, the vast majority of requests use either `GET` or `POST`. These two methods are the only ones considered in this book.

The second token on the request line is the *request Uniform Resource Identifier* (*URI*). This is the URI of the document or other resource being requested. For all practical purposes, this corresponds to the URL without the leading `http://` and host name. In the example of http://www.mycompany.com/mypath.html, the request URI is `/mypath.html`.

| Method | Description |
|---|---|
| `GET` | A simple request to retrieve the resource identified in the URI. |
| `HEAD` | The same as `GET`, except the server doesn't return the requested document. The server only returns the status line and headers. |
| `POST` | A request for the server to accept data that will be written to the client's output stream. |
| `PUT` | A request for the server to store the data in the request as the new contents of the specified URI. |
| `DELETE` | A request for the server to delete the resource named in the URI. |
| `OPTIONS` | A request for information about what request methods the server supports. |
| `TRACE` | A request for the Web server to echo the HTTP request and its headers. |
| `CONNECT` | A documented but currently unimplemented method reserved for use with a tunneling proxy. |

**Table 3-1.** *HTTP Request Methods*

The last token on the line is the HTTP version. This indicates the highest level of the HTTP specification the client application understands. The allowable values are `HTTP/1.0` and `HTTP/1.1`.

After the request line come any request headers. These are key/value pairs, one pair per line, with the key and value separated by a colon (`:`). After the last request header is written, an empty line consisting of only a carriage return and line feed is sent. This informs the server that no more headers follow. Even if no headers exist, this empty line must be sent, so the server doesn't look for any more headers.

Request headers inform the server further about the identity and capabilities of the client. Typical request headers might be

| | |
|---|---|
| `User-Agent` | The vendor and version of the client |
| `Accept` | A list of content types the client recognizes |
| `Content-Length` | The number of bytes of data appended to the request |

A complete list of request and response headers is found in Appendix C.

For HTTP `POST` requests, the request may include data. You see later in Chapter 12 how `POST` data is used to transmit the values of HTML form fields. If data is present, seeing both the `Content-Type` and `Content-Length` request headers used is common.

## Server Acceptance of the Request

When a client connects to the Web server's listening port, the server accepts the connection and handles the request. In most cases, it does so by starting a thread to process the request, so it can continue to service new requests. Handling the request means different things depending on the URI. If the URI represents a static document, the server opens the document file and prepares to copy its contents back to the client. If the URI is a program name, such as a CGI script, servlet, or JSP page, and the server is configured to handle such a request, the server prepares to invoke the program or process.

## The HTTP Response from the Server

However the server processes the request, the result is the same—an HTTP response. Similar to a request, a response consists of up to four parts: a status line, zero or more response headers, an empty line signaling the end of the headers, and the data that makes up the request.

The status line consists of up to three tokens:

- The *HTTP version*. Just as the client indicates the highest version it can understand, so the server indicates its capabilities.
- The *response code*. This is a three-digit numeric code that indicates whether the request succeeded or failed and, if it failed, the reason why. A list of HTTP status codes is found in Appendix C.

- *An optional response description,* which is a human-readable explanation of the response code.

A typical HTTP response status line looks like this

```
HTTP/1.0 200 OK
```

which indicates a successful retrieval of the requested document according to the 1.0 level of the HTTP specification.

After the status line comes the response headers, with an empty line as the delimiter. Like request headers, these indicate the capabilities of the server and identify details about the response data. Appendix C lists valid HTTP response headers.

The last part of the response is the requested data itself, typically an HTML document or image stream. After the data is sent, the server closes its end of the connection.

## Examples

A look at several examples can make this clearer. A simple case of a GET request would be what happens when a URL is typed in a browser address line or a hyperlink is clicked. If you open the URL `http://www.lyricnote.com/simple.html`, the Web browser opens a socket connection to the `www.lyricnote.com` host on port 80, and then writes the following line

```
GET /simple.html HTTP/1.0
```

followed by an empty line. The Web server returns the following:

```
HTTP/1.1 200 OK
Date: Wed, 31 Jan 2001 03:55:43 GMT
Server: Apache/1.3.12 (Win32)
Content-Length: 241
Content-Type: text/html

<HTML>
<BODY>
<H3>Welcome</H3> to <b>The Lyric Note</b>,
the best Internet source for
<UL>
<LI>sheet music
<LI>musical instruments
<LI>books on musical topics
```

```
<LI>music software, and
<LI>musical gift items
</UL>
</BODY>
</HTML>
```

The browser first parses the status line and sees the status code indicates the request was successful. The browser then parses each of the request headers, which inform it 241 bytes of HTML follow. The browser reads the HTML, formats it according to the syntax and semantics of HTML, and displays it in the browser window, as shown in Figure 3-2.

An HTML document may contain references to other resources that need to be loaded when the document is loaded. For example, images are often embedded in the page with the HTML `<img>` tag. JavaScript files or external style sheets may also be required. The Web browser (not the server) recognizes these cases and makes additional requests for the other resources. This bears repeating. The Web server doesn't read through the HTML it serves, recognize an `<img>` tag, and then start sending the bytes of the image file. The Web server simply sends back the resource that was requested in one operation. If, a few milliseconds later, the browser requests an image file, the server returns this in a separate operation. The Web browser does all this under the covers, so the user is unaware several requests are involved.

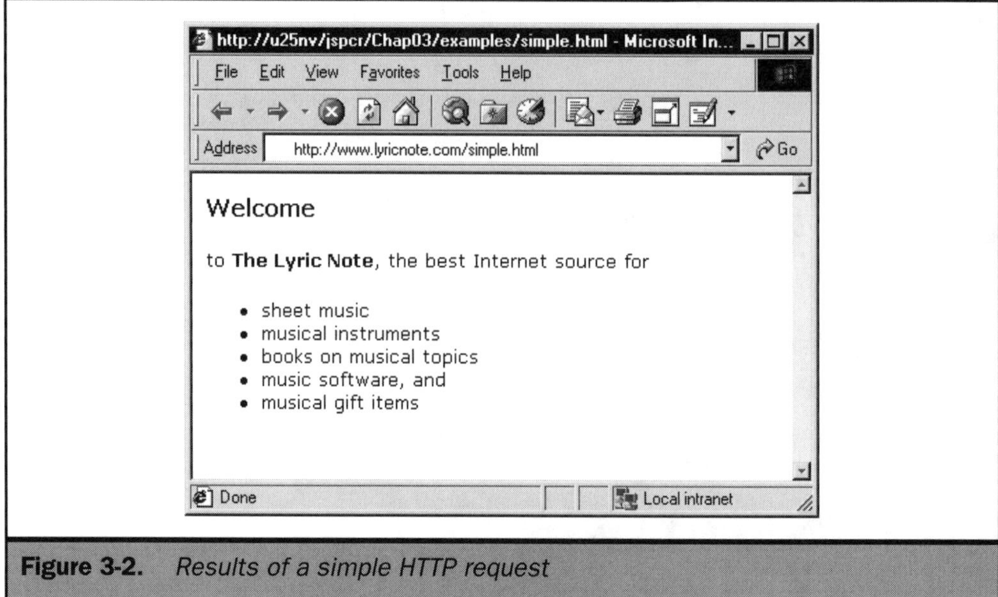


**Figure 3-2.** *Results of a simple HTTP request*

To augment the previous example slightly, suppose you open `http://www.lyricnote.com/compound.html`. The browser again opens a socket connection to `www.lyricnote.com` port 80 and requests the HTML document,

```
GET /compound.html HTTP/1.0
```

which results in the following response:

```
HTTP/1.1 200 OK
Date: Tue, 30 Jan 2001 23:42:16 GMT
Server: Apache/1.3.12 (Win32)
Content-Length: 380
Content-Type: text/html

<HTML>
<HEAD>
<LINK REL="stylesheet" HREF="lyricnote.css">
</HEAD>
<BODY>
<IMG SRC="images/logo.png">
<HR COLOR="#005A9C" ALIGN="LEFT" WIDTH="500">
<H3>Welcome</H3> to <b>The Lyric Note</b>,
the best Internet source for
<UL>
<LI>sheet music
<LI>musical instruments
<LI>books on musical topics
<LI>music software, and
<LI>musical gift items
</UL>
</BODY>
</HTML>
```

As the browser is parsing the HTML, it notices the style sheet request:

```
<LINK REL="stylesheet" HREF="lyricnote.css">
```

and makes a second HTTP request:

```
GET /lyricnote.css HTTP/1.0
```

The Web server retrieves the style sheet and returns it to the client:

```
HTTP/1.1 200 OK
Date: Tue, 30 Jan 2001 23:42:27 GMT
Server: Apache/1.3.12 (Win32)
Connection: Keep-alive, close
Content-Length: 73
Content-Type: text/plain

h3 {
   font-size: 20px;
   font-weight: bold;
   color: #005A9C;
}
```

The browser interprets the style sheet and applies the font size, weight, and color styles to the <H3> tag. Next, it encounters an image tag

```
<IMG SRC="images/logo.png">
```

and makes a request for the logo,

```
GET /images/logo.png HTTP/1.0
```

which causes the Web server to respond with the image data stream:

```
HTTP/1.1 200 OK
Date: Tue, 30 Jan 2001 23:42:44 GMT
Server: Apache/1.3.12 (Win32)
Connection: Keep-alive, close
Content-Length: 1280
Content-Type: text/plain

(Binary image data follows)
```

Finally, the browser renders the completed page, as shown in Figure 3-3.

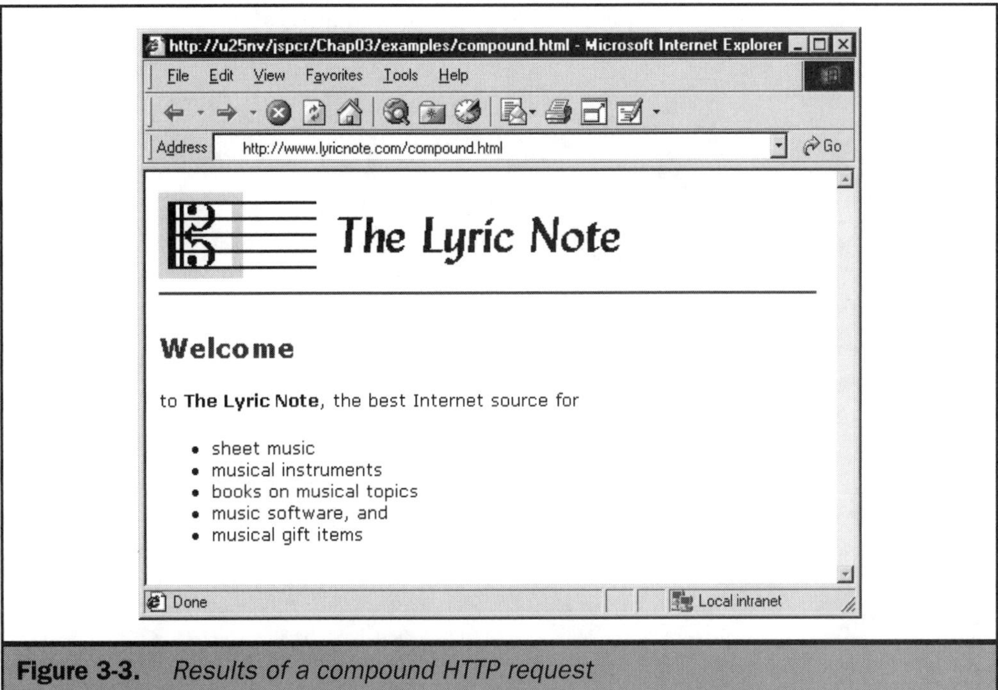


**Figure 3-3.** *Results of a compound HTTP request*

## Summary

This chapter introduces HTTP, the set of rules by which requests are made and responses are returned. Understanding these rules is crucial to proper development and troubleshooting. Important to understand is HTTP is stateless, meaning HTTP doesn't by itself retain knowledge from one request to the next. The JSP environment provides robust ways to remedy this. Another key consideration is that both browsers and servers can be replaced by workalike software. Applications, applets, and programs written in other languages can act as clients and diagnostic tools can play the role of server. Because all they need to do is provide the same HTTP request and response streams a browser and Web server would use, these other applications are indistinguishable from the real thing. You'll exploit this capability in later chapters.

# Chapter 4

## Introduction to Servlets

To understand JavaServer Pages, it's necessary to understand their underlying technology—Java servlets. *Servlets* are Java classes that extend the functionality of a Web server by dynamically generating Web pages. A run-time environment known as a *servlet engine* manages servlet loading and unloading, and works with the Web server to direct requests to servlets and to send output back to Web clients.

Since their introduction in 1997, servlets have become the dominant environment for server-side Java programming and a widely used portal into application servers. They offer several key advantages:

- **Performance** Older technologies such as the *Common Gateway Interface* (*CGI*) typically start a new process to handle each incoming request. In the days when the Web was primarily a repository for academic and scientific research, there wasn't very much traffic and this approach worked well. Servlets, by contrast, are loaded when first requested, and stay in memory indefinitely. The servlet engine loads a single instance of the servlet class and dispatches requests to it using a pool of available threads. The resulting performance improvement is considerable.
- **Simplicity** Client-side Java applets run in a virtual machine provided by the Web browser. This introduces compatibility issues that increase complexity and limit the functionality that applets can provide. Servlets simplify this situation considerably because they run in a virtual machine in a controlled server environment and require only basic HTTP to communicate with their clients. No special client software is required, even with older browsers.
- **HTTP Sessions** Although HTTP servers have no built-in capability to remember details of a previous request from the same client, the Servlet API provides an `HttpSession` class that overcomes this limitation.
- **Access to Java Technology** Servlets, being Java applications, have direct access to the full range of Java features, such as threading, network access, and database connectivity.

JSP pages, which are automatically translated into servlets, inherit all these advantages.

This chapter provides an overview of how servlets work. It examines the primary servlet objects and their API. It discusses the servlet engine, the servlet lifecycle, servlet threading models, and how servlets can maintain persistent state between requests. This chapter also includes an annotated example of a servlet.

## Servlet Lifecycle

Like their client-side applet counterparts, servlets provide methods that are called when specific events occur in a larger context. Programming in this environment involves writing predefined methods (sometimes known as *callback* methods), which are called as required by a managing program.

An applet, for example, provides methods such as `init()`, `start()`, `paint()`, `stop()`, and `destroy()`, which are called by the applet run-time environment in response to actions the user takes. The `java.applet.Applet` base class provides default implementations for all these methods; you only override those that occur during events with which you are concerned. You would write an `init()` method, for instance, if you have GUI components that need to be created.

Similarly, servlets operate in the context of a request and response model managed by a servlet engine. The engine does the following:

- Loads a servlet when it's first requested
- Calls the servlet's `init()` method
- Handles any number of requests by calling the servlet's `service()` method
- When shutting down, calls each servlet's `destroy()` method.

As with applets, there are standard base classes `javax.servlet.GenericServlet` and `javax.servlet.http.HttpServlet` that implement the servlet callback methods. Servlet programming, then, consists of subclassing one of these classes and overriding the necessary method to accomplish the specific task at hand. The following sections examine each of these lifecycle methods.

## init

When a request for a servlet is received by the servlet engine, it checks to see if the servlet is already loaded. If not, the servlet engine uses a class loader to get the particular servlet class required, and then invokes its constructor to get an instance of the servlet. After the servlet is loaded, but before it services any requests, the servlet engine calls an initialization method with the following signature:

```
public void init(ServletConfig config)
   throws ServletException
```

This method is called only once, just before the servlet is placed into service. The `ServletConfig` object provides access to the servlet context (discussed later in this chapter) and to any initialization parameters coded for the servlet. To maintain a reference to the servlet context, the `config` object must be stored as an instance variable, a task that's done by the `init(ServletConfig)` method in `GenericServlet`. For this reason, it's important to call `super.init(config)` within the `init()` method of any subclass.

Inside the `init()` method, the servlet can perform any necessary startup tasks, such as establishing database connections. If any errors occur that make the servlet unable to handle requests, it should throw an `UnavailableException`[1]. This prevents requests from being directed to the servlet.

## service

After the `init()` method completes successfully, the servlet is able to accept requests. By default, only a single instance of the servlet is created, and the servlet engine dispatches each request to the instance in a separate thread. The servlet method that's called has the following signature:

```
public void service(
   ServletRequest request,
   ServletResponse response)
throws ServletException, IOException;
```

The `ServletRequest` object is constructed by the servlet engine and acts as a wrapper for information about the client and the request. This includes the identity of the remote system, the request parameters, and any input stream associated with the request. Similarly, the `ServletResponse` object provides the means for a servlet to communicate its results back to the original requester. It includes methods for opening an output stream and for specifying the content type and length.

As important as the `service()` method is, it's rarely used. The reason for this is most servlets are designed to operate in the HTTP environment, for which there's a specialized `javax.servlet.http` package. Rather than extending `javax.servlet.GenericServlet` directly, most servlets extend its subclass `javax.servlet.http.HttpServlet`. This subclass provides specialized methods corresponding to each HTTP request method: `GET` requests are handled by `doGet()`, `POST` requests by `doPost()`, and so on. The signatures for these methods use HTTP-specific versions of the request and response objects:

```
public void doGet(
      HttpServletRequest request,
```

1 UnavailableException is a subclass of ServletException that can optionally include a number of seconds the servlet is expected to be unavailable. If not specified, the servlet is assumed to be permanently unavailable.

```
        HttpServletResponse response)
    throws ServletException, IOException;
```

The `service(Request, Response)` method in `HttpServlet` casts the request and response objects into their HTTP-specific counterparts, and then calls `service(HttpServletRequest, HttpServletResponse)`, which examines the request and calls the appropriate `doGet()`, `doPost()`, or other method. A typical HTTP servlet, then, includes an override to one or more of these subsidiary methods, rather than an override to `service()`.

### destroy

The servlet specification allows a servlet engine to unload a servlet at any time. This may be done to conserve system resources or in preparation for servlet engine shutdown. The servlet engine notifies each loaded servlet this is about to happen by calling its `destroy()` method. By overriding `destroy()`, you can release any resources allocated during `init()`.

**Note** *Calling `destroy()` yourself won't actually unload the servlet. Only the servlet engine can do this.*

## Example: Kilometers per Liter to Miles per Gallon Servlet

Let's look at a simple servlet. `K2MServlet`, shown in the following, is a servlet that creates a fuel efficiency conversion table that expresses kilometers per liter in terms of miles per gallon.

```
package jspcr.servlets;

import java.io.*;
import java.text.*;
import java.util.*;
import javax.servlet.*;
import javax.servlet.http.*;

/**
* Prints a conversion table of miles per gallon
* to kilometers per liter
*/
```

```
public class K2MServlet extends HttpServlet
{
   private static final DecimalFormat FMT
      = new DecimalFormat("#0.00");

   private static final String PAGE_TOP = ""
      + "<HTML>"
      + "<HEAD>"
      + "<TITLE>Fuel Efficiency Conversion Chart</TITLE>"
      + "</HEAD>"
      + "<BODY>"
      + "<H3>Fuel Efficiency Conversion Chart</H3>"
      + "<TABLE BORDER=1 CELLPADDING=3 CELLSPACING=0>"
      + "<TR>"
      + "<TH>Kilometers per Liter</TH>"
      + "<TH>Miles per Gallon</TH>"
      + "</TR>"
      ;

   private static final String PAGE_BOTTOM = ""
      + "</TABLE>"
      + "</BODY>"
      + "</HTML>" ;

   public void doGet(
         HttpServletRequest request,
         HttpServletResponse response)
      throws ServletException, IOException
   {
      response.setContentType("text/html");
      PrintWriter out = response.getWriter();

      out.println(PAGE_TOP);
      for (double kpl = 5; kpl <= 20; kpl += 1.0) {
         double mpg = kpl * 2.352146;
         out.println("<TR>");
         out.println("<TD>" + FMT.format(kpl) + "</TD>");
         out.println("<TD>" + FMT.format(mpg) + "</TD>");
         out.println("</TR>");
      }
      out.println(PAGE_BOTTOM);
   }
}
```

To start, note the two import statements at the beginning of the program:

```
import javax.servlet.*;
import javax.servlet.http.*;
```

These statements identify to the compiler that we'll use classes from the general and HTTP-specific servlet packages. `import` statements are not strictly required, but they make referring to classes possible without specifying their fully qualified names.

Next, the class declaration:

```
public class K2MServlet extends HttpServlet
```

A servlet is required at a minimum to implement the `javax.servlet.Servlet` interface. To simplify servlet writing, the servlet API provides a basic implementation of this interface called `GenericServlet`. It also supplies an HTTP-specific subclass `HttpServlet`, which is the base class most commonly used for servlets.

```
   public void doGet(
         HttpServletRequest request,
         HttpServletResponse response)
      throws ServletException, IOException
```

Our servlet has no special requirement for startup or termination actions, so it only overrides one method—`doGet()`. This will be invoked from the `HttpServlet` superclass `service()` method if the request method is `GET`.

```
      response.setContentType("text/html");
```

Before writing any results back to the client, we need to specify any HTTP headers we want to send. In our case, the only one is `Content-Type`, which we set to `text/html`.

```
      PrintWriter out = response.getWriter();
```

Creating an HTML page consists of writing HTML statements to an output stream associated with the HTTP request. This output stream can be obtained from the `response` object using either its `getOutputStream()` or `getWriter()` methods, depending on whether a binary stream or character output is to be written, respectively. Important to note is a servlet must chose one or the other of these methods; it cannot call both. Because we're writing ordinary HTML, we'll use `getWriter()` to obtain a character writer.

All that remains is to print the text of our HTML table. For convenience, we've coded the page header and footer in the static string variables PAGE_TOP and PAGE_BOTTOM. We print the table itself in a loop over the desired range of kilometers per liter.

```
out.println(PAGE_TOP);
for (double kpl = 5; kpl <= 20; kpl += 1.0) {
   double mpg = kpl * 2.352146;
   out.println("<TR>");
   out.println("<TD>" + FMT.format(kpl) + "</TD>");
   out.println("<TD>" + FMT.format(mpg) + "</TD>");
   out.println("</TR>");
}
out.println(PAGE_BOTTOM);
```

To run the servlet, we first need to compile it. For this to be successful, the classes in the servlet API must be in the classpath. These classes are typically found in a JAR file distributed with the servlet engine. The official JAR file can also be found at the Apache Jakarta Web site http://jakarta.apache.org.

Next, depending on the servlet engine, it might be necessary to describe the servlet in the Web application deployment descriptor /WEB-INF/web.xml. For a simple servlet, this might consist only of a <servlet> tag with its child <servlet-name> and <servlet-class> elements. In this case, the entry looks like this:

```
<?xml version="1.0" ?>
<web-app>
   ...
   <servlet>
      <servlet-name>K2M</servlet-name>
      <servlet-class>jspcr.servlets.K2MServlet</servlet-class>
   </servlet>
   ...
</web-app>
```

**Note** *<servlet> entries in web.xml must be coded in a specific position with respect to other elements. See Chapter 18 for details or examine the web-app_2.2.DTD.*

In most cases, modifying the web.xml file requires the servlet engine be restarted before any changes take effect.

Finally, the servlet can be invoked using a URL of this form:

```
http://<servername>/<webappname>/servlet/<servletname>
```

The results for this servlet can be seen in Figure 4-1.

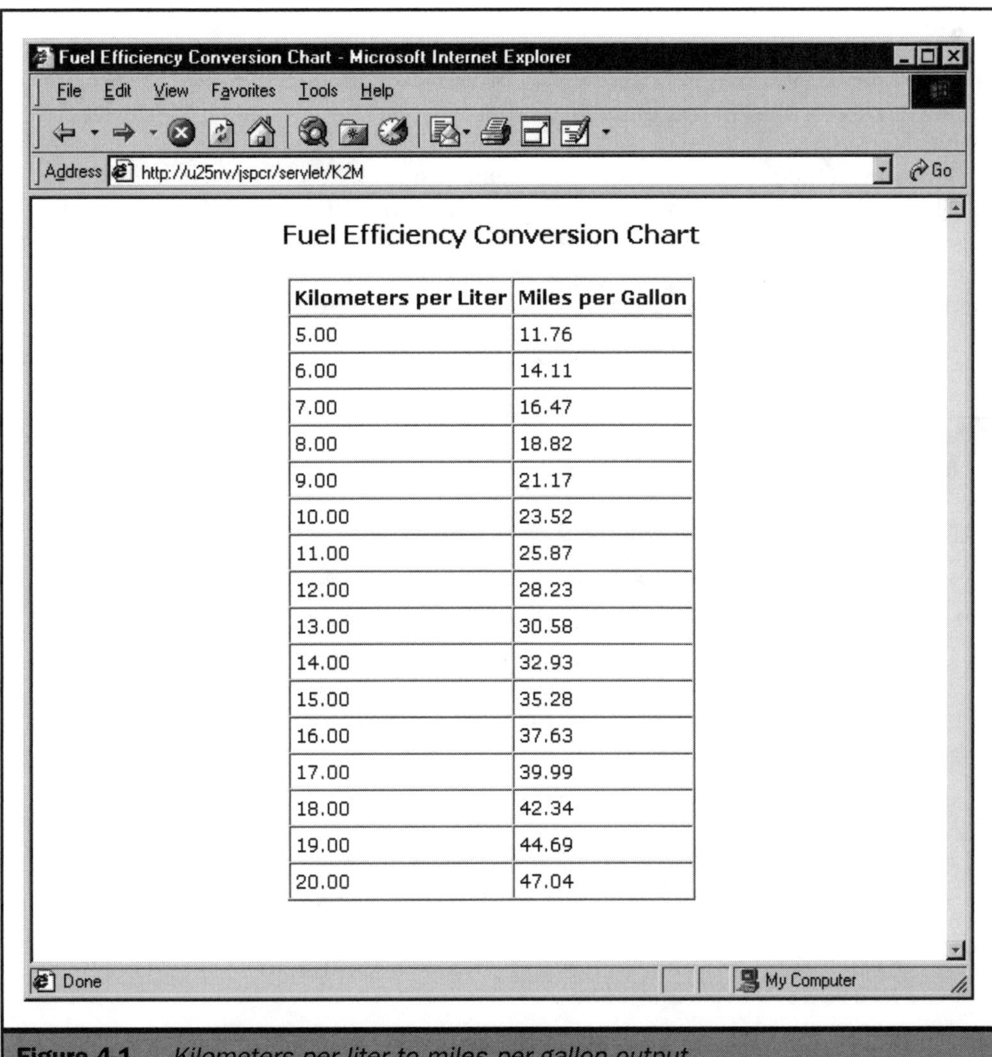


Fuel Efficiency Conversion Chart

| Kilometers per Liter | Miles per Gallon |
|---|---|
| 5.00 | 11.76 |
| 6.00 | 14.11 |
| 7.00 | 16.47 |
| 8.00 | 18.82 |
| 9.00 | 21.17 |
| 10.00 | 23.52 |
| 11.00 | 25.87 |
| 12.00 | 28.23 |
| 13.00 | 30.58 |
| 14.00 | 32.93 |
| 15.00 | 35.28 |
| 16.00 | 37.63 |
| 17.00 | 39.99 |
| 18.00 | 42.34 |
| 19.00 | 44.69 |
| 20.00 | 47.04 |

**Figure 4-1.** *Kilometers per liter to miles per gallon output*

## Servlet Classes

This section outlines several important classes from the `javax.servlet` and `javax.servlet.http` packages. Full details of the servlet API can be found in Appendix A.

## Servlet

The basic servlet abstraction is the `javax.servlet.Servlet` interface, shown in Table 4-1. It prescribes the set of methods that must be implemented by a servlet class for it to be recognized and managed by a servlet engine. Its primary purpose is to supply the lifecycle methods `init()`, `service()`, and `destroy()`.

The servlet API provides a concrete implementation of the `Servlet` interface named `GenericServlet`, described in Table 4-2. This class supplies default implementations of all the interface methods except `service()`. This means you can write a basic servlet simply by extending `GenericServlet` and writing a custom `service()` method.

| Method | Description |
|---|---|
| `void init( ServletConfig config) throws ServletException` | Called once by the servlet engine after a servlet is loaded, just before it's placed into service. If `init()` throws an `UnavailableException`, the servlet is then taken out of service. A servlet should provide some way to store the `config` object to implement the `getServletConfig()` method (see `GenericServlet`). |
| `ServletConfig getServletConfig()` | Returns the `ServletConfig` object passed to the servlet's `init()` method. |
| `void service( ServletRequest request, ServletResponse response) throws ServletException, IOException` | Handles the request described in the `request` object, using the `response` object to return its results to the requester. |
| `String getServletInfo()` | Returns a string that can describe the servlet. Intended for use by administrative tools that need to provide a human-readable description. |
| `void destroy()` | Called by the servlet engine when the servlet is about to be unloaded. |

**Table 4-1.** *Methods in the `servlet` Interface*

| Method | Description |
|---|---|
| `void destroy()` | Writes a log entry consisting of the word "`destroy`". |
| `String getInitParameter (String name)` | Returns the value of the initialization parameter with the specified name. Does so by calling `config.getInitParameter(name)`. |
| `Enumeration getInitParameterNames()` | Returns an `Enumeration` of all the initialization parameters coded for this servlet, calling `config.getInitParameterNames()` to obtain the list. If no initialization parameters were supplied, returns an empty `Enumeration` (not null). |
| `ServletConfig getServletConfig()` | Returns the `ServletConfig` object that was passed to the `init()` method. |
| `ServletContext getServletContext()` | Returns the `ServletContext` referred to in the `config` object. |
| `String getServletInfo()` | Returns an empty string (""). |
| `void init(ServletConfig config) throws ServletException` | Stores the `config` object in an instance variable, writes a log entry consisting of the word "`init`", and then calls the convenience method `init()`. |
| `void init() throws ServletException` | Can be overridden to handle servlet initialization. Automatically called at the end of `init(ServletConfig config)`, after the `config` object has been stored. A concession to servlet authors who, like me, always forget to call `super.init(config)`. |
| `void log(String msg)` | Writes an entry to the servlet log, invoking the servlet context's `log()` method to do so. The servlet's name is added to the beginning of the message text. |

**Table 4-2.** *Methods in the `GenericServlet` Class*

| Method | Description |
|---|---|
| `void log(String msg, Throwable t)` | Writes an entry and a stack trace to the servlet log. This method is also a pass-through to the corresponding method in `ServletContext`. |
| `abstract void service(Request request, Response response) throws ServletException, IOException` | Called by the servlet engine to service the request described by the request object. This is the only abstract method in `GenericServlet`, hence, it's the only one that must be overridden by subclasses. |
| `String getServletName()` | Returns the servlet name as specified in the Web application deployment descriptor (`web.xml`). |

**Table 4-2.** *Methods in the `GenericServlet` Class* (continued)

In addition to the `Servlet` interface, `GenericServlet` also implements `ServletConfig`, which handles initialization parameters and the servlet context, providing convenience methods that delegate to the `ServletConfig` object that was passed to `init()`.

Although the servlet API allows for expansion to other protocols, the current version supports only protocol-independent servlets[2] and HTTP servlets. Because virtually all servlets operate in the Web server environment, few servlets extend `GenericServlet` directly. It's more common for servlets to extend its HTTP-specific subclass `HttpServlet`, described in Table 4-3. See Chapter 3 for an introduction to HTTP.

`HttpServlet` implements `service()` by calling methods specific to the HTTP request method. That is, for `DELETE`, `HEAD`, `GET`, `OPTIONS`, `POST`, `PUT`, and `TRACE`, it calls `doDelete()`, `doHead()`, `doGet()`, `doOptions()`, `doPost()`, `doPut()`, and `doTrace()`, respectively. It also casts the request and response objects used by these methods into their HTTP-specific subclasses, described later in this section.

---

2 What might a protocol-independent servlet be? Perhaps one that doesn't service requests at all, but simply launches background threads from its `init()` method and kills them in `destroy()`. This could be used to emulate Windows NT services or Unix daemon processes.

**Note** *The methods that handle GET, POST, PUT, and DELETE by default return an error indicating the requested method is not supported, so a servlet needs to override the methods it supports explicitly.*

| Method | Description |
|---|---|
| `void doGet(HttpServletRequest request, HttpServletResponse response) throws ServletException, IOException` | Called by the servlet engine to process an HTTP `GET` request. Input parameters, HTTP headers, and the input stream (if any) can be obtained from the `request` object, and response headers and the output stream from the `response` object. |
| `void doPost(HttpServletRequest request, HttpServletResponse response) throws ServletException, IOException` | Called by the servlet engine to process an HTTP `POST` request. No different from `doGet()` from the standpoint of obtaining parameters and input data or returning the response. |
| `void doPut(HttpServletRequest request, HttpServletResponse response) throws ServletException, IOException` | Called by the servlet engine to process an HTTP `PUT` request. The request URI in this case indicates the destination of the file being uploaded. |
| `void doDelete(HttpServletRequest request, HttpServletResponse response) throws ServletException, IOException` | Called by the servlet engine to process an HTTP `DELETE` request. The request URI indicates the resource to be deleted. |
| `void doOptions(HttpServletRequest request, HttpServletResponse response) throws ServletException, IOException` | Called by the servlet engine to process an HTTP `OPTIONS` request. Returns an `Allow` response header indicating the HTTP methods supported by this servlet. It's unlikely that a servlet will need to override this method because the HttpServlet method already implements the functionality required by the HTTP specification. |

**Table 4-3.** *Methods in the `HttpServlet` Class*

| Method | Description |
|---|---|
| `void doTrace(HttpServletRequest request, HttpServletResponse response) throws ServletException, IOException` | Called by the servlet engine to process an HTTP `TRACE` request. Causes the request headers to be echoed as response headers. It's unlikely that a servlet will need to override this method because the HttpServlet method already implements the functionality required by the HTTP specification. |
| `void service(HttpServletRequest request, HttpServletResponse response) throws ServletException, IOException` | An intermediate method called by `service(Request request, Response response)` with HTTP-specific request and response objects. This is the method that actually directs the request to `doGet()`, `doPost()`, and so forth. It shouldn't be necessary to override this method. |
| `void service(Request request, Response response) throws ServletException, IOException` | Casts the request and response objects to their HTTP-specific subclasses and invokes the HTTP-specific `service()` method. |

**Table 4-3.** *Methods in the `HttpServlet` Class* (continued)

## Servlet Request

The `ServletRequest` interface encapsulates the details of the client request. A generic version exists that is protocol-independent and a subinterface exists that is HTTP-specific.

The protocol-independent version shown in Table 4-4 has methods for

- Finding the host name and IP address of the client
- Retrieving request parameters
- Getting and setting attributes
- Getting the input and output streams

| Method | Description |
|---|---|
| `Object getAttribute (String name)` | Returns the request attribute with the specified name, or `null` if it doesn't exist. Attributes can be those set by the servlet engine or those explicitly added with `setAttribute()`. The latter method is useful in connection with a `RequesetDispatcher` object. |
| `Enumeration getAttributeNames()` | Returns an `Enumeration` of the names of all attributes in this request. Returns an empty `Enumeration` if no attributes exist. |
| `String getCharacterEncoding()` | Returns the character encoding used by this request. |
| `int getContentLength()` | Specifies the length of the input stream, if any. If not known, returns -1. |
| `ServletInputStream getInputStream() throws IOException` | Returns the (binary) input stream associated with this request, if any. Either `getInputStream()` or `getReader()` may be called, but not both. |
| `String getParameter (String name)` | Returns the specified input parameter, or `null`, if it doesn't exist. |
| `Enumeration getParameterNames()` | Returns a possibly empty `Enumeration` of the names of all parameters in this request. |
| `String[] getParameterValues (String name)` | Returns an array of values for the specified input parameter name, or `null`, if no values exist. Useful in the case of parameters that can have multiple values (the HTTP `checkbox` element, for example). |
| `String getProtocol()` | Returns the name and version of the protocol used by this request. |

**Table 4-4.** *Methods in the `ServletRequest` Class*

| Method | Description |
|---|---|
| `String getScheme()` | Returns the substring of the request URL up to, but not including, the first colon (`http`, for example). |
| `String getServerName()` | Returns the host name of the server processing the request. |
| `int getServerPort()` | Returns the port number on which the receiving host is listening. |
| `BufferedReader getReader() throws IOException` | Returns a character reader for input data associated with this request. Either this method or `getInputStream()` may be called, but not both. |
| `String getRemoteAddr()` | Returns the numeric IP address of the client host. |
| `String getRemoteHost()` | Returns the name of the client host, if known. |
| `void setAttribute (String name, Object obj)` | Stores a reference to the specified object in the request under the specified name. |
| `void remoteAttribute (String name)` | Removes the specified attribute from the request. |
| `Locale getLocale()` | Returns the client's preferred locale, if known, else `null`. |
| `Enumeration getLocales()` | Returns an `Enumeration` of the client's preferred locales, if known; otherwise, returns the server's preferred locale. |
| `boolean isSecure()` | Returns `true` if the request was made using a secure channel, such as HTTPS. |
| `RequestDispatcher getRequestDispatcher (String name)` | Returns a `RequestDispatcher` object for the specified resource name. See Chapter 8 for details about request dispatching. |

**Table 4-4.** *Methods in the `ServletRequest` Class* (continued)

The HttpServletRequest subinterface in Table 4-5 adds methods to handle

- Reading and writing HTTP headers
- Getting and setting cookies
- Getting path information
- Identifying the HTTP session, if any

| Method | Description |
|---|---|
| String getAuthType() | If the servlet is protected by an authentication scheme, such as HTTP Basic Authentication, returns the name of the scheme. |
| String getContextPath() | Returns the prefix of the URI that designates the servlet context (Web application). |
| Cookie[] getCookies() | Returns an array of the cookies associated with this request. |
| long getDateHeader (String name) | A convenience version of getHeader() that converts its output to a long value suitable for constructing a Date object. |
| String getHeader (String name) | Returns the value of the specified HTTP header, if it was supplied with this request. The name is case-insensitive. |
| Enumeration getHeaderNames() | Returns an Enumeration of the names of all HTTP headers supplied with this request. |
| Enumeration getHeaders (String name) | Returns an Enumeration of the values of all HTTP headers of the specified type supplied with this request. Useful for headers that can have multiple values. |

**Table 4-5.** *Methods in the HttpServletRequest Interface*

| Method | Description |
|---|---|
| `int getIntHeader(String name)` | A convenience version of `getHeader()` that converts its output to an `int` value. |
| `String getMethod()` | Returns the HTTP request method (for example, `GET`, `POST`, and so forth). |
| `String getPathInfo()` | Returns any additional path information specified in the URL. |
| `String getPathTranslated()` | Returns any additional path information specified in the URL, translated into a real path. |
| `String getQueryString()` | Returns the query string—that portion of the URL following the "?", if any. |
| `String getRemoteUser()` | Returns the name of the remote user, if the user has been authenticated, else `null`. |
| `String getRequestedSessionId()` | Returns the session ID returned by the client. |
| `String getRequestURI()` | Returns the portion of the URL beginning with "/" and the context, up to, but not including, any query string. |
| `String getServletPath()` | Returns the substring of the request URI that follows the context. |
| `HttpSession getSession()` | Convenience method that calls `getSession(true)`. |
| `HttpSession getSession(boolean create)` | Returns the current HTTP session, creating a new one if one doesn't exist and the `create` parameter is `true`. |
| `Principal getPrincipal()` | Returns a `java.security.Principal` object representing the current user if the user has been authenticated, else `null`. |

**Table 4-5.** *Methods in the `HttpServletRequest` Interface* (continued)

| Method | Description |
|---|---|
| boolean isRequestedSessionIdFromCookie() | Returns true if the requested session ID was supplied by a Cookie object, false otherwise. |
| boolean isRequestedSessionIdFromURL() | Returns true if the requested session ID was encoded in the request URL, false otherwise. |
| boolean isRequestedSessionIdValid() | Returns true if the session ID returned by the client is still valid. |
| boolean isUserInRole (String role) | Returns true if the currently authenticated user is associated with the specified role. Returns false if not, or if the user isn't authenticated. |

**Table 4-5.** *Methods in the* `HttpServletRequest` *Interface* (continued)

## Servlet Response

The function of the *servlet response* object is to convey results generated by a servlet back to the client that made the request. A `ServletResponse` operates mainly as a wrapper for an output stream, as well as information about its content type and length. It's created by the servlet engine and passed to the servlet as the second parameter of the `service()` method.

Like the servlet request, the servlet response has both generic protocol-independent class and an HTTP-specific one. Table 4-6 describes the methods available in the generic version.

| Method | Description |
|---|---|
| void flushBuffer() throws IOException | Sends the contents of the output buffer to the client. Because HTTP requires headers to be sent before content, calling this method sends the status line and response headers, committing the request. |

**Table 4-6.** *Methods in the* `ServletResponse` *Interface*

| Method | Description |
|---|---|
| `int getBufferSize()` | Returns the buffer size used by the response, or 0 if buffering isn't in effect. |
| `String getCharacterEncoding()` | Returns the name of the character encoding used for the response. Unless explicitly set otherwise, this corresponds to ISO-8859-1. |
| `Locale getLocale()` | Returns the locale used for the response. Unless modified with `setLocale()`, this defaults to the server's locale. |
| `OutputStream getOutputStream() throws IOException` | Returns a stream that can be used to write binary output to be returned to the client. Either this method or `getWriter()` can be called, but not both. |
| `Writer getWriter() throws IOException` | Returns a character writer that can be used to write text output to be returned to the client. Either this method or `getOutputStream()` can be called, but not both. |
| `boolean isCommitted()` | Returns `true` if the status and response headers have already been sent back to the client. Setting headers in the response after it's committed has no effect. |
| `void reset()` | Clears the output buffer as well as any response headers. Causes an `IllegalStateException` if the response has already been committed. |
| `void setBufferSize (int nBytes)` | Sets the minimum buffer size for the response. The actual buffer size may be larger and can be obtained by a call to `getBufferSize()`. If any output has already been written, this method throws an `IllegalStateException`. |

**Table 4-6.** *Methods in the `ServletResponse` Interface* (continued)

| Method | Description |
|---|---|
| `void setContentLength (int length)` | Sets the length of the content body. |
| `void setContentType (String type)` | Sets the content type. In HTTP servlets, this sets the `Content-Type` header. |
| `void setLocale (Locale locale)` | Sets the locale to be used in the response. In HTTP servlets, this may affect the `Content-Type` header value. |

**Table 4-6.** *Methods in the `ServletResponse` Interface* (continued)

The HTTP-specific subinterface `HttpServletResponse` adds methods for manipulating the status code, status message, and response headers. (Appendix C describes HTTP response headers in detail.) This allows it, for example, to be used to send cookies or to redirect the user to another URL. It also provides for encoding the HTTP session ID in URLs written to a Web page. Table 4-7 describes the methods in `HttpServletResponse`.

| Method | Description |
|---|---|
| `void addCookie(Cookie cookie)` | Causes a `Set-Cookie` header to be added to the response. |
| `void addDateHeader (String name, long date)`<br>`void setDateHeader (String name, long date)` | Convenience methods that add a response header with the specified name (or replace all headers of that name) using the specified date value. The long integer date value should be one suitable for the `java.util.Date(long time)` constructor. |
| `void setHeader(String name, String value)` | Sets a response header with the specified name and value. |

**Table 4-7.** *Methods in the `HttpServletResponse` Interface*

| Method | Description |
|---|---|
| `void addIntHeader(String name, int value)`<br>`void setIntHeader(String name, int value)` | Adds a response header with the specified name (or replaces all headers of that name) using the specified integer value. |
| `boolean containsHeader(String name)` | Returns `true` if the response already contains a header by this name. |
| `String encodeRedirectURL(String url)`<br>`String encodeURL(String url)` | Adds the session ID to the URL unless the client is known to accept cookies. The first form should be called only for URLs intended to be used in `sendRedirect()`. Other URLs to be encoded should be passed to `encodeURL()` instead. |
| `void sendError(int status)`<br>`void sendError(int status, String msg)` | Sets the response status code to the specified value (and, optionally, the status message). `HttpServletResponse` defines a complete set of integer constants for the valid status values. |
| `void setStatus(int status)` | Sets the response status code to the specified value. Should only be used for responses that don't indicate an error. Error responses should use `sendError()` instead. |

**Table 4-7.** *Methods in the `HttpServletResponse` Interface* (continued)

Besides additional methods, `HttpServletResponse` also defines integer constants for each possible HTTP response code.

## Servlet Context

A *servlet context* is an interface supplied by the servlet engine to provide services to a Web application. The servlets in the Web application can use the servlet context to get

- The capability to store and retrieve attributes between invocations, and to share these attributes with other servlets.
- The capability to read the contents of files and other static resources in the Web application.
- A means to dispatch requests to each other.
- A facility for logging errors and informational messages.

The servlet context has a name (the name of the Web application it belongs to), which is uniquely mapped to a directory in the file system.

A servlet can get a reference to the servlet context by invoking the `getServletContext()` method on the `ServletConfig` object that was passed to `init()`. If the servlet subclasses `GenericServlet` directly or indirectly, it can use the inherited convenience method `getServetContext()`.[3]

Table 4-8 outlines the methods provided by `ServletContext`.

| Method | Description |
|---|---|
| `Object getAttribute (String name)` `void setAttribute (String name, Object obj)` | Returns the object bound to the specified name in the servlet context or binds an object using the specified name. Such objects are global, from the standpoint of the Web application, because they can be accessed by the same servlet at another time or by any other servlet in the context. |
| `Enumeration getAttributeNames()` | Returns an `Enumeration` of the names of all attributes stored in the servlet context. |

**Table 4-8.** *Methods in the `ServletContext` Interface*

3 JSP pages have it even easier—a reference to the servlet context is automatically stored in the implicit variable `application`.

| Method | Description |
|---|---|
| `ServletContext getContext(String uripath)` | Returns the servlet context that is mapped to another URI. on the same server. The URI must be an absolute path beginning with "/". |
| `String getInitParameter (String name)` | Returns the value of the specified context-wide initialization parameter. This isn't the same as the method of the same name in `ServletConfig`, which applies only to specific servlet for which it is coded. Instead, it's a parameter that applies to all servlets in the context. |
| `Enumeration getInitParameterNames()` | Returns a (possibly empty) `Enumeration` of the names of all the context-wide initialization parameters. |
| `int getMajorVersion()` `int getMinorVersion()` | Returns the major and minor version numbers of the level of the servlet API supported by this context. |
| `String getMimeType (String fileName)` | Returns the MIME type of the specified filename. Typically based on the file extension, rather than the contents of the file itself (which needn't necessarily exist). May return `null` if the MIME type is unknown. |
| `RequestDispatcher getNamedDispatcher (String name)` `RequestDispatcher getRequestDispatcher (String path)` | Returns a `RequestDispatcher` for the servlet or JSP page having the specified name or path, or `null` if the `RequestDispatcher` cannot be created. The path, if specified, must begin with "/" and be relative to the top of the servlet context. |
| `String getRealPath (String path)` | Given a URI, returns the absolute path in the file system the URI corresponds to, or `null` if the mapping cannot be made. |

**Table 4-8.** *Methods in the `ServletContext` Interface* (continued)

| Method | Description |
|---|---|
| URL getResource(String path)<br>InputStream getResourceAsStream (String path) | Returns a URL corresponding to the specified absolute path relative to the servlet context, or an input stream for reading that URL. Returns null if no such resource exists. |
| String getServerInfo() | Returns the name and version number of the servlet engine. |
| void log(String message)<br>void log(String message, Throwable t) | Writes a message to the servlet log, including a stack trace, if a Throwable parameter is supplied. |
| void removeAttribute (String name) | Removes the specified attribute from the servlet context. |

**Table 4-8.** *Methods in the* `ServletContext` *Interface* (continued)

## Threading Models

By default, the servlet engine loads only a single instance of a servlet. Requests serviced by the servlet are run in separate threads, but share the same instance and, therefore, the same instance variables. This fact has several implications, most notably that *instance variables are not thread safe*. For example, look at the following servlet:

```
package jspcr.servlets;

import java.io.*;
import java.sql.*;
import java.util.*;

import javax.servlet.*;
import javax.servlet.http.*;

/**
* Bad example!  Don't try this at home.
*/
public class ColliderServlet extends HttpServlet
```

```
{
   private Connection con;

   public void doGet(
         HttpServletRequest request,
         HttpServletResponse response)
      throws ServletException, IOException
   {
      try {
         Class.forName("sun.jdbc.odbc.JdbcOdbcDriver");
         con = DriverManager.getConnection("jdbc:odbc:usda");
         // ... run some lengthy database operation here
      }
      catch (Exception e) {
         throw new ServletException(e.getMessage());
      }
   }
}
```

Consider what happens when two requests arrive in separate threads a few hundred milliseconds apart. The first one opens the database connection and stores a reference to it in the con instance variable. It then uses the connection to perform a table update or some other database operation. Meanwhile, the second request arrives and opens another connection and stores a reference to it in the same con instance variable. If the first operation finishes and tries to do another database operation, it no longer has its original connection object—it only knows about the second one. Bad things then happen when it tries to use the second connection.

The same type of problem with instance variables can occur in servlets that call other methods from within their service method. If these other methods try to access the servlet request, response, or any object created in the service method that has been saved in an instance variable, there's no way to guarantee a request in another thread won't corrupt the variables by storing references to its own objects in them[4].

The safest approach is simply not to use instance variables, only local variables defined inside the service method.

4 This particular problem can be solved by using a private class (essentially a data structure) to hold all objects of interest, and then passing this class as a parameter to the subsidiary methods.

## SingleThreadModel

Although the single instance multiple thread model is the default, a servlet can change this behavior by implementing `SingleThreadModel`. This interface, which has no methods, informs the servlet engine that it should create a pool of instances and allocate each incoming request to its own instance and thread. This guarantees no two requests *handled by the same instance* will overlap in their execution of the service method. Thus, instance variables can only be affected by one request at a time, making them thread safe. Note, because multiple instances may exist, however, there's nothing to prevent them from executing concurrently in different threads. If they access external resources like files or database connections, therefore, they can still come into conflict. There are few situations in which `SingleThreadModel` solves a problem that couldn't be handled better by other means.

# HTTP Sessions

Although navigating through a Web page may seem like a conversation between client and server, in most cases, it isn't. Typically, a Web client requests an HTML document, which is located by the server and transmitted back to the client. If image links are in the HTML, the client (if it's a Web browser) will make additional requests to the server for each image. If the user clicks a hyperlink in the page, the client issues a new HTTP request for it, but all this happens one request at a time. Between each request, the server moves on to handle other requests, forgetting all about the first client. No back-and-forth exchange of commands and data occurs, only a request followed by a response and a disconnect.[5]

For basic downloading of static documents, this is adequate. However, applications like shopping carts or iterative search engines need to maintain active objects on the server that are associated with particular clients. It may take several requests to build these objects. In this case, a need exists to keep track of to which client the objects are bound.

Several approaches can be used to solve this problem. Most of them involve maintaining the object itself on the server, assigning it a unique key the client is asked to remember. In each subsequent related request, the client passes back the key, which enables the server to reestablish the context.

This is similar to booking an airline ticket over the telephone. The ticket agent asks the customer for her name, address, and flight information, entering all this into a data entry application that assigns a confirmation number, which is reported back

5 HTTP 1.1 does provide a means for connections to persist for a few seconds, so that, for example, HTML and associated images can be downloaded efficiently. This requires both the client and server to know about the capability and request it explicitly. The request/response protocol itself, however, is the same.

to the customer. Later on, if the customer needs to call back and change anything, she supplies the confirmation number, which allows the ticket agent to access and update the original record.

How can the client be induced to remember and supply the key when required? Several means exist:

- **Cookies** The server can send a `Set-Cookie` header in its initial response, with the session ID as the value of the cookie[6]. On subsequent requests, the client can return the value with a `Cookie` header. However, individual users might choose to turn off their browser's cookie capability, so this technique isn't guaranteed to work.
- **Appending the session ID to the URL** For hyperlinks in Web pages created by a dynamic process, the session ID can be encoded as a request parameter in the URL. This doesn't require cookies to be enabled, but it does require every clickable URL to be so encoded. If one is overlooked (an easy thing to do), the session link is lost.
- **Hidden fields** If the application consists of a series of HTML forms using `submit` buttons for navigation, the session ID can be stored as a hidden field that is retrieved with `request.getParameter()`. Obviously, this only works if the forms are all dynamically generated.

## The HttpSession Interface

The servlet API provides a convenient wrapper around these various techniques called an *HTTP Session*. A hashtable-like interface named `javax.servlet.http.HttpSession` has `setAttribute()` and `getAttribute()` methods that store and retrieve objects by name. `HttpSession` provides a session ID key that a participating client stores and returns on subsequent requests in the same session. The servlet engine looks up the appropriates session object and makes it available to the current request. Table 4-9 lists the methods available in `HttpSession`.

---

6 Cookies are name/value pairs sent by a Web server that have a specified life span. Client browsers store cookies and return them automatically to the server each time the browser requests a page from the same domain. More details about cookies can be found in the RFC 2109 specification.

| Method | Description |
|---|---|
| `Object getAttribute (String name)`<br>`void setAttribute (String name, Object value)`<br>`void removeAttribute (String name)` | Stores an object in the session under the specified name, or returns or removes an object by that name that was previously stored. |
| `Enumeration getAttributeNames()` | Returns an `Enumeration` of the names of all attributes currently bound to the session. |
| `long getCreationTime()`<br>`long getLastAccessedTime()` | Returns a long integer representing the date and time at which the session was created or last accessed. The integer is in the form used by the `java.util.Date()` constructor. |
| `String getId()` | Returns the session ID, a unique key assigned by the servlet engine. |
| `int getMaxInactiveInterval()`<br>`void setMaxInactiveInterval (int seconds)` | Sets or returns the maximum number of seconds the session will be kept alive if no interaction occurs with the client. |
| `void invalidate()` | Causes the session to expire and unbinds any objects in it. |
| `boolean isNew()` | Returns `true` if the client hasn't yet joined the session. This is true when the session is first created and the session ID is passed to the client, but the client hasn't made a second request that includes the session ID. |

**Table 4-9.** *Methods in the `HttpSession` Interface*

The API also provides an `HttpSessionBindingListener` interface. Objects that implement this interface must provide `valueBound()` and `valueUnbound()` methods, which get invoked when the objects are added to or removed from an `HttpSession`.

## Summary

Java servlets are extensions to a Web server that allow Web content to be created dynamically in response to a client request. They are managed by a servlet engine, which loads and initializes them, passes them a number of requests for servicing, and then unloads them. Servlets have key advantages over other server-side programming environments:

- Better performance because they remain resident and can run in multiple threads simultaneously
- Simplicity because they require no client software installation other than a Web browser
- Session tracking
- Access to Java technology, including threading, networking, and database connectivity

Servlets operate in a fixed lifecycle, providing callback methods to a servlet engine for being initialized, handling requests, and terminating. The API provides two threading models: the default being a single instance running multiple threads, and the alternative single threaded model.

The principal classes and interfaces in the servlet API are

- The `Servlet` interface, which prescribes the callback methods that must be implemented
- `GenericServlet`, a base class that implements the `Servlet` interface methods
- `HttpServlet`, an HTTP-specific subclass of `GenericServlet`
- `ServletRequest`, which encapsulates information about the client request
- `ServletResponse`, which provides access to an output stream for results to be returned to the client
- The `ServletContext` interface, which allows a group of servlets to interoperate with each other in a Web application

Servlets are the underlying technology for JSP pages. Understanding them is vital to forming the mental model required to develop and debug in the JSP environment.

The Complete Reference

# Chapter 5

## JSP Overview

A *JavaServer page* (*JSP*) is a template for a Web page that uses Java code to generate an HTML document dynamically. JSPs are run in a server-side component known as a JSP container, which translates them into equivalent Java servlets.

For this reason, servlets and JSP pages are intimately related. What's possible in one is, in large part, also possible in another, although each technology has its individual strengths. Because they are servlets, JSP pages have all the advantages of servlets:

- They have better performance and scalability than CGI scripts because they are persistent in memory and multithreaded.
- No special client setup is required.
- They have built-in support for HTTP sessions, which makes application programming possible.
- They have full access to Java technology–network awareness, threads, and database connectivity—without the limitations of client-side applets.

But, in addition, JSP pages have advantages of their own:

- They are automatically recompiled when necessary.
- Because they exist in the ordinary Web server document space, addressing JSP pages is simpler than addressing servlets.
- Because JSP pages are HTML-like, they have greater compatibility with Web development tools.

This chapter provides an overview of JSP as a server-side scripting environment. It describes the JSP container operations and walks through a complete example. Only the basics are covered here; the six chapters of Part II consider JSP pages in-depth.

## How JSP Works

A JSP page exists in three forms:

- **JSP source code** This is the form the developer actually writes. It exists in a text file with an extension of `.jsp`, and consists of a mix of HTML template code, Java language statements, and JSP directives and actions that describe how to generate a Web page to service a particular request.
- **Java source code** The JSP container translates the JSP source code into the source code for an equivalent Java servlet as needed. This source code is typically saved in a work area and is often helpful for debugging.
- **Compiled Java class** Like any other Java class, the generated servlet code is compiled into byte codes in a `.class` file, ready to be loaded and executed.

The JSP container manages each of these forms of the JSP page automatically, based on the timestamps of each file. In response to an HTTP request, the container checks to see if the `.jsp` source file has been modified since the `.java` source was last compiled. If so, the container retranslates the JSP source into Java source and recompiles it.

Figure 5-1 illustrates the process used by the JSP container. When a request for a JSP page is made, the container first determines the name of the class corresponding to the `.jsp` file. If the class doesn't exist or if it's older than the `.jsp` file (meaning the JSP

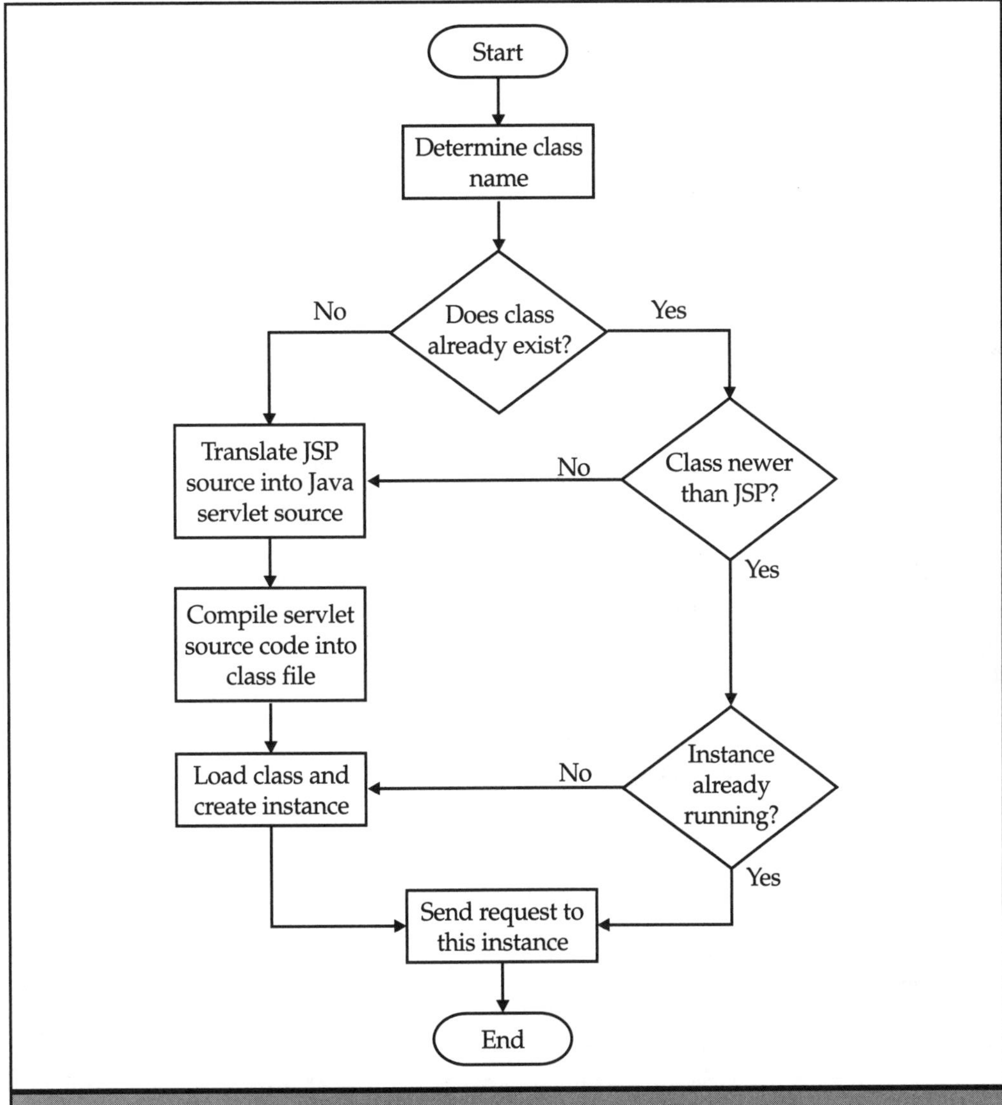


**Figure 5-1.** *Logic used by a JSP container to manage JSP translation*

source has changed since it was last compiled), then the container creates Java source code for an equivalent servlet and compiles it. If an instance of the servlet isn't already running, the container loads the servlet class and creates an instance. Finally, the container dispatches a thread to handle the current HTTP request in the loaded instance.

## A Basic Example

To illustrate how JSP works, let's look at the same example used in the preceding chapter—converting kilometers per liter to miles per gallon. Here's the JSP page:

```
<%@ page session="false" %>
<%@ page import="java.io.*,java.text.*,java.util.*" %>
<%-- Prints a conversion table of miles per gallon
     to kilometers per liter --%>
<%!
   private static final DecimalFormat FMT
      = new DecimalFormat("#0.00");
%>
<HTML>
<HEAD>
<TITLE>Fuel Efficiency Conversion Chart</TITLE>
</HEAD>
<BODY>
<H3>Fuel Efficiency Conversion Chart</H3>
<TABLE BORDER=1 CELLPADDING=3 CELLSPACING=0>
<TR>
<TH>Kilometers per Liter</TH>
<TH>Miles per Gallon</TH>
</TR>
<%
   for (double kpl = 5; kpl <= 20; kpl += 1.0) {
      double mpg = kpl * 2.352146;
%>
<TR>
   <TD><%= FMT.format(kpl)%></TD>
   <TD><%= FMT.format(mpg)%></TD>
</TR>
<%
   }
%>
 </TABLE>
</BODY>
</HTML>
```

Comparing this to the K2MServlet from Chapter 4, first note the JSP is shorter—33 lines versus 55 lines for the servlet. In addition, it looks more like a Web page. Much of the HTML is recognizable as ordinary HTML. Also, to the Java programmer, it's apparent a loop of some kind exists in which the individual rows of the table are produced. Finally, sets of special characters appear to mark the boundaries between Java code and HTML template data. Don't worry if you don't understand what they are—that is covered fully in Chapters 6, 7, and 8.

If you invoke this JSP page from a Web browser, you see the table shown in Figure 5-2, which, not surprisingly, is the same as what the Chapter 4 servlet produced.

To make the JSP-to-servlet relationship clearer, look at the `.java` source code generated by the JSP container. This code will differ greatly, depending on which

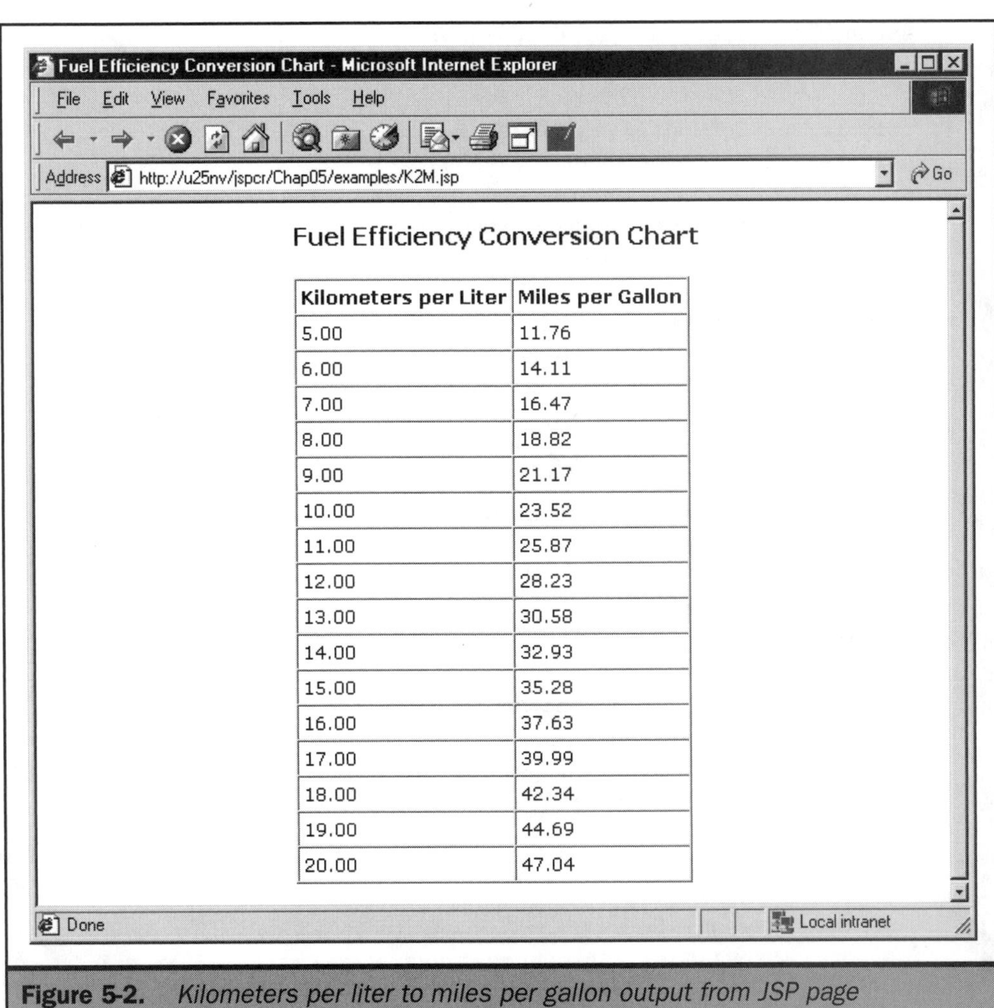


| Kilometers per Liter | Miles per Gallon |
|---|---|
| 5.00 | 11.76 |
| 6.00 | 14.11 |
| 7.00 | 16.47 |
| 8.00 | 18.82 |
| 9.00 | 21.17 |
| 10.00 | 23.52 |
| 11.00 | 25.87 |
| 12.00 | 28.23 |
| 13.00 | 30.58 |
| 14.00 | 32.93 |
| 15.00 | 35.28 |
| 16.00 | 37.63 |
| 17.00 | 39.99 |
| 18.00 | 42.34 |
| 19.00 | 44.69 |
| 20.00 | 47.04 |

**Figure 5-2.** *Kilometers per liter to miles per gallon output from JSP page*

container is used and the implementation approach it takes. The code listed here is what was generated by JRun 3.0 (reformatted slightly for readability):

```
import javax.servlet.*;
import javax.servlet.http.*;
import javax.servlet.jsp.*;
import javax.servlet.jsp.tagext.*;
import allaire.jrun.jsp.JRunJSPStaticHelpers;
import java.io.*;
import java.text.*;
import java.util.*;
public class jrun__Chap05__examples__K2M2ejsp18
   extends allaire.jrun.jsp.HttpJSPServlet
   implements allaire.jrun.jsp.JRunJspPage
{
   private ServletConfig config;
   private ServletContext application;
   private Object page = this;
   private JspFactory __jspFactory
      = JspFactory.getDefaultFactory();

   public void _jspService(
         HttpServletRequest request,
         HttpServletResponse response)
      throws ServletException, java.io.IOException
   {
      if (config == null) {
         config = getServletConfig();
         application = config.getServletContext();
      }
      response.setContentType("text/html; charset=ISO-8859-1");
      PageContext pageContext = __jspFactory.getPageContext
         (this, request, response, null, false, 8192, true);
      JspWriter out = pageContext.getOut();

      try {
         out.print("\r\n<HTML>\r\n"
            + "<HEAD>\r\n"
            + "<TITLE>Fuel Efficiency Conversion Chart</TITLE>\r\n"
            + "</HEAD>\r\n"
            + "<BODY>\r\n"
            + "<H3>Fuel Efficiency Conversion Chart</H3>\r\n"
```

```
            + "<TABLE BORDER=1 CELLPADDING=3 CELLSPACING=0>\r\n"
            + "<TR>\r\n<TH>Kilometers per Liter</TH>\r\n"
            + "<TH>Miles per Gallon</TH>\r\n</TR>\r\n");

         for (double kpl = 5; kpl <= 20; kpl += 1.0) {
            double mpg = kpl * 2.352146;
            out.print("\r\n<TR>\r\n   <TD>");
            out.print(FMT.format(kpl));
            out.print("</TD>\r\n   <TD>");
            out.print(FMT.format(mpg));
            out.print("</TD>\r\n</TR>\r\n");
         }
         out.print("\r\n</TABLE>\r\n</BODY>\r\n</HTML>\r\n");
      }
      catch (Throwable t) {
         if (t instanceof ServletException)
            throw (ServletException) t;
         if (t instanceof java.io.IOException)
            throw (java.io.IOException) t;
         if (t instanceof RuntimeException)
            throw (RuntimeException) t;
         throw JRunJSPStaticHelpers.handleException
            (t, pageContext);
      } finally {
         __jspFactory.releasePageContext(pageContext);
      }
   }
   private static final DecimalFormat FMT
      = new DecimalFormat("#0.00");
   private static final String[] __dependencies__
      = {"/Chap05/examples/K2M.jsp",null};
   private static final long[] __times__ = {980969842306L,0L};
   public String[] __getDependencies()
   {
      return __dependencies__;
   }
   public long[] __getLastModifiedTimes()
   {
      return __times__;
   }
   public int __getTranslationVersion()
   {
```

```
            return 13;
        }
    }
```

A bit mechanical, as if it were generated by a computer program (which, of course, it was), but still recognizable as a servlet, especially the middle part, which differs little from the K2MServlet source code in Chapter 4.

As you see, building a mental model of this process is the key to successful JSP development and debugging. With this backdrop, let's proceed to Part II and explore the elements of JSP more deeply.

# Part II

## Elements of JSP

The next six chapters deal with the syntax and semantics of JSP, giving you the skills necessary to create working code. Topics include basic syntax, scriptlets, expressions, declarations, file inclusion, request forwarding, and specifying page behavior. The concluding chapter provides a detailed tutorial on JSP custom tags.

# Chapter 6

## JSP Syntax and Semantics

The purpose of this chapter is to give an overview of the basic components used in JavaServer Pages, to describe how they are written, and to explain what they do. This chapter reviews the JSP development model, and then introduces each JSP element and considers how the element is used in this overall design. The chapter concludes with an annotated example that illustrates the use of each element. In covering this material, our concern is with the following:

- **Syntax** The coding structure used to represent the element so the JSP compiler recognizes it
- **Semantics** The meaning of the element to the JSP container—what happens when it is used

Each of the JSP elements described in this chapter is covered in greater detail in the remaining chapters of Part II.

## The JSP Development Model

Recall from Chapter 5 that a JSP page exists in three forms:

1. The .jsp source file containing HTML statements and JSP elements
2. The Java source code for a servlet program
3. The compiled Java class

To understand how JSP elements operate, it is important to build a mental model of how these three objects are created and the relationship among them. First, the JSP developer writes a .jsp source file and stores it somewhere in the document file system of a Web server or Web application. In this respect, the .jsp source file is no different from an ordinary HTML file. The URL by which it is known to the network is the same, except its filename ends in .jsp instead of .html. Next, when the .jsp URL is invoked for the first time, the JSP container reads the .jsp file, parses its contents, and generates the source code for an equivalent Java servlet. It then compiles the servlet and creates a .class file. Finally, the JSP container loads the servlet class and uses it to service the HTTP request. The middle step (generating the servlet source code) is repeated for later requests only if the .jsp file has been updated.

In this design, JSP elements can affect how the JSP container operates during two operational phases:

- **Translation time** Generating the Java servlet source code from a .jsp file
- **Request time** Invoking the servlet to handle an HTTP request

Keeping this model in mind can help you understand the syntactical units of a JSP page and what their capabilities might be.

# Components of a JSP Page

A .jsp file can contain JSP elements, fixed template data, or any combination of the two. JSP elements are instructions to the JSP container about what code to generate and how it should operate. These elements have specific start and end tags that identify them to the JSP compiler. Template data is everything else that is not recognized by the JSP container. Template data (usually HTML) is passed through unmodified, so the HTML that is ultimately generated contains the template data exactly as it was coded in the .jsp file.

Three types of JSP elements exist:

- Directives
- Scripting elements, including expressions, scriptlets, and declarations
- Actions

Let's consider each of these elements in more detail.



## Directives

*Directives* are instructions to the JSP container that describe what code should be generated. They have the general form

<%@ *directive-name* [*attribute*="*value*" *attribute*="*value*" ...] %>

Zero or more spaces, tabs, and newline characters can be after the opening <%@ and before the ending %>, and one or more whitespace characters can be after the directive name and between attributes/value pairs. The only restriction is that the opening <%@ tag must be in the same physical file as the ending %> tag.

The JSP 1.1 specification describes three standard directives available in all compliant JSP environments:

- page
- include
- taglib

Although the specification declares that no custom directives can be used in the JSP 1.1 environment, this leaves open the possibility that user-defined directives may be included in a later specification.

The next three sections provide an overview of each of these directives.

## The page Directive

The *page directive* is used to specify attributes for the JSP page as a whole. It has the following syntax:

<%@ page [*attribute*="*value*" *attribute*="*value*" ...] %>

where the attributes are any of those listed in Table 6-1.

| Attribute | Value |
|---|---|
| `language` | The language used in scriptlets, expressions, and declarations. In JSP 1.1, the only valid value for this attribute is java. |
| `extends` | The fully qualified name of the superclass of this JSP page. This must be a class that implements the `HttpJspPage` interface. The JSP specification warns against the use of this attribute without fully understanding its implications. |
| `import` | A comma-separated list of one or more *package*.* names and/or fully qualified class names. This list is used to create corresponding import statements in the generated Java servlet. The following packages are automatically included and need not be specified:<br>java.lang.*<br>java.servlet.*<br>java.servlet.jsp.*<br>java.servlet.http.* |
| `session` | *true* or *false*, indicating whether the JSP page requires an HTTP session. If the value is true, then the generated servlet will contain code that causes an HTTP session to be created (or accessed, if it already exists). The default value is *true*. |
| `buffer` | Specifies the size of the output buffer. Valid entries are *nnn*kb or none, where *nnn* is the number of kilobytes allocated for the buffer. The default value is 8kb. |
| `autoflush` | *true* if the buffer should be automatically flushed when it is full, or *false* if a buffer overflow exception should be thrown. The default value is *true*. |

**Table 6-1.** *Attributes of the Page Directive*

| Attribute | Value |
|---|---|
| isThreadSafe | *true* if the page can handle simultaneous requests from multiple threads, or *false* if it cannot. If *false*, the generated servlet declares that it implements the SingleThreadModel interface. |
| info | A string that will be returned by the page's getServletInfo() method. |
| isErrorPage | *true* if this page is intended to be used as another JSP's error page. In that case, this page can be specified as the value of the errorPage attribute in the other page's page directive. Specifying *true* for this attribute makes the *exception* implicit variable available to this page. The default value is *false*. |
| errorPage | Specifies the URL of another JSP page that will be invoked to handle any uncaught exceptions. The other JSP page must specify isErrorPage="true" in its page directive. |
| contentType | Specifies the MIME type and, optionally, the character encoding to be used in the generated servlet. |

**Table 6-1.** *Attributes of the Page Directive* (continued)



More than one page directive can be in a file and the attributes specified collectively apply to the whole file, but no attribute can be specified more than once, with the exception of the import attribute.

Chapter 10 covers the page directive in more detail.

## The include Directive

The *include directive* merges the contents of another file at translation time into the .jsp source input stream, much like a #include C preprocessor directive. The syntax is

<%@ include file="*filename*" %>

where *filename* is an absolute or relative pathname interpreted according to the current servlet context. Examples would be

```
<%@ include file="/header.html" %>
<%@ include file="/doc/legal/disclaimer.html" %>
<%@ include file="sortmethod" %>
```

The include directive contrasts with the `<jsp:include>` action described later in this chapter, which merges the output of another file at request time into the response output stream. Either element can be used to include standard headers and footers or other common text in JSP pages. Chapter 8 examines both approaches in detail.

## The taglib Directive

The *taglib directive* makes custom actions available in the current page through the use of a tag library. The syntax of the directive is

<%@ taglib uri="*tagLibraryURI*" prefix="*tagPrefix*" %>

where the attributes are those listed here:

| Attribute | Value |
|---|---|
| *tagLibraryURI* | The URL of a Tag Library Descriptor. |
| *tagPrefix* | A unique prefix used to identify custom tags used later in the page. |

For example, if the following directive is used,

```
<%@ taglib uri="/tlds/FancyTableGenerator.tld" prefix="ft" %>
```

and if `FancyTableGenerator.tld` defines a tag named `table`, then the page can contain tags of the following type

```
<ft:table>
...
</ft:table>
```

JSP tag extensions are considered in detail in Chapter 11.

# Comments

The JSP specification provides two means of including comments in a JSP page: one for hidden comments only visible in the JSP page itself and one for comments included in the HTML or XML output generated by the page. The former type has the syntax

```
<%-- This is a hidden JSP comment --%>
```

and the latter looks like this:

```
<!-- This is included in the generated HTML -->
```

When the JSP compiler encounters the start tag `<%--` of a JSP comment, it ignores everything from that point in the file until it finds the matching end tag `--%>`. This means JSP comments can be used to disable (or "comment out") sections of the JSP page. This is a time-honored technique for temporarily enabling and disabling parts of a program without making major modifications to the source code. In addition, however, it means JSP comments cannot be nested because the end tag of an inner comment would be interpreted as marking the end of the outer comment.

The other comment type uses the normal HTML or XML comment tag. Comments of this type are passed through unaltered to the response output stream and are included in the generated HTML. They are invisible in the browser window, but can be seen by invoking the View Source menu option.

If the purpose of a comment is to enlighten the person viewing it, the second comment type seems less useful than the first for two reasons: it is found in HTML generated by a program and it is typically never seen by a human. However, because these HTML comments are computer-generated, they can incorporate version numbers, dates, and other identifying numbers that may be useful to technical support personnel in troubleshooting applications. For example, these three lines included in a JSP page

```
<!--
Remote address was <%= request.getRemoteAddr() %>
-->
```

would record the remote address of the user making a Web request without cluttering the output. If something goes wrong with the application, technical support personnel can instruct the user to view the generated HTML source and report the identifying data.

## Expressions

JSP provides a simple means for accessing the value of a Java variable or other expression and merging that value with the HTML in the page. The syntax is

<%= *exp* %>

where *exp* is any valid Java expression. The expression can have any data value, as long as it can be converted to a string. This conversion is usually done simply by generating an `out.print()` statement. For example, the JSP code

```
The current time is <%= new java.util.Date() %>
```

may generate the servlet code

```
out.write("The current time is ");
out.print( new java.util.Date() );
out.write("\r\n");
```

**Tip** *Understanding what code is generated can help you remember not to put a semicolon inside an expression.*

Chapter 7 discusses expressions in more detail.

## Scriptlets

A *scriptlet* is a set of one or more Java language statements intended to be used to process an HTTP request. The syntax of a scriptlet is

<% *statement*; [*statement*; ...] %>

The JSP compiler simply includes the contents of scriptlet verbatim in the body of the `_jspService()` method. A JSP page may contain any number of scriptlets. If multiple scriptlets exist, they are each appended to the `_jspService()` method in the order in which they are coded. This being the case, a scriptlet may contain an open curly brace that is closed in another scriptlet. Consider the following JSP page, which produces a Fahrenheit to Celsius temperature conversion table:

```
<%@ page import="java.text.*" %>
<TABLE BORDER=0 CELLPADDING=3>
<TR>
   <TH>Degrees<BR>Fahrenheit</TH>
   <TH>Degrees<BR>Celsius</TH>
</TR>
<%
   NumberFormat fmt = new DecimalFormat("###.000");
   for (int f = 32; f <= 212; f += 20) {
      double c = ((f - 32) * 5) / 9.0;
      String cs = fmt.format(c);
%>
   <TR>
      <TD ALIGN="RIGHT"><%= f %></TD>
      <TD ALIGN="RIGHT"><%= cs %></TD>
   </TR>
<%
   }
%>
</TABLE>
```

The example code contains two scriptlets: one for the main body of the loop and one for the closing curly brace. Between the two scriptlets is the HTML markup for a single table row, using JSP expressions to access the values. The generated servlet code converts the scriptlets and what is between them to

```
NumberFormat fmt = new DecimalFormat("###.000");
for (int f = 32; f <= 212; f += 20) {
   double c = ((f - 32) * 5) / 9.0;
   String cs = fmt.format(c);
   out.write("\r\n<TR>\r\n<TD ALIGN=\"RIGHT\">");
   out.print( f );
   out.write("</TD>\r\n");
   out.write("\r\n<TD ALIGN=\"RIGHT\">");
   out.print( cs );
   out.write("</TD>\r\n");
   out.write("</TR>\r\n");
}
```

which produces the following output:

```
 Degrees     Degrees
Fahrenheit  Celsius
   32          .000
   52        11.111
   72        22.222
   92        33.333
  112        44.444
  132        55.556
  152        66.667
  172        77.778
  192        88.889
  212       100.000
```

Scriptlets are explored at length in Chapter 7.

## Declarations

Like scriptlets, *declarations* contain Java language statements, but with one big difference: scriptlet code becomes part of the `_jspService()` method, whereas declaration code is incorporated into the generated source file *outside* the `_jspService()` method. The syntax of a declaration section is

<%! *statement*; [*statement*; ...] %>

ELEMENTS OF JSP

Declaration sections can be used to declare class or instance variables, methods, or inner classes. Unlike scriptlets, they have no access to the implicit objects described in the next section. If you use a declaration section to declare a method that needs to use the request object, for example, you need to pass the object as a parameter to the method.

The following shows an example of a JSP page that uses a declaration section:

```
<%@ page
      errorPage="ErrorPage.jsp"
      import="java.io.*,java.util.*"
%>

<%
   Enumeration enames;
   Map map;
   String title;

   // Print the request headers

   map = new TreeMap();
   enames = request.getHeaderNames();
   while (enames.hasMoreElements()) {
      String name = (String) enames.nextElement();
      String value = request.getHeader(name);
      map.put(name, value);
   }
   printTable(out, map, "Request Headers");

   // Print the session attributes

   map = new TreeMap();
   enames = session.getAttributeNames();
   while (enames.hasMoreElements()) {
      String name = (String) enames.nextElement();
      String value = "" + session.getAttribute(name);
      map.put(name, value);
   }
   printTable(out, map, "Session Attributes");

%>

<%-- Define a method to print a table --%>
```

```
<%!
   private static void printTable
      (Writer writer, Map map, String title)
   {
      // Get the output stream

      PrintWriter out = new PrintWriter(writer);

      // Write the header lines

      out.println("<TABLE BORDER=1 CELLPADDING=3>");
      out.println
         ("<TR><TH COLSPAN=2>" + title + "</TH></TR>");

      // Write the table rows

      Iterator imap = map.entrySet().iterator();
      while (imap.hasNext()) {
         Map.Entry entry = (Map.Entry) imap.next();
         String key = (String) entry.getKey();
         String value = (String) entry.getValue();
         out.println("<TR>");
         out.println("<TD>" + key + "</TD>");
         out.println("<TD>" + value + "</TD>");
         out.println("</TR>");
      }

      // Write the footer lines

      out.println("</TABLE>");
      out.println("<P>");
   }
%>
```

This JSP page collects data for two tables: the HTTP headers passed to the request object and the session attributes. The desired output for each is a nicely formatted HTML table. Of course, the tables could be created while iterating through the data rows, but this would require duplicating the formatting code. Instead, a private static method named `printTable()` is used, passing it a reference to the output stream, a `Map` object containing the key/value pairs, and the table caption.

Chapter 8 discusses declarations in greater detail.

## Implicit Objects

Although scriptlets, expressions, and HTML template data are all incorporated into the `_jspService()` method, the JSP container writes the skeleton of the method itself, initializing the page context and several useful variables. These variables are implicitly available inside scriptlets and expressions (but not declarations). They can be accessed like any other variable, but do not have to be declared first. For example, the `HttpServletRequest` object passed to `_jspService()` is available under the name request, as shown in the following scriptlet:

```
<%
   String accountNumber = request.getParameter("acct");
   if (accountNumber == null) {
      // ... handle the missing account number problem
   }
%>
```

Table 6-2 provides a complete list of implicit variables.

| Variable Name | Value |
|---|---|
| `request` | The `ServletRequest` or `HttpServletRequest` being serviced. |
| `response` | The `ServletResponse` or `HttpServletResponse` that will receive the generated HTML output. |
| `pageContext` | The `PageContext` object for this page. This object is a central repository for attribute data for the page, request, session, and application. |
| `session` | If the JSP page uses an `HttpSession`, it is available here under the name `session`. |
| `application` | The servlet context object. |

**Table 6-2.** *Implicit Variables*

| Variable Name | Value |
|---|---|
| `out` | The character output stream used to generate the output HTML. |
| `config` | The `ServletConfig` object for this servlet context. |
| `page` | A reference to the JSP page itself. |
| `exception` | An uncaught exception that causes the error page to be invoked. This variable is available only to pages with `isErrorPage="true"`. |

**Table 6-2.** *Implicit Variables* (continued)



Additional implicit variables can be created by means of a tag library. See Chapter 11 for discussion of this topic.

## Standard Actions

*Actions* are high-level JSP elements that create, modify, or use other objects. Unlike directives and scripting elements, actions are coded using strict XML syntax

*<tagname* [*attr*="*value*" *attr*="*value*" ...] > ... </*tag-name*>

or, if the action has no body, an abbreviated form:

*<tagname* [*attr*="*value*" *attr*="*value*" ...] />

XML syntax requires the following:

- Every tag must have matching end tag or use the short form /> previously shown
- Attribute values must be placed in quotes
- Tags must nest properly: <A><B> ... </B></A> is legal, but <A><B> ... </A></B> is not.

Seven standard actions are available in all JSP 1.1-compliant environments. These actions are described at length in Chapter 15. Table 6-3 outlines the syntax.

| Tag Name | Description |
|---|---|
| <jsp:useBean> | Declares a Java Bean instance and associates it with a variable name. Syntax is<br><jsp:useBean<br>id="*name*"<br>[ type="*type*" ]<br>[ class="*class*" ]<br>[ beanName="*beanName*" ]<br>[scope="*page* \| *request* \| *session* \| *application*"]><br>...</jsp:useBean> |
| <jsp:setProperty> | Sets the values of one or more properties of a bean previously declared with <jsp:useBean>. Syntax is<br><jsp:setProperty<br>name="*id*"<br>*prop-expression* /><br>where *prop-expression* is one of the following:<br>property="*"<br>property="*propName*"<br>property="*propName*" param="*parameterName*"<br>property="*propName*" value="*value*"<br>property="*propName*" value=<%= *expression* %> |
| <jsp:getProperty> | Returns the value of the specified property of a bean. Syntax is<br><jsp:getProperty name="*id*" property="*name*" /> |
| <jsp:include> | Invokes another resource and merges its output stream with the JSP page output stream. Syntax is<br><jsp:include page="*URL*" flush="true" /><br>or, if parameters need to be passed:<br><jsp:include page="*URL*" flush="true"><br><jsp:param … /><br><jsp:param … /><br>...<br><jsp:param ... /><br></jsp:include> |

**Table 6-3.** *Standard Actions*

| Tag Name | Description |
|---|---|
| `<jsp:forward>` | Forwards this HTTP request to another JSP page or servlet for processing. Syntax is<br><jsp:forward page="*URL*" /><br>or, if parameters need to be passed:<br><jsp:forward page="*URL*"><br><jsp:param ... /><br><jsp:param ... /><br>...<br><jsp:param ... /><br></jsp:forward> |
| `<jsp:param>` | Binds a value to a name and passes the binding to another resource invoked with `<jsp:include>` or `<jsp:forward>`. Syntax is<br><jsp:param name="*name*" value="*value*" /> |
| `<jsp:plugin>` | Used to generate the appropriate HTML linkage for downloading the Java plugin:<br><jsp:plugin<br>type="*bean* \| *applet*"<br>code="*objectCode*"<br>codebase="*objectCodebase*"<br>{ align="*alignment*" }<br>{ archive="*archiveList*" }<br>{ height="*height*" }<br>{ hspace="*hspace*" }<br>{ jreversion="*jreversion*" }<br>{ name="*componentName*" }<br>{ vspace="*vspace*" }<br>{ width="*width*"}<br>{ nspluginurl="*url*" }<br>{ iepluginurl="*url*" } ><br>{ <jsp:params><br>{ <jsp:param name="*name*" value="*value*" /><br>}+</jsp:params> }}</jsp:plugin> |

**Table 6-3.** *Standard Actions* (continued)

## Tag Extensions

In addition to the standard actions listed in Table 6-3, the JSP author can write custom tags to extend JSP functionality of JSP. Chapter 11 is devoted to tag extensions.

# A Complete Example

An example of a JSP page that incorporates all the elements introduced here concludes this chapter. The page is named `Echo.jsp`. Its sole function is to pass back to the client browser an HTML table containing the HTTP request headers the browser sent. The listing is shown in the following:

```
<%@ page import="java.util.*" %>

<HTML>

<HEAD>
<TITLE>Echo</TITLE>
<STYLE>
<jsp:include page="style.css" flush="true"/>
</STYLE>
</HEAD>

<BODY>
<H3>HTTP Request Headers Received</H3>
<TABLE BORDER="1" CELLPADDING="4" CELLSPACING="0">
<%
   Enumeration eNames = request.getHeaderNames();
   while (eNames.hasMoreElements()) {
      String name = (String) eNames.nextElement();
      String value = normalize(request.getHeader(name));
%>
   <TR> <TD><%= name %></TD> <TD><%= value %></TD> </TR>
<%
   }
%>
</TABLE>
</BODY>
</HTML>
<%!
   private String normalize(String value)
   {
```

```
      StringBuffer sb = new StringBuffer();
      for (int i = 0; i < value.length(); i++) {
         char c = value.charAt(i);
         sb.append(c);
         if (c == ';')
            sb.append("<BR>");
      }
      return sb.toString();
   }
%>
```



When `Echo.jsp` is first invoked, it creates the following Java source code:

```
package Chap_00030_00035;

import javax.servlet.*;
import javax.servlet.http.*;
import javax.servlet.jsp.*;
import javax.servlet.jsp.tagext.*;
import java.io.PrintWriter;
import java.io.IOException;
import java.io.FileInputStream;
import java.io.ObjectInputStream;
import java.util.Vector;
import org.apache.jasper.runtime.*;
import java.beans.*;
import org.apache.jasper.JasperException;
import java.util.*;


public class
   _0002fChap_00030_00035_0002fEcho_0002ejspEcho_jsp_5
   extends HttpJspBase
{
   // begin [file="Echo.jsp";from=(27,3);to=(39,0)]
   private String normalize(String value)
   {
      StringBuffer sb = new StringBuffer();
      for (int i = 0; i < value.length(); i++) {
         char c = value.charAt(i);
         sb.append(c);
```

```
            if (c == ';')
               sb.append("<BR>");
         }
         return sb.toString();
      }
      // end

      static {
      }

      public
         _0002fChap_00030_00035_0002fEcho_0002ejspEcho_jsp_5()
      {
      }

      private static boolean _jspx_inited = false;

      public final void _jspx_init() throws JasperException
      {
      }

      public void _jspService(
            HttpServletRequest request,
            HttpServletResponse  response)
         throws IOException, ServletException
      {
         JspFactory _jspxFactory = null;
         PageContext pageContext = null;
         HttpSession session = null;
         ServletContext application = null;
         ServletConfig config = null;
         JspWriter out = null;
         Object page = this;
         String  _value = null;
         try {

            if (_jspx_inited == false) {
               _jspx_init();
               _jspx_inited = true;
            }

            _jspxFactory = JspFactory.getDefaultFactory();
```

```
response.setContentType("text/html");
pageContext = _jspxFactory.getPageContext
   (this, request, response, "", true, 8192, true);

application = pageContext.getServletContext();
config = pageContext.getServletConfig();
session = pageContext.getSession();
out = pageContext.getOut();

// HTML
// begin [file="Echo.jsp";from=(0,32);to=(7,0)]
out.write("\r\n\r\n");
out.write("<HTML>\r\n\r\n");
out.write("<HEAD>\r\n");
out.write("<TITLE>Echo</TITLE>\r\n");
out.write("<STYLE>\r\n");
// end

// begin [file="Echo.jsp";from=(7,0);to=(7,44)]
{
   String _jspx_qStr = "";
   out.flush();
   pageContext.include("style.css" + _jspx_qStr);
}
// end

// HTML
// begin [file="Echo.jsp";from=(7,44);to=(14,0)]
out.write("\r\n");
out.write("</STYLE>\r\n");
out.write("</HEAD>\r\n\r\n");
out.write("<BODY>\r\n");
out.write("<H3>HTTP Request Headers Received");
out.write("</H3>\r\n");
out.write("<TABLE BORDER=\"1\"");
out.write(" CELLPADDING=\"4\"");
out.write(" CELLSPACING=\"0\">\r\n");
// end

// begin [file="Echo.jsp";from=(14,2);to=(19,0)]
Enumeration eNames = request.getHeaderNames();
while (eNames.hasMoreElements()) {
```

```
String name = (String) eNames.nextElement();
String value = normalize(request.getHeader(name));
// end

// HTML
// begin [file="Echo.jsp";from=(19,2);to=(20,12)]
out.write("\r\n    <TR> <TD>");
// end

// begin [file="Echo.jsp";from=(20,15);to=(20,21)]
out.print( name );
// end

// HTML
// begin [file="Echo.jsp";from=(20,23);to=(20,33)]
out.write("</TD> <TD>");
// end

// begin [file="Echo.jsp";from=(20,36);to=(20,43)]
out.print( value );
// end

// HTML
// begin [file="Echo.jsp";from=(20,45);to=(21,0)]
out.write("</TD> </TR>\r\n");
// end
// begin [file="Echo.jsp";from=(21,2);to=(23,0)]

}
// end

// HTML
// begin [file="Echo.jsp";from=(23,2);to=(27,0)]
out.write("\r\n</TABLE>\r\n</BODY>\r\n</HTML>\r\n");
// end

// HTML
// begin [file="Echo.jsp";from=(39,2);to=(40,0)]
out.write("\r\n");
// end
```

```
        }
        catch (Exception ex) {
           if (out.getBufferSize() != 0)
              out.clear();
           pageContext.handlePageException(ex);
        }
        finally {
           out.flush();
           _jspxFactory.releasePageContext(pageContext);
        }
    }
}
```

Let's consider the JSP page and the generated code section by section.



## A Page Directive

The JSP page begins with a page directive indicating the page uses the `java.util` package:

```
<%@ page import="java.util." %>
```

This directive shows up in the servlet source code at the end of its list of imported classes:

```
...
import org.apache.jasper.runtime.*;
import java.beans.*;
import org.apache.jasper.JasperException;
import java.util.*;
```

## A <jsp:include> Action

The page uses a style sheet to set the look and feel of the output. The style sheet is incorporated using a `<jsp:include>` action:

```
<STYLE>
<jsp:include page="style.css" flush="true"/>
</STYLE>
```

The <jsp:include> action causes the following style sheet to be read at request time:

```
body {
   color: #000000;
   background-color: #FEFEF2;
   font: Verdana 9pt;
};
```

## Scriptlet

Two scriptlets are on the page, with HTML template data located before, between, and after them. The HTML data

```
<HTML>

<HEAD>
<TITLE>Echo</TITLE>
...
```

is passed through unchanged by means of write statements:

```
out.write("\r\n");
out.write("<HTML>\r\n\r\n");
out.write("<HEAD>\r\n ");
out.write("<TITLE>Echo</TITLE>\r\n ");
...
```

Then the first scriptlet is simply copied to the servlet:

```
Enumeration eNames = request.getHeaderNames();
while (eNames.HasMoreElements()) {
   String name = (String) eNames.nextElement();
   String value = normalize(request.getHeaderName());
```

Notice the code fragment has an unclosed curly brace on the second line. The matching brace is supplied by the second scriptlet.

## JSP Expressions

During each iteration of the loop, the scriptlet extracts a header name and header value from the request object. Rather than printing these values using `out.write()`, the page author switches back into HTML mode and uses JSP expression tags,

```
%>
   <TR> <TD><%= name %></TD> <TD><%= value %></TD> </TR>
<%
```

which generates the following servlet code:

```
// HTML
// begin [file="Echo.jsp";from=(19,2);to=(20,12)]
out.write("\r\n   <TR> <TD>");
// end

// begin [file="Echo.jsp";from=(20,15);to=(20,21)]
out.print( name );
// end

// HTML
// begin [file="Echo.jsp";from=(20,23);to=(20,33)]
out.write("</TD> <TD>");
// end

// begin [file="Echo.jsp";from=(20,36);to=(20,43)]
out.print( value );
// end

// HTML
// begin [file="Echo.jsp";from=(20,45);to=(21,0)]
out.write("</TD> </TR>\r\n");
// end
```

## A Declaration

Header values that are lists can be very long and cause the table width to be distorted. You can get around this problem by scanning the header value for semicolons and inserting <BR> tags wherever they are found. This function is performed by a method called normalize(), which is found at the end of the JSP file:

```
<%!
   private String normalize(String value)
   {
      StringBuffer sb = new StringBuffer();
      for (int i = 0; i < value.length(); i++) {
         char c = value.charAt(i);
         sb.append(c);
         if (c == ';')
            sb.append("<BR>");
      }
      return sb.toString();
   }
%>
```

As was the case with the two scriptlets, the declaration code is copied verbatim to the generated servlet, except it is not placed inside the `_jspService()` method. Instead, it is written inside the class block, but outside any other method, near the beginning of the servlet:

```
// begin [file="Echo.jsp";from=(27,3);to=(39,0)]
private String normalize(String value)
{
   StringBuffer sb = new StringBuffer();
   for (int i = 0; i < value.length(); i++) {
      char c = value.charAt(i);
      sb.append(c);
      if (c == ';')
         sb.append("<BR>");
   }
   return sb.toString();
}
// end
```

The resulting output is shown in Figure 6-1.

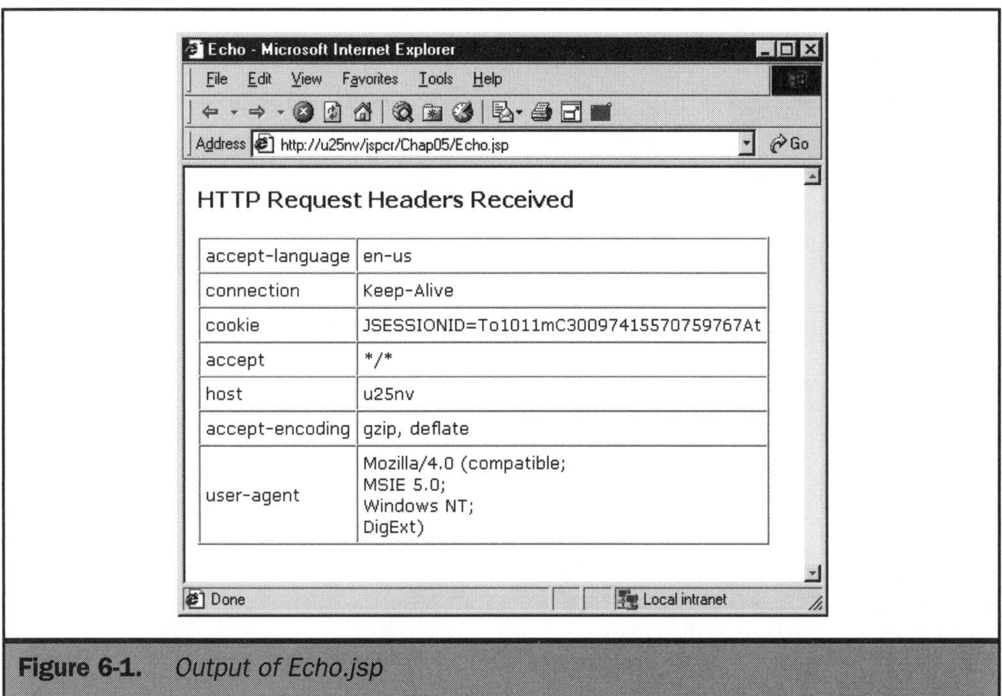


**Figure 6-1.** *Output of Echo.jsp*

## Summary

The JSP development environment provides a means for generating HTML pages dynamically with server-side Java programming. The syntax allows most of the HTML to be coded directly, with sections marked off for Java code that controls the page generation. There is support for including other resources, both static and dynamic. JavaBeans are fully integrated into the framework, and custom tags allow functionality to be encapsulated and made available to nonexpert page authors.

The key point this chapter makes is this: a mental model of the JSP development cycle is crucial to understanding how to create and debug Web applications. Knowledge of what happens at translation time (static resources are included via the `<%@ include %>` directive, for example) versus request time (dynamic request dispatching with `<jsp:include>`) provides insight into which features to use and when to use them. The remaining chapters of Part II discuss each of these features of the application model in more detail.

The Complete Reference

# Chapter 7

## Expressions and Scriptlets

The previous chapter provided an overview of JSP syntax and semantics. While the syntax is not difficult to learn, mastering it doesn't teach you everything you need to know. Understanding JSP requires building a mental model of how it operates—how and when Java source code is generated and when classes are compiled and loaded.

In this chapter, part of that mental model is clarified by exploring two scripting elements: expressions and scriptlets. You see how the JSP container combines template text and JSP scripting elements to generate a Java method that handles user requests. How a JSP page gets access to the Web environment in which it is used, and how it communicates its results, is also examined.

## Expressions

A JSP *expression* is simply a Java[1] language expression in a JSP page set off from its surrounding HTML by the delimiters <%= and %>, as the following shows:

<%= *expression* %>

For example, an expression can be a primitive numeric value,

```
<B>Simple math:</B> 2 + 2 = <%= 2 + 2 %>
```

which produces the output:

**Simple math:** 2 + 2 = 4

or a more elaborate expression involving method calls,

```
The Java virtual machine vendor is
<em><%= System.getProperty("java.vm.vendor") %></em>
```

which produces the output:

The Java virtual machine vendor is *Sun Microsystems Inc.*

1 In theory, JSP pages could be written in other languages, as envisioned in the JSP specification. As of this writing, with a few experimental exceptions, Java is the only supported language. That is why the technology is called JavaServer Pages (JSP), not Language Independent Server Pages (LISP) or Any Old Language Server Pages (AOLSP).

An expression can create new objects and manipulate them. This code creates a `Date` object and passes it to the `format()` method of a new `SimpleDateFormat` object,

```
Today is
<%=
   new java.text.SimpleDateFormat("MMMM d, yyyy")
   .format(new java.util.Date())
%>
```

which produces (on the appropriate day, of course):

Today is June 28, 2001

The Java expression between the <% and %> delimiters can be as complex as desired, the only requirement being it must be capable of being evaluated as a `java.util.String`, either directly or through the invocation of its `toString()` method or a `String.valueOf()` method.

*Expressions must not end in a semicolon. They must consist solely of what can legally appear on the right side of an assignment statement between the equals sign and the ending semicolon.*

## Scriptlets

A *scriptlet* is a set of Java programming statements embedded in an HTML page. The statements are distinguished from their surrounding HTML by being placed between <% and %> markers, as the following shows:

<% *statement; [statement; …]* %>

Whitespace is permitted after the <% and before the %>, so the previous scriptlet could also be written as:

<%<br>*statement;*<br>*[statement; …]*<br>%>

Here is an example of a JSP page that uses a scriptlet to generate a table of ASCII characters:

```
<HTML>
<BODY>
<CENTER>
```

```
<H3>ASCII Table</H3>
<TABLE BORDER="0" CELLPADDING="0" CELLSPACING="0">
<%
   StringBuffer sb = new StringBuffer();
   sb.append("<TR>");
   sb.append("<TH WIDTH=40> </TH>");
   for (int col = 0; col < 16; col++) {
      sb.append("<TH>");
      sb.append(Integer.toHexString(col));
      sb.append("</TH>");
   }
   sb.append("</TR>");
   for (int row = 0; row < 16; row++) {
      sb.append("<TR>");
      sb.append("<TH>");
      sb.append(Integer.toHexString(row));
      sb.append("</TH>");
      for (int col = 0; col < 16; col++) {
         char c = (char)(row * 16 + col);
         sb.append("<TD WIDTH=32 ALIGN=CENTER>");
         sb.append(c);
         sb.append("</TD>");
      }
      sb.append("</TR>");
   }
   out.println(sb);
%>
</TABLE>
</CENTER>
</BODY>
</HTML>
```

There are five lines of HTML, followed by the scriptlet open delimiter <%, a number of lines of Java code, the scriptlet closing delimiter %>, and then the HTML lines needed to close the document. When invoked, the page produces the output shown in Figure 7-1.

The following section describes how these scripting elements are handled by the JSP container.

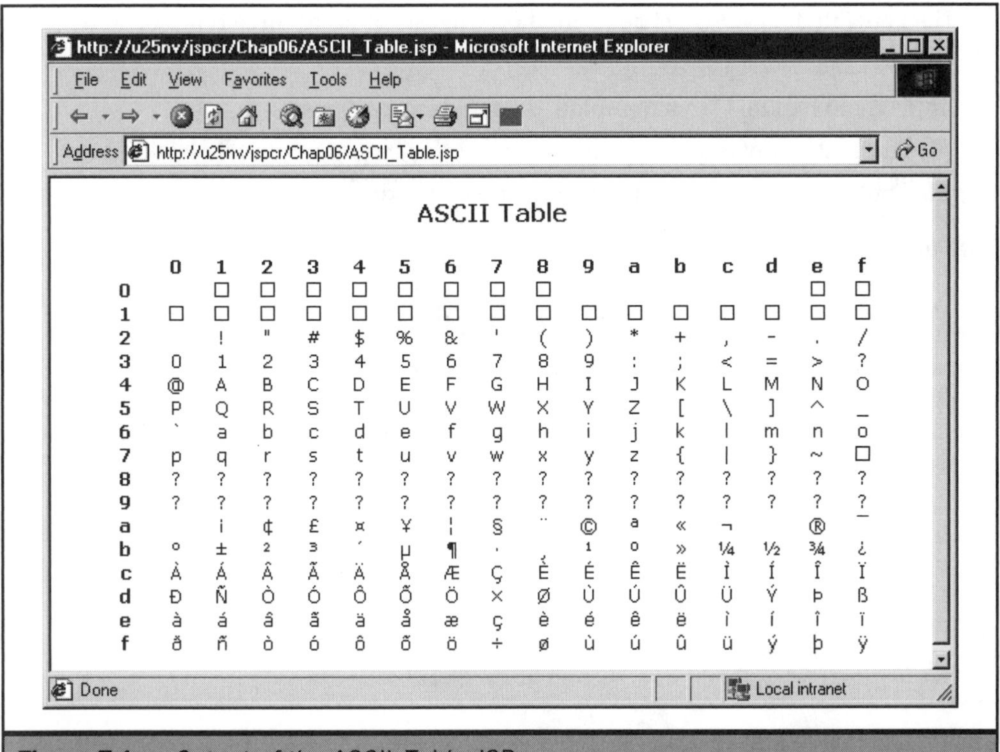


**Figure 7-1.** *Output of the ASCII_Table JSP*



## Expression and Scriptlet Handling by the JSP Container

When it encounters a new or revised JSP page, the JSP container parses it and creates the source code for an equivalent Java servlet[2]. The expressions, scriptlets, and HTML template data found in the page are used by the JSP container to create Java source code for a method named `_jspService()`. This method corresponds to the `service()` method of a servlet, or the more commonly used `doGet()` and `doPost()` methods. `_jspService()` is automatically generated by the container. The JSP author must not define it explicitly.

2 Servlets are discussed at length in Chapter 4.

The generated `_jspService()` method consists of up to three types of statements, depending on the contents of the JSP page:

- Code to handle HTML template data and expressions
- The contents of any scriptlets
- Container-generated initialization and exit code

Let's examine each of these and see how they are handled.

## HTML Template Data and Expressions

Any characters in the JSP page not inside a JSP element (a directive, expression, scriptlet, or action) are considered part of a fixed HTML template. The JSP container creates `out.write()` or `out.print()` statements that write these characters to the response output stream. For example, this code

```
<LI>Cash and Marketable Securities
```

is converted to this:

```
out.write("<LI>Cash and Marketable Securities\r\n");
```

If the HTML template needs to contain any literal <% strings, they must be treated specially to avoid confusing the JSP container. The JSP 1.1 specification indicates this can be done by writing <\% instead of <%. The JSP container generates code to write the intended <% in the output stream.

*JSP containers typically generate one long `out.write()` statement for each uninterrupted stretch of fixed HTML data. The examples in this book take the liberty of breaking long character strings into multiple `out.write()` statements for the sake of readability.*

Besides fixed HTML data, the template also may contain JSP expressions that are evaluated at run time in and printed with an `out.write()` statement. Expressions are considered in the next section.

## Scriptlet Contents

Anything found between <% and %> tags is copied verbatim to the `_jspService()` method. Hence, the lines in a JSP page

```
<TABLE BORDER=0>
<TR><TH>Celsius</TH><TH>Fahrenheit</TH></TR>
<%
```

```
    for (int c = 0; c <= 100; c += 10) {
       int f = 32 + 9*c/5;
       out.print("<TR><TD>" + c + "</TD>");
       out.print("<TD>" + f + "</TD></TR>");
    }
%>
</TABLE>
```



are transformed by the JSP container into the following lines in the `_jspService()` method:

```
// HTML
// begin [file="c2f.jsp";from=(0,0);to=(2,0)]
out.write("<TABLE BORDER=0>\r\n");
out.write("<TR>");
out.write("<TH>Celsius</TH>");
out.write("<TH>Fahrenheit</TH>");
out.write("</TR>\r\n");
// end
// begin [file="c2f.jsp";from=(2,2);to=(8,0)]

for (int c = 0; c <= 100; c += 10) {
   int f = 32 + 9*c/5;
   out.print("<TR><TD>" + c + "</TD>");
   out.print("<TD>" + f + "</TD></TR>");
}
// end
// HTML
// begin [file="c2f.jsp";from=(8,2);to=(10,0)]
out.write("\r\n</TABLE>\r\n");
// end
```

The HTML markup for the table is found in the `out.write()` statements, and the scriptlet contents appear unaltered in the body of the method.

If multiple scriptlets are in a page, they are copied in the order they are encountered. Thus, no functional difference exists between writing this code

```
<%
   for (int i = 0; i < 10; i++) {
      out.println(i);
   }
%>
```

and this,

```
<%   for (int i = 0; i < 10; i++) { %>
<%      out.println(i); %>
<%   } %>
```

except for several newline characters generated in the latter case (which occur because they are technically considered fixed HTML data). Because multiple scriptlets are concatenated and placed into the same method, syntactical units can be started in one scriptlet and completed in another, as illustrated by the opening and closing curly braces in the `for` statement. This also means variables defined in any scriptlet are treated as local variables of the `_jspService()` method, and retain their value from one scriptlet or expression to the next.

## Container-Generated Initialization and Exit Code

In addition to code that the JSP page author writes, `_jspService()` begins and ends with statements that initialize and release objects needed in the method. The exact code generated is implementation-dependent and specific to the JSP container vendor. In the case of the Celsius-to-Fahrenheit example previously given , Tomcat generates the following initialization and exit code:

```
public void _jspService(
         HttpServletRequest request,
         HttpServletResponse  response)
      throws IOException, ServletException
   {
      JspFactory _jspxFactory = null;
      PageContext pageContext = null;
      HttpSession session = null;
      ServletContext application = null;
      ServletConfig config = null;
      JspWriter out = null;
      Object page = this;
      String  _value = null;
      try {
         _jspxFactory = JspFactory.getDefaultFactory();
         response.setContentType("text/html;charset=8859_1");
         pageContext = _jspxFactory.getPageContext
            (this, request, response, "", true, 8192, true);
         application = pageContext.getServletContext();
         config = pageContext.getServletConfig();
```

```
            session = pageContext.getSession();
            out = pageContext.getOut();

            // ... your code appears here ...

        }
        catch (Exception ex) {
            if (out.getBufferSize() != 0)
                out.clearBuffer();
            pageContext.handlePageException(ex);
        }
        finally {
            out.flush();
            _jspxFactory.releasePageContext(pageContext);
        }
    }
```



You can see a number of objects are created before the JSP author's code is added. The meaning of these objects is the subject of the next section.

## Implicit Objects and the JSP Environment

The scriptlets and expressions written in a JSP page do not stand alone as a complete program—they need an environment in which to operate. The JSP container provides this environment and makes it accessible to the page author through what are called *implicit objects*. These objects are created by container-generated statements at the beginning of the `_jspService()` method and are assigned predetermined names that are the same in all JSP pages. Nine of these objects exist, as listed in Table 7-1.

| Object | Description |
|---|---|
| `request` | The `HttpServletRequest` object that was passed to `_jspService()`. |
| `response` | The `HttpServletResponse` object that was passed to `_jspService()`. |

**Table 7-1.** *Implicit Objects Available Within Scriptlets and Expressions*

| Object | Description |
|---|---|
| `pageContext` | A means of accessing page, request, session, or application attributes. |
| `session` | The current `HttpSession` object, if one exists. |
| `application` | The servlet context object. |
| `out` | The `JspWriter` response output stream object. |
| `config` | The servlet configuration object. |
| `page` | A reference to the current instance of the JSP class itself. |
| `exception` | An uncaught exception (valid in error pages only). |

**Table 7-1.** *Implicit Objects Available Within Scriptlets and Expressions* (continued)

These variables can be accessed simply by using their predetermined names like any other variable. One of these variables has already been used in the examples in this chapter—the `JspWriter` `out` variable,

```
<%
out.println("<B>out</B> is an <I>");
out.println(out.getClass().getName());
out.println("</I> object.");
%>
```

which produces the output when run under Tomcat:

**out** is an *org.apache.jasper.runtime.JspWriterImpl* object.

This, of course, is vendor-specific. JRun 3.0 produces

**out** is an *allaire.jrun.jsp.JRunJspWriter* object.

The JSP implicit objects provide the context in which an HTTP request is serviced. The following sections consider each of these objects in detail.

## Request

The `request` variable contains a reference to the `HttpServletRequest` object passed in the first parameter of the generated `_jspService()` method. This object encapsulates the details of the HTTP request generated by the Web browser or other client—its parameters, attributes, headers, and data. Some of its more useful methods[3] are listed in Table 7-2.

## Response

The `response` variable provides access to the other side of the HTTP transaction. This object encapsulates the output returned to the HTTP client, providing the page auth or with a means for setting response headers and the status code. It also has methods for accessing the response output stream, but the JSP specification prohibits directly accessing this stream. All JSP response output must be written using the `out` implicit variable. Methods provided by the `HttpServletResponse` object include those listed in Table 7-3.

| Method | Description |
|---|---|
| String getHeader(String *name*) | Returns the value of the specified HTTP header, or `null` if the header is not present in the request. |
| Enumeration getHeaderNames() | Returns an enumeration of all HTTP headers present in the request. |
| String getParameter(String *name*) | Given the name of a single-valued form parameter, returns its value. |
| Enumeration getParameterNames() | Returns an enumeration of the names of all form parameters passed to this request. |
| HttpSession getSession(boolean *create*) | Returns the current `HttpSession` object. If one does not exist, either creates a new one or returns `null`, depending on the *create* flag. |

**Table 7-2.** *Some Useful Methods of the `request` Object*

3 A complete description of javax.servlet.http.HttpServletRequest and all other classes in the Servlet 2.2 API can be found in Appendix A.

| Method | Description |
| --- | --- |
| boolean isCommitted() | Returns a flag indicating whether the HTTP response has already been returned to the client. |
| void setHeader(String *name*, String *value*) | Sets an HTTP header with the specified name and value. |
| void setStatus(int *sc*) | Sets the HTTP status to the specified value. |

**Table 7-3.** *Some Useful Methods of the `response` Object*

## PageContext

JSP code operates within a hierarchy of environments, as shown in Figure 7-2. A single HTTP request, for example, may be serviced by multiple JSP pages: one that produces heading information and another that generates detailed output. Similarly, multiple HTTP requests may be part of a larger HTTP session that starts with a login request, proceeds through some user selection requests, and then commits the work to a database. Finally, the set of all HTTP sessions in a servlet context may share a connection pool or other common objects.

Each of the layers in this hierarchy can have attributes that apply at that level only. The JSP specification provides for a `PageContext` object that keeps track of attributes at four levels:

- The JSP page
- The HTTP request

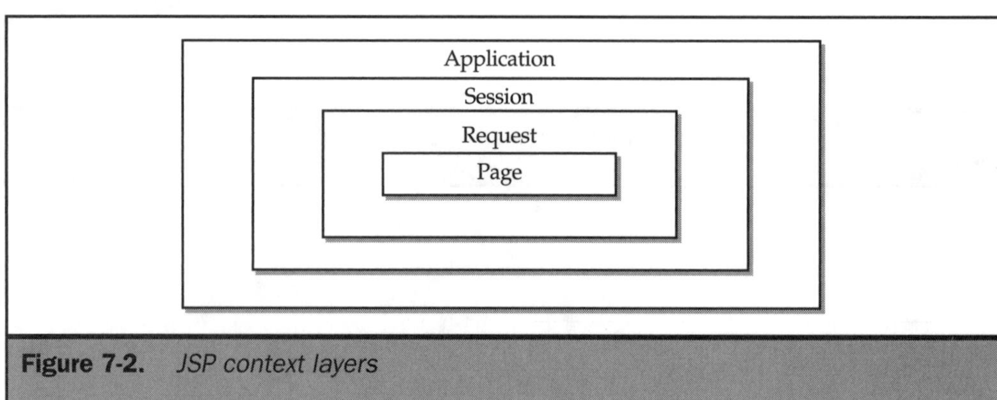


**Figure 7-2.** *JSP context layers*

- The HTTP session
- The overall application

A `PageContext` object is automatically initialized and assigned to a variable named `pageContext` at the beginning of the `_jspService()` method. This object provides search and update capability for attributes at each of the four levels, as described in Table 7-4. It also provides methods that forward requests to other resources and include the output of other resources.



| Method | Description |
|---|---|
| Object findAttribute(String *name*) | Searches for an attribute object with the specified name in the page, request, session, and application scopes, in that order, returning the first one found, or null, if none is found. |
| Object getAttribute(String *name*, int *scope*) | Returns the attribute object with the specified name in the given scope. The *scope* parameter value should be selected from among the PAGE_CONTEXT, REQUEST_CONTEXT, SESSION_CONTEXT, and APPLICATION_CONTEXT constants provided in the `PageContext` class. |
| void removeAttribute(String *name*, int *scope*) | Removes the attribute object having the specified name in the given scope. |
| void setAttribute(String *name*, Object *value*, int *scope*) | Stores an object as a named attribute in the given scope. The *scope* parameter value should be selected from among the PAGE_CONTEXT, REQUEST_CONTEXT, SESSION_CONTEXT, and APPLICATION_CONTEXT constants defined in the `PageContext` class. |

**Table 7-4.** *Some Useful Methods of the `pageContext` Object*

## Session

HTTP is a stateless protocol, which means it doesn't remember from one request to the next anything about previous requests. However, Web applications frequently involve more than one request. For example, an application may begin with some kind of user identification and validation that must be propagated through several other Web pages. The continuity required for this type of application must be provided by something other than the Web server.

Several approaches can be taken to accommodate this need, depending on the requirements of the application. Chapter 14 explores a number of these alternatives in detail, including:

- Hidden fields
- Cookies
- URL rewriting
- HTTP sessions

The last item mentioned is of interest here. An `HttpSession` is a `Hashtable`-like object associated with a single Web browser session. It persists between HTTP requests and can store named objects of any kind. By default, the JSP container creates an `HttpSession` object or accesses the currently active one at the beginning of the `_jspService()` method. This object is assigned to a variable named `session`.

If you do not need to retain objects between requests, you can turn off automatic session creation by specifying `session="false"` in the `page` directive. Doing so can improve performance by reducing the number of objects of which the servlet engine has to keep track. Because a session persists until it times out (typically 30 minutes later) or it is explicitly invalidated, the impact on performance can be considerable.

Table 7-5 outlines several useful methods in the session object.

| Method | Description |
|---|---|
| Object getAttribute(String *name*) | Returns the object with the specified name, if it exists in the session. |
| Enumeration getAttributeNames() | Returns an enumeration of the names of all the objects stored in the session. |
| String getId() | Returns the unique session ID. This ID must be stored by the client (Web browser) between requests and passed back to the JSP container to identify which session is required. |

**Table 7-5.** *Some Useful Methods of the `session` Object*

| Method | Description |
|---|---|
| int getMaxInactiveInterval() | Returns the maximum number of seconds the session stays active between user requests. The JSP container closes the session if no activity occurs over that length of time. |
| void invalidate() | Closes the session and unbinds all its objects. |
| void setAttribute(String *name*, Object *value*) | Stores an object in the session under the specified name. |

**Table 7-5.** *Some Useful Methods of the `session` Object* (continued)



Remember, the `pageContext` object can also be used to get and set attributes in the session in the same manner as the `session.getAttribute()` and `session.setAttribute()` methods.

## Application

The `application` implicit object encapsulates a view of the collection of all servlets, JSP pages, HTML pages, and other resources in a Web application. This object implements the `javax.servlet.ServletContext` interface and is automatically constructed at the beginning of the `_jspService()` method. It provides information about the server version, any application-wide initialization parameters, and the absolute paths of resources within the application. This object also provides a means for logging messages. Some of its more useful methods are described in Table 7-6.

| Method | Description |
|---|---|
| Enumeration getAttributeNames() | Returns an enumeration of the names of all objects stored in the servlet context. |
| Object getAttribute(String *name*) | Returns an object with the specified name that was stored with the application's setAttribute() method. |

**Table 7-6.** *Some Useful Methods of the `application` Object*

| Method | Description |
|---|---|
| String getInitParameter(String *name*) | Returns the value of the specified application-wide initialization parameter. |
| Enumeration getInitParameterNames() | Returns an enumeration of the names of all application-wide initialization parameters. |
| String getRealPath(String *path*) | Converts a path in the context of the Web application to an absolute path in the file system, if possible. |
| URL getResource(String *path*) | Returns the URL (if any) mapped to the specified path in the application. The path must begin with a "/" and is relative to the root of the application. |
| InputStream getResourceAsStream(String *path*) | Similar in operation to getResource(), but returns an opened input stream to the resulting URL. |
| void log(String *msg*) | Writes a message to the log file associated with this application. |

**Table 7-6.** *Some Useful Methods of the `application` Object* (continued)

As is the case with the `page`, `request`, and `session` implicit objects, attributes of the `application` object can be manipulated with methods in the `pageContext` object.

Initialization parameters are discussed in a later section of this chapter.

## Out

The whole purpose of a JSP page is to produce some output and send it back to the user on the other end of the socket connection. As you saw earlier in this chapter, fixed HTML template data and JSP expressions are written by automatically generated `out.write()` and `out.print()` method calls. The `out` variable is initialized with a reference to a `javax.servlet.jsp.JspWriter` object early in the `_jspService()` method. You can have all output generated in this manner or you can write explicitly to the `out` object in scriptlets. Thus, the JSP page

```
<%
   String[] colors = {"red", "green", "blue"};
```

```
   for (int i = 0; i < colors.length; i++) {
%>
<%= colors[i] %> <P>
<%
   }
%>
```

is functionally equivalent to this one:

```
<%
   String[] colors = {"red", "green", "blue"};
   for (int i = 0; i < colors.length; i++) {
      out.println(colors[i] + " <P>");
   }
%>
```



Besides the `write()` methods common to all `java.io.Writer` objects, the `out` object provides methods for querying and manipulating the output buffer, as shown in Table 7-7.

| Method | Description |
|---|---|
| void flush() | Forces buffered data to be written to the output stream. |
| int getBufferSize() | Returns the size of the output buffer in bytes, or 0 if the writer is unbuffered. |
| int getRemaining() | Returns the number of bytes remaining before buffer overflow occurs. |
| void print(*type value*) | A variety of methods to write objects of the specified primitive or object type. No newline character is added at the end. |
| void println(*type value*) | Similar to print(), but adds a newline character at the end. |

**Table 7-7.** *Some Useful Methods of the `out` Object*

## Config

Besides application-wide initialization parameters that are made available through the `application` object, individual servlet mappings (and, therefore, JSP pages) can have initialization parameters. The `config` implicit object provides methods for accessing these parameters, the servlet context (application), and the servlet name, as detailed in Table 7-8.

## Page

The `page` implicit object is a variable containing a reference to the current servlet instance, essentially just an alias for the `this` variable. This object is not typically useful to JSP page authors.

## Exception

The object referred to by the implicit `exception` variable is any instance of `java.lang.Throwable` that has been thrown, but not caught, by a `catch` block in the JSP page. The exception variable is only valid if the `<%@ page %>` directive has the `isErrorPage=`"*true*" attribute. This attribute is discussed in more detail in Chapter 10.

| **Method** | **Description** |
|---|---|
| String getInitParameter(String *name*) | Returns the value of the specified servlet initialization parameter, or null, if the named parameter does not exist. |
| Enumeration getInitParameterNames() | Returns a list of the names of all initialization parameters for this servlet. |
| ServletContext getServletContext() | Returns a reference to the servlet context (same as the *application* implicit variable). |
| String name getServletName() | Returns the name of the generated servlet. |

**Table 7-8.** *Some Useful Methods of the `config` Object*

## Initialization Parameters

Initialization parameters are external name/value pairs that can be read by a JSP page. They can be used in the same manner as string constants, but have the added advantage that they can be modified without requiring the program that uses them to be recompiled. This makes initialization parameters especially useful for storing installation and configuration data, such as HTTP proxy server names, application color schemes, or installation directory names.

These parameters can be specified at the individual JSP and servlet level or for all the JSP pages in an application. In either case, initialization parameters are declared in the application's `web.xml` file[4]. For JSP and servlet level access, this is accomplished by adding one or more `<init-param>` elements to the appropriate `<servlet>` element, as the following shows:

```
<servlet>

   <servlet-name>Food</servlet-name>
   <jsp-file>/Chap07/examples/Food.jsp</jsp-file>

   <init-param>
      <param-name>DRIVER_NAME</param-name>
      <param-value>sun.jdbc.odbc.JdbcOdbcDriver</param-value>
   </init-param>

   <init-param>
      <param-name>DATABASE_URL</param-name>
      <param-value>jdbc:odbc:usda</param-value>
   </init-param>

</servlet>
```

In this example, `Food.jsp` is a JSP page that accesses a database of nutrition information. Rather than containing hardcoded values for the JDBC driver name and database URL, the JSP page gets these values from initialization parameters using the `getInitParameter()` method:

```
   String driverName = getInitParameter("DRIVER_NAME");
   if (driverName == null)
```

4 The web.xml file and other configuration and deployment issues are discussed in Chapter 18.

```
        throw new ServletException
        ("No DRIVER_NAME parameter was specified");

    String databaseURL = getInitParameter("DATABASE_URL");
    if (databaseURL == null)
        throw new ServletException
        ("No DATABASE_URL parameter was specified");

    Class.forName(driverName);
    Connection con = DriverManager.getConnection(databaseURL);
```

Database access parameters are likely needed in several places within a Web application. Rather than having duplicate values in the `web.xml` file, commonly used values can be specified at the application level. This is done with the `<context-param>` element:

```
<context-param>
    <param-name>DRIVER_NAME</param-name>
    <param-value>sun.jdbc.odbc.JdbcOdbcDriver</param-value>
</context-param>

<context-param>
    <param-name>DATABASE_URL</param-name>
    <param-value>jdbc:odbc:usda</param-value>
</context-param>
```

The JSP code for accessing the values is almost the same, except the application object's `getInitParameter()` method is called:

```
String driverName =
        application.getInitParameter("DRIVER_NAME");
    if (driverName == null)
        throw new ServletException
        ("No DRIVER_NAME parameter was specified");

    String databaseURL =
        application.getInitParameter("DATABASE_URL");
```

```
if (databaseURL == null)
   throw new ServletException
   ("No DATABASE_URL parameter was specified");

Class.forName(driverName);
Connection con = DriverManager.getConnection(databaseURL);
```



## Summary

JSP pages provide two means for incorporating Java code in the handling of requests: expressions and scriptlets. JSP *expressions* are simply Java-language expressions that yield a string value (or can be converted into one). Expressions are enclosed in `<%=` and `%>` delimiters. Whatever is between the delimiters is made the argument of an `out.print()` or `out.write()` method. For this reason, expressions must not end in a semicolon. *Scriptlets* are Java code fragments designed to operate inside the `_jspService()` method and are marked by the `<%` and `%>` delimiters. The programming statements in a scriptlet are copied directly into the Java source code of the generated servlet.

To give it linkage to the JSP container, a JSP page has access to a number of implict objects. These are automatically initialized objects that have predefined variable names. These variables are

- `request`
- `response`
- `pageContext`
- `session`
- `application`
- `out`
- `config`
- `page`
- `exception`

The last variable (`exception`) is only available to pages with the `isErrorPage="true"` attribute in their page directive.

The Complete Reference

# Chapter 8

## Declarations

The previous chapter covered JSP expressions and scriptlets. Along with fixed HTML template data, these two element types share a common environment—they exist within the `_jspService()` method of a generated Java servlet. While this is adequate for most request processing, it imposes some restrictions on the servlet's capability. This chapter introduces JSP declarations, which allow the JSP author to write Java code that operates outside the `_jspService()` method.

## What Is a Declaration?

Similar to a scriptlet, a JSP *declaration* consists of Java source code embedded within an HTML page. Declarations are set off from the rest of the page by special opening and closing tags, as the following shows:

<%! *java statements* %>

The syntax of a declaration is identical to that of a scriptlet, with one exception: the opening delimiter is <%!, rather than <%.

Like a scriptlet, the code inside the declaration delimiters is copied verbatim to the generated Java servlet. The essential difference is where the code is placed: scriptlets are copied to the inside of the `_jspService()` method, whereas declarations are written outside the method as top-level members of the enclosing class. Understanding this distinction can help develop your mental model of how JSP works and can help explain unexpected behavior.

### Where Declaration Code Is Generated

An example of how code for a declaration is generated would make this clearer. Consider the following JSP page that uses a scriptlet to display the current time:

```
<%@ page import="java.text.*,java.util.*" %>
<%
   DateFormat fmt = new SimpleDateFormat("hh:mm:ss aa");
   String now = fmt.format(new Date());
%>
The time is <%= now %>
```

The page is stored in a file named `ShowTimeS.jsp` (*S* for *scriptlet*). When this file is invoked, it displays the current time:

```
The time is 09:31:45 PM
```

If the user refreshes the page, the time is incremented, as expected:

```
The time is 09:31:48 PM
The time is 09:31:51 PM
The time is 09:31:53 PM
```

Now consider the same JSP written with a declaration rather than a scriptlet. This page is named `ShowTimeD.jsp` (*D* for *declaration*):

```
<%@ page import="java.text.*,java.util.*" %>
<%!
   DateFormat fmt = new SimpleDateFormat("hh:mm:ss aa");
   String now = fmt.format(new Date());
%>
The time is <%= now %>
```

The only difference between `ShowTimeS.jsp` and `ShowTimeD.jsp` is line two in `ShowTimeD.jsp` starts with <%! instead of <%, making it a declaration rather than a scriptlet.

When `ShowTimeD.jsp` is invoked, it, likewise, displays the current time:

```
The time is 09:32:26 PM
```

But look what happens when the page is refreshed:

```
The time is 09:32:26 PM
The time is 09:32:26 PM
The time is 09:32:26 PM
```

The time is not changing. Why not? The answer can be found in the generated servlet source code for each page. Here is the scriptlet version,

```
import javax.servlet.*;
import javax.servlet.http.*;
import javax.servlet.jsp.*;
import javax.servlet.jsp.tagext.*;
import java.io.PrintWriter;
import java.io.IOException;
import java.io.FileInputStream;
```

```
import java.io.ObjectInputStream;
import java.util.Vector;
import org.apache.jasper.runtime.*;
import java.beans.*;
import org.apache.jasper.JasperException;
import java.text.*;
import java.util.*;


public class ShowTimeS extends HttpJspBase
{
   static
   {
   }

   public ShowTimeS()
   {
   }

   public void _jspService(
         HttpServletRequest request,
         HttpServletResponse  response)
      throws IOException, ServletException
   {
      JspFactory _jspxFactory = null;
      PageContext pageContext = null;
      HttpSession session = null;
      ServletContext application = null;
      ServletConfig config = null;
      JspWriter out = null;
      Object page = this;
      String  _value = null;
      try {
         _jspxFactory = JspFactory.getDefaultFactory();
         response.setContentType("text/html;charset=8859_1");
         pageContext = _jspxFactory.getPageContext
            (this, request, response, "", true, 8192, true);

         application = pageContext.getServletContext();
         config = pageContext.getServletConfig();
         session = pageContext.getSession();
         out = pageContext.getOut();
```

```
         out.write("\r\n");
         DateFormat fmt = new SimpleDateFormat("hh:mm:ss aa");
         String now = fmt.format(new Date());
         out.write("\r\nThe time is ");
         out.print( now );
         out.write("\r\n");
      }
      catch (Exception ex) {
         if (out.getBufferSize() != 0)
            out.clearBuffer();
         pageContext.handlePageException(ex);
      }
      finally {
         out.flush();
         _jspxFactory.releasePageContext(pageContext);
      }
   }
}
```

and here is the declaration version:

```
import javax.servlet.*;
import javax.servlet.http.*;
import javax.servlet.jsp.*;
import javax.servlet.jsp.tagext.*;
import java.io.PrintWriter;
import java.io.IOException;
import java.io.FileInputStream;
import java.io.ObjectInputStream;
import java.util.Vector;
import org.apache.jasper.runtime.*;
import java.beans.*;
import org.apache.jasper.JasperException;
import java.text.*;
import java.util.*;


public class ShowTimeD extends HttpJspBase
{
   DateFormat fmt = new SimpleDateFormat("hh:mm:ss aa");
```

```
String now = fmt.format(new Date());

static
{
}

public ShowTimeD()
{
}

public void _jspService(
      HttpServletRequest request,
      HttpServletResponse  response)
   throws IOException, ServletException
{
   JspFactory _jspxFactory = null;
   PageContext pageContext = null;
   HttpSession session = null;
   ServletContext application = null;
   ServletConfig config = null;
   JspWriter out = null;
   Object page = this;
   String  _value = null;
   try {
      _jspxFactory = JspFactory.getDefaultFactory();
      response.setContentType("text/html;charset=8859_1");
      pageContext = _jspxFactory.getPageContext
         (this, request, response, "", true, 8192, true);

      application = pageContext.getServletContext();
      config = pageContext.getServletConfig();
      session = pageContext.getSession();
      out = pageContext.getOut();

      out.write("\r\n");
      out.write("\r\nThe time is ");
      out.print( now );
      out.write("\r\n");
   }
   catch (Exception ex) {
      if (out.getBufferSize() != 0)
         out.clearBuffer();
```

```
            pageContext.handlePageException(ex);
         }
         finally {
            out.flush();
            _jspxFactory.releasePageContext(pageContext);
         }
      }
   }
```

Other than the program names, the difference between the two servlets is the location of the two scripting lines. In the scriptlet version, they are included in the middle of the `_jspService()` method, making the `fmt` and `now` variables local to that method. In the declaration version, however, they appear as the first entries inside the class. This makes the two variables *instance* variables, which are initialized when the servlet instance is first created and never updated: We will see shortly that this is not only undesirable, it's also dangerous.



## Primary Uses for Declarations

Declarations can contain any valid Java code, but they are most commonly used in three contexts:

- **Variable Declarations** Both class and instance variables can be declared and initialized.
- **Method Definitions** Duplicate or overly complex scriptlet code can be restructured into a main routine that calls other methods.
- **Inner Classes** Additional classes can be defined and made available to scriptlets, expressions, and other declaration code.

The remainder of this chapter considers each of these uses in detail.

## Variable Declarations

As illustrated in the preceding examples, declarations can be used to define and initialize variables. The variables will be available to scriptlets, expressions, and other declarations. These can be class variables (marked with the `static` keyword), as in the following example,

```
<%!
   static final String[] COLORS = {
```

```
         "#CA9A26",
         "#3BF428",
         "#F7E339",
         "#FF40FF",
      };
%>
<%
   for (int i = 0; i < COLORS.length; i++) {
      String color = COLORS[i];
%>
<DIV STYLE="background-color: <%= color%>;
            font-size: 12pt;
            font-weight: bold;">
   This is color <%= color %></DIV>
<% } %>
```

or instance variables, as the following shows, in a file named `vardec2.jsp`:

```
<%! int count; %>
<%
   count = 0;
   for (int i = 0; i < 10; i++) {
%>
Request <%= Integer.toHexString(request.hashCode()) %>
count = <%= ++count %><BR>
<%
      Thread.sleep(250);
   }
%>
```

In either case, the variable declaration is copied verbatim into the generated servlet as a top-level member of the enclosing class.

## Thread Safety and Instance Variables

The instance variable example `vardec2.jsp` contains a subtle flaw. Each time the JSP services a request, it sets the `count` variable to zero, and then enters a loop of ten iterations, incrementing the count and displaying it along with the request object hash code. When first tested, it might look like the output shown in Figure 8-1.

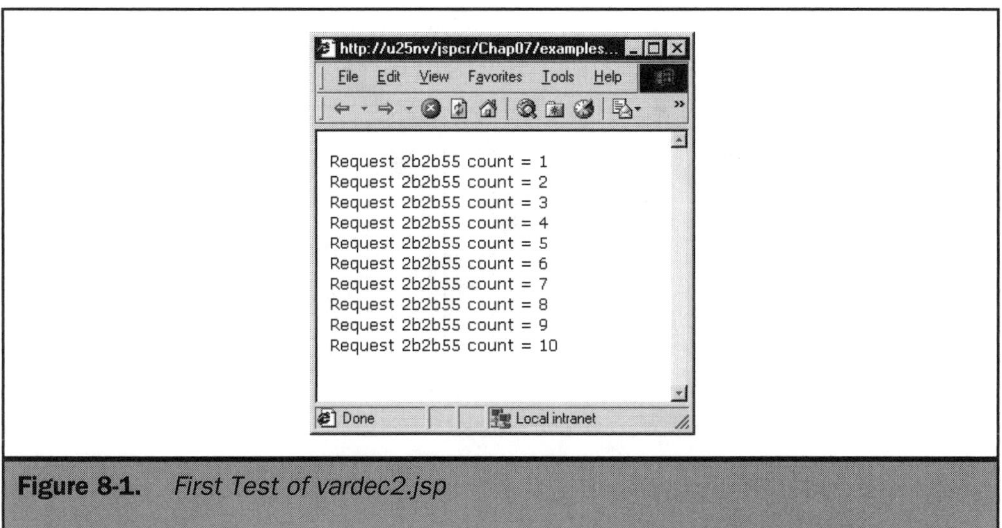


**Figure 8-1.** *First Test of vardec2.jsp*

But look what happens when two people request the JSP page at about the same time (now you know why we added the `Thread.sleep(250)`—to introduce enough of a delay to allow for the collision). Figures 8-2 and 8-3 show two requests being handled simultaneously.

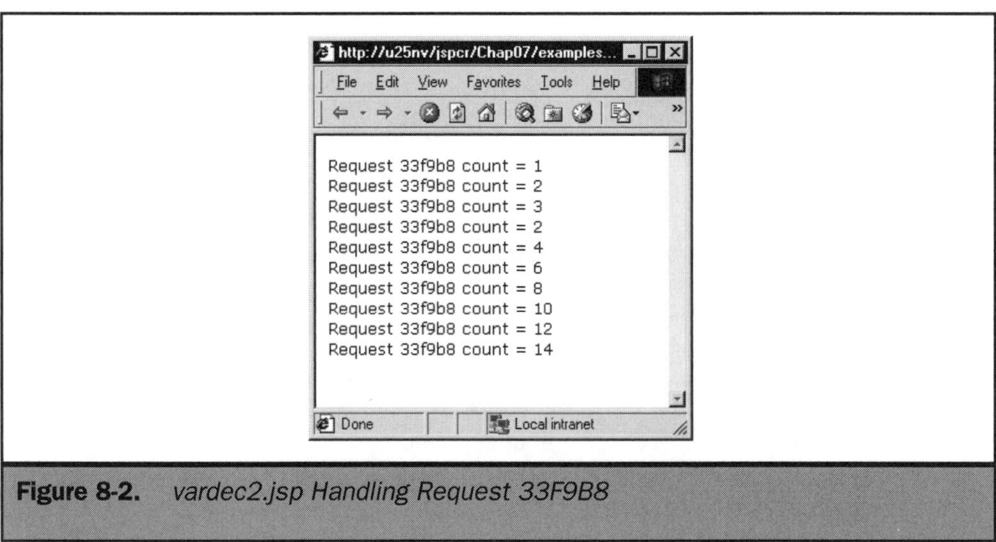


**Figure 8-2.** *vardec2.jsp Handling Request 33F9B8*

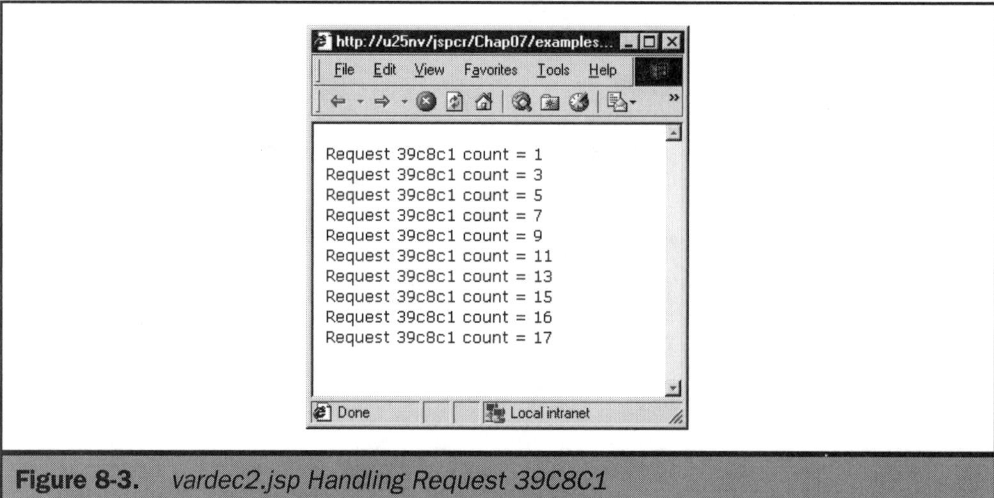


**Figure 8-3.** *vardec2.jsp Handling Request 39C8C1*

The first request starts off normally enough for the first three lines. But then the count drops back to 2, and appears to increment by 2 for the rest of the loop. Similarly, the second request starts at 1, but then skips all the even numbers. An examination of the generated source code shows what the problem is:

```
import javax.servlet.*;
import javax.servlet.http.*;
import javax.servlet.jsp.*;
import javax.servlet.jsp.tagext.*;
import java.io.PrintWriter;
import java.io.IOException;
import java.io.FileInputStream;
import java.io.ObjectInputStream;
import java.util.Vector;
import org.apache.jasper.runtime.*;
import java.beans.*;
import org.apache.jasper.JasperException;

public class vardec2 extends HttpJspBase
{
    // begin [file="vardec2.jsp";from=(0,3);to=(0,15)]
         int count;
    // end
```

```
static
{
}

public vardec2()
{
}

public void _jspService(
      HttpServletRequest request,
      HttpServletResponse  response)
   throws IOException, ServletException
{
   JspFactory _jspxFactory = null;
   PageContext pageContext = null;
   HttpSession session = null;
   ServletContext application = null;
   ServletConfig config = null;
   JspWriter out = null;
   Object page = this;
   String  _value = null;
   try {
      _jspxFactory = JspFactory.getDefaultFactory();
      response.setContentType("text/html;charset=8859_1");
      pageContext = _jspxFactory.getPageContext
         (this, request, response, "", true, 8192, true);

      application = pageContext.getServletContext();
      config = pageContext.getServletConfig();
      session = pageContext.getSession();
      out = pageContext.getOut();

      out.write("\r\n");

      count = 0;
      for (int i = 0; i < 10; i++) {
         out.write("\r\nRequest ");
         out.print( Integer.toHexString(request.hashCode()) );
         out.write("\r\ncount = ");
         out.print( ++count );
         out.write("<BR>\r\n");
         Thread.sleep(250);
```

```
            }
            out.write("\r\n");

        }
        catch (Exception ex) {
            if (out.getBufferSize() != 0)
                out.clearBuffer();
            pageContext.handlePageException(ex);
        }
        finally {
            out.flush();
            _jspxFactory.releasePageContext(pageContext);
        }
    }
}
```

The source of the problem is that count is an instance variable, not a local variable in the _jspService() method. Recall that JSP pages are compiled as servlets, which, by default, run as a single instance with separate threads to handle each request. This being the case, any instance variables are automatically shared between all request-handling threads. In the example, the first request got as far as 3, but then the thread that handled the second request entered _jspService() and reset the shared count variable back to zero. As the loop progressed, the two threads alternated every 125 milliseconds or so, each incrementing the value.

Chapter 14 discusses this problem and explores several solutions. The conclusion presenting itself here is that variable declarations in a JSP page are best used to handle *read-only* variables.

## Method Definitions

A more common use for declarations is to define additional methods. The syntax is no different than for any other method definitions, except for the <%! and %> delimiters:

```
<%!
    public int sum(int a, int b)
    {
        return a + b;
    }
%>
```

As with variable declarations, method definitions are copied verbatim into the generated servlet as top-level members outside the `_jspService()` method:

```
public class methdef1 extends HttpJspBase
{
   // begin [file="methdef1.jsp";from=(0,3);to=(5,0)]

        public int sum(int a, int b)
        {
           return a + b;
        }
   // end

   // ...

   public void _jspService(
         HttpServletRequest request,
         HttpServletResponse  response)
      throws IOException, ServletException
   {
      // ...
   }
}
```

A typical method definition in a JSP declaration would be for a utility method that reformats strings produced by a scriptlet. Consider the following JSP page that displays the value of several system properties in an HTML table:

```
<TABLE BORDER=1 CELLPADDING=3 CELLSPACING=0>
<%
   String[] propNames = {
      "java.awt.printerjob",
      "java.class.path",
      "java.class.version",
      "java.ext.dirs",
      "java.library.path",
   };
   for (int i = 0; i < propNames.length; i++) {
      String name = propNames[i];
      String value = System.getProperty(name);
%>
```

```
<TR>
   <TD ALIGN=LEFT VALIGN=TOP><%= name %></TD>
   <TD ALIGN=LEFT VALIGN=TOP><%= value %></TD>
</TR>
<%
   }
%>
</TABLE>
```

The output of the JSP page is shown in Figure 8-4. The problem with this table is several of the values are quite long, with no embedded spaces. This means the right-hand table cell is too long to be displayed in the window.

A simple solution for this is to shorten the property value strings. One quality the offending members have in common is they consist of a list of several values separated by semicolons. These can be shortened by inserting a <BR> tag after each semicolon, so the list will be displayed on multiple lines. This will make the table width requirement no longer than the longest list entry. This could be done with inline code in the scriptlet,

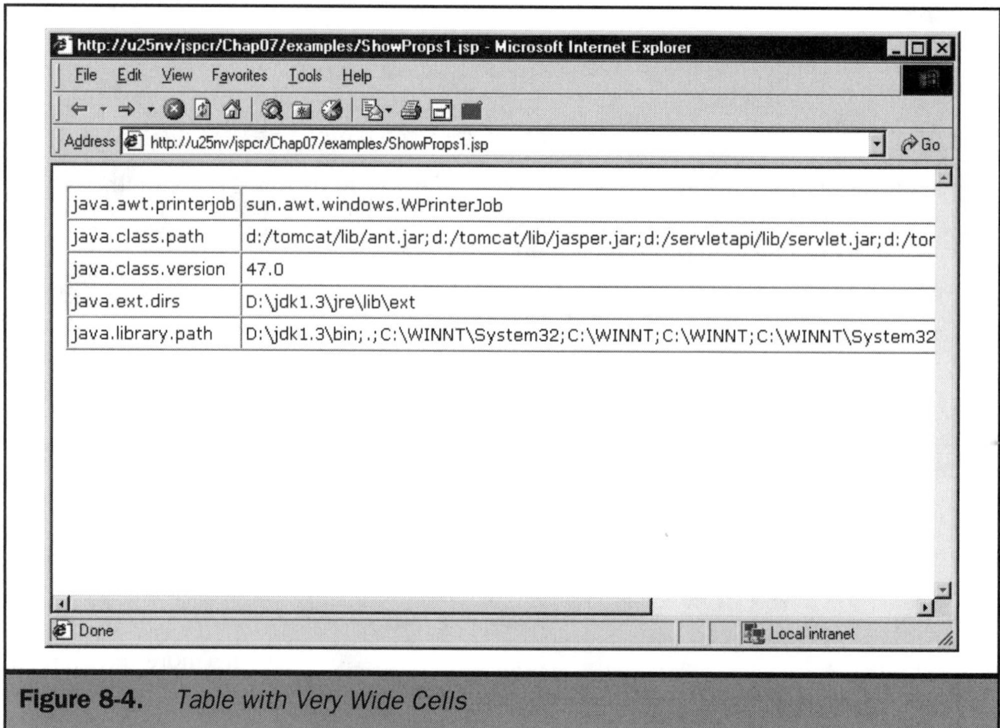


**Figure 8-4.** *Table with Very Wide Cells*

but a more readable solution would be to use a `normalize()` method that applies the necessary transformation. That way, the <%= value %> expression could simply be written <%= normalize(value) %>. The following shows the modified JSP page:

```
<TABLE BORDER=1 CELLPADDING=3 CELLSPACING=0>
<%
   String[] propNames = {
      "java.awt.printerjob",
      "java.class.path",
      "java.class.version",
      "java.ext.dirs",
      "java.library.path",
   };
   for (int i = 0; i < propNames.length; i++) {
      String name = propNames[i];
      String value = System.getProperty(name);
%>
<TR>
   <TD ALIGN=LEFT VALIGN=TOP><%= name %></TD>
   <TD ALIGN=LEFT VALIGN=TOP><%= normalize(value) %></TD>
</TR>
<%
   }
%>
</TABLE>
<%!
   private static final String normalize(String s)
   {
      StringBuffer sb = new StringBuffer();
      for (int i = 0; i < s.length(); i++) {
         char c = s.charAt(i);
         sb.append(c);
         if (c == ';')
            sb.append("<BR>");
      }
      return sb.toString();
   }
%>
```

This time, when the same properties are displayed, the table fits within a more reasonable window size (see Figure 8-5).

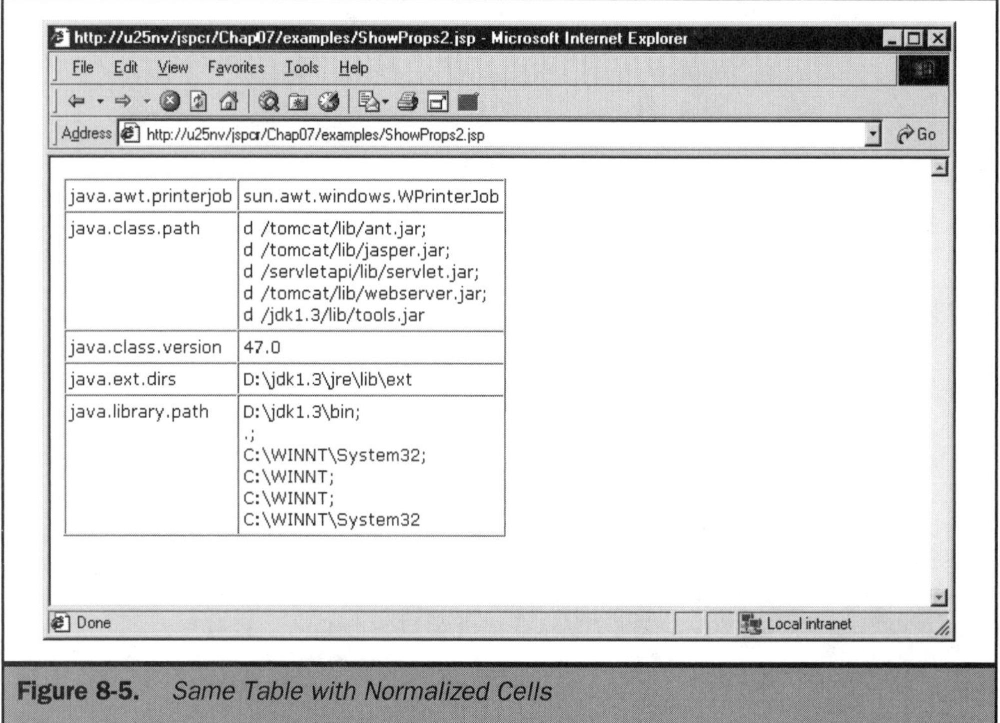


| | |
|---|---|
| java.awt.printerjob | sun.awt.windows.WPrinterJob |
| java.class.path | d /tomcat/lib/ant.jar;<br>d /tomcat/lib/jasper.jar;<br>d /servletapi/lib/servlet.jar;<br>d /tomcat/lib/webserver.jar;<br>d /jdk1.3/lib/tools.jar |
| java.class.version | 47.0 |
| java.ext.dirs | D:\jdk1.3\jre\lib\ext |
| java.library.path | D:\jdk1.3\bin;<br>.;<br>C:\WINNT\System32;<br>C:\WINNT;<br>C:\WINNT;<br>C:\WINNT\System32 |

**Figure 8-5.** *Same Table with Normalized Cells*

# Overriding jspInit and jspDestroy

In the preceding example, the string manipulation could have been done with inline code in the scriptlet, rather than by a method call. In some circumstances, that is not possible. For example, if resources need to be acquired or threads started when a JSP page is loaded, these functions should be performed in the context of the servlet `init()` and `destroy()` methods.

The JSP 1.1 Specification expressly forbids page authors from overriding any of the servlet lifecycle methods directly, including `init()` and `destroy()`[1]. However, it provides two special methods named `jspInit()` and `jspDestroy()` that accomplish the same purpose. These methods are automatically called from within `init()` and `destroy()`, and have empty definitions in the parent JSP page implementation. In

1 JSP 1.1 Specification, Section 3.1. Although some servlet engines do not enforce this restriction, it would be unwise to ignore it.

Tomcat, for example, the base JSP class `org.apache.jasper.runtime.HttpJspBase` defines `init()` and `jspInit()` as follows:

```
public final void init(ServletConfig config)
   throws ServletException
   {
      this.config = config;
      jspInit();
   }

public void jspInit()
{
}
```



Similarly, it defines `destroy()` and `jspDestroy()` as follows:

```
public final void destroy()
{
   jspDestroy();
}
public void jspDestroy()
{
}
```

The use of the `final` keyword ensures `init()` and `destroy()` themselves cannot be overridden. This, in turn, guarantees `jspInit()` and `jspDestroy()` will always be called. To add something to the initialization phase of a JSP, the necessary code should be entered in a JSP declaration[2]:

```
public void jspInit()
{
   TimerThread t = new TimerThread();
   t.start();
}
```

2 Curiously enough, the JSP 1.1 specification makes no provision for throwing an exception from jspInit(), even though init() itself can do so. What can be done if the JSP detects a fatal error during its jspInit() execution is not clear.

## Access to Implicit Objects

Unlike scriptlets and expressions, declarations have no access to the implicit objects described in Chapter 7. The reason for this is apparent when you remember that methods in declarations are defined outside the `_jspService()` method. Therefore, if a declaration method needs access to one or more of these objects, the objects must be passed somehow from `_jspService()`. You can do this in several ways:

- Pass the objects as individual parameters. This is easy to do, but tends to become unwieldy if more than a few parameters are necessary.
- Pass the `pageContext` implicit object as a parameter. From the page context, all the other variables can be accessed indirectly.
- Pass a structure containing all the variables of interest as a single parameter. You see how to do this in the next section.

The second technique (passing the page context) is illustrated in the following code:

```
<%@ page import="java.io.*,java.util.*" %>
<%!
   public void showSessionID(PageContext pc)
      throws IOException
   {
      JspWriter out = pc.getOut();
      HttpSession session = pc.getSession();
      Date created = new Date(session.getCreationTime());
      out.println("The session was created at " + created);
   }
%>
<%
   showSessionID(pageContext);
%>
```

The `showSessionID()` method is able to extract the `JspWriter` and `HttpSession` objects from the page context and use them to write to the current output stream.

## Inner Classes

Just like any other Java class, a JSP page can define inner classes. *Inner classes* are useful for running background threads or encapsulating data structures. When used properly, they can preserve the object-oriented character of a Java program, which can sometimes be lost in an event-driven environment like JSP.

An inner class can be useful as a data structure that holds implict and other variables. The page context acts as a wrapper for other objects in the servlet context, session, request, and page. It also has `getAttribute()` and `setAttribute()` methods for additional user-defined fields, but these must be objects (not primitives like `int` and `double`) and must be cast to the appropriate type when retrieved. An inner class is an alternative that solves the same problem in a type-safe manner. An example of this technique is illustrated in the following:

```
<%@ page import="java.io.*,java.util.*" %>
<%!
   /**
   * Inner class for passing parameters between methods
   */
   class Parameters {
      JspWriter out;
      HttpSession session;
      String url;
   }

   public void showSessionID(Parameters parms)
      throws IOException
   {
      JspWriter out         = parms.out;
      HttpSession session   = parms.session;
      String url            = parms.url;
      Date created = new Date(session.getCreationTime());
      out.println("The session was created at " + created
         + "<P>");
      out.println("The url parameter was " + url);
   }
%>
<%
   Parameters parms = new Parameters();
   parms.out = out;
   parms.session = session;
   parms.url = request.getParameter("url");
   showSessionID(parms);
%>
```

The generated servlet includes both the inner class and the method definition inside the top level of the class, and the scriptlet inside `_jspService()`:

```
import javax.servlet.*;
import javax.servlet.http.*;
import javax.servlet.jsp.*;
import javax.servlet.jsp.tagext.*;
import java.io.PrintWriter;
import java.io.IOException;
import java.io.FileInputStream;
import java.io.ObjectInputStream;
import java.util.Vector;
import org.apache.jasper.runtime.*;
import java.beans.*;
import org.apache.jasper.JasperException;
import java.io.*;
import java.util.*;

public class PassInnerClass extends HttpJspBase
{
   // begin [file="PassInnerClass.jsp";from=(1,3);to=(22,0)]

      /**
      * Inner class for passing parameters between methods
      */
      class Parameters {
         JspWriter out;
         HttpSession session;
         String url;
      }

      public void showSessionID(Parameters parms)
      throws IOException
      {
         JspWriter out          = parms.out;
         HttpSession session    = parms.session;
         String url             = parms.url;
         Date created = new Date(session.getCreationTime());
         out.println("The session was created at " + created
            + "<P>");
```

```
            out.println("The url parameter was " + url);
         }
      // end

      // ...

      public void _jspService(
            HttpServletRequest request,
            HttpServletResponse  response)
         throws IOException, ServletException
      {
         // ...

         // begin [file="PassInnerClass.jsp";from=(23,2);to=(29,0)]

         Parameters parms = new Parameters();
         parms.out = out;
         parms.session = session;
         parms.url = request.getParameter("url");
         showSessionID(parms);

         // end
      }
   }
```



## Summary

Chapter 7 covered scriptlets and expressions. This chapter introduced a third type of scripting element, a JSP *declaration*.

Like a scriptlet, a declaration is used to incorporate Java statements into a JSP page. The key difference between the two is where the JSP container writes the code in the generated servlet. With a scriptlet, the code becomes part of the `_jspService()` method, whereas code in a declaration becomes top-level code in the servlet class. This distinction is important to understand because it affects the context in which the code operates.

Declarations have three primary uses:

- **Variable declarations** Both class and instance variables can be defined, although care must be taken to ensure that write access to the variables is synchronized because servlets, by default, are multithreaded. The most practical use of variable declarations is for static final constants.

- **Method definitions** Additional methods can be added to the generated servlet by means of JSP declarations. Because the generated code is not inside the `_jspService()` method, however, it does not have access to the implicit variables (`request`, `response`, `out`, and so forth). These variables must be explicitly passed to the method if they are to be used. Declarations can be used to override the `jspInit()` and `jspDestroy()` methods.
- **Inner classes** Declarations provide a convenient means for writing inner classes. This chapter describes using an inner class as a data structure for passing a set of variables between methods in the generated servlet.

# Chapter 9

## Request Dispatching

In large-scale Web development projects, having HTTP requests handled by more than one server-side component is often desirable. Several reasons exist for this:

- **Elimination of redundancy** Many features of a Web site are common to all pages, such as headers and footers, navigation bars, and other elements of the look and feel. Rather than duplicate the HTML that generates these features, being able to write them once and use them in a number of places is useful.
- **Separation of content and presentation** Because Java can be used freely in any part of a JSP, you can easily end up with code that both generates information and presents it, perhaps reading from a database, performing calculations, and generating HTML tables. Changing both the logic and the appearance of the page may be necessary later. Such code can quickly become overly complex. What makes more sense is to separate the pure Java code that accesses the database and applies business logic from the JSP code that creates an output Web page.

This chapter examines features of the JSP environment that allow requests to be forwarded and the contents or output of other resources to be included. The chapter also discusses how the `RequestDispatcher` class works and concludes with a comparison of two JSP development models.

## Anatomy of Request Processing

The servlet engine that handles servlet and JSP requests can be part of the Web server itself (referred to as the *in-process* model) or it can run in a separate process. In the latter case, the Web server contains a component referred to as a connector. The *connector* intercepts servlet requests and passes them on to the servlet engine by an implementation-dependent protocol[1]. Other requests are handled by the Web server as usual. Figure 9-1 illustrates this out-of-process model.

When the servlet engine receives a request, it assembles all the details about the request into an `HttpServletRequest` object. These details include the request headers, the URI, the query string, any parameters sent, and so on. Similarly, it initializes an `HttpServletResponse` object that can hold response headers and the response output stream. It then invokes the servlet's `service()` method (the `_jspService()` method, if the servlet is a JSP), passing it references to the two objects, as shown in Figure 9-2.

1 JRun features connectors for several widely used Web servers, and employs a proprietary protocol to communicate requests to its servlet engine. Tomcat uses a protocol known as `ajp12` (developed originally for Apache JServ) to send requests and responses between components.

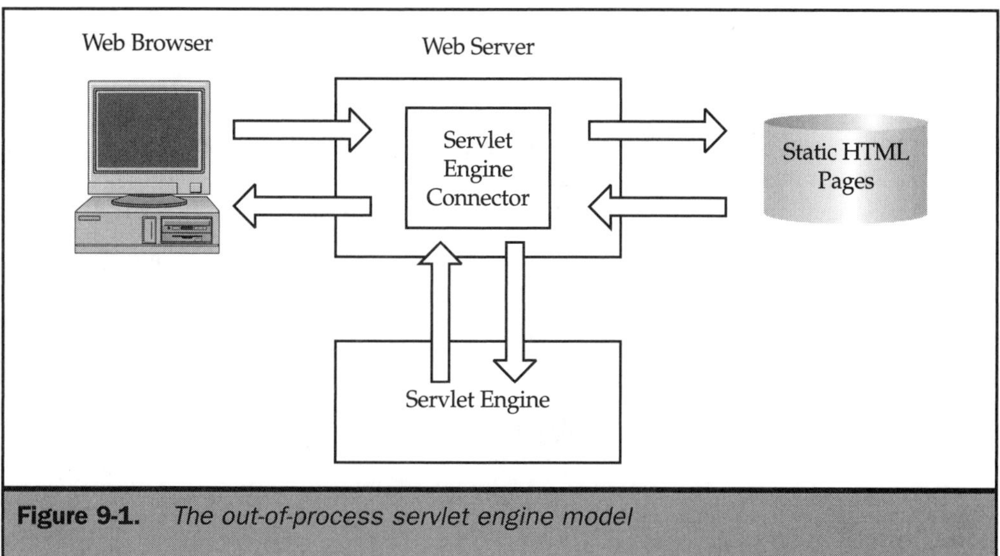


**Figure 9-1.** *The out-of-process servlet engine model*

A simple JSP can extract what it needs from the request object, perform the necessary calculations and other logic, and then create output using the response object. The remainder of this chapter examines how larger and more complex Web applications can operate on these request and response objects, passing them through more than one servlet or JSP.

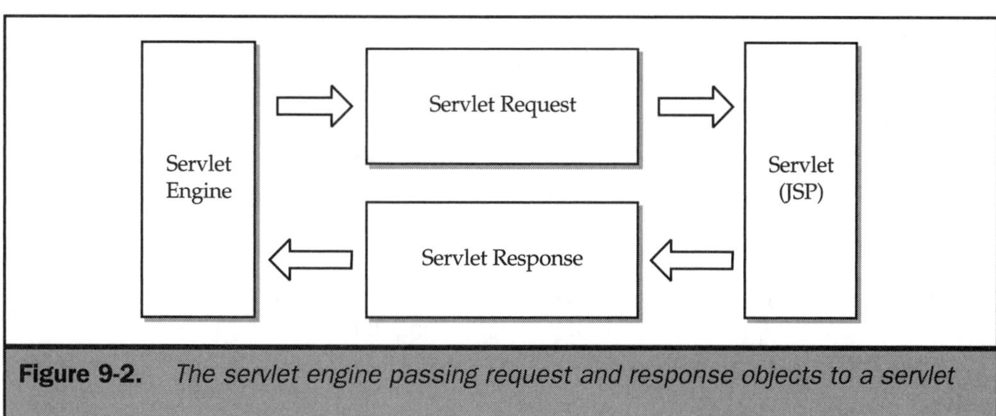


**Figure 9-2.** *The servlet engine passing request and response objects to a servlet*

## Including Other Resources

HTML itself does not have a direct means for including data from other files in its output. This is unfortunate, because a great deal of HTML markup is common to a number of pages in a typical Web site—corporate logos, copyright notices, navigation links, and other features. Besides these static sources of text and images, dynamic content may need to be included. JSP provides two means incorporating such data:

- **The `<%@ include %>` directive** is used to copy static text into the JSP source code before it is transformed into Java servlet source code and compiled. Typically, this text is HTML code, but it can be anything that could appear in a JSP page.
- **The `<jsp:include>` action** causes the servlet engine to invoke another URL and merge its output with that of the original JSP page.

A key point to remember in building a mental model is the `<%@ include %>` directive is performed once, at compilation time, whereas the `<jsp:include>` action is performed each time a request is made. The next two sections describe each of these JSP components and how they operate.

## The include Directive

The syntax of the `include` directive is as follows:

<%@ include file="*filename*" %>

The included filename must be a relative URL specification, meaning it contains only path information, not protocol or server information. As a consequence, only resources in the current servlet context can be included by this means.

If the filename begins with "/", it is considered to be absolute with respect to the top of the servlet context. Otherwise, the filename is considered to be relative to the current JSP page. For example, if a Web application has a `products` subdirectory and the `products/search.jsp` page contains the directive

```
<%@ include file="/includes/header.inc" %>
```

then the file that would be included is `<path>/includes/header.inc`, where `<path>` is the Web application mount point. If, instead, the directive is

```
<%@ include file="includes/header.inc" %>
```

then the file would be `<path>/products/includes/header.inc`.

## How It Works

When a <%@ include %> directive is encountered, the JSP container reads the specified file and merges its contents into the JSP source code currently being parsed. For example, if `flavors.jsp` contains

```
<H3>Flavors</H3>
Our most popular flavors are:
<%@ include file="flavor_list.html" %>
Try them all!
```

and if `flavor_list.html` contains

```
<OL>
<LI>Chocolate
<LI>Strawberry
<LI>Vanilla
</OL>
```

the HTML sent to the Web browser is exactly the same as if `flavors.jsp` contained this:

```
<H3>Flavors</H3>
Our most popular flavors are:
<OL>
<LI>Chocolate
<LI>Strawberry
<LI>Vanilla
</OL>
Try them all!
```

We can see the interleaving of the two files in the servlet source code generated by the Tomcat reference implementation[2]:

```
// begin [file="flavors.jsp";from=(0,0);to=(2,0)]
   out.write("<H3>Flavors</H3>\r\n");
   out.write("Our most popular flavors are:\r\n");
```

2 Generated source code examples have been slightly reformatted for readability.

```
// end

// begin [file="flavor_list.html";from=(0,0);to=(5,0)]
   out.write("<OL>\r\n");
   out.write("<LI>Chocolate\r\n");
   out.write("<LI>Strawberry\r\n");
   out.write("<LI>Vanilla\r\n");
   out.write("</OL>\r\n");
// end

// begin [file="flavors.jsp";from=(2,38);to=(4,0)]
   out.write("\r\nTry them all!\r\n");
// end
```

Other than the filename change in the comment, there is no way to tell that the ordered list was not simply coded in the original JSP page. In this respect, the `<%@ include %>` directive is similar to the C language `#include` preprocessor directive.

## Effect of Changes in an Included File

What happens if the `flavor_list.html` file is modified? The JSP 1.1 specification makes no provision for notifying the JSP container that an included file has changed, although it does not prohibit it, and a robust JSP container should do so. JRun incorporates dependency names and last modification times into the generated source code so it can determine when files are out of date:

```
private static final String[] __dependencies__ = {
   "/Chap09/examples/flavors.jsp",
   "/Chap09/examples/flavor_list.html",
   null
   };

private static final long[] __times__ = {
   958963142531L,
   958961380337L,
   0L
   };
```

The key point to remember is the file included is the file that exists at compilation time because this is when the `<%@ include %>` directive is processed. This is why the filename cannot be a run-time expression. It also means the included file must exist at compilation time.

## Using the include Directive to Copy Source Code

In addition to being used to copy HTML, the `include` directive can be used to include Java source code as a declaration section. For example, a commonly used utility function can be stored in a file and incorporated into a JSP page with the `include` directive. A typical example would be a function that filters out characters with special meaning in HTML and replaces them with symbolic printable equivalents:

```
<%!
public static final String webify(String s)
{
   StringBuffer sb = new StringBuffer();
   int n = s.length();
   for (int i = 0; i < n; i++) {
      char c = s.charAt(i);
      switch (c) {
         case '<': sb.append("&lt;"); break;
         case '>': sb.append("&gt;"); break;
         case '&': sb.append("&amp;"); break;
         case '"': sb.append("&quot;"); break;
         default:  sb.append(c); break;
      }
   }
   return sb.toString();
}
%>
```

Once defined (by being included), this function can be used in scriptlets and expressions in the including JSP page:

```
<%@ include file="webify.jsp" %>

Preformatted text can be coded with the
<%= webify("<PRE> and </PRE>") %> tags.
```

Likewise, constants used throughout an application can be coded in a JSP declaration handled by the `include` directive:

```
<%!
   static final int BORDER = 1;
   static final int CELLPADDING = 3;
   static final int CELLSPACING = 0;
   static final String[] COLORS = {"#C0C0C0", "#E0E0E0"};
%>
```

If the declaration previously shown is stored in the `TableConstants.jsp` file, then a JSP page can generate a table with rows of alternating background colors as follows:

```
<%@ include file="TableConstants.jsp" %>

<TABLE BORDER="<%= BORDER %>"
       CELLPADDING="<%= CELLPADDING %>"
       CELLSPACING="<%= CELLSPACING %>"
       >
<%
   for (int i = 0; i < 10; i++) {
      int x = i+1;
      int xsq = x*x;
%>
<TR BGCOLOR="<%= COLORS[i % 2] %>">
   <TD><%= x %></TD> <TD><%= xsq %></TD>
</TR>
<%
   }
%>
</TABLE>
```

**Note** *Watch for two things when using the include directive for source code declarations. First, the JSP 1.1 specification does not guarantee pages that include code in this manner will be notified if the code changes. Second, the included code uses the namespace of the including page, so care must be exercised to ensure no duplicate variable definitions occur.*

## The <jsp:include> Action

In contrast to the `include` directive, the `jsp:include` action is interpreted each time a request is made. The syntax of this action is

<jsp:include page="*resourcename*" flush="true" />

The included resource name must be a relative URL specification, containing only path information. The resource name is mapped to the current servlet context in the same way as the filename in an `include` directive. If the name begins with "/", it refers to a path beginning at the top of the servlet context; otherwise, it is interpreted as a path relative to the directory containing the calling JSP. The flush attribute (which is mandatory) is used to indicate whether to flush the output `JspWriter` before including the resource. The only valid value in JSP 1.1 is *true*.

## How It Works

The `<jsp:include>` action is parsed by the JSP compiler but, rather than being executed at compilation time, it is converted into Java code that invokes the named resource at request time. The resource can be a static data source, such as an HTML file or a dynamic source, such as a JSP page or a servlet. Returning to our ice cream flavors example, if `flavors.jsp` might contain

```
<H3>Flavors</H3>
Our most popular flavors are:
<jsp:include page="/servlet/FlavorList" flush="true" />
Try them all!
```

where `FlavorList` is a *servlet* that extracts the favorite flavors from a database or some other dynamic source:

```
import java.io.*;
import java.net.*;
import java.sql.*;
import java.util.*;

import javax.servlet.*;
import javax.servlet.http.*;

/**
* Returns the current list of favorite flavors
*/
public class FlavorListServlet extends HttpServlet
{
   public static final String JDBC_DRIVER =
      "sun.jdbc.odbc.JdbcOdbcDriver";

   public static final String URL =
      "jdbc:odbc:IceCream";

   public void doGet(
         HttpServletRequest request,
         HttpServletResponse response)
      throws ServletException, IOException
   {
      PrintWriter out = response.getWriter();
```

```
Connection con = null;
try {

   // Connect to the ice cream database

   Class.forName(JDBC_DRIVER);
   con = DriverManager.getConnection(URL);

   // Run a query to get the top flavors

   Statement stmt = con.createStatement();
   String sql =
      "SELECT  RANK, NAME"
      + "   FROM flavors"
      + "   WHERE (RANK <= 3)"
      + "   ORDER BY RANK"
      ;

   ResultSet rs = stmt.executeQuery(sql);

   // Print as an ordered list

   out.println("<OL>");
   while (rs.next()) {
      int rank = rs.getInt(1);
      String name = rs.getString(2);
      out.println("   <LI>" + name);
   }
   out.println("</OL>");
}
catch (Exception e) {
   e.printStackTrace();
}

// Close the database

finally {
   if (con != null) {
      try {
         con.close();
      }
      catch (SQLException ignore) {}
```

```
            }
        }
    }
}
```

When `flavors.jsp` is invoked, it produces the following output:

```
<H3>Flavors</H3>
Our most popular flavors are:
<OL>
   <LI>Espresso Chip
   <LI>Orange Cream
   <LI>Peanut Butter
</OL>
Try them all!
```



The resulting HTML may look similar, but the underlying mechanism is completely different, as can be seen in the source code of the servlet Tomcat generates:

```
// begin [file="flavors.jsp";from=(0,0);to=(2,0)]
   out.write("<H3>Flavors</H3>\r\n");
   out.write("Our most popular flavors are:\r\n");
// end

// begin [file="flavors.jsp";from=(2,0);to=(2,55)]
   {
      out.flush();
      pageContext.include("/servlet/FlavorList");
   }
// end

// begin [file="flavors.jsp";from=(2,55);to=(4,0)]
   out.write("\r\nTry them all!\r\n");
// end
```

Rather than containing the ordered list of flavors, the JSP invokes the `pageContext.include()` method to run the servlet that accesses the database. The output of the servlet is included in the JSP output and the JSP resumes control. Where the `include` directive was similar to the C language `#include` preprocessor directive, the `<jsp:include>` action is more like a C language function call.

## Restrictions

A JSP page invoked by a `<jsp:include>` action has access to all the implicit objects available to the calling JSP, including the `response` object. It can write to and flush the `out` object, but it cannot set response headers. For example, you can neither specify a different content type nor can you use a `<jsp:include>` action to handle authentication with the `WWW-Authenticate` header. Why not? Because it is too late—the output stream was flushed before the JSP was included, so any headers present have already been written to the client.

## Run-time Features

Because a `<jsp:include>` is evaluated at run time, the page it refers to can be supplied in a run-time expression, rather than being hardcoded. The following JSP page is designed to be a comprehensive view of an HTTP servlet request. Rather than being a long, scrolling list of attribute names and values, the page simulates a tabbed dialog box, with attributes broken down into logical groups and radio buttons along the top used to select which group to show.

```
<%@ page import="java.util.*" %>
<%!
   // Table row colors

   static final String[] COLORS = {"#E0E0E0", "#F0F0F0"};

   // Array of tab codes, labels, and JSP's

   public static final String[][] TABS = {
      {"HD", "Headers", "ShowRequestHeaders.jsp"},
      {"PM", "Parameters", "ShowParameters.jsp"},
      {"SR", "ServletRequest Methods",
         "ShowServletRequestMethodValues.jsp"},
      {"HR", "HttpServletRequest Methods",
         "ShowHttpServletRequestMethodValues.jsp"},
   };
%>
<HTML>
<HEAD>
<TITLE>Show Request</TITLE>
</HEAD>
<BODY>
<H2>Show Request</H2>
<FORM>
<TABLE BORDER=0 CELLPADDING=3 CELLSPACING=0>
```

```
   <%-- Radio buttons for selecting the page --%>

   <TR>
      <TD ALIGN=LEFT>
<%
   String which = request.getParameter("which");
   if (which == null)
      which = TABS[0][0];
   String jspToRun = null;
   for (int i = 0; i < TABS.length; i++) {
      String tabCode  = TABS[i][0];
      String tabLabel = TABS[i][1];
      String tabJSP   = TABS[i][2];
      String CHECKED  = "";
      if (which.equals(tabCode)) {
         CHECKED = "CHECKED";
         jspToRun = tabJSP;
      }
%>
   <INPUT NAME="which"
          TYPE="RADIO"
          VALUE="<%= tabCode %>"
          <%= CHECKED %>
          onClick="this.form.submit()"
          ><%= tabLabel %>
<%
   }
%>
      <P>
      </TD>
   </TR>

   <TR>
      <TD ALIGN=CENTER VALIGN=TOP>

      <%-- Page showing details of the request --%>

      <jsp:include page="<%= jspToRun %>" flush="true" />

      <%-- Resulting table --%>

      <TABLE BORDER=1 CELLPADDING=3 CELLSPACING=0 WIDTH=600>
```

```
        <TR>
           <TH COLSPAN=2 ALIGN=LEFT BGCOLOR="#000000">
              <FONT SIZE="+1" COLOR="#FFFFFF">
              <%= request.getAttribute("_table_title") %>
              </FONT>
           </TH>
        </TR>
        <TR>
           <TH WIDTH=200 ALIGN=LEFT>Name</TH>
           <TH WIDTH=400 ALIGN=LEFT>Value</TH>
        </TR>
        <%
           Map entries = (Map)
              request.getAttribute("_table_entries");
           Iterator iNames = entries.keySet().iterator();
           int row = 0;
           while (iNames.hasNext()) {
              String name = (String) iNames.next();
              Object value = entries.get(name);
        %>
        <TR BGCOLOR="<%= COLORS[row % 2] %>">
           <TD ALIGN=LEFT VALIGN=TOP><B><%= name %></B></TD>
           <TD ALIGN=LEFT VALIGN=TOP><%= value %></TD>
        </TR>
        <%
              row++;
           }
        %>
        </TABLE>
        <P>
        </TD>
     </TR>

</TABLE>
</FORM>
</BODY>
</HTML>
```

The categories available for display are coded in a static `String` array. For each category, a two-character abbreviation exists: a label and the name of a JSP page that will extract the desired data. There are four categories of attributes:

- Request Headers
- Parameters

- Methods in ServletRequest
- Methods in HttpServletRequest

The string array provides all the information needed to generate the page. The radio buttons are contained in a self-referring HTML form and are generated in a loop, with the two-character abbreviation used as the VALUE attribute and the label as the visible text. When a radio button is clicked, the form is submitted, with the value of the button supplying the value of the `which` parameter. Figure 9-3 shows the initial display, which is the request headers category. When another radio button is clicked (for example, the ServletRequest Method button), a different table appears in the body of the table (see Figure 9-4).

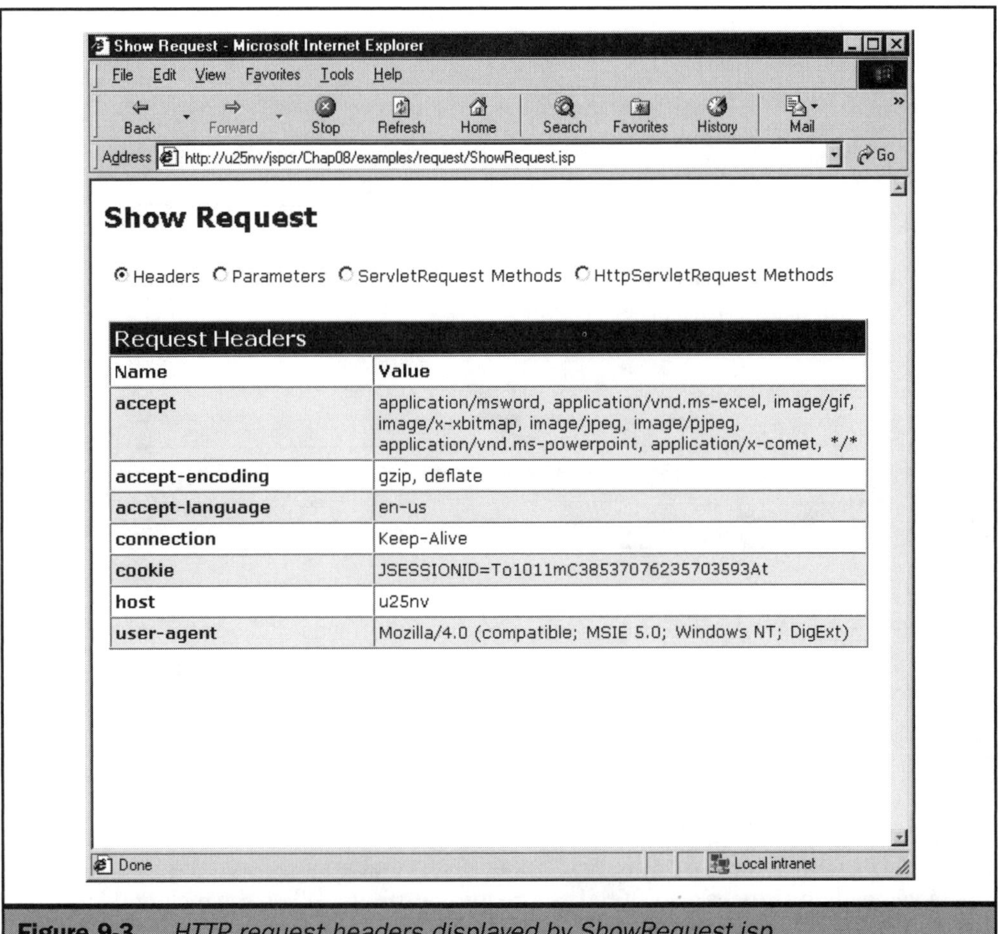


**Figure 9-3.** *HTTP request headers displayed by ShowRequest.jsp*

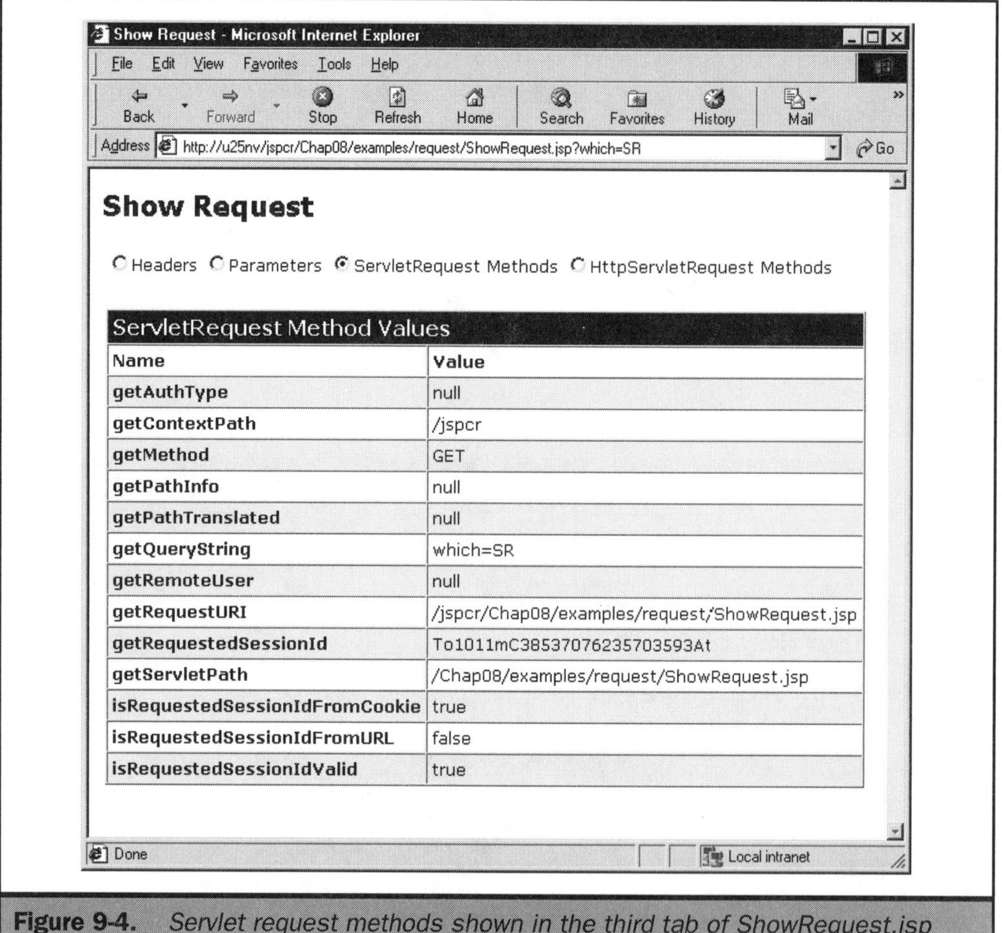


**Figure 9-4.** *Servlet request methods shown in the third tab of ShowRequest.jsp*

The ShowRequest.jsp determines which radio button was clicked and selects the corresponding JSP filename from the string array. This filename is then passed in a JSP expression to the `<jsp:include>` action:

```
<jsp:include page="<%= jspToRun %>" flush="true" />
```

Each of the individual table generating pages creates a list of attribute names and values, and writes them to a `java.util.Map` object that is stored as a request attribute. The table heading string is also stored as a request attribute. When the included JSP completes, the map is retrieved from the request attribute and rendered in an HTML table. The JSP that generates the Request Headers tab is shown in the following:

```
<%@ page import="java.util.*" %>
<%
   Enumeration eNames = request.getHeaderNames();
   if (eNames.hasMoreElements()) {
      String title = "Request Headers";
      Map entries = new TreeMap();
      while (eNames.hasMoreElements()) {
         String name = (String) eNames.nextElement();
         String value = request.getHeader(name);
         entries.put(name, value);
      }
      request.setAttribute("_table_title", title);
      request.setAttribute("_table_entries", entries);
   }
%>
```



This capability to select a page to be included based on run-time information is a useful characteristic of JSP-based Web applications because it allows complex processing to be built on table-driven logic.

## Passing Parameters to the Included JSP

Parameters can be passed to JSP pages that are invoked through `<jsp:include>` actions to provide additional customization. The syntax in this case would be

<jsp:include page="*pageName*" flush="true">
<jsp:param name="*parm1Name*" value="*parm1Value*" />
<jsp:param name="*parm2Name*" value="*parm2Value*" />
</jsp:include>

The parameters are passed to the included JSP the same as ordinary form parameters, and can be retrieved with `request.getParameter(name)`. If the parameter name is the same as one the JSP is already using, both values are passed and can be retrieved as an array of strings using `getParameterValues(name)`.

The following JSP illustrates how this technique can be used. It includes the same page twice, using different parameters each time.

```
<%
   // Diameter of the earth in kilometers

   int distance = 12756;
```

```
%>

<H4>Diameter of the Earth in SI (Metric) Units</H4>
<jsp:include page="ShowDiameter.jsp" flush="true">
   <jsp:param name="dist" value="<%= distance %>" />
   <jsp:param name="units" value="SI" />
</jsp:include>

<H4>Diameter of the Earth in U.S. Customary Units</H4>
<jsp:include page="ShowDiameter.jsp" flush="true">
   <jsp:param name="dist" value="<%= distance %>" />
   <jsp:param name="units" value="US" />
</jsp:include>
```

Two parameters are passed:

- **dist** The distance in kilometers.
- **units** "SI" if metric units are desired, "US" otherwise.

The `ShowDiameter.jsp` page retrieves the kilometer distance, converts it to an integer, and finds the mile equivalent. Then, based on the unit of measure code passed in the units parameter, it displays the distance in either SI or U.S. units.

```
<%
   String dist = request.getParameter("dist");
   int kilometers = Integer.parseInt(dist);
   double miles = kilometers / 1.609344;

   String units = request.getParameter("units");
   if (units.equals("SI")) {
   %> Diameter = <%= kilometers %> km <%
   }
   else {
   %> Diameter = <%= miles %> miles <%
   }
%>
```

Figure 9-5 shows the results.

## Retrieving the Original URI

When a page is invoked in a `<jsp:include>` action, it uses the same request object as its including page, which means `request.getRequestURI()` and

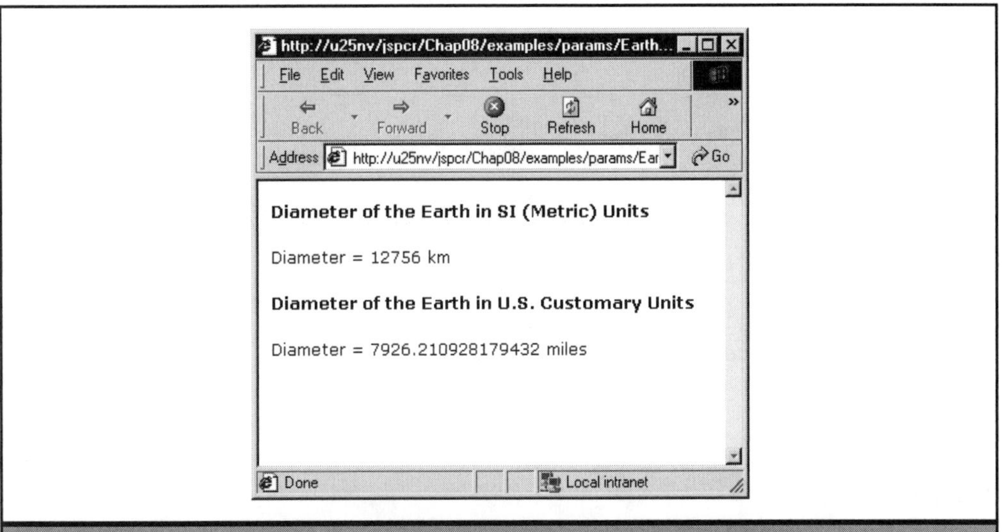


**Figure 9-5.** *A JSP page that includes the same page twice with different parameters*



`request.getServletPath()` return the path to the page originally handling the request, not the current page. The equivalent values for the included page, however, are available as attributes of the request. This is illustrated in `ShowPath1.jsp`:

```
<PRE>
In ShowPath1.jsp:

   request.getRequestURI()
      = <%= request.getRequestURI() %>

   request.getServletPath()
      = <%= request.getServletPath() %>

</PRE>
<jsp:include page="ShowPath2.jsp" flush="true"/>
```

and the page it includes, `ShowPath2.jsp`:

```
<PRE>
In ShowPath2.jsp:

   request.getRequestURI()
```

```
         = <%= request.getRequestURI() %>

      request.getServletPath()
         = <%= request.getServletPath() %>

      javax.servlet.include.request_uri
         = <%= request.getAttribute
         ("javax.servlet.include.request_uri") %>

      javax.servlet.include.servlet_path
         = <%= request.getAttribute
         ("javax.servlet.include.servlet_path") %>
</PRE>
```

The output of the two pages is as follows:

```
In ShowPath1.jsp:

   request.getRequestURI()
      = /jspcr/Chap09/examples/ShowPath1.jsp

   request.getServletPath()
      = /Chap09/examples/ShowPath1.jsp

In ShowPath2.jsp:

   request.getRequestURI()
      = /jspcr/Chap09/examples/ShowPath1.jsp

   request.getServletPath()
      = /Chap09/examples/ShowPath1.jsp

   javax.servlet.include.request_uri
      = /jspcr/Chap09/examples/ShowPath2.jsp

   javax.servlet.include.servlet_path
      = /Chap09/examples/ShowPath2.jsp
```

The set of attributes that can be retrieved in this fashion is listed in Table 9-1.

| Attribute Name | Equivalent Method |
|---|---|
| javax.servlet.include.request_uri | request.getRequestURI() |
| javax.servlet.include.context_path | request.getContextPath() |
| javax.servlet.include.servlet_path | request.getServletPath() |
| javax.servlet.include.path_info | request.getPathInfo() |
| javax.servlet.include.query_string | request.getQueryString() |

**Table 9-1.** *Request Attributes That Describe an Included JSP Page*



## Which Method to Use

The include directive and the <jsp:include> action perform similar functions, and each has its advantages. The decision to use one or the other should take into account whether the inclusion needs to be done at run time. The following table compares the two options:

| Criterion | <%@ include %> | <jsp:include> |
|---|---|---|
| Compilation time | Slower—resource must be parsed | Slightly faster. |
| Execution time | Slightly faster | Slower—resource must be resolved each time. |
| Flexibility | Less—page name is fixed | More—page can be chosen at run time. |

## Forwarding Requests

To facilitate splitting a Web application into content and presentation, the JSP environment provides the `<jsp:forward>` action, which allows requests to be forwarded from one page to another, or to a servlet. The syntax is

```
<jsp:forward page="page" />
```

where `page` is a URI relative to the current page, or an absolute URI with respect to the top of the servlet context. Like `<jsp:include>`, the `<jsp:forward>` action can use a run-time expression for the page name. Similarly, it can pass parameters to the new JSP using the following syntax:

```
<jsp:forward page="page">
<jsp:param name="name_1" value="value_1" />
<jsp:param name="name_2" value="value_2" />
...
<jsp:param name="name_n" value="value_n" />
</jsp:forward>
```

When a `<jsp:forward>` action is executed, the named page is loaded and the current page is terminated. The new page has access to the request and response objects, and is expected to create all the output because the forwarding page cannot write any output. The following table describes what happens when output buffering is or is not enabled, and when the buffer has been filled or not.

| Buffering Enabled | Buffer Filled | Action |
|---|---|---|
| no | N/A | If any output has been written, an IllegalStateException is thrown. |
| yes | no | Buffer is cleared before forwarding. |
| yes | yes | IllegalStateException is thrown. |

The following code shows a typical use for request forwarding—to separate content from presentation. The first JSP page is `GetFoodGroups.jsp`, which reads a list of food groups from the USDA Nutrient Database:

```
<%@ page errorPage="/ErrorPage.jsp" %>
<%@ page import="java.io.*" %>
<%@ page import="java.sql.*" %>
<%@ page import="java.util.*" %>
<%@ page import="jspcr.forward.*" %>
<%
```

```
   // Load the driver class and establish a connection

   Class.forName
      ("sun.jdbc.odbc.JdbcOdbcDriver");

   Connection con = DriverManager.getConnection
      ("jdbc:odbc:usda");

   // Run a database query to get the list of food groups

   Statement stmt = con.createStatement();
   String sql =
        " SELECT   FdGp_Cd, FdGp_Desc"
      + " FROM     fd_group"
   ;
   ResultSet rs = stmt.executeQuery(sql);

   // Store the results as a list of FoodGroup objects

   List fglist = new ArrayList();
   while (rs.next()) {
      String code = rs.getString(1);
      String desc = rs.getString(2);
      FoodGroup fg = new FoodGroup(code, desc);
      fglist.add(fg);
   }

   rs.close();
   stmt.close();
   con.close();

   // Store the list as a request attribute

   request.setAttribute("jspcr.forward.FoodGroups", fglist);

   // Now forward the request

%><jsp:forward page="ShowFoodGroups.jsp" />
```

As the food groups records are read, they are stored in a `List` structure. The list is saved as an attribute in the request. When all the records have been extracted from the database, the request is forwarded to `ShowFoodGroups.jsp`, which retrieves the list and writes it as an HTML table:

```
<%@ page import="java.io.*,java.util.*,jspcr.forward.*" %>

<HTML>
<HEAD>
<TITLE>Show Food Groups</TITLE>
<STYLE>
   body, td {
      background-color: #FFFFFF;
      font: 8pt Sans-Serif;
   }
</STYLE>
</HEAD>
<BODY>
<CENTER>
<H3>Food Groups</H3>

<%--  Get the list of FoodGroup objects
      that was created by database calls --%>

<%
   List fglist = (List) request.getAttribute
      ("jspcr.forward.FoodGroups");
   Iterator igroups = fglist.iterator();
%>

<TABLE BORDER=1 CELLPADDING=3 CELLSPACING=0>
<TR><TH>Code</TH><TH>Description</TH></TR>

<%--  Loop through the list and print each item --%>
<%
   while (igroups.hasNext()) {
      FoodGroup fg = (FoodGroup) igroups.next();
%>
<TR>
   <TD><%= fg.getCode() %></TD>
   <TD><%= fg.getDescription() %></TD>
</TR>
<%
   }
%>
```

```
</CENTER>
</BODY>
</TABLE>
```

`ShowFoodGroups.jsp` has the advantage that it can be tested in isolation, without having to be connected to a database. A stub JSP for testing purposes can be written. As long as it populates the `List` attribute, `ShowFoodGroups.jsp` is unaware that it is not dealing with a database. The results are shown in Figure 9-6.

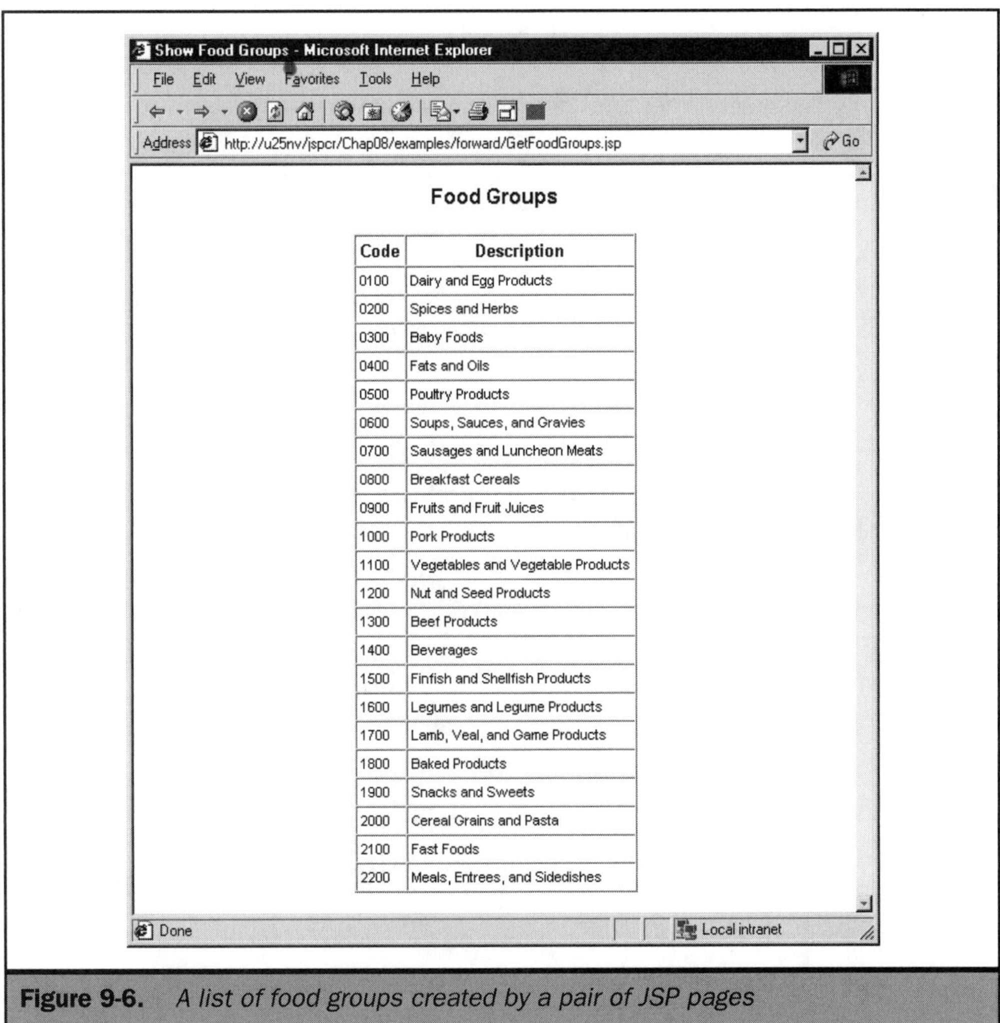


Food Groups

| Code | Description |
|---|---|
| 0100 | Dairy and Egg Products |
| 0200 | Spices and Herbs |
| 0300 | Baby Foods |
| 0400 | Fats and Oils |
| 0500 | Poultry Products |
| 0600 | Soups, Sauces, and Gravies |
| 0700 | Sausages and Luncheon Meats |
| 0800 | Breakfast Cereals |
| 0900 | Fruits and Fruit Juices |
| 1000 | Pork Products |
| 1100 | Vegetables and Vegetable Products |
| 1200 | Nut and Seed Products |
| 1300 | Beef Products |
| 1400 | Beverages |
| 1500 | Finfish and Shellfish Products |
| 1600 | Legumes and Legume Products |
| 1700 | Lamb, Veal, and Game Products |
| 1800 | Baked Products |
| 1900 | Snacks and Sweets |
| 2000 | Cereal Grains and Pasta |
| 2100 | Fast Foods |
| 2200 | Meals, Entrees, and Sidedishes |

**Figure 9-6.** *A list of food groups created by a pair of JSP pages*

## The RequestDispatcher Object

The underlying mechanism for both `<jsp:include>` and `<jsp:forward>` is the `javax.servlet.RequestDispatcher` class. In the food groups example from the previous section, the `<jsp:forward>` action is translated into the following by Tomcat:

```
if (true) {
   out.clear();
   String _jspx_qfStr = "";
   pageContext.forward("ShowFoodGroups.jsp" +  _jspx_qfStr);
   return;
}
```

The Tomcat implementation of `pageContext`, in turn, invokes a `RequestDispatcher` to handle the forwarding:

```
public void forward(String relativeUrlPath)
        throws ServletException, IOException
    {
        String path = getAbsolutePathRelativeToContext(relativeUrlPath);
        context.getRequestDispatcher(path).forward(request, response);
    }
```

You can create a `RequestDispatcher` in three ways:

1. ServletContext.getRequestDispatcher(String *path*)
   - The path must be absolute with respect to the context.
   - A dispatcher for a resource in another servlet context can be created if its context is known. The context can be obtained with context.getContext(*otherContext*).
2. ServletContext.getNamedDispatcher(String *name*)
   - The *name* parameter refers to a servlet alias, rather than a physical pathname.
   - A servlet can get its own name with `config.getServletName()`.
3. ServletRequest.getRequestDispatcher(String *name*)
   - The path can be absolute with respect to the context, or relative with respect to the page. This is the essential difference between this method and the first method.

## Request Dispatching vs. Redirection

Much of what is done by a request dispatcher can also be done by having a JSP or servlet write a "Moved Temporarily" or "Moved Permanently" status code and the URL of the next JSP or servlet written in the Location header. The difference is redirection involves a cooperating client to work, whereas request dispatching is handled entirely on the server side, with no client interaction.



# Model 1 vs. Model 2

These are all handy features, but they are underused if they are only used hit-or-miss for headers and footers. They can, instead, be part of a well-coordinated architecture. If you read JSP newsgroups, you often encounter references to the Model 1 and Model 2 architectures, two different approaches to the structure of a Web application introduced in the original JSP 0.92 specification.

In a Model 1 application, JSP does it all:

- The user requests a JSP page.
- JSP performs calculations, database access, and so forth.
- The JSP page renders its output with HTML.

The Java code necessary to do all this work can be written directly in the form of scriptlets, or it can be contained in JavaBeans.

A Model 2 application follows the *Model-View-Controller* (*MVC*) paradigm. MVC is an object-oriented programming concept prominently featured in the Smalltalk language. It describes a logical partitioning of an application into three parts:

- **Model** is the logical "inner" representation. It had no visible output, no outside representation at all. For this reason, it can be run equally well in a servlet, a standalone GUI, or a batch test program. For example, the model for a chess game may include an array representing the board, numbers representing each of the pieces, and some encoding of the rules.
- **View** is a presentation layer for a model, with little or no programming logic. It reads from already populated structures and displays them. In our chess example, the view would be the screen representation of the game, possibly with alternating colors and ornately carved pieces.
- **Controller** provides user input and directions to a model. In the chess example, the controller would be the keyboard.

In the case of a Model 2 Web application, all user requests are referred to a single URL, a servlet sometimes called a *dispatcher* (the **controller**). This servlet looks in the request's path information for an indication of what it needs to do. There may be a table of actions and names of JSP pages to handle each of them. These action handlers constitute the **model** of the application. They may access a database or perform other calculations, and then populate JavaBeans or other classes with the results. Finally, they invoke JSP pages (the **view**) to present their output.

Which of these models is superior? Model 1 is easier to throw together quickly, but it doesn't scale. Too much is packaged together and it becomes unwieldy as the application grows. Model 2 scales much better and also allows specialists to write different parts of the application:

- Java programmers can write the model and controller.
- User interface specialists can write JSP pages that do nothing but display output.

## Summary

A number of situations exist in which splitting the processing of an HTTP request is advantageous. JSP provides two general capabilities to support this:

- Including other resources, either with `<%@ include %>` or `<jsp:include>`.
- Forwarding a request using `<jsp:forward>`.

Included resources can be either static (like HTML) or dynamic (like a JSP or servlet). The capability to forward requests provides the basis for table-driven applications.

Two general development architectures exist, commonly referred to as Model 1 and Model 2. Model 1 uses JSP pages to accept user input, to access databases as needed, and to format its output. Model 2 follows the MVC paradigm, allowing complex projects to be separated as necessary between groups of people who specialize in one layer or another.

# Chapter 10

## The Page Directive

JSP pages contain not only code that handles requests and generates responses, but instructions to the JSP compiler as well. These instructions are called *directives*. This chapter covers the one most commonly used—the `page` directive. This directive provides a means for setting attributes that affect how the page is interpreted and executed. The syntax is as follows:

<%@ page *attribute="value" attribute="value"* ... %>

where the attributes can be any of the following:

language="*scripting language*"
extends="*className*"
import="*importList*"
session="true | false"
buffer="none | *size*kb"
autoFlush="true | false"
isThreadSafe="true | false"
info="*info_text*"
contentType="*ctinfo*"
errorPage="*error_url*"
isErrorPage="true | false"

The attributes can be specified in any order, and more than one `page` directive can be specified in a compilation unit (the JSP page and any files it includes with the `include` directive). If multiple `page` directives are used, however, they cannot specify the same attribute more than once, with the exception of the `import` attribute.

The remainder of this chapter discusses each of these attributes in detail.

## language

The JSP architecture allows room for it to be extended as a general framework for server-side scripting. For this reason, it supports a `language` attribute in the `page` directive. The value specified (which is `java` by default) applies to all declarations, expressions, and scriptlets in the current translation unit, including any files specified in an `include` directive. All JSP 1.1-compliant containers must support the value `java` for the `language` attribute. No other language is supported in the JSP 1.1 specification, although individual JSP engines may do so.

Although the specification allows for other languages to be used, it imposes some restrictions. The language must support the Java Runtime Environment to the extent that it allows access to the standard implicit object variables, to JavaBeans get and set methods, and to public methods of Java classes.

JRun 3.0 supports both `java` and `javascript` as values for the `language` attribute. When `java` is the language used—either explicitly or implicitly—the scriptlets, expressions, and declarations found in the JSP page are copied to the generated servlet as usual. When `javascript` is specified, there is still a generated Java servlet, but it does not contain the `javascript` code. Instead, the servlet initializes a scripting engine that reads and interprets the original JSP page. For example, if the JSP page looks like this,

```
<%@ page language="java" %>
<%
   int k = 10;
%>
k = <%= k %>
```

then the generated servlet includes the statements,

```
out.print("\r\n");
   int k = 10;
out.print("\r\nk = ");
out.print(k);
out.print("\r\n\r\n");
```

which treats *k* as a Java variable, assigns a value to it, and prints it using the `out` `JspWriter` variable.

By contrast, if the same JSP page uses `javascript` as a value of the `language` attribute,

```
<%@ page language="javascript" %>
<%
   var k = 10;
%>
k = <%= k %>
```

then the generated servlet initializes a JRun-specific scripting engine and invokes its `evaluate` method, as shown in the following:

```
if (scriptEngine == null) {
   try {
      scriptEngine =
         ScriptEngineFactory.getScriptEngine("javascript");
      scriptEngine.init(pageContext);
   } catch (Exception e) {
      throw new ServletException
         ("Error initializing scripting engine.", e);
   }
```

```
}
if (request.getAttribute(SCRIPT_KEY) != null) {
   scriptEngine.init(
      pageContext,
      (String) request.getAttribute(SCRIPT_KEY),
      (String) request.getAttribute(DECLARATION_KEY));
}
scriptEngine.evaluate(pageContext);
```

Obviously, any JSP pages written in a language not explicitly required by the JSP specification most likely won't be portable between JSP containers of different vendors.

## extends

Ordinarily, the JSP container supplies the parent class for any servlet it generates from a JSP page. However, the specification enables you to subclass another parent class of your liking by specifying its fully qualified name in the `extends` attribute of the `page` directive. Doing so would let you provide additional behavior to a family of JSP pages without explicitly coding the behavior in the page.

The JSP specification urges caution when using this capability because it may prevent the JSP container from providing vendor-specific performance and reliability enhancements. For example, the standard JSP parent class used by JRun provides methods for determining dependencies and their last modification times. Similarly, Tomcat implements a parent class that stores a reference to a specialized class loader. If you use a different parent class, it ought to provide important functionality that outweighs these features.

### Required Interfaces for a JSP Superclass

For a class to be used as the superclass for JSP pages, it must implement one of the following interfaces:

- `javax.servlet.jsp.JspPage` A generic interface, not necessarily for use with HTTP. Few servlets implement this interface directly.
- `javax.servlet.jsp.HttpJspPage` Intended for JSP pages that operate under the HTTP protocol, this interface is an extension of `JspPage`.

These interfaces define three methods you must implement, which are described in Table 10-1.

| Method | Description |
|---|---|
| `public void jspInit()` | Method called automatically from the servlet `init()` method when the JSP page is loaded. Although you must implement this method, your implementation needn't do anything. The method is designed as a placeholder to be overridden by JSP page subclasses for any initialization work they need to do. |
| `public void jspDestroy()` | The counterpart of `jspInit()`, this method is automatically called from the servlet's `destroy()` method when a JSP page class is unloaded. |
| `public void _jspService(` *request, response*`) throws ServletException, IOException` | This method is the heart of the JSP request processing logic. It must not be explicitly defined in the JSP page because it is the work of the JSP container to generate the method from the JSP's scriptlets, expressions, and directives. This method is typically declared to be `abstract` in the JSP parent class. |

**Table 10-1.** *Methods Required to Be Declared in JSP Superclasses*



The exact types of the request and response parameters in the `_jspService` method are dictated by the protocol they support. For the HTTP environment, these types are `javax.servlet.http.HttpServletRequest` and `javax.servlet.http.HttpServletResponse`. If you are implementing a different protocol, you need to define request and response classes to be used in the method signature.

`HttpJspPage` extends `JspPage` to provide HTTP-specific behavior. `JspPage`, in turn, extends `javax.servlet.Servlet`, which defines the methods listed in Table 10-2.

| Method | Description |
|---|---|
| `public void init( ServletConfig config) throws ServletException` | A method invoked by the servlet container when a servlet is first loaded. |
| `public ServletConfig getServletConfig()` | Returns the servlet's configuration object, which manages the servlet's initialization parameters and servlet context. |
| `public void service( ServletRequest request, ServletResponse response) throws ServletException, IOException` | Called by the servlet engine to service a request. |
| `public String getServletInfo()` | Returns a description of the servlet. By default, returns an empty string. |
| `public void destroy()` | Called by the servlet engine when a servlet is being unloaded. |

**Table 10-2.** *Methods in the javax.servlet.Servlet Interface*

The JSP superclass must adhere to and implement the JSP protocol. This requires that:

- The `init()` method must call `jspInit()`.
- The `destroy()` method must call `jspDestroy()`.
- The `service()` method must cast its request and response parameters into their protocol-specific classes and invoke `_jspService()`.

This implementation can be direct or the superclass can itself extends a class that provides the implementation, such as `javax.servlet.http.HttpServlet`.

## A JSP Superclass Example

Suitably warned and cautious, if you still want to proceed, this section provides a complete example. Suppose you have a family of JSP pages that all access a common database. If the JSP pages did not have to bother with loading the JDBC driver and establishing a database connection, this might simplify matters. The following servlet can both perform those functions and be used as the parent class of the family of JSP pages.

```
package jspcr.page;

import java.io.*;
import java.sql.*;
import javax.servlet.*;
import javax.servlet.http.*;
import javax.servlet.jsp.*;

/**
* An example of a JSP superclass that can
* be selected with the <CODE>extends</CODE>
* attribute of the page directive.  This servlet
* automatically loads the JDBC-ODBC driver class
* when initialized and establishes a connection
* to the USDA nutrient database.
*/
public abstract class NutrientDatabaseServlet
   extends HttpServlet
   implements HttpJspPage
{
   protected Connection con;

   /**
   * Initialize a servlet with the driver
   * class already loaded and the database
   * connection established.
   */
   public void init(ServletConfig config)
      throws ServletException
   {
      super.init(config);
      try {
         Class.forName("sun.jdbc.odbc.JdbcOdbcDriver");
         con = DriverManager.getConnection("jdbc:odbc:usda");
      }
      catch (Exception e) {
         throw new UnavailableException(e.getMessage());
      }

      jspInit();
   }

   /**
```

```
* Closes the database connection when
* the servlet is unloaded.
*/
public void destroy()
{
   try {
      if (con != null) {
         con.close();
         con = null;
      }
   }
   catch (Exception ignore) {}

   jspDestroy();
   super.destroy();
}

/**
* Called when the JSP is loaded.
* By default does nothing.
*/
public void jspInit()
{
}

/**
* Called when the JSP is unloaded.
* By default does nothing.
*/
public void jspDestroy()
{
}

/**
* Invokes the JSP's _jspService method.
*/
public final void service(
      HttpServletRequest request,
      HttpServletResponse response)
   throws ServletException, IOException
{
   _jspService(request, response);
```

```
   }

   /**
   * Handles a service request
   */
   public abstract void _jspService(
         HttpServletRequest request,
         HttpServletResponse response)
      throws ServletException, IOException;
}
```

In the example, the driver name and database URL are hard-coded. In a production environment, these values should be configurable parameters.

To use `NutrientDatabaseServlet` as a JSP superclass, all that is required is to have the class in the JSP container's classpath and to have the JSP specify its fully qualified name in the `extends` attribute of the `page` directive, as the following shows:

```
<%@ page extends="jspcr.page.NutrientDatabaseServlet" %>

<%--
   This JSP page subclasses the NutrientDatabaseServlet
   parent class, which automatically loads the
   database driver and establishes the connection.
--%>

<%@ page import="java.io.*,java.sql.*" %>
<HTML>
<BODY>
<H3>Food Groups</H3>
<TABLE BORDER=1 CELLPADDING=3 CELLSPACING=0>
<TR><TH>Code</TH><TH>Description</TH></TR>
<%
   // Execute a query

   Statement stmt = con.createStatement();
   String sql = "SELECT * FROM FD_GROUP ORDER BY FDGP_DESC";
   ResultSet rs = stmt.executeQuery(sql);
   while (rs.next()) {
      String code = rs.getString(1);
      String desc = rs.getString(2);
%>
```

```
<TR>
   <TD><%= code %></TD>
   <TD><%= desc %></TD>
</TR>
<%
   }

   // Close the database objects

   rs.close();
   stmt.close();
%>
</TABLE>
</BODY>
</HTML>
```

Notice the JSP does not need to define the `Connection` object. The JSP is a protected variable of the superclass and, therefore, accessible to its subclasses.

## import

The `import` attribute is used to describe the fully qualified names of classes used in the JSP page. This makes it possible for the classes to be referred to by their classes names without the package prefix. This is an optional attribute.

The value of an `import` attribute is a comma-separated list of package names (each terminated with the wildcard string ".*") and/or fully qualified class names. These names are converted directly to import statements in the generated Java servlet. The syntax is fairly flexible. To import all classes in the `java.io`, `java.sql`, and `java.util` packages, for example, you can use any of the following,

```
<%@ page import="java.io.*,java.sql.*,java.util.*" %>
```

or on individual lines (because newlines count as whitespace inside the string),

```
<%@ page import="
   java.io.*,
   java.sql.*,
   java.util.*
   "%>
```

or using separate page directives:

```
<%@ page import="java.io.*" %>
<%@ page import="java.sql.*" %>
<%@ page import="java.util.*" %>
```

All these generate the same Java code, apart from differences in whitespace:

```
import java.io.*;
import java.sql.*;
import java.util.*;
```



Note, importing classes does not involve loading anything; it is simply a shorthand way of letting you use class names inside your Java methods without having to specify the package to which they belong. If you import `java.util.*`, you can write

```
Vector names = new Vector();
```

instead of

```
java.util.Vector names = new java.util.Vector();
```

which affects only the Java compiler, not the run-time class image. You can import thousands of classes, but only those you actually refer to will be required at run time.

The default import list consists of four packages:

- `java.lang`
- `javax.servlet`
- `javax.servlet.http`
- `javax.servlet.jsp`

You do not need to supply an import statement for classes in these packages; you also do not need to qualify them with their package names.

**Note** *Remember, import is the only attribute of the page directive that can be specified more than once.*

## session

The `session` attribute of the page directive indicates whether the page requires an HTTP session. Two values are possible:

- `session="true"` if the page needs an HTTP session. This is the default value.
- `session="false"` if no HTTP session is required. If this is specified, the `session` implicit variable is undefined and will cause a translation error if used.

If your JSP page does not required a session, it is valuable from a performance standpoint to specify `session="false"`, so unnecessary sessions will not be created, using up memory and CPU cycles.

Chapter 14 describes HTTP sessions and session management in detail.

## buffer and autoFlush

The `buffer` and `autoFlush` attributes are used to describe the output buffering model the JSP will employ. The `buffer` attribute can have the value "`none`", indicating all output will be written directly to the servlet response object's output stream, or it can have a integer value with a "kb" suffix. In the latter case, output is stored in memory in a buffer of the specified size. Depending on whether `autoFlush` is "true" or "false", when the buffer is full, either the output will be flushed or a buffer overflow exception will be thrown. The default buffer size is 8kb. Table 10-3 summarizes the results of each combination of values for the two attributes:

| Buffer | AutoFlush | Effect |
|---|---|---|
| none | true | Characters are written to the servlet response output stream as soon as they are generated. |
| none | false | An illegal combination. `autoFlush="false"` is meaningless if buffering is not in effect. |

**Table 10-3.** *Effects of Each Combination of Buffer and AutoFlush*

| Buffer | AutoFlush | Effect |
|---|---|---|
| 8kb | true | An 8,192-byte buffer is used. When this buffer is filled, it is automatically flushed. This is the default value. |
| 8kb | false | An 8,192-byte buffer is used. When this buffer is filled, an exception is thrown. |
| *size*kb | true | A *size* times 1,024-byte buffer is used. When this buffer is filled, it is automatically flushed. |
| *size*kb | false | A *size* times 1,024-byte buffer is used. When this buffer is filled, an exception is thrown. |

**Table 10-3.** *Effects of Each Combination of Buffer and AutoFlush* (continued)



## isThreadSafe

By default, servlet engines load a single instance of a servlet and use a pool of threads to service individual requests. This means two or more threads can be executing the same servlet methods simultaneously. If the servlet has instance variables, and if no provision is made to synchronize access, the threads can collide and interfere with each others' access to the variables.

The servlet API provides a way around this—the SingleThreadModel interface. This interface has no methods; it simply marks a servlet as requiring a dedicated thread for each instance of the servlet[1]. The `isThreadSafe` attribute of the `page` directive provides a means for causing `SingleThreadModel` to be associated with a JSP page.

If you specify `isThreadSafe="true"`, you are asserting that you take care of any possible thread conflicts, so the JSP contain can safely dispatch multiple requests to the servlet simultaneously,

```
<%@ page isThreadSafe="true" %>
```

1 Chapter 14 discusses threading issues in more detail.

which generates the following class signature:

```
public class jrun__Chap10__examples__isThreadSafe__ex12ejsp25
   extends allaire.jrun.jsp.HttpJSPServlet
   implements allaire.jrun.jsp.JRunJspPage
```

If the value is `"false"`, then the JSP container generates a servlet that implements `SingleThreadModel`,

```
<%@ page isThreadSafe="false" %>
```

which generates

```
public class jrun__Chap10__examples__isThreadSafe__ex22ejsp25
   extends allaire.jrun.jsp.HttpJSPServlet
   implements allaire.jrun.jsp.JRunJspPage, SingleThreadModel
```

If not specified, the value of `isThreadSafe` is `"true"`.

**Note** *SingleThreadModel is of limited value because it only prevents thread conflicts within an instance of a servlet. Nothing can prevent the JSP container from loading multiple instances of a servlet, each with a dedicated thread. In this case, competition for external resources like databases and file locks is obviously still unregulated. Careful planning is the only sure design guideline.*

## info

The `info` attribute of the `page` directive lets you specify descriptive information about the JSP page, for example:

<%@ page info="Shopping Cart Checkout Page" %>

The value of this attribute is compiled into the class and is available by means of the servlet's `getServletInfo()` method. This allows servlet engines to provide a useful description for their servlets in an administrative interface.

## contentType

A JSP page ordinarily generates HTML output, but other content types can also be produced. By specifying the `contentType="`*value*`"` attribute in the `page` directive, you can cause an HTTP `Content-Type` header to be returned to the requesting application. Consider the simple JSP page shown in the following:

```
<%@ page contentType="text/plain" %>
Hello, world!
```

Under JRun, the HTTP request and response may look like this:

```
GET /jspcr/Chap10/examples/contentType/ex1.jsp HTTP/1.0

HTTP/1.1 200 OK
Date: Wed, 28 Jun 2000 05:36:33 GMT
Server: Apache/1.3.12 (Win32)
Set-Cookie: jsessionid=7179962170594302;path=/
Expires: Thu, 01 Dec 1994 16:00:00 GMT
Connection: Keep-alive, close
Cache-Control: no-cache="set-cookie,set-cookie2"
Content-Length: 17
Content-Type: text/plain


Hello, world!
```

If the `contentType` attribute is not specified, the request and response will look something like this:

```
GET /jspcr/Chap10/examples/contentType/ex2.jsp HTTP/1.0

HTTP/1.1 200 OK
Date: Wed, 28 Jun 2000 05:40:15 GMT
Server: Apache/1.3.12 (Win32)
Set-Cookie: jsessionid=2106599621708l6161;path=/
Expires: Thu, 01 Dec 1994 16:00:00 GMT
Connection: Keep-alive, close
Cache-Control: no-cache="set-cookie,set-cookie2"
Content-Length: 15
Content-Type: text/html; charset=ISO-8859-1

Hello, world!
```

In addition to the content type, the character set can be specified, using the syntax:

<%@ page contentType="*type/subtype*; charset=*charset*" %>

## errorPage and isErrorPage

If an exception occurs while a JSP page is being evaluated, the servlet engine typically dumps a stack trace to the browser. This may be helpful to the programmer during development, but it is undesirable in a commercial Web application. JSP offers a simple and convenient solution that requires the coordinated use of two attributes: `errorPage` and `isErrorPage`.

A JSP page can indicate that a specific error page should be displayed when it throws an uncaught exception,

<%@ page errorPage="*error_url*" %>

where *error_url* is the URL of another JSP page in the same servlet context. That JSP page must use the following attribute in its `page` directive:

<%@ page isErrorPage="true" %>

An error page has access to the exception through the `exception` implicit variable[2]. It can extract the error message text with `exception.getMessage()`, displaying or logging it as necessary. It can also generate a stack trace with `exception.printStackTrace()`.

The page need not be elaborate. It may simply report the exception:

```
<%@ page isErrorPage="true" session="false"%>

<H3>Application Error</H3>

The error message is:

<B><%= exception.getMessage() %></B>
```

This might be appropriate as a placeholder to be fleshed out later in the development process, adding a corporate logo, for example, as well as instructions for how to proceed.

Because an error page is itself a JSP page, it has access to the servlet context, session (if any), request, and other servlet objects. This makes it possible for the page to capture

2 This is the *only* circumstance in which a JSP page has access to this variable.

diagnostic information, possibly forwarding it to technical support personnel. Here is an example of such an error page:

```
<%@ page isErrorPage="true" session="false"%>

<HTML>
<HEAD><TITLE>Tracking Error Page</TITLE></HEAD>
<BODY>
<CENTER>
<FONT SIZE="+3">
<B><I><U>Monolithic<BR>Technologies Corporation</U></I></B>
</FONT>
<P>
You found a bug we didn't know about:
<B><%= exception.getMessage() %></B>
<P>

<%-- Create a form to submit to Tech Support --%>

<FORM ACTION="/send_diags.jsp">
<INPUT TYPE="submit" VALUE="Please click here">
<P>
to send this information
to our Technical Support department:
<P>

<%-- Supply date, time, and servlet name --%>


<%
   String dateTime       = new java.util.Date().toString();
   String remoteAddr     = request.getRemoteAddr();
   String servletContext = request.getContextPath();

%>
<TABLE BORDER="1" CELLPADDING="3" CELLSPACING="0">
<TR>
   <TD><B>Date and Time:</B></TD>
   <TD><%= dateTime %>
   <INPUT TYPE="hidden"
          NAME="bug.dateTime"
          VALUE="<%= dateTime %>">
```

```
    </TD>
</TR>

<TR>
    <TD><B>Web Client:</B></TD>
    <TD><%= remoteAddr %>
    <INPUT TYPE="hidden"
           NAME="bug.remoteAddr"
           VALUE="<%= remoteAddr %>">
    </TD>
</TR>
<TR>
    <TD><B>Application:</B></TD>
    <TD><%= servletContext %>
    <INPUT TYPE="hidden"
           NAME="bug.servletContext"
           VALUE="<%= servletContext %>">
    </TD>
</TR>
</TABLE>

<%-- Include the stack trace as a hidden field --%>

<INPUT TYPE="hidden" NAME="bug.stackTrace"
       VALUE="<%
java.io.PrintWriter pw = new java.io.PrintWriter(out);
exception.printStackTrace(pw);
       %>"

</FORM>
</CENTER>
</BODY>
</HTML>
```

This page, named `TrackingErrorPage.jsp`, displays the error message associated with the exception, as well as the date, time, IP address of the client, and the Web application name. A button is provided that enables the user to forward this information together with a stack trace to the technical support department (using some other JSP page, not shown here). JSP pages in this application should then include a reference to the error page in its `page` directive:

<%@ page errorPage="TrackingErrorPage.jsp" %>

Figure 10-1 illustrates the results of an exception thrown by an application JSP page that uses this error page.

It is less well known that ordinary servlets can also use this capability. All a servlet needs to do is to emulate what a JSP-generated servlet does

1. Enclose the body of its `doGet()` or `doPost()` method in a `try ... catch` block that catches all exceptions.
2. In the `catch` block, store the exception as an attribute in the request named `javax.servlet.jsp.jspException`.
3. Forward the request to the error page URL using a `RequestDispatcher`.



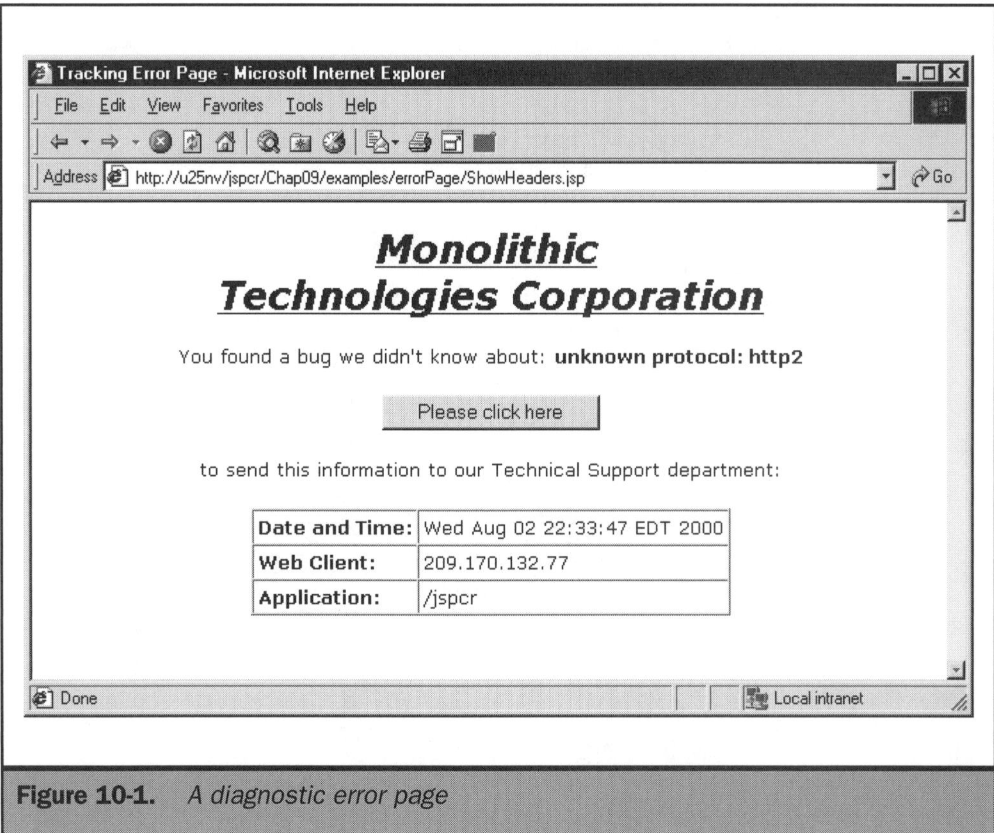


**Figure 10-1.** *A diagnostic error page*

This example shows how this is done:

```
package jspcr.page;

import java.io.*;
import java.net.*;
import java.util.*;

import javax.servlet.*;
import javax.servlet.http.*;

public class BuggyServlet extends HttpServlet
{
   public void doGet(
         HttpServletRequest request,
         HttpServletResponse response)
      throws ServletException, IOException
   {
      try {
         // ... body of servlet here
      }
      catch (Exception e) {

         // A servlet can use the JSP error page
         // mechanism by storing the exception
         // as a request attribute and forwarding
         // the request to the error page.

         request.setAttribute
            ("javax.servlet.jsp.jspException", e);

         getServletContext().getRequestDispatcher
            ("/Chap10/examples/errorPage/TrackingErrorPage.jsp")
            .forward(request, response);
      }
   }
}
```

## Summary

The page directive enables a page author to supply instructions to the JSP container. This chapter describes the operation of each attribute that can be specified:

- `language` The scripting language (`java`, by default)
- `extends` A specialized superclass for the page
- `import` The packages and classes that should be visible to the generated servlet
- `session` Whether to create an HTTP session object
- `buffer` The output buffering model
- `autoFlush` Whether to flush the buffer when full or throw an exception
- `isThreadSafe` Whether to implement `SingleThreadModel`
- `info` A description of the page to be displayed in a development tool
- `contentType` The character encoding used by the JSP response
- `isErrorPage` Whether to supply access to the implicit `exception` variable
- `errorPage` The URL of a page that handles uncaught exceptions

The Complete Reference

# Chapter 11

## JSP Tag Extensions

The JavaServer Pages 1.1 specification significantly enhanced the JSP architecture by making it possible to extend the page authoring environment with custom tags. *Custom tags* are XML-like extensions to the syntax and semantics of a JSP page that are backed by user-written tag handlers. Collections of tags are organized into *tag libraries* that can be packaged as JAR files, enabling their functionality to be easily distributed and installed over any JSP 1.1-compliant servlet engine.

This chapter introduces custom tags, giving an overview of their role and advantages. It gives an extended, step-by-step example of how to write and deploy a custom tag, and then proceeds to the details of tag libraries, the tag library descriptor, the tag extension API, and tag handlers. Several examples of tag environments are explored. The chapter concludes with the implementation of the database query tag given in the first example.

## Why Custom Tags?

Most programmers can write ordinary HTML, and most Web designers can learn to write simple JSP pages. But really good HTML with navigation, browser detection, image handling, and forms interaction requires a knowledgeable author—a specialist.[1] Likewise, Java programming that accesses databases, handles transactions, and communicates with sockets is beyond what could be expected from an HTML author.

Custom tags provide a means for bridging the gap between the two specialties. Java programmers can provide application functionality in convenient packages that Web designers can use as building blocks. While JavaBeans can also encapsulate code, they are most useful as repositories for attributes. Notions of iteration, nesting, or cooperative actions are difficult to express with beans. Custom tags enable a higher-level application-specific approach to JSP development.

For example, a database query written with custom tags might look like the following,

```
<db:connect url="mydatabase">

   <db:runQuery>
      SELECT   *
      FROM     FD_GROUP
      WHERE    FdGp_Desc LIKE '%F%'
      ORDER BY FdGp_Cd
   </db:runQuery>

   <table border="1" cellpadding="3" cellspacing="0">
```

1 Bring up http://www.cnn.com or http://www.msnbc.com and view the HTML source. How much of it do you think you could write?

```
      <tr><th>Food Group Code</th><th>Description</th></tr>
   <db:forEachRow>
      <tr>
         <td><db:getField name="FdGp_Cd"/></td>
         <td><db:getField name="FdGp_Desc"/></td>
      </tr>
   </db:forEachRow>
   </table>

</db:connect>
```



where `connect`, `runQuery`, `forEachRow`, and `getField` are application-oriented custom tags.

All the logic in the previous example could have been written with scriptlets embedded in the JSP page. For example, the equivalent code for the `<db:connect>` tag might include loading the driver class, opening a connection to the database (possibly getting an existing connection from a pool), setting up `Statement` and `ResultSet` objects, and handling any of several exceptions that might be thrown. Also possible would be to incorporate most of the logic in a JavaBean, although scriptlet code would still be required for looping over the result set. Neither alternative is as convenient as packaging the logic into a set of HTML-like tags whose function is readily apparent to both Web designers and servlet developers.

Besides the separation of content and presentation, other benefits of custom tags include:

- **Simplicity** It's significantly easier to express a complex task as a cooperating set of subtasks with their own attributes and control flow than it is to write it as a monolithic block of code. Not only is this easier to code, it's easier to understand. In the previous database query, for example, it's easy to guess correctly what the scope of the database connection is, that an implied result set is created by the `<db:runQuery>` block, and that `<db:forEachRow>` iterates over this result set.
- **Opportunity for code reuse** There may be hundreds of database queries in a Web application. Sharing scriptlet code is difficult without resorting to `<%@ include %>` directives that obscure the logic and may have undesirable side effects. Tag libraries make it easier to package standard code and share it throughout an application.
- **Suitability for authoring tools** *Integrated development environments (IDEs)* can only see scriptlet blocks as blocks of ASCII text. Custom tags, however, by virtue of having a Tag Library Descriptor, lend themselves to being managed by a development tool that can display their descriptions, validate their attributes, and so on.

To get a better idea of how to develop custom tags, let's take a simple example and walk through its development step by step.

# Developing Your First Custom Tag

Resisting the temptation to write a "Hello, World!" tag, we will develop an example of a marginally useful component—a custom tag that retrieves the name and version of the Web server. The implementation of this tag, as well as all the other tags we develop, will follow the same four basic steps:

1. Define the tag.
2. Write the entry in the Tag Library Descriptor.
3. Write the tag handler.
4. Use the tag in a JSP page.

## Step 1—Define the Tag

To start, we need to define the syntax of the tag clearly. This involves answering such questions as:

- What is the name of the tag? As we will see later on, custom tags are always used with a namespace qualifier, so it isn't necessary to make tag name globally unique.
- What attributes does it have? For example, the HTML `<TABLE>` tag has the optional attributes `BORDER`, `CELLPADDING`, `CELLSPACING`, and `WIDTH` (among others). Custom tags can define any numer of required or optional attributes, which are passed to the tag handler when the tag is evaluated.
- Will the tag define scripting variables? The standard action `<jsp:useBean id="xyz" class="jspcr.beans.XYZBean">`, for example, causes a variable named `xyz` of type `jspcr.beans.XYZBean` to be defined. This variable is then available to the `<jsp:getProperty>` and `<jsp:setProperty>` actions, as well as to Java code in any scriptlets or expressions that follow. Custom tags can create scripting variables in the same manner.
- Does the tag do anything special with the body contained between its start and end tags? The HTML `<TABLE>` tag expects table rows and table cells before its terminating `</TABLE>` end tag. Each of these elements rely on information provided by related elements above them in the evaluation stack. Custom tag applications can likewise feature nested tags that cooperatively perform some function. The tag body can also contain non-JSP data (such as SQL statements) that are evaluated by the tag.

In the case of the first example tag, there isn't much to do. We'll call the tag `getWebServer`. It has no attributes because it doesn't need to be configured differently in different JSP pages. The tag defines no scripting variables, simply returning the string containing the Web server name in place of the `getWebServer` tag. Finally, the tag has no body to be considered because its entire function is contained in its start tag.

## Step 2—Create the TLD Entry

A *Tab Library Descriptor* (*TLD*) is an XML document that defines the names and attributes of a collection of related tags. Here is the TLD we will use with the `getWebServer` example tag:

```
<?xml version="1.0" ?>
<taglib>
   <tlibversion>1.0</tlibversion>
   <jspversion>1.1</jspversion>
   <shortname>diag</shortname>
   <tag>
      <name>getWebServer</name>
      <tagclass>jspcr.taglib.diag.GetWebServerTag</tagclass>
      <bodycontent>empty</bodycontent>
   </tag>
</taglib>
```

Later on in this chapter, we will look at TLDs in detail, but the key thing to focus on here is that a TLD maps a tag name

```
      <name>getWebServer</name>
```

to a fully qualified class name:

```
      <tagclass>jspcr.taglib.diag.GetWebServerTag</tagclass>
```

The JSP container uses this mapping to create the appropriate servlet code when it evaluates the custom tag at compile time.

We will give this file the name `diagnostics.tld`. For the purposes of this example, the only thing we need to worry about is copying the file to the right place. A TLD can be placed anywhere in the Web application directory system, but putting it under the `WEB-INF` directory makes sense because it won't be made available for direct public access. By convention, TLDs are usually installed in a directory named `/WEB-INF/tlds`. If there is a Web application named `test`, for example, then diagnostics.tld would be found in /test/WEB-INF/tlds/. Written as a URI relative to the servlet context, this would be /WEB-INF/tlds/diagnostics.tld.

## Step 3—Write the Tag Handler

A tag's action is implemented in a Java class known as a *tag handler*. Instances of tag handlers are created and maintained by the JSP container, and predefined methods in these classes are called directly from a JSP page's generated servlet.

In the sample tag, we need to get the name of the Web server (for example, Apache, Microsoft IIS, Netscape Enterprise, and so forth). The servlet API doesn't provide an obvious way to get this information. The request object tells a lot about the Web client and the servlet context knows about the servlet engine, but neither of these objects appears to know what software product happens to be listening on port 80. However, this information is provided by the Web server itself when it sends the HTTP response back to the Web client. The approach we'll take is to make a dummy HTTP request ourselves within the tag handler, and then extract the server information from the HTTP headers that are returned.

Here is the complete source code for the tag handler:

```
package jspcr.taglib.diag;

import javax.servlet.http.*;
import javax.servlet.jsp.*;
import javax.servlet.jsp.tagext.*;
import java.io.*;
import java.net.*;

/**
* Handler for the "getWebServer" tag
*/
public class GetWebServerTag extends TagSupport
{
   public int doStartTag() throws JspException
   {
      try {

         // Get the request object from the page context

         HttpServletRequest request =
            (HttpServletRequest) pageContext.getRequest();

         // Request information from web server

         URL url = new URL("http",
```

```
                    request.getServerName(),
                    request.getServerPort(),
                    "/");
         URLConnection con = url.openConnection();
         ((HttpURLConnection) con).setRequestMethod("OPTIONS");
         String webserver = con.getHeaderField("server");

         // Write it to the output stream

         JspWriter out = pageContext.getOut();
         out.print(webserver);
      }
      catch (IOException e) {
         throw new JspException(e.getMessage());
      }
      return SKIP_BODY;
   }
}
```

Let's look at the source code in detail to see what we expect it to do.

```
package jspcr.taglib.diag;
```

The first line identifies the package name. It isn't strictly necessary to place the code in a package, but it helps to organized related classes and makes for more meaningful Javadoc documentation. Besides, some JSP engines don't correctly generate `import` statements for custom tags, so classes without a package name can cause compilation errors in the generated servlet.

```
import javax.servlet.http.*;
import javax.servlet.jsp.*;
import javax.servlet.jsp.tagext.*;
import java.io.*;
import java.net.*;
```

Simple tag handlers usually need to import only the `javax.servlet.jsp` and `javax.servlet.jsp.tagext` packages, as well as the `java.io.IOException` class. In this case, we need the `HttpServletRequest` class from `javax.servlet.http`, as well as several classes from `java.net`.

```
public class GetWebServerTag extends TagSupport
```

A tag handler needs to implement either the Tag interface or the BodyTag interface, both of which are in the javax.servlet.jsp.tagext package. BodyTag is a subinterface of Tag. While the tag author is free to implement these interfaces directly, it usually is more convenient to extend one of the default implementation classes TagSupport or BodyTagSupport, overriding only those methods we need for the task at hand. The example tag doesn't support a tag body, so we simply extend the TagSupport class.

```
public int doStartTag() throws JspException
```

This method is called when the start tag is encountered, after any attributes it specifies have been set in the tag handler, but before the body of the tag is processed. In this case, no body and no attributes exist, so all the code will be contained in the doStartTag() method. Note, the method lets you throw a JspException if the code runs into trouble. Because we will be accessing network classes that can throw java.io.IOException, we enclose the entire method in a try ... catch block that converts this to a JspException for handling by the JSP container. Note, likewise, the method returns an integer return code (more about this shortly).

```
HttpServletRequest request =
          (HttpServletRequest) pageContext.getRequest();
```

To send an HTTP request to the Web server, we need to know the host name and port number of the request we received. This information can be found in the request object, which can be obtained from the pageContext object. The observant reader will notice that pageContext is nowhere defined in this class. The reason for this is it's defined as a protected field in the TagSupport superclass, which makes it accessible to subclasses like ours. This variable is set just before doStartTag() is called when the TagSupport.setPageContext() method is called[2].

```
      URL url = new URL("http",
                  request.getServerName(),
                  request.getServerPort(),
                  "/");
      URLConnection con = url.openConnection();
      ((HttpURLConnection) con).setRequestMethod("OPTIONS");
      String webserver = con.getHeaderField("server");
```

2 Reading the source code for TagSupport and BodyTagSupport is helpful. These are fairly small classes, and it's instructive to see where the page context and body content variables come from, and how findAncestorWithClass works. The source is usually available from the same place the servlet.jar classes are obtained.

We use the 4-argument constructor of `java.net.URL` that takes a protocol name, server name, port number, and path, and, from this, we get a `URLConnection` object. Because we don't actually care about the contents of any particular file, we specify the `OPTIONS` method rather than `GET` or `POST`. We could also use `HEAD`, which is essentially the same as `GET`, but returns only headers. Occasionally, however, Web servers report that `HEAD` is not a supported method. `OPTIONS` should work for any `HTTP/1.1`-compliant Web server (after all, its purpose is to return a list of request methods the Web server *does* support). Invoking the connection object's `getHeaderField()` method causes the request to be sent and the appropriate HTTP header in the response to be read.

```
JspWriter out = pageContext.getOut();
out.print(webserver);
```

After capturing the desired information in the `webserver` variable, we can simply write it to the current servlet output stream, which we can obtain from the page context. The effect is that the `getServer` tag used in the JSP Page is replaced by the server information obtained from the HTTP request.

```
return SKIP_BODY;
```

Finally, we exit from the method returning the integer constant `SKIP_BODY`, which is defined in the `Tag` interface. Because we have defined this tag to have no body, there's no need to evaluate it, and the JSP page will throw a run-time exception if any other return code is specified.

## Compiling the Sample Code

This completes the tag handler. The source code file must be named `GetWebServerTag.java`, and its compiled class must have the fully qualified name `jspcr.taglib.diag.GetWebServerTag`. An easy way to ensure this is to create the appropriate set of directories under the Web application's `/WEB-INF/classes` directory,

```
/WEB-INF/classes/jspcr/taglib/diag
```

and place the `.java` source file in the `diag` directory. The program can be compiled from the `/WEB-INF/classes` directory with the command

```
javac jspcr/taglib/diag/GetWebServerTag.java
```

with appropriate provision being made for having the `servlet.jar` file somewhere in the classpath. This should put a `GetWebServerTag.class` file in the same directory as `GetWebServerTag.java`. If this isn't the case, make sure the `package` statement has been entered correctly.

## Step 4—Incorporate the Tag into a JSP Page

At this point, the tag is ready to be used. The following JSP page (`ShowServer.jsp`) demonstrates how this is done:

```
<%@ taglib prefix="diag" uri="/WEB-INF/tlds/diagnostics.tld" %>

<HTML>

<HEAD>
<TITLE>Basic Example of a Custom Tag</TITLE>
</HEAD>

<BODY>
<H3>Basic Example of a Custom Tag</H3>
The web server is <diag:getWebServer/>
</BODY>

</HTML>
```

### The taglib Directive

The first line contains the `taglib` directive:

```
<%@ taglib prefix="diag" uri="/WEB-INF/tlds/diagnostics.tld" %>
```

This directive must appear in the JSP page before any of the custom tags it refers to are used. The top of the page is a good place.

### How to Use the Tag in the JSP Page

The rest of the Web page is traditional HTML, with the exception of the line on which the custom tag is specified:

```
The Web server is <diag:getWebServer/>
```

When `ShowServer.jsp` is first invoked, the JSP container uses information from the `taglib` directive to locate the tag library descriptor and to identify where its tags are used on this page. When the generated servlet receives a request, it produces the following HTML,

```
<HTML>

<HEAD>
```

```
<TITLE>Basic Example of a Custom Tag</TITLE>
</HEAD>

<BODY>
<H3>Basic Example of a Custom Tag</H3>

The web server is Apache/1.3.12 (Win32)

</BODY>

</HTML>
```

depending, of course, on the actual Web server involved. The results are shown in Figure 11-1.

Worth noting is custom tags used in JSP pages must conform to strict XML rules:

1. All tags must be completed, either by a matching end tag,

   ```
   <diag:name>
   ...
   </diag:name>
   ```

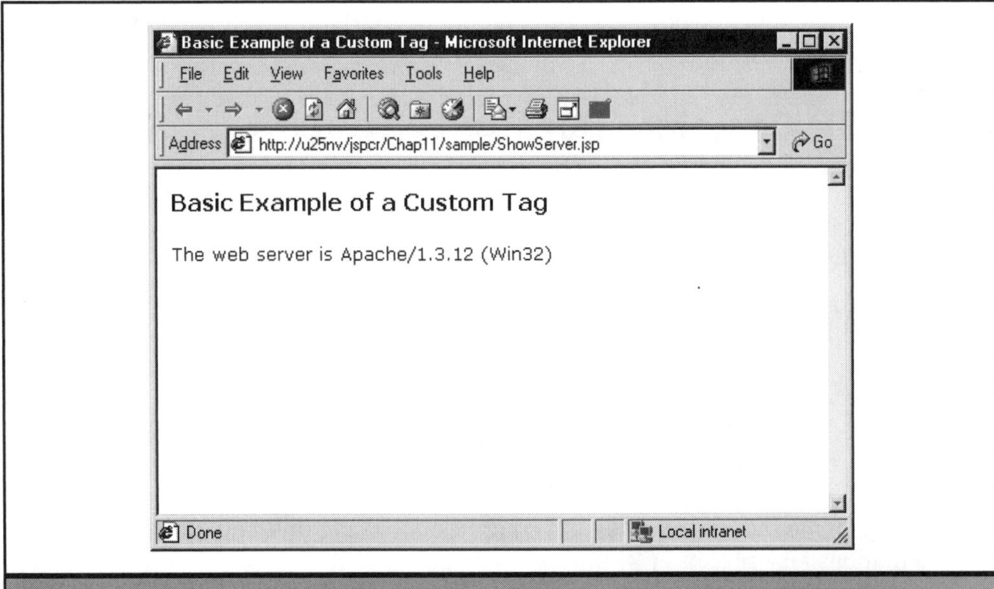


**Figure 11-1.** *Output of a JSP using the custom tag to identify the Web server software*

2. or by the shortcut form, if there's no body:

```
<diag:name/>.
```

3. All attributes must be quoted, even numeric ones:

```
<diag:for id="I" start="1" end="10">
...
</diag:for>
```

4. Nested tags cannot overlap; this

```
<diag:A>
<diag:B>
</diag:A>
</diag:B>
```

   is illegal.

5. Case is significant in tag and attribute names.

# How Tag Handlers Work

A tag handler is a Java class that performs the action of a custom tag by implementing a set of predefined methods that a JSP container calls. In this section, we will learn about the structure of a tag handler, the interfaces it implements, its lifecycle, and how it works with attributes and scripting variables. Wealso look at cooperating and nested tags, and show how they can interact. To start, however, let's review how the JSP container translates and invokes a JSP page.

## What the JSP Container Does

Recall that a JSP page exists in three forms:

- **The `.jsp` file** The original source file the page author writes, which may include HTML, scriptlets, expressions, declarations, action tags, and directives.
- **The `.java` file** Java source code for a servlet that's equivalent to the `.jsp` file. This servlet is generated by the JSP container.
- **The `.class` file** The compiled form of the generated Java servlet.

When a JSP page is requested by an HTTP client, the JSP container checks the modification dates of the `.jsp` and `.java` files. If the `.java` file doesn't exist or if it's older than the `.jsp` file (as it would be if the JSP page had been modified), the JSP container re-creates the Java servlet and compiles it. During this step, the following transformations take place:

- The `<%@ page %>`, `<%@ include %>`, and `<%@ taglib %>` directives supply translation-time information to the JSP container.

- JSP expressions and lines of HTML get translated into out.print() statements inside the _jspService() method in the order they occur.
- Scriptlets are copied verbatim into _jspService().
- Declarations are copied verbatim into the source code outside of _jspService().
- Standard JSP actions such as <jsp:include>, <jsp:useBean>, and <jsp:setProperty> are translated into the run-time logic that performs their function.
- Custom tags are expanded into Java statements that call methods in their corresponding tag handler.



## Tag-Related Code Generated by the Container

The container uses the taglib directives to locate Tag Library Descriptors (TLDs) and to match them to custom tags used in the page based on the tag prefix used. For example, if the directive is

```
<%@ taglib prefix="db"
      uri="/WEB-INF/tlds/database.tld" %>
```

then the container reads the database.tld file to get a list of tags it describes and the name of the tag handler class associated with each one. When it encounters a tag later in the page with a namespace prefix,

```
<db:connect url="mydatabase">
```

it looks for a tag library associated with that prefix that has a tag with the specified name. The container uses information about the tag's structure, which it finds in the TLD, to generate a series of Java statements that accomplish the tag's function. In the case of the db:connect tag previously shown, this would include

1. Code to create an instance of the connect tag handler or obtain one from a pool.
2. Code to pass the connect tag handler a reference to the pageContext object. This is a useful feature because it gives the tag handler access to the JSP page's Request, Response, HttpSession, ServletContext, and output stream objects. It also means the tag handler can get or set attributes at any level the page context manages.
3. Code to pass a reference to the parent tag, if db:connect is nested within another custom tag.
4. A call to the connect tag handler's setUrl() method, passing the "mydatabase" value.
5. A call to a method named doStartTag(), which the connect tag handler implements to perform any action that takes place when its start tag is encountered (more about this shortly).

## What a Tag Handler Does

In the body of a JSP page, a custom tag may look like this:

```
<app:mail from="Accounting Manager" to="Staff" >
   <app:subject>Expense Reports</app:subject>
   Please be sure to submit all expense reports before
   the fifteenth day of the month to allow sufficient
   processing time.  Thanks.
</app:mail>
```

The components of this tag include:

- A start tag `<app:mail ...>` with zero or more attributes
- An end tag `</app:mail>`
- The lines between the start and end tag, known as the *body* of the tag, which may include ordinary text or other JSP statements.[3]

In transforming the tag into servlet code, the container invokes the tag handler for each of these components, using the `pageContext` object to share attributes to the handler. The invocation of these methods is sometimes referred to as the tag handler's *lifecycle*.

For this to work, a tag handler must implement one of two interfaces:

- `javax.servlet.jsp.tagext.Tag` for tags that don't operate on their bodies.
- `javax.servlet.jsp.tagext.BodyTag` for tags that do. `BodyTag` is a subinterface of `Tag`.

These interfaces specify the lifecycle methods the tag handler must provide.

The API also provides two support classes—`TagSupport` and `BodyTagSupport`—that act as the default implementation of the two interfaces. Most tag handlers extend these support classes rather than implementing the interfaces directly, although the interfaces aren't particularly complex. One benefit of using a support class is you can override only the methods you need to change, allowing the support class to handle the rest. In addition, the support class can take care of saving the page context and body content objects in protected variables, so subclasses can simply access them.

---

3 A tag is not required to have a body. A tag may simply perform its function based on the attributes specified in the start tag. In this case, using the shorthand <tag ... /> notation is common.

## Tag Libraries

Custom tags are implemented and distributed in a structure known as a *tag library*, sometimes referred to as a *taglib*. A tag library is a collection of classes and meta-information that includes

- **Tag Handlers** Java classes that implement the functionality of custom tags.
- **Tag Extra Information** Classes that supply the JSP container with logic for validating tag attributes and creating scripting variables.
- **A Tag Library Descriptor (TLD)** An XML document that describes the properties of the individual tags and the tag library as a whole.



The components of a tag library can be installed anywhere they are accessible to the JSP container. The tag handler and tag extra information classes need to be located where they can be found by the JSP container class loader. The tag library descriptor can be anywhere that can be located by a URL. For ease of deployment, however, the JSP 1.1 specification mandates that the JSP container must accept a tag library packaged as a JAR file having a certain fixed structure. In such a JAR file, the classes should be in a directory tree starting at the root that matches their package structure, and the TLD must be a file named `taglib.tld` in the `/META-INF` directory. This means a tag library can be deployed simply by copying its JAR file to the `/WEB-INF/lib` directory. Or, the classes can be unzipped into the `/WEB-INF/classes` directory and the TLD can be placed in another Web-accessible location. This is typically a directory named `/WEB-INF/tlds`, although this is only a convention, not a requirement.

## The Tag Library Descriptor (TLD)

The tag library configuration information needed by a JSP container is stored in a *Tag Library Descriptor* (*TLD*). A TLD is an XML document that describes the individual tags in the library, their tag handlers and attributes, as well as version and identifying information about the library as a whole.

### TLD Elements

The *document type definition* (*DTD*) for a tag library descriptor can be found at `http://java.sun.com/j2ee/dtds/Web-jsptaglibrary_1_1.dtd`. A valid TLD consists of a single `<taglib>` element having certain subelements in a fixed order:

- `tlibversion` is a required element containing the version number of the tag library. This is a dotted decimal number consisting of up to four groups of digits separated by decimal points, such as "1.0", or "1.3.045".

- `jspversion` is an optional element identifying the minimal level of the JSP specification required to support the tag library. For example, for JSP version 1.1, this would be "1.1".
- `shortname` is a short descriptive name that identifies the tag library. A JSP authoring tool might use this name as a default prefix for tags from this library. The DTD prescribes this name should have no white space and must begin with an alphabetic character; however, the restriction about white space seems widely ignored in practice. `shortname` is a required element.
- `uri` is an optional element that defines a unique URI, which identifies this library. This is typically the URL of the location from which the latest version of the taglib can be downloaded.
- `info` is an optional element in which descriptive information about the tag library is entered. This is intended for human viewing in a JSP authoring tool.
- `tag` One or more `tag` entries can be in a TLD. These describe the individual tags that comprise the library.

A `tag` element itself consists of up to six types of subelements:

- `name` The tag name as it will be used in a JSP page. Together with a namespace prefix that identifies the tag library, the name uniquely identifies a tag to the JSP container.
- `tagclass` A required element consisting of the fully qualified name of the tag handler that implements the tag.
- `teiclass` An optional element consisting of the fully qualified name of the *Tag Extra Information* (*TEI*) class used by this tag, if any. A TEI class provides information about scripting variables the tag handler creates, as well as any validations that can be performed on tag attributes.
- `bodycontent` Optionally describes how the tag handler uses its body content. The possible values are

| | |
|---|---|
| `empty` | The tag body must be empty |
| `JSP` | The tag body consists of other JSP elements |
| `tagdependent` | The tag body is interpreted by the tag itself, with no JSP transformations |

- `info` Optional human-readable descriptive information about the tag.
- `attribute` Optional information about attributes that can be coded when the tag is used in a JSP page. This entry is described more fully in the "Defining Tag Attributes" section later in this chapter.

# The taglib Directive

The purpose of the `taglib` directive is to specify the location of the TLD and assign it a short alias (prefix) that distinguishes its tags on this page. Its syntax is as follows:

```
<%@ taglib prefix="tag prefix" uri="taglibURI" %>
```

where the two attributes are

| | |
|---|---|
| *tag prefix* | A name, unique on this page, used to identify tags from this library. If the prefix is `diag`, for example, then any tag from this tag library used on this page should be written as `<diag:xxx>`, where `xxx` is the tag name.<br>The prefix can be any valid XML name token, although Sun Microsystems reserves the prefixes `jsp`, `jspx`, `java`, `javax`, `servlet`, `sun`, and `sunw`. |
| *taglibURI* | The URI of the tag library itself. This can be an absolute path name beginning with / that is interpreted relative to the top of the Web application as in the previous example. Or, it can be a URL that acts as a symbolic name for the TLD. In this case, the name must be mapped to the actual TLD by means of a `<taglib>` entry in the `Web.xml` file. This approach is discussed in the next section. |



## Mapping Tag Libraries in the web.xml File

Suppose the JAR file containing the classes and TLD for version 3.8.2 of a taglib is named `util_v3_8_2.jar` and is deployed in the `/WEB-INF/lib` directory of a Web application. A `taglib` directive can refer to this directly as follows:

```
<%@ taglib
      prefix="util"
      uri="/WEB-INF/lib/util_v3_8_2.jar"
%>
```

Of course, when version 3.8.3 is installed, this means all JSPs that use this tag library must be updated with the new version number.

An alternative to this is to map the physical location of the TLD to a symbolic name that can be used in a `taglib` directive. This is done by adding a `<taglib>`[4] element to

4 Why couldn't they use a different name for this element? The TLD file already has a `<taglib>` element with a completely different meaning. Why afford the poor JSP author such an opportunity for confusion?

the /WEB-INF/web.xml deployment descriptor for this Web application. For the previous example, this element would have the following structure:

```
<taglib>
   <taglib-uri>uri</taglib-uri>
   <taglib-location>
      /WEB-INF/lib/util_v3_8_2.jar
   </taglib-location>
</taglib>
```

where *uri* can be any valid URI, perhaps a file-like mnemonic such as /util-taglib or the URL of a place where the latest version of the taglib can be found. This makes it possible to code the taglib directive as

```
<%@ taglib
      prefix="util"
      uri="http://www.vendor.com/taglibs/util"
%>
```

Note that the URI needn't refer to an actual file. Rather, it's a unique identifier that enables the JSP container to search for in web.xml for the actual file location. Also note, this mapping technique only works for JAR files coded in the prescribed format (TLD in /META-INF/taglib.tld) and some JSP container implementations are known to be buggy in this respect. When in doubt, you can always put the JAR file in /WEB-INF/lib and the TLD in /WEB-INF/tlds, and refer to the /WEB-INF/tlds/filename.tld directly in your JSP page.

# The Tag Handler API

The following section describes the methods associated with the Tag interface and the TagSupport class.

## The Tag Interface

Table 11-1 lists the lifecycle methods that must be supported by classes implementing the Tag interface.

The interface also includes four constants that represent the possible return code from the doStartTag() and doEndTag() methods:

- EVAL_BODY_INCLUDE When returned by doStartTag(), indicates the page implementation servlet should evaluate the tag body.
- SKIP_BODY When returned by doStartTag(), indicates the servlet should ignore the body of this tag.

| Method | Description |
|---|---|
| `public void setPageContext (PageContext ctx)` | The generated servlet calls this method first before requiring the handler to do anything else. The implementing class should save the context variable so it's available at any point in the tag lifecycle. From the page context, the tag handler can access all the JSP implicit objects and can get and set attributes in any scope. |
| `public void setParent (Tag parent)` | Enables a tag to find the tag above it in the evaluation stack. Called immediately after `setPageContext`. |
| `public Tag getParent()` | Returns the parent tag. |
| `public int doStartTag() throws JspException` | Called after the page context, parent, and any attributes coded on the start tag have been set. The return code indicates whether the JSP implementation servlet should evaluate the tag body (`EVAL_BODY_INCLUDE`) or not (`SKIP_BODY`). The method can throw a `JspException` to indicate a fatal error. |
| `public int doEndTag() throws JspException` | Called when the end tag has been encountered. The return code indicates whether the JSP implementation servlet should continue with the rest of the page (`EVAL_PAGE`) or not (`SKIP_PAGE`). The method can throw a `JspException` to indicate a fatal error. |
| `public void release()` | Guaranteed to be called before page exit. Allows the tag handler to release any resources it holds and reset its state so it can be reused, if necessary. |

**Table 11-1.** *Methods in the Tag Interface*

- `EVAL_PAGE` When returned by `doEndTag()`, indicates the rest of the page should be evaluated as usual.
- `SKIP_PAGE` When returned by doEndTag(), indicates the rest of the page should be skipped.

## The TagSupport Class

`javax.servlet.jsp.tagext.TagSupport` is a concrete class that implements the `Tag` interface. In addition to the interface, the `TagSupport` class provides the additional methods listed in Table 11-2.

Extending this class rather than directly implementing the interface is usually advantageous. In addition to providing default implementations for all the required methods and storing the `pageContext` variable, `TagSupport` offers several convenience methods. `findAncestorWithClass()` is particularly useful for supporting nested tags. An *outer tag,* for example, can manage a set of objects as instance variables, providing public accessors that make these objects accessible to *inner tags.* The database tag example later in this chapter illustrates the technique.

# The Tag Handler Life Cycle

The flowchart in Figure 11-2 describes the events in the life of a tag handler. The process shown in the flowchart corresponds to the Java code the JSP container generates for a tag when the JSP page is translated into a servlet. Knowing when each of your

| Method | Description |
|---|---|
| `public static Tag findAncestorWithClass(Tag thisTag, Class cls)` | Looks in the run-time tag stack for the desired parent tag handler. A tag handler can provide methods that child tags within its scope can call. |
| `public void setId(String id)` `public String getId()` | Stores or retrieves the name specified in the `id` attribute. |
| `public void setValue(String name, Object o)` `public Object getValue(String name)` | Stores or retrieves a value under the given name in a local hashtable. |
| `public void removeValue(String name)` | Removes the named value from the local hashtable. |
| `public Enumeration getValues()` | Returns a `java.util.Enumeration` of the keys in the hashtable. |

**Table 11-2.** *Additional Methods in the TagSupport Class*

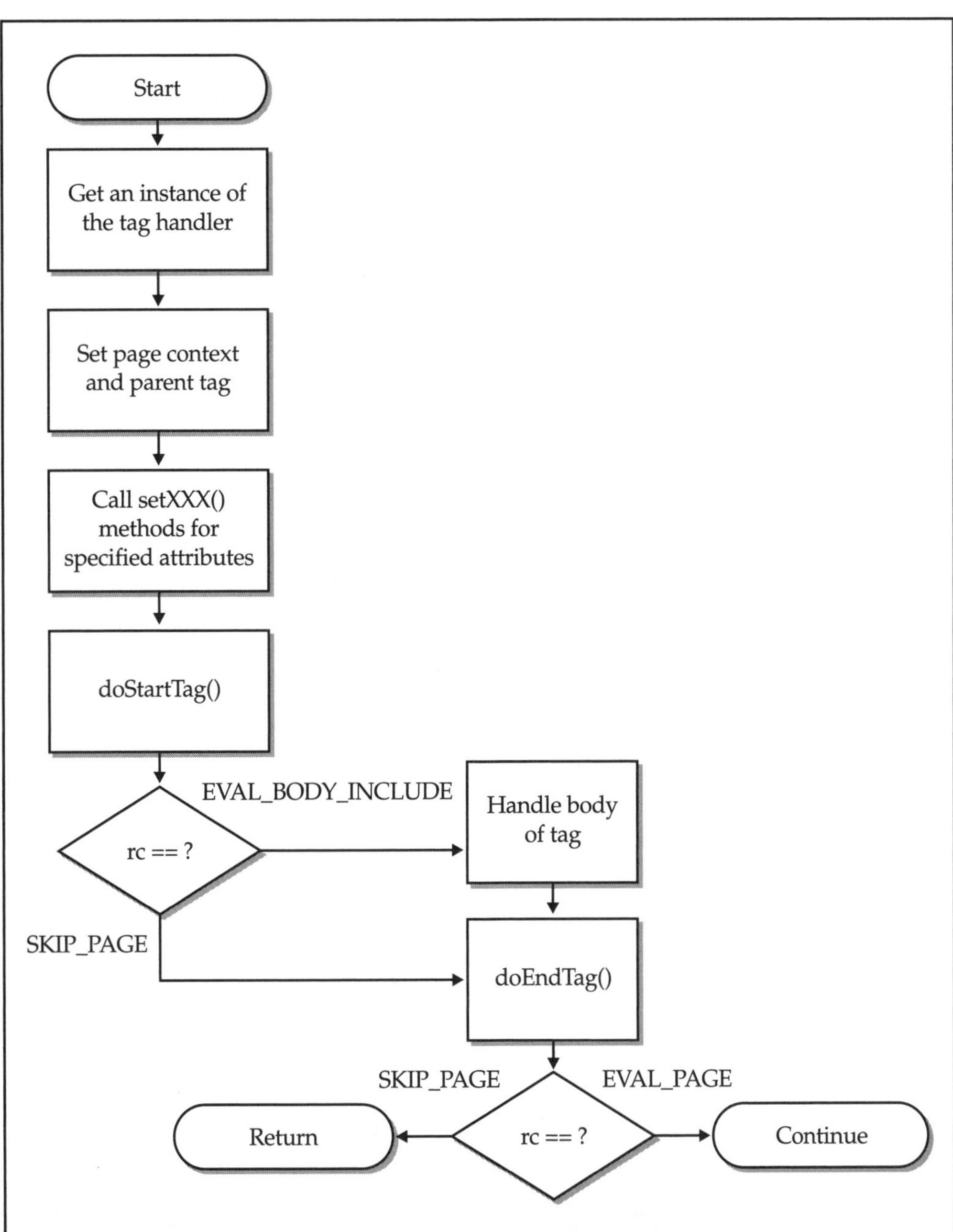


**Figure 11-2.** *Flowchart of the tag handler life cycle*

tag handler methods will be called, and what the state of the page and container will be is important. Understanding this protocol can help you write code that works as you expect. Also important is to remember the tag itself doesn't exist in the generated servlet at run time—the tag has been replaced by equivalent code that sets attributes and calls methods in the tag handler.

Let's consider each step in the flowchart.

## The Flowchart

To start, the generated servlet needs to create an instance of the tag handler class. It usually does so by invoking a method in a factory class that is part of the JSP container. The factory class may maintain a pool of tag handler instances so it can reuse tag handlers that are no longer active.

Next, the tag handler instance is initialized and made aware of the state of the servlet in which it exists. The servlet does this by calling two methods in the tag handler:

| | |
|---|---|
| `setPageContext(PageContext ctx)` | The `PageContext` object contains references to all the JSP implicit object, and provides access to attributes at the page, request, session, and application level. When the servlet calls this method, the tag handler should save the context in an instance variable so it will be available to all the handlers' methods. Note, the `TagSupport` base class does this automatically. |
| `setParent(Tag parent)` | Tags in a JSP page may be nested, that is, contained within the body of another tag. Immediately after `setPageContext()` is called, the servlet calls `setParent()`, passing a reference to the tag that contains this one, if any. If the tag isn't nested, the parameter will be null. Having access to enclosing tags makes it possible for a tag to call methods in any of its parents, which makes cooperative action practical. The `TagSupport` class also saves this variable automatically. |

If a tag supports attributes, the run-time values of these attributes are passed to the tag handler by means of setter methods, which the handler must supply. For example, the database connection tag at the beginning of this chapter

```
<db:connect url="mydatabase">
```

has one attribute, named `url`. Its tag handler must have a method with the signature

```
public void setUrl(String value)
```

that stores the value of the `url` attribute, most likely in a private instance variable. For each attribute *xxx* coded in the start tag, the generated servlet will have a `setXxx(value)` method call. These calls are located immediately after the `setParent()` call.

At this point, the tag handler's `doStartTag()` method is called. The page context and parent tag have already been set, as have all the tag's attributes. The method can read these variables and perform whatever calculations and operations necessary to implement the tag's functionality. It can access the servlet output writer by calling `pageContext.getOut()`. It can change the values of scripting variables in the JSP page by setting attributes in the page context. This is examined in detail later in this chapter, in the section entitled "Defining Scripting Variables." If any fatal errors are encountered, the method should throw a `JspException`.

The `doStartTag()` method must return an integer return code, either `SKIP_BODY` or `EVAL_BODY_INCLUDE`. If the return code from `doStartTag()` is `EVAL_BODY_INCLUDE`, then the body of the tag is handled as usual. If the return code is `SKIP_BODY`, everything in the original JSP page up to this tag's end tag is ignored.

**Note** *SKIP_BODY is the default return code of `doStartTag()` in the `TagSupport` base class, providing a rare instance of where `TagSupport` can actually perform a useful function without being subclassed—you can use it as the handler for a custom tag that "comments out" code. If you make the following entry in a TLD*

```
<tag>
   <name>skip</name>
   <tagclass>javax.servlet.jsp.tagext.TagSupport</tagclass>
   <bodycontent>JSP</bodycontent>
</tag>
```

*then you can surround any part of a JSP page[5] with*

```
<prefix.skip>
...
</prefix.skip>
```

*and it won't be executed at run time.*

After the tag body is either evaluated or ignored, the tag handler's `doEndTag()` method is invoked. Like `doStartTag()`, this method must return an integer return code that indicates how to proceed. If the value is `EVAL_PAGE`, the rest of the page is evaluated; if it's `SKIP_PAGE`, the servlet code executes an immediate return from `_jspService()`.

5 Well, not *any* part. Scriptlets, expressions, standard actions, and HTML template data will be suppressed if they are inside the `skip` tag body, but you cannot use tags *inside* a scriptlet, expression, or declaration.

## An Example of Generated Code

The interaction between the generated servlet and a tag handler becomes clearer when we look at an example. Let's develop an enhanced version of the getWebServer tag from earlier in the chapter, one that lets us specify any header name, rather than hard coding the choice of the Server header. To do this, the tag will accept an *attribute* called name. The following section discusses tag attributes at length but, for the purposes of this example, all we need to know is the attribute is described in the TLD and communicated to the tag handler using its setName() method. This tag will be called getWebServerHeader. The TLD requires a small addition:

```
<tag>
   <name>getWebServerHeader</name>
   <tagclass>jspcr.taglib.diag.GetWebServerHeaderTag</tagclass>
   <bodycontent>empty</bodycontent>
   <attribute>
      <name>name</name>
      <required>true</required>
      <rtexprvalue>true</rtexprvalue>
   </attribute>
</tag>
```

The name attribute is defined as a required field and its value can be supplied by a request time expression if desired, rather than being coded as a literal.

Not surprisingly, the tag handler is almost identical to the one for getWebServer. Here's the source code for the getWebServerHeader tag handler:

```
package jspcr.taglib.diag;

import javax.servlet.http.*;
import javax.servlet.jsp.*;
import javax.servlet.jsp.tagext.*;
import java.io.*;
import java.net.*;

/**
* Handler for the "getWebServerHeader" tag
*/
public class GetWebServerHeaderTag extends TagSupport
{
   private String name;

   /**
```

```
   * Sets the name property.  A call to this method
   * is automatically generated by the JSP container
   * when a tag with the name attribute is used in
   * a JSP page.
   */
   public void setName(String name)
   {
      this.name = name;
   }

   public int doStartTag() throws JspException
   {
      try {

         // Get the request object from the page context

         HttpServletRequest request =
            (HttpServletRequest) pageContext.getRequest();

         // Request information from web server

         URL url = new URL("http",
                     request.getServerName(),
                     request.getServerPort(),
                     "/");
         URLConnection con = url.openConnection();
         ((HttpURLConnection) con).setRequestMethod("OPTIONS");

         // Extract the requested header

         String header = con.getHeaderField(name);

         // Write it to the output stream

         JspWriter out = pageContext.getOut();
         out.print(header);
      }
      catch (IOException e) {
         throw new JspException(e.getMessage());
      }
      return SKIP_BODY;
   }
}
```

The main difference is the addition of the name attribute. This required a name variable and a setName() method be created. Then, rather than

```
String webserver = con.getHeaderField("server");
```

you have

```
String header = con.getHeaderField(name);
```

where name is the value coded in the JSP tag.

In the JSP page, we'll use the old tag to get the Web server product name and the new tag to get the Allow header. Because the tag handler makes an HTTP request using the OPTIONS method, the server should return an Allow header that lists the request methods it will accept. Here is the updated page, named ShowServerHeader.jsp:

```
<%@ taglib prefix="diag" uri="/WEB-INF/tlds/diagnostics.tld" %>

<HTML>

<HEAD>
<TITLE>Custom Tag with Attributes</TITLE>
</HEAD>

<BODY>
<H3>Custom Tag with Attributes</H3>

Request methods supported by this instance of
<diag:getWebServer/>
are
<H4><diag:getWebServerHeader name="allow"/></H4>
</BODY>

</HTML>
```

When ShowServerHeader.jsp is run, it produces the output shown in Figure 11-3.

Let's examine part of the _jspService() method servlet that the JSP container (JRun 3.0, in this example) generated for ShowServerHeader.jsp. The source code

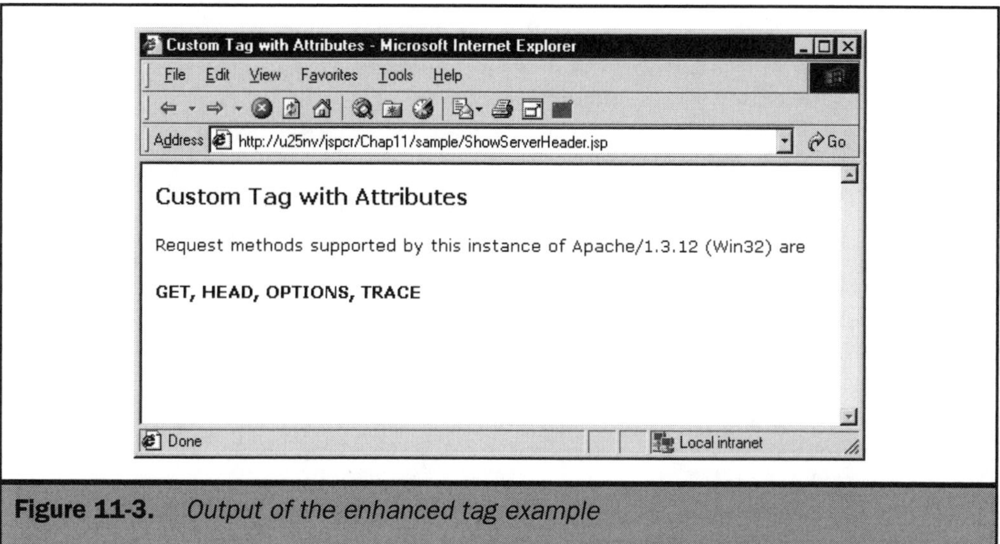


**Figure 11-3.** *Output of the enhanced tag example*



has been reformatted and modified slightly for clarity. Note, you needn't write this; it's what the JSP container generates based on your JSP page and TLD definition.

```
PageContext pageContext = __jspFactory.getPageContext
   (this, request, response,  null, true, 8192, true);
JspWriter out = pageContext.getOut();

try {

   out.print("\r\n\r\n"
      + "<HTML>\r\n\r\n"
      + "<HEAD>\r\n"
      + "<TITLE>Custom Tag with Attributes</TITLE>\r\n"
      + "</HEAD>\r\n\r\n"
      + "<BODY>\r\n"
      + "<H3>Custom Tag with Attributes</H3>\r\n\r\n"
      + "Request methods supported by this instance of"
      + "\r\n");
```

```
    GetWebServerTag tag1 = (GetWebServerTag)
       JRunJSPStaticHelpers.createTagHandler
          (pageContext, "GetWebServerTag");

    tag1.setPageContext(pageContext);
    tag1.setParent(null);
    tag1.doStartTag();

    if (tag1.doEndTag() == Tag.SKIP_PAGE) {
       return;
    }

    out.print("\r\n"
       + "are\r\n"
       + "<H4>");

    GetWebServerHeaderTag tag2 = (GetWebServerHeaderTag)
       JRunJSPStaticHelpers.createTagHandler
          (pageContext, "GetWebServerHeaderTag");

    tag2.setPageContext(pageContext);
    tag2.setParent(null);
    tag2.setName("allow");
    tag2.doStartTag();

    if (tag2.doEndTag() == Tag.SKIP_PAGE) {
       return;
    }

    out.print("</H4>\r\n\r\n</BODY>\r\n\r\n</HTML>\r\n");

 }
```

Near the beginning of `_jspService()`, the servlet creates and initializes its page context:

```
PageContext pageContext = __jspFactory.getPageContext
   (this, request, response,  null, false, 8192, true);
```

The `JspFactory` has a `getPageContext()` method that takes a reference to the current servlet, the request and response objects, the URL for the error page (if any), a flag indicating whether the page needs an HTTP session, the output buffer size, and a flag indicating whether the buffer should be autoflushed. The method returns an initialized page context that encapsulates all these objects.

```
JspWriter out = pageContext.getOut();
```

Having initialized a page context object, the servlet uses it to obtain a reference to the response output writer. The tag handler can use this same method call to do its own output to the page, if desired. The issue becomes slightly more complicated for tag handlers that interact with their body content, as we will see in the next section.



```
GetWebServerTag tag1 = (GetWebServerTag)
   JRunJSPStaticHelpers.createTagHandler
      (pageContext, "GetWebServerTag");
```

After printing the page headings, the servlet creates an instance of the tag handler, using a static method in a helper class. This helper class may use a pool of tag handler instances or perform other optimizations—the JSP specification doesn't dictate how this should be done. This affords servlet engine vendors the opportunity to distinguish their product's performance and functionality.

```
tag1.setPageContext(pageContext);
tag1.setParent(null);
```

As the flowchart in Figure 11-2 indicates, the generated servlet then calls the tag handler's `setPageContext()` and `setParent()` methods. No parent tag exists in this case, so the parameter value is `null`.

```
tag1.doStartTag();
```

With the page environment thus fully described to the tag handler, its `doStartTag()` method is called. Note, no return code is captured, even though `doStartTag()` returns one. The reason for this is the TLD indicates the `getWebServer` tag has no body (`<bodycontent>empty</bodycontent>`), so no conditional code is generated to handle it. The JSP container is able to optimize the code rather than checking a meaningless return value.

```
if (tag1.doEndTag() == Tag.SKIP_PAGE) {
   return;
}
```

The doEndTag() method can return either EVAL_PAGE or SKIP_PAGE. The effect of each becomes clear when we see that SKIP_PAGE simply causes a return from the _jspService() method.

After printing the intervening HTML, the servlet begins work on the second tag:

```
GetWebServerHeaderTag tag2 = (GetWebServerHeaderTag)
   JRunJSPStaticHelpers.createTagHandler
      (pageContext, "GetWebServerHeaderTag");

tag2.setPageContext(pageContext);
tag2.setParent(null);
tag2.setName("allow");
tag2.doStartTag();
```

The only difference between the handling of this tag and the previous one results because the getWebServerHeader tag has a name attribute. This is transformed into a call to the tag handler's setName() method just before doStartTag() is called. The end tag is handled the same, with its return code determining whether to exit from the _jspService() method or continue.

## Defining Tag Attributes

A custom tag can have any number of *attributes*, which are name/value pairs coded in the start tag when it's used in a JSP page. For example, the tag shown in the following

```
<opera:role name="Papageno" range="baritone"
            description="a bird-catcher"/>
```

has three attributes: name, range, and description. Attributes may be required or optional, and their values can be coded as string literals or supplied at request time using JSP expressions (if the tag allows this).

For each attribute a tag supports, its tag handler must supply two things:

- An instance variable to store the attribute
- One or more set*Attrname*() methods, where *Attrname* is the attribute name with the first letter capitalized.

For the previous example tag, the tag handler might look like this:

```
/**
* RoleTag
```

```
*/
public class RoleTag extends TagSupport
{
   // Three attributes:

   private String name;
   private String range;
   private String description;

   // ... and their setter methods:

   public void setName(String nameFromJSPTag)
   {
      name = nameFromJSPTag;
   }

   public void setRange(String rangeFromJSPTag)
   {
      range = rangeFromJSPTag;
   }

   public void setDescription(String descriptionFromJSPTag)
   {
      description = descriptionFromJSPTag;
   }

   public int doStartTag() throws JspException
   {
      try {
         JspWriter out = pageContext.getOut();
         out.println("<TR>");
         out.println("<TD>" + name + "</TD>");
         out.println("<TD>" + range + "</TD>");
         out.println("<TD>" + description + "</TD>");
         out.println("</TR>");
      }
      catch (IOException e) {
         throw new JspException(e.getMessage());
      }
      return SKIP_BODY;
   }
}
```

The JSP container generates code in the JSP servlet to take attribute values coded in a custom tag and sends them to the tag handler. It does this by calling the `setAttrname()` methods for each attribute. This is done after the page context and parent tag have been set, but just before `doStartTag()` has been called. For example, if a JSP page uses the `<opera:role>` tag as follows

```
<%@ page session="false" %>
<%@ taglib prefix="opera" uri="/WEB-INF/tlds/opera.tld" %>

<HTML>
<HEAD><TITLE>The Magic Flute</TITLE></HEAD>

<BODY>
<H2>The Magic Flute</H2>
<H3>Dramatis Personae</H3>
<TABLE BORDER="1" CELLPADDING="3" CELLSPACING="0">
<TR><TH>Role</TH><TH>Range</TH><TH>Description</TH>

<opera:role name="Tamino" range="Tenor"
            description="an Egyptian prince"/>

<opera:role name="Pamina" range="Soprano"
            description="daughter of the Queen of the Night"/>

<opera:role name="Papageno" range="Baritone"
            description="a bird-catcher"/>

<opera:role name="Queen of the Night" range="Soprano"
            description="die Sternflammende Königin"/>

<opera:role name="Sarastro" range="Bass"
            description="High Priest of Isis and Osiris"/>

</TABLE>
</BODY>
</HTML>
```

then the generated servlet (again using JRun as the container) would handle each of the `<opera:role>` tags with code similar to the following:

```
RoleTag roleTag = (RoleTag)
   JRunJSPStaticHelpers.createTagHandler
   (pageContext, "RoleTag");
```

```
    roleTag.setPageContext(pageContext);
    roleTag.setParent(null);

    roleTag.setRange("Baritone");
    roleTag.setName("Papageno");
    roleTag.setDescription("a bird-catcher");

    roleTag.doStartTag();
```

The property setter method is all that's required for a tag to support an attribute, but more information can be specified in the TLD. In the `<tag>` element, there can be any number of `<attribute>` elements in the following form:

```
<attribute>
    <name>attributeName</name>
    <required>true|false</required>
    <rtexprvalue>true|false</rtexprvalue>
</attribute>
```

Only the attribute name is required; the other two elements are optional and default to `false`.

If `<required>true</required>` is specified, then the attribute must be coded everywhere the tag is used or a fatal translation error will occur. Otherwise, the attribute is optional. The tag handler should take care to handle the case where the attribute hasn't been specified, in which case the instance variable will be null.

If `<rtexprvalue>true</rtexprvalue>` is specified, then the attribute value may be specified with a request time expression. Attributes coded in this manner have the form

```
attribute="<%= scriptlet_expression %>"
```

where the quotes may include nothing but the JSP expression. In addition to making it possible to supply a value for the attribute at run time, this also causes the type of the expression to be preserved. In other words,

```
date="<%= new java.util.Date() %>"
```

would result in the generated servlet code

```
    tag.setDate(new java.util.Date());
```

which would cause the tag handler's `public void setDate(Date date)` method to be invoked, rather than `public void setDate(String date)`.

Here is an example of a custom tag with two optional attributes, each of which can be specified with request time expressions.

```
<x:formattedDate date="date" format="format"/>
```

The date attribute should be specified at a `java.util.Date` object in a request time expression, but the format can be either a `java.text.SimpleDateFormat` or the format string that `SimpleDateFormat` uses. The TLD would look like this:

```
<?xml version="1.0" ?>
<taglib>

   <tlibversion>1.0</tlibversion>
   <jspversion>1.1</jspversion>
   <shortname>util</shortname>

   <tag>
      <name>formattedDate</name>
      <tagclass>jspcr.taglib.util.FormattedDateTag</tagclass>
      <bodycontent>empty</bodycontent>
      <info>
         Returns a date formatted using the specified format.
         If no date is specified, uses current date.
         Default date format is MM/dd/yyyy
      </info>

      <attribute>
         <name>date</name>
         <required>false</required>
         <rtexprvalue>true</rtexprvalue>
      </attribute>

      <attribute>
         <name>format</name>
         <required>false</required>
         <rtexprvalue>true</rtexprvalue>
      </attribute>
   </tag>

</taglib>
```

Here is the tag handler:

```
package jspcr.taglib.util;

import javax.servlet.jsp.*;
import javax.servlet.jsp.tagext.*;
import java.io.*;
import java.text.*;
import java.util.*;

/**
* FormattedDateTag
*/
public class FormattedDateTag extends TagSupport
{
   // The date attribute

   private Date date;
   public void setDate(Date date)
   {
      this.date = date;
   }

   // The format attribute

   private SimpleDateFormat format;
   public void setFormat(String fmtstr)
   {
      format = new SimpleDateFormat(fmtstr);
   }
   public void setFormat(SimpleDateFormat fmt)
   {
      format = fmt;
   }

   /**
   * Prints the date when the start tag is encountered
   */
   public int doStartTag() throws JspException
   {
      // Get date attribute, defaulting to current date
```

```
        Date date = this.date;
        if (date == null)
           date = new Date();

        // Get date format attribute, defaulting
        // to month/day/year

        SimpleDateFormat format = this.format;
        if (format == null)
           format = new SimpleDateFormat("MM/dd/yyyy");

        // Format and print

        try {
           pageContext.getOut().print(format.format(date));
        }
        catch (IOException e) {
           throw new JspException(e.getMessage());
        }

        return SKIP_BODY;
     }
  }
```

Note two `setFormat()` methods exist: one takes a `java.text.SimpleDateFormat`; another takes a string and creates a `SimpleDateFormat` from it. The method for which the JSP container generates servlet code depends on whether the tag is coded with a request time expression. Here is an example of how the tag can be used:

```
<%@ page session="false" %>
<%@ page import="java.util.*,java.text.*" %>
<%@ taglib prefix="x" uri="/WEB-INF/tlds/util.tld" %>

<%
   Calendar gc = new GregorianCalendar(1931, 6, 25);
   Date then = gc.getTime();
   SimpleDateFormat fmt =
      new SimpleDateFormat("MMMMM d, yyyy");
%>
```

```
The date was
<x:formattedDate date="<%= then %>" format="<%= fmt %>" />.
```

When used in the preceding JSP page, the tag produces the output

```
The date was July 25, 1931.
```



# The Body Tag Handler API

Simple tags are useful components that perform their function entirely within their start tag. However, the real power of custom tags results from their capability to interact with their tag body. This makes it possible for a custom tag to

- Post-process its body text, perhaps sorting it, making an HTML table from it, or filtering out characters like "<" and ">", replacing them with their HTML-safe equivalents "`<`" and "`>`".
- Define new implicit objects and create scripting variables for them.
- Cooperate with nested tags to perform complex operations.

Tags that operate on their body are an extension of the tags discussed so far in this chapter. They implement a subinterface of `javax.servlet.jsp.tagext.Tag`, known as `javax.servlet.jsp.tagext.BodyTag`. As was the case with the `TagSupport` class, a base class implementation of `BodyTag` also exists, called `BodyTagSupport`.

## BodyContent

When the JSP container generates code for a tag that has a body, it saves and restores the object that represents the current servlet output writer. Before the body of the tag is processed, a new output writer is created—this one an instance of the `BodyContent` class. While the body is being evaluated, the `out` scripting variable as well as the value returned by `pageContext.getOut()` both refer to the new writer object. If several levels of nesting exist, the writers are saved on a stack, so each level has its own writer.

`BodyContent` is a subclass of `javax.servlet.jsp.JspWriter`, but differs from its superclass, in that its contents aren't automatically written to the servlet output stream. Instead, they're accumulated in what amounts to a string buffer. After the tag body is completed, the original `JspWriter` is restored, but the `BodyContent` object is still available in `doEndTag()` in the `bodyContent` variable. Its contents can be retrieved with its `getString()` or `getReader()` methods, modified as necessary, and written to the restored `JspWriter` output stream to be merged with the page output. Table 11-3 lists the additional methods that `BodyContent` provides.

| Method | Description |
|---|---|
| `public void flush() throws IOException` | Overrides the `JspWriter.flush()` method so it always throws an exception. Flushing a BodyContent writer isn't valid because it isn't connected to an actual output stream to which it could be written. |
| `public void clearBody()` | Resets the `BodyContent` buffer to empty. This can be useful if the body is being written to the enclosing writer in `doAfterBody()`. |
| `public Reader getReader()` | Returns a reader for the body content after it has been evaluated. This reader can be passed to other classes that can process a `java.io.Reader`, such as `StreamTokenizer`, `FilterReader`, or an XML parser. |
| `public String getString()` | Returns a string containing the body content after it has been evaluated. |
| `public void writeOut(Writer w)` | Writes the body content to the specified output writer. |
| `public JspWriter getEnclosingWriter()` | Returns the writer object (possibly another `BodyContent`) next higher in the stack. |

**Table 11-3.** *Additional Methods in the BodyContent Class*

Why does the JSP container create this elaborate structure for custom tag output? We already learned the JSP container allows output to be post-processed and filtered, but it's also because not all body content is intended to produce output. For example, in the earlier database query

```
<db:runQuery>
   SELECT   *
   FROM     FD_GROUP
   WHERE    FdGp_Desc LIKE '%F%'
   ORDER BY FdGp_Cd
</db:runQuery>
```

the body is not HTML at all, but a character string representing an SQL statement. This would presumably be read with the `BodyContent.getString()` method and passed to a JDBC statement object whose output would be written to the Web page. This is automatically possible because the `BodyContent` object stores its output in a buffer rather than writing it.

## The BodyTag Interface

Tags that interact with their body content have a slightly more complex life cycle, so they require a few more methods in their tag handlers. For this reason, an extension of the `Tag` interface called `BodyTag` exists, which inherits all the methods required by `Tag`, but adds three new ones having to do with body handling. Table 11-4 describes the interface.

In addition to the three new methods, the `BodyTag` interface also defines one new integer constant:

- `EVAL_BODY_TAG` When returned by `doStartTag()`, causes a new BodyContent object to be created and associated with this tag handler. When returned by `doAfterBody()`, causes the JSP servlet to evaluate the body again after updating any scripting variables controlled by this tag. This makes it possible for a tag handler to loop through a list of elements, evaluating the body for each one.

| Method | Description |
|---|---|
| `public void setBodyContent(BodyContent out)` | Invoked by the JSP servlet after the current `JspWriter` has been pushed and a new `BodyContent` writer has been created. This occurs just after `doStartTag()`. |
| `public void doInitBody() throws JspException` | A lifecycle method called after `setBodyContent()`, but just before the body is evaluated. If the body is evaluated multiple times, this method is called only once. |
| `public int doAfterBody() throws JspException` | A lifecycle method called after the body has been evaluated, but while the `BodyContent` writer is still active. This method must return either `EVAL_BODY_TAG` or `SKIP_BODY`. If the return code is `EVAL_BODY_TAG`, the body is evaluated again and `doAfterBody()` is called again. |

**Table 11-4.** *Methods in the BodyTag Interface*

*In addition to SKIP_BODY, doStartTag() can return either EVAL_BODY_INCLUDE or EVAL_BODY_TAG, both of which indicate the body should be processed. However, tag handlers that implement BodyTag cannot return EVAL_BODY_INCLUDE, and tag handlers that don't implement BodyTag cannot return EVAL_BODY_TAG. Both of these actions cause run-time exceptions.*

## The BodyTagSupport Class

As was the case with the `Tag` interface, `BodyTag` has a default implementation class called `javax.servlet.jsp.tagext.BodyTagSupport`. This class extends `TagSupport`, but with a few subtle changes. Table 11-5 describes the public methods implemented by `BodyTagSupport`.

Body tag handlers are free to implement the `BodyTag` interface directly, but `BodyTagSupport` is usually a more convenient base class.

| Method | Description |
|---|---|
| `public int doStartTag() throws JspException` | Overrides `doStartTag()` in `TagSupport`, returning `EVAL_BODY_TAG` by default instead of `SKIP_BODY`. |
| `public int doEndTag() throws JspException` | Invokes `doEndTag()` in `TagSupport`, returning its result. |
| `public void setBodyContent (BodyContent out)` | Stores the new body content object in a protected variable named `bodyContent`. Subclasses can access this variable directly. |
| `public void doInitBody() throws JspException` | Does nothing by default. Intended to be overridden by subclasses that need to perform initialization before the body is evaluated. |
| `public int doAfterBody() throws JspException` | Called by the JSP servlet after each time the body has been evaluated. The body content object is still active. This method must return either `SKIP_BODY` or `EVAL_BODY_TAG`, which causes the body to be evaluated again and `doAfterBody()` to be called again. |

**Table 11-5.** *Methods in BodyTagSupport*

| Method | Description |
|---|---|
| `public void release()` | Sets the `bodyContent` variable to `null`, and then calls `super.release()`. An overriding method must call `super.release()` as well, otherwise `bodyContent` may not be available for garbage collecting. |
| `public BodyContent getBodyContent()` | Returns the `bodyContent` variable. Subclasses already have access to the protected variable, but this method allows unrelated tag handler classes to send output to this body content. |
| `public JspWriter getPreviousOut()` | A convenience method that calls `getEnclosingWriter()` on the `bodyContent` variable and returns the result. |

**Table 11-5.** *Methods in BodyTagSupport* (continued)



# The Body Tag Handler Life Cycle

Figure 11-4 depicts the slightly more complex life cycle of tag handlers that interact with their body.

The following section describes each event in the life cycle flowchart.

## The Flowchart

The first few steps down to `doStartTag()` are no different than they were in Figure 11-2. The first difference is in the handling of the return code from this method. `doStartTag()` in a body tag handler can return either `SKIP_BODY`, which causes an immediate branch to `doEndTag()`, or `EVAL_BODY_TAG`, which starts the chain of events that handle the tag body.

When `EVAL_BODY_TAG` is returned from `doStartTag()`, the JSP servlet[6] invokes the page context's `pushBody()` method, which does three things:

1. Saves the current `JspWriter` on a stack.

6 The term *JSP servlet* in this section refers to the servlet generated by the JSP container based on the JSP page source code.

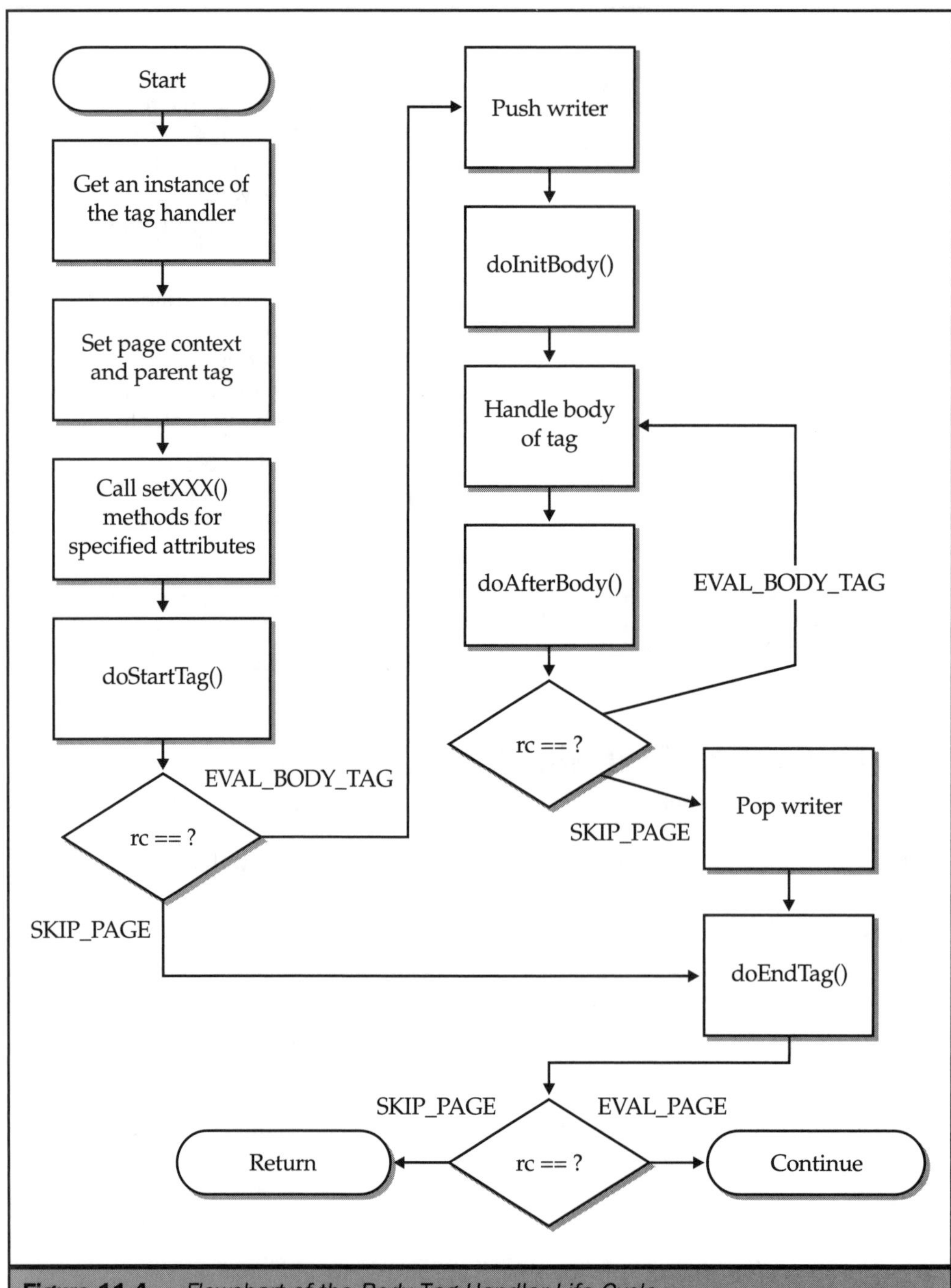


**Figure 11-4.** *Flowchart of the Body Tag Handler Life Cycle*

2. Creates a new `BodyContent` object and stores it in the page context's attributes in page scope under the name `out`.
3. Assigns the new `BodyContent` object to the JSP page implicit variable `out`.

After this, the JSP servlet calls the tag handler's `setBodyContent()` method with the new writer.

Next, the tag handler's `doInitBody()` method is called to handle any necessary initialization before the body is evaluated. This initialization could also be done in `doStartTag()`, but the new `BodyContent` object isn't available there yet. `doInitBody()` isn't called if no body is in the tag, and can throw a `JspException` if it detects any fatal errors.

At this point, the servlet handles the body of the tag as it normally would, writing its output to the `BodyContent` object. The processing depends on the value of the `<bodycontent>` element of the tag in the TLD. Three possible values exist for this element:

- `empty` The tag body must be empty.
- `JSP` Scriptlets, expressions, and template HTML are evaluated as usual. If any other custom tags are within the scope of the body, they are also evaluated, the same as they would be if used elsewhere on the page. If any of these have tag handlers that implement `BodyTag`, then the process is done recursively—the current `BodyContent` is pushed, a new `BodyContent` is assigned to the inner tag, and so on.
- `tagdependent` The contents of the body are written verbatim to the `BodyContent`. Scriptlets and expressions appear in their original JSP source form, rather than being interpreted by the JSP container.

After handling the body, the servlet invokes the tag handler's `doAfterBody()` method. If the tag handler wants to write its body content to the enclosing `JspWriter` at this time, it can do so, as follows

```
JspWriter out = bodyContent.getEnclosingWriter();
out.println(bodyContent.getString());
bodyContent.clear();
```

or, as

```
JspWriter out = bodyContent.getEnclosingWriter();
bodyContent.writeOut(out);
bodyContent.clear();
```

ELEMENTS OF JSP

If the body content isn't too large, it may be easier to wait until `doEndTag()`, and then write the body content in one operation.

The `doAfterBody()` method can return one of two possible return codes:

- `SKIP_BODY` proceeds with the rest of the page.
- `EVAL_BODY_TAG` causes the body to be evaluated again, followed by the `doAfterBody()` method. This would typically be done if an array or enumeration is being processed, with the next element in the array or enumeration being assigned to a scripting variable at each iteration.

When the `doAfterTag()` finally returns `SKIP_BODY`, the loop (if any) is exited. The body content is now completed, so the process of creating it is reversed:

1. A call to `pageContent.popBody()` retrieves the immediately previous `JspWriter`.
2. The writer is assigned back to the `out` scripting variable.

Finally, the `doEndTag()` method is called, allowing the tag handler to send its content back to the output stream. At this point, pageContext.getOut() refers to the original writer, the same one that existed before the tag was processed. However, the body content is still available in the protected `bodyContent` variable. It can be written to the servlet output stream as follows

```
JspWriter out = pageContext.getOut();
out.println(bodyContent.getString());
```

or simply

```
bodyContent.writeOut(pageContext.getOut());
```

`doEndTag()` should return either `SKIP_PAGE`, to cause the rest of the JSP page to be ignored, or `EVAL_PAGE`, to cause the page to be evaluated as usual.

Before we can give a detailed example of generated code for a body tag, we first need to understand how a tag handler interacts with scripting variables.

## Defining Scripting Variables

JSP page authors are familiar with scripting variables—these often are Java variables defined in a scriptlet or a `<jsp:useBean>` action. For example, in the scriptlet at the beginning of this code,

```
<%
   String[] flavors = {"Chocolate", "Strawberry", "Vanilla"};
   for (int i = 0; i < flavors.length; i++) {
%>
<LI>Flavor <%= i %> is <%= flavors[i] %>
<%
   }
%>
```

the integer variable *i* and the string array variable *flavors* are defined, and are later available for use by other scriptlets and expressions on the page. Similarly, in this JSP page,

```
<jsp:useBean id="m1" class="Meteor"/>
<jsp:setProperty name="m1"
      property="bane"
      value="The atmosphere"/>
Ahhhh! <%= m1.getBane() %>! Ahhhh!
```

the `<jsp:useBean>` action causes a variable named `m1` of class `Meteor` to be defined. This is used by the `<jsp:setProperty>` action that follows and is available to the expression on the last line.

Custom tags can also define scripting variables in their tag handlers and, as in the previous examples, the variables are then available to scriptlets, expressions, and other tags on the same page. The mechanism for defining such variables is the `TagExtraInfo` class.



## The TagExtraInfo Class

A tag that needs to define variables or perform validation on its attributes needs to define a class that extends the `TagExtraInfo` class. This subclass is associated with the custom tag in the TLD:

```
<tag>
   <name>mytag</name>
   <tagclass>mypackage.MyTagHandler</tagclass>
   <teiclass>mypackage.MyTagTEI</teiclass>
   ...
</tag>
```

The TEI comes into play during JSP translation time. When the JSP parser reads a `taglib` directive, it loads the associated tag and TEI class names for each tag from the TLD. Then, when a tag is parsed, methods in its TEI are invoked that get information about scripting variables and validations. By overriding these methods in a TEI subclass, a tag author can create variables and verify the tag attributes are valid. Table 11-6 lists the methods available in the `TagExtraInfo` class.

The method of primary interest is `getVariableInfo()`. This method is called by the JSP parser at page translation time and is expected to return an array of `VariableInfo` objects. `VariableInfo` is essentially only a data structure having four fields:

- `varName` The name of the variable to be created.
- `className` The fully qualified name of the variable's class.
- `declare` A boolean variable that is `true` if the JSP parser should create an actual definition for the variable (as opposed to assuming a variable of that class will have already been defined earlier in the servlet).
- `scope` An integer indicating the point at which the variable should be defined (or considered active).

| Method | Description |
|---|---|
| `public VariableInfo[] getVariableInfo(TagData data)` | Based on the list of attribute names and values in the `data` parameter, constructs an array of `VariableInfo` objects that describe the name, type, existence, and scope of each scripting variable to create. |
| `public boolean isValid(TagData data)` | Called by the JSP parser at page translation time. Given a list of attribute names and values, the method can validate them individually and in combination with each other. Returns `true` if the attributes are valid, `false` otherwise. The default implementation simply returns `true`. |
| `public void setTagInfo(TagInfo info)` | Sets the `TagInfo` object used by this class. |
| `public TagInfo getTagInfo()` | Returns the TagInfo object used by this class. |

**Table 11-6.** *The TagExtraInfo Class*

Three possible values exist for `scope` and each is represented by a constant defined in `VariableInfo`:

- `AT_BEGIN` The variable is defined when the start tag is encountered and remains visible for the rest of the page. This is the visibility of the `id` variable defined by `<jsp:useBean>`, for example.
- `AT_END` The variable is defined after the end tag and remains visible for the rest of the page.
- `NESTED` The variable is only defined within scope of the body of the tag.



## Example: The enumerate Tag

To illustrate the use of a TEI class, develop a tag named `enumerate`, which loops over a `java.util.Enumeration`, making each element in turn available as a scripting variable in the tag body. Here is the TLD definition for the tag:

```
<tag>
   <name>enumerate</name>
   <tagclass>jspcr.taglib.util.EnumerateTag</tagclass>
   <teiclass>jspcr.taglib.util.EnumerateTEI</teiclass>
   <bodycontent>JSP</bodycontent>
   <info>
      Iterates tag body through an enumeration
   </info>

   <attribute>
      <name>enumeration</name>
      <required>true</required>
      <rtexprvalue>true</rtexprvalue>
   </attribute>
</tag>
```

The tag takes one required attribute named `enumeration`. The type of this attribute is a `java.util.Enumeration`, so its value must be supplied by a request-time expression. The tag handler takes care of the actual iteration using the `Enumeration.hasMoreElements()` and `nextElement()` methods:

```
package jspcr.taglib.util;

import javax.servlet.jsp.*;
import javax.servlet.jsp.tagext.*;
import java.io.*;
```

```
import java.util.*;

/**
* EnumerateTag
*/
public class EnumerateTag extends BodyTagSupport
{
   // Enumeration attribute

   private Enumeration list;
   public void setEnumeration(Enumeration list)
   {
      this.list = list;
   }

   public int doStartTag() throws JspException
   {
      // Do not evaluate the body if the list is empty

      if (list.hasMoreElements()) {

         // Create a scripting variable named "element"
         // that contains the value of the current
         // element of the enumeration

         pageContext.setAttribute
            ("element", list.nextElement());

         return EVAL_BODY_TAG;
      }
      return SKIP_BODY;
   }

   public int doAfterBody() throws JspException
   {
      // Get next element.  This will be assigned
      // to the scripting variable named "element"

      if (list.hasMoreElements()) {

         pageContext.setAttribute
            ("element", list.nextElement());
```

```
            return EVAL_BODY_TAG;
         }

         // If no more elements, exit from the loop

         return SKIP_BODY;
      }

      public int doEndTag() throws JspException
      {
         // getOut() now refers to the original JspWriter

         try {
            bodyContent.writeOut(pageContext.getOut());
         }
         catch (IOException e) {
            throw new JspException(e.getMessage());
         }

         return EVAL_PAGE;
      }
   }
```



Notice as each element of the enumeration is processed, it is stored in the page context as an attribute under the name `element`.

To make the current element available as a scripting variable, we employ a TEI class:

```
package jspcr.taglib.util;

import javax.servlet.jsp.*;
import javax.servlet.jsp.tagext.*;

/**
* EnumerateTEI
*/
public class EnumerateTEI extends TagExtraInfo
{
   public VariableInfo[] getVariableInfo(TagData tagData)
   {
      return new VariableInfo[] {
```

```
            new VariableInfo(
               "element",               // Variable name
               "java.lang.Object",      // Class
               true,                    // Create a declaration?
               VariableInfo.NESTED      // Scope
            )
         };
      }
   }
```

The `getVariableInfo()` method in this case returns an array of length 1 containing a `VariableInfo` object for the desired scripting variable. The constructor declares that

- The variable name should be `element`.
- Its class should be `java.lang.Object`.
- The JSP parser should generate a declaration for the variable.
- The variable should be visible to the JSP page throughout the evaluation of the body, but not afterward.

The following `EnumTest.jsp` page shows the tag in action:

```
<%@ page session="false" %>
<%@ page import="java.util.*" %>
<%@ taglib prefix="util" uri="/WEB-INF/tlds/util.tld" %>

<%--
      The scriptlet below loads the properties object.
      It could just as easily be loaded from a file.
--%>
<%
   Properties flavors = new Properties();
   flavors.setProperty("Vanilla", "The perennial favorite");
   flavors.setProperty("Chocolate", "Rich and smooth");
   flavors.setProperty("Strawberry", "Dazzling and fruity");
%>

<TABLE BORDER="1" CELLPADDING="3" CELLSPACING="0">
<TR><TH>Flavor</TH><TH>Description</TH></TR>

<%--
      The enumerate tag will evaluate its body
```

```
      for each item in the properties object.
--%>

<util:enumerate enumeration="<%= flavors.propertyNames() %>">
<%
   String description = flavors.getProperty((String) element);
%>
<TR>
   <TD><%= element %></TD>
   <TD><%= description %></TD>
</TR>
</util:enumerate>

</TABLE>
```



The enumerate tag appears near the end of the file. Its value is assigned from the java.util.Enumeration returned by flavors.propertyNames(). Notice the element variable has no visible declaration—it's an implicit variable with a fixed name, similar to request, response, session, and other implicit variables defined everywhere in the JSP environment. The page uses element twice, once in a scriptlet, where it's used to get a property value, and once in a JSP expression, where its string value is printed in an HTML table.

Let's examine the servlet code generated by JRun for the enumerate tag. Comparing this to the flowchart shown in Figure 11-4 can be helpful.

```
EnumerateTag enumTag = (EnumerateTag)
   JRunJSPStaticHelpers.createTagHandler
      (pageContext, "EnumerateTag");

enumTag.setPageContext(pageContext);
enumTag.setParent(null);
enumTag.setEnumeration( flavors.propertyNames() );
```

The JSP page specified the value of the enumeration attribute with

```
enumeration="<%= flavors.propertyNames() %>"
```

This is passed on to the tag handler with a call to its setEnumeration() method. Next, the generated servlet invokes doStartTag() and checks its return code. Recall the doStartTag() reads the first element of the enumeration and stores it in the page context with setAttribute("element", list.nextElement()).

```
int rc = enumTag.doStartTag();
JRunJSPStaticHelpers.checkStartVal
   ("EnumerateTag", rc, BodyTag.EVAL_BODY_TAG, 24);
```

If the enumeration isn't empty, the `doStartTag()` method returns `EVAL_BODY_TAG`, which triggers the first pass through evaluating the body:

```
if (rc == BodyTag.EVAL_BODY_TAG) {

   out = pageContext.pushBody();

   enumTag.setBodyContent((BodyContent)out);
   enumTag.doInitBody();

   do {
      java.lang.Object element =
         (java.lang.Object)
            pageContext.getAttribute("element");
```

After setting up the nested body content and calling `doInitBody()`, the servlet enters a `do while` loop. The first statement of the loop is a `getAttribute()` for the `element` variable, which was just set in `doStartTag()`.

```
      out.print("\r\n");

      String description =
         flavors.getProperty((String) element);

      out.print("\r\n<TR>\r\n   <TD>");

      out.print(element);
      out.print("</TD>\r\n   <TD>");

      out.print(description);
      out.print("</TD>\r\n</TR>\r\n");

   }
   while (enumTag.doAfterBody() == BodyTag.EVAL_BODY_TAG);
```

The `element` variable is then used to print the table entry, and then `doAfterBody()` is called. `doAfterBody()` repeats the logic, which gets the next element, and sets it as the `element` attribute in `pageContext`. As long as elements are available, doAfterBody() returns EVAL_BODY_TAG, which causes the next loop iteration, assigning a new value to element as it runs.

```
      out = pageContext.popBody();
   }

   if (enumTag.doEndTag() == Tag.SKIP_PAGE) {
      if (true)
         return;
   }
```

Finally, after the enumeration is exhausted, doAfterBody() returns SKIP_BODY and the loop terminates. The previous JspWriter is popped from the stack, and doEndTag() dumps the result shown in Figure 11-5.

## Synchronizing Scripting Variables

When a scripting variable is defined in a TEI, the JSP container generates servlet code not only to define the variable, but also to synchronize it with its value inside the tag handler. Recall the tag handler uses pageContext.setAttribute() to assign the desired value. The generated servlet code has a corresponding pageContext.getAttribute() statement that assigns the value to the scripting variable after each of the "do" methods in the tag life cycle. Which variables get

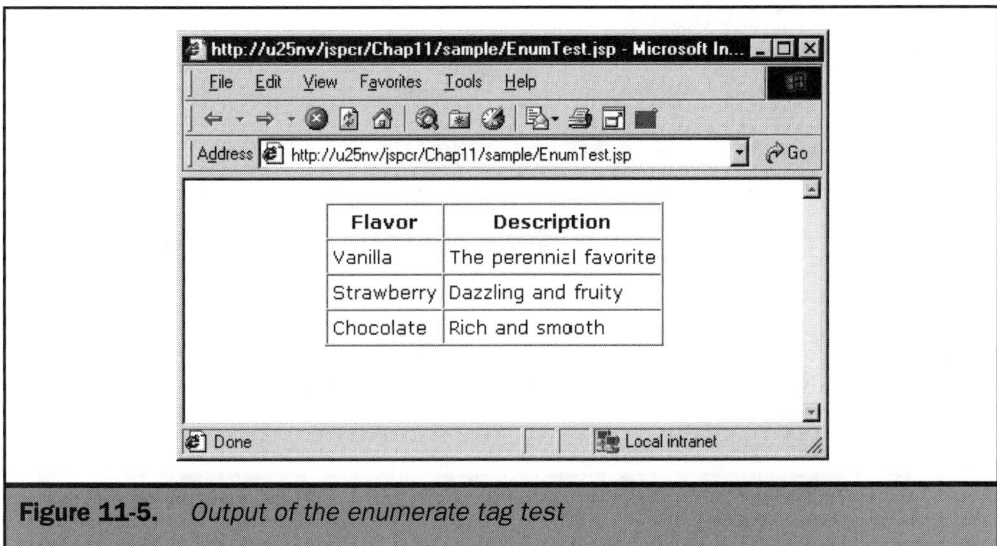


**Figure 11-5.** *Output of the enumerate tag test*

updated in this manner depends on their scope as defined in the TEI. Table 11-7 describes the assignment:

### Validating Tag Attributes

In addition to defining scripting variables, the TEI provides the `public boolean isValid(TagData data)` method in which tag attributes can be validated. In this method, you can extract the list of attribute names and values from the `data` parameter and check whether their values are valid. If not, you can return `false` to cause a page compilation error. For example, if a tag has several attributes, each of which is optional, but one of which must be specified, you cannot specify that semantic using the `<attribute>` elements in the TLD alone. The `isValid()` method is your only opportunity to do so.

To navigate through the list of attributes, you can call methods in the `TagData` parameter that is passed to `isValid()`. Table 11-8 lists some of the methods available.

One drawback of the `isValid()` method, however, is no obvious way exists to emit a meaningful error message. Either the tag as a whole is valid or it isn't.

## Cooperating Tags

Custom tags can interact with each other to perform useful operations. One approach commonly used is described as *syntactic scoping,* in which a tag handler calls methods in its parent classes. This section gives an extended example of the techniques.

### Using Syntactic Scoping

Recall that tags can be nested, that is, a tag can be used in the body of another tag. The `TagSupport` class provides the means for a tag handler to find the tag handlers of its

| Method | Scope of Variables Synchronized |
|---|---|
| `doStartTag()` | `AT_BEGIN, NESTED` |
| `doInitBody()` | `AT_BEGIN, NESTED` |
| `doAfterBody()` | `AT_BEGIN, NESTED` |
| `doEndTag()` | `AT_BEGIN, NESTED, AT_END` |

**Table 11-7.** *How Scope of Scripting Variables Affects Synchronization*

| Method | Description |
| --- | --- |
| `public void String getId()` | Returns the name of the ID attribute, if it was specified. |
| `public Object getAttribute(String name)` | Given an attribute name, returns the attribute value as an `Object`. If the attribute's value is unknown at translation time (that is, it is specified with a request time expression), this method returns `TagData.REQUEST_TIME_VALUE`. |
| `public String getAttributeString(String name)` | Given an attribute name, returns the attribute value as a `java.lang.String`, if possible. |
| `public Enumeration getAttributes()` | Returns an enumeration of the tag attribute names. Used in conjunction with `getAttribute()`, this can allow stepping through a list of all attribute/value pairs. |

**Table 11-8.** *Some Useful Methods in TagData*



enclosing tags using its `findAncestorWithClass()` method. This is a static method that takes two parameters—a reference to the current tag handler (`this`) and the class of the parent tag of interest:

```
OuterTag ot = (OuterTag)
   findAncestorWithClass(this, OuterTag.class);
if (ot == null)
   throw new JspException("No outer tag found");
```

Once the parent tag is found, all its public methods can be called directly. The following section illustrates how this technique can be used.

## Example: The switch Tag

We can use syntactic scoping to emulate the Java language `switch ... case` construct. We need three tags:

- `switch` The outer tag whose body defines the scope of the switch logic. This tag has a `value` attribute that defines the condition to be tested and determines which case block should be executed.

- `case` A tag representing one possible case block. We will give it two attributes: one to specify an exact value to match, another to specify a substring. A third attribute specifies whether the comparison should be case-sensitive. We use a TEI class `isValid()` method to verify only one of the first two attributes is specified.
- `default` The block to be executed if none of the other case blocks succeed.

Here are the TLD entries we need:

```
<tag>
   <name>switch</name>
   <tagclass>jspcr.taglib.util.SwitchTag</tagclass>
   <bodycontent>JSP</bodycontent>
   <info>
      The enclosing tag for a switch/case block
   </info>

   <attribute>
      <name>value</name>
      <required>true</required>
      <rtexprvalue>true</rtexprvalue>
   </attribute>
</tag>

<tag>
   <name>case</name>
   <tagclass>jspcr.taglib.util.CaseTag</tagclass>
   <teiclass>jspcr.taglib.util.CaseTEI</teiclass>
   <bodycontent>JSP</bodycontent>
   <info>
      A case block to be included in the body of a switch
   </info>

   <attribute>
      <name>match</name>
      <required>false</required>
      <rtexprvalue>true</rtexprvalue>
   </attribute>

   <attribute>
      <name>contains</name>
      <required>false</required>
```

```
         <rtexprvalue>true</rtexprvalue>
      </attribute>

      <attribute>
         <name>caseSensitive</name>
         <required>false</required>
         <rtexprvalue>true</rtexprvalue>
      </attribute>
   </tag>

   <tag>
      <name>default</name>
      <tagclass>jspcr.taglib.util.DefaultTag</tagclass>
      <bodycontent>JSP</bodycontent>
      <info>
         The default case included in the body of a switch
      </info>
   </tag>
```

The logic isn't particularly complicated. The `switch` tag provides public accessor methods for its `value` property and for a boolean `completed` property, which keeps track of whether a case block has matched the value and claimed the switch. Here is the tag handler:

```
package jspcr.taglib.util;

import javax.servlet.jsp.*;
import javax.servlet.jsp.tagext.*;

/**
* A tag that emulates the switch ... case construct.
* Within the body of this statement there can be
* any number of case tag, including one default tag.
* The first one that matches the text is executed,
* and the rest are bypassed.
*/
public class SwitchTag extends TagSupport
{
   // The value attribute.  This is the text that
   // case statements will compare to.
```

```
    private String value;
    public void setValue(String value)
       { this.value = value; }
    public String getValue()
       { return value; }

    // A flag that indicates whether the switch statement
    // is complete.  This happens when one of the case
    // statements matches the value and is executed.

    private boolean complete;
    public void setComplete(boolean complete)
       {this.complete = complete; }
    public boolean isComplete()
       { return complete; }

    /**
    * No real setup is required.  All this method
    * needs to do is return EVAL_BODY_INCLUDE
    */
    public int doStartTag() throws JspException
    {
       return EVAL_BODY_INCLUDE;
    }
}
```

The `case` tag is also fairly simple. It finds its enclosing `switch` tag using `findAncestorWithClass()`.The `case` tag first calls the `switch` tag's `isComplete()` method to see whether any other case has already claimed the switch. If so, it returns `SKIP_BODY`, so its body isn't executed. Otherwise, it calls the `switch` tag's `getValue()` method to retrieve the string to match. If the match succeeds, the `case` tag claims the `switch` with `setComplete(true)` and returns `EVAL_BODY_INCLUDE`. Here is the tag handler listing:

```
package jspcr.taglib.util;

import javax.servlet.jsp.*;
import javax.servlet.jsp.tagext.*;

/**
* The body of this tag will be executed if it
```

```
* satisfies the condition specified in its attributes
* with respect to the value of the enclosing switch tag
*/
public class CaseTag extends TagSupport
{
   // Value of an exact string to be matched

   private String match;
   public void setMatch(String match)
      { this.match = match; }

   // Value of a substring that could be contained
   // in the switch tag's value

   private String contains;
   public void setContains(String contains)
      { this.contains = contains; }

   // Value of a boolean flag that indicates whether
   // the match or comparison should be case sensitive.

   private boolean caseSensitive;
   public void setCaseSensitive(String flag)
   {
      caseSensitive = new Boolean(flag).booleanValue();
   }

   public int doStartTag() throws JspException
   {
      // Find the enclosing switch tag so that we
      // can call its methods

      SwitchTag switchTag = (SwitchTag)
         findAncestorWithClass(this, SwitchTag.class);

      // If the switch has already been satisfied,
      // skip the body of this statement

      if (switchTag.isComplete())
         return SKIP_BODY;

      // Test for an exact match, if the match attribute
```

```
    // was specified

    if (match != null) {

       String parentValue = switchTag.getValue();
       if (!caseSensitive)
          parentValue = parentValue.toUpperCase();

       String thisValue = match;
       if (!caseSensitive)
          thisValue = thisValue.toUpperCase();

       // If exact match, claim the switch

       if (parentValue.equals(thisValue)) {
          switchTag.setComplete(true);
          return EVAL_BODY_INCLUDE;
       }

       // Otherwise, ignore the body

       return SKIP_BODY;
    }

    // Test for an substring match, if the contains attribute
    // was specified

    if (contains != null) {

       String parentValue = switchTag.getValue();
       if (!caseSensitive)
          parentValue = parentValue.toUpperCase();

       String thisValue = contains;
       if (!caseSensitive)
          thisValue = thisValue.toUpperCase();

       // If parent value contains this substring,
       // claim the switch

       if (parentValue.indexOf(thisValue) != -1) {
          switchTag.setComplete(true);
          return EVAL_BODY_INCLUDE;
```

```
            }

            // Otherwise, ignore the body

            return SKIP_BODY;
         }

         return SKIP_BODY;
      }
   }
```

The TEI verifies that either the `match` attribute or the `contains` attribute have been specified, but not both:

```
package jspcr.taglib.util;

import javax.servlet.jsp.*;
import javax.servlet.jsp.tagext.*;

/**
* Validates the attributes of a case tag
*/
public class CaseTEI extends TagExtraInfo
{
   public boolean isValid(TagData tagData)
   {
      // The tag must contain either the match attribute
      // or the contains attribute, but not both.

      boolean noMatch =
         (tagData.getAttribute("match") == null);

      boolean noContains =
         (tagData.getAttribute("contains") == null);

      return (noMatch != noContains);
   }
}
```

The `default` tag handler works just like `case`, except its match condition is always true. `default` doesn't work exactly like its Java counterpart because it's not guaranteed to be executed last, unless it happens to be coded last. Here is the source code:

```
package jspcr.taglib.util;

import javax.servlet.jsp.*;
import javax.servlet.jsp.tagext.*;

/**
* The body of this tag will be executed if no other
* case tag has been encountered that satisfied
* the enclosing switch tag.
*/
public class DefaultTag extends TagSupport
{
   public int doStartTag() throws JspException
   {
      // Find the enclosing switch tag so that we
      // can call its methods

      SwitchTag switchTag = (SwitchTag)
         findAncestorWithClass(this, SwitchTag.class);

      // If the switch has already been satisfied,
      // skip the body of this statement

      if (switchTag.isComplete())
         return SKIP_BODY;

      // Otherwise, claim the switch

      switchTag.setComplete(true);
      return EVAL_BODY_INCLUDE;
   }
}
```

Used together, these tags can test a condition and execute the desired block. This JSP page illustrates their use:

```
<%@ page session="false" %>
<%@ taglib prefix="util" uri="/WEB-INF/tlds/util.tld" %>

<%
```

```
   String value = request.getParameter("value");
   if (value == null)
      value = "B";
%>
<H3>The value is <%= value %></H3>
<util:switch value="<%= value %>">

   <util:case match="A">
      <H3>The match="A" case block was selected</H3>
   </util:case>

   <util:case contains="B">
      <H3>The contains="B" case block was selected</H3>
   </util:case>

   <util:default>
      <H3>None of the case blocks were selected</H3>
   </util:default>

</util:switch>
```



When we run the JSP page with a parameter value of `A`, we get the results shown in Figure 11-6. With a value of `beauty` (containing *B*, case-insensitive), the results are as shown in Figure 11-7. Finally, if the value is `C`, which matches none of the case blocks, the resulting page is Figure 11-8.

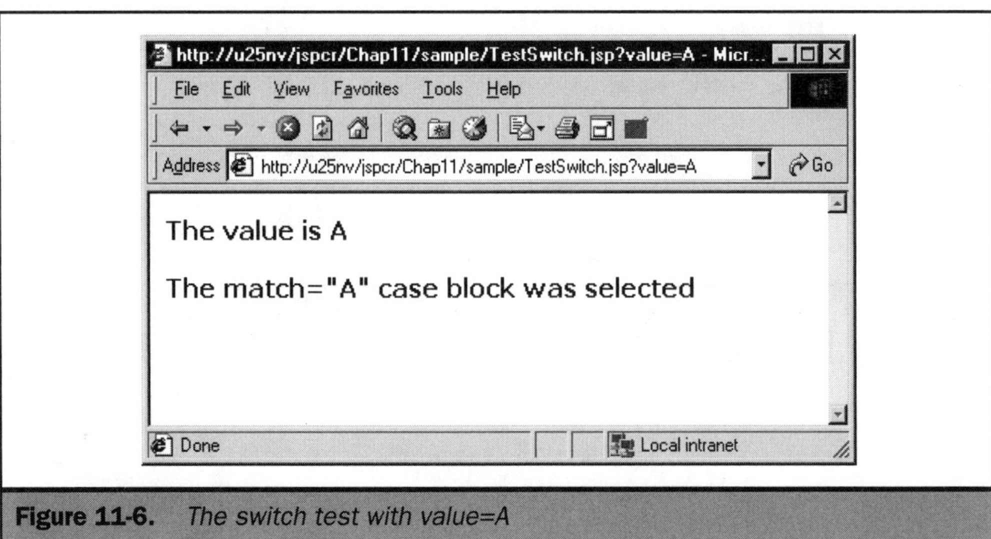


**Figure 11-6.** *The switch test with value=A*

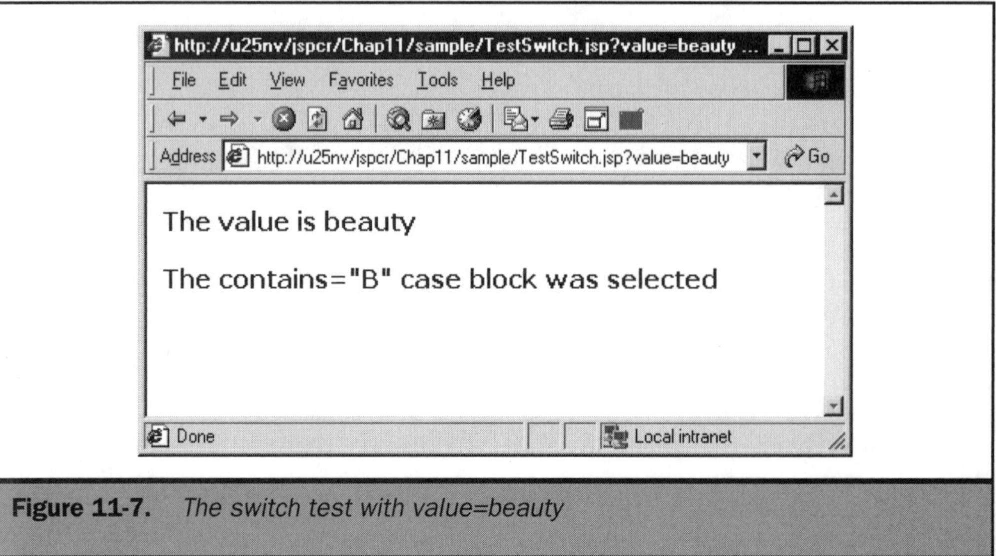


**Figure 11-7.** *The switch test with value=beauty*

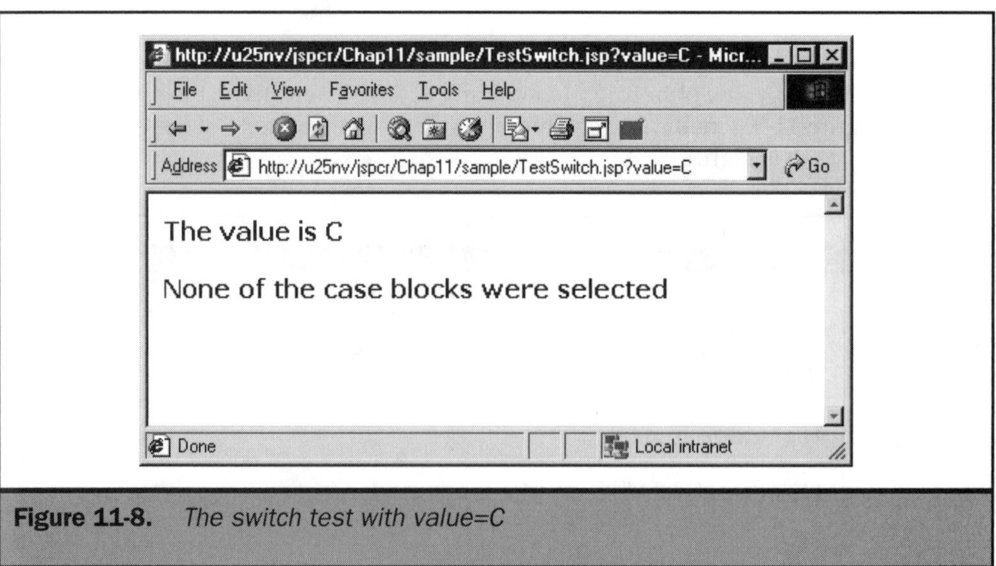


**Figure 11-8.** *The switch test with value=C*

# Implementation of the DatabaseQuery Example

This chapter concludes with the implementation of the database query example that was described at the beginning:

```
<db:connect url="mydatabase">

   <db:runQuery>
      SELECT    *
      FROM      FD_GROUP
      WHERE     FdGp_Desc LIKE '%F%'
      ORDER BY FdGp_Cd
   </db:runQuery>

   <table border="1" cellpadding="3" cellspacing="0">
      <tr><th>Food Group Code</th><th>Description</th></tr>
   <db:forEachRow>
      <tr>
         <td><db:getField name="FdGp_Cd"/></td>
         <td><db:getField name="FdGp_Desc"/></td>
      </tr>
   </db:forEachRow>
   </table>

</db:connect>
```

## The Necessary Tags

Four cooperating tags exist:

| | |
|---|---|
| `connect` | Opens a database connection and manages implicit `Statement` and `ResultSet` objects |
| `runQuery` | Reads an SQL statement in its body and tells the `connect` tag to execute it |
| `forEachRow` | An iterator over the `ResultSet` |
| `getField` | Retrieves the current value of the named field |

## The Tag Library Descriptor

The TLD for these tags is shown here:

```
<tag>
      <name>connect</name>
      <tagclass>jspcr.taglib.jdbc.ConnectTag</tagclass>
      <bodycontent>JSP</bodycontent>
      <info>Opens a database connection and manages
            a Statement and ResultSet object</info>

      <attribute>
         <name>url</name>
         <required>true</required>
         <rtexprvalue>true</rtexprvalue>
      </attribute>

   </tag>
```

The `connect` tag opens a connection and manages a `Statement` and `ResultSet` object. These aren't exposed as scripting variables; they're only accessible through other tags in this library. The connection is closed when the end tag is encountered. The syntax is

<db:connect url="*mydatabase*">

The driver class name could easily be added as another attribute. I made it implicit here to simplify the JSP.

```
<tag>
   <name>runQuery</name>
   <tagclass>jspcr.taglib.jdbc.RunQueryTag</tagclass>
   <bodycontent>JSP</bodycontent>
   <info>Reads and executes the SQL statement
         in the tag body</info>
</tag>
```

The `runQuery` tag reads an SQL statement from its body and executes it using the Statement object created by the enclosing connect tag. It can only be used in the body of a `connect` tag. The syntax of the runQuery tag is

<db:runQuery>*sql statement*</db:runQuery>

The result set is also managed by the `connect` tag.

```
   <tag>
      <name>forEachRow</name>
      <tagclass>jspcr.taglib.jdbc.ForEachRowTag</tagclass>
      <bodycontent>JSP</bodycontent>
      <info>Iterates over the current result set</info>
   </tag>
```

The `forEachRow` tag iterates over the current result set, so the `getField` tag can access its values. This can only be used the body of a connect tag after a `runQuery` tag. Its syntax is

<db:forEachRow>
...
</db:forEachRow>

```
<tag>
      <name>getField</name>
      <tagclass>jspcr.taglib.jdbc.GetFieldTag</tagclass>
      <bodycontent>empty</bodycontent>
      <info>Retrieves a field
         from the current result set row</info>

      <attribute>
         <name>name</name>
         <required>true</required>
         <rtexprvalue>true</rtexprvalue>
      </attribute>

   </tag>
```

The `getField` tag reads a field from the current result set row and returns its value as a String. this can only appear in the body of a `forEachRow` tag. Its syntax is

<db:getField name="*fieldName*" />

## The Tag Handlers

Four tag handlers need to be developed. Because no scripting variables are defined, we don't need any TEI classes.

## Connect

The connect tag takes a database URL as an attribute, so the tag handler needs an instance variable and a setUrl() method:

```
package jspcr.taglib.jdbc;

import javax.servlet.jsp.*;
import javax.servlet.jsp.tagext.*;
import java.io.*;
import java.sql.*;

/**
* ConnectTag
*/
public class ConnectTag extends TagSupport
{
   public static final String DRIVER_CLASS
      = "sun.jdbc.odbc.JdbcOdbcDriver";

   // ============================================
   //    Tag attributes
   // ============================================

   private String url;

   public void setUrl(String url)
   {
      this.url = url;
   }
```

It defines the Connection, Statement, and ResultSet objects and provides public accessor methods for each, as well as a public runQuery() method:

```
   // ============================================
   //    JDBC objects managed by this tag
   // ============================================

   private Connection con;
   private Statement stmt;
   private ResultSet rs;

   public Connection getConnection() { return con; }
```

```
public Statement getStatement() { return stmt; }
public ResultSet getResultSet() { return rs; }

/**
* Runs a query
* @param sql an SQL statement
*/
public void runQuery(String sql)
   throws SQLException
{
   rs = stmt.executeQuery(sql);
}
```

The whole database operation is contained between the start and end tags, so the two lifecycle methods manage startup and shutdown:

```
// ============================================
//    Lifecycle methods
// ============================================

/**
* Loads the driver class, opens a database
* connection, and creates a Statement object
*/
public int doStartTag() throws JspException
{
   con = null;
   try {
      Class.forName(DRIVER_CLASS);
      con = DriverManager.getConnection(url);
      stmt = con.createStatement();
   }
   catch (Exception e) {
      throw new JspException(e.getMessage());
   }
   return EVAL_BODY_INCLUDE;
}

/**
* Closes the connection and other JDBC objects
*/
public int doEndTag() throws JspException
```

```
    {
       try {
          if (rs != null) {
             rs.close();
             rs = null;
          }
          if (stmt != null) {
             stmt.close();
             stmt = null;
          }
          if (con != null) {
             con.close();
             con = null;
          }
       }
       catch (SQLException e) {
          throw new JspException(e.getMessage());
       }
       return EVAL_PAGE;
    }
}
```

## RunQuery

The `runQuery` tag does three things:

- Extracts an SQL statement from its body.
- Finds the enclosing connect tag.
- Executes the connect.runQuery() method.

The source code is listed here:

```
package jspcr.taglib.jdbc;

import javax.servlet.jsp.*;
import javax.servlet.jsp.tagext.*;
import java.io.*;
import java.sql.*;
import java.util.*;

/**
* RunQueryTag
```

```
*/
public class RunQueryTag extends BodyTagSupport
{
   /**
   * Reads the SQL statement in the body of the tag
   * and asks the connect tag to execute it.
   */
   public int doEndTag() throws JspException
   {
      // Get the SQL to be run

      String sql = bodyContent.getString();
      if (sql == null)
         throw new JspException
         ("No SQL statement found in body of runQuery tag");

      sql = sql.trim();
      if (sql.equals(""))
         throw new JspException
         ("Empty SQL statement found in body of runQuery tag");

      // Locate the enclosing connect tag

      ConnectTag connectTag = (ConnectTag)
         findAncestorWithClass(this, ConnectTag.class);
      if (connectTag == null)
         throw new JspException
         ("runQuery must be used in the body of a connect tag");

      // Tell the connect tag to run the query

      try {
         connectTag.runQuery(sql);
      }
      catch (SQLException e) {
         throw new JspException(e.getMessage());
      }

      // Normal return

      return EVAL_PAGE;
   }
}
```

## ForEachRow

This is an iterator tag, similar to the enumerate tag described earlier in this chapter. Like runQuery, it first gets a reference to the connect tag using findAncestorWithClass(). From the connect tag handler instance, it can get the result set using getResultSet(). Using a private convenience method called incrementRow(), it advances the result set to the next row. Either doStartTag() or doAfterBody() can detect the end of the result set and return SKIP_BODY accordingly.

```
package jspcr.taglib.jdbc;

import javax.servlet.jsp.*;
import javax.servlet.jsp.tagext.*;
import java.io.*;
import java.sql.*;

/**
* ForEachRowTag
*/
public class ForEachRowTag extends BodyTagSupport
{
   private ConnectTag connectTag;

   /**
   * Sets up for the first iteration of the result set
   */
   public int doStartTag() throws JspException
   {
      connectTag = (ConnectTag)
         findAncestorWithClass(this, ConnectTag.class);
      if (connectTag == null)
         throw new JspException
         ("forEachRow must be in the body of a connect tag");
      return incrementRow();
   }

   /**
   * After each row has been evaluated,
   * increment the result set and indicate
   * when end is reached.
   */
   public int doAfterBody() throws JspException
```

```
{
   return incrementRow();
}

/**
* When end tag is reached, dump the results
*/
public int doEndTag() throws JspException
{
   try {
      pageContext.getOut().print(bodyContent.getString());
   }
   catch (IOException e) {
      throw new JspException(e.getMessage());
   }
   return EVAL_PAGE;
}

/**
* Convenience method for getting the next row.
* Used by both <CODE>doStartTag</CODE>
* and <CODE>doAfterBody</CODE>.
* Returns EVAL_BODY_TAG if a row exists,
* SKIP_BODY otherwise.
*/
private int incrementRow() throws JspException
{

   ResultSet rs = connectTag.getResultSet();

   if (rs == null)
      throw new JspException
      ("No result set found - no query has been run");

   // Get the next row or indicate that there are no rows

   boolean hasNext = false;
   try {
      hasNext = rs.next();
   }
   catch (SQLException e) {
      throw new JspException(e.getMessage());
```

```
        }

        return (hasNext) ? EVAL_BODY_TAG : SKIP_BODY;
    }

}
```

## GetField

Like its counterparts `runQuery` and `forEachRow`, `getField` uses public methods in the enclosing `connect` tag. It extracts the specified field value from the `ResultSet` and sends it to the current output writer.

```
package jspcr.taglib.jdbc;

import javax.servlet.jsp.*;
import javax.servlet.jsp.tagext.*;
import java.io.*;
import java.sql.*;

/**
* GetFieldTag
*/
public class GetFieldTag extends TagSupport
{
    private String name;

    public void setName(String name)
    {
        this.name = name;
    }

    /**
    * Returns the value of the specified
    * field in the result set as a string.
    */
    public int doEndTag() throws JspException
    {
```

```
      // Get the enclosing Connect tag

      ConnectTag connectTag = (ConnectTag)
         findAncestorWithClass(this, ConnectTag.class);
      if (connectTag == null)
         throw new JspException
         ("getField must be in the body of a connect tag");

      // Get its current result set

      ResultSet rs = connectTag.getResultSet();
      if (rs == null)
         throw new JspException
         ("No result set exists - no query has been run");

      try {

         // Get the specified field and write it
         // to the output stream

         String value = rs.getString(name);
         JspWriter out = pageContext.getOut();
         out.print(value);
      }
      catch (SQLException e) {
         throw new JspException(e.getMessage());
      }
      catch (IOException e) {
         throw new JspException(e.getMessage());
      }

      // Normal completion

      return SKIP_BODY;
   }
}
```

When the database query is run, it produces the results shown in Figure 11-9.

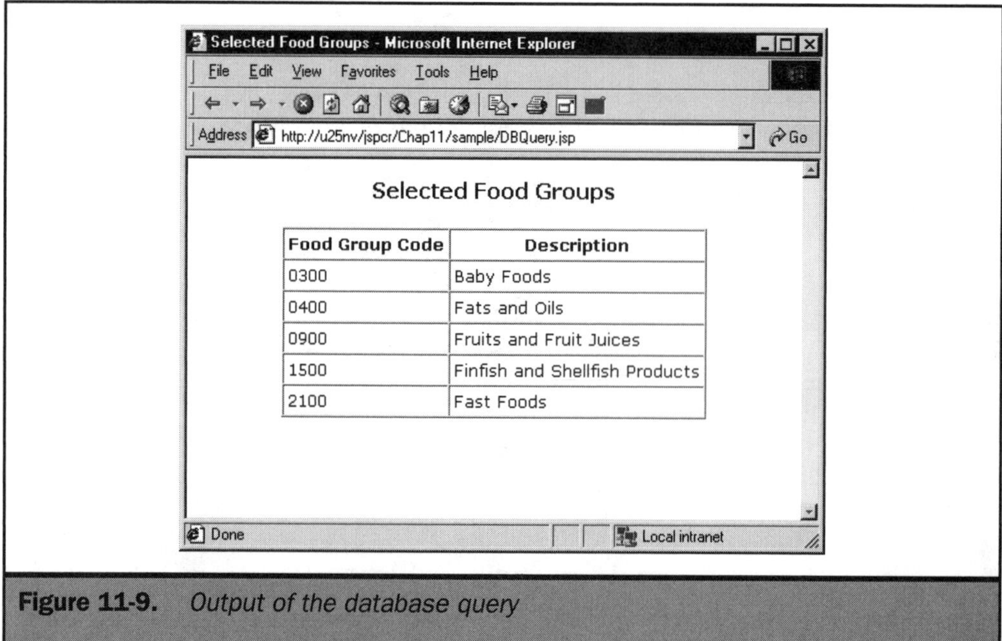


**Figure 11-9.** *Output of the database query*

## Summary

Custom tags are an elegant, robust method of extending the JSP authoring environment, allowing development teams to provide a toolkit of application-specific JSP tags that can be used by page designers who aren't proficient in Java programming. A tag's functionality is implemented by a Java class called a *tag handler,* which provides methods that are called by the JSP container at various points in the tag's life cycle. Sets of related tags can cooperate to accomplish complex tasks. Collections of tag handlers and configuration information are packaged in *tag libraries,* which have a vendor-independent structure and can be deployed with a minimum of effort.

The Complete Reference

# Part III

## JSP in Action

This section looks at how JSP works with major components of the Java environment. After gaining a background in HTML forms and JDBC database access, you'll examine advanced topics such as session management, threading, JavaBeans, and XML. Chapters 17 and 18 cover debugging and deploying Web applications, respectively, and Chapter 19 presents a complete case study incorporating techniques from throughout the book.

# Chapter 12

## HTML Forms

Most applications need user input at some point and, in the Web environment, this input usually comes from HTML forms. Like their paper counterparts, HTML forms consist of a set of labels and entry fields arranged in a logical sequence. When a user fills out a form and clicks the Submit button, the entry field names and values are transmitted to a program associated with the Web server for processing. Figure 12-1 illustrates a typical form.

HTML provides a basic set of elements or input controls that can accommodate a wide range of data entry requirements. The set includes

- **Text entry elements** Rectangular boxes for single line or multiple line input.
- **Selection menus** Lists of options displayed in a drop-down list box. These can have an external form displayed on the screen and an internal code value associated with the selected item or items.

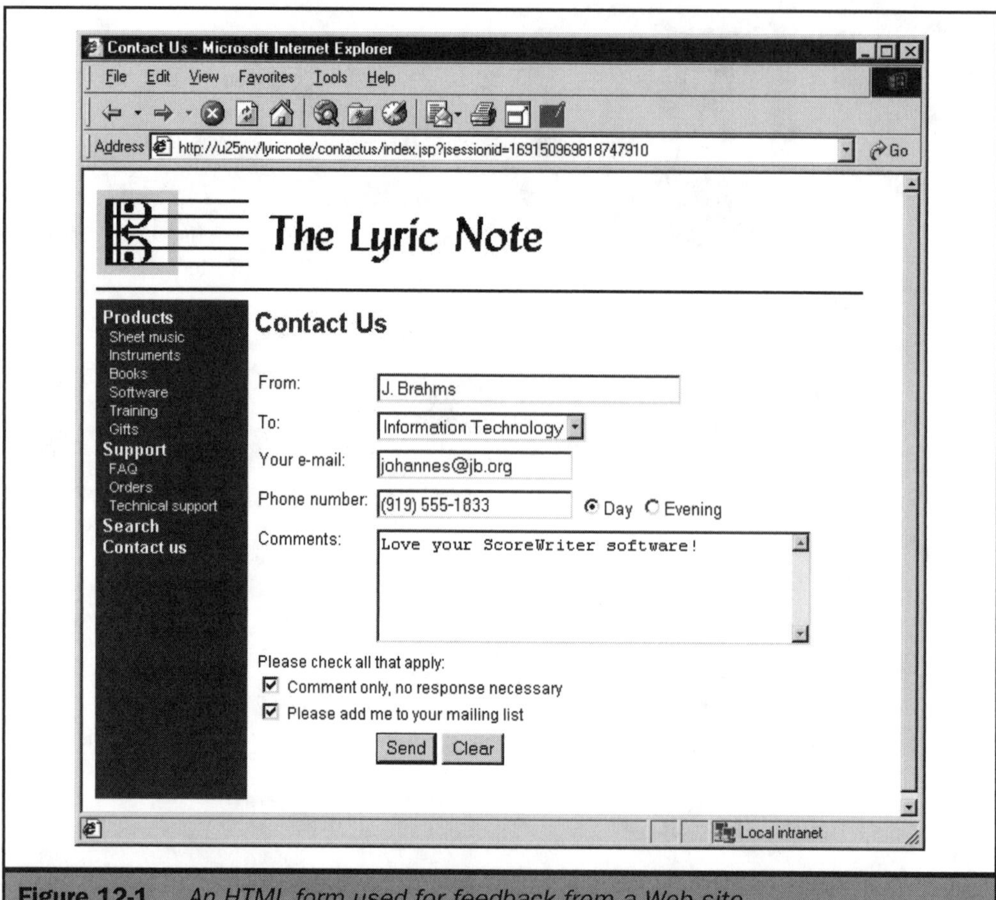


**Figure 12-1.** *An HTML form used for feedback from a Web site*

- **Buttons** Rectangular controls that simulate a pushbutton on a control panel. These are most often used to initiate a command, such as to submit a form or clear the input fields.
- **Check boxes** Small squares that can be either checked or unchecked, on or off. Check boxes can be used to specify options that have yes or no values.
- **Radio buttons** Similar to check boxes, radio buttons indicate yes or no values. However, they usually occur in mutually exclusive groups, so selecting one causes all the others to be unselected.
- **File selection elements** Controls that enable a user to specify the name of a file to be uploaded. Typically, this control includes a Browse button that causes a file selection dialog box to pop up.
- **Hidden elements** Nonvisual elements used to create parameters with constant values.

The set of elements that can be used in an HTML form is standardized and formally documented in the HTML specification (available at http://www.w3.org/TR/html4/). This specification is the work of the *World Wide Web Consortium* (W3C), which updates it periodically as new features emerge. As might be expected, not all browsers implement all features. This chapter uses HTML 4.01 as the basis for describing how forms work, but features mainly those elements and attributes that are widely supported.

This chapter describes elements used in HTML forms, how they are used, and how browsers render them. It discusses how forms are validated and submitted. The chapter then briefly examines the server side of forms handling.



## The FORM Element

The `FORM` element is the basic structure behind HTML forms and has three main purposes:

- To group input elements together syntactically
- To identify a server-side program that handles the form processing
- To specify what data values are to be sent and in what form

A `FORM` element is described in HTML with the `<FORM>` tag. The syntax of this element is shown here:

```
<FORM
      action="uri"
      method="method"
      enctype="content type"
      accept-charset="charsets"
```

```
        accept="content types"
        name="form name">
...
</FORM>
```

The attributes and their values are described in the following section.

## Attributes of the FORM Element

Of the six attributes listed, the only required one is `action`. In practice, attributes other than `action` and `method` are rarely used. Here are the definitions of each attribute.

### The action Attribute

When a form is completed and the user clicks the Submit button, the Web browser creates an HTTP request that packages all the form data and sends it to a program on some Web server. This program is specified in the `action` attribute.

The value of the `action` attribute must be an HTTP *Uniform Resource Identifier* (*URI*). (See http://www.ietf.org/rfc/rfc2396.txt for the formal definition of a URI.) This means it has the form

```
[http://<servername>][/]<path>
```

To submit the form, the Web browser opens a socket connection to the specified server (which defaults to the server from which the HTML page was downloaded) and makes an HTTP request using the specified path. The path typically points to a servlet, JSP page, or CGI program. This program receives the HTTP request and the form data, either in the URI itself or in an input stream, depending on the HTTP method used (see the following `method`).

Specifying a query string on the URI is possible. In this case, the parameter(s) encoded in the query string is merged with those specified in the body of the form. This is usually unnecessary because a hidden field can accomplish the same purpose.

### The method Attribute

The HTTP protocol provides a number of request types used for file transfer, download, delete, and diagnostic operations. Of these, only GET and POST are valid for use in HTML forms. The `method` attribute is where this is specified.

An HTTP GET or POST request is ordinarily interpreted by the Web server as a request to retrieve the document named in the URI. When the Web server has been configured to handle servlets, CGI programs, or other server-side scripting environments, it interprets requests for those resources as requests to invoke them as programs. The output produced by such a program (typically an HTML document) is sent back to the requester, the same as if it were a static document requested by name.

The difference between the GET and POST methods when used in an HTML form is in how they supply input data to the server process:

- **GET** Form values are appended to the URI as a query string
- **POST** Form values are supplied in the input stream

Although either method can be used, and the servlet API makes the choice fairly transparent, several characteristics should be taken into account. Because GET requests cause input values to be appended to the request URI, they are visible as name/value pairs on the browser address line and in Web server logs. This makes GET undesirable for sending sensitive data like passwords. Moreover, some servers and browsers may have restrictions on the length of URL's they can handle. In addition, GET requests are described in the HTTP specification as *idempotent*, which means they can safely be repeated without undesirable side effects. Under certain circumstances, this means a server can tell a client to reuse its existing copy of a resource rather than sending it a new copy. This is usually not what you want as a response from form input. For these reasons, POST is usually a better choice for the request method.

The `method` attribute is optional. If not specified, GET is used by default. The value of the attribute can be specified in either uppercase or lowercase.

## The enctype Attribute

Form input values can be transmitted to the server in several different ways. The method of encoding the values into a data stream is described as the *content type*, and is specified in the `enctype` attribute when the POST method is used. Two commonly used encodings exist

- `application/x-www-form-urlencoded`
- `multipart/form-data`

***`application/x-www-form-urlencoded`*** If not specified (and it usually isn't), the value of the `enctype` attribute is `application/x-www-form-urlencoded`. (See RFC 1738, available at http://www.freesoft.org/CIE/RFC/1738/index.htm, for a complete discussion of URL encoding.) This encoding technique involves the following steps:

1. Replace all nonblank special characters[1] in input element names or values with `%`*xx*, where *xx* is the two-digit hexadecimal value of the corresponding ASCII character code.
2. Replace any spaces with a plus (`+`) `sign.`

1 Some disagreement exists about which characters these are. RFC 1738 describes them as any nonalphanumeric character other than "`$-_.+!*'(),`". However, Internet Explorer, Netscape Navigator, and java.net.URLEncoder limit the exclusions to only "`-_.*`". At any rate, because both the encoding and decoding are done by programs that agree, this isn't a real problem.

JSP IN ACTION

3. Combine each resulting pair of names and values with an equals (=) sign between them.
4. Connect the resulting `name=value` strings in the order they occur in the form, separating them with ampersands (&).

The server process unwinds the encoding by reversing each step, recovering the original parameter names and values.

For example, if a form contains an input field named `product`, with a value of "Great Music@Home", and another field named `quantity`, with a value of 3, the encoded string would be

```
product=Great+Music%40Home&quantity=3
```

The purpose of URL encoding is to make it safe to append character strings to a URL. If spaces, quotation marks, or other delimiter characters appear in a URL, they may confuse programs that process them.

***multipart/form-data*** `multipart/form-data` is a newer approach used primarily to support file uploading. (RFC 2388 (http://www.ietf.org/rfc/rfc2388.txt) describes the use of multipart/form-data with HTML forms.) In this encoding, each input field and its value are sent in their own block in the input stream. A special delimiter string called a *boundary* marks the beginning and end of each block. The boundary is a pseudorandom string chosen by the Web browser and is specified in the `Content-Type` header. Within each block are one or more HTTP headers, followed by a blank line, and then a line containing the value of the input field. The field name is passed in the `Content-Disposition` header.

So, using the previous example, if a form contains the input fields `product` with a value of "Great Music@Home" and `quantity` with a value of 3, the browser would create an HTTP request that contains something like this:

```
POST /someURI HTTP/1.0
Content-Type: multipart/form-data;boundary=7d025a324c0138
Content-Length: 178

--7d025a324c0138
Content-Disposition: form-data; name="product"

Great Music@Home
--7d025a324c0138
```

```
Content-Disposition: form-data; name="quantity"

3
--7d025a324c0138--
```

The main disadvantage of `multipart/form-data` encoding is it isn't directly supported in the current servlet API. That is, the individual field names cannot be retrieved with `getParameterNames()`, and their values cannot be read with `getParameterValues()`. Reading and parsing the input stream to obtain this information is necessary.

## The accept-charset Attribute

A *character set* in HTTP use is a set of rules for converting a set of bytes to a set of characters. The most widely used character set is ISO-8859-1, a superset of ASCII that maps the additional byte values in the range 127-255. If the `accept-charset` is used, it should contain a list of character set values separated by commas or blanks.

The purpose of `accept-charset` is to indicate which character sets the server program can interpret and process. In practice, however, this attribute is rarely used and, indeed, seems to be ignored by Internet Explorer and Netscape Navigator.

## The accept Attribute

A `FORM` tag can indicate the content types its server-side handler program is designed to accept. If specified, the `accept` attribute must contain a comma-separated list of content types, such as `text/html`, or `image/jpg`. This is only a hint to the Web browser, however, and the browser is free to ignore it (which most do).

## The name Attribute

A form can have a name by which it is referred to in `<SCRIPT>` sections elsewhere in the document. For example, in the following form:

```
<form
   method="post"
   action="diag/ShowParms.jsp"
   name="prodform"
   onsubmit="return checkform();"
<pre>
Product: <input type="text" name="product"
Quantity: <input type="text" name="quantity"
</pre>
</form>
```

where `checkform()` is a JavaScript function that validates form input fields, `checkform()` can read the values of the two input fields as `document.prodform.product.value` and `document.prodform.quantity.value`, respectively.

The HTML specification deprecates the `name` attribute in favor of the `id` attribute, however, `id` isn't yet recognized by the JavaScript document object model. `name` is still a better choice if you need to integrate your form with JavaScript.

# Form Input Elements

Within the body of a `<FORM>...</FORM>` tag, the individual data fields are described. The HTML consists of descriptive labels for each field and the appropriate HTML tags that create the required controls. Visual layout is usually accomplished with an HTML table, so field labels and controls are horizontally and vertically aligned. The following HTML produced the form shown in Figure 12-1:

```
<form method="post" action="diag/ShowParms.jsp">
<table border="0" cellpadding="3" cellspacing="0">

   <tr valign="top">
      <td>From:</td>
      <td><input name="from" type="text" size=32></td>
   </tr>

   <tr valign="top">
      <td>To:</td>
      <td>
         <select name="to" size=1>
            <option value="CS">Customer Service
            <option value="EX">Executive
            <option value="FI">Finance
            <option value="HR">Human Resources
            <option value="IT">Information Technology
            <option value="MK">Marketing
            <option value="FA">Facilities
            <option value="PC">Purchasing
            <option value="SP">Shipping
         </select>
      </td>
   </tr>

   <tr valign="top">
```

```
        <td>Your e-mail:</td>
        <td><input name="email" type="text" size=20></td>
    </tr>

    <tr valign="top">
        <td>Phone number:</td>
        <td>
        <input name="phone" type="text" size=20>
        <input name="dayphone" type="radio" value="1" checked>Day
        <input name="dayphone" type="radio" value="0">Evening
        </td>
    </tr>

    <tr valign="top">
        <td>Comments:</td>
        <td>
        <textarea name="comments" rows=5 cols=40></textarea>
        </td>
    </tr>

    <tr valign="top">
        <td colspan=2>
        <font size=-1>
        Please check all that apply: <br>
        <input name="category" type="checkbox" value="1">
            Comment only, no response necessary <BR>
        <input name="category" type="checkbox" value="2">
            Please add me to your mailing list
        </font>
        </td>
    </tr>

    <tr valign="top">
        <td> </td>
        <td>
            <input type="submit" value="Send">
            <input type="reset" value="Clear">
        </td>
    </tr>

    <input type="hidden" name="remoteHost"
```

```
value="209.170.132.238">
   <input type="hidden" name="userAgent"
value="Mozilla/4.0 (compatible; MSIE 5.0; Windows NT; DigExt)">
</table>

</form>
```

We use this form in the examples throughout this section.

Four sets of HTML tags are used to create form input elements:

- `<INPUT>` A generic tag used for several specific element types.
- `<SELECT>` and `<OPTION>` Used to create a menu or a drop-down list box.
- `<TEXTAREA>` Used for multiline text input.
- `<BUTTON>` Used to create submit, reset, and general purpose pushbuttons. This tag isn't yet widely supported and, for this reason, will not be covered here.

## Elements Created with the INPUT Tag

The HTML `INPUT` tag is used for a number of element types. It has a large number of attributes, many of which are specific to only certain field types. The following syntax diagram describes those attributes common to most types:

```
<INPUT
     type="text | password | checkbox | radio | submit |
     reset | file | hidden | image | button"
     name="name"
     value="value"
     size="size">
```

where the attributes are defined as follows:

- **type="*type*"** indicates the specific field type to be used. If not specified, defaults to text.
- **name="*name*"** is used to assign an identifier to the field so it can be manipulated by scripts or style sheets. This is also the name by which the field can be retrieved by the server program.
- **value="*value*"** can be used to assign an initial value to the field.
- **size="*size*"** indicates its visual width, either in pixels or characters (for text fields).

In addition to these attributes, `INPUT` tags can specify event handlers that invoke scripting actions in the browser when certain events occur. The value of the event handler attribute is a snippet of scripting code, typically JavaScript. Event handler attributes are named after the event they handle, with a prefix of "on":

- **onfocus** occurs when a user tabs to the field or clicks the mouse in the field, so it receives the keyboard focus.
- **onblur** occurs when a user tabs or clicks out of the field, so it loses the keyboard focus.
- **onselect** occurs when some text is selected (not supported by Netscape Navigator).
- **onchange** occurs when a user changes the control's value, and then commits the change by tabbing or clicking out of the field.

When a form is submitted, the browser extracts the name and value of each control, converts these according to the encoding type specified (or implied) on the `<FORM>` tag, and sends the resulting data stream to the server process.

The following sections consider each `<INPUT>` type:

## Text

This is the simplest and most common `<INPUT>` type, used for entering a single line of text. Its syntax is as follows:

```
<INPUT
    type="text"
    name="name"
    value="value"
    size="size"
    maxlength="maxlength">
```

with the attributes having the following meanings:

- **type="`text`"** indicates this is a text control.
- **name="*name*"** specifies a name by which scripts can refer to this control. This is also the name by which the text can be retrieved by the server program.
- **value="*value*"** can be used to assign an initial text value. This attribute is useful when a form appears on the same page as the output of the form processing program.
- **size="*size*"** specifies the display width. If not specified, the browser chooses a default size, which may be unsuitable. Specifying a preferred size is best.
- **maxlength="*maxlength*"** sets a limit on the number of characters that can be typed into the field.

A TEXT input element is typically displayed as a rectangular box. For example, the HTML shown here,

```
<tr valign="top">
   <td>From:</td>
   <td><input name="from" type="text" size=32></td>
</tr>
```

might be rendered like this:

From: J. Brahms

## Password

A variation on the `text` control is the `password` control. The only difference is the characters a user types aren't visible onscreen. Instead, a mask character, such as an asterisk, is displayed for each character typed. The syntax of the password input tag is shown here:

<INPUT<br>
type="`password`"<br>
name="*name*"<br>
value="*value*"<br>
size="*size*"<br>
maxlength="*maxlength*">

with the attributes having the same meaning as they do for the text input tag.

A password input element is also typically displayed as a rectangular box. For example, the HTML shown here, used in a technical support application

```
<tr valign="top">
   <td>Support ID:</td>
   <td><input name="suppid" type="password" size=10></td>
</tr>
```

might be rendered like this:

Support ID:

**Note** *This is a minimal form of security, designed simply to prevent prying eyes from seeing what is typed in a password field. The characters transmitted to the server process, however, are those the user originally typed, not the asterisks. Using a password control doesn't encrypt or otherwise hide the value of the field, except visually as it is typed.*

## Checkbox

A *check box control* is used to present an option that's either true or false. Its syntax is shown here,

```
<INPUT
    type="checkbox"
    name="name"
    value="value"
    checked>
```

with the attributes defined as follows:

- **type="checkbox"** indicates this is a check box control.
- **name="*name*"** specifies a name by which scripts can refer to this check box. This is also the name by which the check box value can be retrieved by the server program. A group of check boxes can have the same name if they represent multiple values of the same field, which aren't mutually exclusive.
- **value="*value*"** can be used to specify the value returned when this box is checked. If not specified, the value defaults to the two character string `on`. `(That's on, not true, 1, yes, or checked.)`
- **checked**, if present, indicates the check box has an initial selected state.

A check box supports one additional event handler attribute:

- **onclick** occurs when the user clicks the check box;

and it does not support the `onchange` event.

A check box is usually rendered as a small square box, with a check mark present or absent, reflecting the boolean value of the control. For example, the HTML shown here,

```
<tr valign="top">
   <td colspan=2>
   <font size=-1>
   Please check all that apply: <br>
   <input name="category" type="checkbox" value="1">
      Comment only, no response necessary <BR>
   <input name="category" type="checkbox" value="2">
      Please add me to your mailing list
```

```
        </font>
        </td>
    </tr>
```

might look like this:

Please check all that apply:

☑ Comment only, no response necessary

☑ Please add me to your mailing list

## Radio

A *radio control,* like a check box, is used to present an option that is either true or false. The difference is, a group of radio buttons are mutually exclusive in operation. When one is clicked, any others with the same name attribute are cleared. In this respect, they operate like the buttons on a car radio—when one is pushed in, any others are pushed out. The syntax of the radio control is shown here

```
<INPUT
      type="radio"
      name="name"
      value="value"
      checked>
```

with the attributes defined as follows:

- **type="radio"** indicates this is a radio button control.
- **name="*name*"** specifies a name by which scripts can refer to this radio button. This is also the name by which the radio button value can be retrieved by the server program. A group of radio buttons can have the same name, if they represent mutually exclusive values of the same field.
- **value="*value*"** specifies the value returned with the form when this button is in a selected state. This is a required attribute.
- **checked**, if present, indicates this radio button is the initially selected one of the group.

Like the check box, a radio button supports the `onclick` event, but not `onchange`.

A radio button is usually rendered as a small circle, with an inner dot present or absent, reflecting the Boolean value of the control. For example, the HTML shown here,

```
<tr valign="top">
      <td>Phone number:</td>
```

```
    <td>
    <input name="phone" type="text" size=20>
    <input name="dayphone" type="radio" value="1" checked>Day
    <input name="dayphone" type="radio" value="0">Evening
    </td>
</tr>
```

might look like this:

Phone number: (919) 555-1833 Day Evening

## Submit

To submit a form to the server, there must be a way of indicating the user is done entering data. This is the role played by the `submit` input type. A Submit button is unlike other controls because it ordinarily does not contribute to the data stream sent to the server. Here is the Submit button's syntax,

```
<INPUT
    type="submit"
    name="name"
    value="value">
```

with the attributes defined as follows:

- **type="`submit`"** indicates this is a submit control.
- **name="*name*"** specifies a name by which scripts or the server program can refer to this Submit button. This is normally unnecessary from the standpoint of the server because it's clear the Submit button must have been clicked or else the form wouldn't have been submitted. It can be useful, however, if several Submit buttons are in the form and each one has a different value.
- **value="*value*"** specifies the value displayed on the button (and returned with the form, if the name attribute is also present). If not specified, defaults to "Submit Query" in Internet Explorer 5.x and Netscape Communicator 4.75. Other browsers may supply a different default.

This control supports the `onclick` event, but not `onchange`.

A Submit button is usually rendered as a rectangular pushbutton with the text specified in the `value` attribute. For example, if a Submit button is coded like this,

```
<input type="submit" value="Send">
```

it might appear like this:

Send

## Reset

Closely related to Submit is Reset, which is used to set all controls in the form back to their initial values. Like the Submit button, Reset does not contribute to the data stream sent to the server. Its syntax is,

<INPUT<br>
    type="`reset`"<br>
    value="*value*">

with the attributes defined as follows:

- **type="`reset`"** indicates this is a reset control.
- **value="*value*"** specifies the value displayed on the button (and returned with the form, if the name attribute is also present). If not specified, defaults to "Reset".

This control supports the `onclick` event, but not `onchange`.

A Reset button is usually rendered as a rectangular pushbutton with the text specified in the `value` attribute. For example, if a Submit button is coded like this,

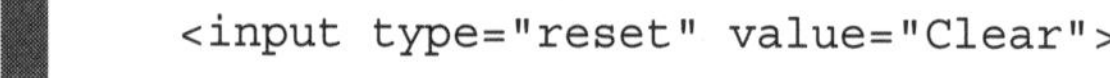

```
<input type="reset" value="Clear">
```

it might appear like this:

## File

Some applications call for files to be uploaded to the server. For example, technical support applications may handle stack traces sent in by users. Bulletin board systems may accept file submissions. Web pages that are front ends to applications like these can use the `file` input control. Here is its syntax,

<INPUT<br>
    type="`file`"<br>
    name="*name*"<br>
    size="*size*">

with its attributes defined as follows:

- **type="`file`"** indicates this is a file control.
- **name="*name*"** specifies a name by which scripts can refer to this file control. This is also the name by which the field will be known to the server program, although in a different format, as you soon see.
- **size="*size*"** indicates the visual width of the file name input field.

A file control is typically rendered as a text field with an associated Browse button. The filename can be entered directly in the text field, or the user can click the button to use a file selection dialog box:

Two changes must be made to a form for it to use the file control:

- The request method *must* be `POST`.
- The encoding type (specified in the `enctype` attribute in the `<FORM>` tag) *must* be `multipart/form-data`.

If these conditions aren't met, the control is still displayed, but is treated like an ordinary text input field—all that will be sent to the server is the filename.

More significant changes also must be made to the server program. It must be able to extract the file contents, as well as the other nonfile parameter values, using the `multipart/form-data` encoding format discussed earlier in this chapter.

**Note** *Limitations can also be imposed by the Web server on the size of files that can be uploaded. The purpose of these restrictions is to prevent denial of service attacks that use huge files to bring down the Web server.*

As an example of a file upload application, suppose LyricNote.com sponsors a contest in which users can upload MIDI files of their own musical compositions[2]. The winner(s) of the contest would receive music software products that LyricNote sells. Figure 12-2 shows the input form.

2 *MIDI* (*Musical Instrument Digital Interface*) uses a file format in which musical notes are described rather than actually recorded. Their content is re-created by MIDI-compatible instruments or media players.

The following HTML generates the form:

```
<form method="post"
      action="http://u25nv/lyricnote/servlet/midi_contest"
      enctype="multipart/form-data"
      >
<table border="0" cellpadding="3" cellspacing=0>
   <tr valign="top">
      <td colspan="2">
         Are you a budding composer?
         Submit a MIDI file of your own composition
         for a chance to win a copy of <B>ScoreWriter 4.5</B>.
         Click
         <A HREF="product/midi_contest/rules.html">here</A>
         for official rules.
      </td>
   </tr>

   <tr valign="top">
      <td>Your name:</td>
      <td><input name="name" type="text" size=32></td>
   </tr>

   <tr valign="top">
      <td>Your e-mail:</td>
      <td><input name="email" type="text" size=20></td>
   </tr>

   <tr valign="top">
      <td>Title of composition:</td>
      <td><input name="title" type="text" size=48></td>
   </tr>

   <tr valign="top">
      <td>MIDI file name:</td>
      <td><input type="file" name="midifile" size=32></td>
   </tr>

   <tr valign="top">
      <td> </td>
      <td>
         <input type="submit" value="Send">
```

```
            <input type="reset" value="Clear">
         </td>
      </tr>

   </table>
   </form>
```

When the form is submitted, the browser generates an HTTP request with a data stream in `multipart/form-data` format that contains, in part, the following:

```
Content-Type: multipart/form-data;
   boundary=---------------------------7d01012174012c
Content-Length: 1507

-----------------------------7d01012174012c
Content-Disposition: form-data; name="name"

S. Vetter
-----------------------------7d01012174012c
Content-Disposition: form-data; name="email"

vetter@lyricnote.com
-----------------------------7d01012174012c
Content-Disposition: form-data; name="title"

It-B-Gone
-----------------------------7d01012174012c
Content-Disposition: form-data; name="midifile";
filename="C:\my_midi_files\Itbgon.mid"
Content-Type: audio/mid

MThd... (binary data not shown)
-----------------------------7d01012174012c--
```

We can see the four input fields are present, each in their own blocks delimited by the boundary string. Each block has a `Content-Disposition` header that specifies the field name. The last block, which contains the uploaded file, also has a `filename` attribute on its `Content-Disposition` header that gives the original file name on the client system, as well as a `Content-Type` header, which indicates the file data is in a binary format known as `audio/mid`. The server program can parse the data stream and extract the field values and file content.

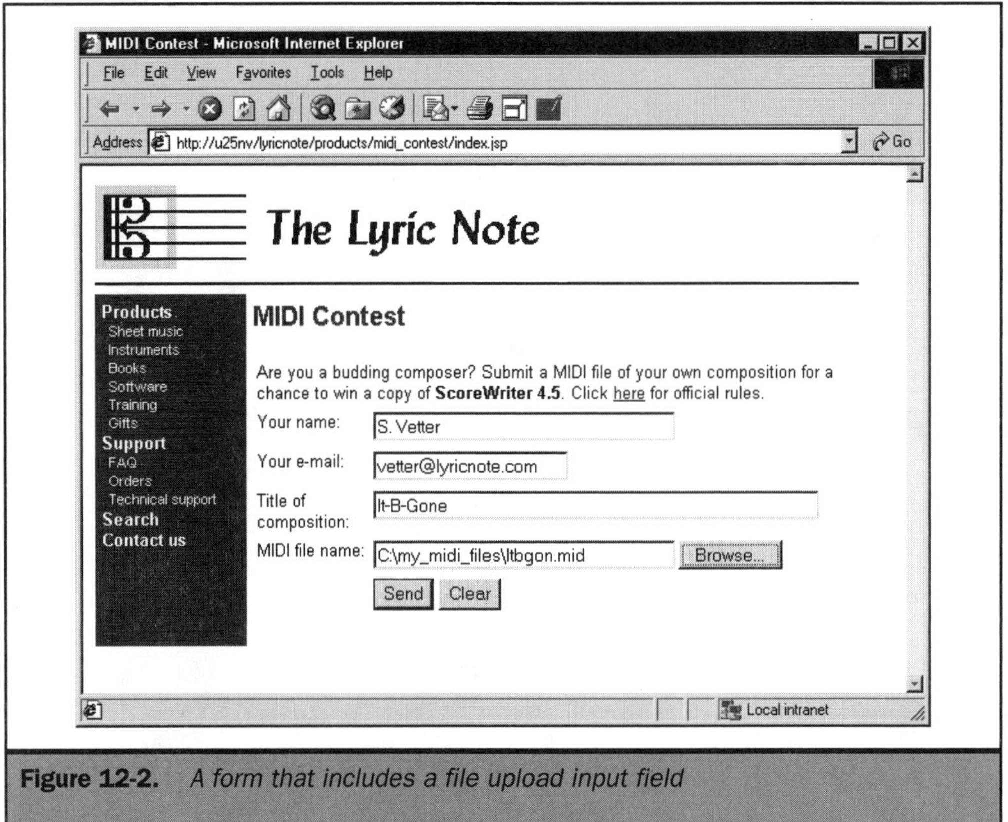


**Figure 12-2.** *A form that includes a file upload input field*

## Hidden

Not all input comes from the user, at least not directly. Some forms may use constants that are hard coded or dynamically generated. An `INPUT` element with `type="hidden"` can be used for this purpose. Its syntax is shown here,

```
<INPUT
    type="hidden"
    name="name"
    value="value">
```

and the attributes have the following meanings:

- **type="hidden"** indicates this is a hidden control.
- **name="*name*"** specifies a name by which scripts can refer to this control. This is also the name by which the text can be retrieved by the server program.

- **value="*value*"** must be used to assign an initial text value.

As you might guess, a hidden field has no visual representation. Its only purpose is to create a parameter with a constant value. This might be a transaction code of some kind, which a dispatching servlet would use as a key to a table of other classes. More often, though, a hidden field has a value that's dynamically generated by the servlet or a JSP page that created the HTML. For example,

```
<input type="hidden" name="remoteHost"
   value="<%= request.getRemoteHost() %>">

<input type="hidden" name="userAgent"
   value="<%= request.getHeader("user-agent") %>">
```

would store the IP address or host name on which the Web browser is running and a string identifying the browser software and version number as hidden fields in the form. These fields might be useful to technical support people working on a problem with the form.

## Image

An *image* can be used as an input field in which the user clicks with the mouse rather than typing with the keyboard. The information in this case is the location within the image of where the mouse click occurred. The `image` input type can be used for this purpose. Its syntax is shown here,

```
<INPUT
    type="image"
    name="name"
    src="imageurl">
```

and the attributes have the following meanings:

- **type="`image`"** indicates this is an image control.
- **name="*name*"** specifies a name by which scripts can refer to this control. This is also the name by which a mouse click location can be retrieved by the server program.
- **src="*imageurl*"** is the URL of an image file.

Two parameters are created in the data stream for an image control, one each for the *x* and *y* coordinates of the click. The coordinates are given in units of pixels and are relative to the top-left corner of the image, which is (0, 0). The parameter names are composed of the image control name with "`.x`" or "`.y`" appended. For example, a form might contain an image of a staff of musical notation and invite the user to click the desired note:

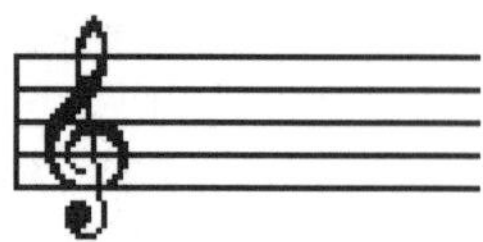


If the image input control were coded like this,

```
<input type="image" name="staff" src="images/clef/tcstaff.png">
```

and if the user clicked the note C above middle C, approximately at (108, 40), the resulting data stream would be this:

```
staff.x=108&staff.y=40
```

Clicking an image control causes the form to be submitted. It isn't necessary for the user to click the Submit button.

## Button

Besides the Submit and Reset buttons, a generic Button input type exists. Its syntax is shown here,

```
<INPUT
    type="button"
    name="name"
    value="value">
```

with the attributes defined as follows:

- **type="button"** indicates this is a button control.
- **name="*name*"** specifies a name by which scripts can refer to this button.
- **value="*value*"** specifies the value displayed on this button.

For this control to be useful, it must define the `onclick` event handler attribute. A JavaScript function can then refer to the button name and value.

## Elements Created with select and option

The `select` and `option` tags can be used together to create a scrollable list of menu items. Referring to the customer feedback example in Figure 12-1, the user selects the destination of the form from a drop-down list. The HTML used to create this list is shown here:

```
<select name="to" size=1>
   <option value="CS">Customer Service
   <option value="EX">Executive
   <option value="FI">Finance
   <option value="HR">Human Resources
   <option value="IT">Information Technology
   <option value="MK">Marketing
   <option value="FA">Facilities
   <option value="PC">Purchasing
   <option value="SP">Shipping
</select>
```

The syntax of the `select` tag is shown here,

<select name="*name*" size="*number*"multiple> *options* </select>

where the attributes mean the following:

- **name="*name*"** assigns a name by which the server program can refer to the list.
- **size="*number*"** indicates the number of elements visible at one time; the height of the list box. If the number is 1, the list is a drop-down menu.
- **multiple**, if specified, lets the user select more than one item.

Note, the `<select>` tag must be closed by a `</select>`.

The heart of the `select` list is the set of `option` tags with their associated values and descriptions. Frequently, such lists are dynamically generated from a database query. The `option` tag has the following syntax,

<option value="*value*" selected> *text* </option>

where

- **value="*value*"** specifies the value returned with the form, if this item is selected. If this attribute isn't specified, the body of the option tag is returned.
- **selected**, if present, preselects the item.

The text between the start and end tags (referred to as the *body*) is what's actually displayed in the list box. The closing `</option>` tag isn't required and is frequently omitted.

When the form is submitted, the value of the selected item is the value associated with the `select` element. In the previous example, if the user selected the last item in the list, the value returned in the data stream would be this:

```
to=SP
```

If the `multiple` attribute is specified on the `<select>` tag, and the user selects multiple items, the parameter name then appears multiple times in the data stream associated with different values. So, if the user had selected not only shipping, but finance and marketing as well, the data stream would look like this:

```
to=FI&to=MK&to=SP
```

## The textarea Element

Whereas the `text` and `password` input fields are single-line only, the `textarea` element can accept multiple lines. This makes the `textarea` element useful for entering comments or other free-form text, which could be longer than one line. Both a height and width can be specified, and scrollbars are added by the browser as necessary. The syntax of `textarea` is as follows,

<textarea name="*name*" rows="*number*" cols="*number*">
... *text* ...
</textarea>

where

- **name="*name*"** assigns the name by which this field will be known to scripts and the server program.
- **rows="*number*"** specifies the number of rows in the visible height of the text area. This is *not* a limit on the number of rows that can actually be in the list box, it's only a limit on how many rows are displayed at a time as the list is scrolled.
- **cols="*number*"** specifies the width in characters of the visible width of the text area. This is *not* a limit on the number of columns that can actually be in the list box, only its display width.

# Form Validation

User interface programming is inherently complex. The amount of code devoted to validating input fields is often greater than what performs the actual function. Required fields have to be checked to ensure they are nonempty, and optional fields must have default values assigned. All fields may need to be validated against a set of acceptable values or algorithms. The validity of some fields may depend on the values of others.

All this validation can be done by the server program, but the back-and-forth network traffic may make it too expensive in terms of response time. For this reason, validation is better done on the client using a scripting language such as JavaScript. A wide variety of JavaScript books are available, so I won't go into any detail about how JavaScript works, other than to present a complete example.

## The Contact Us Form with Validation

Let's add some minimal validation to the "Contact Us" form example shown in Figure 12-1. You need to do three things.

### Setting the Trigger

First, you need to force some code to be executed when the form is submitted. To do this, set the `onsubmit` attribute in the form tag:

```
<form method="post"
      action="diag/ShowParms.jsp"
      onsubmit="return validate(this);">
```

The string specified in the onsubmit attribute is evaluated before the form is submitted. Only if it evaluates to `true` is the form actually submitted. In principle, the validation code could be entered directly as the `onsubmit` attribute value, but it's simpler to call a function and return its value. This also makes adding new code easier as validation requirements change.

### Adding a Script Block

To incorporate JavaScript statements into the HTML you generate, you must enclose them in `<SCRIPT> ... </SCRIPT>` tags. To ensure these tags have been loaded and evaluated, placing them in the `<HEAD> ... </HEAD>` section of the HTML is best.

## Writing the Validation Functions

The third step is to write the validation functions themselves:

```
function validate(frm) {
   if (!hasData(frm.from.value)) {
      alert("Please type your name in the 'From:' box");
      return false;
   }
   return true;
}

function hasData(s) {
   if (s == null)
      return false;
   var n = s.length;
   for (var i = 0; i < n; i++) {
      var c = s.charAt(i);
      switch (c) {
         case ' ':
         case '\t':
         case '\n':
            continue;
         default:
            return true;
      }
   }
   return false;
}
```

Two functions are shown here:

- `validate(frm)` Given a reference to the form, performs all necessary validations and returns true if no errors are found.
- `hasData(s)` A utility function that returns true if the specified string has at least one non-whitespace character.

The only field you can really validate is the user name. In this example, you simply verify it's nonblank. If the user doesn't enter anything in the field, the result is as shown in Figure 12-3.

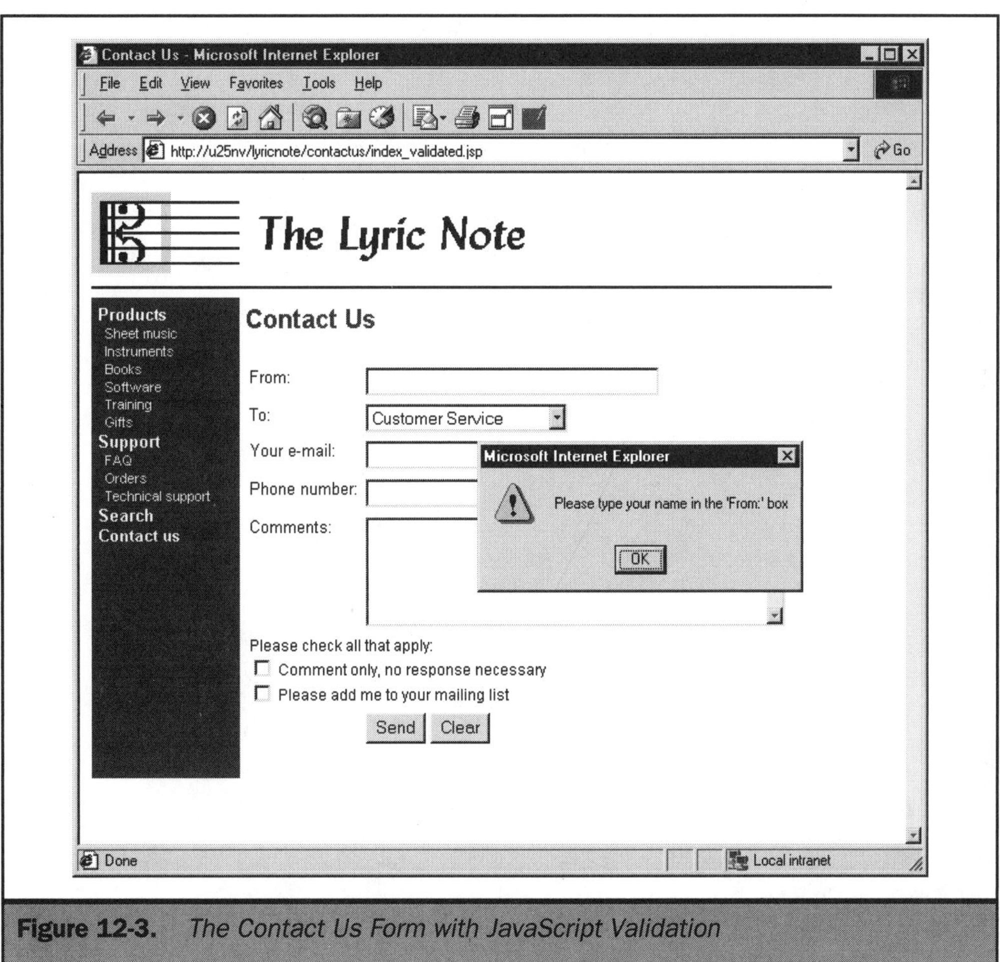


**Figure 12-3.** *The Contact Us Form with JavaScript Validation*



## The Server Side of Forms Handling

A variety of models for handling forms are on the server side. The case study in Chapter 19 examines this question in-depth. For illustrative purposes, you develop a simple JSP page that only collects the request parameters and formats them in a readable HTML table. The server program is ShowParms.jsp, which is used in the Contact Us example:

```
<%@ page import="java.io.*,java.util.*" %>
<%@ taglib prefix="lyric" uri="/WEB-INF/tlds/taglib.tld" %>

<html>
<head>
<title>Parameter Values</title>
<base href="<lyric:baseURL/>">
<link rel="stylesheet" href="styles/diag.css">
</head>

<body>
<center>
<table border="1" cellpadding="3" cellspacing="1" width="600">
<tr>
<td colspan="2" align="center" class="header">
Parameter Values
</td>
</tr>
<tr><th>Name</th><th>Value</th></tr>
<%
   int currentRow = 0;
   Enumeration eNames = request.getParameterNames();
   while (eNames.hasMoreElements()) {
      String name = (String) eNames.nextElement();
      String[] values = request.getParameterValues(name);
      for (int i = 0; i < values.length; i++) {
         String value = values[i];
         currentRow++;
         String rowClass = "row" + (currentRow % 2);
%>
<tr valign="top">
<td align="right" class="<%= rowClass %>"><B><%= name %></B></td>
<td align="left"  class="<%= rowClass %>"> <%= value %> </td>
</tr>
<%
      }
   }
%>
```

```
</table>
</center>
</body>
</html>
```

The program opens with two directives:

```
<%@ page import="java.io.*,java.util.*" %>
<%@ taglib prefix="lyric" uri="/WEB-INF/tlds/taglib.tld" %>
```

A tag library is declared and assigned the prefix "`lyric`". You use only one tag from it, the one that returns the base URL of the Web application. When used in the HTML `<BASE>` tag, it makes creating relative and absolute links easier to the images, style sheets, and other resources in the application.

```
<base href="<lyric:baseURL/>">
```

The heart of the program is the call to `getParameterNames()`, which returns an enumeration of the form field names, and the subsequent loop over these names, retrieving their respective values with `getParameterValues(Striing name)`.

```
   Enumeration eNames = request.getParameterNames();
   while (eNames.hasMoreElements()) {
      String name = (String) eNames.nextElement();
      String[] values = request.getParameterValues(name);
      ...
   }
```

When the form in Figure 12-1 is submitted to `ShowParms.jsp`, the results are as shown in Figure 12-4.

## Summary

HTML forms provide a GUI environment that's easy for users to work with and easy to handle in a server program. Controls exist for text entry, menu selection, and Boolean selections, such as check boxes and radio buttons. With an alternate encoding type, forms can support the client side of file uploading. Constant values can be specified in hidden fields. Forms can be validated with client-side functions written in JavaScript,

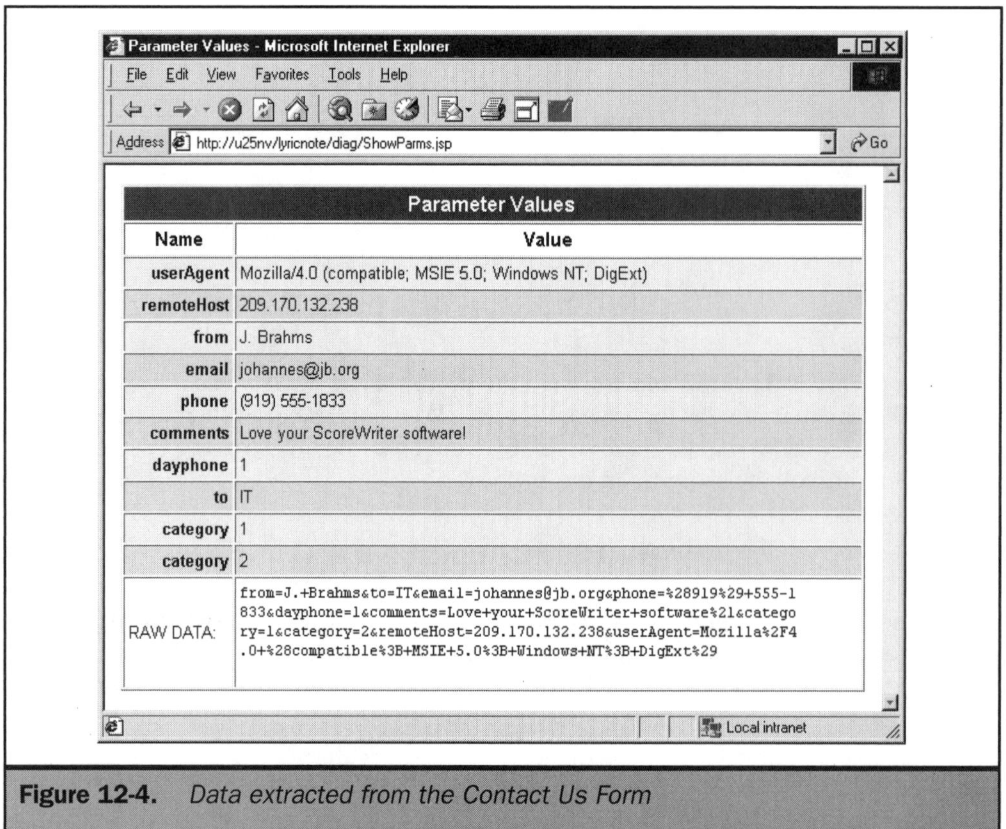


**Figure 12-4.** *Data extracted from the Contact Us Form*

which saves network transmission and processing time. Server programs, whether JSP pages or servlets, can use the servlet API to retrieve parameter names and values, and to return the results to the browser that submitted the form.

# Chapter 13

## Database Access

The corporate database is the heart of the business and most JSP pages of any consequence need access to it. Web sites for online retailers make their catalogs available for browsing. Theater Web pages may list show times and movie infor mation. Search engines prompt for keywords and return sets of matching links.

In addition to read-only access, many JSP pages act as front-ends to applications that store data as well. In a shopping cart checkout function, lists of items to be ordered must be converted into transactions that are processed by other systems: order fulfillment, shipping, and accounting.

Java provides a comprehensive and general-purpose means for handling database use with a technology known as JDBC[1]. *JDBC* makes communication possible with a wide variety of database management systems using SQL[2]. This chapter contains an overview of JDBC and how it can be used in Web-based applications. It covers JDBC drivers, how to connect to a database, how to execute SQL statements, and how to read their results. It describes JDBC's mechanisms for robust transaction handling and connection pooling. The concluding section discusses new features in JDBC 2.0 and beyond.

## Overview of JDBC

JDBC is an application programming interface between Java programs and database management systems. Like Oracle's *Oracle Call Interface* (*OCI*) or Microsoft's *Open Database Connectivity* (*ODBC*), JDBC is a call-level interface. This means a program uses method or function calls to access its features, as opposed to embedded SQL statements, which are translated by a precompiler.

A programmer uses a Java class known as a *JDBC driver* to connect to a database. Hundreds of JDBC drivers exist—at least one for each widely used database, whether commercial or shareware. A special JDBC driver, known as the *JDBC-ODBC bridge,* makes using ODBC as an intermediary possible, which makes the vast number of ODBC drivers usable from JDBC.

The great advantage of JDBC is it provides a standard interface to all database management systems. JDBC queries that work on an Oracle database require little or no changes to work with DB2, or SQL Server, or any other database. The few differences that remain usually have to do with data type names and support for certain operation types. Even these differences can usually be resolved programmatically using metadata provided by the JDBC connection.

JDBC also eases the transition from legacy systems to Web-enabled applications. Embedded SQL products, which have been around since the early 1980s, for the most part use SQL statements and operations that can be duplicated by JDBC calls. The

---

1 According to Sun Microsystems, JDBC is not an acronym. In particular, it does not stand for Java Database Connectivity.

2 Structured Query Language (SQL) is a topic large enough to fill several books. One of the best is *SQL: The Complete Reference*, by James R. Groff & Paul N. Weinberg, published by Osborne/McGraw-Hill, ISBN 0-07-211845-8.

syntax and semantics of SQL statements in a batch mainframe COBOL application require few changes when the applications are converted to Java.

## Basic JDBC Operations

Working with JDBC isn't difficult. Depending on the task to be performed, usually only four steps are required:

1. Load a JDBC driver for your DBMS. This typically involves only a `Class.forName()` statement specifying the driver class name.
2. Use that driver to open a connection to a particular database. This is done with a call to a static `getConnection(`*`url`*`)` method to the `DriverManager` class. The `url` argument is in a specific form that indicates the driver type and the data source to use.
3. Issue SQL statements through the connection. Once the connection is established, it can be used to create `Statement` objects through which SQL commands can be made.
4. Process result sets returned by the SQL operations. The `ResultSet` interface provides methods to step through each row and get the values of each column.

Figure 13-1 illustrates these four steps.

With JDBC 2.0, a bit more flexibility occurs. Using *Java Naming and Directory Interface (JNDI)*, an application can look up a `DataSource` object by name from a naming service, rather than hard-coding the driver class name and database URL. Additionally, JDBC 2.0 result sets have more capabilities. They can be accessed in random order rather than sequentially from start to finish. They can be updated and have the updates propagated back to the underlying table. They can also be dynamically linked to their base table(s) so changes there are reflected concurrently in the result set. Figure 13-2 shows the basic steps involved in JDBC 2.0 database access.

## Essential JDBC Classes

The JDBC interface is contained in the `java.sql` and `javax.sql` packages.[3] It consists mainly of interfaces rather than concrete classes because each vendor's implementation is specific to their particular database protocol. The core API in `java.sql` consists of 16 interfaces, 8 classes, and 4 exception types. The Optional Package API adds another 12 interfaces and 2 classes. Many of these classes are of interest primarily to JDBC driver developers. A smaller subset of these is more commonly used, as outlined in the following:

- **`Connection`** An active link to a database through which a Java program can read and write data, as well as explore the database structure and capabilities.

3 javax.sql contains the JDBC 2.0 Optional Package API, formerly known as the JDBC 2.0 Standard Extension API.

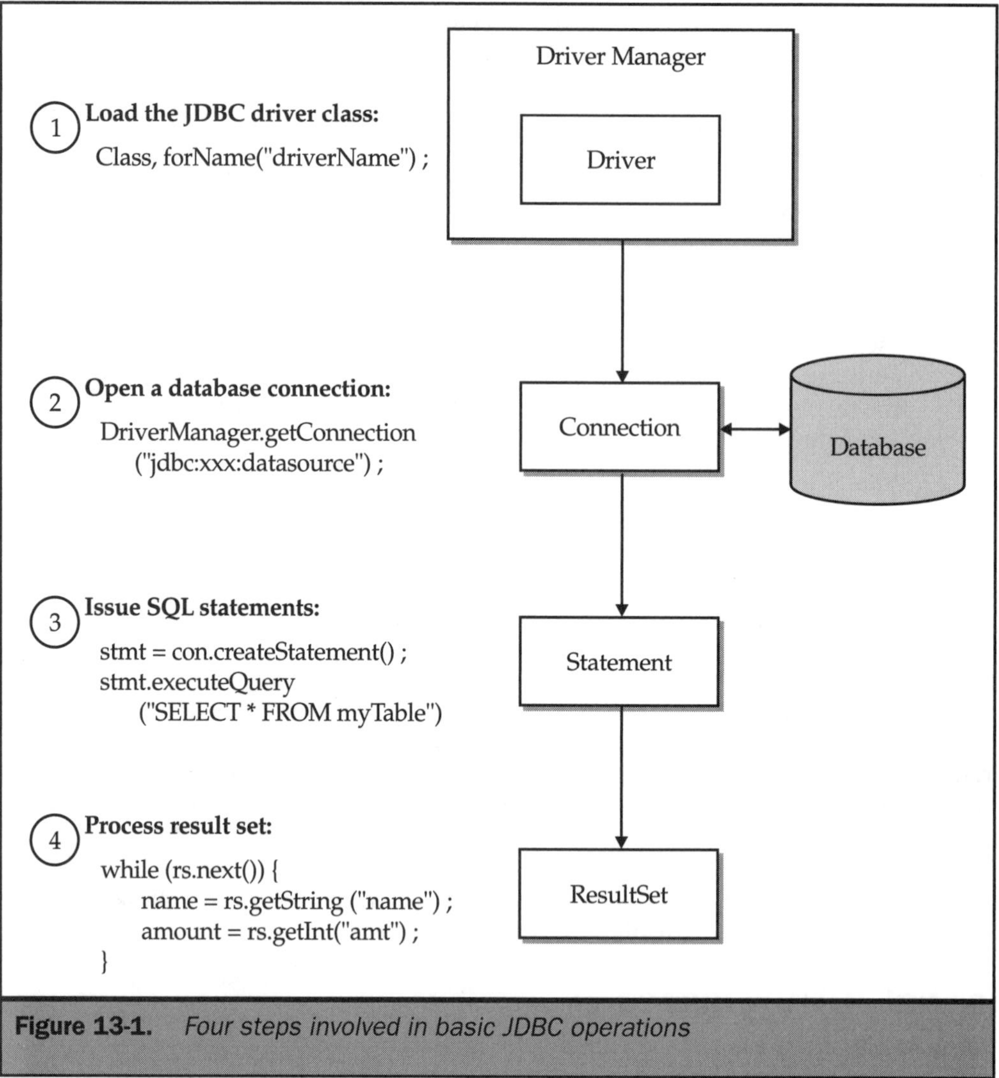


**Figure 13-1.** *Four steps involved in basic JDBC operations*

A `Connection` object is created either by a call to `DriverManager.getConnection()` or `DataSource.getConnection()`, in JDBC 2.0.

- **`Statement`** An object that allows SQL statements to be sent through a connection and retrieves the result sets and update counts they produce. Three types of statements exist, each one a specialization of its predecessors:
  - **Statement** Used to execute static SQL strings. A Statement is created with Connection.createStatement().

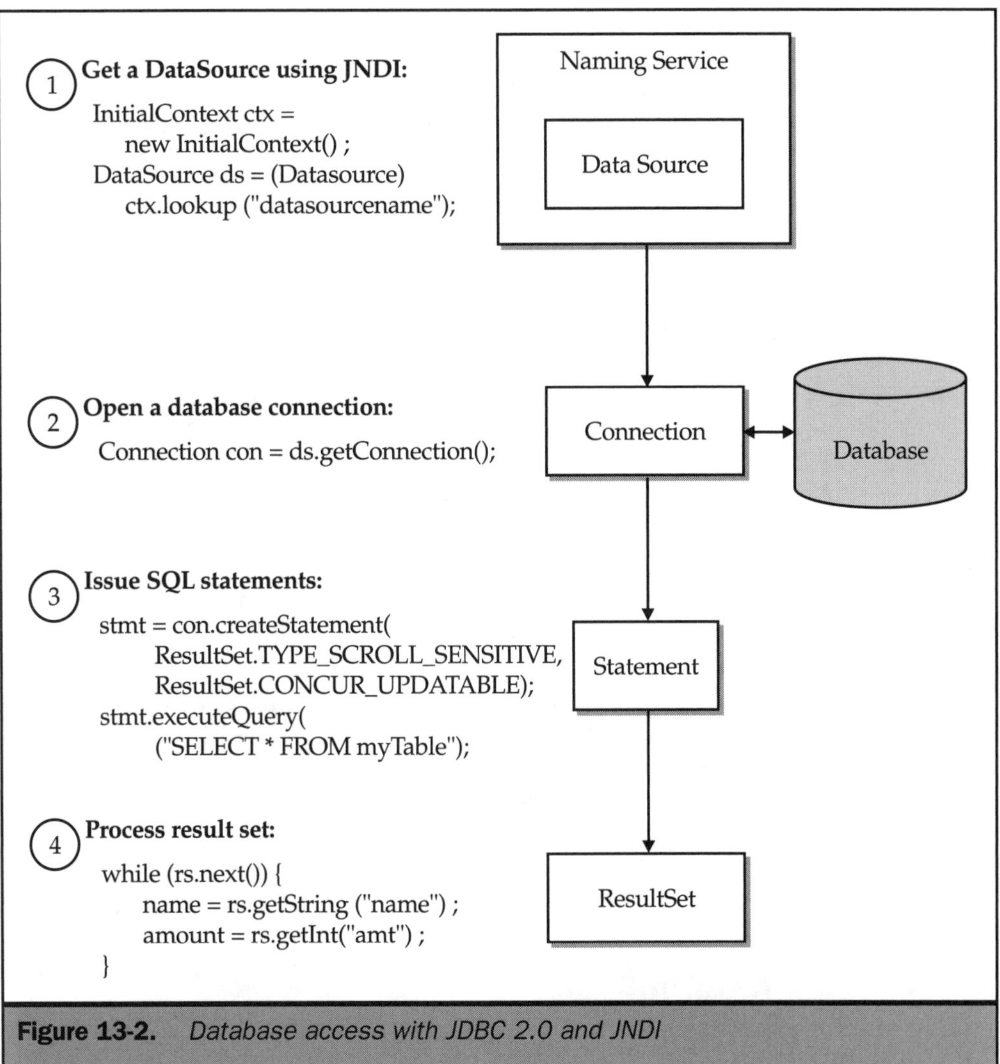


**Figure 13-2.** *Database access with JDBC 2.0 and JNDI*

- **PreparedStatement** An extension of Statement that uses precompiled SQL, possibly with dynamically set input parameters.. PreparedStatement objects are often used in a loop with SQL insert operations. They are created with Connection.prepareStatement(*sqlstring*).
- **CallableStatement** A PreparedStatement that invokes a stored procedure. Not all database management systems support stored procedures but, for those that do, CallableStatement provides a standard invocation syntax.

- **`ResultSet`** An ordered set of table rows produced by an SQL query or a call to certain metadata functions. A `ResultSet` is most often encountered as the return value of a `Statement.executeQuery(`*sqlstring*`)` method call. The JDBC API provides a `next()` method for iterating through the rows of a `ResultSet` and `getXXX()` methods for extracting the column values, where `XXX` is the Java data type. JDBC 2.0 adds a number of methods for randomly accessing and updating rows.
- **`DatabaseMetaData`** An interface containing numerous methods that provide information about the structure and capabilities of a database. The `DatabaseMetaData` object is returned by the `getMetaData()` method of a `Connection` object.
- **`ResultSetMetaData`** An interface that describes the columns of a `ResultSet`. This can be obtained by calling the result set's `getMetaData()` method. It contains methods that describe the number of columns, as well as each column's name, display size, data type, and class name.
- **`DriverManager`** An interface that registers JDBC drivers and supplies connections that can handle specific JDBC URLs. The only method commonly used is the static `DriverManager.getConnection()`, in one of its three forms, which returns an active `Connection` object bound to the specified JDBC URL.
- **`SQLException`** The base exception class used by the JDBC API. `SQLException` has methods that can supply the `SQLState` value any vendor-specific error code. It can also be linked to another `SQLException` if more than one exception occurred.

One of the stated goals of the JDBC API was it should be simple and easy to master. Learning these seven classes and three or four of their main methods can easily be done in a few days, which has helped to make JDBC a popular and well-accepted technology.

## A Simple JDBC Example

Let's consider an example of JDBC used in a JSP page. Our hypothetical LyricNote company maintains an internal employee database containing two tables: `departments` and `employees`. These tables were created with the following SQL:

```
CREATE TABLE departments (
   deptno       char(2),
   deptname     char(40),
   deptmgr      char(4)
)
```

and

```
CREATE TABLE employees (
   deptno      char(2),
   empno       char(4),
   lname       char(20),
   fname       char(20),
   hiredate    date,
   ismgr       bit,
   deptno      char(2),
   title       char(50),
   email       char(32),
   phone       char(4)
)
```

Our example JSP page displays a list of departments identifying their manager's name, title, telephone number, and e-mail address. The SQL to assemble this list is as follows:

```
SELECT   D.deptname, E.fname, E.lname, E.title, E.email, E.phone
FROM     departments D, employees E
WHERE    D.deptmgr = E.empno
ORDER BY D.deptname
```

The D and E prefixes are pseudotable names used to qualify column names, so the DBMS can distinguish which table supplies which columns.

The complete JSP source code is

```
<%@ page session="false" %>
<%@ page import="java.sql.*" %>
<%@ page import="java.util.*" %>

<HTML>
<HEAD>
<TITLE>Department Managers</TITLE>
</HEAD>
<BODY>
<img src="images/lyric_note.png" border=0><p>
<hr color="#000000">
<H2>Department Managers</H2>
<%
```

```
    String DRIVER = "org.enhydra.instantdb.jdbc.idbDriver";
    String URL =
       "jdbc:idb:d:/lyricnote/WEB-INF/database/internal/db.prp";

    // Open a database connection

    Class.forName(DRIVER);
    Connection con = null;
    try {

       con = DriverManager.getConnection(URL);

       // Get department manager information

       String sql = ""
          + " SELECT   D.deptname, E.fname, E.lname,"
          + "          E.title, E.email, E.phone"
          + " FROM     departments D, employees E"
          + " WHERE    D.deptmgr = E.empno"
          + " ORDER BY D.deptname"
          ;

       Statement stmt = con.createStatement();
       ResultSet rs = stmt.executeQuery(sql);
%>
<DL>
<%
       while (rs.next()) {
          String dept  = rs.getString(1);
          String fname = rs.getString(2);
          String lname = rs.getString(3);
          String title = rs.getString(4);
          String email = rs.getString(5);
          String phone = rs.getString(6);
%>
<DT><B><%= dept %></B></DT>
<DD>
   <%= fname %> <%= lname %>, <%= title %><BR>
   (919) 555-0822 x<%= phone %>, <%= email %>
</DD>
<%
       }
```

```
            rs.close();
            rs = null;

            stmt.close();
            stmt = null;
        }
        finally {
            if (con != null) {
                con.close();
            }
        }
%>
</DL>
</BODY>
</HTML>
```



Let's examine each section.

To begin with, three page directives exist

```
<%@ page session="false" %>
<%@ page import="java.sql.*" %>
<%@ page import="java.util.*" %>
```

We explicitly request no HTTP session should be created. This should be done in all JSP pages that don't require access to a session because it saves the server resources required to establish and maintain a session.

After the HTML that creates the page headings, a scriptlet interrogates the LyricNote internal database and displays the results. It begins with the declaration of two string constants that define the JDBC driver name and database URL. For convenience, keep this information isolated in a declarations section for ease of modification:

```
    String DRIVER = "org.enhydra.instantdb.jdbc.idbDriver";
    String URL =
        "jdbc:idb:d:/lyricnote/WEB-INF/database/internal/db.prp";
```

This example uses the InstantDB[4] database and connects to the LyricNote internal database, whose `Properties` file is `db.prp`.

---

4 *InstantDB* is a free, all-Java relational DBMS available from http://instantdb.enhydra.org/index.html. InstantDB has a number of advanced features and supports JDBC 2.0.

The real work begins with the next statements:

```
    Class.forName(DRIVER);
    Connection con = null;
    try {
       con = DriverManager.getConnection(URL);
```

The `Class.forName()` call causes the JDBC driver class to be loaded. According to the JDBC specification, drivers should include a static initialization section that causes an instance to be created and registered with the driver manager. Some older drivers fail to do this and, in that case, invoking the newInstance() method on the driver class is necessary. The `DriverManager` class provides the actual connection in response to the call to its static `getConnection()` method.

Note, the con variable that holds a reference to the connection is declared and assigned a `null` value. Then the rest of the page is enclosed in a `try {...}` block followed by

```
finally {
      if (con != null) {
         con.close();
      }
   }
```

The reason for this is, once opened, the connection needs to be closed, regardless of whether any errors occur or exceptions are thrown. This can be guaranteed by the `finally { ... }` block. Including a `catch` block is unnecessary; in our case, the default exception handler is good enough.

Once the connection is established, the SQL query can be run. For this, we call the `Connection` object's `createStatement()` method to obtain a `Statement` object, on which we can invoke the `executeQuery()` method.

```
    String sql = ""
       + " SELECT   D.deptname, E.fname, E.lname,"
       + "          E.title, E.email, E.phone"
       + " FROM     departments D, employees E"
       + " WHERE    D.deptmgr = E.empno"
       + " ORDER BY D.deptname"
       ;

    Statement stmt = con.createStatement();
    ResultSet rs = stmt.executeQuery(sql);
```

`executeQuery()` returns a `ResultSet`. Our listing simply reads each row of this set by invoking its `next()` method in a loop:

```
   while (rs.next()) {
         String dept  = rs.getString(1);
         String fname = rs.getString(2);
         String lname = rs.getString(3);
         String title = rs.getString(4);
         String email = rs.getString(5);
         String phone = rs.getString(6);
%>
<DT><B><%= dept %></B></DT>
<DD>
   <%= fname %> <%= lname %>, <%= title %><BR>
   (919) 555-0822 x<%= phone %>, <%= email %>
</DD>
<%
      }
```

Inside the loop, we extract each column value with the `ResultSet.getString` `(`*columnNumber*`)` method, and then format and print the department name, manager name, title, telephone number, and e-mail lines.

Finally, we close all the JDBC objects we created and set their references to `null`, so they can be garbage collected.

```
      rs.close();
      rs = null;

      stmt.close();
      stmt = null;
```

The `Connection` object is closed in the `finally { ... }` block previously discussed. The finished product is shown in Figure 13-3.

## JDBC Drivers

To insulate programs from the specifics of particular database protocols, JDBC uses a middle layer composed of a `DriverManager` class and one or more JDBC drivers. A *driver* is Java class, usually supplied by the database vendor, which implements the `java.sql.Driver` interface. The primary function of the driver is to connect to a database and return a `java.sql.Connection` object.

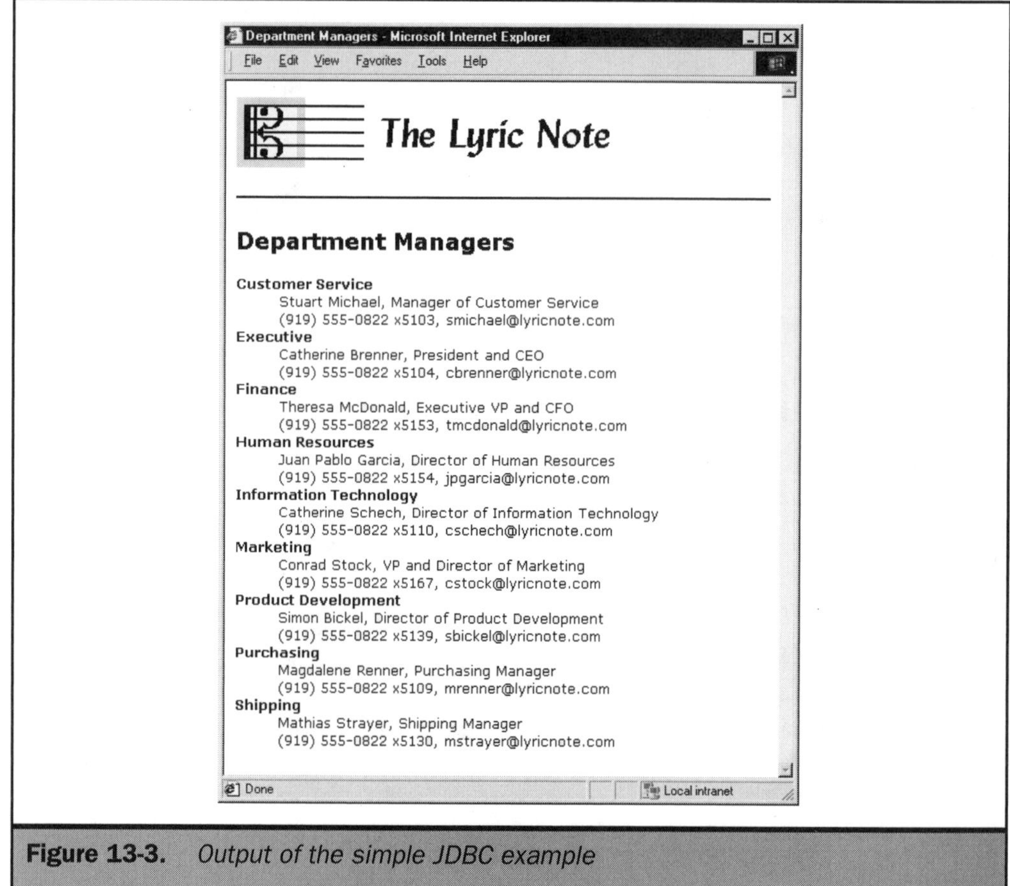


**Figure 13-3.** *Output of the simple JDBC example*

Drivers aren't called directly by application programs. Instead, they're registered with the `DriverManager`, which determines the appropriate driver for a particular connection request and makes the connection through it.

Hundreds of JDBC drivers exist, covering virtually all database management systems. Most of them can be downloaded from vendor Web sites. A searchable list can be found at http://industry.java.sun.com/products/jdbc/drivers.

The next section discusses the four JDBC driver types, the special case of the JDBC-ODBC bridge, and the mechanics of registering a driver.

## Driver Types

The JDBC specification classifies drivers as being one of four types, according to their architecture. These types are

- **Type 1—JDBC-ODBC bridge** Drivers of this type connect to databases through an intermediate ODBC driver. Several drawbacks are involved with this approach, so Sun describes it as being experimental and appropriate for use only where no other driver is available. Both Microsoft and Sun provide type 1 drivers.
- **Type 2—Native API, partly Java** Similar to a JDBC-ODBC bridge, type 2 drivers use native methods to call vendor-specific API functions. These drivers are also subject to the same limitations as the JDBC-ODBC bridge, in that they require native library files to be installed on client systems, which must be configured to use them.
- **Type 3—Pure Java to database middleware** Type 3 drivers communicate using a network protocol to a middleware server, which, in turn, communicates to one or more database management systems.
- **Type 4—Pure Java direct to database** Drivers of this type call directly into the native protocol used by the database management system.

The architecture of each of the four driver types is shown in Figure 13-4.

What difference does the driver type make? From the standpoint of the application programmer, not much. The classifications mean more to the system architect. Type 1 and type 2 drivers require native code to be installed and configured on client systems. Type 4 drivers may not be suitable if the DBMS is behind a firewall. Likewise, each of the four driver types has its own performance characteristics, but the application programming interface is exactly the same in all four cases.



## The JDBC-ODBC Bridge

The type 1 JDBC-ODBC bridge driver requires special considerations. As we have seen, several problems are involved in using it. First, the JDBC-ODBC bridge driver is limited to the capabilities of the underlying ODBC driver, which is single threaded and may, therefore, perform poorly under a heavy load. Also, it requires native code library `JdbcOdbc.dll` to be installed on the client system. Finally, to be of any use, the JDBC-ODBC bridge driver requires an ODBC data source to be configured. These restrictions make it unsuitable for applets intended for use on the external internet. Sun recommends the bridge should only be used for experimental purposes when no other JDBC driver is available.

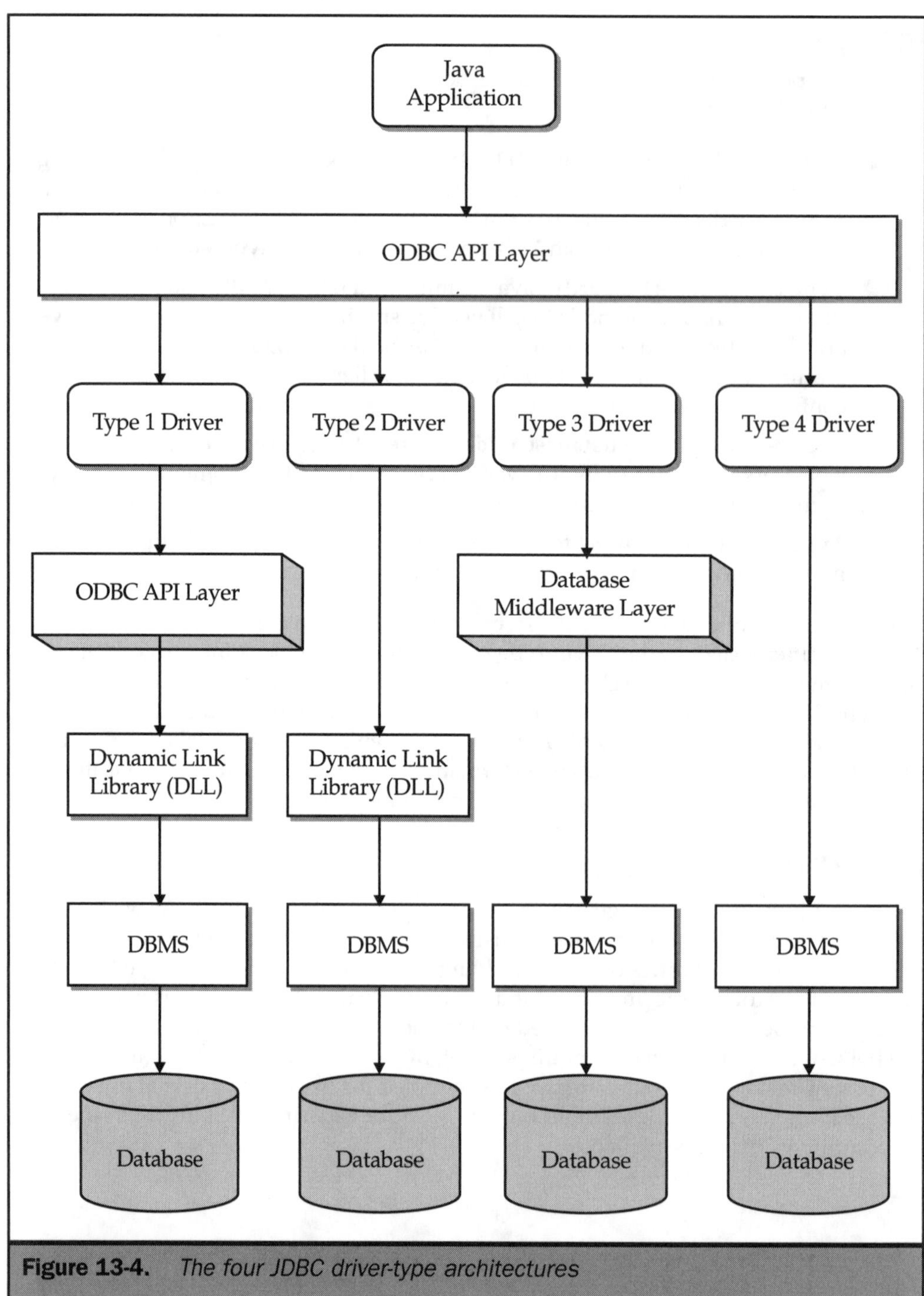


**Figure 13-4.** *The four JDBC driver-type architectures*

On the other hand, the JDBC-ODBC bridge offers several significant advantages. Because JSP pages aren't operating in the applet environment, they have none of these limitations. ODBC is widely supported, so using the bridge makes possible accessing a wide variety of existing systems for which data sources are already configured. Likewise, ODBC-enabled database products, such as Microsoft Access and FoxBase, are widely available. These features make the JDBC-ODBC bridge a good choice for low-volume Web applications and a useful tool for learning JDBC.

To use the JDBC-ODBC bridge in a Java application, a suitable ODBC data source must be configured. On Windows systems, this is done through the Control Panel ODBC Data Sources application. The data source should be configured as a System DSN, not a User DSN, because the JSP engine is typically running under a system user profile. The driver class name is `sun.jdbc.odbc.JdbcOdbcDriver` if the Sun JVM is being used or `com.ms.jdbc.odbc.JdbcOdbcDriver` for the Microsoft virtual machine. The database URL used in the `getConnection()` statement is `jdbc:odbc:`*dsn*, where *dsn* is the data source name.

Microsoft supplies ODBC drivers for its Access database product, as well as dBase, Excel, FoxPro, and a number of others, including a text driver that can use ordinary text files (.txt and .csv) as a simple database system.



## Registering a Driver

For a JDBC driver to be used, it must first be registered with the driver manager. You can accomplish this in several ways, but each involves calling `DriverManager.registerDriver()`.

The most common approach is simply to load the driver class:

```
try {
   Class.forName("MyJdbcDriver");
}
catch (ClassNotFoundException e) {
   // Report the exception
}
```

A driver class loaded in this fashion should create an instance of itself and register it with the driver manager, using logic similar to the following:

```
static {
   PrintStream log = DriverManager.getLogStream();
   if (log != null)
      log.println("MyJdbcDriver class loaded");
   MyJdbcDriver driver = new MyJdbcDriver();
   try {
      DriverManager.registerDriver(driver);
   }
```

```
      catch (SQLException e) {
         if (log != null)
            log.println("Unable to register driver");
      }
   }
```

Some older drivers have been known to omit this step, doing the registration in their constructor instead. In that case, creating an instance of the driver is necessary, using the following method[5]:

```
   try {
      Class.forName("MyJdbcDriver");
   }
   catch (ClassNotFoundException e) {
      // Report the exception
   }
   catch (InstantiationException e) {
      // Report the exception
   }
   catch (IllegalAccessException e) {
      // Report the exception
   }
```

Another approach to driver registration is to put the driver name in the `jdbc.drivers` system property. This is a colon-delimited list of driver class names, which `DriverManager` loads during its initialization. For example, a standalone Java application that uses this approach might be invoked as follows:

```
   java -Djdbc.drivers=org.enhydra.instantdb.jdbc.idbDriver MyPGM
```

Some JDBC driver vendors, notably Oracle, recommend explicitly creating an instance of the driver and registering it with the driver manager:

```
   DriverManager.registerDriver(
      new oracle.jdbc.driver.OracleDriver());
```

JDBC 2.0 allows connections to be made through a `DataSource` object that is registered with a JNDI service provider. JRun 3.0, for example, provides a means for defining JDBC data sources at the Web server level, as well as a quick online test

---

5 A tedious workaround, isn't it? You could simply catch `Exception` itself, but that always leaves you open to applying the wrong logic to exceptions you didn't anticipate.

for connectivity. The advantage of this approach is driver class names and database URL's are stored in the naming service, rather than being hard coded in application programs. Only the data source name is required. The sample JSP page associated with Figure 13-3 earlier in this chapter could have its connection logic replaced with the following:

```
InitialContext ctx = new InitialContext();
DataSource ds = (DataSource) ctx.lookup
   ("java:comp/env/jdbc/lyricnote_internal");

Connection con = null;
try {
   con = ds.getConnection();
   ...
}
finally {
   if (con != null)
      con.close();
}
```

**Note** *JSP pages using a DataSource for JDBC connections must import* `javax.sql.*` *and* `javax.naming.*` *or else fully qualify the references to InitialContext and DataSource.*

Another advantage of using a `DataSource` is other advanced database features like connection pooling and distributed transactions can be implemented entirely with changes to bindings in the naming service. No changes to the JSP source code are required.



## Connecting to a Database

After a driver is loaded and registered, it can be used to create database connections. `DriverManager` provides three methods for doing this:

`getConnection(String` *url*`)`
`getConnection(String` *url*`, String` *userID*`, String` *password*`)`
`getConnection(String` *url*`, Properties` *prop*`)`

Internally, `DriverManager` uses the same private worker method to handle each of these methods.

The driver manager maintains a list of registered drivers. When its `getConnection()` method is invoked, it interrogates each driver in turn to see if it will accept the specified URL. The driver manager does this by calling the driver's `connect()` method, which returns either `null` if the driver cannot accept the URL or an active `Connection` object if it can.

As noted previously, JDBC 2.0 allows `DataSource` to be used instead of `DriverManager` to establish connections. In this case, the URL parameter isn't used, because it's stored in the naming service.

## The JDBC Database URL

The key argument to DriverManager.getConnection() is a *JDBC URL*, which is a string with three components separated by semicolons:

*<protocol>* : *<subprotocol>* : *<subname>*

where

- *protocol* is always `jdbc`.
- *subprotocol* is a vendor-specific string that identifies the driver to be used. The driver indicates whether it can handle that subprotocol when asked by the driver manager. For example, the JDBC-ODBC bridge uses the reserved value `odbc` as its subprotocol. This value is intended to be unique across all driver vendors. Sun Microsystems acts as an informal registrar of JDBC subprotocols.
- *subname* identifies the specific database to connect to. This string contains whatever the driver needs to identify the database. It may also contain connection parameters the database needs.

Examples of JDBC URLs are

```
jdbc:odbc:usda
```

This would indicate an ODBC data source named `usda` that is accessed by the JDBC-ODBC bridge driver.

```
jdbc:idb:c:/path/database.prp
```

InstantDB interprets the *subname* to be a properties file that describes the database location and characteristics.

```
"jdbc:oracle:thin:@"
   + "(DESCRIPTION="
   + "(ADDRESS=(HOST=u25nv)"
   + "(PROTOCOL=tcp)"
   + "(PORT=4311))"
   + "(CONNECT_DATA=(SID=music)))"
```

This is a lengthy connection string that might be used with the Oracle thin client driver.

As was the case with driver registration, JDBC 2.0 makes possible using a `DataSource` from a naming service to hide the details of the JDBC URL.

# The Statement Interfaces

The SQL language consists of statements that create, manipulate, and extract data from a relational database. JDBC provides an object-oriented representation of these SQL statements that encapsulates their text, execution status, and results. Not surprisingly, this representation is called the `java.sql.Statement` interface. Statement objects send SQL commands to a database, which can be any of the following types:

- A data definition command such as `CREATE TABLE` or `CREATE INDEX`
- A data manipulation command such as `INSERT` or `UPDATE`
- A `SELECT` statement for performing a query

Data manipulation commands return a count of the number of rows modified, whereas a `SELECT` statement returns a set of rows known as a result set.

The `Statement` interface has two specialized subinterfaces that extend its capabilities: `PreparedStatement`, which uses precompiles SQL, and `CallableStatement`, which invokes stored procedures. The following section discusses all three types of statements and how they are used.



## Statement

The base interface is `java.sql.Statement`. Because this is an interface, it doesn't have a constructor; instead, it's obtained from the connection object with `Connection.createStatement()`. A typical example follows

```
Connection con = null;
try {
   con = DriverManager.getConnection(URL);
   Statement stmt = con.createStatement();
   ...
   stmt.close();
}
finally {
   if (con != null)
      con.close();
}
```

JDBC 2.0 introduces an additional form of `createStatement()` that takes parameters indicating where its result sets should be scrollable or not and whether they reflect concurrent changes in the underlying table. The section on result sets later in this chapter describes these features in more detail.

Once a statement is created, it can be used to execute commands. Four methods exist for doing this: `executeUpdate`, `executeQuery`, `execute`, and `executeBatch`. The choice of which method to use depends on the expected results:

- **`executeUpdate`** is intended for use with the SQL `INSERT`, `UPDATE`, or `DELETE` statements, or with data definition statements such as `CREATE TABLE`. It returns a count of the number of rows updated.
- **`executeQuery`** is used to execute an SQL `SELECT` statement and to return a result set.
- **`execute`** can be used for either purpose, but is intended for those statements that return either an update count, multiple result sets, or some combination. It returns a boolean flag that indicates whether its result was an update count or a result set. Additional methods are available that navigate through results.
- **`executeBatch`** allows multiple update statements to be executed in a batch. The update counts are returned in an array.

The following examples illustrate each of these methods.

## The executeUpdate Method

In this example, an erroneous product description is corrected with an SQL UPDATE statement invoked by the `executeUpdate` method.

```
import java.sql.*;

public class UpdateExample
{
   public static void main(String[] args)
      throws ClassNotFoundException, SQLException
   {
      String DRIVER = "org.enhydra.instantdb.jdbc.idbDriver";
      String URL = "jdbc:idb:"
         + "D:/lyricnote/WEB-INF/database/products/db.prp";

      Class.forName(DRIVER);
      Connection con = null;
      try {
         con = DriverManager.getConnection(URL);
         Statement stmt = con.createStatement();
         int nRows = stmt.executeUpdate(
              " UPDATE   products"
            + " SET      description ="
            + "'Telemann: Concerto No. 1 in F for Two Horns'"
```

```
            + " WHERE    itemcode = '022370'"
            );
         System.out.println(nRows + " rows updated");
         stmt.close();
      }
      finally {
         if (con != null)
            con.close();
      }
   }
}
```

When successfully executed, the program prints "1 rows updated".

## The executeQuery Method

To see that the erroneous listing was corrected, this example uses a SELECT statement to display all sheet music titles in the product catalog that are Telemann concertos:

```
import java.sql.*;

public class QueryExample
{
   public static void main(String[] args)
      throws ClassNotFoundException, SQLException
   {
      String DRIVER = "org.enhydra.instantdb.jdbc.idbDriver";
      String URL = "jdbc:idb:"
         + "D:/lyricnote/WEB-INF/database/products/db.prp";

      Class.forName(DRIVER);
      Connection con = null;
      try {
         con = DriverManager.getConnection(URL);
         Statement stmt = con.createStatement();
         ResultSet rs = stmt.executeQuery(
              " SELECT   itemcode, description"
            + " FROM     products"
            + " WHERE    prodtype = 'SM'"
            + " AND      description like 'Telemann%'"
            + " AND      description like '%Concerto%'"
         );
         while (rs.next()) {
            String itemCode = rs.getString(1);
```

```
            String description = rs.getString(2);
            System.out.println(itemCode + " " + description);
         }
         rs.close();
         stmt.close();
      }
      finally {
         if (con != null)
            con.close();
      }
   }
}
```

When run, it produces the corrected output:

```
022340 Telemann: Double Viola Concerto in G
022350 Telemann: Viola Concerto in G
022360 Telemann: Concerto for Horn Quartet
022370 Telemann: Concerto No. 1 in F for Two Horns
```

The process of getting values from the result set is explained later in this chapter.

## The execute Method

Although the `execute` method can be used for either queries or updates, it's strictly necessary only for operations that may return multiple results. The `Statement` interface provides methods for determining what has been returned and for processing the results. The most common use for `execute` is for processing unknown SQL strings, such as in this example, which reads and processes SQL statements from a file:

```
import java.io.*;
import java.sql.*;

public class ExecuteExample
{
   public static void main(String[] args)
      throws ClassNotFoundException, SQLException, IOException
   {
      String DRIVER = "org.enhydra.instantdb.jdbc.idbDriver";
      String URL = "jdbc:idb:"
         + "D:/lyricnote/WEB-INF/database/products/db.prp";
```

```
Class.forName(DRIVER);
Connection con = null;
try {
   con = DriverManager.getConnection(URL);
   Statement stmt = con.createStatement();

   // Read SQL statements from a file

   BufferedReader in =
      new BufferedReader(
      new FileReader("executeExample.sql"));

   while (true) {
      String line = in.readLine();
      if (line == null)
         break;

      // Execute statement

      boolean hasResultSet = stmt.execute(line);
      while (true) {

         if (hasResultSet) {
            ResultSet rs = stmt.getResultSet();
            System.out.println("Processing result set");
            // ... process result set
            rs.close();
         }
         else {
            int count = stmt.getUpdateCount();
            if (count == -1)
               break;
            System.out.println("Processing update count");
            // ... process update count
         }

         // See if there are any more results

         hasResultSet = stmt.getMoreResults();
      }
   }
   stmt.close();
```

```
            in.close();
         }
         finally {
            if (con != null)
               con.close();
         }
      }
   }
```

The initial return code from execute is a boolean value that is true if the statement execution produced a result set. If not, the update count can be obtained with Statement.getUpdateCount(). If the update count is -1, then no more results exist. Otherwise, the Statement.getMoreResults() method can be called to cycle through the next result set or update count. It returns a boolean value with the same interpretation as the one returned by execute.

## The executeBatch Method

JDBC 2.0 introduced the capability to submit a group of update statements to be executed as a batch. In some cases, this can represent a significant performance improvement. The methods used in connection with batch updates are these:

- **clearBatch** resets a batch to the empty state.
- **addBatch** adds an update statement to the batch.
- **executeBatch** submits the batch and collects update counts.

Not all drivers support batch updates. Those that do indicate this by returning true from their DatabaseMetaData.supportsBatchUpdates() method.

One driver that does implement this is the JDBC-ODBC bridge with Microsoft Access. In the following example, the LyricNote composers Access database is updated with a table of composers who lived to at least the age of 90.

```
import java.io.*;
import java.sql.*;
import java.util.*;

public class BatchUpdateExample
{
   public static void main(String[] args)
      throws ClassNotFoundException, SQLException, IOException
   {
      Class.forName("sun.jdbc.odbc.JdbcOdbcDriver");
```

```
Connection con = null;
try {

   // Connect to the composers database

   con = DriverManager.getConnection
      ("jdbc:odbc:composers");
   Statement stmt = con.createStatement();

   // Clear the existing table and create a new one

   stmt.executeUpdate("DROP TABLE over90");
   stmt.executeUpdate(
         " CREATE TABLE over90"
       + " ("
       + "    lastName    VARCHAR(20),"
       + "    firstName   VARCHAR(20),"
       + "    age         INTEGER"
       + " )"
   );

   // Set up for handling all-or-nothing transaction

   con.setAutoCommit(false);

   // Add insert statements to a batch

   stmt.clearBatch();

   stmt.addBatch("INSERT INTO over90 VALUES"
      + "('Rodrigo','Joaquin',99)");
   stmt.addBatch("INSERT INTO over90 VALUES"
      + "('Gossec','Francois-Joseph',96)");
   stmt.addBatch("INSERT INTO over90 VALUES"
      + "('Ruggles','Carl',96)");
   stmt.addBatch("INSERT INTO over90 VALUES"
      + "('Widor','Charles-Marie',94)");
   stmt.addBatch("INSERT INTO over90 VALUES"
      + "('Sibelius','Jean',93)");
   stmt.addBatch("INSERT INTO over90 VALUES"
      + "('Copland','Aaron',91)");
   stmt.addBatch("INSERT INTO over90 VALUES"
```

```
               + "('Auber','Daniel Francois',90)");
            stmt.addBatch("INSERT INTO over90 VALUES"
               + "('Stravinsky','Igor',90)");

            // Execute the batch and check the update counts

            int[] counts = stmt.executeBatch();

            boolean allGood = true;
            for (int i = 0; i < counts.length; i++)
               if (counts[i] != 1)
                  allGood = false;

            // Commit or roll back the transaction

            if (allGood) {
               System.out.println
                  ("Transaction successful with "
                  + counts.length + " statements committed");
               con.commit();
            }
            else {
               System.out.println("Transaction failed");
               con.rollback();
            }

            // Done

            stmt.close();
         }
         finally {
            if (con != null)
               con.close();
         }
      }
   }
```

Setting off the connection's `autoCommit` flag enables us either to commit or rollback the batch update as a whole.

## PreparedStatement

`java.sql.PreparedStatement` is a subinterface of `Statement` that uses precompiled SQL. This may result in performance improvements if the statement is used repeatedly. A `PreparedStatement` differs from `Statement` in that its `execute` methods don't take a SQL string as a parameter. Instead, the SQL string is specified when the `PreparedStatement` is created, as shown here:

```
PreparedStatement pstmt = con.prepareStatement(sqlstring);
```

The string to be executed may contain substitution parameters, which are indicated by the presence of a question mark (?) in the string. These parameters act as placeholders in the statement and must be filled in with values before they are executed. To do this, the API provides a number of `setXXX()` methods, where `XXX` is the Java data type.

The batch update example, which created and loaded a table of composers who lived to at least the age of 90, could also be written with a `PreparedStatement` that is executed in a loop, as shown here:

```
import java.io.*;
import java.sql.*;
import java.util.*;

public class PreparedStatementExample
{
   public static void main(String[] args)
      throws ClassNotFoundException, SQLException, IOException
   {
      String DRIVER = "sun.jdbc.odbc.JdbcOdbcDriver";
      String URL = "jdbc:odbc:composers";

      Connection con = null;
      try {

         // Load the driver class

         Class.forName(DRIVER);

         // Connect to the database

         con = DriverManager.getConnection(URL);

         // Create the new table
```

```
Statement stmt = con.createStatement();
try {
stmt.executeUpdate("DROP TABLE OVER90");
}
catch (SQLException ignore){}
stmt.executeUpdate(
      " CREATE TABLE over90"
    + " ("
    + "    lastName     VARCHAR(20),"
    + "    firstName    VARCHAR(20),"
    + "    age          INTEGER"
    + " )"
);
stmt.close();
stmt = null;

// Prepare a statement to do inserts into the table

PreparedStatement pstmt = con.prepareStatement(
   "INSERT INTO over90 VALUES(?, ?, ?)"
);

// Read composer names and ages from a file
// that uses tabs to separate the fields

BufferedReader in =
   new BufferedReader(
   new FileReader("over90.txt"));

while (true) {
   String line = in.readLine();
   if (line == null)
      break;

   // Split the line into the last name, first name
   // and age tokens

   StringTokenizer st = new StringTokenizer(line, "\t");
   if (st.countTokens() != 3)
      throw new IOException ("Expected 3 fields");
```

```
            String lastName = st.nextToken();
            String firstName = st.nextToken();
            int age = Integer.parseInt(st.nextToken());

            // Set the parameters in the prepared statement

            pstmt.setString(1, lastName);
            pstmt.setString(2, firstName);
            pstmt.setInt(3, age);

            // Update the record

            pstmt.executeUpdate();
            System.out.println(
            "Added record for " + firstName + " " + lastName);
         }

         in.close();

         pstmt.close();
         pstmt = null;

      }
      finally {
         if (con != null)
            con.close();
      }
   }
}
```

Consider several key points in the code. First, the statement needs to be created with substitution parameters:

```
   PreparedStatement pstmt = con.prepareStatement(
      "INSERT INTO over90 VALUES(?, ?, ?)"
   );
```

Three question marks are here, one for each column in the table. Notice no difference exists in use between numeric and string parameters. Both are coded simply as question marks, with no embedded quotes or apostrophes needed.

To use the values that were read from the file in the `INSERT` statement, employ the `setString()` and `setInt()` methods:

```
pstmt.setString(1, lastName);
pstmt.setString(2, firstName);
pstmt.setInt(3, age);
```

The first parameter to the `setXXX()` methods is the column number, which starts at 1 for the first column, 2 for the second, and so on. The second parameter is the value to be inserted.

`setXXX()` methods exist for all data types, as well as two special ones: `setObject()` and `setNull()`. Type conversions into any JDBC data type can be made with `setObject()`, which takes a third parameter:

`pstmt.setObject(int` *column*`, Object` *value*`, int` *typeNumber*`)`

where *typeNumber* is an static integer constant defined in `java.sql.Types`. Similarly, `setNull()` can be used to store the appropriate null type in a parameter:

`pstmt.setNull(int` *column*`, int` *typeNumber*`)`

## Using Prepared Statements to Avoid Dynamic Syntax Errors

While the primary motivation for using prepared statements is performance, another subtle advantage exists. Suppose you want to make a JSP page that can run queries against the LyricNote product database. The page includes a form in which a search argument can be entered. This argument is extracted from the request parameters and an SQL statement is then constructed on the fly. Here is part of the JSP page showing how the SQL is constructed:

```
ResultSet rs = stmt.executeQuery(
  " SELECT   itemcode, description"
   + " FROM     products"
   + " WHERE    prodtype = 'SM'"
   + " AND      description like '%" + searchFor + "%'"
   );
```

When the JSP page is used to search for works by Stravinsky, it returns the results shown in Figure 13-5.

If, however, you search specifically for Stravinsky's *L'Histoire du Soldat*, you get the nasty error screen shown in Figure 13-6.

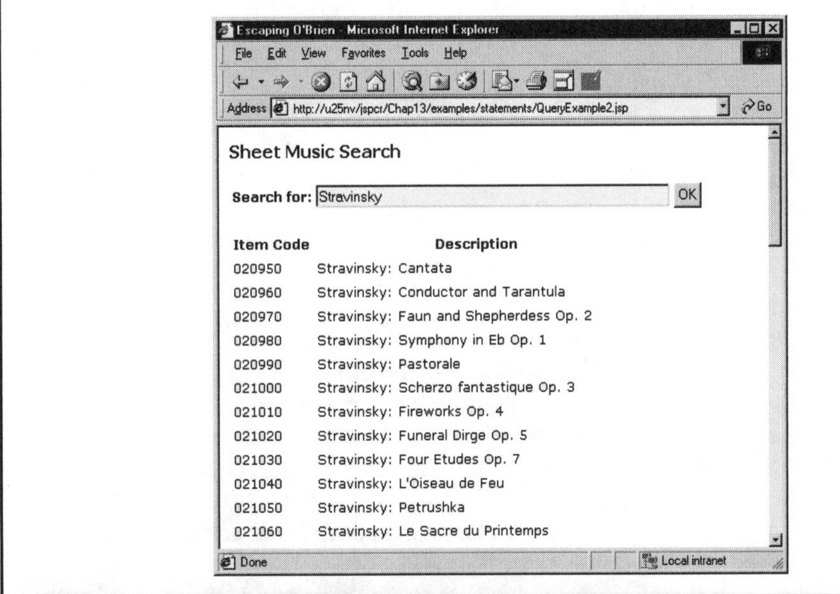


**Figure 13-5.** *Normal output of QueryExample2.jsp*

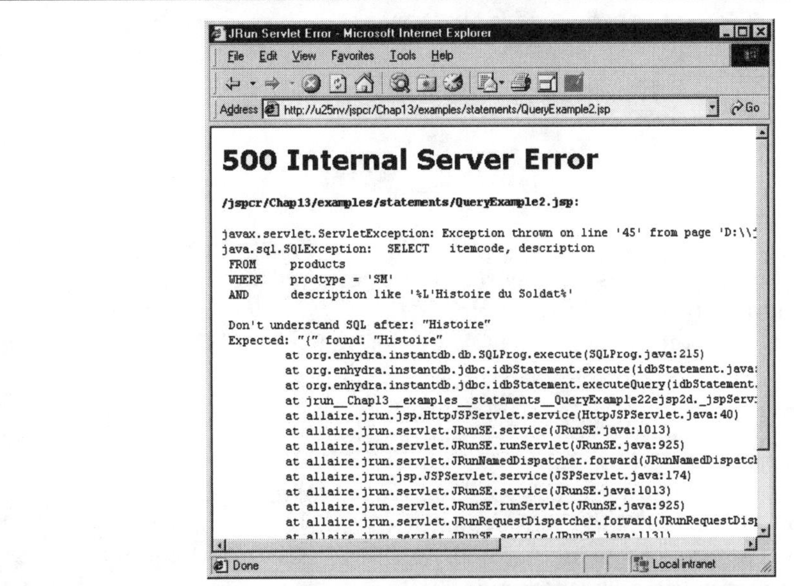


**Figure 13-6.** *Syntax error caused by an unescaped apostrophe*

What happened? The explanation can be found in the error message:

```
javax.servlet.ServletException
java.sqlSQLException:  SELECT   itemcode, description
 FROM     products
 WHERE    prodtype = 'SM'
 AND      description like '%L'Histoire du Soldat%'

Don't understand SQL after: "Histoire"
```

The word *L'Histoire* has an embedded apostrophe, so when the `LIKE` clause is evaluated, it terminates too soon, viewing `'%L'` as the operand it is trying to match. Whatever follows is parsed as if it were SQL, which causes the error.

This problem can be avoided by scanning user input for embedded apostrophes and replacing them with a safe alternative, but this is more complicated than it sounds. This technique, referred to as *escaping characters,* varies in different databases and SQL dialects. A JDBC-architected way exists to indicate the escape character, but this adds complexity everywhere user input has to be handled.

A simpler and cleaner way to handle this is to use a `PreparedStatement` with a substitution parameter. The code that needs to be changed is this:

```
PreparedStatement pstmt = con.prepareStatement(
     " SELECT   itemcode, description\n"
   + " FROM     products\n"
   + " WHERE    prodtype = 'SM'\n"
   + " AND      description like ?"
);
pstmt.setString(1, "%" + searchFor + "%");
ResultSet rs = pstmt.executeQuery();
```

The operand of the `LIKE` clause is now simply a question mark and the search argument is now added dynamically at run time. The query now works with any type of input, regardless of its meaning in SQL, as seen in Figure 13-7.

## CallableStatement

A further refinement of `PreparedStatement` is embodied in `java.sql.CallableStatement`. This interface is used to invoke stored procedures, if the database supports them[6]. Oracle, for example, allows procedures to be written in PL/SQL. Queries written in Microsoft Access can be invoked through the JDBC-ODBC bridge as stored procedures.

---

6 Few, if any, noncommercial databases support stored procedures.

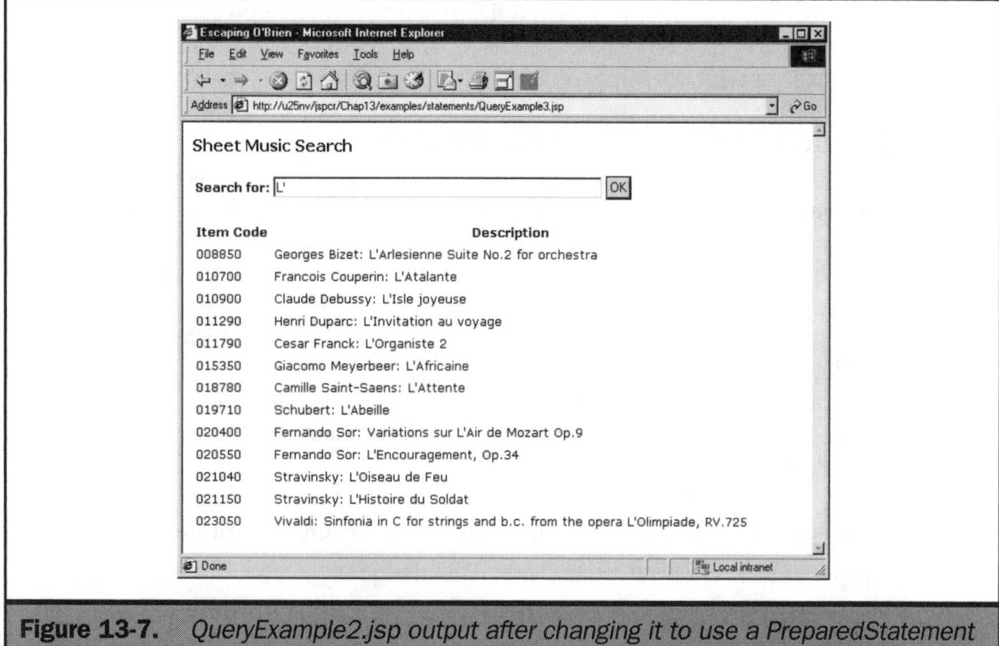


**Figure 13-7.** *QueryExample2.jsp output after changing it to use a PreparedStatement*



Like its immediate superinterface `PreparedStatement`, a `CallableStatement` is created with an explicit command string that gets precompiled:

`CallableStatement cstmt = con.prepareCall(`*escapeString*`);`

It also uses question marks to indicate substitution parameters. The syntax of a stored procedure call used with `CallableStatement` is as follows:

`{? = call `*procedureName*`(?, ?, ..., ?)}`

If there is no return value from the procedure, the "`? =`" should be omitted. Similarly, if there are no input parameters, the "`(?, ?, ..., ?)`" is not used.

Because `CallableStatement` extends `PreparedStatement`, it uses the same methods for setting substitution parameter values:

```
String sql = "{call myproc(?, ?)}";
CallableStatement cstmt = con.prepareCall(sql);
cstmt.setString(1, "New York");
cstmt.setDouble(2, "19.73");
cstmt.executeQuery();
```

If any of the parameters are OUT or INOUT, their types must be registered with `CallableStatement.registerOutParameter()` before the call is executed. Their values can be retrieved with the same `getXXX()` methods used by `PreparedStatement`.

## Stored Procedures in Microsoft Access

Microsoft Access supports queries written in SQL or developed with its own design wizard. These queries can be invoked by name using the JDBC-ODBC bridge and a `CallableStatement`. Figure 13-8 shows the design view of a query that creates a list of composers born during a specified year interval. The beginning and ending years are input parameters to the query.

When run using 1891–1900 as the year interval, 12 records are selected. The results are shown in Figure 13-9.

This query can be run from a JSP page using `CallableStatement`, as illustrated in the following listing. The steps the JSP page performs are as follows:

1. Prompts for the beginning and ending year in an HTML form.
2. Connects to the Access database through the JDBC-ODBC bridge.
3. Creates a `CallableStatement` that calls the query.
4. Sets the beginning and ending year parameter from the form values.

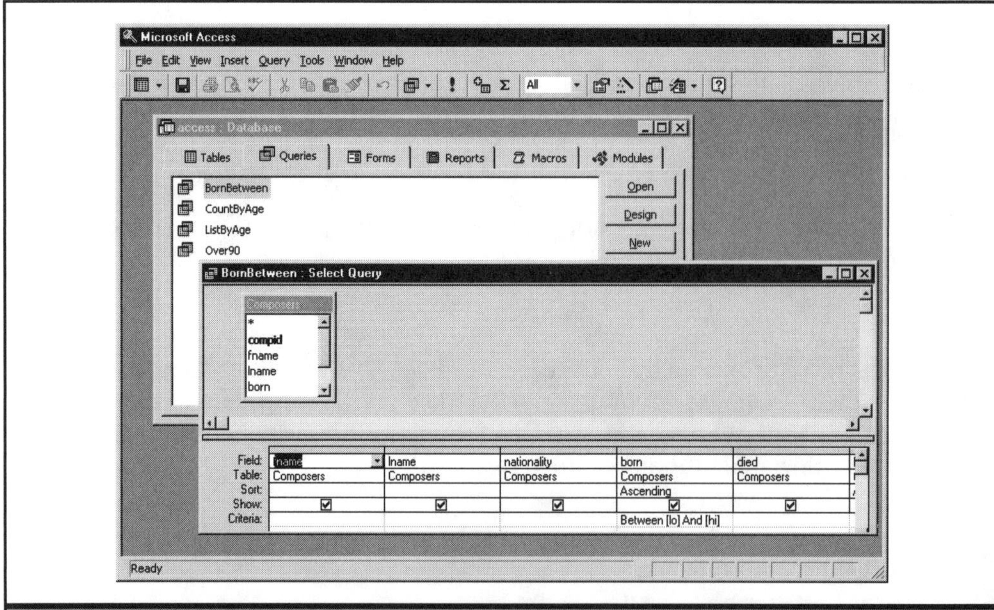


**Figure 13-8.** *Design view of the BornBetween query*

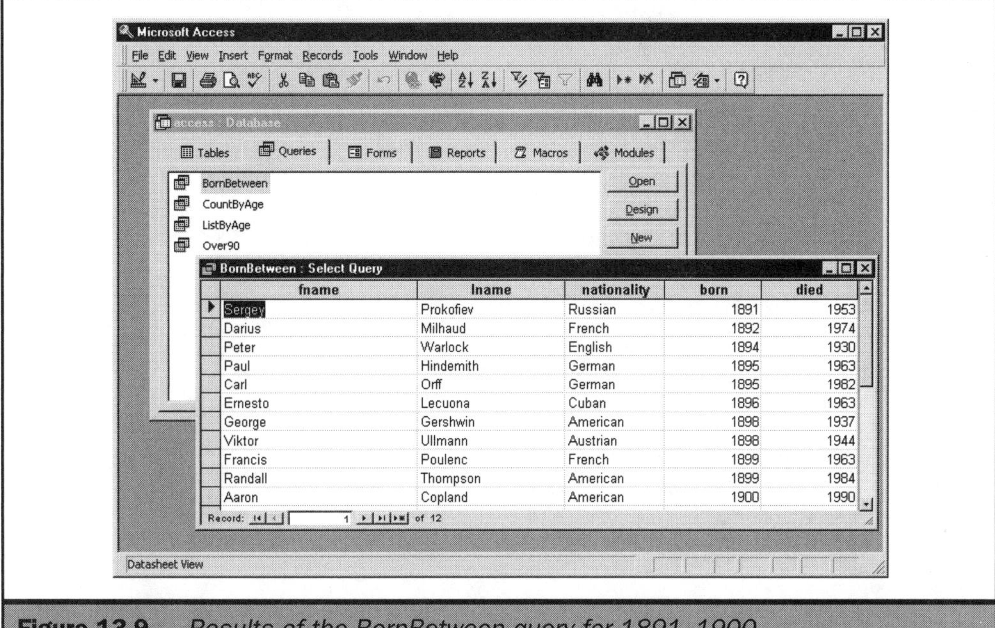


| fname | lname | nationality | born | died |
|---|---|---|---|---|
| Sergey | Prokofiev | Russian | 1891 | 1953 |
| Darius | Milhaud | French | 1892 | 1974 |
| Peter | Warlock | English | 1894 | 1930 |
| Paul | Hindemith | German | 1895 | 1963 |
| Carl | Orff | German | 1895 | 1982 |
| Ernesto | Lecuona | Cuban | 1896 | 1963 |
| George | Gershwin | American | 1898 | 1937 |
| Viktor | Ullmann | Austrian | 1898 | 1944 |
| Francis | Poulenc | French | 1899 | 1963 |
| Randall | Thompson | American | 1899 | 1984 |
| Aaron | Copland | American | 1900 | 1990 |

**Figure 13-9.** *Results of the BornBetween query for 1891–1900*



5. Executes the query.
6. Displays the results in an HTML table.

```
<%@ page session="false" %>
<%@ page import="java.sql.*" %>
<%
   // Prompt for beginning and ending years

   String sLo = request.getParameter("lo");
   if (sLo == null)
      sLo = "";
   String sHi = request.getParameter("hi");
   if (sHi == null)
      sHi = "";
%>
   <H3>Select Composers by Year Born</H3>
   <FORM>
   <TABLE>
   <TR>
      <TD>Year range:
```

```
            <INPUT TYPE="TEXT" NAME="lo" SIZE=4 VALUE="<%= sLo %>">
            and
            <INPUT TYPE="TEXT" NAME="hi" SIZE=4 VALUE="<%= sHi %>">
            <INPUT TYPE="SUBMIT" VALUE="Search">
         </TD>
      </TR>
      </TABLE>
      </FORM>
   <%
      if (!sLo.equals("") && (!sHi.equals(""))) {

         int lo = Integer.parseInt(sLo);
         int hi = Integer.parseInt(sHi);

         // Load the driver

         Class.forName("sun.jdbc.odbc.JdbcOdbcDriver");
         Connection con = null;
         try {

            // Connect to the composers database

            con = DriverManager.getConnection
               ("jdbc:odbc:lyricnote_internal");

            // Set up callable procedure

            String sql = "{call BornBetween(?, ?)}";
            CallableStatement cstmt = con.prepareCall(sql);
            cstmt.setInt(1, lo);
            cstmt.setInt(2, hi);
            ResultSet rs = cstmt.executeQuery();
   %>
      <P>
      <TABLE BORDER=1 CELLPADDING=3 CELLSPACING=0>
      <TR>
         <TH>Name</TH>
         <TH>Nationality</TH>
         <TH>Lived</TH>
      </TR>
   <%
            // Print the result set
```

```
            while (rs.next()) {
               String fname = rs.getString(1);
               String lname = rs.getString(2);
               String nationality = rs.getString(3);
               int yearBorn = rs.getInt(4);
               int yearDied = rs.getInt(5);
%>
   <TR>
      <TD><%= fname %> <%= lname %></TD>
      <TD><%= nationality %></TD>
      <TD><%= yearBorn %>-<%= yearDied %></TD>
   </TR>
<%
            }
%>
   </TABLE>
<%
            rs.close();
            rs = null;
            cstmt.close();
            cstmt = null;
         }
         finally {
            if (con != null) {
               con.close();
               con = null;
            }
         }
   }
%>
```

The results are as shown in Figure 13-10.

Of course, because the query itself is SQL-based, couldn't you just execute the equivalent SQL inside the JSP page with an ordinary `Statement`? Perhaps, but several good reasons exist why you may choose not to do this:

- The query has already been written and tested in the native Microsoft Access environment. Hundreds of queries may already be developed, with little justification for conversion.
- If the query is modified in its original form, the changes are automatically reflected in the Web-based version.
- The query may use database features that work within Access, but aren't supported through the ODBC and JDBC-ODBC bridge layers.

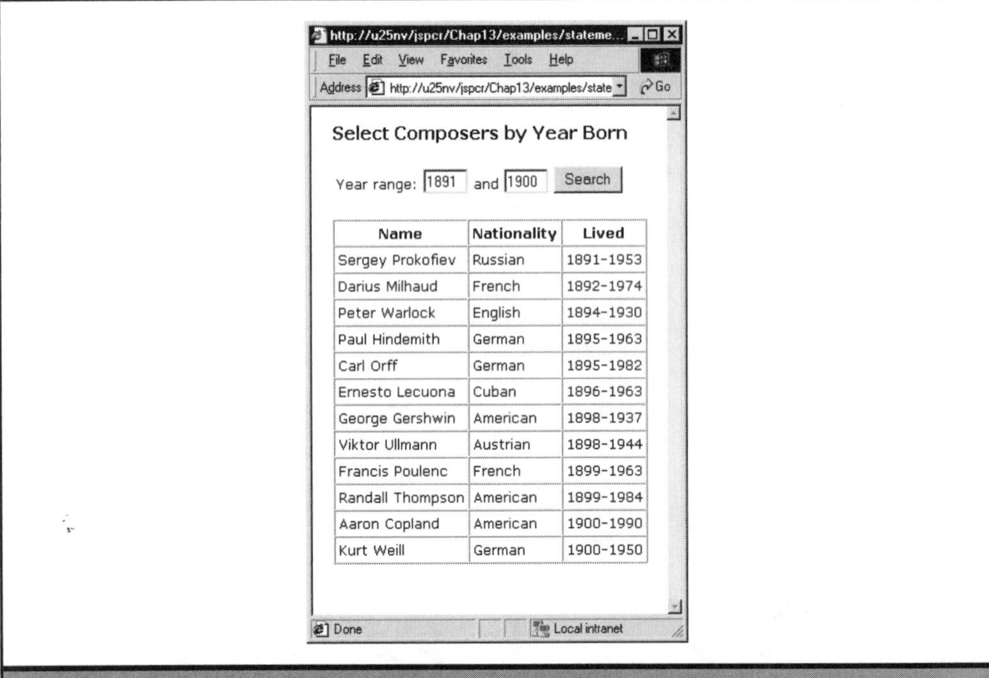


| Name | Nationality | Lived |
|---|---|---|
| Sergey Prokofiev | Russian | 1891-1953 |
| Darius Milhaud | French | 1892-1974 |
| Peter Warlock | English | 1894-1930 |
| Paul Hindemith | German | 1895-1963 |
| Carl Orff | German | 1895-1982 |
| Ernesto Lecuona | Cuban | 1896-1963 |
| George Gershwin | American | 1898-1937 |
| Viktor Ullmann | Austrian | 1898-1944 |
| Francis Poulenc | French | 1899-1963 |
| Randall Thompson | American | 1899-1984 |
| Aaron Copland | American | 1900-1990 |
| Kurt Weill | German | 1900-1950 |

**Figure 13-10.** *Web-based version of the BornBetween query for 1891–1900*

## Result Sets

A *result set* is an ordered list of table rows, represented in JDBC with the `java.sql.ResultSet` interface. Result sets are produced by `executeQuery()` or by certain metadata method calls. Once it is created, the data in a result set can be extracted as follows:

1. Move to the desired row, by calling the `ResultSet.next()` method or by one of the richer set of methods provided by JDBC 2.0—`absolute()`, `relative()`, `next()`, `previous()`, `first()`, `last()`, `beforeFirst()`, or `afterLast()`.
2. Retrieve desired column values with `ResultSet.getXXX(columnNumber)` or `ResultSet.getXXX(columnName)`, where `XXX` is the JDBC data type.

The following is a simple example, with a JSP page that searches the LyricNote composer database for those born in Ireland:

```
<%@ page session="false" %>
<%@ page import="java.sql.*" %>
```

```
<HTML>
<HEAD>
<TITLE>Irish Composers</TITLE>
</HEAD>
<BODY>
<H3>Irish Composers</H3>
<TABLE BORDER=0 CELLPADDING=3 CELLSPACING=1>
<%
   // JDBC driver name and database URL can be stored
   // in web.xml as context parameters so that they
   // do not have to be hard-coded.

   String DRIVER = application.getInitParameter("jdbc.driver");
   String URL = application.getInitParameter("jdbc.url.internal");

   // Load the driver

   Class.forName(DRIVER);

   Connection con = null;
   try {

      // Connect to the database

      con = DriverManager.getConnection(URL);
      Statement stmt = con.createStatement();

      // Create a query to select Irish composers

      String sql =
         "SELECT lname, fname, born, died"
         + " FROM composers"
         + " WHERE nationality = 'Irish'";

      // Execute the query to create a result set

      ResultSet rs = stmt.executeQuery(sql);

      // Loop through each row of the result set

      while (rs.next()) {

         // Extract the two string values and two
         // integer values from the current row
```

```
            String lastName = rs.getString(1);
            String firstName = rs.getString(2);
            int born = rs.getInt(3);
            int died = rs.getInt(4);

            // Print a table row with the values
%>
<TR>
   <TD><%= firstName %> <%= lastName %></TD>
   <TD><%= born %>-<%= died %></TD>
</TR>
<%
         }

         // After last row is printed, close the result set
         // and the statement

         rs.close();
         stmt.close();
      }

      // Always close the connection

      finally {
         if (con != null) {
            con.close();
            con = null;
         }
      }
%>
</TABLE>
</BODY>
</HTML>
```

A `ResultSet` object is created when the `Statement` executes a query. The JSP page reads each row by using the `next()` method, and then extracts each column value with `getString()` or `getInt()`. The results are shown in Figure 13-11.

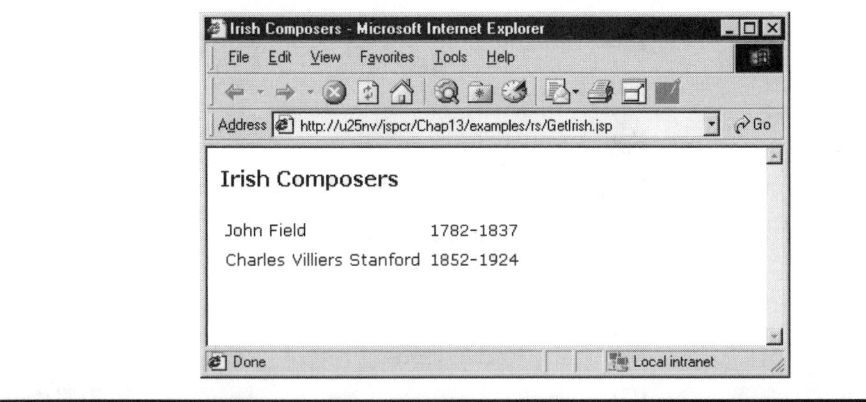


**Figure 13-11.** *A simple example of result set processing*

A number of `getXXX()` methods can be called on a `ResultSet` object. Table 13-1 contains the complete list.

Two versions of each `getXXX()` method exist: one that takes an integer column number (1, 2, ...) and one that takes a column name string. Accessing columns by number can be slightly more efficient, although column names make maintenance easier when the order of fields changes.



| Method | Description |
|---|---|
| `getArray` | Returns an SQL array. |
| `getAsciiStream` | Returns an opened java.io.InputStream of ASCII characters. Translation to ASCII (if necessary) is handled by the JDBC driver. |
| `getBigDecimal` | Returns a `java.math.BigDecimal`. |
| `getBinaryStream` | Returns an opened `java.io.InputStream`. No translation is done on the stream. |
| `getBlob` | Returns a `java.sql.Blob` (*Binary Large Object*). |
| `getBoolean` | Returns a `boolean` value. |

**Table 13-1.** *getXXX() Methods Provided by ResultSet*

| Method | Description |
|---|---|
| `getByte` | Returns a single byte. |
| `getBytes` | Returns an array of bytes. |
| `getCharacterStream` | Returns a `java.io.Reader` character stream. |
| `getClob` | Returns a `java.sql.Clob` (*Character Large Object*). |
| `getDate` | Returns a `java.sql.Date`. Note, this is a subclass of `java.util.Date`. |
| `getDouble` | Returns a double value. |
| `getFloat` | Returns a float value. |
| `getInt` | Returns an integer value. |
| `getLong` | Returns a long integer value. |
| `getObject` | Returns a `java.lang.Object`. |
| `getRef` | Returns a `java.sql.Ref`, which is a reference to a SQL structured type value. |
| `getShort` | Returns a short integer value. |
| `getString` | Returns a string. |
| `getTime` | Returns a `java.sql.Time` value. |
| `getTimestamp` | Returns a `java.sql.Timestamp` value, which includes time in nanoseconds. |

**Table 13-1.** *getXXX() Methods Provided by ResultSet* (continued)

JDBC 2.0 introduced significant new features in result sets, which are discussed in the next three sections.

## Scrollable Result Sets

Originally, result sets could only be navigated in one direction (forward) and starting at only one point (the first row). With JDBC 2.0, the programmer has a great deal more flexibility. The cursor (row pointer) can be manipulated as if it were an array index. Methods exist for reading both forward and backward, for starting from any row, and for testing the current cursor location. Table 13-2 lists the available navigation methods.

| Method | Description |
|---|---|
| `boolean next()` | Advances the cursor to the next row. |
| `boolean previous()` | Moves the cursor back one row. |
| `boolean first()` | Moves the cursor to the first row. |
| `boolean last()` | Moves the cursor to the last row. |
| `void beforeFirst()` | Moves the cursor before the first row, usually in anticipation of calling `next()`. |
| `void afterLast()` | Moves the cursor after the last row, usually in anticipation of calling `previous()`. |
| `boolean absolute(int row)` | Moves the cursor to the specified row. Specifying a negative number moves the cursor relative to the end of the result set; `absolute(-1)` is the same as `last()`. |
| `boolean relative(int row)` | Moves the cursor forward or backward the number of rows specified. |
| `boolean isBeforeFirst()` | True if the cursor is before the first row. |
| `boolean isAfterLast()` | True if the cursor is after the last row. |
| `boolean isFirst()` | True if the cursor is positioned on the first row. |
| `boolean isLast()` | True if the cursor is positioned on the last row. |

**Table 13-2.** *JDBC 2.0 Navigation Methods for Scrollable Result Sets*



To use scrollable result sets, the `Statement` object must be created with parameters that indicate the specific capabilities requested. For this reason, a new form of the `Connection.createStatement()` method exists

```
public Statement createStatement
(int resultSetType, int resultSetConcurrency)
throws SQLException
```

where *resultSetType* is the type of scrolling to be used and *resultSetConcurrency* indicates whether the result set can be updated. Both parameters take their values from constants in `ResultSet`, as shown in Table 13-3.

| Constant | Meaning |
|---|---|
| TYPE_FORWARD_ONLY | JDBC 1.0-style navigation in which the cursor starts at the first row and can only move forward. |
| TYPE_SCROLL_INSENSITIVE | All cursor positioning methods are enabled; the result set doesn't reflect changes made by others in the underlying table. |
| TYPE_SCROLL_SENSITIVE | All cursor positioning methods are enabled; the result set reflects changes made by others in the underlying table. |
| CONCUR_READ_ONLY | The result set won't be updatable. |
| CONCUR_UPDATABLE | Rows and be added and deleted, and columns can be updated. |

**Table 13-3.** *Constants in ResultSet that Can Be Used to Describe Scrollable Result Sets*

The following JSP page is an example of using a scrollable result set to display only the last page of a potentially lengthy query.

```
<%@ page import="java.sql.*" %>
<%@ page import="java.text.*" %>
<%!
   public static final DecimalFormat PRICE_FMT
      = new DecimalFormat("$#,###.00");
%>
<HTML>
<HEAD>
<TITLE>Scrollable Example</TITLE>
</HEAD>
<BODY>
<IMG SRC="images/lyric_note.png" BORDER=0><P>
<HR COLOR="#000000">
<%
   // Get driver name and database URL from configuration
   // parameters stored in web.xml

   String DRIVER = application.getInitParameter("jdbc.driver");
   String URL    = application.getInitParameter("jdbc.url");
```

```
    // Load the driver

    Class.forName(DRIVER);

    Connection con = null;
    Statement stmt = null;
    ResultSet rs   = null;

    try {

       // Connect to the database

       con = DriverManager.getConnection(URL);

       // Open a statement that supports scrollable result sets

       stmt = con.createStatement(
                     ResultSet.TYPE_SCROLL_INSENSITIVE,
                     ResultSet.CONCUR_READ_ONLY);

       // Execute the query

       rs = stmt.executeQuery(
               " SELECT   itemcode, price, description"
             + " FROM     products"
             + " WHERE    prodtype = 'IN'"
             + " ORDER BY description"
          );

       // Calculate number of rows

       rs.last();
       int nRows = rs.getRow();

       // Back up ten rows

       rs.relative(-10);

       // Now print last page of result set
%>
<H3>
```

```
    Musical Instruments
    - Items <%= rs.getRow() + 1 %> through <%= nRows %>
</H3>
<TABLE BORDER=1 CELLPADDING=3 CELLSPACING=0>
<TR><TH>Item</TH><TH>Price</TH><TH>Description</TH></TR>
<%
        while (rs.next()) {
            String itemcode = rs.getString(1);
            double price = rs.getLong(2) / 100.0;
            String description = rs.getString(3);
%>
<TR>
    <TD><%= itemcode %></TD>
    <TD ALIGN="RIGHT"><%= PRICE_FMT.format(price) %></TD>
    <TD><%= description %></TD>
</TR>
<%
        }
    }
    finally {
        if (rs != null) { rs.close(); rs = null; }
        if (stmt != null) { stmt.close(); stmt = null; }
        if (con != null) { con.close(); con = null; }
    }
%>
</TABLE>
</BODY>
</HTML>
```

The `Statement` object is opened so the result sets it creates are scrollable, but not updatable. Having these properties, the `ResultSet` can be asked how many rows it contains, which wasn't possible in JDBC 1.0. By positioning the cursor at the last row and issuing a `relative(-10)` method call, the last ten rows in the result set can be isolated and printed. Figure 13-12 shows the results.

## Updatable Result Sets

With JDBC 2.0, updating columns in a result set is possible, both to add new rows and to delete existing rows. In each of these cases, the corresponding rows in the underlying table are then also updated.

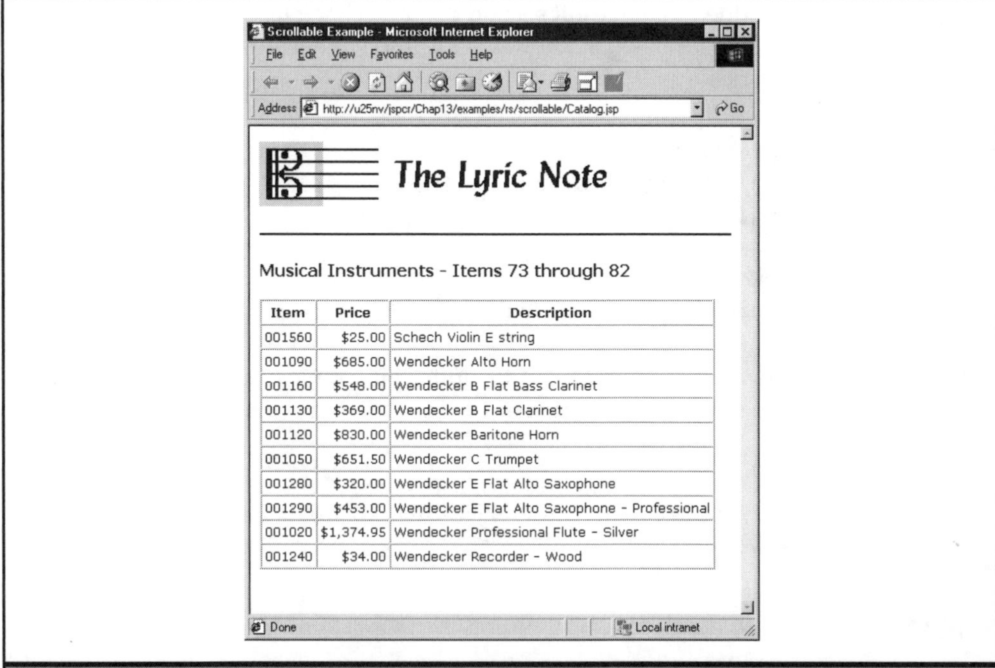


**Figure 13-12.** *Showing the last page of a lengthy query using a scrollable result set*



For a result set to be updated, it must have been produced by a `Statement` object created with a concurrency type of `ResultSet.CONCUR_UPDATABLE`. JDBC 2.0 provides `updateXXX()` methods, where `XXX` is the JDBC data type, similar to the existing `getXXX()` methods. These methods take a column number or column name parameter, and a value parameter, as illustrated in the following example:

```
double mySalary = rs.getDouble("SALARY");
mySalary *= 2.0;
rs.updateDouble("SALARY", mySalary);
rs.updateString("HOME_PHONE", unlisted);
rs.updateRow();
```

The updated values aren't automatically replicated in the underlying table until `updateRow()` is called. The updates can be canceled explicitly with `ResultSet.cancelRowUpdates()` if `updateRow()` hasn't yet been called or implicitly if a cursor movement method is called before `updateRow()`.

New rows can be added to the result set and the underlying table with `insertRow()`. This involves a special cursor position known as the *insert row*. The following example illustrates how this works:

```
rs.moveToInsertRow();
rs.setString("employeeid", "M1205");
rs.setString("firstName", "Maria");
rs.setString("lastName", "Alicia");
rs.insertRow();
rs.moveToCurrentRow();  // Return to where we were
```

In like fashion, rows in a result set and its underlying table can be deleted with `deleteRow()`. To do so, the cursor must be positioned at the row to be deleted, as shown here:

```
rs.last(); // Delete the last row
rs.deleteRow();
```

## RowSets

The `javax.sql` package contains a `RowSet` interface, which extends and generalizes `java.sql.ResultSet` so it can be detached from its database connection. This can be useful for *Personal Digital Assistant* (*PDA*) applications that cannot easily maintain a connection and have a limited amount of memory. At press time, RowSets are still in their infancy. Sun Microsystems has three early access implementations of the interface that can be used to explore their capabilities:

- **`CachedRowSet`** A serializable, disconnectable RowSet that can be populated from a JDBC result set.
- **`JdbcRowSet`** A connected RowSet also populated from a JDBC result set, which behaves according to the JavaBeans model.
- **`WebRowSet`** A subclass of `CachedRowSet` that can write its contents as an XML document.

# Using Metadata

JDBC provides a rich set of *metadata*—data about data—for database connections and result sets. This section describes these two interfaces, how instances of them are obtained, and highlights of what information they can provide.

## Database Metadata

Information about a JDBC connection can be obtained with `Connection.getMetaData()`. This method returns an instance of `java.sql.DatabaseMetaData`, an interface that has more methods (149 in all) than any other class or interface in the `java.sql` or `javax.sql` packages. These methods describe the features the database supports, what tables it contains, and what columns are in these tables. Using metadata, differences in the SQL language and capabilities of database systems can be minimized.

Viewing all the information a `DatabaseMetaData` object provides can be instructional. Because so many methods are in the interface, coding all the individual calls by hand is tedious. For this purpose, using reflection to list all the metadata methods programmatically, and then invoke each one and print the results, is easier. The following JSP page (`MetadataExplorer.jsp`) illustrates the technique:

```
<%@ page session="false" %>
<%@ page import="java.sql.*" %>
<%@ page import="java.util.*" %>
<%@ page import="java.lang.reflect.*" %>
<%
   // Get required driver name parameter

   String driverName = request.getParameter("driverName");
   if (driverName == null)
      driverName = "";
   driverName = driverName.trim();
   if (driverName.equals(""))
      throw new ServletException("No driverName parameter");

   // Get required database URL parameter

   String url = request.getParameter("url");
   if (url == null)
      url = "";
   url = url.trim();
   if (url.equals(""))
      throw new ServletException("No url parameter");

   // Get optional userID parameter

   String userID = request.getParameter("userID");
   if (userID == null)
      userID = "";
```

```
userID = userID.trim();

// Get optional password parameter

String password = request.getParameter("password");
if (password == null)
   password = "";
password = password.trim();
// Load the driver

Class.forName(driverName);
Connection con = null;
try {

   // Open the database connection and get the metadata

   con = DriverManager.getConnection(url, userID, password);
   DatabaseMetaData md = con.getMetaData();

   // Use reflection to get a list of methods that the
   // metadata class supports.  Select only public methods
   // that take no parameters and that return either
   // a string or a boolean.

   Class mdclass = md.getClass();
   Method[] methods = mdclass.getDeclaredMethods();
   Map methodMap = new TreeMap();

   for (int i = 0; i < methods.length; i++) {
      Method method = methods[i];

      // Public methods only

      if (!Modifier.isPublic(method.getModifiers()))
         continue;

      // with no parameters

      if (method.getParameterTypes().length > 0)
         continue;

      // that return String or boolean
```

```
            Class returnType = method.getReturnType();
            if ((returnType != java.lang.Boolean.TYPE) &&
                (returnType != java.lang.String.class))
               continue;

            // Add selected methods to sorted map

            methodMap.put(method.getName(), method);
         }
%>
<HTML>
<HEAD>
<TITLE>Metadata Explorer</TITLE>
<LINK REL="stylesheet" HREF="style.css">
</HEAD>
<BODY>
<CENTER>
<H3>
Metadata Explorer for
<%= md.getDatabaseProductName() %>
<%= md.getDatabaseProductVersion() %>
<BR>
[<%= driverName %>]
</H3>
<TABLE BORDER=0 CELLPADDING=3 CELLSPACING=1>
<TR CLASS="header">
   <TH CLASS="header">Method</TH>
   <TH CLASS="header">Value</TH>
</TR>
<%
      // Generate the table

      int row = 0;
      Iterator im = methodMap.keySet().iterator();
      while (im.hasNext()) {
         String methodName = (String) im.next();
         Object methodValue = null;

         Method method = (Method) methodMap.get(methodName);

         // Invoke the method and get the result
```

```
            try {
               Object[] noParameters = new Object[0];
               methodValue = method.invoke(md, noParameters);
            }
            catch (Exception ignore) {}

            // Display the results

            row++;
            String rowClass = "row" + (row % 2);
%>
<TR CLASS="<%= rowClass %>">
   <TD><%= methodName %></TD>
   <TD><%= formatLine(methodValue) %></TD>
</TR>
<%
      }
   }
   finally {
      if (con != null)
         con.close();
   }
%>
</TABLE>
</CENTER>
</BODY>
</HTML>
<%!
   /**
   * Formats an object in an HTML-friendly way,
   * making sure it doesn't exceed 48 characters
   * in width.
   */
   private static String formatLine(Object obj)
   {
      if (obj == null)
         return "";

      StringBuffer out = new StringBuffer();
      StringBuffer line = new StringBuffer();
      StringTokenizer st =
```

```
            new StringTokenizer(obj.toString(), ",;", true);

        while (st.hasMoreTokens()) {
            if (line.length() > 48) {
                out.append(line.toString());
                out.append("<BR>");
                line = new StringBuffer();
            }
            line.append(st.nextToken());
        }
        out.append(line.toString());

        return out.toString();
    }
%>
```

This JSP page is designed to be invoked from an HTML form that supplies the driver name, JDBC URL, user ID, and password fields, as shown in Figure 13-13.

When run against a Microsoft Access database using the JDBC-ODBC bridge, the MetadataExplorer produces the output partially listed in Figure 13-14. The complete listing is contained in Table 13-4.



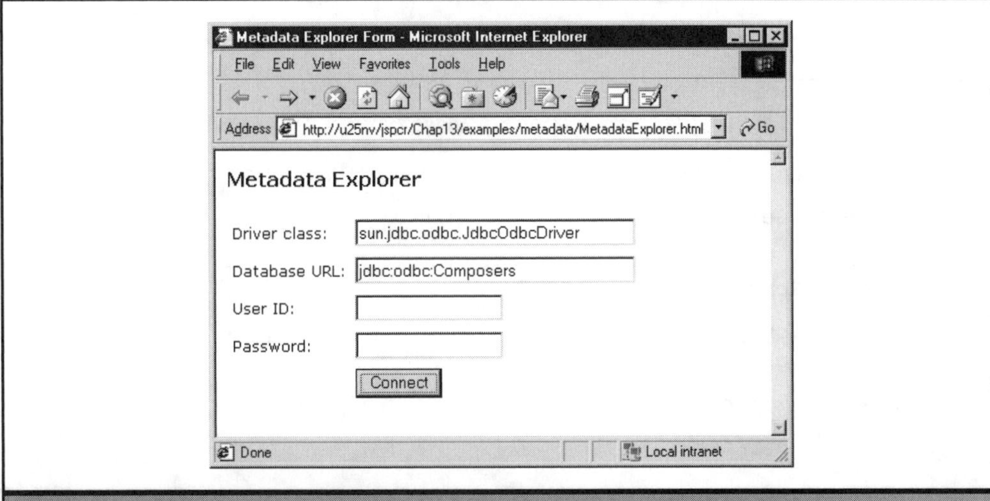


**Figure 13-13.** *Parameter input form for MetadataExplorer.jsp*

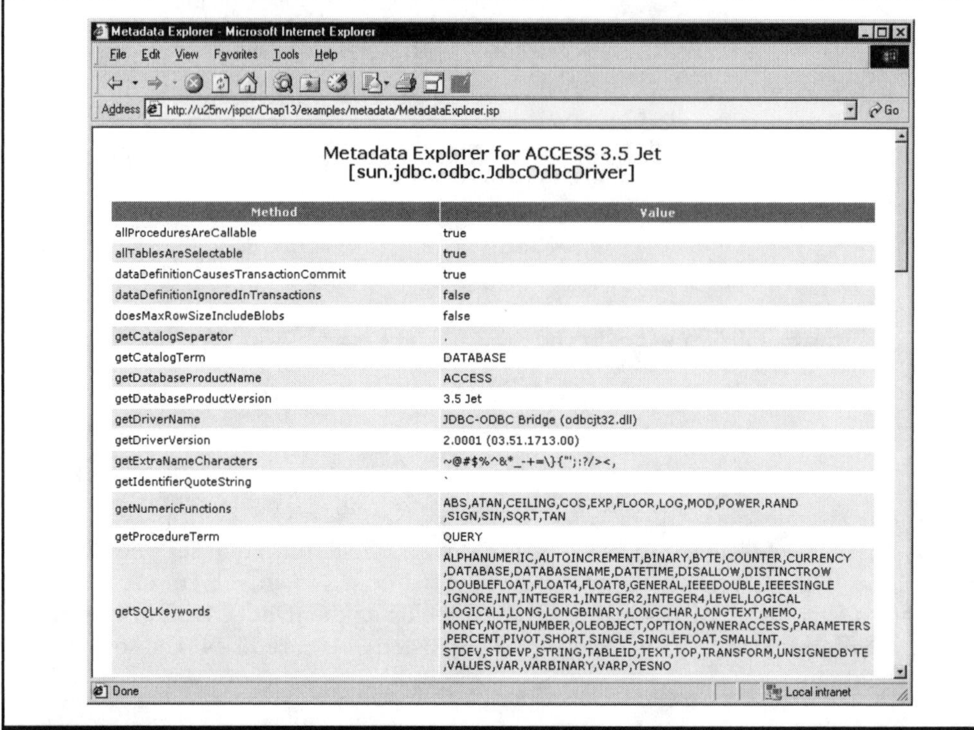


**Figure 13-14.** *MetadataExplorer used with a Microsoft Access database*

| Method | Value |
|---|---|
| `allProceduresAreCallable` | True |
| `allTablesAreSelectable` | True |
| `dataDefinitionCausesTransactionCommit` | True |
| `dataDefinitionIgnoredInTransactions` | False |
| `doesMaxRowSizeIncludeBlobs` | False |
| `getCatalogSeparator` | . |

**Table 13-4.** *Metadata from Microsoft Access Database*

| Method | Value |
|---|---|
| getCatalogTerm | DATABASE |
| getDatabaseProductName | ACCESS |
| getDatabaseProductVersion | 3.5 Jet |
| getDriverName | JDBC-ODBC Bridge (odbcjt32.dll) |
| getDriverVersion | 2.0001 (03.51.1713.00) |
| getExtraNameCharacters | ~@#$%^&*_-+=\}{"';:?/><, |
| getIdentifierQuoteString | ` |
| getNumericFunctions | ABS, ATAN, CEILING, COS, EXP, FLOOR, LOG, MOD, POWER, RAND, SIGN, SIN, SQRT, TAN |
| getProcedureTerm | QUERY |
| getSQLKeywords | ALPHANUMERIC, AUTOINCREMENT, BINARY, BYTE, COUNTER, CURRENCY, DATABASE, DATABASENAME, DATETIME, DISALLOW, DISTINCTROW, DOUBLEFLOAT, FLOAT4, FLOAT8, GENERAL, IEEEDOUBLE, IEEESINGLE, IGNORE, INT, INTEGER1, INTEGER2, INTEGER4, LEVEL, LOGICAL, LOGICAL1, LONG, LONGBINARY, LONGCHAR, LONGTEXT, MEMO, MONEY, NOTE, NUMBER, OLEOBJECT, OPTION, OWNERACCESS, PARAMETERS, PERCENT, PIVOT, SHORT, SINGLE, SINGLEFLOAT, SMALLINT, STDEV, STDEVP, STRING, TABLEID, TEXT, TOP, TRANSFORM, UNSIGNEDBYTE, VALUES, VAR, VARBINARY, VARP, YESNO |
| getSchemaTerm | \ |
| getStringFunctions | ASCII, CHAR, CONCAT, LCASE, LEFT, LENGTH, LOCATE, LOCATE_2, LTRIM, RIGHT, RTRIM, SPACE, SUBSTRING, UCASE |

**Table 13-4.** *Metadata from Microsoft Access Database* (continued)

| Method | Value |
|---|---|
| `getSystemFunctions` | CURDATE, CURTIME, DAYOFMONTH, DAYOFWEEK, DAYOFYEAR, HOUR, MINUTE, MONTH, NOW, SECOND, WEEK, YEAR |
| `getURL` | jdbc:odbc:Composers |
| `getUserName` | admin |
| `isCatalogAtStart` | True |
| `isReadOnly` | False |
| `nullPlusNonNullIsNull` | False |
| `nullsAreSortedAtEnd` | False |
| `nullsAreSortedAtStart` | False |
| `nullsAreSortedHigh` | False |
| `nullsAreSortedLow` | True |
| `storesLowerCaseIdentifiers` | False |
| `storesLowerCaseQuoted Identifiers` | False |
| `storesMixedCaseIdentifiers` | False |
| `storesMixedCaseQuoted Identifiers` | True |
| `storesUpperCaseIdentifiers` | False |
| `storesUpperCaseQuoted Identifiers` | False |
| `supportsANSI92EntryLevelSQL` | True |
| `supportsANSI92FullSQL` | False |
| `supportsANSI92IntermediateSQL` | False |
| `supportsAlterTableWith AddColumn` | True |
| `supportsAlterTableWith DropColumn` | True |
| `supportsBatchUpdates` | True |
| `supportsCatalogsInData Manipulation` | True |

**Table 13-4.** *Metadata from Microsoft Access Database* (continued)

| Method | Value |
|---|---|
| supportsCatalogsInIndex Definitions | True |
| supportsCatalogsInPrivilege Definitions | False |
| supportsCatalogsInProcedure Calls | False |
| supportsCatalogsInTable Definitions | True |
| supportsColumnAliasing | True |
| supportsConvert | True |
| supportsCoreSQLGrammar | False |
| supportsCorrelatedSubqueries | True |
| supportsDataDefinitionAndData ManipulationTransactions | True |
| supportsDataManipulation TransactionsOnly | False |
| supportsDifferentTable CorrelationNames | False |
| supportsExpressionsInOrderBy | True |
| supportsExtendedSQLGrammar | False |
| supportsFullOuterJoins | False |
| supportsGroupBy | True |
| supportsGroupByBeyondSelect | True |
| supportsGroupByUnrelated | False |
| supportsIntegrity EnhancementFacility | False |
| supportsLikeEscapeClause | False |
| supportsLimitedOuterJoins | False |
| supportsMinimumSQLGrammar | True |
| supportsMixedCaseIdentifiers | True |
| supportsMixedCaseQuoted Identifiers | False |

**Table 13-4.** *Metadata from Microsoft Access Database* (continued)

| Method | Value |
|---|---|
| supportsMultipleResultSets | False |
| supportsMultipleTransactions | True |
| supportsNonNullableColumns | False |
| supportsOpenCursorsAcross Commit | False |
| supportsOpenCursorsAcross Rollback | False |
| supportsOpenStatements AcrossCommit | True |
| supportsOpenStatements AcrossRollback | True |
| supportsOrderByUnrelated | False |
| supportsOuterJoins | True |
| supportsPositionedDelete | False |
| supportsPositionedUpdate | False |
| supportsSchemasInData Manipulation | False |
| supportsSchemasInIndex Definitions | False |
| supportsSchemasInPrivilege Definitions | False |
| supportsSchemasInProcedure Calls | False |
| supportsSchemasInTable Definitions | False |
| supportsSelectForUpdate | False |
| supportsStoredProcedures | True |
| supportsSubqueriesIn Comparisons | True |
| supportsSubqueriesInExists | True |
| supportsSubqueriesInIns | True |

**Table 13-4.** *Metadata from Microsoft Access Database* (continued)

| Method | Value |
|---|---|
| supportsSubqueriesIn Quantifieds | True |
| supportsTableCorrelationNames | True |
| supportsTransactions | True |
| supportsUnion | True |
| supportsUnionAll | True |
| usesLocalFilePerTable | False |
| usesLocalFiles | True |

**Table 13-4.** *Metadata from Microsoft Access Database* (continued)



## ResultSetMetadata

In addition to `DatabaseMetaData` for database connections, `ResultSetMetaData` also gets information about the columns of a result set. This interface consists of one method to get the number of columns—`getColumnCount()`—and 20 other methods that describe individual columns.

To obtain a `ResultSetMetaData` object, a program invokes the `ResultSet.getMetaData()` method., and then invokes its methods, passing it a column number parameter. As is the case with `ResultSet`, the column numbers start with 1.

Table 13-5 describes the methods available in `ResultSetMetaData`.

| Method | Description |
|---|---|
| getColumnCount() | Returns the number of columns in each row of the result set. |
| getCatalogName(int col) | Returns the catalog name of the table from which the specified column is drawn. |
| getColumnClassName(int col) | Returns the fully qualified Java type name of the specified column. |

**Table 13-5.** *Methods Available in `ResultSetMetaData`*

| Method | Description |
|---|---|
| `getColumnDisplaySize(int col)` | Returns the maximum display width for the specified column. |
| `getColumnLabel(int col)` | Returns the label for the specified column. |
| `getColumnName(int col)` | Returns the name of the specified column. |
| `getColumnType(int col)` | Returns the type of the specified column in a form corresponding to java.sql.Types. |
| `getColumnTypeName(int col)` | Returns the column data type as a string. |
| `getPrecision(int col)` | Returns number of decimal positions. |
| `getScale(int col)` | Returns the number of digits to the right of the decimal point. |
| `getSchemaName(int col)` | Returns the schema name of the column's table. |
| `getTableName(int col)` | Returns the name of the column's underlying table. |
| `isAutoIncrement(int col)` | True if the column is automatically numbered. |
| `isCaseSensitive(int col)` | True if the column's case matters. |
| `isCurrency(int col)` | True if the column is a cash value. |
| `isDefinitelyWritable(int col)` | True if a write to the specified column will definitely succeed. |
| `isNullable(int col)` | Returns a constant indicating whether the column can have a null value. |
| `isReadOnly(int col)` | True if the result set is read-only. |
| `isSearchable(int col)` | True if this column can be used in a where clause. |
| `isSigned(int col)` | True if the column value is signed numeric. |
| `isWritable(int col)` | True if a write to the specified column may succeed. |

**Table 13-5.** *Methods Available in `ResultSetMetaData` (continued)*

## New Features in JDBC 2.0 and Beyond

JDBC 2.0 was originally referred to as the JDBC 2.0 Standard Extension API and has now been renamed as the JDBC 2.0 Optional Package API. This is included in the JDBC 2.1 core API package that ships with the Java 2 Standard Edition. A number of its new features were discussed throughout this chapter, which include:

- **DataSource** JDBC driver names and URLs can be stored in a name service and retrieved using JNDI.
- **Connection pooling** A data source provider can offer connection pooling, allowing connections to be activated and recycled, usually with a significant performance improvement. This capability is configured entirely in the naming service and requires no changes to applications.
- **Scrollable result sets** JDBC 1.0 allowed only forward navigation through a result set starting at the first record. JDBC 2.0 provides methods for forward and backward navigation, as well as relative and absolute cursor positioning.
- **RowSets** Disconnected result sets can be made to conform to the JavaBeans model.
- **BatchUpdates** Transactions can be grouped and sent to the database as a unit.

The first public draft of JDBC 3.0 was released for public review in September 2000. Its new features include

- Enhanced control of commit/rollback transaction boundaries
- Configurability for connection pools
- Better interface to parameters in prepared and callable statements



## Summary

Almost all nontrivial JSP applications require access to a database. Java provides a standard API known as JDBC. JDBC allows a wide variety of database systems to be accessed using standard SQL statements in an object-oriented framework. To use JDBC, a driver must be available for the database. Drivers exist for virtually all commercial databases, as well as a JDBC-ODBC bridge for using ODBC data sources.

Only a few key objects exist in JDBC, which makes it easy to learn. The `Connection` object maintains an active link to a database. The three types of `Statement` object allow SQL statements to be executed through the connection and capture the results in a `ResultSet` object. A large volume of information about connections and result sets can be obtained from the `DatabaseMetaData` and `ResultSetMetaData` objects.

JDBC has continued to evolve through several releases with enhanced features and promises to continue as the dominant database access technology for Java programming.

# Chapter 14

## Session and Thread Management

*Hypertext Transfer Protocol* (*HTTP*) was originally designed for distributing documents and images over the *World Wide Web* (*WWW*). As such, it uses a fairly simple communication model. A client makes a request for a document, the server responds with the document or some error code, and the transaction is complete. The server doesn't retain any knowledge of the request. The next time the client makes a request, the server has no way of distinguishing it from any other client. For this reason, HTTP is said to be a *stateless* protocol.

Unfortunately, few applications fit this single request/response model. In most cases, several requests are required for any meaningful work to be done. For example, an application may have one Web page that prompts for a user ID and password, and then a search page that requests key words to look up in a product database, followed by a list of matching products, a detailed product information page, a shopping cart checkout page, and an order summary page. Each of these pages depends on the previous pages and also depends on the server knowing the state of the application for that client at that time. What's worse, the user on the client end of the application may go forward or backward through the pages, or go to another Web page entirely, never telling the server that the session is over or what to do with any partial work. A related difficulty is that some server processes take a long time—longer than a Web server can afford to wait if it's to maintain reasonable performance.

These aren't new problems. *Common Gateway Interface* (*CGI*) programs and online transaction processing systems have been dealing with these same issues for years. The techniques applied in those environments still work in the Servlet/JSP environment, but the Java Servlet API has a built-in mechanism that provides a clean, easy-to-use solution: HTTP sessions.

This chapter explores two key aspects of making the JSP model fit the application model: session management and thread management. It discusses four techniques for session tracking, focusing primarily on the HTTP session API, examining how sessions are created, how they manage objects, and how they are terminated. The chapter then explores Java's built-in support for multithreaded applications and the available servlet threading models, concluding with a section covering application considerations with respect to object lifecycle and visibility.

## Session Tracking

Because the Web server doesn't remember clients from one request to the next, the only way to maintain a session is for clients to keep track of it. You can accomplish this in two basic ways:

- Have the client remember all session-related data and send it back to the server as needed.

- Have the server maintain all the data, assign an identifier to it, and have the client remember the identifier.

The first approach is simple to implement and requires no special capabilities on the part of the server. This approach can entail transmitting large amounts of data back and forth, however, which might degrade performance. Another problem is server-side objects, such as database and network connections, have to be reinitialized with every request. For these reasons, this approach is best suited for long-term persistence of small amounts of data, such as user preferences or account numbers.

The second approach offers more functionality. Once a server initiates a session and the client accepts it, the server can build complex, active objects and maintain large amounts of data, requiring only a key to distinguish between sessions. Most of the discussions in this chapter focus on this approach.

So, how can we get the client to remember data and return it to the Web server? Four techniques are commonly used

- Hidden fields
- URL rewriting
- Cookies
- The HTTP session API

The following sections describe each technique in detail.



## Hidden Fields

HTML forms support input elements with a type of `HIDDEN`. *Hidden fields* are passed along with other form parameters in the HTTP request sent to the Web server, but they don't have any visual representation. They serve only to include literals or constant values with a request. A similar technique is used with CICS and mainframe transaction monitors to supply transaction codes. In principle, hidden fields can be used in ordinary HTML Web pages but, for session tracking purposes, they must be used in dynamically generated Web pages created by server processes like CGI, servlets, or JSP.

Hidden fields are well suited to back-and-forth conversational applications that don't require a great deal of data storage or object initialization. An example would be the well-known number-guessing game included in the Tomcat examples folder. This game selects a random integer between 1 and 100, and then asks the user to guess it. After each guess, the game tells the user whether the guess was too low, too high, or exactly right.

The JSP presented in the following is a game that does the opposite: it asks the user to think of a number between 1 and 100, and then guesses the number, relying on the user to indicate whether each guess is too low, too high, or exactly right.[1] This JSP uses a binary search to find the number.

```
<%@ page session="false" %>
<H3>Number Guess Guesser</H3>
<%
   int wayLo = 1 - 1;
   int wayHi = 100 + 1;
   int state = 0;
   String parm = request.getParameter("state");
   if (parm != null)
      state = Integer.parseInt(parm);

   switch (state) {
      case 0: {   // Initial screen
%>
<FORM>
Think of a number between
<%= wayLo + 1 %> and <%= wayHi - 1 %>,
and I'll try to guess it.<P>
Click OK when ready.<P>
<INPUT TYPE="submit" VALUE="OK">
<INPUT TYPE="hidden" NAME="lo" VALUE="<%= wayLo %>">
<INPUT TYPE="hidden" NAME="hi" VALUE="<%= wayHi %>">
<INPUT TYPE="hidden" NAME="numGuesses" VALUE="0">
<INPUT TYPE="hidden" NAME="state" VALUE="1">
</FORM>
<%
         break;
      }
      case 1: {   // First guess
         int numGuesses = 1 + Integer.parseInt
            (request.getParameter("numGuesses"));
         int lo = Integer.parseInt(request.getParameter("lo"));
         int hi = Integer.parseInt(request.getParameter("hi"));
         int guess = (hi + lo)/2;
```

1 If you play these programs against each other in separate windows, you can watch them politely comment on each other's progress.

```
%>
<FORM>
My first guess is <%= guess %>. How did I do?<P>
<INPUT TYPE="radio"
       NAME="result"
       VALUE="-1" onClick="submit()"> Too low
<INPUT TYPE="radio"
       NAME="result"
       VALUE="0" onClick="submit()"> Exactly right
<INPUT TYPE="radio"
       NAME="result"
       VALUE="1" onClick="submit()"> Too high
<P>
<INPUT TYPE="hidden" NAME="lo" VALUE="<%= lo %>">
<INPUT TYPE="hidden" NAME="hi" VALUE="<%= hi %>">
<INPUT TYPE="hidden" NAME="numGuesses" VALUE="<%= numGuesses %>">
<INPUT TYPE="hidden" NAME="state" VALUE="2">
</FORM>
<%
         break;
      }
      case 2: {   // After first guess
         int numGuesses = 1 + Integer.parseInt
            (request.getParameter("numGuesses"));
         int lo = Integer.parseInt(request.getParameter("lo"));
         int hi = Integer.parseInt(request.getParameter("hi"));
         int result =
            Integer.parseInt(request.getParameter("result"));
         int guess = (hi + lo)/2;

         if (result < 0) {
            lo = guess;
            guess = (hi + lo)/2;
         }
         else if (result > 0) {
            hi = guess;
            guess = (hi + lo)/2;
         }

         if (result != 0) {
%>
<FORM>
```

```
<%
   if (lo > wayLo)
      out.println(lo + " is too low.<BR>");
   if (hi < wayHi)
      out.println(hi + " is too high.<BR>");
   if ((hi - lo) > 1) {
%>
My next guess is <%= guess %>. How did I do?<P>
<INPUT TYPE="radio"
       NAME="result"
       VALUE="-1" onClick="submit()"> Too low
<INPUT TYPE="radio"
       NAME="result"
       VALUE="0" onClick="submit()"> Exactly right
<INPUT TYPE="radio"
       NAME="result"
       VALUE="1" onClick="submit()"> Too high
<P>
<INPUT TYPE="hidden" NAME="lo" VALUE="<%= lo %>">
<INPUT TYPE="hidden" NAME="hi" VALUE="<%= hi %>">
<INPUT TYPE="hidden" NAME="numGuesses" VALUE="<%= numGuesses %>">
<INPUT TYPE="hidden" NAME="state" VALUE="2">
</FORM>
<%
   }
   else {
      String[] text = {
         "Are we cheating?",
         "Did we forget our number?",
         "Perhaps we clicked the wrong button?",
         "What happened?",
         "What gives?",
      };
      String message = text[(int)(Math.random() * text.length)];
%>
<FORM>
<%= message %><P>
<INPUT TYPE="SUBMIT" VALUE="Start Over">
</FORM>
<%
```

```
   }
         }
         else {
            numGuesses--;
%>
<FORM>
I win, and after only <%= numGuesses %> guesses!<P>
Do you want to try again?<P>
<INPUT TYPE="SUBMIT" VALUE="Start Over">
</FORM>
<%
         }
         break;
      }
   }
%>
```



The JSP page uses a hidden field named `state` to keep track of what's happening in the game. Based on the state, it displays the appropriate form:

- **State 0** The initial form explains the game and sets up the variables to be used. These include the state, the number of guesses, the highest value known to be too low, and the lowest value known to be too high. The variables are all stored as hidden fields in the form.
- **State 1** After the user clicks the OK button, the program retrieves the too-low and too-high parameters and uses the average of the two as its next guess. The form presents the user with three radio buttons to indicate whether the guess is too low, too high, or exactly right. The low and high values, the user result selection, and the incremented number of guesses are stored again as hidden fields.
- **State 2** Based on what the user specified in the radio buttons, the program updates either the too-low or the too-high value with the new upper or lower bound. If the guess was exactly right, the program congratulates itself and prompts for whether to play again. Otherwise, it displays the known upper and lower bounds and its next guess, as shown in Figure 14-1.

The problem with hidden fields is they can only be used in HTML forms. If the user clicks a hyperlink and leaves the page, the hidden fields are lost, unless the technique described in the next section—URL rewriting—is also employed.

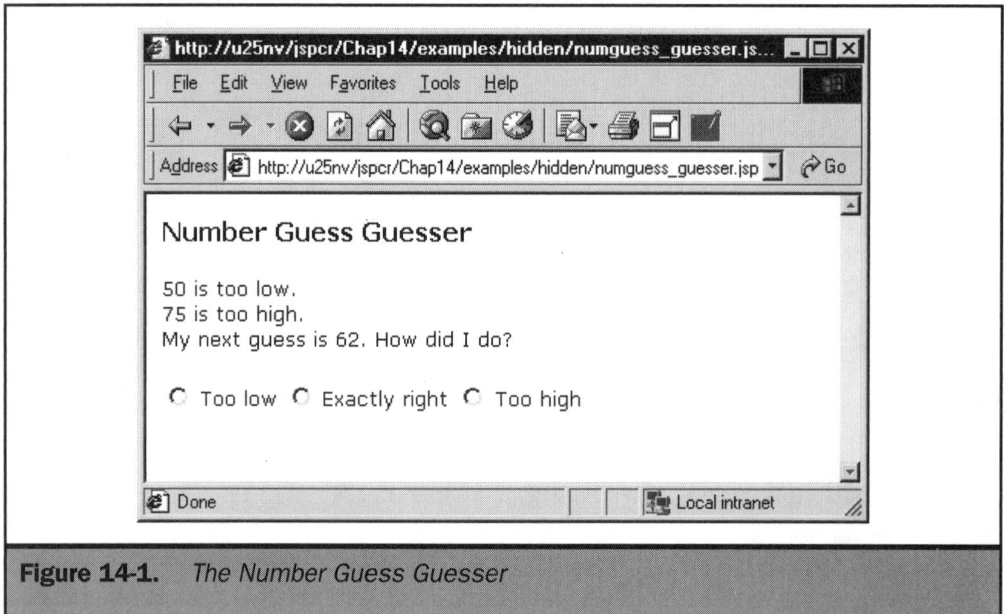


**Figure 14-1.** *The Number Guess Guesser*

## URL Rewriting

A URL can have parameters appended to it that are sent along with the request to the Web server. These parameters are name/value pairs having the following syntax:

`http://server/MyPage.jsp?`*name1=value1&name2=value2*`&...`

When the JSP page receives the request, it can read the values with

```
String value1 = request.getParameter("name1");
String value2 = request.getParameter("name2");
...
```

Dynamically generated Web pages can take advantage of this facility to store session data in URLs that are written to the page as hyperlinks. This allows the client to remind the server of all values necessary to put the server application into the required state.

A simple example would be a counter that indicates the number of times a user has accessed a page during the current session, as shown in the following listing:

```
<%@ page session="false" %>
<HTML>
<HEAD>
```

```
<TITLE>Page Counter Using URL Rewriting</TITLE>
</HEAD>
<BODY>
<H3>Page Counter Using URL Rewriting</H3>
<%
   int count = 0;
   String parm = request.getParameter("count");
   if (parm != null)
      count = Integer.parseInt(parm);
   if (count == 0) {
%> This is the first time you have accessed this page. <%
   }
   else if (count == 1) {
%> You have accessed the page once before.<%
   }
   else {
%> You have accessed the page <%= count %> times before.<%
   }
%>
<P> Click
<A HREF="Counter.jsp?count=<%=count + 1 %>"
   >here</A> to visit the page again.
</BODY>
</HTML>
```



When the user requests the page for the first time using nothing but the basic URL, no `count` parameter exists and, therefore, the integer `count` variable is set to zero:

At the bottom of the page is a hyperlink that invokes the same `counter.jsp` page again but, this time, with a `count` parameter with a value one greater than the current count:

Each time the page is reinvoked, the counter is updated and the message changes:

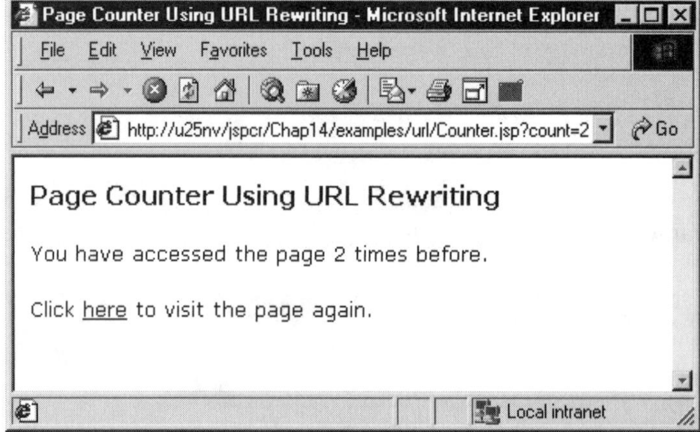


This technique is guaranteed to work in all browser environments and security settings, but that's about its only advantage. The technique tends to degrade performance if large amounts of data are stored. The URLs can become very large, possibly exceeding the size accepted by the Web server. Additionally, the URLs aren't secure, being visible in the browser address window and in Web server logs. The requirement that every URL on the page has to be rewritten entails a lot of tedious code and it's easy to overlook a URL in the process. Nevertheless, for simple applications, URL rewriting is reliable and easy to implement.

Note, manually appending parameters to hyperlink URLs isn't commonly done. More common is to use the HTTP Session API to do the URL rewriting and, in this case, only a session ID is appended.

## Cookies

The most widely used technique for persistent client data storage involves HTTP cookies. A *cookie* is a small, named data element the server passes to a client with a `Set-Cookie` header as part of the HTTP response. The client is expected to store the cookie and return it to the server with a `Cookie` header on subsequent requests to the same server. Along with the name and value, the cookie may contain

- An expiration date, after which the client is no long expected to retain the cookie. If no date is specified, the cookie expires as soon as the browser session ends.
- A domain name, such as `servername.com`, which restricts the subset of URLs for which the cookie is valid. If unspecified, the cookie is returned with all requests to the originating Web server.
- A path name that further restricts the URL subset.
- A `secure` attribute, which, if present, indicates the cookie should only be returned if the connection uses a secure channel, such as SSL.

Details of the original cookie specification can be found at http://home.netscape.com/newsref/std/cookie_spec.html.

Figure 14-2 illustrates how cookies are set and retrieved with HTTP requests and responses. First, the Web browser requests a page from the Web server. No cookies are involved at this point. When the server responds with the requested document, it sends a `Set-Cookie` header assigning the value `fr` to a cookie named `language`. The cookie is set to expire in one year. The browser reads this header, extracts the cookie information, and stores the name/value pair in its cookie cache, along with the Web server's domain and default path. Later, when the user visits the page again, the browser recognizes it previously received a cookie from this server and the cookie hasn't yet expired, and, therefore, sends the cookie back to the server.

One advantage of cookies over other persistence schemes is they can retain their values after the browser session is over, even after the client computer is rebooted. This makes cookies well suited for maintaining users' preferences, such as language. The application shown in the following enables the user to select the desired language by clicking a hyperlink. The selection causes two cookies to be sent to the client: one for language and one for country. The next time the user visits the site, the browser

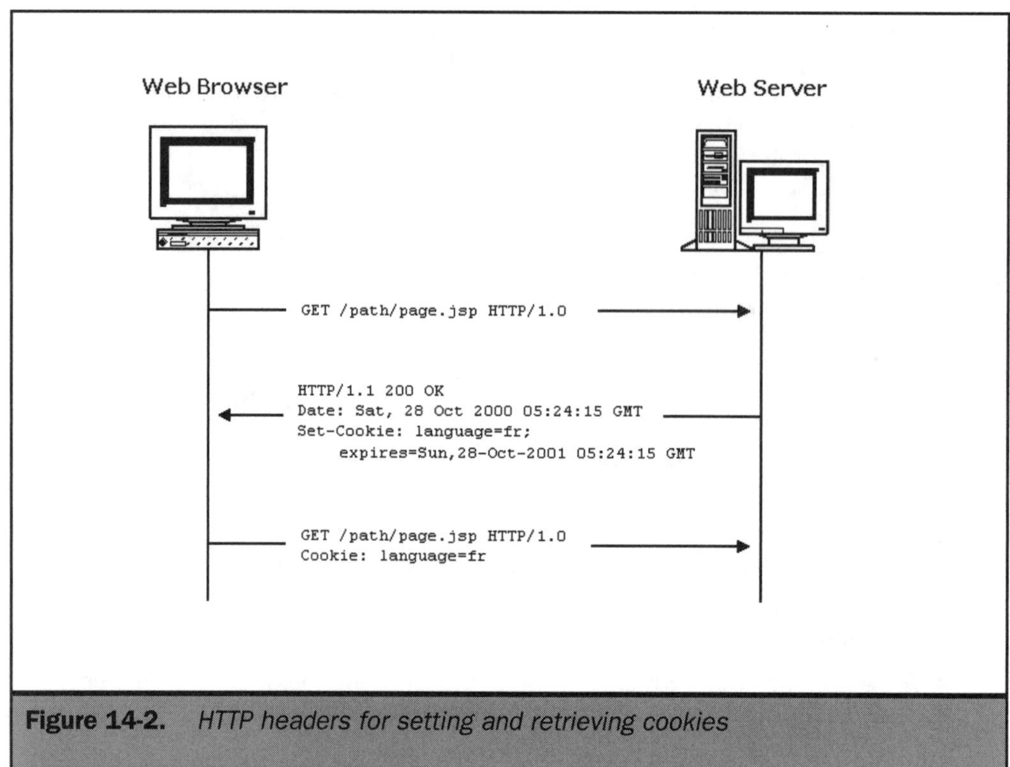


**Figure 14-2.** *HTTP headers for setting and retrieving cookies*

automatically sends the cookies back to the server and the user's preferred language is used in the page.

```
<%@ page session="false" %>
<%@ page import="java.util.*" %>
<jsp:include page="getLocale.jsp" flush="true"/>
<%
   ResourceBundle RB =
      (ResourceBundle) request.getAttribute("RB");
%>
<HTML>
<HEAD>
<TITLE>Using Cookies to Store Preferences</TITLE>
</HEAD>
<BODY>
<IMG SRC="images/lyric_note.png"><P>
```

```
<HR>
<jsp:include page="languageBar.jsp" flush="true"/>
<H3><%= RB.getString("greeting") %></H3>
</BODY>
</HTML>
```

The main application page `index.jsp` uses `<jsp:include>` to invoke a utility JSP page that scans the request headers for existing cookies and returns a resource bundle[2] for the appropriate language. Here is the utility page, `getLocale.jsp`:

```
<%@ page session="false" %>
<%@ page import="java.util.*" %>
<%
   // Look through cookies for language and country

   String language = null;
   String country  = null;

   Cookie[] cookies = request.getCookies();
   if (cookies != null) {
      for (int i = 0; i < cookies.length; i++) {
         Cookie cookie = cookies[i];
         String name = cookie.getName();
         if (name.equals("language"))
            language = cookie.getValue();
         if (name.equals("country"))
            country = cookie.getValue();
      }
   }

   // Get locale-specific resources

   Locale locale = null;
```

2 A `java.util.ResourceBundle` object is a means for a program to retrieve messages and other strings in different languages so the program can be used in multiple locales without requiring any changes. Several implementations of `ResourceBundle` exist, the most common of which uses an ordinary `.properties` file to store the message text.

```
    if (language != null && country != null)
       locale = new Locale(language, country);
    if (locale == null)
       locale = Locale.getDefault();

    ResourceBundle RB = ResourceBundle.getBundle
       ("jspcr.sessions.welcome", locale);

    // Store the resource bundle as an attribute of the request

    request.setAttribute("RB", RB);
%>
```

getLocale.jsp uses request.getCookies() to get an array of all the cookies in the request. It looks through the list for the language and country cookies. If getLocale.jsp finds them, it creates a java.util.Locale for that language and country. If the cookies aren't found (which is the case the first time the user visits the page), it uses the default locale. Either way, it loads the resource bundle associated with this application and locale, and then stores the bundle as a request attribute. After it returns from the <jsp:include>, index.jsp retrieves the resource bundle and uses ResourceBundle.getString() to get the translated text.

index.jsp calls another utility page—named languageBar.jsp—to create the language selection hyperlinks. Stored in each hyperlink is the URL for the main page (including any parameters), as well as the language and country codes. Here is languageBar.jsp:

```
<%@ page session="false" %>
<%@ page import="java.util.*" %>
<%
    String thisURL = HttpUtils.getRequestURL(request).toString();
    thisURL = java.net.URLEncoder.encode(thisURL);

    Object[][] locales = {
       {new Locale("en", "US"), "English"},
       {new Locale("de", "DE"), "Deutsch"},
       {new Locale("es", "ES"), "Español"},
       {new Locale("fr", "FR"), "Français"},
       {new Locale("it", "IT"), "Italiano"},
    };

    for (int i = 0; i < locales.length; i++) {
```

```
      Locale locale = (Locale) locales[i][0];
      String name   = (String) locales[i][1];

      StringBuffer sb = new StringBuffer();
      if (i > 0)
         sb.append(" | ");
      sb.append("<A HREF=\"setPreferences.jsp?cameFrom=");
      sb.append(thisURL);
      sb.append("&language=");
      sb.append(locale.getLanguage());
      sb.append("&country=");
      sb.append(locale.getCountry());
      sb.append("\"");
      sb.append(">");
      sb.append(name);
      sb.append("</A>");
      out.println(sb);
   }
%>
```

The hyperlinks invoke `setPreferences.jsp`, which generates the appropriate language and country cookies, and then adds them to the outgoing response header. Next, the JSP redirects the browser back to the calling page, as shown in the following:

```
<%@ page session="false" %>
<%
   // Set cookies for language and country

   final int ONE_YEAR = 60 * 60 * 24 * 365;
   String[] parms = { "language", "country" };
   for (int i = 0; i < parms.length; i++) {
      String name = parms[i];
      String value = request.getParameter(name);
      if (value != null) {
         Cookie cookie = new Cookie(name, value);
         cookie.setMaxAge(ONE_YEAR);
         response.addCookie(cookie);
      }
   }
```

```
// Redirect back to the calling JSP

   String cameFrom = request.getParameter("cameFrom");
   if (cameFrom == null)
      cameFrom = request.getContextPath();
   response.sendRedirect(cameFrom);
%>
```

The `index.jsp` page originally comes up in the default locale, as shown in Figure 14-3. If the user clicks the French hyperlink, the `setPreferences.jsp` page is invoked, which redirects the browser back to `index.jsp`, this time with cookies attached. The result is the French version of the page, seen in Figure 14-4. If the user visits the site the next day, the language preference is remembered and applied.

The main problem with cookies is users can and do turn off their browser's cookie support, usually for privacy reasons. This means the application must be prepared to do its work some other way if it cannot use cookies.

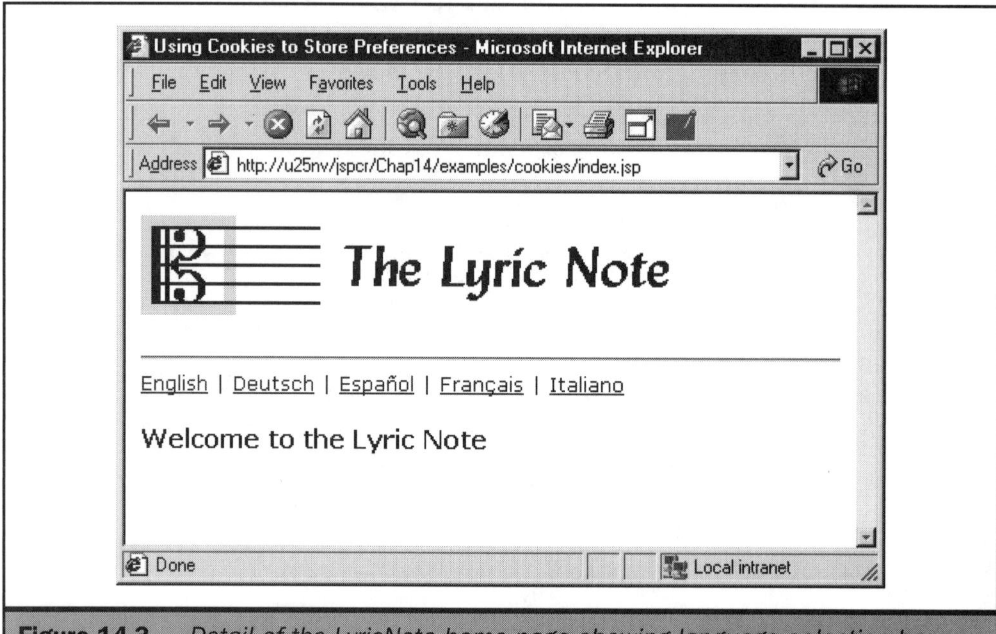


**Figure 14-3.** *Detail of the LyricNote home page showing language selection bar*

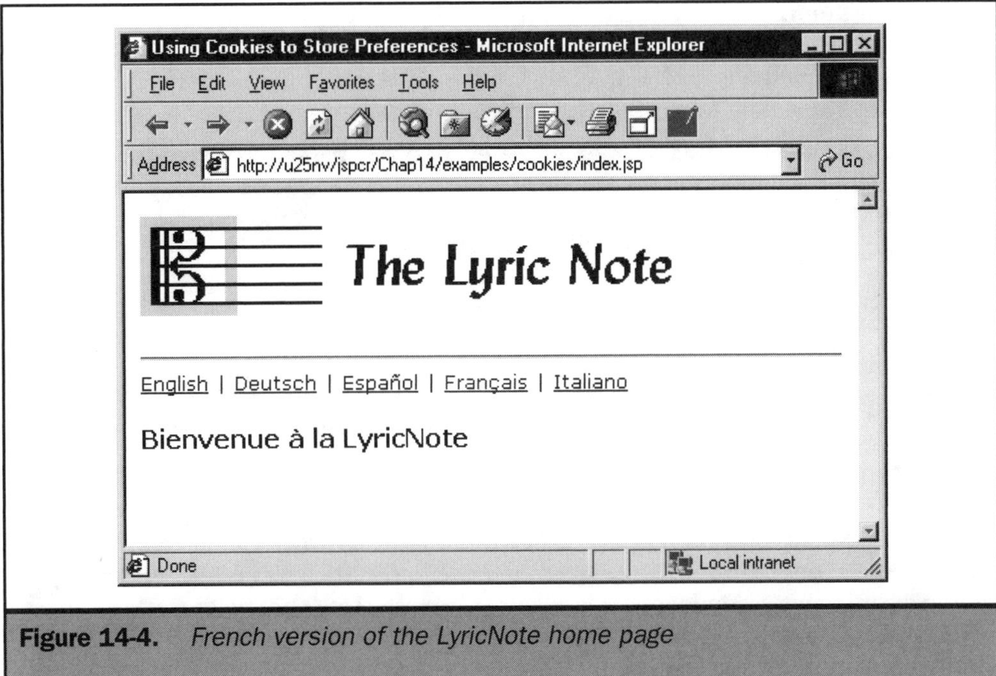


**Figure 14-4.** *French version of the LyricNote home page*



## The Session API

So far, we've examined two general approaches to session tracking, both of which involve the client remembering the state:

- Have the client store all session data and return it to the server with each request.
- Have the client store a session identifier and have the server handle the rest.

While the first method may be easier to implement, the second, in general, offers more flexibility and scalability. We have seen that hidden fields, URL rewriting, and cookies can all be used to support either method, to some extent. But most servlets and JSP pages that need to use sessions can take advantage of a higher-level approach: the *HttpSession* API.

Three classes are in the `javax.servlet.http` package that comprise the session API:

- **`HttpSession`** An interface that acts like a `Map` or `Hashtable`, able to store and retrieve objects by name. A session is created by a call to `HttpServletRequest.getSession()` and persists until it times out or is shut down by a servlet participating in the session. Incoming HTTP requests that carry the session identifier are automatically associated with the session

- **HttpSessionBindingListener** An interface that allows an object to know when it has been stored in a session or removed from one. The interface has two callback methods, `valueBound()` and `valueUnbound()`, which the object must implement to receive the binding notifications.
- **HttpSessionBindingEvent** An event object passed to the `valueBound()` and `valueUnbound()` methods of an `HttpSessionBindingListener`. The event has methods for returning the session and the name under which the listener was bound to the session.

## Creating Sessions

A servlet indicates it wants to use a session by calling the `getSession()` or `getSession(boolean create)` methods in `HttpServletRequest`, as shown here:

```
HttpSession session = request.getSession(true);
```

The getSession() method with no parameters is a convenience method that simply calls `getSession(true)`. The `create` parameter indicates whether the servlet engine should create a new session if one doesn't already exist. If the parameter is `false`, the servlet can only operate on an existing session. In either case, the request is examined to see if it contains a valid session ID. If so, the servlet container returns a reference to the session object, which can then be used to store and retrieve session attributes.

In a JSP page, session creation is automatic, unless is it suppressed in the `page` directive. At the beginning of the `_jspService()` method in the generated servlet, the `PageContext` object is created and initialized. As part of the initialization, the `JspFactory.getPageContext()` method calls `request.getSession(true)`. The newly created or accessed session is returned to the generated servlet when it calls `pageContext.getSession()`. The session is then accessible to the rest of the JSP page as the implicit variable `session`, as the following shows:

```
public void _jspService(
        HttpServletRequest request,
        HttpServletResponse response)
    throws ServletException, IOException
  {
    PageContext pageContext = _jspFactory.getPageContext
       (this, request, response, null, true, 8192, true);

    JspWriter out = pageContext.getOut();
    HttpSession session = pageContext.getSession();
    ...
  }
```

If a JSP page doesn't need to use a session, it should suppress the automatic creation in the page directive:

```
<%@ page session="false" %>
```

This relieves the servlet engine from having to create and maintain a session when it isn't needed. The memory requirements for unnecessary sessions can be significant.

When the session is first created, the client (Web browser) doesn't yet know about it. When the session ID has been sent to the client and the client sends it back in the next request, the client is said to *join* the session. A servlet or JSP page can detect whether this has happened with the `isNew()` method:

```
HttpSession session = request.getSession();
if (session.isNew()) {
   // Create an empty shopping cart
}
```

`session.isNew()` is true if the session is newly created and the client hasn't yet been informed or if the client has been informed, but chooses not to participate.

## Session Tracking Mechanisms

The servlet engine tries to use cookies to keep track of the session ID. In the HTTP response written by a servlet that created a session, a `Set-Cookie` header containing the session ID is in a cookie named `JSESSIONID`[3].

```
Set-Cookie: JSESSIONID=rkbg6z27j1;Path=/jspcr
```

If the client accepts the cookie, the client returns it in subsequent requests:

```
Cookie: JSESSIONID=rkbg6z27j1
```

If this happens, the client request can be associated with the session with no special considerations on the part of the servlet. If the client doesn't accept cookies, however, the session is lost. To prevent this, the servlet API has a fallback mechanism. It uses URL rewriting if cookies fail. This is slightly more complicated for the programmer because it means all URLs written by the servlet must have the session ID appended.

---

3 This is prescribed by the Servlet 2.2 API specification. Some servlet engines use a different value.

But, because this is unnecessary and expensive if the client accepts cookies, the URL rewriting should only be done if you definitely know the cookie method fails. Fortunately, the servlet API has methods that encapsulate all this logic. The `HttpServletResponse` class has `encodeURL()` and `encodeRedirectURL()` methods that add the session ID to a URL only if necessary:

```
String myURL = response.encodeURL("/servlet/nextServlet");
out.println("Click <A HREF='"
   + myURL + "'>here</A>"
   + " to continue");
```

`encodeRedirectURL()` should be used with URLs passed to the `response.sendRedirect()` method and `encodeURL()` with all others.

When the `encodeURL()` method is used, the session ID is always embedded in the URL when `session.isNew()` is true. After the first response from the client, the servlet engine determines whether the session ID was returned in a cookie. If not, the servlet engine continues to append the ID to URLs passed through `encodeURL()`. Otherwise, it switches to using cookies only and `encodeURL()` returns unmodified URL strings. This makes testing all the possibilities unnecessary for the programmer.

## Storing and Retrieving Objects from Sessions

Objects are bound to a session with the `setAttribute()` method:

```
session.setAttribute("jspcr.sessions.myapp.user", userID);
```

The name under which an object is bound can be any unique string. Because sessions are shared between all servlets and JSP pages in the current HTTP session, however, it makes sense to use a name that won't conflict with other applications. Most common is to choose names with a prefix that's the package name or fully qualified class name of the servlet or JSP page.

Any kind of object can be stored in a session, but because sessions may be serialized, a good idea is to have session objects implement `java.io.Serializable`. Note, too, only objects can be stored, not primitives like `int`, `char` or `double`. To store these primitives, you must use their object wrappers `Integer`, `Character`, or `Double`.

Objects can be retrieved from a session with the `getAttribute()` method:

```
String userID = (String) session.getAttribute(
   "jspcr.sessions.myapp.user");
```

Like a `Map` or `Hashtable`, a session stores only objects, so when they're retrieved, they must be cast into the appropriate type. Primitives contained in wrapper classes must be extracted by the methods provided in the wrapper class:

```
Integer countObject = (Integer) getAttribute("count");
int count = countObject.intValue();
```

Usually, if you stored an attribute in a session, you know its name and type, and you can request it directly in this manner. You can also get a list of attribute names, however, from the `getAttributeName()` method:

```
out.println("Objects in this session:");
out.println("<PRE>");
Enumeration enames = session.getAttributeNames();
while (enames.hasMoreElements()) {
   String name = (String) enames.nextElement();
   Object value = session.getAttribute(name);
   out.println(name + " = " + value);
}
out.println("</PRE>");
```

When an object is no longer needed, it can be removed from the session with `removeAttribute()`:

```
session.removeAttribute("jspcr.sessions.myapp.user");
```

This happens automatically when the session is closed, but situations may occur when an attribute needs to be removed earlier than this.



## Destroying Sessions

Once created, a session ordinarily persists until it times out or is shut down. *Timeout* refers to the maximum length of time between requests that the session will remain valid. This is an important consideration because the server has no way of knowing whether a client has finished working with a session, other than by being told explicitly or by waiting a fixed length of time.

The default timeout interval can be set in the deployment descriptor `web.xml`:

```
<web-app>
   ...
   <session-config>
      <session-timeout> 30 </session-timeout>
   </session-config>
   ...
</web-app>
```

The interval is specified as a number of minutes, 30 being the default. The value entered here applies to all sessions in the application unless they individually override it.

Some applications that use scarce resources like database connections may choose to time out sooner. These applications can use the `setMaxInactiveInterval()` method to select a shorter time period:

```
session.setMaxInactiveInterval(180);
```

The argument supplied to `setMaxInactiveInterval()` is a number of seconds[4]. The previous example uses 180 seconds or three minutes. The current value can be obtained with `getMaxInactiveInterval()`. If a negative value is specified, the session never times out.

In some cases, a definite end to the session can be provided. In these cases, the `invalidate()` method can be used:

```
session.invalidate();
```

This method marks the session as being inactive and unbinds all objects bound to it. For example, in a shopping cart application that uses a session to store items being ordered, after the checkout logic writes the order to a database, the session should be destroyed so, if the user purchases more items, the old session contents won't still be there.

## Examples Revisited

The session API can handle all the session tracking tasks described earlier in this chapter. In this section, you learn how the hidden fields, URL rewriting, and cookies examples can be done using the same session API approach.

### Hidden Fields Example—The Number Guesser

The number guesser developed in the hidden fields section can be simplified by moving all the hidden fields into an object stored in an HTTP session. The object in this example is an inner class named `Parameters`, which is defined near the top of the JSP page, but it could just as easily be an externally defined class.

```
<%@ page session="true" %>
<H3>Number Guess Guesser</H3>
<%!
```

4 The API is a little inconsistent here. Why use minutes in the deployment descriptor and seconds in the session API?

```
   public static final int WAY_LO = 0;
   public static final int WAY_HI = 101;
   public static final String PARMSKEY
      = "jspcr.sessions.numguess.parameters";

   // Inner class containing state variables

   public class Parameters {
      int lo;
      int hi;
      int numGuesses;
      int state;
   }
%>
<%
   Parameters parms=(Parameters) session.getAttribute(PARMSKEY);
   if (parms == null) {
      parms = new Parameters();
      parms.state = 0;
      session.setAttribute(PARMSKEY, parms);
   }

   switch (parms.state) {
      case 0: {   // Initial screen
%>
<FORM>
Think of a number between
<%= WAY_LO + 1 %> and <%= WAY_HI - 1 %>,
and I'll try to guess it.<P>
Click OK when ready.<P>
<INPUT TYPE="submit" VALUE="OK">
</FORM>
<%
         parms.lo = WAY_LO;
         parms.hi = WAY_HI;
         parms.numGuesses = 0;
         parms.state = 1;
         break;
      }
      case 1: {   // First guess
         parms.numGuesses++;
         int guess = (parms.hi + parms.lo)/2;
```

```
%>
<FORM>
My first guess is <%= guess %>. How did I do?<P>
<INPUT TYPE="radio"
       NAME="result"
       VALUE="-1" onClick="submit()"> Too low
<INPUT TYPE="radio"
       NAME="result"
       VALUE="0" onClick="submit()"> Exactly right
<INPUT TYPE="radio"
       NAME="result"
       VALUE="1" onClick="submit()"> Too high
</FORM>
<P>
<%
         parms.state = 2;
         break;
      }
      case 2: {    // After first guess
         parms.numGuesses++;
         int result =
            Integer.parseInt(request.getParameter("result"));
         int guess = (parms.hi + parms.lo)/2;

         if (result < 0) {
            parms.lo = guess;
            guess = (parms.hi + parms.lo)/2;
         }
         else if (result > 0) {
            parms.hi = guess;
            guess = (parms.hi + parms.lo)/2;
         }

         if (result != 0) {
%>
<FORM>
<%
   if (parms.lo > WAY_LO)
      out.println(parms.lo + " is too low.<BR>");
   if (parms.hi < WAY_HI)
      out.println(parms.hi + " is too high.<BR>");
   if ((parms.hi - parms.lo) > 1) {
```

```
%>
My next guess is <%= guess %>. How did I do?<P>
<INPUT TYPE="radio"
       NAME="result"
       VALUE="-1" onClick="submit()"> Too low
<INPUT TYPE="radio"
       NAME="result"
       VALUE="0" onClick="submit()"> Exactly right
<INPUT TYPE="radio"
       NAME="result"
       VALUE="1" onClick="submit()"> Too high
</FORM>
<%
   }
   else {
      String[] text = {
         "Are we cheating?",
         "Did we forget our number?",
         "Perhaps we clicked the wrong button?",
         "What happened?",
         "What gives?",
      };
      String message = text[(int)(Math.random() * text.length)];
      session.removeAttribute(PARMSKEY);
%>
<FORM>
<%= message %><P>
<INPUT TYPE="SUBMIT" VALUE="Start Over">
</FORM>
<%
   }
         }
         else {
            parms.numGuesses--;
%>
<FORM>
I win, and after only <%= parms.numGuesses %> guesses!<P>
Do you want to try again?<P>
<INPUT TYPE="SUBMIT" VALUE="Start Over">
</FORM>
<%
            session.removeAttribute(PARMSKEY);
```

```
            }
            break;
        }
    }
%>
```

The logic remains the same, but where hidden fields were written to the HTML form, their values are now stored in the `Parameter` object that's bound to the session.

## URL Rewriting Example—The Page Counter

Similarly, the page counter developed in the URL rewriting section can use an HTTP session to store the count variable. Because `int` is a primitive, use the `Integer` object wrapper and call its `intValue()` method to get the actual value.

```
<%@ page session="true" %>
<HTML>
<HEAD>
<TITLE>Page Counter Using HTTP Session</TITLE>
</HEAD>
<BODY>
<H3>Page Counter Using HTTP Session</H3>
<%
   if (session.getAttribute("count") == null)
      session.setAttribute("count", new Integer(0));

   int count=((Integer) session.getAttribute("count")).intValue();

   switch (count) {
      case 0:
%> This is the first time you have accessed this page. <%
         break;
      case 1:
%> You have accessed the page once before.<%
         break;
      default:
%> You have accessed the page <%= count %> times before.<%
         break;
   }

   session.setAttribute("count", new Integer(count+1));
%>
```

```
<P>
Click
<A HREF="<%= response.encodeURL("Counter.jsp") %>">here</A>
to visit the page again.
</BODY>
</HTML>
```

Each time the page is refreshed, the count is incremented and stored in the session in a new `Integer` wrapper. Note, the hyperlink the user clicks to redisplay the page uses `response.encodeURL()` to ensure the session tracking works, regardless of whether the user accepts cookies.

## Cookies Example—Language Preference

In the Cookies section, you learned how an application could allow a user to indicate his language preference, so the rest of the Web pages in that session were displayed in that language. The application used cookies so the preference would persist even between sessions. If that persistence isn't a requirement, the same thing can be done with the session API.

The main `index.jsp` page changes little. It still uses a resource bundle for message text, but now it gets it as a session attribute, rather than a request attribute. In addition, note the page directive now has `session="true"`.

```
<%@ page session="true" %>
<%@ page import="java.util.*" %>

<%-- Get the appropriate resource bundle from the session --%>

<jsp:include page="getLocale.jsp" flush="true"/>
<%
   ResourceBundle RB = (ResourceBundle)
      session.getAttribute("RB");
%>

<HTML>
<HEAD>
<TITLE>Using Session API to Store Language Preference</TITLE>
</HEAD>
<BODY>
<IMG SRC="images/lyric_note.png"><P>
<HR>
```

```
<%-- Show a row of hyperlinks with language choices --%>

<jsp:include page="languageBar.jsp" flush="true"/>

<%-- Display greeting in appropriate language --%>

<H3><%= RB.getString("greeting") %></H3>

</BODY>
</HTML>
```

The included modules—`getLocale.jsp` and `setPreferences.jsp`—are where the real change takes place. `setPreferences` can now do the actual loading of the appropriate resource bundle, based on the language and country parameters it receives

```
<%@ page session="true" %>
<%@ page import="java.util.*" %>
<%
   // Get parameters for language and country

   String language = request.getParameter("language");
   String country = request.getParameter("country");

   // Get locale-specific resources

   Locale locale = null;
   if (language != null && country != null)
      locale = new Locale(language, country);
   if (locale == null)
      locale = Locale.getDefault();

   ResourceBundle RB = ResourceBundle.getBundle
      ("jspcr.sessions.welcome", locale);

   // Store the resource bundle as an attribute in the session

   session.setAttribute("RB", RB);

   // Redirect back to the calling JSP

   String cameFrom = request.getParameter("cameFrom");
```

```
   if (cameFrom == null)
      cameFrom = request.getContextPath();

   cameFrom = response.encodeRedirectURL(cameFrom);

   response.sendRedirect(cameFrom);
%>
```

The resource bundle is stored as a session attribute and the user is redirected back to the original page. Note, the "cameFrom" URL is passed through the `encodeRedirectURL()` method, in case cookies are turned off.

The `getLocale` JSP page can now simply look in the session for the resource bundle or use the default bundle if none is found

```
<%@ page session="true" %>
<%@ page import="java.util.*" %>
<%
   // Get the existing resource bundle from the session,
   // if one exists

   ResourceBundle RB = (ResourceBundle)
      session.getAttribute("RB");

   // If not, use the default resource bundle

   if (RB == null) {
      RB = ResourceBundle.getBundle("jspcr.sessions.welcome");
      session.setAttribute("RB", RB);
   }
%>
```

The `languageBar.jsp` page only needs to make one change in two places. Because it writes URLs for the main page and `setPreferences.jsp`, it needs to pass the URLs through `response.encodeURL()` so session tracking works even if cookies are turned off:

```
<%@ page session="true" %>
<%@ page import="java.util.*" %>
<%
   String thisURL = HttpUtils.getRequestURL(request).toString();
   // Encode the session ID into the URL, if necessary
```

```
    thisURL = response.encodeURL(thisURL);
    thisURL = java.net.URLEncoder.encode(thisURL);

    Object[][] locales = {
       {new Locale("en", "US"), "English"},
       {new Locale("de", "DE"), "Deutsch"},
       {new Locale("es", "ES"), "Español"},
       {new Locale("fr", "FR"), "Français"},
       {new Locale("it", "IT"), "Italiano"},
    };

    for (int i = 0; i < locales.length; i++) {

       Locale locale = (Locale) locales[i][0];
       String name   = (String) locales[i][1];

       StringBuffer sb = new StringBuffer();
       if (i > 0)
          sb.append(" | ");
       sb.append("<A HREF=\"");

       // Encode the session ID into the generated URL

       StringBuffer sb2 = new StringBuffer();
       sb2.append("setPreferences.jsp?cameFrom=");
       sb2.append(thisURL);
       sb2.append("&language=");
       sb2.append(locale.getLanguage());
       sb2.append("&country=");
       sb2.append(locale.getCountry());
       String url = sb2.toString();
       url = response.encodeURL(url);

       sb.append(url);
       sb.append("\"");
       sb.append(">");
       sb.append(name);
       sb.append("</A>");
       out.println(sb);
    }
%>
```

## Session Binding Listeners

The session API provides a means for objects to keep track of when they are added or removed from a session. An object that wants to receive notification of these events can implement the `HttpSessionBindingListener` interface. Implementing classes must provide two methods:

- `public void valueBound(HttpSessionBindingEvent event)`
- `public void valueUnbound(HttpSessionBindingEvent event)`

In each case, an instance of `HttpSessionBindingEvent` is passed to the methods. The event parameter has methods for retrieving the session and for determining the name by which the object was bound to the session.

The main advantage gained by session binding listeners is they can free the resources they acquire, regardless of whether the client explicitly closes the application or the session times out. This makes the interface useful for managing database connections. JDBC 2.0 provides for connection pooling, but many drivers don't yet implement it. In this case, a session-resident connection that knows enough to disconnect itself is a workable alternative.

The following example illustrates the technique. `BoundConnection` is a wrapper around a `java.sql.Connection` object and implements `HttpSessionBindingListener`, so it can close the connection after it's no longer in use.

```
package jspcr.jdbc;

import java.io.*;
import java.sql.*;
import java.text.*;
import java.util.*;
import javax.servlet.*;
import javax.servlet.http.*;

/**
* A wrapper for a <CODE>Connection</CODE>
* object that is aware it is in an HTTP session.
* This enables it to shut down the connection
* when the session is destroyed.
*/
public class BoundConnection
   implements HttpSessionBindingListener, Serializable
{
```

```
private transient Connection connection;

/**
* Creates a new <CODE>BoundConnection</CODE> object
* for the specified connection.
* @param con the connection
*/
public BoundConnection(Connection con)
{
   this.connection = con;
}

/**
* Returns the underlying connection
*/
public Connection getConnection()
{
   return connection;
}

/**
* Called when the <CODE>BoundConnection</CODE>
* is stored in an HTTP session
* @param event the binding event
*/
public void valueBound(HttpSessionBindingEvent event)
{
   trace("bound", event);
}

/**
* Called when the <CODE>BoundConnection</CODE>
* is removed from an HTTP session
* @param event the unbinding event
*/
public void valueUnbound(HttpSessionBindingEvent event)
{
   if (connection != null)
      try {
         connection.close();
         connection = null;
      }
      catch (SQLException e) {
```

```
            e.printStackTrace();
         }
      trace("unbound", event);
   }

   /**
   * Prints a trace message
   */
   private void trace(String s, HttpSessionBindingEvent event)
   {
      HttpSession session = event.getSession();

      java.util.Date now =
         new java.util.Date(System.currentTimeMillis());
      java.util.Date last =
         new java.util.Date(session.getLastAccessedTime());

      SimpleDateFormat fmt = new SimpleDateFormat("hh:mm:ss");
      StringBuffer sb;

      sb = new StringBuffer();
      sb.append("TRACE: ");
      sb.append(fmt.format(now));
      sb.append(" session ");
      sb.append(session.getId());
      sb.append(" last accessed time ");
      sb.append(fmt.format(last));
      System.err.println(sb.toString());

      sb = new StringBuffer();
      sb.append("TRACE: ");
      sb.append(fmt.format(now));
      sb.append(" session ");
      sb.append(session.getId());
      sb.append(" connection " );
      sb.append(s);
      System.err.println(sb.toString());
   }
}
```

The BoundConnection constructor stores a Connection object as a private instance variable and makes it available through a getConnection() method. BoundConnection implements the two HttpSessionBindingListener methods:

valueBound() and valueUnbound(). In each of them, it writes a trace message, so a record exists of when the connection is bound or unbound. The key feature is the valueUnbound() method, which closes the underlying connection.

**Note** *The BoundConnection object implements Serializable because sessions may be serialized, especially in distributable applications. This makes marking the Connection instance variable as transient necessary so the servlet container won't attempt to serialize it. The caller of getConnection(), therefore, needs to check the value returned for null and, if necessary, create a new BoundConnection.*

A JSP page that uses BoundConnection can, therefore, invoke it when the session begins, giving it a newly opened database connection. When a BoundConnection is stored in the session, its valueBound() method is triggered. Subsequent requests in the same session can simply retrieve the BoundConnection from the session and call its getConnection() method to get the underlying java.sql.Connection. The reusable connect.jsp module shown in the following implements this logic.

```
<%@ page import="java.sql.*" %>
<%@ page import="jspcr.jdbc.*" %>
<%
   // If there is not already a connection bound to this
   // session, create one

   if (session.getAttribute("bcon") == null) {

      String driver =
         application.getInitParameter("jdbc.driver");
      String url =
         application.getInitParameter("jdbc.url.internal");

      Class.forName(driver);
      Connection con = DriverManager.getConnection(url);

      // Bind the connection to this session

      BoundConnection bcon = new BoundConnection(con);
      session.setAttribute("bcon", bcon);

      // Set the timeout interval to three minutes

      session.setMaxInactiveInterval(180);
   }
%>
```

In addition to creating the BoundConnection when necessary, connect.jsp sets the session timeout interval to three minutes.

The application shown in the following uses a BoundConnection to provide quick access for repeated database queries. ComposerSearch.jsp prompts for a nationality and century, and then searches the LyricNote composer database and displays the results. It includes connect.jsp to do the actual connection and session binding work.

```
<%@ page session="true" %>
<%@ page import="jspcr.jdbc.*" %>
<%@ page import="java.sql.*" %>
<%
   // Get form parameters or use defaults

   String nationality = request.getParameter("nationality");
   if (nationality == null)
      nationality = "";

   String yearRange = request.getParameter("yearRange");
   if (yearRange == null)
      yearRange = "1901-2000";
%>
<HTML>
<HEAD>
<TITLE>Composer Search</TITLE>
</HEAD>
<BODY>
<CENTER>
<H3>Composer Search</H3>
<FORM METHOD="POST">
<B>Nationality:</B>
<INPUT TYPE="TEXT" NAME="nationality" VALUE="<%= nationality %>">
<B>Century:</B>
<SELECT NAME="yearRange">
<%
   // Create the century option list

   for (int century = 16; century <= 20; century++) {
      int fromYear = (century - 1) * 100 + 1;
      int toYear = century * 100;
      StringBuffer sb = new StringBuffer();
      sb.append("<OPTION");
      if (yearRange.startsWith("" + fromYear))
         sb.append(" SELECTED");
```

```
        sb.append(" VALUE='");
        sb.append(fromYear);
        sb.append("-");
        sb.append(toYear);
        sb.append("'>");
        sb.append(century);
        sb.append("th Century</OPTION>");
        out.println(sb);
    }
%>
</SELECT>
<INPUT TYPE="SUBMIT" VALUE="Search">
</FORM>
<%
    // If values were entered in the form, display results

    if (!nationality.equals("")) {
%>

<%-- Get the bound connection --%>

<jsp:include page="connect.jsp" flush="true"/>

<TABLE BORDER=0 CELLPADDING=1 CELLSPACING=1>
<%
        BoundConnection bcon = (BoundConnection)
           session.getAttribute("bcon");
        Connection con = bcon.getConnection();
        String sql = ""
           + " SELECT   lname, fname, born, died"
           + " FROM     composers"
           + " WHERE    nationality = ?"
           + " AND      ((born between ? and ?)"
           + " OR       (died between ? and ?))"
           + " ORDER BY born, lname"
           ;
        PreparedStatement pstmt = con.prepareStatement(sql);

        int fromYear = Integer.parseInt(yearRange.substring(0, 4));
        int toYear = Integer.parseInt(yearRange.substring(5));

        pstmt.setString(1, nationality);
```

```
        pstmt.setInt(2, fromYear);
        pstmt.setInt(3, toYear);
        pstmt.setInt(4, fromYear);
        pstmt.setInt(5, toYear);
        ResultSet rs = pstmt.executeQuery();
        while (rs.next()) {
           String lname = rs.getString(1);
           String fname = rs.getString(2);
           int born = rs.getInt(3);
           int died = rs.getInt(4);
%>
<TR>
   <TD><%= fname %> <%= lname %></TD>
   <TD><%= born %>-<%= died %></TD>
</TR>
<%
        }
        rs.close();
        pstmt.close();
%>
</TABLE>
<%
   }
%>
</CENTER>
</BODY>
</HTML>
```

To access the session-resident connection, all the application must do is retrieve the `bcon` session attribute, cast it to a `BoundConnection`, and call its `getConnection()` method. Notice it's unnecessary to close the connection explicitly. This is done automatically when three minutes have expired with no further requests from the client. The resulting Web page, seen in Figure 14-5, can be used for repeated queries with a new connection required only for the first one.

The trace entries in the System.err log show the `BoundConnection` lifecycle in the HTTP session:

```
TRACE: 07:55:00 session 8720188469 last accessed time 07:55:00
TRACE: 07:55:00 session 8720188469 connection bound
TRACE: 07:59:38 session 8720188469 last accessed time 07:56:38
TRACE: 07:59:38 session 8720188469 connection unbound
```

JSP IN ACTION

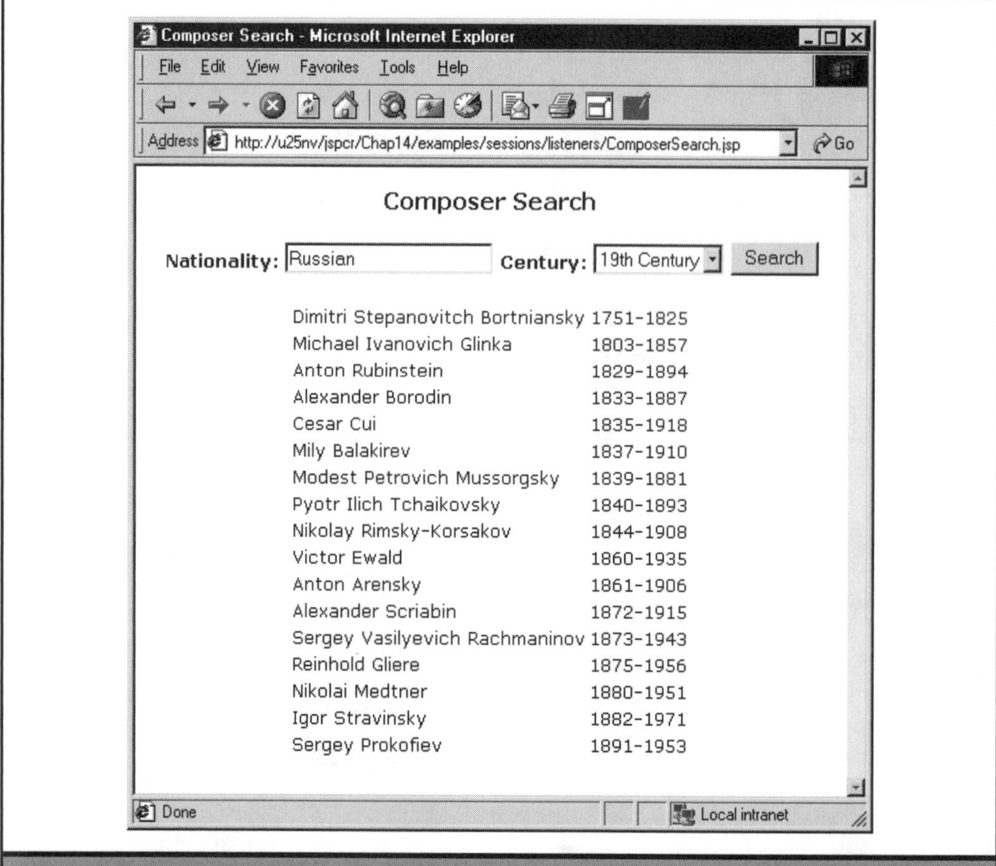


**Figure 14-5.** *A Web database query that uses BoundConnection*

The connection was bound to the session at 07:55:00 and used one or more times, the last time being 07:56:38. Three minutes later, at 07:59:38, the session timed out, unbinding the `BoundConnection` object. This, in turn, caused the `valueUnbound()` method to be called, which closed the underlying connection.

## Thread Management

Servlets and JSP pages have a significant advantage over older server-side technologies because they are loaded into memory and run as single instances in a multithreaded environment. This benefit comes with a tradeoff, however. The multithreaded model introduces difficulties that don't exist in simpler application models. For example, if a servlet has instance variables, they can potentially be accessed simultaneously from different requests. If both requests write to the variables, their values may be unpredictable.

Fortunately, because the servlet engine is written in Java, it can take advantage of Java's built-in support for multithreaded applications. In this section, you learn about some basic threading concepts, examine two servlet threading models, and consider an efficient multithreaded application.

# Threading Concepts

A *thread* is a single sequential flow of control with its own stack and program counter. Programs that use multiple threads appear to be doing more than one thing at a time. A thread is able to operate independently of other threads in the same process while, at the same time, sharing all the process objects.

The Web server itself is an example of where threads can be useful. A simple Web server operates as follows:

1. Creates a `ServerSocket` and invokes its `accept()` method to wait for HTTP clients requests.
2. Gets the client `Socket` object returned by the `accept()` method and starts a separate thread to handle its request.
3. Returns to Step 1 to accept more requests at the same time the last one is being processed by the other thread.

Java in general (not only in JSP pages) makes creating and using multiple threads easy. Both the language and the class libraries are built from the ground up with threads in mind. `java.lang.Object`, the ultimate base class of all objects, has methods for synchronizing thread operations, which are inherited by every Java object.

A thread is represented by an instance of the `java.lang.Thread` class. A new `Thread` object isn't actually associated with an underlying operating system thread until its `start()` method is called, which allows its characteristics (name, priority, and so forth) to be set before it starts. After `start()` is called, an operating system thread is created by the Java virtual machine and this thread begins executing the thread's `run()` method. A `Thread` continues to run until its `run()` method returns or its `interrupt()` method is called.

## Creating and Starting Threads

Three techniques are available for starting new threads. The first is to subclass `Thread` and override its `run()` method. Objects of this class can then be created and started individually. The following `Example1.java` illustrates this technique. It uses a subclass of `Thread` called `CounterThread` to count to eight, printing the thread name and time for each iteration, and waiting a random length of time between iterations.

```
import java.text.*;
import java.util.*;

/**
* A class that demonstrates simple multithreading
*/
public class Example1
{
   public static void main(String[] args)
   {
      /**
      * Create, name, and start two counter threads
      */

      Thread t1 = new CounterThread();
      t1.setName("A");
      t1.start();

      Thread t2 = new CounterThread();
      t2.setName("B");
      t2.start();
   }
}

/**
* A thread that counts to eight, waiting
* a random length of time between iterations.
*/
class CounterThread extends Thread
{
   /**
   * Date format used in message. Includes milliseconds.
   */

   public static final SimpleDateFormat FMT
      = new SimpleDateFormat("hh:mm:ss.SSS aa");

   /**
   * Starts the run method in a new thread
   */
   public void start()
   {
      System.out.println("Starting " + getName());
```

```
        super.start();
    }

    /**
    * Where the counter loop takes place.
    */
    public void run()
    {
        for (int i = 0; i < 8; i++) {
            try {
                sleep((long) (Math.random() * 500 + 100));
            }
            catch (InterruptedException e) {
                break;
            }
            System.out.println
                (FMT.format(new Date())
                + " Thread " + getName()
                + ": Count = " + i);
        }
        System.out.println("Leaving " + getName());
    }
}
```



The mainline launches two CounterThread instances named A and B. The following program output shows both threads execute simultaneously and occasionally overlap in their iterations:

```
Starting A
Starting B
09:55:40.465 PM Thread B: Count = 0
09:55:40.545 PM Thread A: Count = 0
09:55:40.615 PM Thread B: Count = 1
09:55:40.846 PM Thread A: Count = 1
09:55:41.056 PM Thread B: Count = 2
09:55:41.346 PM Thread B: Count = 3
09:55:41.366 PM Thread A: Count = 2
09:55:41.687 PM Thread A: Count = 3
09:55:41.717 PM Thread B: Count = 4
09:55:41.847 PM Thread B: Count = 5
09:55:41.967 PM Thread B: Count = 6
```

```
09:55:42.017 PM Thread A: Count = 4
09:55:42.137 PM Thread B: Count = 7
Leaving B
09:55:42.268 PM Thread A: Count = 5
09:55:42.428 PM Thread A: Count = 6
09:55:42.848 PM Thread A: Count = 7
Leaving A
```

The second technique is to have a class implement the `Runnable` interface. In this case, the class must provide its own `run()` method and also create a `Thread` object to do the actual work. The class must pass a reference to itself (using the `this` variable) in the `Thread` constructor. The following `Example2.java` shows this technique in operation. Modeled closely after `Example1`, it creates two threads and passes each of them its `this` variable. Note, both threads can run the same run() method simultaneously.

```
import java.text.*;
import java.util.*;

/**
* A class that demonstrates simple multithreading
* using the Runnable interface.
*/
public class Example2 implements Runnable
{
   public static void main(String[] args)
   {
      new Example2();
   }

   public Example2()
   {
      /**
      * Start two Runnable threads each using this run method.
      */

      Thread t1 = new Thread(this);
      t1.setName("A");
      t1.start();

      Thread t2 = new Thread(this);
      t2.setName("B");
```

```
      t2.start();
   }

   /**
   * Date format used in message. Includes milliseconds.
   */

   public static final SimpleDateFormat FMT
      = new SimpleDateFormat("hh:mm:ss.SSS aa");

   /**
   * Where the counter loop takes place.
   */
   public void run()
   {
      Thread t = Thread.currentThread();
      System.out.println("Starting " + t.getName());
      for (int i = 0; i < 8; i++) {
         try {
            t.sleep((long) (Math.random() * 500 + 100));
         }
         catch (InterruptedException e) {
            break;
         }
         System.out.println
            (FMT.format(new Date())
            + " Thread " + t.getName()
            + ": Count = " + i);
      }
      System.out.println("Leaving " + t.getName());
   }
}
```

The output from `Example2` is similar to the output from `Example1`:

```
Starting main
Starting A
10:10:54.269 PM Thread A: Count = 0
10:10:54.299 PM Thread main: Count = 0
10:10:54.620 PM Thread main: Count = 1
```

```
10:10:54.690 PM Thread A: Count = 1
10:10:54.980 PM Thread main: Count = 2
10:10:55.180 PM Thread A: Count = 2
10:10:55.351 PM Thread A: Count = 3
10:10:55.461 PM Thread main: Count = 3
10:10:55.671 PM Thread A: Count = 4
10:10:55.811 PM Thread A: Count = 5
10:10:56.042 PM Thread main: Count = 4
10:10:56.272 PM Thread main: Count = 5
10:10:56.382 PM Thread A: Count = 6
10:10:56.753 PM Thread main: Count = 6
10:10:56.773 PM Thread A: Count = 7
Leaving A
10:10:56.943 PM Thread main: Count = 7
Leaving main
```

One disadvantage of using the `Runnable` interface is it's a class with only one `run()` method and so can only perform one kind of background operation, no matter how many threads it creates. An application that does animation and also listens to a socket or input stream, for instance, cannot do so by implementing `Runnable`.

Java 2 introduced a third technique for starting threads, the `java.util.Timer` and `java.util.TimerTask` classes. The `Timer` class acts as a scheduler of delayed or repeated tasks. These tasks must extend the `TimerTask` class and provide a `run()` method. Tasks are scheduled for execution with the `Timer.scheduleTask()` method in one of its several forms. Unlike in the other two approaches, the `TimerTask run()` method doesn't normally contain an execution loop because `Timer` can automatically schedule repeated task execution. The following `Example3.java` shows the counter example done with `Timer` and `TimerTask`.

```
import java.text.*;
import java.util.*;

/**
* A class that demonstrates simple multithreading
* using <CODE>java.util.Timer</CODE>
*/
public class Example3
{
   public static void main(String[] args)
   {
      /**
```

```
        * Create a timer to control the timer tasks
        */
        Timer timer = new Timer();

        /**
        * Create two timer tasks and schedule
        * their execution at half-second intervals,
        * delaying the second one's start by 250 ms
        */
        TimerTask t1 = new CounterTimerTask("A");
        timer.schedule(t1, 0, 500);

        TimerTask t2 = new CounterTimerTask("B");
        timer.schedule(t2, 250, 500);
    }
}

/**
* A TimerTask that counts to eight
*/
class CounterTimerTask extends TimerTask
{
    /**
    * Date format used in message. Includes milliseconds.
    */

    public static final SimpleDateFormat FMT
        = new SimpleDateFormat("hh:mm:ss.SSS aa");

    private String name;
    private int counter;

    public CounterTimerTask(String name)
    {
        this.name = name;
        this.counter = 0;
    }

    /**
    * Where the counter loop takes place.
    */
    public void run()
```

```
      {
         if (counter == 0)
            System.out.println("Starting " + name);

         System.out.println
            (FMT.format(new Date())
            + " Thread " + name
            + ": Count = " + counter);

         counter++;
         if (counter >= 8) {
            System.out.println("Leaving " + name);
            cancel();
         }
      }
   }
```

The `CounterTimerTask` object keeps track of the number of times it has been called and invokes its own `cancel()` method when it reaches the iteration limit. Because `Example3` uses a fixed schedule for each task, the counter messages alternate in approximate quarter-second intervals:

```
Starting A
10:57:44.209 PM Thread A: Count = 0
Starting B
10:57:44.460 PM Thread B: Count = 0
10:57:44.710 PM Thread A: Count = 1
10:57:44.961 PM Thread B: Count = 1
10:57:45.211 PM Thread A: Count = 2
10:57:45.461 PM Thread B: Count = 2
10:57:45.712 PM Thread A: Count = 3
10:57:45.962 PM Thread B: Count = 3
10:57:46.212 PM Thread A: Count = 4
10:57:46.463 PM Thread B: Count = 4
10:57:46.713 PM Thread A: Count = 5
10:57:46.963 PM Thread B: Count = 5
10:57:47.214 PM Thread A: Count = 6
10:57:47.464 PM Thread B: Count = 6
10:57:47.715 PM Thread A: Count = 7
Leaving A
10:57:47.965 PM Thread B: Count = 7
Leaving B
```

## Synchronizing Threads

Multithreaded applications often have operations that must be performed by only one thread at a time or operations that require multiple threads to act cooperatively. To accomplish this, a means for protecting critical sections of code must exist, so two threads don't run them simultaneously.

To see why this is necessary, consider the following example of a program that issues invoice numbers to a billing application. The last invoice number used is stored in a text file. A new invoice number is assigned in a method that reads the file, adds one to the invoice number, and writes it back to disk. The program starts five threads to simulate multiple online users accessing the invoice numbering routine at random times. The invoice handling in this demonstration consists of simply printing the name of the thread and the invoice number it has been assigned. See if you can spot the bug:

```
import java.io.*;
import java.net.*;
import java.util.*;

/**
* An illustration of a thread synchronization problem
*/
public class SynchTest implements Runnable
{
   public static void main(String args[])
   {
      new SynchTest();
   }

   /**
   * Creates a new SynchTest object that starts
   * five invoice handling threads.
   */
   public SynchTest()
   {
      Thread[] threads = {
         new Thread(this, "A"),
         new Thread(this, "B"),
         new Thread(this, "C"),
         new Thread(this, "D"),
         new Thread(this, "E"),
      };
      for (int i = 0; i < threads.length; i++)
         threads[i].start();
   }
```

```
/**
* Simulates handling ten invoices. This method
* will be run by each of the five threads.
*/
public void run()
{
   try {
      for (int i = 0; i < 10; i++) {
         handleInvoice();
         Thread.sleep((long) (Math.random()*500));
      }
   }
   catch (InterruptedException ignore) {
   }
   catch (IOException e) {
      e.printStackTrace();
   }
}

/**
* The invoice handling method (with a subtle bug)
*/
public void handleInvoice()
   throws IOException
{
   Thread t = Thread.currentThread();

   // Get the last used invoice number from invoice.dat

   BufferedReader in =
      new BufferedReader(
      new FileReader("invoice.dat"));
   int invoiceNumber = Integer.parseInt(in.readLine());
   in.close();

   // Add 1 to get the current invoice number

   invoiceNumber++;
   System.out.println
      (t.getName() + " handles invoice " + invoiceNumber);
```

```
        // Update the invoice number

        PrintWriter out =
           new PrintWriter(
           new FileWriter("invoice.dat"));
        out.println(invoiceNumber);
        out.flush();
        out.close();
     }
  }
```

The program may run several times without any problems, assigning consecutive invoice numbers to each thread. But after a while, output like the following appears:

```
A handles invoice 68401
B handles invoice 68402
C handles invoice 68403
D handles invoice 68404
E handles invoice 68405
E handles invoice 68406
D handles invoice 68407
A handles invoice 68408
D handles invoice 68409
B handles invoice 68410
B handles invoice 68411
E handles invoice 68412
C handles invoice 68412
B handles invoice 68413
D handles invoice 68414
E handles invoice 68415
B handles invoice 68416
B handles invoice 68417
A handles invoice 68418
```



Invoice number 68412 appears twice in the list, assigned to both thread E and thread C. What happened?

The problem is this: during the time interval from when the invoice number is read to when it is rewritten in the `invoice.dat` file, it's possible for another thread executing the same method to read the file and get the old number. This thread can then increment it and update the file, but it can then have a duplicate invoice number.

To prevent this, Java provides a means for getting an exclusive lock on an object respected by all threads. This locking mechanism is called *synchronization* and is triggered by the keyword `synchronized`. Individual blocks of code can be synchronized using the following syntax:

```
synchronized (object) {
  // code to be synchronized
}
```

where *object* is a reference to any object. Entire methods can be synchronized by using the `synchronized` keyword as a method modifier, for example,

```
public synchronized void myMethod() {
   // code to be synchronized
}
```

which is functionally equivalent to the following:

```
public void myMethod() {
   synchronized(this) {
      // code to be synchronized
   }
}
```

When a thread encounters a synchronized block, it first attempts to obtain the lock on the specified object. If the thread is successful, it executes the block and releases the lock. If the thread cannot obtain the lock, it waits until the lock is available, acquires the lock for itself, executes the block, and releases the lock. The Java virtual machine ensures these operations are performed by only one thread at a time.

In the invoice handling example, the duplicate invoice problem can be eliminated[5] by synchronizing the `handleInvoice()` method:

```
public synchronized void handleInvoice() throws IOException
{
   // Read the file, increment the invoice number,
   // and update the file.
   ...
}
```

5 Of course, synchronization does nothing to prevent some other Java class or some process running outside the Java virtual machine from updating the `invoice.dat` file. The example assumes you have exclusive control over the file.

For the sake of performance, it's important not to synchronize any more code than necessary because this forces threads to walk single file through the synchronized section. The entire `handleInvoice()` needn't be synchronized, just the code from where the file is opened for reading to where it's closed for writing.

# Servlet Threading Models

The servlet API takes advantage of Java's built-in support for multithreading to ensure responsive request handling and good throughput. In doing so, it offers some flexibility in how threads are used. The process whereby requests are dispatched to one or more threads is called the *servlet threading model*. You can choose from two models:

- Multiple threads running a single servlet instance, which is the *default threading model.*
- Multiple instances, each running in their own thread. This is referred to as the *single thread model.*

Let's consider the implications of operating in each model.

## Default Threading Model

In the default model, only a single instance of the servlet (or JSP) is loaded.[6] The servlet engine maintains a pool of threads, assigning them to requests as they arrive. Each thread runs the appropriate service method, typically doget() or dopost(). During periods of peak activity, many requests may be running simultaneously through the same servlet methods but, because each thread has its own instruction pointer and stack for local variables, no conflict occurs between requests. Figure 14-6 illustrates the default model, showing three requests being handled by three threads.

The default model provides good throughput, but some restrictions exist. Because there is only one servlet instance, only one copy of any instance variable exists. If no precautions are taken and the code allows the variables to be written, one thread can overwrite a value needed by another. In Figure 14-6, for example, Request 2 is running at the same time as both Request 1 and Request 3. If they are all in the `doGet()` method writing to an instance variable and, later, reading it, their writes and reads could possibly overlap. Also, if the `doGet()` or `doPost()` method calls subroutines, it must pass all necessary objects as parameters because it cannot rely on instance variables to retain their value from the time they are written until the time the subroutine reads them.

For this reason, avoid using instance variables, unless they are read-only. This may sound like a restriction, but it's simply a different point-of-view. The real unit of work,

6 Technically, one instance per servlet name. Several servlet names may be associated with the same servlet class in the `web.xml` deployment descriptor. See Chapter 18 for details.

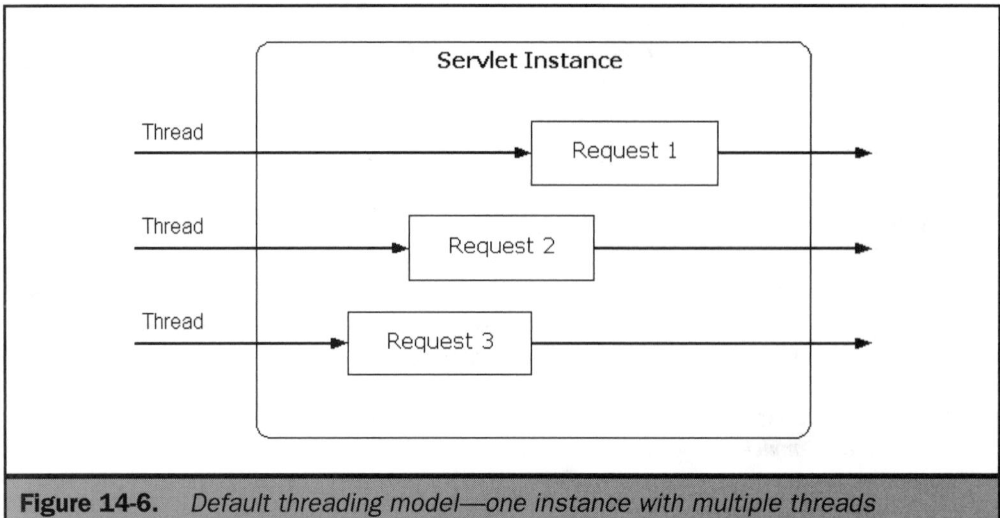


**Figure 14-6.** *Default threading model—one instance with multiple threads*

after all, is the request, not the servlet instance. Objects of any kind can be stored as request attributes in a completely thread-safe manner:

```
public void doGet(
      HttpServletRequest request,
      HttpServletResponse response)
   throws ServletException, IOException
{
   ...
   openConnection(request);
   runQuery(request);
   ...
}

public void openConnection(HttpServletRequest request)
   throws SQLException
{
   request.setAttribute
      ("connection", DriverManager.getConnection(...));
}
```

```
public void runQuery(HttpServletRequest request)
   throws SQLException
{
   Connection con = (Connection)
      request.getAttribute("connection");
   Statement stmt = con.createStatement();
   ResultSet rs = stmt.executeQuery("SELECT ...");
   request.setAttribute("resultSet", rs);
}
```

Likewise, you can synchronize critical sections of code in a servlet method, although care must be exercised to avoid synchronizing too much and adversely affecting performance.

## Single Threaded Model

The alternative to the default model is the single threaded model. In this environment, the servlet engine guarantees only one request at a time is running the service method of a servlet instance. To use this model, a servlet must implement the `SingleThreadModel` interface. No methods are in this interface; it simply marks the servlet as requiring this threading treatment. In a JSP page, this model is selected by means of the `page` directive:

```
<%@ page isThreadSafe="false" %>
```

This causes the generated servlet to specify it implements `SingleThreadModel`.

Only one thread at a time can execute the `doGet()` or `doPost()` method of a single threaded servlet, so this means instance variables are threadsafe. But the servlet engine is free to create as many instances of the servlet as it needs to maintain adequate performance. This mode of operation is illustrated in Figure 14-7, which shows Request 3 waiting until Request 1 is completely finished before it runs, but Request 2 running in a different instance at the same time as the others.

`SingleThreadModel` is the source of much confusion. You can find messages posted to Java newsgroups complaining that network or database connections aren't properly isolated, despite the fact that they're used in a servlet that implements `SingleThreadModel`. And it's easy to see why: the only thing that's made thread safe is the servlet instance itself. But, because multiple instances exist, external resources aren't protected from simultaneous access.

Finding any compelling advantages afforded by the single threaded model is difficult. Given a little planning and judicious synchronization, the default model is usually a better choice.

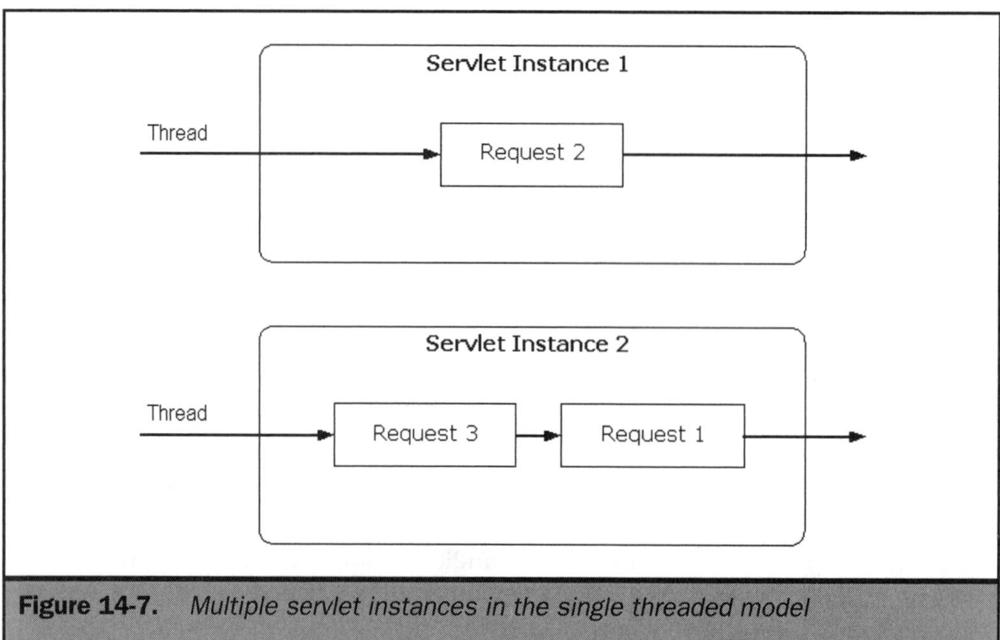


**Figure 14-7.** *Multiple servlet instances in the single threaded model*

## Multithreaded Applications

A number of server-side environments exist where multiple threads are particularly useful. One is running an automatically started background process, not attached to any specific request, similar to a Unix daemon or a Windows NT service. This can easily be done in a servlet environment, using the following technique:

1. Have the `init()` method start a thread that performs the desired task. This may consist of opening a socket to service requests or periodically reading a Web page for dynamically updated data, such as stock quotes or news headlines. Maintain a reference to the thread in the servlet context.
2. Use the `doGet()` method strictly for commands, administrative tasks, and status reporting. Providing a command that can shut down or restart the background thread is usually desirable.
3. In the `destroy()` method, close the thread after releasing any resources it's using.

The servlet (or JSP) can be designated as `load-on-startup` in the deployment descriptor, so it runs whenever the servlet engine is running, without requiring a user to be logged on. Because the servlet engine itself can typically be run as a daemon or service, this amounts to being able to write such processes as Java servlets.

Another beneficial use of multithreading is for handling long-running requests, such as complex data analysis or other project-like requests. If a client requests a server process that takes a considerable amount of time, both the client and the servlet engine simply wait until it finishes. This needn't be the case, though.

Consider how print spooling works. A user can click the Print button in a word processing application and experience only a slight pause while the print request is queued. Usually, some message about which printer has received the request appears and possibly a job ID identifying the print request. The spooled output then waits on a queue for the printer to become available, but the user is free to continue writing the document or to perform any other tasks. Those other tasks may include monitoring the print queue status, holding and releasing jobs, changing their priority, canceling them, and so forth.

A JSP page can operate similarly. Instead of running a complex task in the current thread, it can be run by launching a background thread, keeping a reference to the thread as a session attribute. The user can receive notification that the request has been queued and is being serviced. The JSP page may also provide displays that show the status of the request and enable the user to hold, release, or cancel it. When the request completes, the JSP page can provide a hyperlink that enables the results to be viewed. Extremely long-running requests handled by extremely clever JSP pages might even have their results e-mailed to the user.



## Long Running Requests with Status Messages

A variation on this technique can be used to provide the user with a status screen indicating the request is being processed, which is replaced by the results when the request is complete. The key to the technique is using a background session-scoped thread to do the work and using the `<META HTTP-EQUIV="REFRESH">` HTML tag to have the Web browser automatically monitor the status.

In the following example, the user is logging on and requesting authentication by means of time-consuming simulated database operation. While the authentication request is being processed, the user sees an "Authenticating, please wait..." message. When the request is complete, this message is replaced with the results of the authentication. Meanwhile, the servlet engine is free to handle other requests without waiting for the authentication request to complete.

The basic conversation between client and server in this session is as follows:

**Client:** Please authenticate me. UserID=MyUserID, password=MyPassword
**Server:** OK, call me back in two seconds for status.
**Client:** (*two seconds later*) Are you done?
**Server:** No, call me back in two seconds for status
**Client:** (*two seconds later*) Are you done?
**Server:** No, call me back in two seconds for status
**Client:** (*two seconds later*) Are you done?
**Server:** Yes, you are authenticated (*or not*).

The user needn't request the updated status manually. HTML provides a client-side automatic means of periodically updating a page:

```
<META HTTP-EQUIV="REFRESH" CONTENT="seconds; URL=url">
```

The presence of this <META> tag in an HTML document causes the browser to wait the specified number of seconds, and then redirect to the specified URL. This feature is commonly used to indicate a Web site has moved and the user is going to be automatically forwarded to the new address.

The following JSP implements this protocol using a background worker thread that simulates the database authentication delay.

```
<%--
   Authenticator.jsp

      A JSP page that displays status messages during a
      long-running request and does not tie up server
      resources waiting for the request to complete.
--%>
<%

   // See if there is an authentication worker thread running

   WorkerThread worker = (WorkerThread)
      session.getAttribute("worker");

   // If not, create a new one and start the authentication

   if (worker == null) {
      String userID = request.getParameter("userID");
      String password = request.getParameter("password");
      worker = new WorkerThread(userID, password);
      session.setAttribute("worker", worker);
   }

   // Now display either the "please wait" screen
   // or the "user authenticated" screen

   if (!worker.isDone()) {
      String url = HttpUtils.getRequestURL(request).toString();
      url = response.encodeURL(url);
%>
```

```
<HTML>
<HEAD>
<TITLE>Please Wait</TITLE>
<META HTTP-EQUIV="REFRESH" CONTENT="2; URL=<%= url %>">
</HEAD>
<BODY>
Authenticating, please wait...
</BODY>
</HTML>
<%
   }
   else {
%>
<HTML>
<HEAD><TITLE>Done</TITLE></HEAD>
<BODY>
Authentication complete.
<%= worker.isAuthenticated() ? " You pass!" : " You fail!" %>
</BODY>
</HTML>
<%
      // Done with worker

      session.invalidate();
   }
%>
<%!
/**
* A background thread that performs a potentially
* long-running task (authentication from a database).
*/
public class WorkerThread implements Runnable
{
   private boolean done;
   private boolean authenticated;
   private Thread kicker;

   public WorkerThread(String userID, String password)
   {
      done = false;
```

```
         authenticated = false;
         kicker = new Thread(this);
         kicker.start();
      }

      public boolean isDone()
      {
         return done;
      }

      public boolean isAuthenticated()
      {
         return authenticated;
      }

      public void run()
      {
         // Do the work here

         try {

            // Pretend to do something that takes five seconds

            for (int i = 0; i < 5; i++)
               Thread.sleep(1000);

            // Randomly authenticate 80% of all users

            authenticated = (Math.random() > 0.2);

            // We are done

            done = true;
         }
         catch (InterruptedException ignore) {}
         finally {
            kicker = null;
         }
      }
   }
%>
```

## Application Considerations

The JSP environment offers rich set of alternatives for mapping application characteristics to the HTTP environment. The main consideration is *object scope*, that is, the period of time during which an attribute is valid. The page context defines four scopes:

- page
- request
- session
- application

Each scope has its own lifecycle and attributes can be stored in any of them. Objects in a particular scope are accessible to both JSP pages and servlets in the same servlet context. The task of the developer is to choose the object scope that matches the object use requirements.

*Page scope* is equivalent to the lifetime of the `_jspService()` method in a single JSP page. A user ID string, for example, can be given this page scope as follows:

```
pageContext.setAttribute
   ("userID", userID, PageContext.PAGE_SCOPE);
```

or simply

```
pageContext.setAttribute("userID", userID);
```

Corresponding `getAttribute()` methods exist for retrieving the object.

Why bother storing objects in the page context with page scope when they are already accessible simply as Java variables? The main context for this is JSP custom tags, which use the page context to communicate between tag handlers and the JSP page. See Chapter 11 for details about JSP custom tags.

*Request scope* is almost the same as page scope, but it includes other JSP pages or servlets invoked by `<jsp:include>` or `<jsp:forward>`. Attributes can be set in the request directly

```
request.setAttribute("userID", userID);
```

or by means of the page context:

```
pageContext.setAttribute
   ("userID", userID, PageContext.REQUEST_SCOPE);
```

The effect of the two method calls is identical; the `pageContext.setAttribute()` method simply calls `request.setAttribute()`. Request scope is appropriate for objects associated with a single request, possibly set in a servlet and used in a JSP page to which a `RequestDispatcher` forwards the request.

*Session scope* is used by multiple requests that identify themselves with the same session ID and are associated with an active `HttpSession` with that ID. Attributes can be set in the `session` object directly

```
session.setAttribute("userID", userID);
```

or by means of the page context:

```
pageContext.setAttribute
   ("userID", userID, PageContext.SESSION_SCOPE);
```

Session scope is appropriate when all three of the following requirements are present:

- The application requires multiple HTTP requests
- Data needs to persist between requests
- One or more server-side objects must persist in a particular state across requests

As considered in this chapter, alternatives like hidden fields, URL rewriting, and cookies exist when HTTP sessions aren't required.

*Application scope* is the common namespace for all servlets and JSP pages in a Web application. It persists between requests automatically, no session is required. Static initialization parameters can be set in application scope by using `<context-param>` in the `web.xml` deployment descriptor:

```
<context-param>
   <param-name>jdbc.driver</param-name>
   <param-value>sun.jdbc.odbc.JdbcOdbcDriver</param-value>
</context-param>

<context-param>
   <param-name>jdbc.url</param-name>
   <param-value>jdbc:odbc:composers</param-value>
</context-param>
```

These static parameters can be retrieved in a servlet or JSP page with the servlet context `getInitParameter()` method:

```
String driver = application.getInitParameter("jdbc.driver");
String url = application.getInitParameter("jdbc.url");
```

Objects can be stored in and retrieved from application scope with the same methods as the other three scopes

```
pageContext.setAttribute
   ("userID", userID, PageContext.APPLICATION_SCOPE);
```

or

```
application.setAttribute("userID", userID);
```

Application scope is most useful for objects that need to persist between requests, for objects that must be visible to all users of the application, or for objects that need to be shared between other servlets and JSP pages.

## Summary

The Web application model doesn't automatically map into the HTTP protocol. HTTP is *stateless,* not remembering anything about the client from one request to the next. The Web browser environment also introduces complications—in an application, each page depends on its predecessors, but a user may browse pages out of order and leave an application without signaling she is done.

The solution to the problem is to have the client (browser) remember certain details and remind the server each time it makes a request. This can involve the client managing all the data but, in practice, it's more common to see the client remember only an identifier of some kind and have the server use that to retrieve the rest of the data from a database. This virtual conversation (virtual because no persistent connection is involved) is commonly called a *session.*

This chapter deals with four techniques for session management:

- **Hidden fields in HTML forms** These are simple to use, but can only be transmitted with an HTML form. If the user clicks a hyperlink, the hidden fields (and, therefore, the session) are lost.
- **URL rewriting** This involves appending the session identifier to all URLs generated by the JSP page. Performance-wise, this technique can be expensive.
- **Cookies** Small named data elements are sent to the client and returned to the server when the page is revisited. Cookies have the advantage that they can persist for an arbitrary length of time, even after the client computer is turned off. The disadvantage is some users turn off cookie support because of concerns for privacy.

- **The session API** The servlet engine can create an `HttpSession` object that acts as a repository for named objects that persist between requests from the same client in the same application. The client remembers the ID of the session either with cookies or URL rewriting. The servlet engine determines which of these techniques the client accepts and adjusts accordingly.

Sessions can be shut down programmatically or they can time out according to a configurable period of inactivity. The session API provides a means for objects to know when they have been bound or unbound from a session.

JSP pages, because they run in a pure Java environment, have full access to Java's support for multithreaded applications. This chapter discusses basic thread concepts, such as how to create, start, and synchronize them, and then considers the two servlet threading models. Two examples of Web applications using multiple threads are presented.

Even though dynamic content wasn't planned for in the original HTTP protocol, the protocol has proved to be quite capable of extension. Building on this flexibility, the session API provides the framework for making HTTP work in the Web application environment.

# Chapter 15

## JSP and JavaBeans

Great advances in hardware and electronics technology have been made possible by component engineering. Instead of starting with bare circuits, engineers can assemble tested modules in novel ways to create higher-level functionality. Component-based programming extends this idea to the realm of software. In the Java world, this means *JavaBeans*.

This chapter describes the JavaBeans programming model and how beans surface their properties to classes that use them. It explains the interface provided for using beans in a JSP page. The chapter concludes with a complete example illustrating the operation of a customizable weather-reporting bean in a JSP page.

## What Is a JavaBean?

The definition of a bean is purposely broad. A *bean* is simply a Java class that meets two requirements:

- It has a zero-argument constructor.
- It implements `Serializable` or `Externalizable` to make it persistent.

By this definition, most classes are already beans or can be converted with little effort. No required context for running beans exists other than the Java virtual machine. This allows properly constructed beans to be used in any Java environment—applets, servlets, JSP pages, or standalone Java applications.

### Bean Properties

In addition, most beans have properties. *Properties* are attributes of the bean for which the bean provides read and/or write methods. All access to the bean's properties must be done through these methods; the underlying data field (if there is one) is private. Part of the JavaBeans programming model is the naming convention used for these methods. Unless you make special provision through a `BeanInfo` class, the read method for a property is a public method named `get`*<PropertyName>*`()`, where *<PropertyName>* is the name of the property with the first letter converted to uppercase. Similarly, the write method, if there is one, is named `set`*<PropertyName>*`()`.

The following example is a JavaBean named `Mortgage`, which encapsulates the parameters that describe a mortgage loan:

```
package jspcr.beans.mortgage;

import java.io.*;

public class Mortgage implements Serializable
{
   private double principal;
```

```
private double rate;
private int term;

/**
* Returns the principal.
*/
public double getPrincipal()
{
   return principal;
}

/**
* Sets the principal.
* @param principal the principal.
*/
public void setPrincipal(double principal)
{
   this.principal = principal;
}

/**
* Returns the annual interest rate
*/
public double getRate()
{
   return rate;
}

/**
* Sets the interest rate.
* @param rate the annual interest rate as a percentage.
*/
public void setRate(double rate)
{
   this.rate = rate;
}

/**
* Returns the term in months.
*/
public int getTerm()
{
   return term;
```

```
    }

    /**
    * Sets the term.
    * @param term the term in months.
    */
    public void setTerm(int term)
    {
       this.term = term;
    }

    /**
    * Returns the amortization factor, the amount of the
    * monthly payment that will pay all principal and
    * interest within the specified period of time.
    */
    public double getPayment()
    {
       if (rate == 0)
          throw new IllegalArgumentException
          ("No interest rate specified");

       double mrate = rate / 1200.0;

       double fv = Math.pow((1 + mrate), term);
       double numer = principal * mrate * fv;
       double denom = fv - 1.0;
       return round(numer / denom);
    }

    /**
    * Utility method that rounds a currency amount to
    * the nearest 1/100 of the currency unit.
    */
    public static final double round(double x)
    {
       return ((double) ((long) (x * 100.0 + 0.5))) / 100.0;
    }
}
```

The `Mortgage` bean has four properties:

- **principal** The amount of money borrowed.
- **rate** The annual interest rate expressed as a percentage. For example, 6 percent would be entered as 6.0.
- **term** The number of months over which payments are to be made on the loan.
- **payment** A read-only property.

Notice private data fields exist for the first three properties, but not for the fourth, which is calculated on demand. This underscores that what counts is the existence of the get and set methods. These methods are the only face the bean shows to the outside world.

Classes interested in changes in a bean's state can implement one of the many `EventListener` interfaces. When a class is registered as an event listener, it receives callbacks when events of interest happen in the bean. This makes it possible for beans to act cooperatively to accomplish larger tasks. The AWT and Swing GUI architectures make extensive use of this event model. Beans used in server-side environments, however, tend to be used mainly as property repositories and don't typically implement support for event listeners.

## Persistence

That being the case, a bean must provide some way for its state to persist in between times in which it is active, even in different Java virtual machines. This is accomplished by having the bean implement either the `Serializable` or the `Externalizable` interface.

*Serialization* refers to the process of converting objects to a stream of bytes that can be stored in a file or transmitted across a network. The complementary process of reassembling the objects from the byte stream is called *deserialization*. The Java API provides `ObjectOutputStream` and `ObjectInputStream` classes designed for this purpose.

An object is serialized by being written to an `ObjectOutputStream` with the output stream's `writeObject()` method. For example, a program that contains a `Mortgage` bean can serialize it as follows:

```
OutputStream fileOut = new FileOutputStream("mortgage.ser");
ObjectOutputStream objOut = new ObjectOutputStream(fileOut);
objOut.writeObject(mortgageBean);
objOut.flush();
fileOut.close();
```

Later, this or any other program can reconstitute the `Mortgage` bean from the `mortgage.ser` file using the `readObject()` method of an `ObjectInputStream`:

```
InputStream fileIn = new FileInputStream("mortgage.ser");
ObjectInputStream objIn = new ObjectInputStream(fileIn);
```

```
Mortgage mortgageBean = null;
try {
   mortgageBean = (MortgageBean) objIn.readObject();
}
catch (ClassNotFoundException e) {
   // handle exception
}
```

In these two code snippets, only one object is being serialized, and it's being serialized to a file. Serializing multiple objects is just as easy; there are simply multiple calls to `objOut.writeObject()`. As long as the program that deserializes the object(s) knows the correct number of objects and their types, it can read them with multiple calls to `objIn.readObject()`. Similarly, the backing stream needn't be a file—it can be a socket, a byte array, or punched cards, if the virtual machine supports them.

Note: the `Mortgage` class needn't do anything special to be serialized; it only needs to implement the `Serializable` interface. Ordinarily, the servlet engine takes care of all the logic needed to store session and application beans when the servlet engine is terminated, and restoring them when it's restarted.

One exception exists, however. Not all objects are serializable. For example, a database connection cannot be put into suspended animation and reawakened later. Its very nature requires it to be in communication with a corresponding object in the database management system. Likewise, threads are tied to underlying operating system threads and cannot simply be dematerialized and rematerialized. In these cases, the object containing nonserializable objects must provide a means for them to be reconnected or restarted. Moreover, it must declare variable references to those objects with the keyword `transient` to prevent the normal serialization process from attempting to handle them.

A class that contains `transient` objects should restore them by providing a method with this signature:

```
private void readObject(ObjectInputStream in)
   throws IOException
```

In the `readObject()` method, the class should first call `defaultReadObject()` to restore the serializable data fields, and then perform whatever logic is necessary to initialize the transient fields. Typically, this restoration is done by calling another method, which can also be called from the constructor, to avoid duplicate code.

An example can help clarify this:

```
import java.io.*;
```

```
public class CounterBean implements Runnable, Serializable
{
   private transient Thread thread;
   private int count;

   /**
   * Creates a new CounterBean, initializes its count
   * to zero, and starts the counting thread
   */
   public CounterBean()
   {
      count = 0;
      start();
   }

   /**
   * Restores this CounterBean from an object stream
   * and restarts the thread
   */
   private void readObject(ObjectInputStream in)
      throws IOException
   {
      try {

         // Call this first to restore all the
         // non-transient fields

         in.defaultReadObject();
      }
      catch (ClassNotFoundException e) {
         throw new IOException(e.getMessage());
      }

      // Restart the thread

      start();
   }

   /**
```

```
    * Provides a means to shut down the thread
    */
    public void interrupt()
    {
       if (thread != null)
          thread.interrupt();
    }

    /**
    * Starts the counting thread. This method
    * is called both from the constructor when
    * the object is first created and from the
    * readObject method when the object is deserialized.
    */
    private void start()
    {
       if (thread == null) {
          thread = new Thread(this);
          thread.setPriority(Thread.MIN_PRIORITY);
          thread.start();
       }
    }

    /**
    * Increments and prints the value of the counter
    * every second.
    */
    public void run()
    {
       try {
          for (;;) {
             Thread.sleep(1000);
             count++;
             System.out.println(count);
          }
       }
       catch (InterruptedException e) {}
    }
}
```

The CounterBean class uses a background thread to print the value of a counter at one-second intervals. The class is serializable, but the thread isn't, so logic exists for restarting the thread when the class is deserialized. Note, the thread variable is declared with the transient keyword. The class has two entry points: its constructor and the readObject() method. Both entry points call start(), which creates and starts a thread to handle the counter logic. The thread continues to run until it's interrupted.

A program that uses this counter bean can invoke it by its constructor, serialize it, and then deserialize it with the thread apparently picking up where it left off:

```
import java.io.*;

/**
* A class that uses CounterBean. If a serialized
* version exists, it will deserialize that. Otherwise,
* it will create a new CounterBean.
*/
public class CBTest
{
   public static void main(String[] args)
      throws IOException, ClassNotFoundException
   {
      CounterBean bean = null;

      // If a serialized version exists, load it

      File file = new File("counter.ser");
      if (file.exists()) {
         System.out.println("Deserializing bean");
         FileInputStream fileIn = new FileInputStream(file);
         ObjectInputStream objIn = new ObjectInputStream(fileIn);
         bean = (CounterBean) objIn.readObject();
         objIn.close();
         fileIn.close();
      }

      // Otherwise, create a new bean

      else {
         System.out.println("Creating new bean");
```

```
            bean = new CounterBean();
         }

         // Let the bean run until the user presses the
         // enter key

         BufferedReader in =
            new BufferedReader(
            new InputStreamReader(
            System.in));

         System.out.println("Press Enter to terminate program");
         in.readLine();
         bean.interrupt();

         // Serialize the bean

         System.out.println("Serializing bean");
         FileOutputStream fileOut = new FileOutputStream(file);
         ObjectOutputStream objOut = new ObjectOutputStream(fileOut);
         objOut.writeObject(bean);
         objOut.flush();
         objOut.close();
         fileOut.close();
      }
   }
```

Instead of implementing `Serializable`, a bean may implement `Externalizable` for its persistence scheme. An `Externalizable` object handles its own reading and writing from object streams, using whatever format it chooses. It must provide `readExternal(ObjectInput)` and `writeExternal(ObjectOutput)` methods for this purpose. But, because `Serializable` objects can supply their own `readObject()` methods using any format desired, `Externalizable` offers few advantages and isn't widely used.

## JSP Actions

As you've seen, JavaBeans are also Java classes and, as such, can be created and manipulated in JSP pages using scriptlets, declarations, and expressions. The JSP specification provides special support for beans that makes them scriptable at a higher level, however. This support consists of three standard actions:

**`<jsp:useBean>`** For declaring, instantiating, and initializing beans

**`<jsp:setProperty>`** For setting bean properties

**`<jsp:getProperty>`** For retrieving bean property values

The following sections discuss each of these actions.

## <jsp:useBean>

A `<jsp:useBean>` tag creates or deserializes a bean and associates it with a scripting variable. The syntax is as follows:

```
<jsp:useBean id="name" scope="scope" typespec/>
```

or

```
<jsp:useBean id="name" scope="scope" typespec>
  <body>
</jsp:useBean>
```

where *name*, *scope*, and *typespec* are defined in the following.

### The <jsp:useBean> id Attribute

The *name* specified in the `id` attribute is an identifier used as the attribute name for the bean object in the specified scope and declared as a Java scripting variable in the JSP page. Because this value is a scripting variable, it is case-sensitive and must conform to Java naming rules for identifiers. This value is used in the `name` attribute of the `<jsp:setProperty>` and `<jsp:getProperty>` actions to indicate to which of possibly several beans the action applies.

### The <jsp:useBean> scope Attribute

*scope* designates the namespace in which the bean exists. These are the same scopes maintained by the `PageContext` object. Possible values are

- **`PAGE`** Valid for the duration of this JSP page. This is the default scope.
- **`REQUEST`** Valid for the remainder of the JSP page and for any other resources servicing this request through a `<jsp:forward>` or `<jsp:include>` action.

JSP IN ACTION

- **SESSION** Valid during the execution of any JSP page or servlet in this HTTP session.
- **APPLICATION** Valid in any JSP page or servlet in this Web application (servlet context).

Beans in any of these scopes can be accessed with the `getAttribute()` and `setAttribute()` methods of the `pageContext` variable. Beans in the `request`, `session`, or `application` namespaces can be accessed in servlets with the `getAttribute()` and `setAttribute()` methods of the `ServletRequest`, `HttpSession`, and `ServletContext` classes, respectively.

## The <jsp:useBean> type Specification

The type specification consists of some combination of the `class`, `type`, and `beanName` attributes. Combinations of these attributes allow flexibility in what the `useBean` action does. At least one of `class` and `type` must be specified, and `beanName` cannot be used if `class` is specified. This means the valid combinations are

- `type` only
- `class` only
- `type` and `class`
- `type` and `beanName`

The type specification allows new beans to be created, serialized beans to be reused, or existing beans to be incorporated into the JSP bean framework. Further capabilities arise from the fact that `<jsp:useBean>` can have a body of JSP code. The code in the body of the `<jsp:useBean>` tag (typically one or more `<jsp:setProperty>` actions and scriptlets) is only executed if the bean is newly instantiated in the current request.

The exact operation of the `<jsp:useBean>` tag is best explained graphically. The flowcharts in this section describe how the tag is evaluated in each of the four cases listed previously.

**Only type attribute Specified** A bean may implement several interfaces, with only one of them important to the operation of the bean in a given JSP page. The desired interface can be entered in the `type` attribute. When only the `type` is specified, the JSP engine defines a scripting variable of that type, and then looks in the specified scope for an attribute whose name matches the given `id`. If the JSP engine finds a matching object, it casts the object into the specified type and assigns it to the variable. Otherwise, if it cannot find the object, the JSP engine throws an `InstantiationException`. This process is illustrated in Figure 15-1.

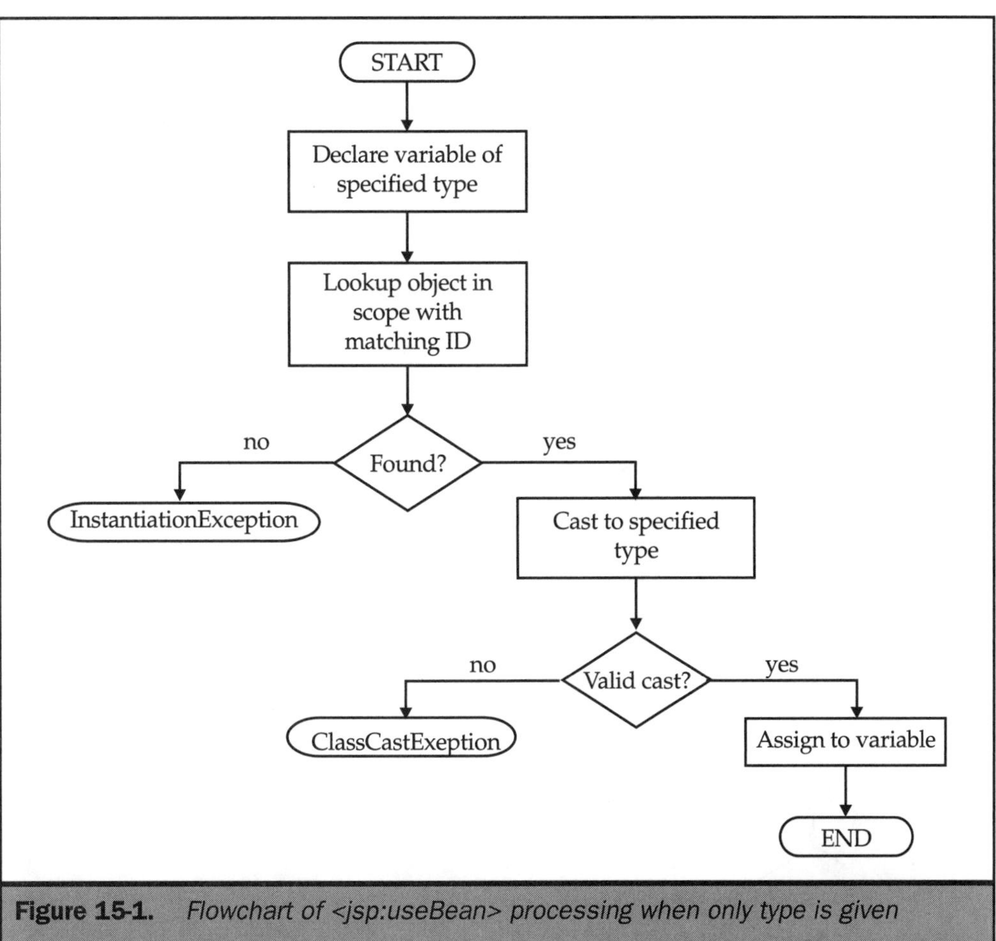


**Figure 15-1.** *Flowchart of <jsp:useBean> processing when only type is given*



**Only class attribute Specified** If a specific bean class is required, the class attribute should be specified. Again, the JSP engine declares a variable of the class and looks in the specified scope for an attribute with a matching name. If it finds one, the JSP engine casts the object into the specified class and assigns it to the variable. Otherwise, the JSP engine creates a new object of the specified class, assigns this to the variable, and sets it as an attribute in the scope. If the `<jsp:useBean>` tag has a body, the body is then evaluated. This process is shown in Figure 15-2.

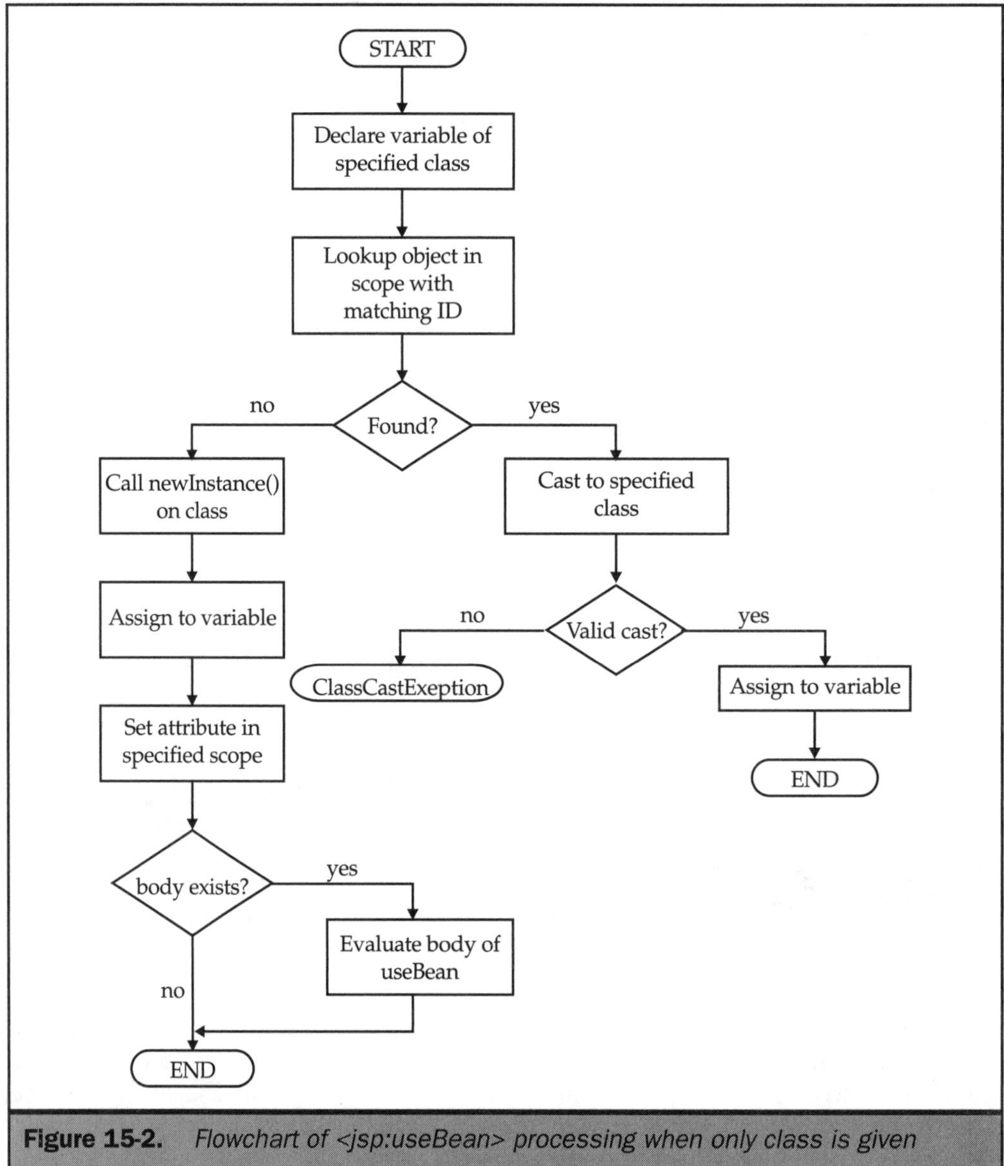


**Figure 15-2.** *Flowchart of <jsp:useBean> processing when only class is given*

**Both type and class Specified** A closely related situation is where a specific bean class is desired, but only a particular interface will be used. In this case, the processing is the same as the previous case, except the variable type and the casting operations use the type, not the class. Figure 15-3 shows the algorithm.

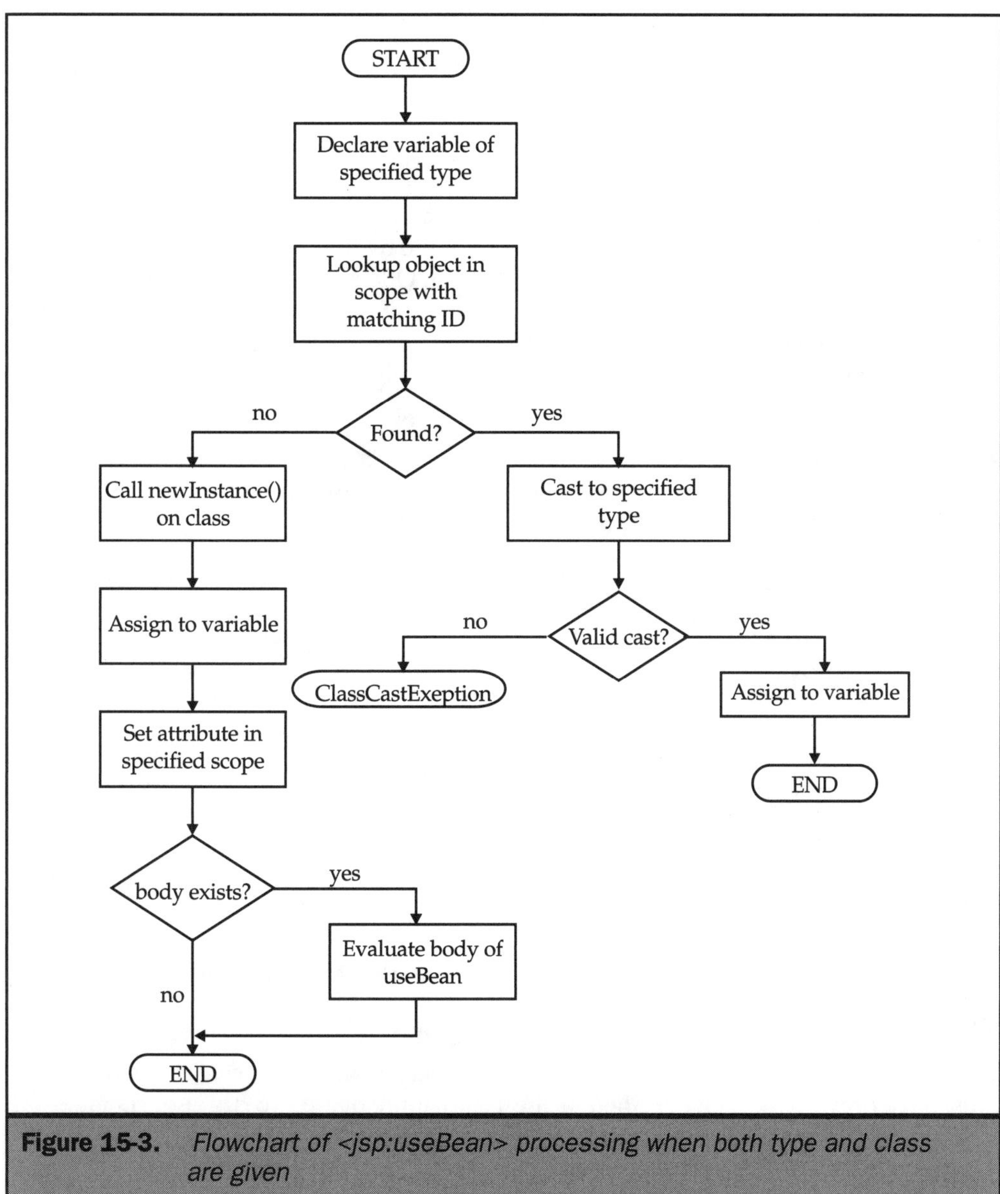


**Figure 15-3.** *Flowchart of <jsp:useBean> processing when both type and class are given*



**Type and beanName Specified** When an already serialized bean is to be imported into the JSP environment (such as the Mortgage or CounterBean beans described earlier in the chapter), the `type` and `beanName` attributes should be used. The `beanName` must be in the form used by `Beans.instantiate(ClassLoader loader, String name)`. The name is first converted to a filename, as follows:

- Periods are converted to "/"
- `.ser` is appended to the end

So, for example, `jspcr.beans.mortgage.Mortgage` is converted to `jspcr/beans/mortgage/Mortgage.ser`. If a file by that name can be found by the class loader, it's deserialized to obtain the object. Otherwise, the original name is treated as a class name and the class loader tries to create an instance of the named class. In either case, the new bean is assigned to a scripting variable of the specified `id` and stored as an attribute in the appropriate scope. The process is illustrated in Figure 15-4.

## <jsp:setProperty>

The `<jsp:setProperty>` action assigns values to bean properties based on values in the JSP page. The syntax can be any of the four following forms:

```
<jsp:setProperty name="name" property="property" value="value" />
```

or

```
<jsp:setProperty name="name" property="property" param="param" />
```

or

```
<jsp:setProperty name="name" property="property" />
```

or

```
<jsp:setProperty name="name" property="*" />
```

where *name*, *property*, *param*, and *value* are as described in the following sections.

### The <jsp:setProperty> name Attribute

The `name` attribute identifies the bean whose properties should be set. The name must have previously been specified as the `id` attribute of a `<jsp:useBean>` tag.

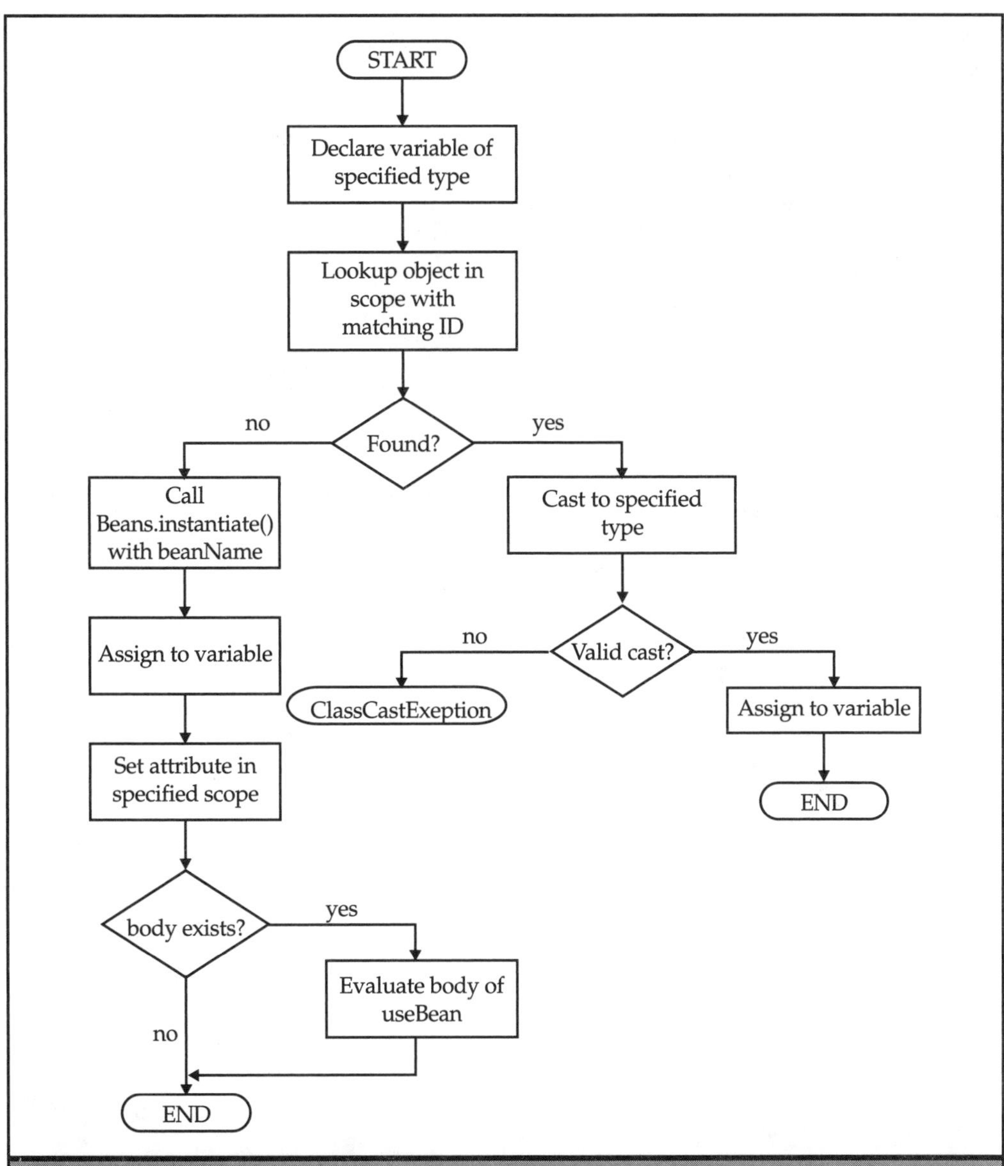


**Figure 15-4.** *Flowchart of <jsp:useBean> processing when type and beanName are specified*

## The <jsp:setProperty> property Attribute

Once the particular bean has been identified, the name of the property or properties to be set must be specified. This is the role of the `property` attribute. This attribute can be either a property name or the special value *. If this attribute is a name, then the bean must have a corresponding set method for that property. For example, in our `Mortgage` bean, `setPrincipal()`, `setRate()`, and `setTerm()` methods exist, which are used to set the `principal`, `rate`, and `term` properties, respectively.

If the property attribute is *, then the list of the bean's settable properties is compared with a list of parameters in the current request. Wherever a match occurs, the `set` method is invoked with the corresponding request parameter. So, for example, if an HTML form contains these fields

```
<FORM ACTION="DoMortgage.jsp">
Principal: <INPUT TYPE="TEXT" NAME="principal"><BR>
Annual Interest Rate: <INPUT TYPE="TEXT" NAME="rate"><BR>
Term in months: <INPUT TYPE="TEXT" NAME="term"><BR>
<INPUT TYPE="SUBMIT">
</FORM>
```

and `DoMortgage.jsp` has the following actions:

```
<jsp:useBean id="loan" class="jspcr.beans.mortgage.Mortgage">
<jsp:setProperty name="loan" property="*"/>
</jsp:useBean>
```

Then the `setProperty` line has the same effect as these lines

```
<jsp:setProperty
        name="loan"
        property="principal"
        value="<%= request.getParameter("principal") %>"/>

<jsp:setProperty
        name="loan"
        property="rate"
        value="<%= request.getParameter("rate") %>"/>

<jsp:setProperty
        name="loan"
```

```
        property="term"
        value="<%= request.getParameter("term") %>"/>
```

but with the benefit of requiring fewer lines of code and involving fewer chances for error.

This is also the effect achieved by specifying the property name, but no `value` or `param` attribute. In this case, the property value is assigned from the corresponding request parameter.

*If `property` attribute is *, or if neither `value` nor `param` is specified, and the request parameter is null or the empty string, then the corresponding bean property is not modified.*

## The <jsp:setProperty> param Attribute

Mapping request parameters to bean properties is possible when their names are different by using the `param` attribute in `<jsp:setProperty>`. If the `param` attribute is specified, the request parameter by that name is assigned to the property named in the `property` attribute[1].

## The <jsp:setProperty> value Attribute

The `value` attribute specifies the value to be assigned to the bean property. If the attribute is omitted, then the corresponding request parameter value is used, as previously described. Otherwise, the value can be specified as a string or as a JSP expression in the form `<%= expression %>`. The latter syntax is known as a *request time attribute expression.*

If the value is a literal string, then the bean property must have the `java.lang.String` type or it must be a primitive type (`boolean`, `byte`, `char`, `double`, `int`, `float`, `long`) or the corresponding object wrapper type (`Boolean`, `Byte`, `Char`, `Double`, `Integer`, `Float`, `Long`). The nonstring types are converted from string using the object wrapper `valueOf` methods. So, for example, the `Mortgage` property `rate`, with its setter method

```
public void setRate(double x)
{
   this.rate = x;
}
```

1 Normally, you have more latitude in assigning names to form variables than you do to bean properties because forms are rarely shared between applications. So why make it hard on yourself when you can simply use the same name in the form as you do in the bean?

JSP IN ACTION

can be invoked as follows:

```
<jsp:setProperty name="loan" property="rate" value="8.75"/>
```

The JSP translator then creates code to set the property like this:

```
loan.setRate(Double.valueOf("8.75").doubleValue());
```

If a request time expression is used to supply the value

```
<jsp:setProperty name="loan" property="rate"
   value="<%= LIBOR.getSixMonthLiborRate() + 0.05 %>"/>
```

then the JSP translator uses introspection to find the property type and casts the expression into that type:

```
loan.setRate((double) (LIBOR.getSixMonthLiborRate() + 0.05));
```

### <jsp:getProperty>

Bean property values can be retrieved with the `<jsp:getProperty>` action. This action has the form

```
<jsp:getProperty name="name" property="property" />
```

where *name* is the bean with the corresponding `id` attribute, and *property* is the name of the property desired. The property name must be a literal string, not a request time expression. When the `<jsp:getProperty>` tag is evaluated at run time, the value of the corresponding bean property is converted to a string and written to the JSP output stream.

## A Complete Example—Personalization with Beans

Let's put all these elements together and consider a complete example. Many portal Web sites customize the content and presentation of the page according to the user's preferences. This personalization may take the form of hyperlinks to products and information related to previous interests the user has expressed. MSNBC, for example, displays local weather and stock prices of the user's choice. The idea behind this is the user is less likely to leave the site to find this information if it's always there on the home page.

We (the LyricNote Web designers) have decided to add information like this to the home page. The first piece to be added is a line of local weather information, customized by the user to report the weather for the desired local area.

## Getting Weather Data from the Web

The first thing we need is a source of weather information. In the United States, this is readily available from the National Weather Service, an organization of the National Oceanic and Atmospheric Administration. Their Web pages provide weather data, forecasts, current conditions, weather maps, storm predication, and a wealth of other weather information. Although they are designed to be accessed through a Web browser by a human user, these Web pages can just as easily be read as a URL input stream by a Java program.

To do this, we create a weather `Observation` bean. `Observation` uses an airport code as the key to a National Weather Service Web site that reports current weather observations for that location. The bean has five properties, as listed in Table 15-1:

Most of these properties have only `get` methods because their values should be set internally as the bean parses the National Weather Service Web page. The only property that can be set is the airport code. Calling the `setAirportCode()` tells the bean to get the latest readings and update its other properties.

From the airport code, the bean constructs the URL to the specific Web page with that airport's weather readings. It then opens the URL input stream and parses the HTML that flies by for the specific properties it needs: location, time, and temperature.



| Property | Access | Description |
|---|---|---|
| airportCode | read/write | The three-character code for the airport at which the weather is measured. Setting this property instructs the bean to go to the weather Web site to get the latest readings. |
| URL | read-only | The URL for the National Weather Service Web page that contains this airport's readings. |
| location | read-only | The airport name. |
| time | read-only | The date and time of the observation. |
| temperature | read-only | The temperature in degrees Celsius. |

**Table 15-1.** *Properties of the Weather Observation Bean*

**Note** *This is the weak link in the chain. A Web page produced by an outside source is obviously subject to change, so whatever heuristics are used to parse it must be reviewed and updated periodically. This "Web mining" technique is most useful when it is based on internal Web sites for which the format is positively known. However, many governmental and commercial Web sites are computer-generated and present information in a fairly regular form.*

```
package jspcr.beans.weather;

import java.io.*;
import java.net.*;
import java.text.*;
import java.util.*;

/**
* A bean that extracts weather information from
* the U. S. National Weather Service web site
*/
public class Observation implements Serializable
{
   /**
   * The base URL for National Weather Service data
   */
   private static final String BASEURL =
      "http://weather.noaa.gov/weather/current";

   /**
   * Date format used for parsing observation time
   */
   private static final SimpleDateFormat DATEFMT =
      new SimpleDateFormat("MMM dd, yyyy - hh:mm aa zzz");

   /**
   * Airport code
   */
   private String airportCode;

   /**
   * Full name of location
   */
   private String location;
```

```
/**
* Time of observation
*/
private Date time;

/**
* Temperature in degrees Celsius
*/
private Double temperature;

// ==========================================
//    Bean accessor methods
// ==========================================

/**
* Returns the airport code
*/
public String getAirportCode()
{
   return airportCode;
}

/**
* Sets the airport code, which
* causes the bean to be reloaded.
* @param airportCode the airportCode.
*/
public void setAirportCode(String airportCode)
   throws IOException
{
   this.airportCode = airportCode;
   loadFromURL(getURL());
}

/**
* Returns the location.
*/
public String getLocation()
{
   return location;
}
```

```
/**
* Sets the location.
* @param location the location.
*/
protected void setLocation(String location)
{
   this.location = location;
}

/**
* Returns the time.
*/
public Date getTime()
{
   return time;
}

/**
* Sets the time.
* @param time the time.
*/
protected void setTime(Date time)
{
   this.time = time;
}

/**
* Returns the temperature.
*/
public double getTemperature()
{
   return (temperature == null)
            ? 0
            : temperature.doubleValue();
}

/**
* Sets the temperature.
* @param temperature the temperature.
*/
protected void setTemperature(double temperature)
{
```

```
      this.temperature = new Double(temperature);
   }

   /**
   * Returns the URL of the NWS web page that contains
   * current weather conditions at the airport
   */
   public URL getURL() throws MalformedURLException
   {
      StringBuffer sb = new StringBuffer();

      sb.append(BASEURL);
      sb.append("/K");
      sb.append(airportCode.toUpperCase());
      sb.append(".html");

      return new URL(sb.toString());
   }

   // ============================================
   //    Web page parsing routines
   // ============================================

   /**
   * Loads the weather data from a URL
   */
   protected void loadFromURL(URL url)
      throws IOException
   {
      load(url.openStream());
   }

   /**
   * Parses an HTML input stream to extract a weather
   * observation. Note that this uses heuristics to
   * determine where each data element can be found
   * in the HTML. As such, it is subject to change.
   */
   protected void load(InputStream stream) throws IOException
   {
      location = null;
      time = null;
```

```
      temperature = null;

      BufferedReader in =
         new BufferedReader(
         new InputStreamReader(stream));

      for (;;) {
         String line = in.readLine();
         if (line == null)
            break;

         if (location == null)
            parseLocation(line);
         if (time == null)
            parseTime(line);
         if (temperature == null)
            parseTemperature(line);
      }
      in.close();
   }

   /**
   * Searches the current line for the location
   */
   protected void parseLocation(String line)
   {
      final String TOKEN1 = "<TITLE>";
      final String TOKEN2 = "-";
      final String TOKEN3 = "</TITLE>";

      int p = line.indexOf(TOKEN1);
      if (p != -1) {
         p += TOKEN1.length();
         p = line.indexOf(TOKEN2, p);
         if (p != -1) {
            p += TOKEN2.length();
            int q = line.indexOf(TOKEN3);
            if (q != -1) {
               String token = line.substring(p, q).trim();
               StringTokenizer st =
                  new StringTokenizer(token, ",");
               token = st.nextToken();
               token = st.nextToken();
```

```
            setLocation(token);
         }
      }
   }
}

/**
* Searches the current line for the time
*/
protected void parseTime(String line)
{
   final String TOKEN1 = "<OPTION SELECTED>";
   final String TOKEN2 = "<OPTION>";

   int p = line.indexOf(TOKEN1);
   if (p != -1) {
      p += TOKEN1.length();
      int q = line.indexOf(TOKEN2, p);
      if (q != -1) {
         String token = line.substring(p, q).trim();
         Date date = DATEFMT.parse
            (token, new ParsePosition(0));
         if (date != null)
            setTime(date);
      }
   }
}

/**
* Searches the current line for the temperature
*/
protected void parseTemperature(String line)
{
   final String TOKEN1 = "(";
   final String TOKEN2 = "C)";

   int q = line.lastIndexOf(TOKEN2);
   if (q != -1) {
      int p = line.lastIndexOf(TOKEN1);
      if (p != -1) {
         p += TOKEN1.length();
         String token = line.substring(p, q).trim();
         try {
```

```
                setTemperature(Double.parseDouble(token));
            }
            catch (NumberFormatException e) {
                e.printStackTrace();
            }
        }
    }
}

}
```

The heart of the bean is the `load()` method, which parses the input stream looking for the location, time, and temperature. Figure 15-5 shows a typical National Weather Service Web page for weather conditions at the Raleigh-Durham International Airport in North Carolina.

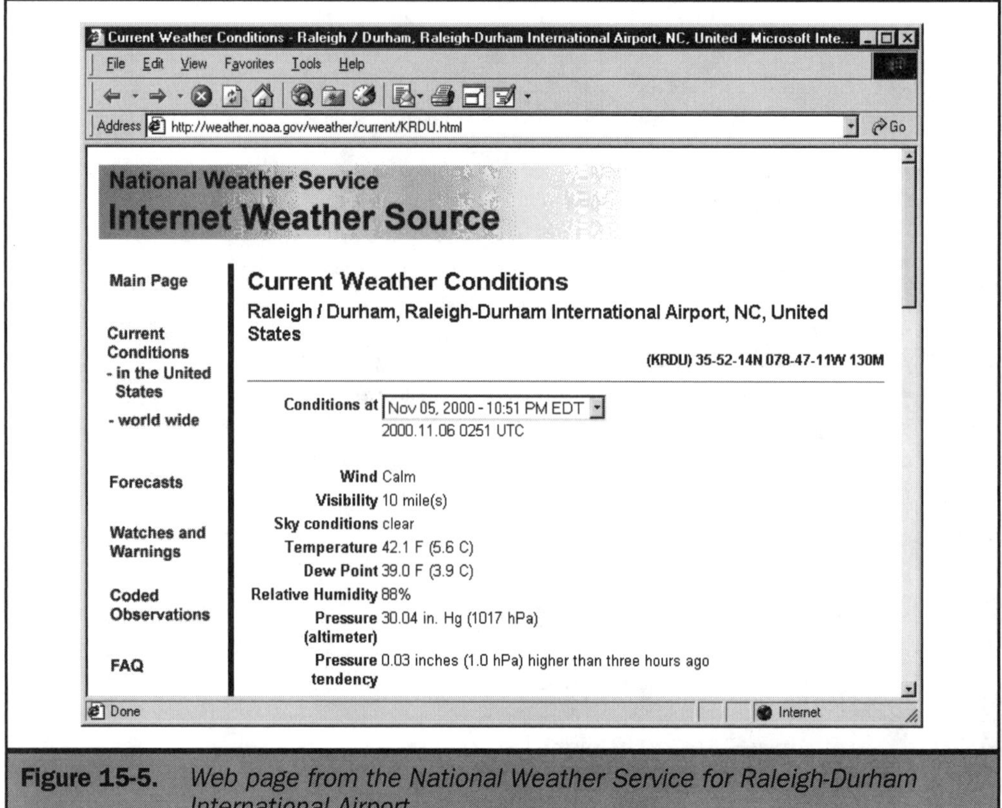


**Figure 15-5.** *Web page from the National Weather Service for Raleigh-Durham International Airport*

The HTML that produces the Web page contains all the information we need, if we can find reliable rules for extracting it. The `location` property turns out to be fairly simple because it's enclosed in the HTML `<TITLE> ...</TITLE>` tags:

```
<HTML>
<HEAD>
<TITLE>Current Weather Conditions - Raleigh / Durham,
Raleigh-Durham International Airport, NC,
United States </TITLE>
```

(The title is all on one line in the HTML; it is folded here for readability). The `parseLocation()` method tests the current line to see if it contains the `<TITLE>` and `</TITLE>` tokens. If so, the text between the tokens is extracted and the second comma-delimited field is used as the location name.

The `time` property is located between the only pair of `<OPTION SELECTED>` and `<OPTION>` tags in the document:

```
<TD><FONT FACE="Arial,Helvetica"><FORM>
<SELECT><OPTION SELECTED> Nov 05, 2000 - 10:51 PM EDT
<OPTION> Nov 05, 2000 - 09:51 PM CDT
<OPTION> Nov 05, 2000 - 08:51 PM MDT
<OPTION> Nov 05, 2000 - 07:51 PM PDT
<OPTION> Nov 05, 2000 - 06:51 PM ADT
<OPTION> Nov 05, 2000 - 05:51 PM HDT
</SELECT><BR> 2000.11.06 0251 UTC
</FORM></FONT></TD>
```

(Again, the HTML has been wrapped for readability. The original HTML is all on one line.) We use the `parse()` method in `SimpleDateFormat` to convert the date and time into a `java.util.Date`.

The `temperature` property occurs in the Web page in this form:

```
<TR VALIGN=TOP>
<TD ALIGN=RIGHT BGCOLOR="#FFFFFF"><B><FONT COLOR="#0000A0">
<FONT FACE="Arial,Helvetica">Temperature</FONT></FONT></B></TD>
<TD><FONT FACE="Arial,Helvetica">  42.1 F (5.6 C)
</FONT></TD>
</TR>
```

This property is slightly more difficult to isolate because the keyword `Temperature` appears on the previous line. We take a simpler approach, looking for the first line ending in `(...C)` and parsing the string between the parentheses for the degrees Celsius.

The rest of the class consists mainly of the appropriate get and set methods for each of the properties.

## The LyricNote Portal

Now we have a bean that hides all the messy details of finding Web pages and parsing HTML, and simply presents a means of getting current weather conditions given an airport code. The bean reduces the process to the complexity of a function call, hardly more difficult than finding the cosine of an angle by calling `Math.cos()`. We can now put this bean to work in our portal Web page.

Our strategy is now to record the user's location preference (airport code) with a persistent cookie. Each time the Web page is displayed, the airport code is retrieved from the cookie and is used to initialize an `Observation` bean. The resulting location, time, and temperature are displayed unobtrusively on a line under the logo at the top of the page. In addition, the line contains a hyperlink that enables the user to select a new airport code. The following shows a portion of the portal JSP:

```
<%@ page session="false" %>
<HTML>
<HEAD>
<TITLE>LyricNote Portal</TITLE>
<LINK REL="stylesheet" HREF="style.css">
</HEAD>
<BODY>
<IMG SRC="images/lyric_note.png">
<HR COLOR="#000000">

<%-- Get weather cookie --%>

<%
   String airportCode = "RDU";
   Cookie[] cookies = request.getCookies();
   if (cookies != null) {
      for (int i = 0; i < cookies.length; i++) {
         Cookie cookie = cookies[i];
         if (cookie.getName().equals("airportCode")) {
            airportCode = cookie.getValue();
            break;
         }
      }
   }
```

```
%>

<%-- Get the weather observation bean for that location --%>

<jsp:useBean id="wobs" class="jspcr.beans.weather.Observation">
<jsp:setProperty
   name="wobs"
   property="airportCode"
   value="<%= airportCode %>"/>
</jsp:useBean>

<%-- Show weather information --%>

<SPAN CLASS="whiteOnBlue"> Weather </SPAN>
<SPAN CLASS="blueOnWhite">
<jsp:getProperty name="wobs" property="location"/>
<jsp:getProperty name="wobs" property="time"/>
<jsp:getProperty name="wobs" property="temperature"/> C&deg;
</SPAN>
<A CLASS="whiteOnBlue" HREF="AirportSelection.html">
 Select City 
</A>
<HR COLOR="#000000">

<%-- Show the rest of the web page --%>

</BODY>
</HTML>
```



The array of cookies returned with the HTTP request is scanned for a cookie whose name is `airportCode`. If this cookie exists, its value is substituted for the default airport code (RDU, for Raleigh/Durham North Carolina). Next, the `Observation` bean is declared

```
<jsp:useBean id="wobs" class="jspcr.beans.weather.Observation">
```

and initialized with the selected airport code:

```
<jsp:setProperty
   name="wobs"
```

```
    property="airportCode"
    value="<%= airportCode %>"/>
```

All that remains is to extract the bean properties and to write them to the output stream:

```
<jsp:getProperty name="wobs" property="location"/>
<jsp:getProperty name="wobs" property="time"/>
<jsp:getProperty name="wobs" property="temperature"/> C&deg;
```

Figure 15-6 shows the resulting display.

If the user clicks the `Select City` hyperlink, a list of airports for which weather data is known to be available is presented, as seen in Figure 15-7. This isn't a JSP page, only a simple HTML form that invokes the proper cookie-setting JSP.

The form `action` attribute points to `SetAirportCode.jsp`, which is a nonvisual JSP page that sends the new airport code cookie to the user and redirects back to the portal page, as shown in the following code.

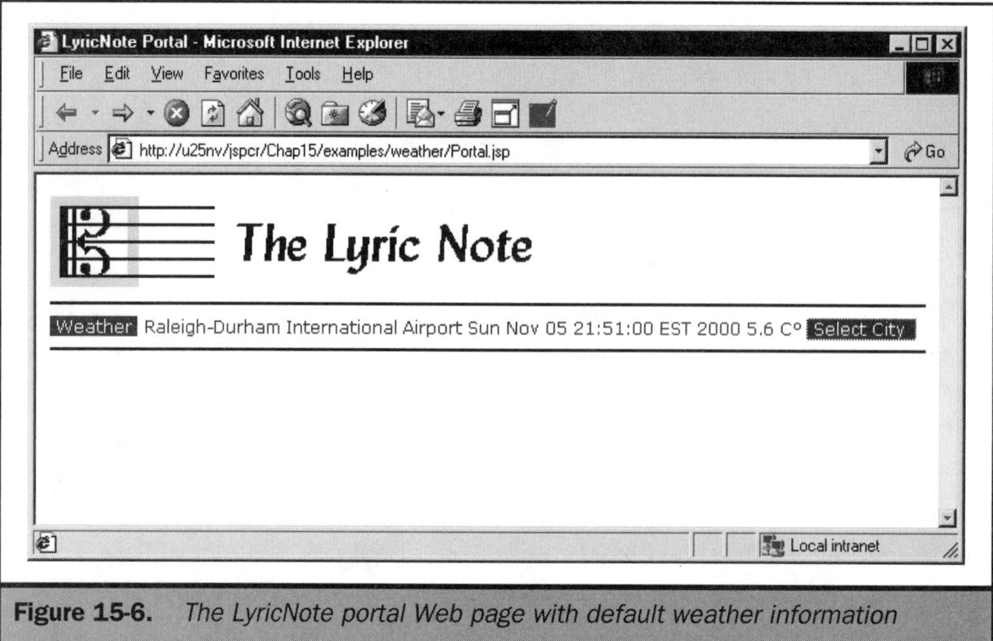


**Figure 15-6.** *The LyricNote portal Web page with default weather information*

```
<%@ page session="false" %>
<%
   String airportCode = request.getParameter("airportCode");
   if (airportCode != null) {
      Cookie cookie = new Cookie("airportCode", airportCode);
      final int ONE_YEAR = 60 * 60 * 24 * 365;
      cookie.setMaxAge(ONE_YEAR);
      response.addCookie(cookie);
   }
   response.sendRedirect("Portal.jsp");
%>
```

If the Web user happens to be located in Roswell, New Mexico (or interested in weather conditions for landing there), and chooses the appropriate line in the airport selection box, the airport code cookie value is set to `ROW`. All subsequent requests through the LyricNote portal cause the `Observation` bean to retrieve weather conditions at Roswell Industrial Air Center Airport (see Figure 15-8).



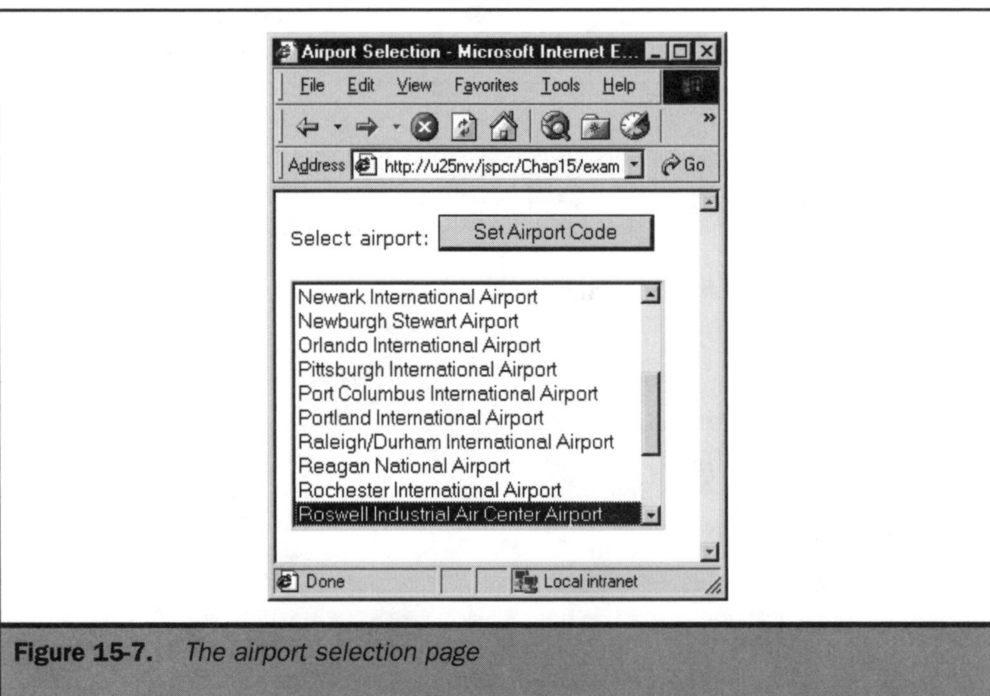


**Figure 15-7.** *The airport selection page*

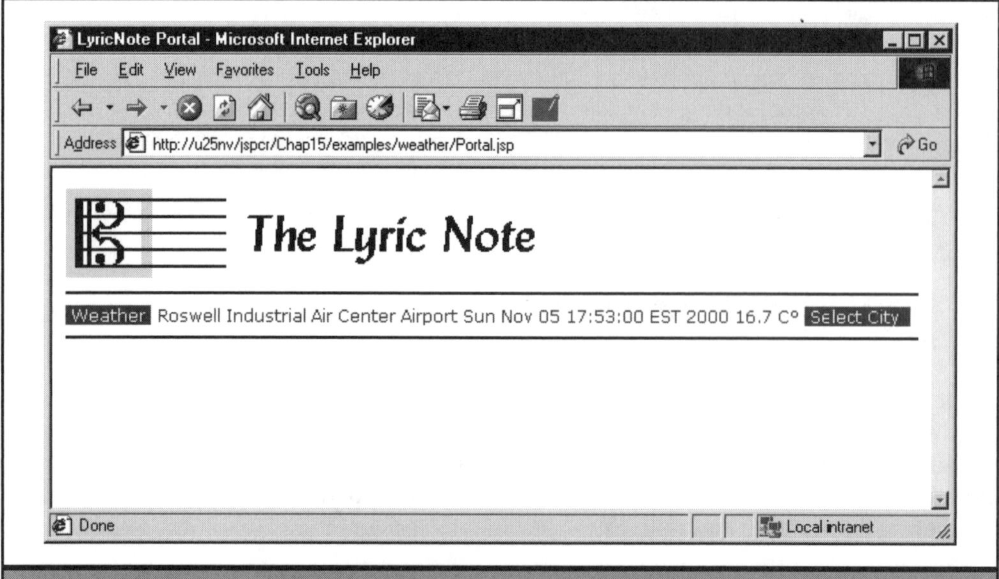


**Figure 15-8.** *The LyricNote portal Web page with updated weather information*

## Summary

Component-based programming in the Java architecture uses JavaBeans. The beans programming model uses public `get` and `set` methods to access private bean properties, event listeners to link other classes to the state of a bean, and serialization to make beans persistent.

The JSP programming environment provides standard tags for declaring and accessing beans:

- `<jsp:useBean>`
- `<jsp:setProperty>`
- `<jsp:getProperty>`

The `useBean` tag can declare, instantiate, and initialize a bean. This tag has a variety of attribute combinations that enable the bean to be extracted from an existing namespace, created as a new instance, or restored from a serialized object. The namespaces supported are page scope, request scope, session scope, or application scope.

`setProperty` and `getProperty` are used to store and retrieve properties from a bean. In addition to literal string values, properties can be set from both form parameters and request time expressions.

JavaBeans offer significant advantages in the JSP environment. They can be written and tested in isolation, and then reused in applet, servlet, and standalone application contexts. JavaBeans also reduce the amount of Java code exposed in JSP scriptlets and declarations. In conjunction with cookies, custom tags, and other advanced JSP techniques, JavaBeans provide a reliable, productive base for developing useful Web applications.

# Chapter 16

## JSP and XML

Since its origin in the World Wide Web Consortium (W3C) in 1996 and its adoption as a W3C recommendation in 1998, the *Extensible Markup Language* (*XML*) has established itself as the universal language for structured data storage and interchange. XML is used for Web site content management, business to business data exchange, and applications as diverse as architecture, financial reporting, and music. In addition to applications, XML tools and extensions are finding their way into all aspects of programming.

This chapter examines some ways in which XML can be incorporated into Web applications. After an overview section, it discusses the two XML parser models, and then XSL transformations. All three technologies are illustrated in three solutions to the same HTML creation task.

## XML Overview

XML is a system of describing structured data with a user-defined set of markup tags. XML isn't a language itself, but a system of defining special-purpose languages. It looks superficially like HTML, which marks sections of a Web document with predefined `<UL>`, `<LI>`, `<TABLE>`, and other tags. The difference is HTML has a fixed set of tags, whereas XML enables you to design any set of tags necessary to describe your data.

For example, a song for voice and piano might be represented in part like this:

```
<?xml version="1.0"?>
<song>
   <title>The Birds</title>
   <words-by>Hilaire Belloc</words-by>
   <music-by>Benjamin Britten</music-by>

   <track name="Voices">
      <time-signature>2/2</time-signature>
      <tempo>Andante con moto</tempo>
      <measure>
         <rest duration="1"/>
      </measure>
      <measure>...</measure>
   </track>

   <track name="Piano">
      <time-signature>2/2</time-signature>
      <tempo>Andante con moto</tempo>
      <measure>
         <note duration="8" value="e" octave="2"/>
         <note duration="8" value="g#" octave="2"/>
```

```
            <note duration="8" value="c#" octave="3"/>
            <note duration="8" value="g#" octave="3"/>
            <note duration="2" value="f#" octave="3"/>
        </measure>
        <measure>...</measure>
    </track>
</song>
```

Note, this representation of the song is entirely structural—it has nothing to do with how the song will appear. Indeed, the same XML document might be used for generating the printed sheet music and for synthesizing the tones in a MIDI player.

## The Problem XML Solves

Earlier text-processing formats often didn't distinguish between content and presentation. RTF, for example, has codes for structural data like tables and lists, as well as for fonts and graphics. HTML suffers from the same problem. Elements like `<table>`, `<tr>`, and `<td>` with specific width and height attributes are commonly used to influence physical layout in a Web page, rather than for grouping related items in tabular format.

The problem with this approach is, as new output formats are needed, the formatting information contained in the document becomes useless. And, worse, tags originally designed to convey structural information are misused, simply for their side effects, such as using `<UL>` to cause indentation.

XML, by contrast, focuses entirely on structure. Specific data elements can be clearly identified and extracted by text search applications. If an XML document needs to be rendered on a Web browser, it can be programmatically converted to HTML using an XSL style sheet. If the document needs to be used in a transaction processing system, it can be parsed by an XML parser, which extracts the specific fields that make up the transaction. The XML document can be browsed as a tree structure or collapsed into relational database tables. So long as the application using the document knows the language in which it's written, the application can find and extract the data it needs.



## XML Syntax

XML is simple, and the rules governing its syntax are easy to learn. An XML document consists of elements, each of which has a start tag, a body, and an end tag, as the following illustrates:

```
<tempo>Andante con moto</tempo>
```

The *start tag* <tempo> consists of a tag name enclosed in the less-than and greater-than characters. The *end tag* </tempo> is the same as the start tag, but with a forward slash following the opening greater-than character. The *body* consists of everything between the start tag and the end tag. This may include ordinary text or other XML elements.

A start tag may include *attributes*, which are name="*value*" pairs coded inside the start tag after the name, but before the closing greater-than character:

```
<track name="voices"> ... </track>
```

Attributes in XML *must* be enclosed in single or double quotes.

If the body of an element is empty, an abbreviated form of the start and end tags can be used. In this form, the forward slash from the end tag is moved into the start tag just before the closing greater-than character, and then the body and end tags are omitted. Therefore, the following two forms are functionally equivalent:

```
<rest duration="1"></rest>
<rest duration="1"/>
```

Elements can be nested inside each other to any depth

```
<song>
   <track>
      <measure>...</measure>
   </track>
</song>
```

but their end tags must appear in the exact opposite order in which the start tags appear. That is, elements cannot overlap. The following is illegal:

```
<B><I>Do not do this!</B></I>
```

A well-formed XML document, therefore, consists of exactly one outer element, called the *document element*, which may contain any number of properly nested inner elements.

For complete details on XML syntax, consult the XML 1.0 specification, second edition, found in the W3C Recommendation of October 6, 2000. This document can be found at http://www.w3.org/TR/REC-xml.

## The Document Type Definition

XML isn't just a free-form group of tags, however. Clearly, applications that use an XML document for input need to know what elements it can contain, how these elements can be nested or repeated, what attributes are allowed, and so on. Likewise, applications that generate XML documents (as well as humans composing documents with a text editor) need to know the same structural information. This is the role of the *document type definition* (*DTD*).

A DTD is the definition of the tags and attributes allowed in a specific document type. For example, a DTD for memo documents might define the <memo>, <from>, <to>, <subject>, <text>, and <paragraph> tags, indicate <paragraph> elements can only appear inside <text> elements, and <from> and <to> are required, while the rest are optional. Then applications that generate memo documents can ensure they only generate syntactically correct versions. Likewise, validation tools can read human-generated memo documents and determine whether they adhere to the syntax. This means applications on the receiving end can be relied on to understand the document and process it correctly.

An XML document indicates the DTD it uses and where to find it with a <!DOCTYPE> tag immediately before the document element:

```
<?xml version="1.0"?>
<!DOCTYPE song SYSTEM "song.dtd">
<song>
...
</song>
```

The DTD can also be embedded in the document itself

```
<?xml version="1.0"?>
<!DOCTYPE song [
...
]>
<song>
...
</song>
```

or it can be kept in a public repository:

```
<?xml version="1.0"?>
<!DOCTYPE song PUBLIC publicid URL>
<song>
...
</song>
```

A DTD isn't required but, if present, the document must adhere to it. In the language of the XML specification, a document is said to be *well formed*, if it adheres to the syntactical rules (all elements closed, no nested elements, all attributes in quotes). If the document has a DTD, it is said to be *valid*, if it is well formed and adheres to the DTD.

The DTD for our song document type looks like this:

```
<!ELEMENT   song      (title?,words-by?,music-by?,track+)>
<!ELEMENT   title     (#PCDATA)>
<!ELEMENT   words-by  (#PCDATA)>
<!ELEMENT   music-by  (#PCDATA)>
<!ELEMENT   track     (time-signature|tempo|measure)*>
<!ATTLIST   track
   name     CDATA     #IMPLIED>
<!ELEMENT   time-signature (#PCDATA)>
<!ELEMENT   tempo     (#PCDATA)>
<!ELEMENT   measure   (note|rest)+>
<!ELEMENT   note      EMPTY>
<!ATTLIST   note
   duration CDATA     #IMPLIED
   value    CDATA     #IMPLIED
   octave   (1|2|3|4|5|6|7|8) #REQUIRED>
<!ELEMENT   rest      EMPTY>
<!ATTLIST   rest
   duration CDATA     #IMPLIED>
```

A DTD consists of a list of elements and attributes. Each element definition gives the element name followed by a rigorous description of the elements it can contain, their order, whether they are required, and whether they can be repeated. This description may take several forms:

- Ordinary text is indicated as (#PCDATA), for *parsed character data.*
- Allowable subelements are listed in order, separated by commas.
- Mutually exclusive elements are separated by the logical OR symbol |.
- Subelements and parenthesized lists of subelements can be followed by a repetition count: ? meaning zero or one occurrences, * for zero or more, and + for one or more.
- Elements that cannot contain a body are described as EMPTY.

For example, the <song> element is allowed to contain the optional <title>, <words-by>, and <music-by> elements, followed by one or more <track> elements:

```
<!ELEMENT   song      (title?,words-by?,music-by?,track+)>
```

Note, the subelements, if present, must occur only in the order specified. The <measure> element is defined as containing at least one <note> or <rest> element, followed by any number of repetitions of <note> or <rest>:

```
<!ELEMENT   measure   (note|rest)+>
```

and the <time-signature> element may contain only ordinary text:

```
<!ELEMENT   tempo     (#PCDATA)>
```

The attributes an element can have are listed in an <!ATTLIST> tag containing the element name, followed by groups of three tokens for each attribute, designating the attribute name, type, and default value. For example, the <note> element is described in the following as having optional duration and value attributes, as well as a required octave attribute that can take integer values from 1 to 8:

```
<!ATTLIST   note
   duration CDATA     #IMPLIED
   value    CDATA     #IMPLIED
   octave   (1|2|3|4|5|6|7|8) #REQUIRED>
```

If the DTD syntax looks intimidating, don't worry. Unless you're a document definition specialist, you'll rarely be called on to write one. The informal description given in this section is intended to give you the basic ability to read a DTD. For a rigorous definition, consult the XML specification.

*The ability to read a DTD is useful in understanding the web.xml deployment descriptor. The structure and content of web.xml is defined in the web-app_2_2.dtd (or later versions) listed in the Servlet API specification. If you need to know where to define initialization parameters for a servlet, for example, the DTD shows they must be coded in the <servlet> block, just after <servlet-class> and before <load-on-startup>.*

## XML Parsers

To use an XML document in an application, you need to parse it. An XML *parser* reads a document and separates it into start tags, attributes, body contents, and end tags. The parser has an application programming interface that enables you to extract the elements you need without the complexity of interpreting the input stream yourself.

Two generally accepted XML parser models exist:

- **DOM** Document Object Model
- **SAX** Simple API for XML

The following sections consider each of these models.

# Document Object Model (DOM)

The *Document Object Model* (*DOM*) is the W3C standard representation of a document in memory. Rather than just strings of text, DOM represents a document as a tree of nodes. The tree can be traversed in any order, nodes can be added and deleted, and the modified DOM tree can be saved as a new document.

The DOM specification has different versions, referred to as *levels*. *DOM Level 1* was the core feature set, providing the means for creating and accessing document elements. *DOM Level 2*, which was approved as a W3C recommendation on November 13, 2000, adds support for namespaces.

DOM isn't just a standard, but an *Application Programming Interface* (*API*) as well. The W3C publishes a list of interfaces that comprise the `org.w3c.dom` package. Different vendors, then, supply parsers that implement these interfaces. Popular DOM parsers include Xerces, from the Apache Software Foundation, and JAXP, from Sun Microsystems.

The DOM API consists of four categories of classes and interfaces:

- Nodes
- Node collections
- Metadata
- Exceptions

## Node Interfaces

The basic unit of interest in DOM is the *node*. Everything in an XML document—individual elements, attributes in a start tag, comments, element text, and the document as a whole—are all nodes. Table 16-1 lists the methods in the `Node` interface.

| Method | Description |
|---|---|
| `Node appendChild(Node newChild) throws DOMException` | Adds a new child node to the current node. |
| `Node cloneNode(boolean deep)` | Makes a copy of the node. If `deep` is true, recursively clones all subtrees under this node. Otherwise, clones the current node. |
| `NamedNodeMap getAttributes()` | Returns the named attributes of this node, if the node is an `Element`. Otherwise, returns `null`. |

**Table 16-1.** *Methods in the Node Interface*

| Method | Description |
|---|---|
| NodeList getChildNodes() | Returns the list of all immediate child nodes. |
| Node getFirstChild() | Returns the first child node, or null, if this node isn't an Element. |
| Node getLastChild() | Returns the last child node, or null, if this node isn't an Element. |
| Node getNextSibling() | Returns the next child of the same parent, or null, if the parent node isn't an Element. |
| String getNodeName() | Returns the name of the node, for named nodes types like Element, Attr, and Entity. For unnamed types like Text, CDATAsection, and Comment, returns #text, #cdata-section, and #comment, respectively. |
| int getNodeType() | Returns an integer constant that indicates this node's specific type. The value returned is one of the following constants defined in the Node interface:<br>ATTRIBUTE_NODE<br>CDATA_SECTION_NODE<br>COMMENT_NODE<br>DOCUMENT_FRAGMENT_NODE<br>DOCUMENT_NODE<br>DOCUMENT_TYPE_NODE<br>ELEMENT_NODE<br>ENTITY_NODE<br>ENTITY_REFERENCE_NODE<br>NOTATION_NODE<br>PROCESSING_INSTRUCTION_NODE<br>TEXT_NODE |

**Table 16-1.** *Methods in the Node Interface* (continued)

| Method | Description |
| --- | --- |
| `String getNodeValue()` | For attributes and text-type nodes, returns the text, otherwise `null`. |
| `Document getOwnerDocument()` | Returns the `Document` node for the document in which this node occurs. |
| `Node getParentNode()` | Returns the immediate parent node, or `null`, if this is a `Document`, `DocumentFragment`, or `Attr` node. New nodes that haven't yet been added to a document may also have a `null` parent node. |
| `Node getPreviousSibling()` | Returns the previous child of the same parent, or `null`, if the parent node isn't an `Element`. |
| `boolean hasChildNodes()` | Returns `true` if this node has a nonempty list of child nodes. |
| `Node insertBefore(Node child, Node beforeNode)` | Inserts a new child node before the specified node. `beforeNode` may be null, in which case the child node is appended to the end of the list. |
| `Node removeChild(Node child) throws DOMException` | Removes the specified node from the list of child nodes. Throws an exception if the node isn't a child of the current node. |
| `Node replaceChild(Node newChild, Node oldChild) throws DOMException` | Removes `oldChild` and replaces it with `newChild`. Throws an exception if the node isn't a child of the current node. |
| `void setNodeValue(String value) throws DOMException` | Sets the value of the current node. |

**Table 16-1.** *Methods in the Node Interface* (continued)

In DOM Level 2, Node has two new methods—isSupported() and hasAttributes()—and now contains the normalize() method, which was previously part of the Element interface.

Node has 13 specialized subinterfaces that correspond to particular nodes types, which can appear in an XML document. These interfaces are listed in Table 16-2.

| Interface | Description |
|---|---|
| Attr | An attribute of an Element node. Attr has methods for retrieving the name and value of the attribute. In DOM Level 2, the Attr interface includes a getOwnerElement() method. |
| CDATASection | A text node enclosed with the <![CDATA[ ... ]]> escape syntax in the XML document. CDATA sections are parsed verbatim without being evaluated. They allow document content to contain characters and strings that, otherwise, would be interpreted as XML. |
| CharacterData | A common superinterface for the three text-containing node types: Text, Comment, and CDATASection. Provides methods for getting and setting the character contents, as well as determining the length of the data. |
| Comment | A node containing an XML comment. The Comment value doesn't include the <!-- and --> delimiters, only the text of the comment, including whitespace. |
| Document | The Document node represents the XML document as a whole. Only one Document node is in a DOM instance. DOM Level 2 adds support for namespaces to the Document interface. |

**Table 16-2.** *Subinterfaces of Node for Specific Node Types*

| Interface | Description |
|---|---|
| `DocumentFragment` | A temporary node used to build a subtree of a `Document` node. This interface has no methods. |
| `DocumentType` | A node representing the `<!DOCTYPE>` element at the beginning of the document. This interface provides methods for getting the DTD name, entities, and notations defined in the DTD. |
| `Element` | The most common subinterface of `Node`. Represents an XML start tag, body, and end tag. In addition to the methods it inherits from `Node`, `Element` has methods for setting and retrieving the attributes that appear in the start tag. In DOM Level 2, `Element` includes numerous namespace-aware methods. |
| `Entity` | An external component used in an XML document, such as an image file. DOM level 1 provides only minimal support for this node type. |
| `EntityReference` | A reference (name or pointer) to an unevaluated Entity. This interface acts simply as a placeholder in the document; it defines no methods. |
| `Notation` | Represents a notation declared in the DTD. Notations describe the format of external entities. |
| `ProcessingInstruction` | A processor-specific instruction in the XML document. Processing instructions employ the syntax `<?`*<target> [<data>]*`?>`. |
| `Text` | A `Text` node contains the character content of an element body. |

**Table 16-2.** *Subinterfaces of Node for Specific Node Types* (continued)

## Node Collection Interfaces

Various DOM API methods return collections of nodes, either ordered lists or maps of names to nodes. Two interfaces represent these collections: `NodeList`, shown in Table 16-3, and `NamedNodeMap`, in Table 16-4.

| Method | Description |
|---|---|
| `int getLength()` | Returns the number of nodes in the list. |
| `Node item(int n)` | Returns the *n*th node in the list, where nodes are numbered 0, 1, ... |

**Table 16-3.** *Methods Defined by the NodeList Interface*

| Method | Description |
|---|---|
| `int getLength()` | Returns the number of nodes in the list. |
| `Node item(int n)` | Returns the *n*th node in the list, where nodes are numbered 0, 1, ... |
| `Node getNamedItem(String name)`<br>`void setNamedItem(Node item)`<br>`void removeNamedItem(String name)` | Gets, sets, or removes the node having the specified name. `getNamedItem()` returns `null` if the node doesn't exist in the collection. |

**Table 16-4.** *Methods Defined by the NamedNodeMap Interface*



The `NamedNodeMap` interface in DOM Level 2 supports qualified item names in namespaces.

## Node Metadata

XML features can be version-specific. To determine the DOM configuration, DOM has an interface that enables you to query which features it supports. This interface is named `DOMImplementation`. Currently, it consists of a single method

boolean hasFeature(String *feature*, String *version*)

which returns `true` if the specified level of the specified feature is supported. DOM Level 2 adds two new methods to `DOMImplementation` to support creating documents.

## Exceptions

DOM defines a single exception class named `DOMException`. This is a subclass of `RuntimeException`, which means the compiler won't require methods that can throw this exception to declare it or to enclose it in a try/catch block.

## DOM Use

A typical DOM-oriented application creates an instance of a DOM parser, and then instructs it to parse an XML input source to create the DOM tree. Once the tree is created, the application can navigate through it, examining its contents and extracting what it needs.

The means for instantiating the parser are implementation-specific. It can be created directly with the `new` operator. A higher level approach is available with the *Java API for XML (JAXP)* wrapper defined by Sun Microsystems. Under JAXP, an application creates an instance of `DocumentBuilderFactory`, optionally sets its `namespaceAware` and/or `validating` properties, and then uses the factory to obtain an instance of the parser. The factory finds a DOM parser class that matches the required features.

So, to parse an XML document with DOM, an application can do this:

```
DocumentBuilderFactory factory =
   DocumentBuilderFactory.newInstance();
DocumentBuilder builder = factory.newDocumentBuilder();
Document document = builder.parse(fileName);
Element root = document.getDocumentElement();
```

Let's look at an example of XML parsing with DOM in a JSP page. The following XML document was extracted from the LyricNote product catalog, possibly as the result of a database query. It consists of a list of musical instruments identified by a product code. For each instrument, the document contains the price, the quantity on hand, the name of the manufacturer, and a product description. The list is abbreviated here; the full list has 82 entries.

```
<?xml version="1.0"?>

<!DOCTYPE products PUBLIC "-//jspcr//products//EN"
   "http://u25nv/jspcr/Chap16/examples/products/products.dtd">

<products>

   <product code="001000">
      <product-type>IN</product-type>
```

```
      <price>537.00</price>
      <on-hand>48</on-hand>
      <manufacturer>Clemens-Altman</manufacturer>
      <description>Silver Flute - Student</description>
   </product>

   <product code="001010">
      <product-type>IN</product-type>
      <price>876.00</price>
      <on-hand>83</on-hand>
      <manufacturer>Gabriel</manufacturer>
      <description>Silver Flute</description>
   </product>

   ...

   <product code="001790">
      <product-type>IN</product-type>
      <price>165.50</price>
      <on-hand>94</on-hand>
      <manufacturer>Roush and Sons</manufacturer>
      <description>Cello case (1/2 size)</description>
   </product>

</products>
```



The JSP parses the document and extracts only products whose manufacturer is `Clemens-Altman`. It arranges this subset in an HTML table, with columns for the product code, the description, and the price. Because the document consists of a set of product elements, a logical approach is to parse the document and convert it into a collection of `Product` objects. The `Product` object will have fields corresponding to the XML elements in each product block. Having the `Product` object help with the parsing also makes sense. Because DOM creates a tree, you can simply locate each `<product>` element, create a `Product` object, and call its `load()` method, passing the DOM element as a parameter.

The following shows the `Product` object. In addition to its `load()` method, `Product` contains `get` and `set` methods for each of its private fields.

```
package jspcr.xml.samples;

import org.w3c.dom.*;
```

```
public class Product
{
   private String code;
   private String productType;
   private double price;
   private int onHand;
   private String manufacturer;
   private String description;

   /**
   * Load the product data from a DOM element
   */
   public void load(org.w3c.dom.Element element)
   {
      code = element.getAttribute("code");
      for (Node node = element.getFirstChild();
            node != null;
            node = node.getNextSibling())
      {
         // Select only element nodes

         if (node.getNodeType() != Node.ELEMENT_NODE)
            continue;

         String tagName = node.getNodeName();

         // product-type

         if (tagName.equals("product-type")) {
            String text = node.getFirstChild().getNodeValue();
            productType = text.trim();
         }

         // price

         else
         if (tagName.equals("price")) {
            String text = node.getFirstChild().getNodeValue();
            price = Double.parseDouble(text.trim());
         }
```

```
         // on-hand

         else
         if (tagName.equals("on-hand")) {
            String text = node.getFirstChild().getNodeValue();
            onHand = Integer.parseInt(text.trim());
         }

         // manufacturer

         else
         if (tagName.equals("manufacturer")) {
            String text = node.getFirstChild().getNodeValue();
            manufacturer = text.trim();
         }

         // description

         else
         if (tagName.equals("description")) {
            String text = node.getFirstChild().getNodeValue();
            description = text.trim();
         }
      }
   }
  // Not shown here - get and set methods
}
```

- The code field is easy to get because it's an attribute of the product element. All you have to do is call element's `getAttribute("code")` method. The other fields are slightly more complicated because their values are in text nodes beneath subelements of product. Our approach is to loop through the child nodes of the product element, comparing the node name in each to the field names you need to populate. This loop can be done several ways: Call the `getChildNodes()` method on the product element, which returns a `NodeList` object. The `NodeList` has a `getLength()` method, which tells us the node count, and an `item(int index)` method, which returns the node at the specified index within the list.
- Call the product element's `getFirstChild()` method, and then each child's `getNextSibling()` method in turn until it returns `null`.

Our code uses the second method.

To get the text node values, you can take advantage of the fact that each data element has no subelements, just parsed character data. Therefore, you can call each data element's `getFirstChild()` method and know you'll get a text node. The text itself is available from the `getNodeValue()` method.Armed with the XML-aware product element, you can now parse the product catalog XML document and perform our query. Here is the JSP page:

```
<%@ page session="false" %>
<%@ page import="java.io.*" %>
<%@ page import="java.net.*" %>
<%@ page import="java.text.*" %>
<%@ page import="javax.xml.parsers.*" %>
<%@ page import="jspcr.xml.samples.*" %>
<%@ page import="org.w3c.dom.*" %>
<%@ page import="org.xml.sax.*" %>
<%
   long stime = System.currentTimeMillis();
%>
<HTML>
<HEAD>
<TITLE>(DOM) Clemens-Altman Musical Instruments</TITLE>
</HEAD>
<BODY>
<CENTER>
<H3>Clemens-Altman Musical Instruments</H3>
<H4>(Powered by DOM Level 1)</H4>
<TABLE BORDER="1" CELLPADDING="3" CELLSPACING="0">
<TR>
   <TH>Product Code</TH>
   <TH>Description</TH>
   <TH>Price</TH>
</TR>
<%
   // Get a new document builder

   DocumentBuilderFactory factory =
      DocumentBuilderFactory.newInstance();
   DocumentBuilder builder = factory.newDocumentBuilder();

   // Define the input source to be an XML document named
   // "instruments.xml" in the same directory as this JSP
```

```
StringBuffer requestURL = HttpUtils.getRequestURL(request);
URL jspURL = new URL(requestURL.toString());
URL url = new URL(jspURL, "instruments.xml");
InputSource is = new InputSource(url.openStream());

// Load the document

Document document = builder.parse(is);
Element root = document.getDocumentElement();
root.normalize();

// Define currency formatter

NumberFormat fmt = NumberFormat.getCurrencyInstance();

// Select product code, description, and price
// where manufacturer = "Clemens-Altman"

for (
   Node node = root.getFirstChild();
   node != null;
   node = node.getNextSibling())
{
   // Ignore everything but product elements

   if (node.getNodeType() != Node.ELEMENT_NODE)
      continue;

   Element productElement = (Element) node;
   if (!productElement.getTagName().equals("product"))
      continue;

   // Load the product object

   Product product = new Product();
   product.load(productElement);

   // See if the manufacturer is "Clemens-Altman"

   String text = product.getManufacturer();
   if (!text.equals("Clemens-Altman"))
```

```
            continue;

         // Get the product code, price, and item name

         String code = product.getCode();
         String description = product.getDescription();
         double price = product.getPrice();
%>
<TR>
   <TD><%= code %></TD>
   <TD><%= description %></TD>
   <TD ALIGN="RIGHT"><%= fmt.format(price) %></TD>
</TR>
<%
   }
%>
</TABLE>
<P>
<%
   long etime = System.currentTimeMillis();
   double elapsed = (etime - stime)/1000.0;
%>
<EM>Elapsed time: <%= elapsed %> seconds</EM>
</CENTER>
</BODY>
</HTML>
```

After generating the table headings, the JSP page creates an instance of the DOM `DocumentBuilder` using the JAXP approach:

```
DocumentBuilderFactory factory =
   DocumentBuilderFactory.newInstance();
DocumentBuilder builder = factory.newDocumentBuilder();
```

The product catalog XML document is in a file named `instruments.xml` in the same directory as the JSP page. You can locate that using the `HttpUtils` `getRequestURL()` method for the JSP URL, and then use the two-argument URL constructor to get the XML file as a URL:

```
StringBuffer requestURL = HttpUtils.getRequestURL(request);
```

```
    URL jspURL = new URL(requestURL.toString());
    URL url = new URL(jspURL, "instruments.xml");
    InputSource is = new InputSource(url.openStream());
```

InputSource is a convenience class that wraps a byte stream, a character stream, or a filename.

With the document builder and input source defined, you are ready to parse:

```
    Document document = builder.parse(is);
    Element root = document.getDocumentElement();
```

The root <products> element is available from the document.getDocumentElement() method.

Now, loop through the immediate children of the <products> element searching for <product> elements. Although looking at the XML document suggests you won't find anything else, this isn't the case. Text nodes are separating each <product> block.

```
for (
        Node node = root.getFirstChild();
        node != null;
        node = node.getNextSibling())
    {
        if (node.getNodeType() != Node.ELEMENT_NODE)
            continue;
        Element productElement = (Element) node;
        if (!productElement.getTagName().equals("product"))
            continue;
```

Once you find a <product> element, you can create a Product object and have it navigate the subelements looking for what it needs:

```
        Product product = new Product();
        product.load(productElement);
```

At this point, you can get everything you need from the Product object. You can determine if its manufacture is Clemens-Altman and print it in the table if this is so. The results are shown in Figure 16-1.

The main advantage of DOM as a parsing model is it provides random access to all parts of the document structure. This is made possible by its biggest disadvantage, though—the entire document must be read and parsed before any part of it is accessible through the DOM API. For large documents, this overhead can be significant.

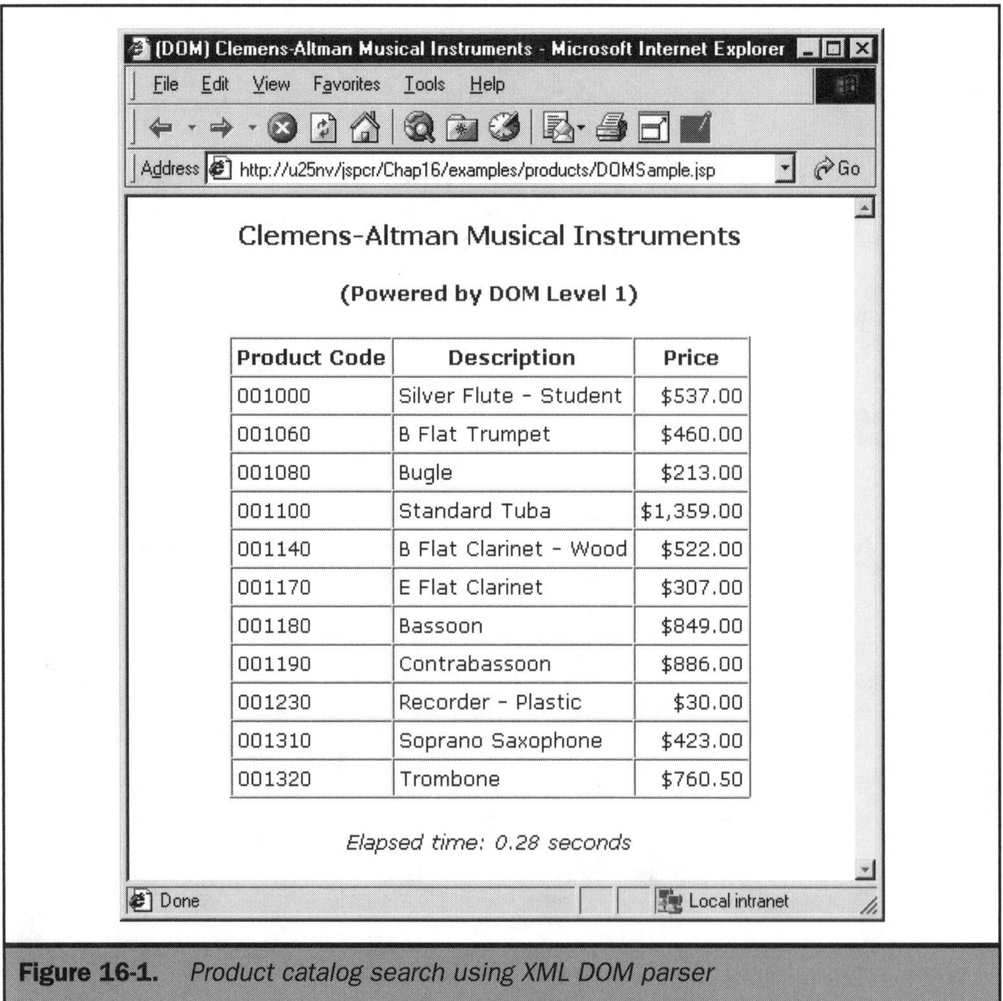


**Figure 16-1.** *Product catalog search using XML DOM parser*

## Simple API for XML (SAX)

SAX provides a different approach to parsing. Rather than creating a tree from an XML document, a SAX parser reads through the file and notifies registered listeners when certain parsing events occur. These events include

- The beginning of a document
- Reading a start tag at the beginning of a new element
- Reading an end tag at the end of an element

- Reading text in the body of an element
- Reading comments
- Reaching the end of a document

A SAX interface defines methods for all these events. An application that wants to handle particular events can implement one or more of the methods, and then register as a handler for the document. When the events occur, the handler's method(s) are then invoked with values from the element currently being parsed. This makes SAX ideal for filtering-type applications that require little or no document context.

Like DOM, the SAX API continues to evolve. SAX 1.0 emerged in May 1998 from design discussions on the XML-DEV mailing list. The SAX 2.0 specification was published in May 2000. While SAX isn't an official W3C specification, it's widely accepted and usually offered alongside DOM in most parsers. In fact, DOM parsers are often built over SAX parsers and the JAXP `DocumentBuilder` interface for DOM uses several SAX classes.

## The SAX Parser

The basic SAX interface is `Parser`. An implementation of the SAX API would supply a concrete class that implements `Parser`. This interface defines methods that register the various handler classes to be used and defines two forms of the `parse()` method, as shown in Table 16-5.

| Method | Description |
|---|---|
| `void parse(InputSource is) throws SAXException, IOException` | Causes the parser to begin parsing the document supplied by the specified input source. |
| `void parse(String systemId) throws SAXException, IOException` | Causes the parser to begin parsing the document referred to in the specified system ID. This can be a filename or a fully resolved URL. |
| `void setDocumentHandler (DocumentHandler handler)` | Registers a document handler for this parser. |
| `void setDTDHandler(DTDHandler handler)` | Registers a DTD handler for this parser. |

**Table 16-5.** *Methods in the SAX Parser Interface*

| Method | Description |
|---|---|
| `void setEntityResolver(EntityResolver resolver)` | Registers an entity resolver for this parser. An `EntityResolver` can be used to locate external entities in custom ways. |
| `void setErrorHandler(ErrorHandler handler)` | Registers an error handler for custom error handling. |
| `void setLocale(Locale locale) throws SAXException` | Specifies the locale to be used for errors and warnings. |

**Table 16-5.** *Methods in the SAX Parser Interface* (continued)

## Handlers

Four interfaces handle parsing events:

- `DocumentHandler` defines callback methods for the start and end of a document, for the start and end of every XML element, for the text of the document, and for whitespace, comments, and processing instructions.
- `ErrorHandler` defines callbacks for fatal, recoverable, and warning errors.
- `EntityResolver` allows custom handling of external entities, such as document type definitions.
- `DTDHandler` receives notifications of notation declarations and unparsed entity declarations in a document type definition.

Of these, you'll most often employ only the first, `DocumentHandler`. An application can implement this interface, and then register itself with the parser using the `setDocumentHandler()` method to begin receiving callbacks. The methods in `DocumentHandler` are described in Table 16-6.

In addition to the four handler interfaces, the SAX API provides a default implementation—named `HandlerBase`—for all four of them. An application would typically subclass `HandlerBase` and implement only those necessary methods. Often, this consists of just the `startElement()`, `characters()`, and `endElement()` methods.

| Method | Description |
|---|---|
| `void characters(char[] ch, int start, int len) throws SAXException` | This method is called with the XML parser and reads character data in the text of an element. The character data is passed in the `ch` array starting at `start` for length `len`. Conveniently, a `java.lang.String` constructor uses these same three fields. |
| `void endDocument() throws SAXException` | Called when the parser has finished parsing a document. |
| `void endElement(String name) throws SAXException` | Called when the end tag for the current element is parsed. The tag name is passed as a parameter. |
| `void ignorableWhitespace(char[] ch, int start, int len) throws SAXException` | This method is called with the XML parser and reads nonsignificant character data. The character data is passed in the `ch` array starting at `start` for length `len`. |
| `void processingInstruction(String target, String data) throws SAXException` | Called when a processing instruction is encountered. |
| `void setDocumentLocator(Locator locator)` | Informs the document handler about the `Locator` to be used during parsing. `Locator` provides line and column number information useful during parsing errors. |
| `void startDocument() throws SAXException` | Called when the parser starts parsing a new document. |
| `void startElement(String name, AttributeList attrs) throws SAXException` | Called when the parser encounters the beginning of a new element tag. The parameters passed include the tag name and the name/value attribute pairs. |

**Table 16-6.** *Methods Defined by DocumentHandler*

## SAX Use

A typical SAX-oriented application creates an instance of a SAX parser, registers the document handler, and then invokes the `parse()` method to start the parsing and callbacks. In this section, you develop the same product catalog example you did for DOM. You still use the `Product` object, but only to store the product properties, not to do any parsing.

```
<%@ page session="false" %>
<%@ page import="java.io.*" %>
<%@ page import="java.net.*" %>
<%@ page import="java.text.*" %>
<%@ page import="java.util.*" %>
<%@ page import="javax.xml.parsers.*" %>
<%@ page import="jspcr.xml.samples.*" %>
<%@ page import="org.xml.sax.*" %>
<%
   long stime = System.currentTimeMillis();
%>
<HTML>
<HEAD>
<TITLE>(SAX 1.0) Clemens-Altman Musical Instruments</TITLE>
</HEAD>
<BODY>
<CENTER>
<H3>Clemens-Altman Musical Instruments</H3>
<H4>(Powered by SAX 1.0)</H4>
<TABLE BORDER="1" CELLPADDING="3" CELLSPACING="0">
<TR>
   <TH>Product Code</TH>
   <TH>Description</TH>
   <TH>Price</TH>
</TR>
<%
   // Get a new SAX parser

   SAXParserFactory factory = SAXParserFactory.newInstance();
   SAXParser parser = factory.newSAXParser();

   // Define the input source to be an XML document named
   // "instruments.xml" in the same directory as this JSP
```

```
   StringBuffer requestURL = HttpUtils.getRequestURL(request);
   URL jspURL = new URL(requestURL.toString());
   URL url = new URL(jspURL, "instruments.xml");
   InputSource is = new InputSource(url.openStream());

   // Parse the input source

   parser.parse(is, new ProductParser(out));
%>
</TABLE>
<P>
<%
   long etime = System.currentTimeMillis();
   double elapsed = (etime - stime)/1000.0;
%>
<EM>Elapsed time: <%= elapsed %> seconds</EM>
</CENTER>
</BODY>
</HTML>
<%!

// Inner class that parses the XML input source

class ProductParser extends HandlerBase
{
   private Product product;
   private StringBuffer buffer;
   private JspWriter out;
   private NumberFormat fmt;

   public ProductParser(JspWriter out)
   {
      this.out = out;
      buffer = new StringBuffer();
      fmt = NumberFormat.getCurrencyInstance();
   }

   /**
   * Called when a start tag is encountered
   */
   public void startElement(String name, AttributeList attrs)
```

```
      throws SAXException
   {
      if (name.equals("product")) {
         product = new Product();
         product.setCode(attrs.getValue("code"));
      }
      buffer = new StringBuffer();
   }

   /**
   * Accumulates characters from text nodes
   */
   public void characters(char[] ch, int start, int len)
      throws SAXException
   {
      buffer.append(ch, start, len);
   }

   /**
   * Called when an end tag is encountered
   */
   public void endElement(String name)
      throws SAXException
   {
      String text = buffer.toString().trim();
      if (name.equals("price"))
         product.setPrice(Double.parseDouble(text));
      else if (name.equals("manufacturer"))
         product.setManufacturer(text);
      else if (name.equals("description"))
         product.setDescription(text);
      else if (name.equals("product")) {
         if (product.getManufacturer().equals("Clemens-Altman")) {
            try {
               String[] lines = {
                  "<TR>",
                  "<TD>", product.getCode(), "</TD>",
                  "<TD>", product.getDescription(), "</TD>",
                  "<TD ALIGN='RIGHT'>",
                  fmt.format(product.getPrice()), "</TD>",
                  "</TR>",
```

```
                  };
                  for (int i = 0; i < lines.length; i++)
                     out.println(lines[i]);
               }
               catch (IOException e) {
                  throw new SAXException(e.getMessage());
               }
            }
         }
      }
   }
%>
```

Like DOMBuilderFactory and DOMBuilder, SAXParserFactory and SAXParser can be invoked through JAXP:

```
SAXParserFactory factory = SAXParserFactory.newInstance();
SAXParser parser = factory.newSAXParser();
```

Remember, the SAX technique is to implement DocumentHandler (or extend HandlerBase) and provide callbacks for the parsing event methods of interest. An inner class can be used to do that. The JAXP parse() method registers our ProductParser class as the document handler, and then starts parsing:

```
parser.parse(is, new ProductParser(out));
```

The ProductParser class is interested in three events:

- startElement  At the beginning of a new <product> element, you need to create a Product object and store the code attribute in it.
- characters  As text flies by, you accumulate it in a StringBuffer.
- endElement  At the end of an element, you assign its value from the StringBuffer, if it's one of the product fields. If this is the end of a <product> element, you can print the product in the HTML table, clear your buffers, and wait for the next product to be parsed.

The resulting HTML table is shown in Figure 16-2. Note the difference in elapsed time from the DOM version in Figure 16-1.

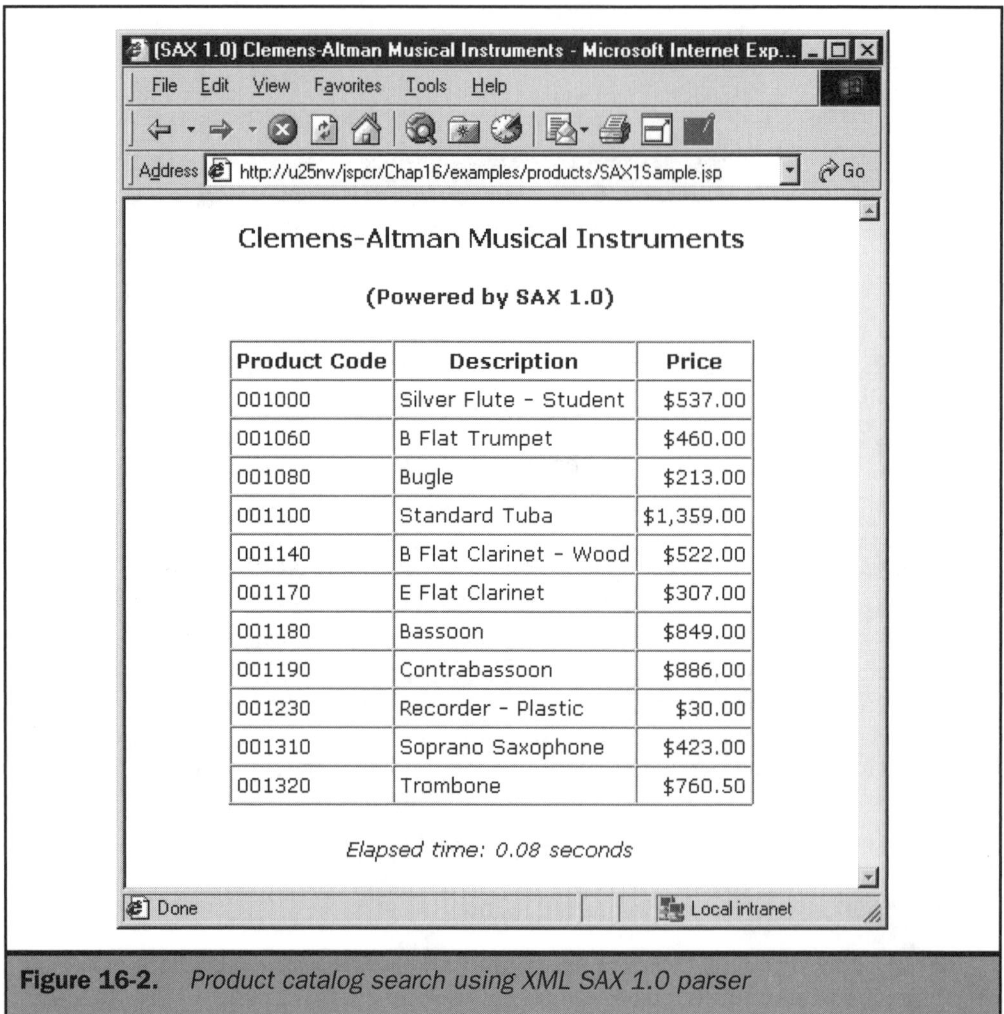


**Figure 16-2.** *Product catalog search using XML SAX 1.0 parser*

## SAX 2.0

An updated SAX specification was adopted in May 1998. The main improvement in SAX 2.0 is support for namespaces. *Namespaces* are groups of tags with a common prefix that distinguishes them from other tags that may have the same name without the prefix. This allows packages of XML tags to be defined without worrying about colliding with similarly named tags.

In API terms, SAX 2.0 deprecates the `Parser`, `DocumentHandler`, and `AttributeList` interfaces, replacing them with the namespace-aware `XMLReader`, `ContentHandler`, and `Attributes` interfaces, respectively.

**Note** *As you might expect, not all XML products have caught up to the latest DOM and SAX levels. As of November 2000, JAXP doesn't yet support SAX 2.0, except in an early access package. The Xerces-J 1.2.1 release supports SAX 2.0 by itself, but not through the Xerces version of JAXP, which is still only for SAX 1.0. Check the Sun, W3C, and xml.apache.org Web sites for updated versions.*

In SAX 2.0, our product catalog JSP page looks like this:

```
<%@ page session="false" %>
<%@ page import="java.io.*" %>
<%@ page import="java.net.*" %>
<%@ page import="java.text.*" %>
<%@ page import="java.util.*" %>
<%@ page import="jspcr.xml.samples.*" %>
<%@ page import="org.xml.sax.*" %>
<%@ page import="org.xml.sax.helpers.*" %>
<%
   long stime = System.currentTimeMillis();
%>
<HTML>
<HEAD>
<TITLE>(SAX 2.0) Clemens-Altman Musical Instruments</TITLE>
</HEAD>
<BODY>
<CENTER>
<H3>Clemens-Altman Musical Instruments</H3>
<H4>(Powered by SAX 2.0)</H4>
<TABLE BORDER="1" CELLPADDING="3" CELLSPACING="0">
<TR>
   <TH>Product Code</TH>
   <TH>Description</TH>
   <TH>Price</TH>
</TR>
<%
   // Get a new SAX parser

   XMLReader parser = new org.apache.xerces.parsers.SAXParser();
   DefaultHandler handler = new ProductParser(out);
   parser.setContentHandler(handler);
   parser.setErrorHandler(handler);

   // Define the input source to be an XML document named
```

```
   // "instruments.xml" in the same directory as this JSP

   StringBuffer requestURL = HttpUtils.getRequestURL(request);
   URL jspURL = new URL(requestURL.toString());
   URL url = new URL(jspURL, "instruments.xml");
   InputSource is = new InputSource(url.openStream());

   // Parse the input source

   parser.parse(is);
%>
</TABLE>
<P>
<%
   long etime = System.currentTimeMillis();
   double elapsed = (etime - stime)/1000.0;
%>
<EM>Elapsed time: <%= elapsed %> seconds</EM>
</CENTER>
</BODY>
</HTML>
<%!

// Inner class that parses the XML input source

class ProductParser extends DefaultHandler
{
   private Product product;
   private StringBuffer buffer;
   private JspWriter out;
   private NumberFormat fmt;

   public ProductParser(JspWriter out)
   {
      this.out = out;
      buffer = new StringBuffer();
      fmt = NumberFormat.getCurrencyInstance();
   }

   /**
   * Called when a start tag is encountered
   */
```

```
public void startElement(
      String namespaceURI,
      String localName,
      String qName,
      Attributes attrs)
   throws SAXException
{
   if (qName.equals("product")) {
      product = new Product();
      product.setCode(attrs.getValue("code"));
   }
   buffer = new StringBuffer();
}

/**
* Accumulates characters from text nodes
*/
public void characters(char[] ch, int start, int len)
   throws SAXException
{
   buffer.append(ch, start, len);
}

/**
* Called when an end tag is encountered
*/
public void endElement(
      String namespaceURI,
      String localName,
      String qName)
   throws SAXException
{
   String text = buffer.toString().trim();
   if (qName.equals("price"))
      product.setPrice(Double.parseDouble(text));
   else if (qName.equals("manufacturer"))
      product.setManufacturer(text);
   else if (qName.equals("description"))
      product.setDescription(text);
   else if (qName.equals("product")) {
      if (product.getManufacturer().equals("Clemens-Altman")) {
         try {
```

```
                 String[] lines = {
                    "<TR>",
                    "<TD>", product.getCode(), "</TD>",
                    "<TD>", product.getDescription(), "</TD>",
                    "<TD ALIGN='RIGHT'>",
                    fmt.format(product.getPrice()), "</TD>",
                    "</TR>",
                 };
                 for (int i = 0; i < lines.length; i++)
                    out.println(lines[i]);
              }
              catch (IOException e) {
                 throw new SAXException(e.getMessage());
              }
           }
        }
     }
}
%>
```

The essential differences are in how the parser is invoked

```
   XMLReader parser = new org.apache.xerces.parsers.SAXParser();
   DefaultHandler handler = new ProductParser(out);
   parser.setContentHandler(handler);
   parser.setErrorHandler(handler);
```

and in the callback method signatures:

```
   public void startElement(
         String namespaceURI, String localName, String qName,
         Attributes attrs)
      throws SAXException
   ...
   public void endElement(
         String namespaceURI, String localName, String qName)
      throws SAXException
```

As seen in Figure 16-3, the resulting output is produced slightly faster than in SAX 1.0.

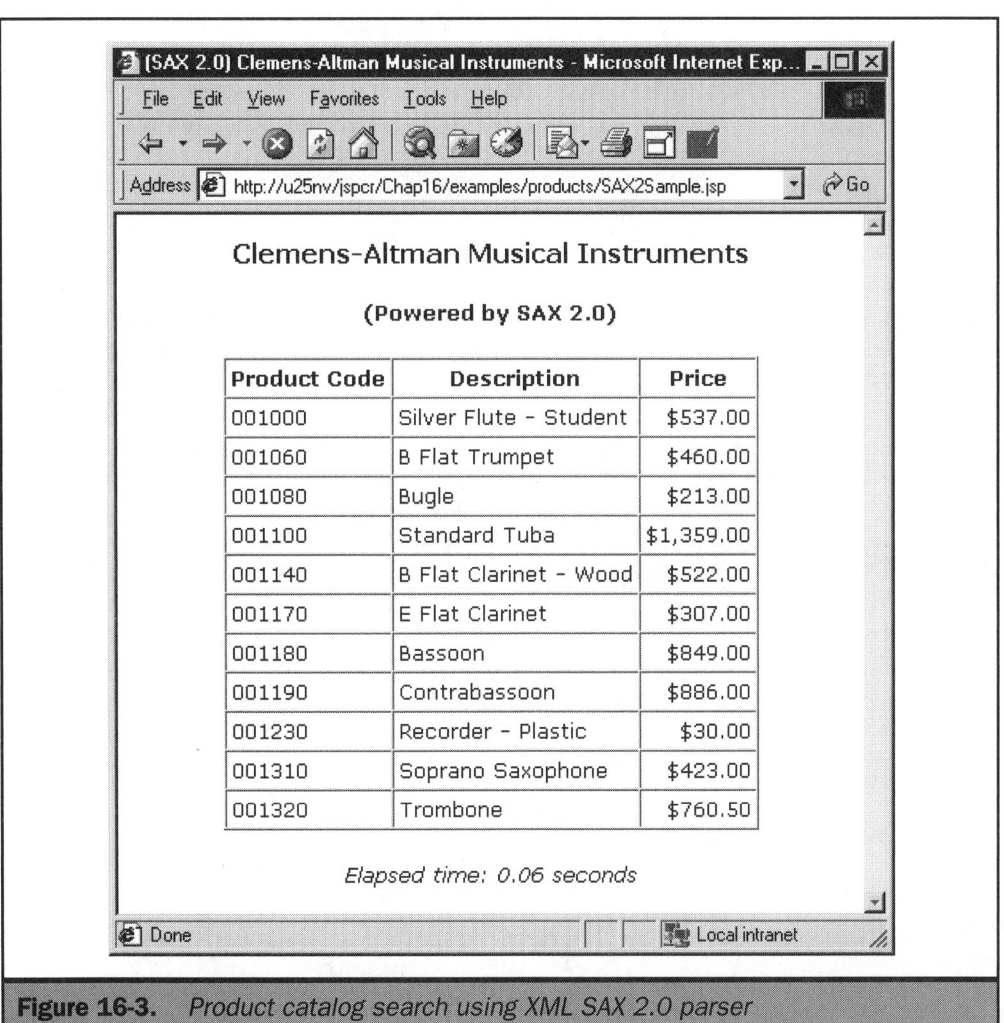


**Figure 16-3.** *Product catalog search using XML SAX 2.0 parser*

SAX offers a number of advantages over DOM. It's much simpler and easier to learn, has much smaller memory use, and doesn't require an entire document to be loaded. Nearly all XML parsers have a SAX interface; fewer have a DOM interface. SAX is also well suited for reading ill-formed documents (like most HTML).

## XSL Transformations with XSLT

As noted earlier, XML is designed purely to identify document structure, not document appearance. Obviously, though, XML and HTML are closely related, and XML documents can be converted to HTML. When this happens, style information can be added. This is the role of *Extensible Stylesheet Language* (*XSL*).

XSL is a language for designing style sheets. An XSL style sheet systematically describes which formatting elements are applied to which elements in an XML source document to product the desired HTML output. Not surprisingly, an XSL style sheet itself is an XML document.

Although XSL was originally designed for style sheet purposes, it became apparent that it could also be used for general XML structure transformations. This manipulation is performed by an *XSL transformation* processor (*XSLT*). XSLT is defined in a W3C recommendation dated November 1999 (see http://www.w3.org/TR/xslt.html). Popular XSLT processors are available from the Apache Software Foundation (Xalan), Microsoft (MSXML), Michael Kay (Saxon), and James Clark (XT).

XSLT is a broad topic, and the subject of numerous books and articles. This book only gives you a basic introduction, just enough to let you read an XSLT style sheet, if you need to do so.

XSLT uses an XML document called an *XSL style sheet* to describe what it modifies and how. In the style sheet are one or more templates, which identify the particular XML elements they're designed to transform, and then provide a set of literals and nested XSL statements that indicate the format of the output. The key XSLT instructions are listed in Table 16-7.

| Instruction | Description |
|---|---|
| `<xsl:stylesheet>` | The outermost document element in an XSL style sheet. Required attributes are `xmlns:xsl` (the namespace for XSL tags) and `version`. |
| `<xsl:template>` | Identifies a template block. Optional attribute is `match`, which specifies which XML element the template matches. A rich variety of ways exists to express the match value. See the XSLT specification for details. |

**Table 16-7.** *Highlights of XSLT Instructions*

| Instruction | Description |
|---|---|
| `<xsl:apply-templates>` | Causes the processor to seek other elements to match. Optional attribute is `select`, which specifies a subset of elements in the same language as the `<xsl:template>` `match` attribute. |
| `<xsl:value-of>` | Causes the processor to substitute the value of the specified element. Optional attribute is select, which operates the same as in `<xsl:apply-templates>` |

**Table 16-7.** *Highlights of XSLT Instructions* (continued)



## XSLT in Action

We can do the same example in XSLT that we used to illustrate DOM and SAX. Here's the XSL style sheet:

```
<?xml version="1.0"?>

<xsl:stylesheet
   xmlns:xsl="http://www.w3.org/1999/XSL/Transform"
   version="1.0">

<xsl:output method="html"/>

<xsl:template match="/">
<TABLE BORDER="1" CELLPADDING="3" CELLSPACING="0">
<TR>
   <TH>Product Code</TH>
   <TH>Description</TH>
   <TH>Price</TH>
</TR>
<xsl:apply-templates
   select="//product[manufacturer='Clemens-Altman']"/>
</TABLE>
</xsl:template>
```

```
<xsl:template match="//product">
<TR>
   <TD><xsl:value-of select="@code"/></TD>
   <TD><xsl:value-of select="description"/></TD>
   <TD ALIGN="RIGHT">
      <xsl:value-of select="price"/>
   </TD>
</TR>
</xsl:template>

</xsl:stylesheet>
```

The document element matches the / template, so the HTML used on either side of the HTML table is coded in the body of this template. In place of the table, there's a call back into the XSLT processor:

```
   <xsl:apply-templates
      select="//product[manufacturer='Clemens-Altman']"/>
```

The value of the `select` attribute indicates any product elements one level down from the document root that have a manufacturer attribute with a value of `Clemens-Altman` will be matched.

So, as the document is parsed, each product element that matches the criteria is passed to the `//product` template. This template stands for a single row in the table. It adds the `<TR><TD>...</TD></TR>` tags and fills them in with document element text:

```
   <TD><xsl:value-of select="@code"/></TD>
```

The previous line extracts the value of an attribute named `code` in the current node.

```
   <TD><xsl:value-of select="description"/></TD>
```

This line extracts the text value of the `<description>` tag.

The JSP page is easy. Beyond generating the outer HTML, all it does is create an instance of the XSLT processor and start it running:

```
<%@ page session="false" %>
<%@ page import="java.io.*" %>
```

```
<%@ page import="java.net.*" %>
<%@ page import="org.xml.sax.*" %>
<%@ page import="org.apache.xalan.xslt.*" %>
<%
   long stime = System.currentTimeMillis();
%>
<HTML>
<HEAD>
<TITLE>(XSLT) Clemens-Altman Musical Instruments</TITLE>
</HEAD>
<BODY>
<CENTER>
<H3>Clemens-Altman Musical Instruments</H3>
<H4>(Powered by XSLT)</H4>
<%
   // Create an instance of the XSLT processor

   XSLTProcessor p = XSLTProcessorFactory.getProcessor();

   // Create the XML input and XSL URL's

   StringBuffer requestURL = HttpUtils.getRequestURL(request);
   URL jspURL = new URL(requestURL.toString());
   URL inURL  = new URL(jspURL, "instruments.xml");
   URL xslURL = new URL(jspURL, "XSLTSample.xsl");

   // Process the stylesheet

   p.process(
      new XSLTInputSource(inURL.openStream()),
      new XSLTInputSource(xslURL.openStream()),
      new XSLTResultTarget(out)
      );

   out.flush();
%>
<P>
<%
   long etime = System.currentTimeMillis();
   double elapsed = (etime - stime)/1000.0;
```

```
%>
<EM>Elapsed time: <%= elapsed %> seconds</EM>
</CENTER>
</BODY>
</HTML>
```

The results are shown in Figure 16-4.

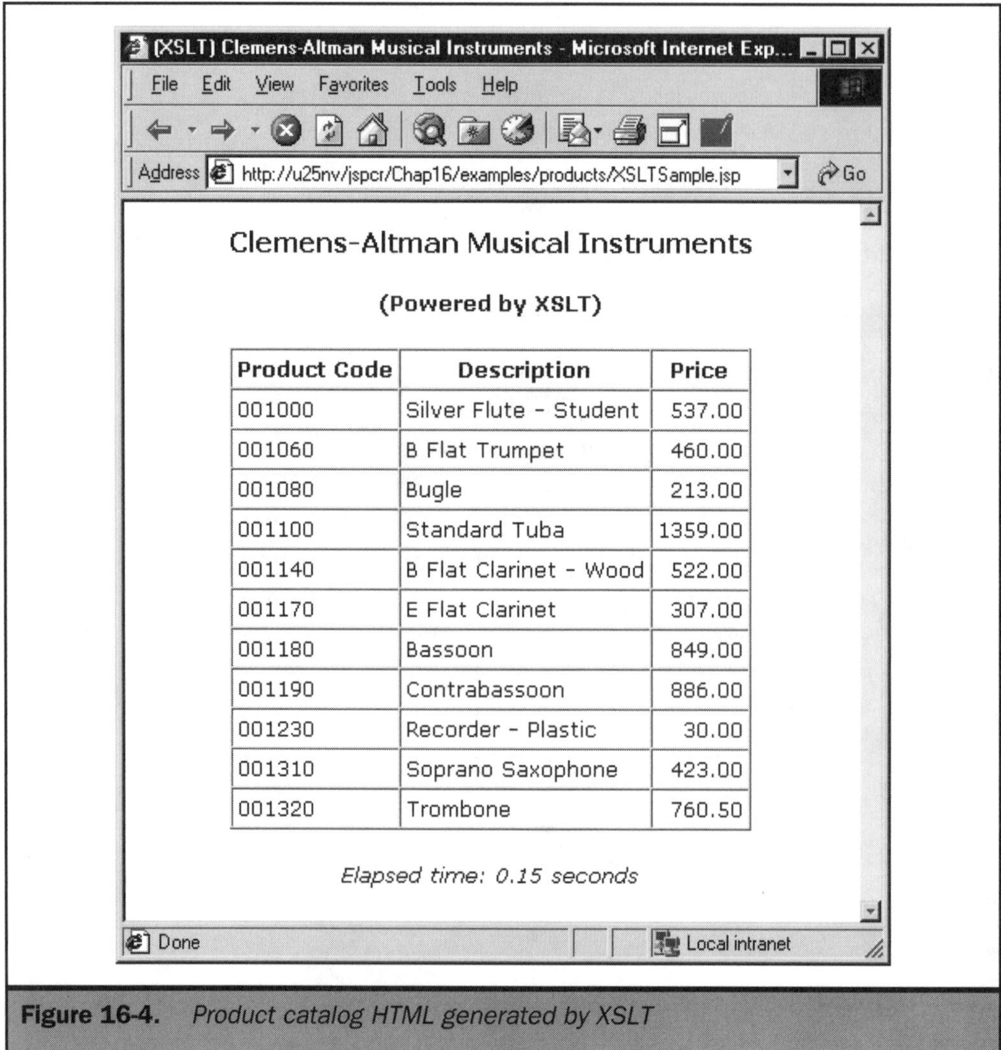


| Product Code | Description | Price |
|---|---|---|
| 001000 | Silver Flute - Student | 537.00 |
| 001060 | B Flat Trumpet | 460.00 |
| 001080 | Bugle | 213.00 |
| 001100 | Standard Tuba | 1359.00 |
| 001140 | B Flat Clarinet - Wood | 522.00 |
| 001170 | E Flat Clarinet | 307.00 |
| 001180 | Bassoon | 849.00 |
| 001190 | Contrabassoon | 886.00 |
| 001230 | Recorder - Plastic | 30.00 |
| 001310 | Soprano Saxophone | 423.00 |
| 001320 | Trombone | 760.50 |

**Figure 16-4.** *Product catalog HTML generated by XSLT*

This example ran the XSL transformation on the server. Passing XML and the style sheet over the Web and running the transformation on the client is already possible. Internet Explorer 5.0 introduced direct support for XML and XSL style sheets. Unfortunately, the XSLT specification was only in beta form when Microsoft added these features. Since then, the XSLT language has changed and a number of features are incompatible with Microsoft's version. Expecting these difficulties to be resolved in the future is logical.

## Summary

XML is becoming the universal language for structured data storage and interchange. Using human-readable text files and simple grammatical rules, XML captures not only data but metadata, information about the structure of the data. Hundreds of applications are being written or converted to use XML as their input and/or output. The XML specifications and those for its related technologies are managed by the World Wide Web Consortium , usually referred to as W3C.

To read XML, you need a parser. Two primary parser models are in general use:

- **Document Object Model (DOM)** Models an XML document as a tree of nodes. The DOM API provides methods for navigating a DOM tree in an arbitrary order: forward, backward, through siblings.
- **Simple API for Java (SAX)** Event-driven parser model that invokes callback methods in registered handlers.

XML can be transformed using an XSLT processor and an XSL style sheet.

There's no question that XML applications will multiply greatly in the future. JSP can be an enabling technology for these applications.

# Chapter 17

## JSP Testing and Debugging

Debugging techniques are frequently glossed over in programming tutorials, but are indispensable in application development. While programming can be systematic and code is easily borrowed from other programs, debugging is often viewed as a process of random trial-and-error changes that may or may not fix a problem.

The Web application environment presents its own unique difficulties. Because applications are split into server and client components, request handling involves multiple cooperating processes. As a result, errors are hard to reproduce, especially if they occur intermittently.

In this chapter, you see testing and debugging can be as systematic as development. The chapter outlines basic testing and debugging techniques that can be applied and develops several tools that can be helpful.

# Building a Mental Model

The key to systematic debugging is understanding how the application is designed to work. This means knowing what components are involved, how they interact, and what their expected behavior is. This makes it possible to isolate the failing component and determine what can account for the error.

## Translation and Compilation

For example, you know a JSP page exists in three forms, as illustrated in Figure 17-1:

1. **JSP Source Code** This is what a developer creates—a `.jsp` file containing scriptlets, expression, directives, and HTML template code.
2. **Generated Servlet Source Code** When a JSP page is first requested or whenever it is requested after any changes to its `.jsp` file, the JSP container translates it into an equivalent Java servlet.
3. **Compiled Servlet Class** After the JSP page is translated into servlet source code, it is compiled to produce a Java `.class` file.

Errors can occur at any point during this process. A careful examination of the error message and a knowledge of where the intermediate forms exist can help us zero in on the cause.

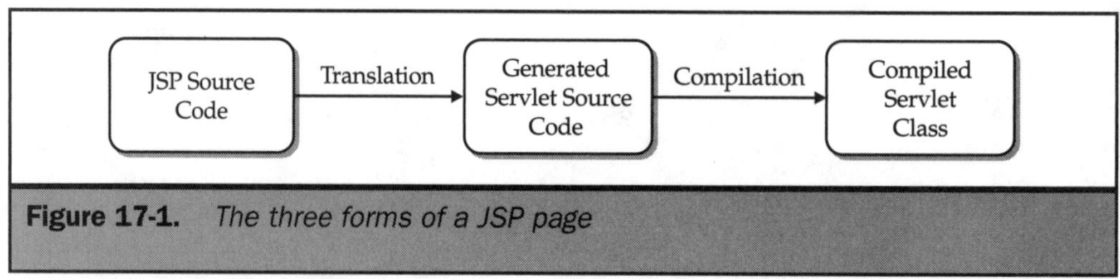


**Figure 17-1.** *The three forms of a JSP page*

**Note** *Careful reading of error messages is crucial, but you can't read them if they aren't there. Internet Explorer 5.x by default substitutes its own error page when a 500 level (internal servlet) error occurs. Presumably, this is intended to protect end users from frightening stack traces, but it makes things difficult for the developer. You can turn off this feature by selecting the Tools | Internet Options menu item, and then selecting the Advanced tab. A check box entitled "Show friendly HTTP error messages" is under the Browsing section of the tree. If you deselect this option, you can see full stack traces and any other data sent by a servlet exception.*

For example, suppose you have a custom tag named `timer` that keeps track of how long its body takes to execute. The tag handler is a class named `TimerTag`, which takes a snapshot of the current system time in its `doStartTag()` and `doEndTag()` methods and creates a scripting variable with the result.

```
import javax.servlet.jsp.*;
import javax.servlet.jsp.tagext.*;
import java.io.*;
import java.net.*;
import java.util.*;

/**
* A tag handler for a custom tag that keeps track
* of how long its body takes to execute
*/
public class TimerTag extends TagSupport
{
   private long startTime;
   private long endTime;

   /**
   * Starts the timer
   */
   public int doStartTag() throws JspException
   {
      startTime = System.currentTimeMillis();
      return EVAL_BODY_INCLUDE;
   }

   /**
   * Stops the timer and calculates the elapsed time
   * in seconds. This is stored as a page context
   * attribute using the ID variable name
   */
   public int doEndTag() throws JspException
```

```
    {
       endTime = System.currentTimeMillis();
       double elapsed = (endTime - startTime)/1000.0;
       pageContext.setAttribute(getId(), new Double(elapsed));
       return EVAL_PAGE;
    }
}
```

A typical use might be to see how long it takes to create a JDBC connection, as shown in the following JSP code:

```
<%@ page session="false" %>
<%@ page import="java.sql.*" %>
<%@ taglib prefix="debug" uri="/WEB-INF/tlds/debug.tld" %>
<debug:timer id="t1">
<%
   Connection con = null;
   try {
      Class.forName("sun.jdbc.odbc.JdbcOdbcDriver");
      con = DriverManager.getConnection("jdbc:odbc:usda");
   }
   finally {
      if (con != null)
         con.close();
   }
%>
</debug:timer>
Connecting to the database took <%= t1 %> seconds.
```

When this JSP page is run under JRun 3.0, it works. But under Tomcat 3.2, it produces the following error message:

```
Error: 500
Location:/jspcr/Chap17/examples/Timer.jsp
Internal Servlet Error:
org.apache.jasper.JasperException:
Unable to compile class for JSP
D:\tomcat\work\localhost_8080%2Fjspcr\_0002fChap_00031_00037
_0002fexamples_0002fTimer_0002ejspTimer_jsp_0.java:70:
Class Chap_00031_00037.examples.TimerTag not found.
      TimerTag _jspx_th_debug_timer_0 = new TimerTag();
      ^
```

Looking at the message carefully, you can find several clues about the nature of the error. First, it reports the location of the JSP page. This tells you Tomcat was able to find the JSP source code. Next, the message text says *Jasper* (the Tomcat JSP translator) was unable to compile a JSP servlet class and gives the name of the generated `.java` source file. This means translation from `.jsp` to `.java` completed and the java compiler was invoked, but failed. So you know this isn't a run-time error. This isn't due to a problem with the JDBC-ODBC driver, so it must be a compilation error with the generated servlet source code.

Having isolated the failing component, you can understand the rest of the error message. The generated servlet on line 70 creates an instance of `TimerTag()` and stores it in the `_jspx_th_debug_timer_0` variable. This is the line that gets the error message "`Class Chap_00031_00037.examples.TimerTag not found.`" So the java compiler (not the JSP translator or the servlet engine) was unable to find a class. If you can figure out why, you're done.

The compiler might not find a class for several reasons. The class may not have been compiled or its `.class` file may not exist in the classpath. But a careful examination of the error message points to a different reason. Notice exactly which class the compiler is looking for: `Chap_00031_00037.examples.TimerTag`. Where did that package name come from? Looking back at the tag handler source code, you can see no `package` statement and, in the TLD, the fully qualified class name is simply `TimerTag`. This accounts for why the class isn't found—the compiler isn't looking for it under the correct name.

But why is the compiler looking for a class with that package name? Because this is a compile issue, you need to look at the `.java` file to determine the source of the problem. The location of this file is servlet engine-dependent, but you can tell from the error message it's under the `work` subdirectory of the Tomcat root. Working your way down through the Web application subdirectories, you find the servlet source file. The first few lines show what the problem is

```
package Chap_00031_00037.examples;

import javax.servlet.*;
import javax.servlet.http.*;
import javax.servlet.jsp.*;
...
import org.apache.jasper.JasperException;
import java.sql.*;

public class ... extends HttpJspBase {
    ...
}
```

The generated servlet has a `package` statement and a number of `import` statements. From your general Java knowledge, you know classes can be referred to without their fully qualified package name if an `import` statement supplies the rest of the name. If none of the imported packages contain a referenced class name, the compiler assumes it's in the same package as the class being compiled. Therefore, the `TimerTag` class referred to on line 70 of the generated servlet (remember the error message?) is looked up in each of the imported packages, where it isn't found, and is then treated as if it were a class in the servlet's own package: `Chap_00031_00037.examples`. End of mystery.

But this leaves two questions:

- Why does this work in JRun?
- How can you fix the problem?

The first question is easy to answer if you look at JRun's version of the generated servlet:

```
// Generated by JRun, do not edit

import javax.servlet.*;
import javax.servlet.http.*;
import javax.servlet.jsp.*;
import javax.servlet.jsp.tagext.*;
import allaire.jrun.jsp.JRunJSPStaticHelpers;
import java.sql.*;

public class jrun__Chap17__examples__Timer2ejsp1a
   extends allaire.jrun.jsp.HttpJSPServlet
   implements allaire.jrun.jsp.JRunJspPage
{
   ...
}
```

The JRun JSP translator doesn't generate a `package` statement, so the generated servlet is in the default unnamed package. This is the same package the tag handler is in, so there's no conflict when the servlet uses the unadorned class name:

```
   TimerTag timer__4_1 = (TimerTag)
      JRunJSPStaticHelpers.createTagHandler
         (pageContext, "TimerTag");
```

Now, how can you fix the error under Tomcat? One way is to supply an `import` statement for `TimerTag`, so the java compiler knows not to try to associate it with any other package. You don't have access to the generated servlet, only to the JSP source, which means you could place this statement in your JSP:

```
<%@ page import="TimerTag" %>
```

While this would work, it's an unsatisfactory solution because it would have to be done in every JSP page that uses the tag. Apart from the problem of remembering to do this, it isn't even clear to the maintenance programmer why this class is being imported—no visible references exist to it.

A better solution is to assign a package name to the tag handler. If the full class name is `jspcr.debug.TimerTag`, then line 70 becomes

```
jspcr.debug.TimerTag _jspx_th_debug_timer_0
   = new jspcr.debug.TimerTag();
```

and no ambiguity occurs.

**Note** *A helpful way to separate compilation and run-time errors is to precompile the JSP page. The JSP 1.1 specification requires compliant JSP containers to do this when a page is invoked with a request parameter named "`jsp_precompile`". The JSP container translates the JSP page into servlet source code and compiles the servlet, but won't cause it to service the request. This needn't be done from a browser; it can be done from a batch Java application that simply creates a URL for the request (including the "`jsp_precompile`" parameter) and calling its `openStream()` method.*



## Testing in Isolation

Given that isolating the failing component is the key to debugging, making this easy to do is important. Walking through the mental flowchart and identifying both what *should* be happening and what is *actually* happening should be possible. When the problem area is isolated, it should be possible to test the failing component by itself, verifying each step of its operation.

To do this, you need to start from a known state. If you've changed several sections of code, recompiled some beans, and modified a deployment descriptor, you may well find the solution, but you may not see different results because of partial initializations and leftover classes. To avoid this, you can do the following:

- **Delete old copies of translated JSP servlets and classes.** A JSP file is only translated when it's newer than its corresponding servlet and class file, but modules it depends on may change without triggering its retranslation. Changes to files included with the `<%@ include %>` directive, for example, aren't guaranteed to cause the including JSP page to be retranslated. Some JSP containers do this, but the specification doesn't require it.

- **Delete serialized sessions.** Some JSP containers save sessions to persistent storage during shutdown, and then restore them when the JSP container is started again. JRun, for example, writes serialized sessions to the `/WEB-INF/sessions` directory. If you make changes to classes and recompile them, you may have an old version of the class deserialized when you bring the servlet engine back up.
- **Restart the Web server and servlet engine.** While this may not be strictly necessary in all cases, this step lets you be certain all initializations are done properly. Changes to `web.xml` and tag library descriptors, for example, may only be detected during startup.

Once you're sure of the application state, you can provide it with known input and follow it through the process. The servlet log provides a central collection point for messages from the servlet engine, and from individual servlets and JSP pages. You can write a message to the log with the `log()` method[1], the same as you would use `System.out.println()`. Particularly in JSP pages, it's easy to add a few log messages, test, add a few more based on the results of that test, and so on. Writing messages to the servlet log provides a better execution trace than trying to write to the servlet output stream, which may be corrupted and disappear before you can analyze it.

## Debugging Tools

Most commercial *integrated development environments* (*IDEs*) provide some kind of debugger that enables you to step through the execution of a Java class, examining and, possibly changing, the values of variables. The JDK includes a command line debugger named `jdb`, which performs these same functions, more or less. While these tools can be useful, they have several drawbacks when used to debug JSP code.

To begin with, JSP pages don't map closely to their byte code equivalents. They may consist of scriptlets, directives, expressions, HTML, and custom tags. If you're really interested in line-by-line execution tracing, you would need to debug with the generated servlet source code, not the `.jsp` file.

In addition, JSP classes are loaded and run in a separate virtual machine controlled by the servlet engine, possibly linked to a Web server. To debug an individual class, starting the whole servlet engine in debug mode is necessary. You need to verify all the same classpath entries are active, the same ports are used, and so on. Given that you can even figure out how to do this, it tends to make the debug environment very

1 This is a method in the `ServletContext` class, but it's also available as a convenience method of `GenericServlet`, from which most JSP pages derive. `log()` is preferable to `System.out.println()` because it's vendor-independent and provided by all servlet containers.

different from the actual run-time environment. Likewise, substantial timing differences between the two environments may cause timeouts and race conditions that have nothing to do with the problem being debugged.

In practical terms, you can do little with a line-by-line debugger that you can't do with the `log()` method (or `System.out.println()`, for that matter). Any variable you might examine at a breakpoint can just as easily be written to the servlet log. You can stop execution at any point and produce a stack trace simply by throwing an exception. Given JSP's automatic compilation and the browser refresh button, you can probably do several iterations with new message points faster than you can start the IDE and bring up the servlet engine in debug mode.

In this section, you learn to develop three tools that are less intrusive and better adapted to the HTTP request-handling environment. Used in conjunction with `log()` method for execution tracing, they can help both in isolating errors and verifying fixes.

## Capturing Form Parameters

When an HTML form is used to send request parameters to a JSP or servlet, an obvious testing requirement is being able to know what parameters it sends and what their value is. This isn't always obvious. If a `<SELECT>` element allows multiple selections, what is the value of the request parameter? If a `TEXT` input element isn't filled in, will it be passed as a blank or null? What about check boxes that don't specify a `VALUE` attribute?

An easy way to find out is to use a debugging JSP page that captures the request parameters and displays them as name/value pairs in tabular form. The following JSP page (`Echo.jsp`) shows how this can be done:

```
<%@ page session="false" %>
<%@ page import="java.util.*" %>
<HTML>
<HEAD><TITLE>Form Parameters</TITLE></HEAD>
<BODY>
<H3>Form Parameters</H3>
<TABLE BORDER="1" CELLPADDING="3" CELLSPACING="0">
<TR><TH WIDTH=200>Name</TH><TH WIDTH=200>Value</TH></TR>
<%
   Enumeration enames = request.getParameterNames();
   while (enames.hasMoreElements()) {
      String name = (String) enames.nextElement();
      String[] values = request.getParameterValues(name);
      if (values != null) {
         for (int i = 0; i < values.length; i++) {
            String value = values[i];
%><TR><TD><%= name %></TD><TD><%= value %></TD></TR><%
```

```
            }
        }
    }
%>
</TABLE>
</BODY>
</HTML>
```

`Echo.jsp` gets a list of all the parameter names from the `request` object, and then loops through the list and prints the name and value(s) of each one. The only wrinkle is a parameter may have more than one value. For example, groups of check boxes can have the same name but different `value` attributes. The servlet API takes care of this, however, by providing a `getParameterValues()` method in the request object that returns an array of values.

Figure 17-2 shows an HTML form with several types of input elements. The JSP page that generates the form is listed in the following:

```
<%@ page session="false" %>
<HTML>
<HEAD>
<TITLE>Job Application</TITLE>
</HEAD>
<BODY>
<H3>Please Indicate Your Qualifications</H3>

<FORM ACTION="/dailyplanet/apphandler.jsp" METHOD="POST">

<INPUT
   TYPE="hidden"
   NAME="locale"
   VALUE="<%= request.getLocale() %>"
   >
<TABLE BORDER="0" CELLPADDING="3" CELLSPACING="0">
   <TR>
      <TD>
         <INPUT TYPE="checkbox" NAME="speed">
         Faster than a speeding bullet
         <BR>
         <INPUT TYPE="checkbox" NAME="power">
         More powerful than a locomotive
         <BR>
```

```
            <INPUT TYPE="checkbox" NAME="flight">
            Able to leap tall buildings with a single bound
            <BR>
         </TD>
      </TR>
      <TR><TD>Name: <INPUT TYPE="text" NAME="name">
      <INPUT TYPE="submit" VALUE="Submit"></TD></TR>
   </TABLE>

   </FORM>
   </BODY>
   </HTML>
```

This form enables job applicants to describe their qualifications using a set of check boxes. Additionally, the user's locale is captured as a hidden field, so responses can be sent in the user's preferred language. Ordinarily, this form is processed by `/dailyplanet/apphander.jsp`. To handle this input properly, `apphandler.jsp` needs to know the format in which the request parameters will be sent. Without peeking, would you know the default format of the check box values because they don't specify a `VALUE` attribute?

This is easy to determine. By substituting `ACTION="Echo.jsp"` for `ACTION="dailyplanet.jsp"`, you can capture the output of the form and test it using several different browsers and combinations of values. If you do this for the form values in Figure 17-2, you get the table shown in Figure 17-3.



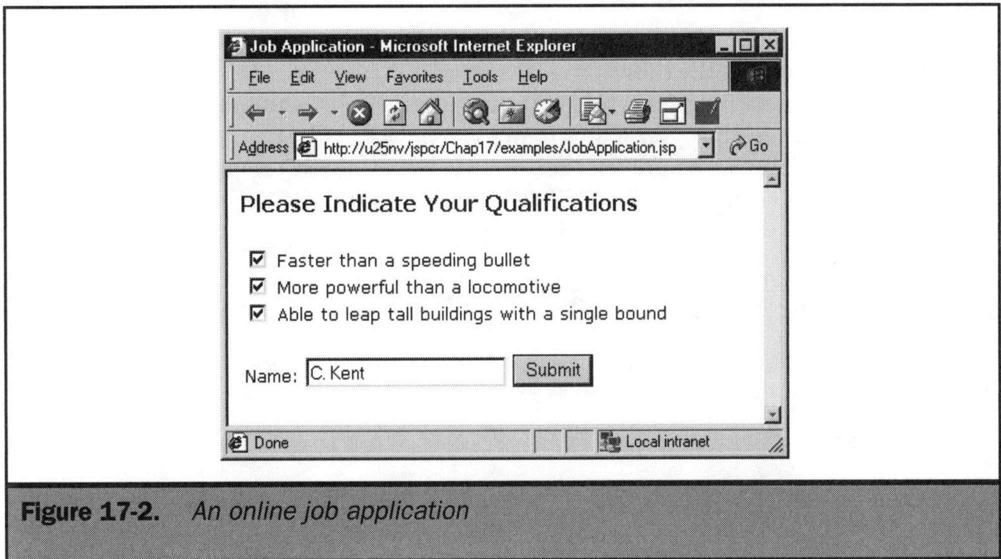


**Figure 17-2.** *An online job application*

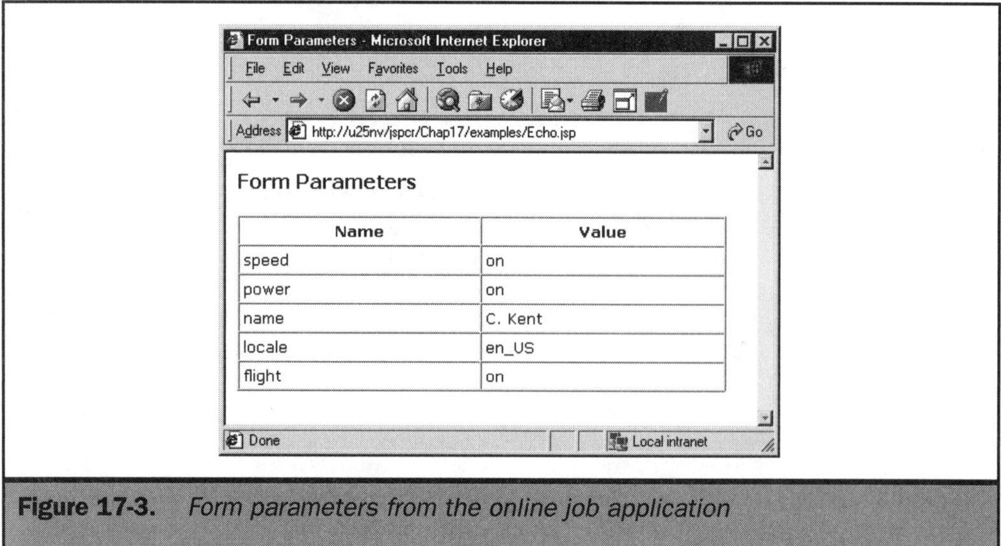


| Name | Value |
|---|---|
| speed | on |
| power | on |
| name | C. Kent |
| locale | en_US |
| flight | on |

**Figure 17-3.** *Form parameters from the online job application*

`Echo.jsp` can be enhanced to show more information about the request, such as the request headers, cookies, and request attributes. The main advantage of `Echo.jsp` is it requires no change to the server-side component that processes the form. All it takes is a quick one-line change to the `<FORM>` element in the HTML document or JSP page that submits the form.

# A Debugging Web Client

The `Echo.jsp` server enables you to see what the Web client produces. The other side of the transaction is how the processing servlet or JSP page responds. Debugging the server side component is easier when you can view its input and output in isolation, rather than after a Web browser manipulates it.

This is easier than you might suspect. A Web server doesn't require a Web browser, only something that can produce an HTTP request in ordinary ASCII form. Telnet invoked on port 80 works perfectly well for this:

```
% telnet www.lyricnote.com 80
Trying...
Connected to www.lyricnote.com.
Escape character is '^]'.
GET / HTTP/1.0

HTTP/1.1 200 OK
...
```

Unfortunately, the default Telnet client on Windows systems is GUI-based and awkward to use for this purpose. The GUI window doesn't scroll and automatically clears its text after the request is processed. And the Windows client doesn't handle the Unix line-ending convention properly.

Duplicating the HTTP request functionality with a standalone console-mode Java application is easy enough, however. `WebClient.java`, listed in the following, is a simple Web client designed to be called from a command line:

```
import java.io.*;
import java.net.*;
import java.util.*;

public class WebClient
{
   /**
   * Mainline.
   * Reads command line parameters and creates a new
   * <CODE>WebClient</CODE> object.
   */
   public static void main(String[] args)
      throws Exception
   {
      String host = "localhost";
      int port = 80;

      for (int i = 0; i < args.length; i++) {
         String arg = args[i];
         if (arg.startsWith("-")) {
            if (arg.equals("-host")) {
               if (++i >= args.length)
                  throw new RuntimeException
                  ("no argument for " + arg);
               host = args[i];
            }
            else if (arg.equals("-port")) {
               if (++i >= args.length)
                  throw new RuntimeException
                  ("no argument for " + arg);
               try {
                  port = Integer.parseInt(args[i]);
               }
               catch (NumberFormatException e) {
```

```
                  throw new RuntimeException
                  ("Invalid port number [" + args[i] + "]");
               }
            }
            else {
               System.out.println("Invalid argument: " + arg);
               showUsage();
               System.exit(0);
            }
         }
         else {
            showUsage();
            System.exit(0);
         }
      }

      new WebClient(host, port);
   }

   /**
   * Displays the calling syntax
   */
   public static void showUsage()
   {
      String[] text = {
         "usage: java WebClient"
         + " [-host <hostName>]"
         + " [-port <portNumber>]",
      };
      for (int i = 0; i < text.length; i++)
         System.out.println(text[i]);
   }

   /**
   * Creates and runs the web client
   * @param host the HTTP server
   * @param port the server port number
   * @exception IOException if a socket error occurs
   */
   public WebClient(String host, int port)
      throws IOException
   {
```

```
int contentLength = 0;

// Open a socket to the web host

Socket socket = new Socket(host, port);

// Read input from user and echo it to web host

BufferedReader in =
   new BufferedReader(
   new InputStreamReader(System.in));

PrintWriter out =
   new PrintWriter(socket.getOutputStream());

// First line - request

String line = in.readLine();
out.println(line);

// Header lines

for (;;) {

   // Read and echo the line

   line = in.readLine();
   if (line == null)
      throw new IOException("Unexpected EOF");
   line = line.trim();
   out.println(line);

   // End of headers

   if (line.equals(""))
      break;

   // Otherwise, this is a header

   int p = line.indexOf(": ");
   if (p == -1)
      throw new IOException
```

```
            (line + " is not a valid header line");

        String name = line.substring(0, p).trim();
        String value = line.substring(p+1).trim();

        if (name.equalsIgnoreCase("Content-Length")) {
            try {
                contentLength = Integer.parseInt(value);
            }
            catch (NumberFormatException e) {
                throw new IOException
                ("Invalid content length " + value);
            }
        }
    }

    // Read <contentLength> bytes of content

    if (contentLength > 0) {
        StringBuffer sb = new StringBuffer();
        for (;;) {
            line = in.readLine();
            if (line == null)
                break;
            sb.append(line);
            int len = sb.length();
            if (len < contentLength)
                continue;
            if (len > contentLength)
                sb.setLength(contentLength);
            break;
        }

        // Write data to output stream

        out.print(sb.toString());
    }

    out.flush();

    // The server is now working on the request.
    // Read its output and dump to stdout
```

```
         in =
            new BufferedReader(
            new InputStreamReader(
            socket.getInputStream()));

         out = new PrintWriter(System.out);

         for (;;) {
            line = in.readLine();
            if (line == null)
               break;
            out.println(line);
         }

         // Close files

         in.close();
         out.close();
         socket.close();
      }
   }
```



WebClient's calling syntax is

`java WebClient [-host` *<hostName>*`] [-port` *<portNumber>*`]`

When started, it opens a socket connection to the specified host (default is `localhost`), and then waits for an HTTP request and optional headers to be entered from the keyboard. Each line entered by the user is sent out over the socket. Input terminates when a blank line is entered. This signals to the HTTP server that no more headers will be sent and the request is complete, except possibly for data being sent with a `POST` request.

After the request is sent and processed, the server sends back a response, which is echoed to the console. A typical exchange might be

```
D:\jspcr\Chap17\examples>java WebClient
POST /jspcr/Chap17/examples/Echo.jsp HTTP/1.0
Content-type: application/x-www-form-urlencoded
Content-length: 53

speed=on&power=on&flight=on&name=C.+Kent&locale=en_US
HTTP/1.1 200 OK
```

```
Date: Tue, 05 Dec 2000 03:59:35 GMT
Server: Apache/1.3.12 (Win32)
Connection: Keep-alive, close
Content-Length: 434
Content-Type: text/html; charset=ISO-8859-1



<HTML>
<HEAD>
<TITLE>Form Parameters</TITLE>
</HEAD>
<BODY>
<H3>Form Parameters</H3>
<TABLE BORDER="1" CELLPADDING="3" CELLSPACING="0">
<TR><TH WIDTH=200>Name</TH><TH WIDTH=200>Value</TH></TR>

<TR><TD>flight</TD><TD>on</TD></TR>

<TR><TD>speed</TD><TD>on</TD></TR>

<TR><TD>power</TD><TD>on</TD></TR>

<TR><TD>name</TD><TD>C. Kent</TD></TR>

<TR><TD>locale</TD><TD>en_US</TD></TR>

</TABLE>
</BODY>
</HTML>
```

## Tracing HTTP Requests

To troubleshoot a Web application effectively, you must be able to monitor how it makes requests and receives responses. You already saw that Java classes can act both as a Web client and a Web server. In this section, you develop a monitoring tool that performs both functions, acting as the middleman between the client and server, as illustrated in Figure 17-4. When this tracer tool is plugged into a Web application, its server component listens for HTTP requests, logs their headers, and then forwards them to the real Web server. Its client component then receives the Web server's response, logs the headers, and sends the response back to the client. Neither the client nor the server is aware of the tracer's presence in the loop.

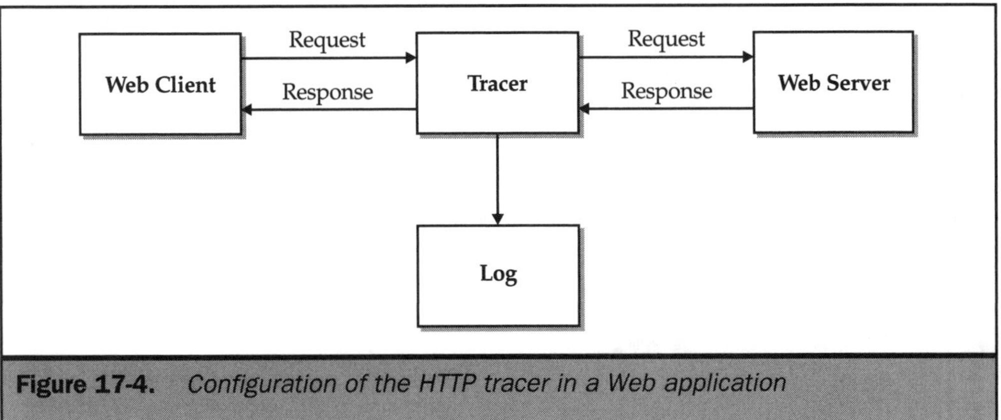


**Figure 17-4.** *Configuration of the HTTP tracer in a Web application*

The tool consists of two main components:

- A Web server proxy that listens for HTTP requests.
- A request handler that copies the client request to the server and the response back to the client, logging headers in both directions.

The following lists the first component (`Tracer.java`).

```
package http;

import java.io.*;
import java.net.*;
import java.util.*;

/**
* Acts as a proxy web server, capturing requests
* and responses and echoing the headers to a
* log stream.
*/
public class Tracer extends Thread implements Logger
{
   public static final int DEFAULT_PORT = 8601;

   private String host;
   private int port;
   private int tracerPort;
   private PrintWriter logWriter;
```

```
// ============================================
//    Class methods
// ============================================

/**
* Mainline
*/
public static void main(String[] args)
   throws IOException
{
   String opt_host = null;
   String opt_port = null;
   String opt_tracerPort = null;
   String opt_log = null;

   try {
      for (int i = 0; i < args.length; i++) {
         String arg = args[i];

         if (!arg.startsWith("-"))
            throw new IllegalArgumentException
            ("Unknown argument ["
            + arg + "]. Use -h for help");

         // -h for help

         String keyword = arg.substring(1);
         if (keyword.equals("h") ||
             keyword.equals("help"))
         {
            showUsage();
            return;
         }

         // -host <hostname>

         if (keyword.equals("host")) {
            if (++i >= args.length)
               throw new IllegalArgumentException
               (arg + " but no argument");
            opt_host = args[i];
         }
```

```
      else

      // -port <hostname>

      if (keyword.equals("port")) {
         if (++i >= args.length)
            throw new IllegalArgumentException
            (arg + " but no argument");
         opt_port = args[i];
      }
      else

      // -tracerPort <hostname>

      if (keyword.equals("tracerPort")) {
         if (++i >= args.length)
            throw new IllegalArgumentException
            (arg + " but no argument");
         opt_tracerPort = args[i];
      }
      else

      // -log <filename>

      if (keyword.equals("log")) {
         if (++i >= args.length)
            throw new IllegalArgumentException
            (arg + " but no argument");
         opt_log = args[i];
      }
      else
         throw new IllegalArgumentException
         ("Unrecognized option " + arg);
   }

   // Verify that there is no port conflict

   int testTracerPort = (opt_tracerPort == null)
      ? DEFAULT_PORT
      : Integer.parseInt(opt_tracerPort);

   int testHostPort = (opt_port == null)
```

```
            ? RequestHandler.DEFAULT_PORT
            : Integer.parseInt(opt_port);

         if (testTracerPort == testHostPort)
            throw new IllegalArgumentException
            ("Cannot assign port and tracerPort both to "
            + testHostPort);
      }
      catch (IllegalArgumentException e) {
         System.err.println(e.getMessage());
         return;
      }

      // Create the tracer

      Tracer tracer = new Tracer();

      // Set its properties, if any

      if (opt_host != null)
         tracer.setHost(opt_host);

      if (opt_port != null)
         tracer.setPort(Integer.parseInt(opt_port));

      if (opt_tracerPort != null)
         tracer.setTracerPort
            (Integer.parseInt(opt_tracerPort));

      if (opt_log != null)
         tracer.setLogWriter(new FileWriter(opt_log));

      tracer.start();
   }

   /**
   * Displays calling syntax
   */
   public static final void showUsage()
   {
      String[] text = {
         "",
         "usage: java http.Tracer [options]",
```

```
            "",
            "where options are:",
            "",
            "-host          <hostName>  "
               + "(defaults to "
               + RequestHandler.DEFAULT_HOST + ")",
            "-port          <hostPort>  "
               + "(defaults to "
               + RequestHandler.DEFAULT_PORT + ")",
            "-tracerPort  <localPort> "
               + "(defaults to "
               + DEFAULT_PORT + ")",
            "-log           <fileName>  "
               + "(defaults to System.out)",
         };
         for (int i = 0; i < text.length; i++)
            System.out.println(text[i]);
      }

      // ============================================
      //    Instance methods
      // ============================================

      public void run()
      {
         // Set defaults if not otherwise specified

         if (tracerPort == 0)
            tracerPort = DEFAULT_PORT;

         if (logWriter == null)
            logWriter = new PrintWriter(System.out);

         // Start proxy server

         try {
            log("M: Opening tracer server on tracerPort "
               + tracerPort);
            ServerSocket server = new ServerSocket(tracerPort);

            // Loop forever
```

```
            for (;;) {

               // Wait for connection

               log("M: Waiting for connections");
               Socket client = server.accept();
               log("M: Connection received from " + client);

               // Dispatch it to a request handler thread

               RequestHandler rh = new RequestHandler(client);
               rh.setLogger(this);
               if (host != null)
                  rh.setHost(host);
               if (port != 0)
                  rh.setPort(port);
               rh.start();
            }
         }
         catch (IOException e) {
            e.printStackTrace();
         }
      }

      // ============================================
      //    Implementation of Logger
      // ============================================

      /**
      * Writes a message to the log
      * @param message the message
      */
      public synchronized void log(String message)
      {
         logWriter.println(message);
         logWriter.flush();
      }

      // ============================================
      //    Accessors
      // ============================================
```

```
/**
* Returns the host.
*/
public String getHost()
{
   return host;
}

/**
* Sets the host.
* @param host the host.
*/
public void setHost(String host)
{
   this.host = host;
}

/**
* Returns the port.
*/
public int getPort()
{
   return port;
}

/**
* Sets the port.
* @param port the port.
*/
public void setPort(int port)
{
   this.port = port;
}

/**
* Returns the tracerPort.
*/
public int getTracerPort()
{
   return tracerPort;
}
```

```
    /**
    * Sets the tracerPort.
    * @param tracerPort the tracerPort.
    */
    public void setTracerPort(int tracerPort)
    {
       this.tracerPort = tracerPort;
    }

    /**
    * Returns the logWriter.
    */
    public Writer getLogWriter()
    {
       return logWriter;
    }

    /**
    * Sets the logWriter.
    * @param logWriter the logWriter.
    */
    public void setLogWriter(Writer logWriter)
       throws IOException
    {
       this.logWriter = new PrintWriter(logWriter);
    }
}
```

The `Tracer` mainline parses the command line, which supports four options:

- `-host` *<hostname>* The name of the target Web server host. If not specified, this defaults to `localhost`.
- `-port` *<portnumber>* The port number on the target Web server. The default is 80, which is the default HTTP port number.
- `-tracerPort` *<portnumber>* The local port number on which the tracer itself runs. The default is 8601. This port number must be included in the URL to be traced. For example, if an HTML form has an `ACTION` attribute of http://www.lyricnote.com/search/ProductSearch.jsp, then it should be changed to http://www.lyricnote.com:8601/search/ProductSearch.jsp. This is the only change that must be made to hook up the tracer to any application.
- `-log` *<filename>* The name of a file to which the HTTP headers is to be written. Log messages go to `System.out` if this option isn't specified.

After validating the command line options, the mainline creates a `Tracer` object, sets its properties, and starts it.

The `run()` method creates a `java.net.ServerSocket` and begins listening for client connections. When a connection is accepted, `run()` creates a request-handling thread to process the transaction. You examine this component shortly. A log message is written for each of these steps.

Both `Tracer` and `RequestHandler` write log messages. Because the log may be redirected by a command line option, each component needs a handle to the log output stream. You can accomplish this by defining a `Logger` interface that `Tracer` implements. `RequestHandler` is passed a reference to `Tracer` in its role as `Logger`. To make clear which component sent the message, each message begins with either `C:` for client, `S:` for server, or `M:` for the tracer middleman.

The second component of the tool, `RequestHandler`, acts as a Web client to the target Web server, passing it the request line, request headers, and any request data stream it obtains from the real Web client, logging headers as it goes. `RequestHandler` then turns around and copies the response line, response headers, and response data to the client.

```
package http;

import java.io.*;
import java.net.*;
import java.util.*;

/**
* A proxy HTTP server that handles a single request
*/
public class RequestHandler extends Thread
{
   public static final String DEFAULT_HOST = "localhost";
   public static final int DEFAULT_PORT = 80;

   private Socket client;
   private Logger logger;
   private String host;
   private int port;

   // ===========================================
   //    Constructors
   // ===========================================

   /**
```

```
* Creates a new <CODE>RequestHandler</CODE>
* for the specified client
*/
public RequestHandler(Socket client)
{
   this.client = client;
}

// ============================================
//    Instance methods
// ============================================

/**
* Copies the request from the client to the server
* and copies the response back to the client.
*/
public void run()
{
   try {

      // Open a socket to the web server

      if (host == null)
         host = DEFAULT_HOST;
      if (port <= 0)
         port = DEFAULT_PORT;

      Socket server = new Socket(host, port);

      // Open I/O streams to the client

      InputStream cin =
         new BufferedInputStream(client.getInputStream());
      OutputStream cout =
         new BufferedOutputStream(client.getOutputStream());

      // Open I/O streams to the server

      InputStream sin =
         new BufferedInputStream(server.getInputStream());
```

```
OutputStream sout =
   new BufferedOutputStream(server.getOutputStream());

// Copy request line and headers from client to server,
// echoing to logger if specified. Stop after the
// first empty line (end of headers)

int contentLength = 0;
StringBuffer sb = new StringBuffer();
for (;;) {

   // Read a byte from client
   // and copy it to server

   int c = cin.read();
   sout.write(c);

   // Ignore CR at end of line

   if (c == '\r')
      continue;

   // If LF, process the line

   if (c == '\n') {
      String line = sb.toString();
      sb = new StringBuffer();

      // Log the line

      logger.log("C: " + line);

      // If this is an empty line,
      // there are no more headers

      if (line.length() == 0)
         break;

      // If it is a content length header,
      // save the content length
```

```
            int p = line.indexOf(":");
            if (p != -1) {
               String key = line.substring(0, p).trim();
               String value = line.substring(p+1).trim();
               if (key.equalsIgnoreCase("content-length"))
                  contentLength = Integer.parseInt(value);
            }
         }

         // Otherwise, append char to string buffer

         else
            sb.append((char) c);
      }
      sout.flush();

      // If content length was specified, read input stream
      // and copy to server

      if (contentLength > 0) {
         for (int i = 0; i < contentLength; i++) {
            int c = cin.read();
            sout.write(c);
         }
         sout.flush();
      }

      // Echo the response back to the client

      sb = new StringBuffer();
      for (;;) {

         // Read a byte from server
         // and copy it to client

         int c = sin.read();
         cout.write(c);

         // Ignore CR at end of line

         if (c == '\r')
            continue;
```

```
      // If LF, process the line

      if (c == '\n') {
         String line = sb.toString();
         sb = new StringBuffer();

         // Log the line

         logger.log("S: " + line);

         // If this is an empty line,
         // there are no more headers

         if (line.length() == 0)
            break;
      }

      // Otherwise, append char to string buffer

      else
         sb.append((char) c);
   }
   cout.flush();

   // Copy remaining bytes to client

   int bytesCopied = 0;
   for (;;) {
      int c = sin.read();
      if (c == -1)
         break;
      cout.write(c);
      bytesCopied++;
   }
   if (bytesCopied > 0)
      cout.flush();

   // Close streams and sockets

   cin.close();
   cout.close();
```

```
         client.close();

         sin.close();
         sout.close();
         server.close();
      }
      catch (IOException e) {
         e.printStackTrace();
      }
   }

   // ==============================================
   //    Accessors
   // ==============================================

   /**
   * Returns the client.
   */
   public Socket getClient()
   {
      return client;
   }

   /**
   * Returns the logger.
   */
   public Logger getLogger()
   {
      return logger;
   }

   /**
   * Sets the logger.
   * @param logger the logger.
   */
   public void setLogger(Logger logger)
   {
      this.logger = logger;
   }
```

```
   /**
   * Returns the host.
   */
   public String getHost()
   {
      return host;
   }

   /**
   * Sets the host.
   * @param host the host.
   */
   public void setHost(String host)
   {
      this.host = host;
   }

   /**
   * Returns the port.
   */
   public int getPort()
   {
      return port;
   }

   /**
   * Sets the port.
   * @param port the port.
   */
   public void setPort(int port)
   {
      this.port = port;
   }
}
```



The heart of `RequestHandler` is its `run()` method, which opens a client socket to the Web server, and then opens the socket's input and output streams. Likewise, it opens input and output streams for the Web client. `run()` method then reads the request line and request headers, looking for a blank line that signals the end of the headers. As each header is read, it is logged and passed on to the Web server. If a `Content-Length` header is found, its value is noted. After the blank line at the end of the headers, if the content length is non-zero, the request handler reads that many bytes from the client input stream and copies them to the server. The same process is then repeated in reverse for the server's response, except the Content-Length header is ignored and the server's output is read and copied until the end of the file.

An example of where the `Tracer` tool can be useful is HTTP authentication. Much of what makes this work happens under the covers of both the browser and the Web server. An examination of the HTTP headers can make it clear.

HTTP basic authentication works like this:

- A Web user requests a document protected by HTTP basic authentication.
- The Web browser formats an HTTP request and sends it to the Web server.
- The server refuses the request, setting the status code to 401 (Authorization Required) and sending a `WWW-Authenticate` header specifying the authentication type and the realm.
- The browser gets the 401 response code and searches its cache to see if the user has already logged in to this realm during this session. If the user hasn't logged in, the browser prompts for the user ID and password.
- The credentials, obtained either from this prompt or from the browser session cache, are Base64-encoded[2] and the original request is retransmitted, this time with an `Authorization` header.
- The server sees the `Authorization` header, verifies whether the user is authorized to retrieve the document, and then returns either the document or another 401 response line.

Here's what `Tracer` reports for this process[3]:

```
M: Opening tracer server on tracerPort 8601
M: Waiting for connections
M: Connection received from Socket
   [addr=ppp-1-247.dialup.lyricnote.com/209.165.213.47,
   port=1180,localport=8601]
M: Waiting for connections
```

2 Base64 encoding converts a byte stream to readable ASCII characters so control characters in the bytes don't interfere with the server operations. RFC 2068 describes the algorithm. Note, however, this isn't encryption, only a character transformation that can easily be reversed. For this reason, HTTP Basic Authentication is not particularly secure and should only be used for internal applications where the security risks are acceptable.

3 The log is reformatted slightly for readability.

The tracer server started by opening a server socket on port 8601. It blocked on the server socket's `accept()` method waiting for clients to connect. Once a connection was received, a request handler was started and the tracer server resumed listening for other client requests.

```
C: GET /logviewer/index.jsp HTTP/1.1
C: Accept: application/msword, application/vnd.ms-excel, ...
C: Accept-Language: en-us
C: Accept-Encoding: gzip, deflate
C: User-Agent: Mozilla/4.0 (compatible; Windows NT 4.0)
C: Host: u25nv:8601
C: Connection: Keep-Alive
C:
```

The request handler read the request line and six headers, echoing them to the Web server.

```
S: HTTP/1.1 401 Authorization Required
S: Date: Tue, 05 Dec 2000 22:28:22 GMT
S: Server: Apache/1.3.12 (Win32)
S: WWW-Authenticate: Basic realm="Servlet Administrators"
S: Keep-Alive: timeout=15, max=100
S: Connection: Keep-Alive
S: Transfer-Encoding: chunked
S: Content-Type: text/html; charset=iso-8859-1
S:
```

The Web server refused the request, returning a 401 status code (Authorization Required) and a `WWW-Authenticate` header specifying the authentication type was `Basic` and the realm was "`Servlet Administrators`". The Web browser prompted the user for the user ID ("`wolfgang`") and password ("`papageno`") for that realm and reissued the request:

```
M: Connection received from Socket
   [addr=ppp-1-247.dialup.lyricnote.com/209.165.213.47,
   port=1184,localport=8601]
M: Waiting for connections

C: GET /logviewer/index.jsp HTTP/1.1
C: Accept: application/msword, application/vnd.ms-excel, ...
C: Accept-Language: en-us
```

```
C: Accept-Encoding: gzip, deflate
C: User-Agent: Mozilla/4.0 (compatible; Windows NT 4.0)
C: Host: u25nv:8601
C: Connection: Keep-Alive
C: Authorization: Basic d29sZmdhbmc6cGFwYWdlbm8=
C:

S: HTTP/1.1 200 OK
S: Date: Tue, 05 Dec 2000 22:28:37 GMT
S: Server: Apache/1.3.12 (Win32)
S: Connection: Keep-alive, Keep-Alive
S: Content-Length: 142
S: Keep-Alive: timeout=15, max=100
S: Content-Type: text/html; charset=ISO-8859-1
S:
```

This time, the request included an `Authorization` header with the Base64-encoded credentials. And, this time, the server accepted the request and sent back the document.

## Summary

Testing and debugging are indispensable parts of application development. While programming is systematic and amenable to design patterns, debugging is often haphazard and performed by trial and error changes. This chapter highlighted two key aspects of a systematic debugging methodology:

- Building a mental model of the components and their interactions
- Isolating the failing component

Three tools that can assist in this methodology were presented:

- `Echo.jsp` A JSP page that captures parameters produced by an HTML form
- `WebClient` A standalone application that simulates a Web browser
- `Tracer` A standalone application that intercepts and logs HTTP requests

With sufficient forethought and design for testability, debugging can be as systematic as application development.

The Complete Reference

# Chapter 18

## Deploying Web Applications

Installing and configuring Web applications has historically been a completely vendor-specific task. Apache JServ, for example, used both `.properties` files and files containing Apache directive extensions to configure its servlet zones and their attributes. Early versions of JRun came with a raft of `.properties` files used to indicate how many servers existed, what ports they used, their classpaths, what servlets aliases they recognized, which servlets should be preloaded, and so on. The JSWDK reference implementation used a custom XML format for this purpose.

A certain amount of diversity is inevitable because servlet engines are, after all, different implementations with their own particular features. But that part of the configuration task is limited. The part that describes and interacts with servlets themselves is fairly regular and can be standardized with great benefit. This is precisely what happened in connection with the introduction of Web applications in the Servlet 2.2 API.

This chapter describes the structure of a Web application and how to move it out of the development environment and into a production environment.

## The Web Application Environment

A collection of cooperating resources mapped to a common area of the Web server namespace is referred to by the Servlet 2.2 and JSP 1.1 API specifications as a *Web application*. This collection may include servlets, JSP pages, HTML files, images, supporting classes, and configuration data.

For example, the LyricNote Web site might contain several Web applications:

- `products` This would include the product catalog database, images, a search engine, a shopping cart application for customer orders, and Web pages that describe product categories.
- `support` This application would provide JSP pages for customers to report problems and ask questions, defect tracking servlets, servlets for generating e-mail, and classes that interact with a knowledge base.
- `internal` MIS applications such as conference room bookings, job postings, and company newsletters would live here, in a mixture of servlets, JSP pages, and ordinary HTML.

### Directory Structure

A Web application has a prescribed directory structure that all compliant servlet engines understand. The structure is illustrated in Figure 18-1. The top level, or *application root*, contains HTML documents, JSP pages, images, and any other resources that make up the *content* of the application. Any number of subdirectories, which also

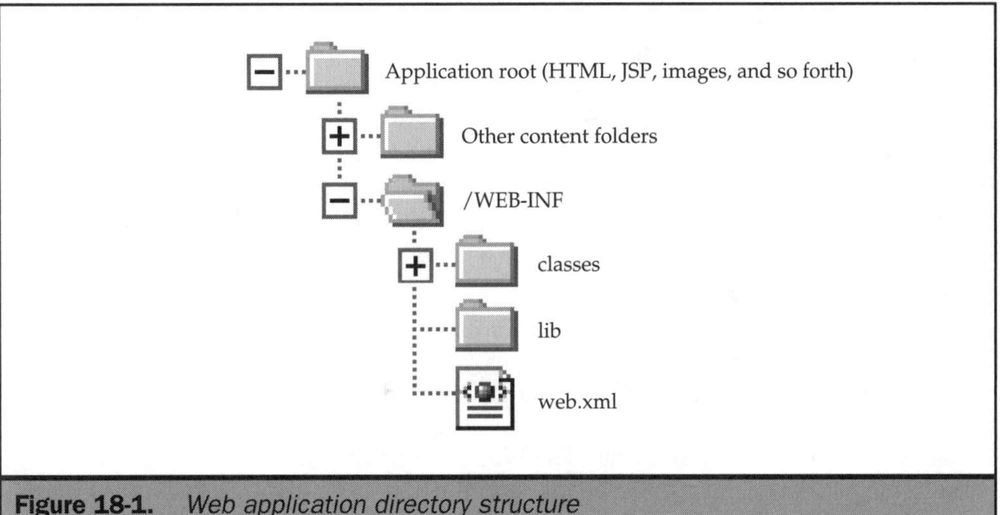


**Figure 18-1.** *Web application directory structure*



contain application content, can be under the root, much like folders in the document tree of a Web server.

The root directory also contains a special directory named `WEB-INF`. This directory and its subdirectories aren't visible to application users. Instead, they contain servlets, classes, `.jar` files, and configuration data that make up the operational parts of the application. Three entries of note are in `WEB-INF`:

- `classes` This directory contains servlets and other classes. These classes are automatically found by the servlet class loader, as if they were in the application classpath. `classes` may have subdirectories that correspond to the package structure, the same as any other directory in a classpath.
- `lib` Similar to `classes`, but contains `.jar` files. Classes in any .jar file in this directory are automatically made available to the class loader without having to be listed explicitly in some classpath.
- `web.xml` This is an XML document referred to as the *deployment descriptor*. It has a rigorously defined vendor-independent structure and is used to configure the servlets and other resources that make up the Web application. You examine `web.xml` in greater detail later in this chapter.

Other files and subdirectories may be in `WEB-INF`, although the Servlet API specification doesn't define any particular ones. One subdirectory commonly used is `tlds`, which contains Tag Library Descriptors for JSP custom tags. Because entries in this subdirectory are visible to application classes, but not to Web users, `WEB-INF` is often used for vendor-specific purposes. JRun, for example, creates a subdirectory named `jsp` that contains the Java source code and compiled classes for servlets generated from JSP pages. JRun also creates a subdirectory named `sessions`, which holds serialized versions of any HTTP sessions that are active when the servlet engine is brought down. In general, `WEB-INF` is suitable for any data you want to use in a Web application while keeping it hidden from direct access by users.

## Resource Mapping

Web servers have a document root directory that primarily contains HTML files. In Apache, for example, this is *<apache root>*`/htdocs`. Microsoft *Internet Information Server* (*IIS*) uses `inetpub/wwwroot`. When a URL is clicked in a Web browser, the browser breaks it down into its server and path components and generates an HTTP request to the server for the specified resource. The Web server, when it receives the request, extracts the path from the request header and translates it into a path relative to the document root directory. For example, if the URL is

```
http://www.lyricnote.com/products/index.html
```

the browser opens an HTTP connection to the `www.lyricnote.com` host and sends it a request starting with the line

```
GET /products/index.html HTTP/1.0
```

If the Web server is Apache and is installed at `/usr/local/Apache`, then the file sent back is

```
/usr/local/Apache/htdocs/products/index.html
```

If the server is Microsoft IIS and is installed at `c:\inetpub`, then the file requested is

```
c:\inetpub\wwwroot\products\index.html
```

A Web application also has a document root directory, as you've seen, but this root can be anywhere in the file system. The servlet engine, when it recognizes an HTTP request is for a servlet or JSP page, extracts the Web application name from the URL and maps the rest to a resource within that application. For example, if the URL is

```
http://www.lyricnote.com/products/contest/rules.jsp
```

then the servlet engine creates a request for /contest/rules.jsp and passes it to the products Web application.[1] Servlets are handled similarly. A URL like

```
http://www.lyricnote.com/products/servlet/Counter
```

gets passed to the products Web application as a request for the Counter servlet.[2]

URLs used in a servlet or JSP page within an application to refer to another resource within the application don't use the application name. For example, if the rules.jsp page needs to include the output of the Counter servlet dynamically, it uses this statement

```
    <jsp:include page="/servlet/Counter" flush="true"/>
```

not this statement

```
    <jsp:include page="/products/servlet/Counter" flush="true"/>
```

The same applies to URLs used by <jsp:include>, the <%@ include %> directive, the <%@ taglib %> directive, and methods that create RequestDispatcher objects. The rule for interpreting these relative URL's is this:

- If the URL begins with /, it's interpreted as being relative to the application root directory.
- If it doesn't begin with /, it's interpreted as being relative to the current JSP page.

This brings up a subtle difficulty, however. URLs in a JSP page used as hyperlinks, form actions, style sheet links, or image sources are interpreted by the browser, not the server. If the LyricNote home page is a JSP page with a link to /products/contest/rules.jsp, the link cannot be hardcoded with the products application name. Why not? Because the application name isn't necessarily going to be products. This depends entirely on where the system administrator chose to install the Web application. It could have been mounted as product_test or staging_area or anything else. Only when the application is actually running can a JSP page know the name, which can be obtained from the request.getContextPath() method.



1 Strictly speaking, the portion of the URL that constitutes the Web application name can be a multilevel string like /products/test/Wednesday, but it's more common for a single token to be used.

2 The <servlet-mapping> element of the deployment descriptor can be used to map any URL substring to a particular servlet. Shown here are the default mappings.

You can get around this in several ways. The JSP page can write every URL as a JSP expression concatenating `request.getContextPath()` with the rest of the URL, but this gets to be tedious and clutters up the code unnecessarily. A more elegant approach is to use the HTML `<BASE>` element to assign a context to the page:

```
<HTML>
<HEAD>
<BASE HREF="http://www.lyricnote.com/products/">
</HEAD>
<BODY>
<A HREF="contest/rules.jsp">View the contest rules</A>
</BODY>
</HTML>
```

With the `<BASE>` statement, the Web browser can interpret any nonabsolute URLs relative to the `HREF` attribute. Thus, `contest/rules.jsp` becomes `http://www.lyricnote.com/products/contest/rules.jsp`.

Of course, you aren't done yet. You still need to figure out the `BASE HREF` at run time. The `HREF` attribute needs to be a complete URL, not just an absolute path from the server, so you need a number of details. The URL may start with `https`, if the connection uses SSL. A port number may exist, not just the default port 80. Fortunately, the `request` object can provide all this information. The following scriptlet solves the problem in a general way.

```
<%
   String   scheme   = request.getScheme();
   String   server   = request.getServerName();
   int      port     = request.getServerPort();
   String   path     = request.getContextPath();

   StringBuffer sb = new StringBuffer();
   sb.append(scheme);
   sb.append("://");
   sb.append(server);
   if ((port != -1) && (port != 80)) {
      sb.append(":");
      sb.append(port);
   }
   sb.append(path);
   sb.append("/");
```

```
    String baseURL = sb.toString();
%>
<BASE HREF="<%= baseURL %>">
```

## The Servlet Context

Within a Web application, servlets and JSP pages can share data and functionality through a common object known as the *servlet context*. This is an object that implements the `javax.servlet.ServletContext` interface. The servlet context serves a number of useful purposes:

- **Object sharing** Both servlets and JSP pages can store objects by name in the servlet context, so they can be retrieved by other servlets and JSP pages. These bindings persist as long as the application is active.
- **Initialization parameters** Constants used throughout the application can be specified in the deployment descriptor and accessed through methods in the servlet context. This permits configuration details—such as database URLs and driver class names—to be specified outside any compiled Java code.
- **Request dispatching** Servlets can forward requests to other servlets and JSP pages or include their output in the current output stream. The servlet context provides methods for creating request dispatchers using either a path or a servlet name.
- **Message logging** The servlet context has access to the servlet log and can be used to write messages in a vendor-independent way.

See Table 4-8 for a complete description of the methods provided by the servlet context.

In a JSP page, the servlet context object is automatically available in the `application` implicit variable. In a servlet, it can be obtained with the `getServletContext()` method.

# The Web Archive (war) File

Described so far is the run-time structure of a Web application. For deployment, this structure must be collapsed into a single file called a *Web archive* (*war*) file. This is nothing more than a `.jar` file with a different extension (`.war`), whose top level corresponds to the root of the Web application.

To use a concrete example, consider the `products` Web application, shown in Figure 18-2. Its root directory contains an `index.jsp` file and four content

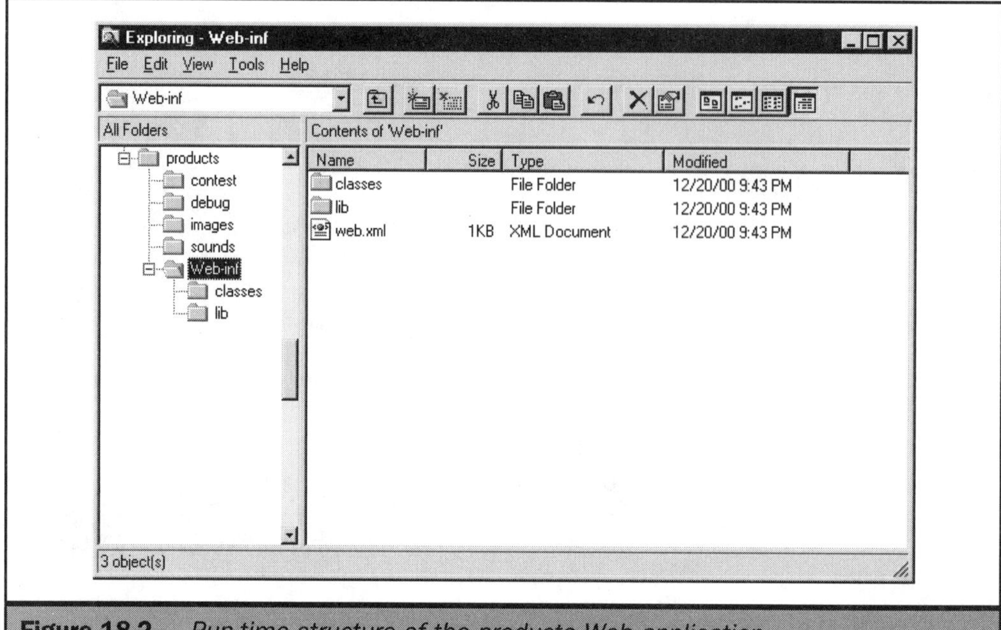


**Figure 18-2.** *Run-time structure of the products Web application*

subdirectories: `contest`, `debug`, `images`, and `sounds`. In addition, it contains a `WEB-INF` directory with the required `classes` and `lib` subdirectories, as well as the `web.xml` deployment descriptor.

To create the `.war` file, go to the products directory and use the JDK `jar` command line tool:

```
D:\lyricnote\products>jar -cvf products.war *
added manifest
adding: contest/(in = 0) (out= 0)(stored 0%)
adding: contest/contest.url(in = 184) (out= 125)(deflated 32%)
adding: contest/index.jsp(in = 1890) (out= 739)(deflated 60%)
adding: debug/(in = 0) (out= 0)(stored 0%)
adding: debug/AddProduct.jsp(in = 400) (out= 240)(deflated 40%)
adding: debug/AddProduct2.jsp(in = 543) (out= 292)(deflated 46%)
adding: debug/Example1.jsp(in = 153) (out= 119)(deflated 22%)
adding: debug/Example1.url(in = 76) (out= 78)(deflated -2%)
adding: images/(in = 0) (out= 0)(stored 0%)
```

```
adding: index.jsp(in = 782) (out= 392)(deflated 49%)
adding: sounds/(in = 0) (out= 0)(stored 0%)
adding: sounds/BIRDS.MID(in = 3494) (out= 1138)(deflated 67%)
adding: sounds/ITBGON.MID(in = 975) (out= 478)(deflated 50%)
adding: WEB-INF/(in = 0) (out= 0)(stored 0%)
adding: WEB-INF/classes/(in = 0) (out= 0)(stored 0%)
adding: WEB-INF/lib/(in = 0) (out= 0)(stored 0%)
adding: WEB-INF/web.xml(in = 46) (out= 37)(deflated 19%)
```

See the JDK documentation for complete details about the `jar` tool.

The resulting file `products.war` is ready to be deployed. All Servlet 2.2-compliant servlet engines are required to accept a `.war` file directly and construct the corresponding Web application. The specific means for installing the file are, as you might expect, vendor-specific. Tomcat, the reference implementation, allows `.war` files simply to be dropped into the *<tomcat_home>*`/webapps` directory. When Tomcat is restarted, the `.war` file is then unpacked and validated, and the new application is available. Commercial servlet engines usually provide a GUI administration tool for this job. JRun offers a deployment wizard in its management console (shown in Figure 18-3) for deploying applications from a `.war` file.

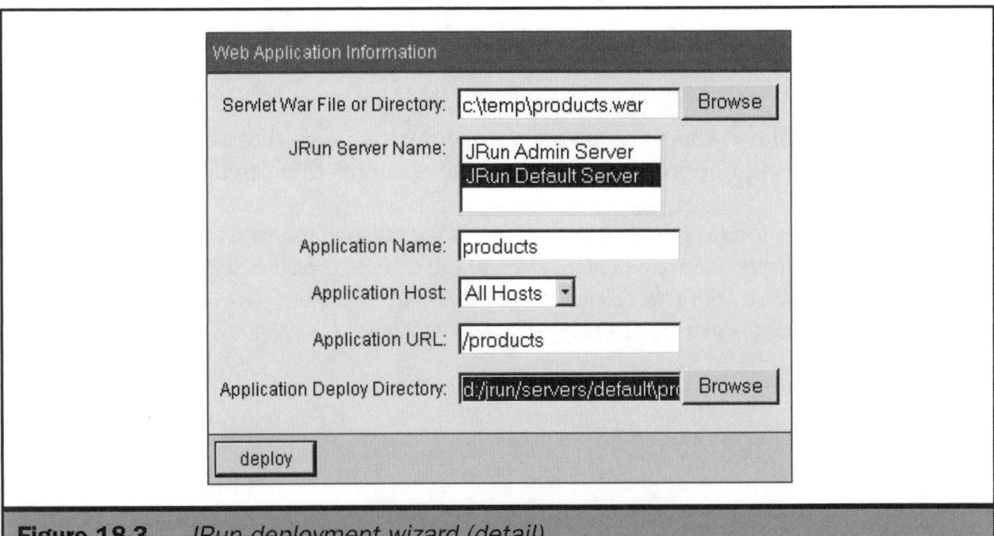


**Figure 18-3.** *JRun deployment wizard (detail)*

## The Deployment Descriptor—web.xml

The `web.xml` file in the `WEB-INF` directory is referred to as the *deployment descriptor*. This is an XML document in a strictly defined format that specifies the configuration of the Web application. Among other things, it can be used to describe

- Servlets aliases, mappings, and initialization parameters
- Session timeout limits
- Global parameters to be made available throughout the application
- Security configuration
- Mime types

Because this file is an XML document, its format is described with a *document type definition*, or *DTD*. The DTD is named `web-app_`*x.y*`.dtd`, where *x.y* is the servlet API specification version, such as 2.2. It is published by Sun Microsystems and can be downloaded at http://java.sun.com/j2ee/dtds/web-app_2_2.dtd.

The simplest possible `web.xml` file looks like this:

```
<?xml version="1.0"?>
<!DOCTYPE web-app PUBLIC
   "-//Sun Microsystems, Inc.//DTD Web Application 2.2//EN"
   "http://java.sun.com/j2ee/dtds/web-app_2_2.dtd">
<web-app>
</web-app>
```

In the body of the `<web-app>` element are other elements that describe the application configuration. Table 18-1 lists the elements that can be used.

**Note**

*Any elements used inside the `<web-app>` body must be specified exactly in the order listed. If multiple occurrences of an element are allowed, they must all occur together, not intermingled with other elements. For example, all `<servlet>` elements must occur before any `<servlet-mapping>` elements.*

| Element | Contents |
|---|---|
| <web-app> | This is the top-level element. It may contain any of the following subelements, in the order shown:<br><icon> (optional)<br><display-name> (optional)<br><description> (optional)<br><distributable> (optional)<br><context-param> (zero or more)<br><servlet> (zero or more)<br><servlet-mapping> (zero or more)<br><session-config> (optional)<br><mime-mapping> (zero or more)<br><welcome-file-list> (optional)<br><error-page> (zero or more)<br><taglib> (zero or more)<br><resource-ref> (zero or more)<br><security-constraint> (zero or more)<br><login-config> (optional)<br><security-role> (zero or more)<br><env-entry> (zero or more)<br><ejb-ref> (zero or more) |
| <icon> | Allows developer to specify the relative location within the application of icon files, in either JPEG or GIF format. These icons can be used by a GUI administration to represent the application. It may contain either of the following elements, or both:<br><small-icon> (optional)<br><large-icon> (optional) |

**Table 18-1.** *Contents of the web.xml Deployment Descriptor*

| Element | Contents |
|---|---|
| <small-icon> | A 16 × 16 icon image filename. |
| <large-icon> | A 32 × 32 icon image filename. |
| <display-name> | A short name for the parent element (<web-app> or <servlet>), which can be used by administrative tools. |
| <description> | A description of the parent element that can be used by administrative tools. This element can appear in several different contexts in this file. |
| <distributable> | If specified, indicates this application is designed to run in multiple distributed servlet containers. |
| <context-param> | Defines an application-wide initialization parameter. Contains the following subelements:<br><param-name> (required)<br><param-value> (required)<br><description> (optional) |
| <param-name> | A parameter name. |
| <param-value> | A parameter value. |
| <servlet> | Defines a servlet and all its associated configuration. May contain the following subelements, in this order:<br><icon> (optional)<br><servlet-name> (required)<br><display-name> (optional)<br><description> (optional)<br><servlet-class> or <jsp-file><br>(must specify one or the other)<br><init-param> (zero or more)<br><load-on-startup> (optional)<br><security-role-ref> (zero or more) |

**Table 18-1.** *Contents of the web.xml Deployment Descriptor* (continued)

| Element | Contents |
|---|---|
| <servlet-name> | The name by which a servlet is known to the servlet container. Note, multiple `<servlet>` elements with different servlet names may specify the same servlet class. In that case, the servlet engine creates multiple instances of the servlet. A servlet may call the `getServletName()` method in `GenericServlet` or `ServletConfig` to determine its name. |
| <servlet-class> | The fully qualified name of the servlet class. |
| <jsp-file> | The full path to a JSP file relative to the root of the Web application. |
| <init-param> | Defines a servlet initialization parameter. Contains the following subelements:<br>`<param-name>` (required)<br>`<param-value>` (required)<br>`<description>` (optional) |
| <load-on-startup> | If specified, this element indicates the servlet should be preloaded when the servlet engine starts. This means the servlet's `init()` method will be called and the servlet will then be available for requests. The value of this element (if any) can be an integer specifying the relative order in which this servlet should be started, if several exist. |
| <servlet-mapping> | Specifies which URL patterns should be mapped to which servlet names. Must contain the following subelements:<br>`<servlet-name>` (required)<br>`<url-pattern>` (required). |
| <url-pattern> | Indicates a pattern that must be matched by a substring of a URL for this servlet to be invoked. The pattern may include the wildcard character `*`. |

**Table 18-1.** *Contents of the web.xml Deployment Descriptor* (continued)

| Element | Contents |
|---|---|
| <session-config> | Defines session configuration parameters. May include the <session-timeout> subelement. |
| <session-timeout> | The default number of minutes with no activity the servlet engine allows before HTTP sessions are terminated. |
| <mime-mapping> | Defines the MIME type implied by a file extension. Must contain the following elements: <extension> (required) <mime-type> (required). |
| <extension> | A suffix of a filename that indicates its type. For example, png is used to indicate a Portable Network Graphics file. |
| <mime-type> | The MIME type associated with a particular file extension. For example, image/png is used to indicate a Portable Network Graphics file. |
| <welcome-file-list> | A list of zero or more <welcome-file> elements. When a request is made for a URL that is a directory, the servlet engine tries each welcome file in turn. |
| <welcome-file> | The default file to be used to service a request in a directory if no filename is specified in the URL. Examples would be index.html, or index.jsp. |
| <taglib> | Used to define a URL mapping for a JSP tag library. Must contain the following subelements: <taglib-uri> (required) <taglib-location> (required) |
| <taglib-uri> | A string of characters intended to be used in the uri attribute of a <%@ taglib %> directive. Although a URL or path is often specified here, it needn't point to an actual Web resource. It serves only as a unique identifier that JSP pages can use to map taglib directives to *tag library descriptors* (*TLDs*). |

**Table 18-1.** *Contents of the web.xml Deployment Descriptor* (continued)

| Element | Contents |
|---|---|
| <taglib-location> | A URI relative to the Web application root directory at which a tag library descriptor (TLD) can be found. For example, `/WEB-INF/tlds/mytags.tld`. |
| <error-page> | Maps an HTTP response code or exception type to a servlet, JSP page, or HTML file that will be invoked by default when error occurs. Contains the following subelements:<br><error-code> or <exception-type><br>(one or the other is required)<br><location> (required) |
| <error-code> | An HTTP response code to be mapped to an error page. |
| <exception-type> | A fully qualified Java exception class name. |
| <location> | The URI of a servlet, JSP page, or HTML file used as an error page. |
| <resource-ref> | Contains information used to set up a J2EE resource factory. May contain the following subelements:<br><description> (optional)<br><res-ref-name> (required)<br><res-type> (required)<br><res-auth> (required). |
| <res-ref-name> | Specifies the name of a resource factory reference. |
| <res-type> | Specifies the Java class name of the data source associated with a resource factory. |
| <res-auth> | Indicates the source of the credentials supplied to a resource factory. Two possible values exist: `SERVLET`—The Web application supplies the value programmatically. `CONTAINER`—Credentials supplied by the container. |

**Table 18-1.** *Contents of the web.xml Deployment Descriptor* (continued)

| Element | Contents |
|---|---|
| <security-constraint> | Defines the security constraints to be applied to one or more resource collections. May contain the following subelements:<br><web-resource-collection> (one or more)<br><auth-constraint> (optional)<br><user-data-constraint> (optional) |
| <web-resource-collection> | Defines a set of resources in the Web application to which security constraints can be applied. May contain the following subelements:<br><web-resource-name> (required)<br><description> (optional)<br><url-pattern> (zero or more)<br><http-method> (zero or more) |
| <web-resource-name> | The name by which a Web resource can be referred. |
| <http-method> | An HTTP method type (for example, GET, POST, and so forth). |
| <user-data-constraint> | Specifies how data transmitted to and from the application should be protected. May contain the following subelements:<br><description> (optional)<br><transport-guarantee> (required) |
| <transport-guarantee> | Allowed values are<br>NONE—application doesn't require transport guarantees.<br>INTEGRAL—requires that data cannot be altered in transit.<br>CONFIDENTIAL—requires that data cannot be read in transit. |
| <auth-constraint> | Specifies a list of role names treated collectively in a <security-constraint> element. May contain the following subelements:<br><description> (optional)<br><role-name> (zero or more) |

**Table 18-1.** *Contents of the web.xml Deployment Descriptor* (continued)

| Element | Contents |
|---|---|
| <role-name> | A name used to identify a role in which an authenticated user may be logged in. This is the same value specified in the `request.isUserInRole()` method to allow conditional execution of parts of a servlet by users in different roles. |
| <login-config> | Specifies the type of login configuration. May include the following subelements:<br><auth-method> (optional)<br><realm-name> (optional)<br><form-login-config> (optional). |
| <realm-name> | A realm name used in HTTP Basic Authentication. |
| <form-login-config> | Specifies the resources used in form-based login. Must contain the following subelements:<br><form-login-page> (required)<br><form-error-page> (required) |
| <form-login-page> | Specifies the name of a resource (HTML file, JSP page, servlet) that prompts for user name and password. This page must adhere to the following requirements:<br>1. The form must use METHOD="POST" and ACTION="j_security_check".<br>2. The user name field must be named j_username.<br>3. The password field must be named j_password. |
| <form-error-page> | Specifies the name of a resource (HTML file, JSP page, servlet) displayed when the form-based login isn't successful. |
| <auth-method> | Specifies the authentication method used. Four legal values exist<br>BASIC<br>DIGEST<br>FORM<br>CLIENT-CERT<br>Not all servlet engines support all methods. |

**Table 18-1.** *Contents of the web.xml Deployment Descriptor* (continued)

JSP IN ACTION

| Element | Contents |
|---|---|
| <security-role> | Declares a security role name valid for use in a <security-constraints> element. May contain the following subelements:<br><description> (optional)<br><role-name> (required) |
| <security-role-ref> | Creates a mapping between a role name and an alias for it. May contain the following subelements:<br><description> (optional)<br><role-name> (required)<br><role-link> (required)<br>This allows servlets to use the role link in the request.isUserInRole() method and have that name equated to the actual role name. Thereafter, if the application is modified to use a different role name, the servlet needn't be modified. |
| <role-link> | A symbolic name used by a servlet to refer to an actual role name. |
| <env-entry> | Used to define the J2EE environment entry. May contain the following subelements:<br><description> (optional)<br><env-entry-name> (required)<br><env-entry-value> (optional)<br><env-entry-type> (required) |
| <env-entry-name> | The J2EE environment entry name relative to the JNDI java:comp/env context. |
| <env-entry-value> | The value of the J2EE environment entry. |
| <env-entry-type> | Must be one of the following:<br>java.lang.Boolean<br>java.lang.String<br>java.lang.Integer<br>java.lang.Double<br>java.lang.Float |

**Table 18-1.** *Contents of the web.xml Deployment Descriptor* (continued)

| Element | Contents |
|---|---|
| <ejb-ref> | Defines a reference to an *Enterprise Java Bean* (*EJB*). May contain the following subelements:<br><description> (optional)<br><ejb-ref-name> (required)<br><ejb-ref-type> (required)<br><home> (required)<br><remote> (required)<br><ejb-link> (optional) |
| <ejb-ref-name> | The JNDI name of an EJB reference. |
| <ejb-ref-type> | The Java class of the EJB. |
| <home> | The fully qualified name of the class that's the EJB's home interface. |
| <remote> | The fully qualified name of the class that's the EJB's remote interface. |
| <ejb-link> | The name of an EJB in an encompassing J2EE application to which this EJB is linked. |

**Table 18-1.** *Contents of the web.xml Deployment Descriptor* (continued)



## Sample Deployment Descriptor

Table 18-1 looks formidable but, fortunately, most deployment descriptors use only a tiny fraction of the possible elements. The following listing shows a typical web.xml file:

```
<?xml version="1.0"?>

<!DOCTYPE web-app PUBLIC
   "-//Sun Microsystems, Inc.//DTD Web Application 2.2//EN"
   "http://java.sun.com/j2ee/dtds/web-app_2_2.dtd">

<web-app>

   <context-param>
      <param-name>JDBC.DRIVER</param-name>
      <param-value>
```

```
            org.enhydra.instantdb.jdbc.idbDriver
         </param-value>
      </context-param>

      <context-param>
         <param-name>JDBC.URL</param-name>
         <param-value>
            jdbc:idb:d:/lyricnote/WEB-INF/db.prp
         </param-value>
      </context-param>

      <servlet>
         <servlet-name>Sample</servlet-name>
         <servlet-class>
            jspcr.servlets.SampleServlet
         </servlet-class>
         <init-param>
            <param-name>message</param-name>
            <param-value>Hello, world</param-value>
         </init-param>
      </servlet>

      <servlet>
         <servlet-name>daytime</servlet-name>
         <servlet-class>
            jspcr.services.daytime
         </servlet-class>
         <load-on-startup>1</load-on-startup>
      </servlet>

   </web-app>
```

This deployment descriptor contains four elements: two context parameters and two servlet declarations. The context parameters define constants available to all servlets and JSP pages in the Web application. In this case, they define a JDBC driver class and a database URL. Servlets and JSP pages can retrieve these values with the servlet context `getInitParameter()` method. Because this type of information frequently changes and, typically, varies in different installations, being able to describe it here rather than hard coding it in a Java class is convenient.

Two servlets are defined. The first one, named `Sample`, refers to the `jspcr.servlets.SampleServlet` class and has one initialization parameter. This allows the servlet to be called with a URL similar to the following

```
http://www.lyricnote.com/products/servlet/Sample
```

without requiring the full servlet class name to be specified. The second servlet, named `daytime`, uses the `<load-on-startup>` element to cause it to be preloaded when the servlet engine starts.

The Servlet 2.2 API specification provides other sample deployment descriptors. Likewise, most servlet engines come with examples of this file.

## Summary

With the advent of the Servlet 2.2 specification, Web application deployment has become standardized and vendor-independent. The specification describes a standard directory structure that contains the Web content, as well as configuration information and class directories. The configuration is specified in an XML document named `web.xml` and known as the *deployment descriptor*. The directory structure is mirrored in the *web archive* (`.war`) file format. Deploying a Web application and moving it from one servlet engine to another usually requires little more than installing the `.war` file and invoking the servlet engine's deployment tool.

# Chapter 19

## Case Study: A Product Support Center

Our hypothetical Internet music store, LyricNote.com, sells a variety of musical products: sheet music, musical instruments, books on musical topics, gift items, and music software. Support for these products involves taking orders over the phone, checking order status, resolving billing questions, and providing technical support for software. The last item is the focus of this chapter.

In this case study, you develop a Web-based system for managing the product support center. Users of the system can report and track product defects, log comments about them, and route them to the appropriate parties.

In the interest of clarity, this application doesn't include all the validations, user controls, or management reporting that a real production system might have. It does, however, illustrate many of the techniques described throughout the book and provide a model for further development.

## Process Flow

To start, let's consider the environment in which the system is going to operate. The process flow is shown in Figure 19-1.

When a customer calls to report a software problem, the first available call center agent answers the phone. This *call center agent* may route the call to sales or customer service, if the problem isn't software-related. Otherwise, the agent verifies the customer is entitled to support, meaning the customer is a valid purchaser of the specified product. The agent creates a problem report and tells the customer to expect a call from product support.

The problem report is routed to the product support specialist for the product for which the defect is being reported. Each *product support specialist* has a queue of open problem reports and, when a new problem is received, the specialist calls the customer to get more details, trying to determine if this is a customer problem or a code problem. Customer problems may involve lack of required hardware or software, or failure to install the product properly. In these cases, the product support person helps the customer resolve the problem to the extent possible, and then closes the problem report.

If the problem is code-related, it may be that other customers have encountered it and a fix already exists. If so, the fix is documented in the knowledge base, which the product support person can search by appropriate keywords. The patch or procedure necessary to fix the problem is sent to the customer via e-mail or made available over the Web.

If the problem isn't found in the knowledge base, it's routed to the developer listed as the primary support for the product. The *developer* analyzes the problem and attempts to reproduce it. It may be the product is working as designed, in which case the defect is rerouted back to product support marked "not a bug." Otherwise, the developer tries to isolate the bug and to develop a fix. After unit testing the fix, the developer routes the problem to quality assurance. The problem report may be updated to indicate how to reproduce the problem and where to get the code patch necessary to fix it.

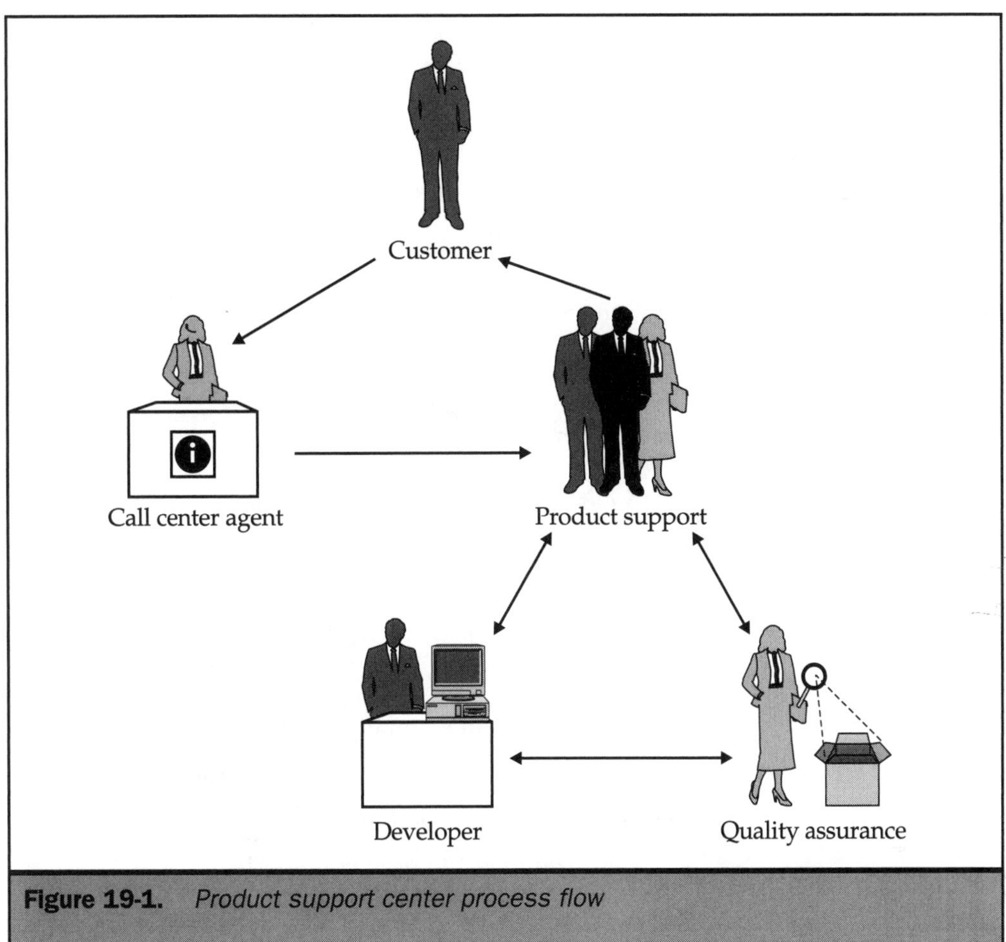


**Figure 19-1.** *Product support center process flow*

The *quality assurance* support person for the product receives the problem report from development and tests the fix. This is an integration test, in which the effect of the new code on existing systems is examined. If the fix introduces other problems or fails to pass all the established test cases, the problem is rerouted to development. Otherwise, the fix is routed to product support, so the customer can be contacted and supplied with the new code.

At any point, system users can look up the status of a particular problem, add comments to it, and route the problem to its next destination. To be most effective, each routing would be accompanied by e-mail sent to the new problem owner. That part isn't developed here, deferring the topic to Chapter 21, which examines the Java Mail API.

To summarize, the system users and their functions are as follows:

| | |
|---|---|
| **Call center agent** | Verifies customer entitlement |
| | Enters new problems |
| | Can look up status of existing problems |
| **Product support** | Receives incoming problem reports from call center |
| | Can view outstanding problems by product |
| | Interviews customer |
| | Updates problem status |
| | Adds comments |
| | Routes problem to development |
| **Developer** | Receives problem reports from product support |
| | Can view outstanding problems by product |
| | Analyzes problem and develops fix |
| | Adds comments to problem report |
| | Routes problem to quality assurance |
| **Quality assurance** | Receives problem reports and fixes from development |
| | Performs integration test |
| | Adds comments to problem report |
| | Routes fixed problems to product support |
| | May route problem back to developer if tests fail |

In addition, management can view problem status at any time and can access reports showing quality statistics, such as time in queues, bugs reported per product, and outstanding bugs by developer. These reports aren't included in this application, but could be developed from the problem database.

## Data Model

Table 19-1 describes the database tables that contain all the data necessary to record and track problems.

| Table Name | Description | Fields |
|---|---|---|
| `customer` | A list of customers who have bought LyricNote products. | customerID<br>customer name<br>phone |
| `product` | A list of products and their support personnel. | productID<br>product name<br>product support person<br>lead developer<br>lead tester |
| `custprod` | A list of customer/product pairs indicating which customer bought which product. | customerID<br>productID<br>date purchased |
| `problems` | The main record of a reported problem. | problemID<br>description<br>severity (1=high, 2=medium, 3=low)<br>date reported<br>date resolved (if closed)<br>customerID<br>productID |
| `problog` | A log of events in the life of a reported problem. | problemID<br>timestamp<br>eventID<br>comments |
| `employees` | Users of the system, including call center agents, product support, developers, and testers. | employeeID<br>name<br>other fields (not used here) |

**Table 19-1.** *Data Model for Product Support Application*



## Developing the System

JSP is a convenient development environment. Pages get automatically compiled when necessary and URLs map easily to directory locations. Inside a JSP page, you can use any mix of HTML and Java you like, which gives you a great deal of flexibility.

Unfortunately, these same advantages mean ordinary JSP applications don't scale well. As more Java code is embedded in JSP pages, keeping track of it becomes increasingly more difficult. Unlike Java classes that can be compiled and unit tested, JSP scriptlet code cannot easily be separated from its container. Being consistent over large stretches of Java-strewn HTML is also difficult. You may start out using beans to do most of the work, and then find they don't do quite what you need, leading you to cheat with a little extra Java buried in the HTML. These problems are compounded if the application makes free use of the `<%@ include %>` directive.

What's needed in larger applications is a better way to separate code into components with clear responsibilities. For your product support system, you use the *Model-View-Controller* (*MVC*) design.

## Model-View-Controller Architecture

The idea behind MVC is the visual aspects of a system should be isolated from the internal workings, which, in turn, should be separate from the mechanism that starts and controls the internals. The MVC architecture was first prominently adopted by Smalltalk and its practitioners, but is now a widely used design pattern. Figure 19-2 illustrates how MVC works.

The *model* refers to code that manages the abstract internal state and operations of the system. It handles database access and most business logic. The model has no visual component, providing instead an application programming interface that's accessible to other parts of the system. This makes it possible to write a driver program that can test and debug the model from a simple command line interface.

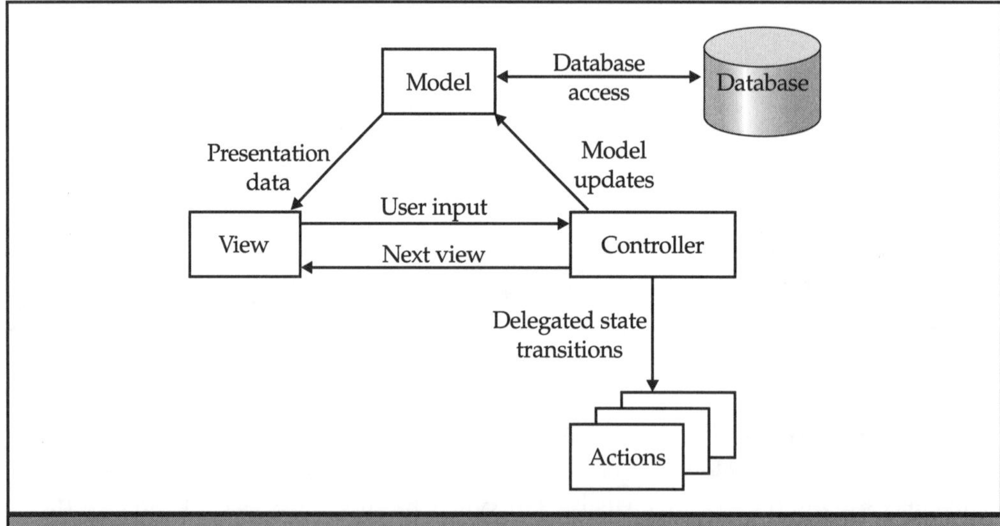


**Figure 19-2.** *The Model-View-Controller architecture*

In a chess game, for example, the model might consist of a set of objects representing the pieces and a simple 8 × 8 array to hold them. The model could have methods that indicate whose turn it is to move, that evaluate whether a given move is legal, and that move pieces from one array element to another. The model would *not* have code that provides any visual representation of the board.

The *view* is the presentation layer of the system. It does no database access and contains no business logic. What little nonvisual code the view has is limited to presentation logic, such as looping over an array of objects to be displayed. By design, a model can be associated with more than one view, perhaps a *graphical user interface* (*GUI*) and a printed report. For example, a Web-based, two-player game could have one view for each player, both attached to the same model. This wouldn't require any changes to the model because the model is unaware of how it is being displayed.

In the case of the chess game, the view would contain code to draw the board and the pieces, list the moves, and show the clock. It wouldn't know anything about the rules of chess, whose turn it was, or even the locations of the pieces. The view would call methods in the model to keep track of all this. Even though GUI code is often complex, all a view has to worry about is its visual aspects. Testing and debugging is straightforward because a stub version of the model can be used to exercise all parts of the view.

The *controller* is what manipulates the model according to user input. Based on the current view, the state of the model, and the actions taken by the user, the controller calls the model API to update the model state and select the next view. Roughly speaking, the controller handles input *from* the user, whereas the view handles output going *to* the user[1]. The chess game might have two controllers—one that conveys the human player's moves, and one that chooses the computer's moves.

In this product support system, the model consists of ordinary Java classes (not servlets and not network-oriented). Simple JSP pages are used as the view and the controller is a single servlet with some supporting classes.



## Model Classes

Let's start by examining the product support system model. It consists of three sets of classes:

- Classes that represent business objects, roughly corresponding to tables in the database
- The application container and interface classes
- A testing framework

These classes collectively make up the `com.lyricnote.support.model` package. In addition to maintaining the application state, the model contains all

1 The role of the controller is sometimes handled by the view in a simpler Model-View architecture.

the code that accesses the database, using a session-aware wrapper class to ensure database resources are properly managed.

## Business Objects

Six classes encapsulate business entities used in the data model:

- `com.lyricnote.support.model.Customer`
- `com.lyricnote.support.model.Product`
- `com.lyricnote.support.model.CustomerProduct`
- `com.lyricnote.support.model.Employee`
- `com.lyricnote.support.model.Problem`
- `com.lyricnote.support.model.ProblemLog`

The following sections list the source code for each of these classes and describe their operation.

**Customer Class** The first class in the package is the `Customer` class, which represents a person or company that has bought LyricNote products and is eligible for product support. The class contains the customer name and phone number, as well as a unique customer identifier. The identifier is composed of the first four letters of the customer's last name, followed by the first and last letters of the customer's first name, ending with a two-digit unique numeric suffix. The class is shown in the following listing:

```
package com.lyricnote.support.model;

import java.io.*;
import java.sql.*;
import java.util.*;

/**
* A person or company that has bought LyricNote products.
*/
public class Customer implements Serializable
{
   private String customerID;
   private String name;
   private String phone;

   /**
   * Factory method to create a customer record
   * from the current row of a result set.
```

```
* @param rs a result set from the customer table
* @exception SQLException if a database error occurs
*/
public static Customer load(ResultSet rs)
   throws SQLException
{
   Customer customer = new Customer();
   String value = null;

   value = rs.getString(1);
   if (value != null)
      customer.setCustomerID(value);

   value = rs.getString(2);
   if (value != null)
      customer.setName(value);

   value = rs.getString(3);
   if (value != null)
      customer.setPhone(value);

   return customer;
}

/**
* Returns the object as a CSV string
*/
public String toString()
{
   StringBuffer sb = new StringBuffer();

   if (getCustomerID() != null)
      sb.append(Util.quote(getCustomerID()));

   sb.append(",");
   if (getName() != null)
      sb.append(Util.quote(getName()));

   sb.append(",");
   if (getPhone() != null)
      sb.append(Util.quote(getPhone()));
```

```
      return sb.toString();
   }

   // ============================================
   //    Property accessor methods
   // ============================================

   /**
   * Returns the customerID.
   */
   public String getCustomerID()
   {
      return customerID;
   }

   /**
   * Sets the customerID.
   * @param customerID the customerID.
   */
   public void setCustomerID(String customerID)
   {
      this.customerID = customerID;
   }

   /**
   * Returns the name.
   */
   public String getName()
   {
      return name;
   }

   /**
   * Sets the name.
   * @param name the name.
   */
   public void setName(String name)
   {
      this.name = name;
   }

   /**
```

```
    * Returns the telephone number
    */
    public String getPhone()
    {
       return phone;
    }

    /**
    * Sets the telephone number.
    * @param phone the phone.
    */
    public void setPhone(String phone)
    {
       this.phone = phone;
    }
}
```

In addition to the getter and setter methods for each property, the `Customer` class contains a `toString()` method that returns a comma-separated-values string and a class method named `load()`. The `load()` method creates a `Customer` object from a `customer` table row in an SQL result set. This method is used in the model application classes to simplify retrieving a collection of `Customer` objects from the database.

The `Util.quote()` method in the `toString()` method is discussed later in this chapter in the Application Objects section.



**Product Class** Next is the `Product` class, representing a row in the `product` table. Its properties consist of a unique product identifier, the product name, and the employee numbers of the product's primary support person, its lead developer, and its lead tester. The class is show in the following listing.

```
package com.lyricnote.support.model;

import java.io.*;
import java.sql.*;
import java.util.*;

/**
* A software product supported by the Product
* Support system.
*/
public class Product implements Serializable
```

```
{
   private String productID;
   private String name;
   private String productSupport;
   private String developer;
   private String tester;

   /**
   * Factory method to create a product record
   * from the current row of a result set.
   * @param rs a result set from the product table
   * @exception SQLException if a database error occurs
   */
   public static Product load(ResultSet rs)
      throws SQLException
   {
      Product product = new Product();
      String value = null;

      value = rs.getString(1);
      if (value != null)
         product.setProductID(value);

      value = rs.getString(2);
      if (value != null)
         product.setName(value);

      value = rs.getString(3);
      if (value != null)
         product.setProductSupport(value);

      value = rs.getString(4);
      if (value != null)
         product.setDeveloper(value);

      value = rs.getString(5);
      if (value != null)
         product.setTester(value);

      return product;
   }
```

```
/**
* Returns the object as a CSV string
*/
public String toString()
{
   StringBuffer sb = new StringBuffer();

   if (getProductID() != null)
      sb.append(Util.quote(getProductID()));

   sb.append(",");
   if (getName() != null)
      sb.append(Util.quote(getName()));

   sb.append(",");
   if (getProductSupport() != null)
      sb.append(Util.quote(getProductSupport()));

   sb.append(",");
   if (getDeveloper() != null)
      sb.append(Util.quote(getDeveloper()));

   sb.append(",");
   if (getTester() != null)
      sb.append(Util.quote(getTester()));

   return sb.toString();
}

// ===========================================
//    Property accessor methods
// ===========================================

/**
* Returns the product ID.
*/
public String getProductID()
{
   return productID;
}

/**
```

```
* Sets the product ID.
* @param product the product ID.
*/
public void setProductID(String productID)
{
   this.productID = productID;
}

/**
* Returns the product name.
*/
public String getName()
{
   return name;
}

/**
* Sets the product name.
* @param name the product name.
*/
public void setName(String name)
{
   this.name = name;
}

/**
* Returns the productSupport ID.
*/
public String getProductSupport()
{
   return productSupport;
}

/**
* Sets the productSupport ID.
* @param productSupport the productSupport.
*/
public void setProductSupport(String productSupport)
{
   this.productSupport = productSupport;
}
```

```
    /**
    * Returns the developer ID.
    */
    public String getDeveloper()
    {
       return developer;
    }

    /**
    * Sets the developer ID.
    * @param developer the developer.
    */
    public void setDeveloper(String developer)
    {
       this.developer = developer;
    }

    /**
    * Returns the tester ID.
    */
    public String getTester()
    {
       return tester;
    }

    /**
    * Sets the tester ID.
    * @param tester the tester.
    */
    public void setTester(String tester)
    {
       this.tester = tester;
    }
}
```



Like the `Customer` class, `Product` contains getter and setter methods for each of its properties, as well as the customized `toString()` method and the factory method for loading a `Product` object from a result set row.

**CustomerProduct Class** A key responsibility of the call center agent is to verify *customer entitlement*, meaning the person reporting the problem is a valid customer and has purchased the specified product. This is indicated by the existence of a record linking the customer and product in the custprod table. The class corresponding to this table is CustomerProduct, shown in the following listing:

```
package com.lyricnote.support.model;

import java.io.*;
import java.sql.ResultSet;
import java.sql.SQLException;
import java.util.*;

/**
* A customer/product pair whose existence indicates
* that the customer bought the specified product.
*/
public class CustomerProduct implements Serializable
{
   private String customerID;
   private String productID;
   private Date datePurchased;

   /**
   * Factory method to create a customer/product record
   * from the current row of a result set.
   * @param rs a result set from the customer table
   * @exception SQLException if a database error occurs
   */
   public static CustomerProduct load(ResultSet rs)
      throws SQLException
   {
      CustomerProduct custprod = new CustomerProduct();

      custprod.setCustomerID(rs.getString(1));
      custprod.setProductID(rs.getString(2));
      custprod.setDatePurchased(rs.getDate(3));

      return custprod;
   }

   /**
   * Returns the object as a CSV string
   */
   public String toString()
   {
```

```
      StringBuffer sb = new StringBuffer();

      sb.append(getCustomerID());
      sb.append(",");
      sb.append(getProductID());
      sb.append(",");
      sb.append(Util.dateFormat(getDatePurchased()));

      return sb.toString();
   }

   // ============================================
   //    Property accessor methods
   // ============================================

   /**
   * Returns the customerID.
   */
   public String getCustomerID()
   {
      return customerID;
   }

   /**
   * Sets the customerID.
   * @param customerID the customerID.
   */
   public void setCustomerID(String customerID)
   {
      this.customerID = customerID;
   }

   /**
   * Returns the productID.
   */
   public String getProductID()
   {
      return productID;
   }

   /**
   * Sets the productID.
```

```
        * @param productID the productID.
        */
       public void setProductID(String productID)
       {
          this.productID = productID;
       }

       /**
       * Returns the datePurchased.
       */
       public Date getDatePurchased()
       {
          return datePurchased;
       }

       /**
       * Sets the datePurchased.
       * @param datePurchased the datePurchased.
       */
       public void setDatePurchased(Date datePurchased)
       {
          this.datePurchased = datePurchased;
       }
    }
```

`CustomerProduct` has fields containing the customer ID, the product ID, and the date the product was purchased. This information comes from product registration mail-in cards, or manual input, not shown here.

Like the `Customer` and `Product` classes, `CustomerProduct` has getter and setter methods, a `toString()` method to create a comma-separated-values string, and a factory method for loading objects from the database.

**Employee Class** Associated with each product is a product support person, a lead developer, and a lead tester. Information about these employees is contained in the `employee` table and encapsulated in the `Employee` class, listed here:

```
package com.lyricnote.support.model;

import java.io.*;
import java.sql.ResultSet;
import java.sql.SQLException;
import java.util.*;
```

```
/**
* A LyricNote employee that uses the Product Support system.
*/
public class Employee implements Serializable
{
   private String employeeID;
   private String name;
   private Date dateHired;
   private boolean isManager;
   private String departmentID;
   private String title;
   private String email;
   private String phone;

   /**
   * Factory method to create an employee record
   * from the current row of a result set.
   * @param rs a result set from the employee table
   * @exception SQLException if a database error occurs
   */
   public static Employee load(ResultSet rs)
      throws SQLException
   {
      Employee employee = new Employee();

      employee.setEmployeeID(rs.getString(1));
      employee.setName(rs.getString(2));
      employee.setDateHired(rs.getDate(3));
      employee.setIsManager(rs.getBoolean(4));
      employee.setDepartmentID(rs.getString(5));
      employee.setTitle(rs.getString(6));
      employee.setEmail(rs.getString(7));
      employee.setPhone(rs.getString(8));

      return employee;
   }

   /**
   * Returns the object as a CSV string
   */
   public String toString()
   {
      StringBuffer sb = new StringBuffer();
```

```
      sb.append(getEmployeeID());
      sb.append(",");
      sb.append(Util.quote(getName()));
      sb.append(",");
      sb.append(Util.dateFormat(getDateHired()));
      sb.append(",");
      sb.append(getIsManager());
      sb.append(",");
      sb.append(getDepartmentID());
      sb.append(",");
      sb.append(Util.quote(getTitle()));
      sb.append(",");
      sb.append(getEmail());
      sb.append(",");
      sb.append(getPhone());

      return sb.toString();
   }

   // ============================================
   //    Property accessor methods
   // ============================================

   /**
   * Returns the employee ID.
   */
   public String getEmployeeID()
   {
      return employeeID;
   }

   /**
   * Sets the employee ID.
   * @param employeeID the employee ID.
   */
   public void setEmployeeID(String employeeID)
   {
      this.employeeID = employeeID;
   }

   /**
   * Returns the employee name.
   */
```

```
public String getName()
{
   return name;
}

/**
* Sets the employee name.
* @param name the employee name.
*/
public void setName(String name)
{
   this.name = name;
}

/**
* Returns the dateHired.
*/
public Date getDateHired()
{
   return dateHired;
}

/**
* Sets the dateHired.
* @param dateHired the dateHired.
*/
public void setDateHired(Date dateHired)
{
   this.dateHired = dateHired;
}

/**
* Returns the isManager flag.
*/
public boolean getIsManager()
{
   return isManager;
}

/**
* Sets the isManager flag.
* @param isManager the isManager flag.
```

```
   */
   public void setIsManager(boolean isManager)
   {
      this.isManager = isManager;
   }

   /**
   * Returns the department ID.
   */
   public String getDepartmentID()
   {
      return departmentID;
   }

   /**
   * Sets the department ID.
   * @param departmentID the department ID.
   */
   public void setDepartmentID(String departmentID)
   {
      this.departmentID = departmentID;
   }

   /**
   * Returns the title.
   */
   public String getTitle()
   {
      return title;
   }

   /**
   * Sets the title.
   * @param title the title.
   */
   public void setTitle(String title)
   {
      this.title = title;
   }

   /**
   * Returns the email.
```

```
    */
    public String getEmail()
    {
       return email;
    }

    /**
    * Sets the email.
    * @param email the email.
    */
    public void setEmail(String email)
    {
       this.email = email;
    }

    /**
    * Returns the phone.
    */
    public String getPhone()
    {
       return phone;
    }

    /**
    * Sets the phone.
    * @param phone the phone.
    */
    public void setPhone(String phone)
    {
       this.phone = phone;
    }
}
```



Unlike some of the other tables, the `employee` table is used in more than just the product support system. For this reason, it contains more fields than are used in product support, as shown here:

- `employeeID` A unique four-digit employee number
- `name` The employee name
- `dateHired` The employee's date of hire
- `isManager` A boolean variable, which is true if the employee is a manager

- `departmentID` The code of the department to which the employee belongs
- `title` Job title
- `email` E-mail address
- `phone` Telephone extension

The `Employee` class (shown in the following listing) encapsulates a row in the `employee` table.

```
package com.lyricnote.support.model;

import java.io.*;
import java.sql.ResultSet;
import java.sql.SQLException;
import java.util.*;

/**
* A LyricNote employee that uses the Product Support system.
*/
public class Employee implements Serializable
{
   private String employeeID;
   private String name;
   private Date dateHired;
   private boolean isManager;
   private String departmentID;
   private String title;
   private String email;
   private String phone;

   /**
   * Factory method to create an employee record
   * from the current row of a result set.
   * @param rs a result set from the employee table
   * @exception SQLException if a database error occurs
   */
   public static Employee load(ResultSet rs)
      throws SQLException
   {
      Employee employee = new Employee();

      employee.setEmployeeID(rs.getString(1));
```

```
        employee.setName(rs.getString(2));
        employee.setDateHired(rs.getDate(3));
        employee.setIsManager(rs.getBoolean(4));
        employee.setDepartmentID(rs.getString(5));
        employee.setTitle(rs.getString(6));
        employee.setEmail(rs.getString(7));
        employee.setPhone(rs.getString(8));

        return employee;
    }

    /**
    * Returns the object as a CSV string
    */
    public String toString()
    {
        StringBuffer sb = new StringBuffer();

        sb.append(getEmployeeID());
        sb.append(",");
        sb.append(Util.quote(getName()));
        sb.append(",");
        sb.append(Util.dateFormat(getDateHired()));
        sb.append(",");
        sb.append(getIsManager());
        sb.append(",");
        sb.append(getDepartmentID());
        sb.append(",");
        sb.append(Util.quote(getTitle()));
        sb.append(",");
        sb.append(getEmail());
        sb.append(",");
        sb.append(getPhone());

        return sb.toString();
    }

    // ===========================================
    //    Property accessor methods
    // ===========================================

    /**
```

```
   * Returns the employee ID.
   */
   public String getEmployeeID()
   {
      return employeeID;
   }

   /**
   * Sets the employee ID.
   * @param employeeID the employee ID.
   */
   public void setEmployeeID(String employeeID)
   {
      this.employeeID = employeeID;
   }

   /**
   * Returns the employee name.
   */
   public String getName()
   {
      return name;
   }

   /**
   * Sets the employee name.
   * @param name the employee name.
   */
   public void setName(String name)
   {
      this.name = name;
   }

   /**
   * Returns the dateHired.
   */
   public Date getDateHired()
   {
      return dateHired;
   }

   /**
```

```
* Sets the dateHired.
* @param dateHired the dateHired.
*/
public void setDateHired(Date dateHired)
{
   this.dateHired = dateHired;
}

/**
* Returns the isManager flag.
*/
public boolean getIsManager()
{
   return isManager;
}

/**
* Sets the isManager flag.
* @param isManager the isManager flag.
*/
public void setIsManager(boolean isManager)
{
   this.isManager = isManager;
}

/**
* Returns the department ID.
*/
public String getDepartmentID()
{
   return departmentID;
}

/**
* Sets the department ID.
* @param departmentID the department ID.
*/
public void setDepartmentID(String departmentID)
{
   this.departmentID = departmentID;
}
```

```
/**
* Returns the title.
*/
public String getTitle()
{
   return title;
}

/**
* Sets the title.
* @param title the title.
*/
public void setTitle(String title)
{
   this.title = title;
}

/**
* Returns the email.
*/
public String getEmail()
{
   return email;
}

/**
* Sets the email.
* @param email the email.
*/
public void setEmail(String email)
{
   this.email = email;
}

/**
* Returns the phone.
*/
public String getPhone()
{
   return phone;
}
```

```
   /**
   * Sets the phone.
   * @param phone the phone.
   */
   public void setPhone(String phone)
   {
      this.phone = phone;
   }
}
```

The Employee class has the toString() and load() methods, described earlier.

**Problem Class** The heart of the system is the set of reported problems. In the database, each problem consists of two types of records: one that represents the problem as a whole, and another that represents each event in the life of the problem, from when it is reported until it's closed. The static problem data is contained in the Problem class, listed here.

```
package com.lyricnote.support.model;

import java.io.*;
import java.sql.ResultSet;
import java.sql.SQLException;
import java.util.*;

/**
* A software problem supported by the Problem
* Support system.
*/
public class Problem implements Serializable
{
   private String problemID;
   private String description;
   private int severity;
   private java.util.Date dateReported;
   private java.util.Date dateResolved;
   private String customerID;
   private String productID;

   /**
   * Factory method to create a problem record
```

```
    * from the current row of a result set.
    * @param rs a result set from the problem table
    * @exception SQLException if a database error occurs
    */
    public static Problem load(ResultSet rs)
       throws SQLException
    {
       Problem problem = new Problem();

       problem.setProblemID(rs.getString(1));
       problem.setDescription(rs.getString(2));
       problem.setSeverity(rs.getInt(3));
       problem.setDateReported(rs.getTimestamp(4));
       problem.setDateResolved(rs.getTimestamp(5));
       problem.setCustomerID(rs.getString(6));
       problem.setProductID(rs.getString(7));

       return problem;
    }

    /**
    * Returns the object as a CSV string
    */
    public String toString()
    {
       StringBuffer sb = new StringBuffer();

       sb.append(getProblemID());
       sb.append(",");
       sb.append(getDescription());
       sb.append(",");
       sb.append(getSeverity());
       sb.append(",");
       sb.append(Util.dateTimeFormat(getDateReported()));
       sb.append(",");
       sb.append(Util.dateTimeFormat(getDateResolved()));
       sb.append(",");
       sb.append(getCustomerID());
       sb.append(",");
       sb.append(getProductID());

       return sb.toString();
    }
```

```
/**
* Closes the problem
*/
public void close()
{
   setDateResolved(Util.toTimestamp(new Date()));
}

// ============================================
//    Property accessor methods
// ============================================

/**
* Returns the problemID.
*/
public String getProblemID()
{
   return problemID;
}

/**
* Sets the problemID.
* @param problemID the problemID.
*/
public void setProblemID(String problemID)
{
   this.problemID = problemID;
}

/**
* Returns the description.
*/
public String getDescription()
{
   return description;
}

/**
* Sets the description.
* @param description the description.
*/
public void setDescription(String description)
{
```

```
      this.description = description;
   }

   /**
   * Returns the severity.
   */
   public int getSeverity()
   {
      return severity;
   }

   /**
   * Sets the severity.
   * @param severity the severity.
   */
   public void setSeverity(int severity)
   {
      this.severity = severity;
   }

   /**
   * Returns the dateReported.
   */
   public java.util.Date getDateReported()
   {
      return dateReported;
   }

   /**
   * Sets the dateReported.
   * @param dateReported the dateReported.
   */
   public void setDateReported(java.util.Date dateReported)
   {
      this.dateReported = dateReported;
   }

   /**
   * Returns the dateResolved.
   */
   public java.util.Date getDateResolved()
   {
```

```
    return dateResolved;
}

/**
* Sets the dateResolved.
* @param dateResolved the dateResolved.
*/
public void setDateResolved(java.util.Date dateResolved)
{
    this.dateResolved = dateResolved;
}

/**
* Returns the customerID.
*/
public String getCustomerID()
{
    return customerID;
}

/**
* Sets the customerID.
* @param customerID the customerID.
*/
public void setCustomerID(String customerID)
{
    this.customerID = customerID;
}

/**
* Returns the productID.
*/
public String getProductID()
{
    return productID;
}

/**
* Sets the productID.
* @param productID the productID.
*/
public void setProductID(String productID)
```

```
    {
       this.productID = productID;
    }
}
```

A `Problem` object consists of the following fields:

- `problemID` A unique problem identifier, assigned by the system
- `description` A brief description of the problem for display in the GUI
- `severity` The call center agent's assessment of how critical the problem is to the customer, with 1=high, 2=medium, 3=low
- `dateReported` The date and time at which the problem was reported to the call center
- `dateResolved` If the problem is closed, this contains the date and time at which it was closed. The value is `null` otherwise.
- `customerID` The eight-character customer identifier
- `productID` The unique product identifier

**ProblemLog Class** The events in a problem's lifecycle are modeled by rows in the `problog` table, which contains the following columns:

- `problemID` The problem identifier, to allow for joining the `problog` and `problem` tables.
- `logtime` A timestamp generated by the database system. This, combined with the problem ID, constitute the unique key for this problem log entry.
- `eventID` A three-character code indicating the nature of the problem log event. Event ID codes are taken from the following list:

  `COM`–Comment
  `RPS`–Routed to product support
  `RPD`–Routed to product development
  `RQA`–Routed to quality assurance
  `CNB`–Closed—not a bug
  `CCP`–Closed—customer problem
  `CFX`–Closed—fixed

- `comments` Comments entered by the person making this log entry.

The system uses the `ProblemLog` class, shown in the following listing, to represent a row in the `problog` table.

```
package com.lyricnote.support.model;

import java.io.*;
import java.sql.ResultSet;
import java.sql.SQLException;
import java.util.*;

/**
* An update to a reported problem.
*/
public class ProblemLog implements Serializable
{
   private String problemID;
   private java.util.Date logTime;
   private String eventID;
   private String comments;

   /**
   * Factory method to create a problem record
   * from the current row of a result set.
   * @param rs a result set from the problem table
   * @exception SQLException if a database error occurs
   */
   public static ProblemLog load(ResultSet rs)
      throws SQLException
   {
      ProblemLog probLog = new ProblemLog();

      probLog.setProblemID(rs.getString(1));
      probLog.setLogTime(rs.getTimestamp(2));
      probLog.setEventID(rs.getString(3));
      probLog.setComments(rs.getString(4));

      return probLog;
   }

   /**
   * Returns the object as a CSV string
   */
   public String toString()
   {
```

```
      StringBuffer sb = new StringBuffer();

      sb.append(getProblemID());
      sb.append(",");
      sb.append(Util.dateTimeFormat(getLogTime()));
      sb.append(",");
      sb.append(getEventID());
      sb.append(",");
      sb.append(getComments());

      return sb.toString();
   }

   // ============================================
   //    Property accessor methods
   // ============================================

   /**
   * Returns the problemID.
   */
   public String getProblemID()
   {
      return problemID;
   }

   /**
   * Sets the problemID.
   * @param problemID the problemID.
   */
   public void setProblemID(String problemID)
   {
      this.problemID = problemID;
   }

   /**
   * Returns the logTime.
   */
   public java.util.Date getLogTime()
   {
      return logTime;
   }

   /**
```

```
   * Sets the logTime.
   * @param logTime the logTime.
   */
   public void setLogTime(java.util.Date logTime)
   {
      this.logTime = logTime;
   }

   /**
   * Returns the eventID.
   */
   public String getEventID()
   {
      return eventID;
   }

   /**
   * Sets the eventID.
   * @param eventID the eventID.
   */
   public void setEventID(String eventID)
   {
      this.eventID = eventID;
   }

   /**
   * Returns the comments.
   */
   public String getComments()
   {
      return comments;
   }

   /**
   * Sets the comments.
   * @param comments the comments.
   */
   public void setComments(String comments)
   {
      this.comments = comments;
   }
}
```

## Application Objects

The business objects represent the individual entities known by the system. For the purposes of the model, other objects represent the application as a whole. Classes in this category include the following:

- `com.lyricnote.support.model.Model`
- `com.lyricnote.support.model.WebModel`
- `com.lyricnote.support.model.Util`

The following sections list the source code for each of these classes and describe their operation.

**Model Class** During the operation of the system, the business objects reside in an application container class named `Model`. This class exposes an API that allows the controller to manipulate it and the view to extract data from it. One `Model` object exists for each user session, so model state is threadsafe.

`Model` is a fairly large class. Let's list a section at a time, so you can examine it in detail.

```
package com.lyricnote.support.model;

import java.io.*;
import java.sql.*;
import java.util.*;

/**
* The model component in the Model-View-Controller architecture
* of the product support application. The model is designed
* to be used in a dedicated HTTP session with a single user,
* however, there is no HTTP-specific code. This allows the
* model to be tested by a batch driver.
*/
public class Model implements Serializable
{
   // Configuration fields

   private String problemIDFile;
   private String jdbcDriver;
   private String databaseURL;
   private transient Connection con;

   // Customer fields

   private List customers;
```

```
private String customerID;

// Product fields

private List products;
private String productID;

// Problem fields

private List problems;
private String problemID;

// Problem log fields

private List problemLogs;
```

`Model` contains instance variables that represent the state of the application. These variables fall into the following categories:

- **Configuration fields** These include the name of the file containing the next available problem ID number, the name of the JDBC driver used to access the database, the database URL, and the database connection object.
- **Customer fields** The model supports an alphabetic search for customer names. The results of the most recent search are stored in a `java.util.List` of `Customer` objects. This list is exposed as a property and made available with the `getCustomers()` method. In addition, the model has a `customerID` property, which supplies an implicit ID for several methods that require it.
- **Product fields** Like the customer fields, instance variables exist for the current product search results and the current product ID.
- **Problem fields** The model has instance variables for the current list of `Problem` objects and the currently selected problem.
- **Problem log fields** Likewise, there's a `java.util.List` for the list of `ProblemLog` objects associated with the current problem.

```
// ============================================
//    Configuration and database methods
// ============================================

/**
* Assigns a globally unique problem ID
*/
```

```
public static synchronized String assignProblemID
   (String problemIDFile)
{
   String id = null;
   try {

      // Read the next available ID

      BufferedReader in =
         new BufferedReader(
         new FileReader(problemIDFile));
      id = in.readLine();
      in.close();

      // Increment it and rewrite the file

      String prefix = id.substring(0, 1);
      int suffix = Integer.parseInt(id.substring(1));
      suffix++;
      String newID = "0000000" + String.valueOf(suffix);
      newID = newID.substring(newID.length() - 7);
      newID = prefix + newID;

      PrintWriter out =
         new PrintWriter(
         new FileWriter(problemIDFile));
      out.println(newID);
      out.flush();
      out.close();
   }
   catch (IOException e) {
      e.printStackTrace();
   }
   finally {
      return id;
   }
}

/**
* Creates a new connection using the currently
* specified JDBC driver and URL
* @exception SQLException if the connection fails
```

```
   * or if it already exists
   */
   public void connect()
      throws SQLException
   {
      if (isConnected())
         throw new SQLException("Already connected");

      // Verify that the driver and URL have been specified

      if (jdbcDriver == null)
         throw new SQLException("No jdbcDriver property");

      if (databaseURL == null)
         throw new SQLException("No databaseURL property");

      // Load the driver

      try {
         Class.forName(jdbcDriver).newInstance();
      }
      catch (ClassNotFoundException e) {
         throw new SQLException
         (jdbcDriver + " class could not be loaded");
      }

      // Open the connection

      con = DriverManager.getConnection(databaseURL);
   }

   /**
   * Closes the current connection
   */
   public void disconnect()
   {
      // Close the connection

      if (con != null) {
         try {
            con.close();
         }
```

```
        catch (SQLException ignore) {}
        finally {
           con = null;
        }
     }
  }

  /**
  * Returns true if there is an active connection
  */
  public boolean isConnected()
  {
     return (con != null);
  }

  /**
  * Returns the jdbcDriver.
  */
  public String getJdbcDriver()
  {
     return jdbcDriver;
  }

  /**
  * Sets the jdbcDriver.
  * @param jdbcDriver the jdbcDriver.
  */
  public void setJdbcDriver(String jdbcDriver)
  {
     this.jdbcDriver = jdbcDriver;
  }

  /**
  * Returns the databaseURL.
  */
  public String getDatabaseURL()
  {
     return databaseURL;
  }

  /**
  * Sets the databaseURL.
  * @param databaseURL the databaseURL.
  */
```

```
public void setDatabaseURL(String databaseURL)
{
   this.databaseURL = databaseURL;
}

/**
* Returns the problemIDFile.
*/
public String getProblemIDFile()
{
   return problemIDFile;
}

/**
* Sets the problemIDFile.
* @param problemIDFile the problemIDFile.
*/
public void setProblemIDFile(String problemIDFile)
{
   this.problemIDFile = problemIDFile;
}
```



The model contains a set of methods that handle data sources. The first is `assignProblemID(String problemIDFile)`. This is a class method that reads the next available problem ID from a file, and then rewrites the file with an incremented number. The method is synchronized, so the generated IDs are unique. There are get and set methods for the problem ID file name[2].

Database connections are managed with three methods:

- `void connect()`
- `void disconnect()`
- `boolean isConnected()`

The `connect()` method uses the model's `JdbcDriver` and `databaseURL` properties to open a JDBC connection to the database. These properties are set from context parameters specified in the `web.xml` deployment descriptor. The `disconnect()` method closes the connection, and the `isConnected()` method exposes a means for testing whether a database connection exists.

---

2 The file name is stored as an instance variable, but the method that uses it is a class method. This is why it must be passed as a parameter. The reason is the model can be run from the Web or from a command-line test shell. The file would likely be in different locations in each case.

**Note** *The connect() and disconnect() methods provide the capability of connecting to a database, but they don't choose when and how to do so. In fact, the model itself has no logic for handling this. This is the task of the controller object, as you will see.*

```
// ==============================================
//    Customer methods
// ==============================================

/**
* Returns the customer object corresponding to
* the current customer ID
* @exception SQLException if a database error occurs
*/
public Customer getCustomer()
   throws SQLException
{
   // Verify that a connection exists

   if (!isConnected())
      throw new SQLException("No connection");

   // Verify that there is a current customer ID

   if (customerID == null)
      throw new SQLException("No customer ID");

   PreparedStatement pstmt = null;
   ResultSet rs = null;
   Customer customer = null;

   try {

      // Prepare the query SQL

      pstmt = con.prepareStatement
      ("select * from customers where customerID = ?");
      pstmt.setString(1, customerID);

      // Execute the query

      rs = pstmt.executeQuery();
      if (rs.next())
```

```
            customer = Customer.load(rs);
      }
      finally {
         if (rs != null)
            rs.close();
         if (pstmt != null)
            pstmt.close();
      }

      // Return the customer

      return customer;
   }

   /**
   * Returns the current customer search results
   */
   public List getCustomers()
   {
      return customers;
   }

   /**
   * Uses the specified customer search argument to query
   * the database for matching customers. Creates a list
   * of customer objects.
   * @param searchArgument the search argument
   * @exception SQLException if a database error occurs
   */
   public void customerSearch(String searchArgument)
      throws SQLException
   {
      // Verify that a connection exists and that
      // the search argument has been specified

      if (!isConnected())
         throw new SQLException("No connection");

      PreparedStatement pstmt = null;
      ResultSet rs = null;
      customers = null;
```

```
      try {

         // Prepare the query SQL

         pstmt = con.prepareStatement(
            "select *"
            + " from customers"
            + " where name like ?"
            + " order by name"
         );
         searchArgument = searchArgument.trim();
         searchArgument = "%" + searchArgument + "%";
         pstmt.setString(1, searchArgument);

         // Execute the query and copy the results
         // to a List

         rs = pstmt.executeQuery();
         customers = new LinkedList();
         while (rs.next()) {
            customers.add(Customer.load(rs));
         }
      }
      finally {
         if (rs != null)
            rs.close();
         if (pstmt != null)
            pstmt.close();
      }
   }

   /**
   * Returns the customerID.
   */
   public String getCustomerID()
   {
      return customerID;
   }

   /**
   * Sets the customerID.
   * @param customerID the customerID.
```

```
   */
   public void setCustomerID(String customerID)
   {
      this.customerID = customerID;
   }
```

There are get and set methods for the current customer ID, and a method for retrieving from the database the `Customer` object having that ID. The `getCustomer()` method illustrates the function of the `Customer.load()` method in extracting a `Customer` object from a result set. The `customerSearch()` method selects `Customer` objects from the `customer` table whose name field matches a specified search argument. The resulting `java.util.List` is stored as an instance variable and can be retrieved with `getCustomers()`.

```
   // ============================================
   //    Product methods
   // ============================================

   /**
   * Returns the product object corresponding to
   * the current product ID
   * @exception SQLException if a database error occurs
   */
   public Product getProduct()
      throws SQLException
   {
      // Verify that a connection exists

      if (!isConnected())
         throw new SQLException("No connection");

      // Verify that a current product ID exists

      if (productID == null)
         throw new SQLException("No product ID");

      PreparedStatement pstmt = null;
      ResultSet rs = null;
      Product product = null;

      try {
```

```
         // Prepare the query SQL

         pstmt = con.prepareStatement
         ("select * from products where productID = ?");
         pstmt.setString(1, productID);

         // Execute the query

         rs = pstmt.executeQuery();
         if (rs.next())
            product = Product.load(rs);
      }
      finally {
         if (rs != null)
            rs.close();
         if (pstmt != null)
            pstmt.close();
      }

      // Return the product

      return product;
   }

   /**
   * Returns the current product search results
   */
   public List getProducts()
   {
      return products;
   }

   /**
   * Uses the specified product search argument to query
   * the database for matching products. Creates a list
   * of product objects.
   * @param searchArgument the search argument
   * @exception SQLException if a database error occurs
   */
   public void productSearch(String searchArgument)
      throws SQLException
   {
```

```
   // Verify that a connection exists and that
   // the search argument has been specified

   if (!isConnected())
      throw new SQLException("No connection");

   PreparedStatement pstmt = null;
   ResultSet rs = null;
   products = null;

   try {

      // Prepare the query SQL

      pstmt = con.prepareStatement(
         "select *"
         + " from products"
         + " where name like ?"
         + " order by name"
      );
      searchArgument = searchArgument.trim();
      searchArgument = "%" + searchArgument + "%";
      pstmt.setString(1, searchArgument);

      // Execute the query and copy the results
      // to a List

      rs = pstmt.executeQuery();
      products = new LinkedList();
      while (rs.next())
         products.add(Product.load(rs));
   }
   finally {
      if (rs != null)
         rs.close();
      if (pstmt != null)
         pstmt.close();
   }
}

/**
* Returns the productID.
```

```
    */
    public String getProductID()
    {
       return productID;
    }

    /**
    * Sets the productID.
    * @param productID the productID.
    */
    public void setProductID(String productID)
    {
       this.productID = productID;
    }
```

Exactly parallel to the customer methods, product methods get and set the current product ID, retrieve the corresponding `Product` object, select products matching a search string, and retrieve the selection.

```
    // ============================================
    //    Customer/product methods
    // ============================================

    /**
    * Returns a list of CustomerProduct objects
    * for the current customer.
    * @exception SQLException if a database error occurs
    */
    public List getCustomerProducts()
       throws SQLException
    {
       // Verify that a connection exists

       if (!isConnected())
          throw new SQLException("No connection");

       // Verify that a current customer ID exists

       if (customerID == null)
          throw new SQLException("No customer ID");

       PreparedStatement pstmt = null;
       ResultSet rs = null;
```

```
      List list = null;

      try {

         // Prepare the query SQL

         pstmt = con.prepareStatement(
            "select *"
            + " from custprod"
            + " where customerID = ?"
            + " order by datePurchased desc"
         );
         pstmt.setString(1, customerID);

         // Execute the query and populate the list

         rs = pstmt.executeQuery();
         list = new LinkedList();
         while (rs.next())
            list.add(CustomerProduct.load(rs));
      }
      finally {
         if (rs != null)
            rs.close();
         if (pstmt != null)
            pstmt.close();
      }

      // Return the list

      return list;
   }
```

When a customer ID has been selected and stored in the model, the `custprod` table can be searched for products purchased by that customer. The resulting list of `CustomerProblem` objects is sorted in descending order by date purchased and returned to the caller.

```
   // ==========================================
   //    Employee methods
   // ==========================================
```

```
/**
* Returns the employee object corresponding to
* the specified employee ID
* @param employeeID the employee ID
* @exception SQLException if a database error occurs
*/
public Employee getEmployee(String employeeID)
   throws SQLException
{
   // Verify that a connection exists

   if (!isConnected())
      throw new SQLException("No connection");

   PreparedStatement pstmt = null;
   ResultSet rs = null;
   Employee employee = null;

   try {

      // Prepare the query SQL

      pstmt = con.prepareStatement
      ("select * from employees where employeeID = ?");
      pstmt.setString(1, employeeID);

      // Execute the query

      rs = pstmt.executeQuery();
      if (rs.next())
         employee = Employee.load(rs);
   }
   finally {
      if (rs != null)
         rs.close();
      if (pstmt != null)
         pstmt.close();
   }

   // Return the employee

   return employee;
}
```

`Employee` objects can be retrieved from the database by calling `getEmployee()`, passing it the employee ID. This is primarily useful for displaying employee names for the three support IDs in the `Product` object.

```
// =============================================
//    Problem methods
// =============================================

/**
* Factory method to create a new problem record
* and add it to the database
*/
public void newProblem() throws SQLException
{
   if (getCustomerID() == null)
      throw new SQLException
      ("No customer ID");

   if (getProductID() == null)
      throw new SQLException
      ("No product ID");

   Problem problem = new Problem();

   String fileName = getProblemIDFile();
   problemID = assignProblemID(fileName);
   problem.setProblemID(problemID);
   problem.setDescription("");
   problem.setSeverity(2);
   problem.setDateReported(new java.util.Date());
   problem.setCustomerID(getCustomerID());
   problem.setProductID(getProductID());

   // Add to database

   PreparedStatement pstmt = null;
   try {
      pstmt = con.prepareStatement
      ("insert into problems values(?, ?, ?, ?, ?, ?, ?)");
      pstmt.setString(1, problemID);
      pstmt.setString(2, problem.getDescription());
      pstmt.setInt(3, problem.getSeverity());
      pstmt.setTimestamp
         (4, Util.toTimestamp(problem.getDateReported()));
```

JSP IN ACTION

```
         pstmt.setNull(5, Types.TIMESTAMP);
         pstmt.setString(6, problem.getCustomerID());
         pstmt.setString(7, problem.getProductID());
         pstmt.executeUpdate();
      }
      finally {
         if (pstmt != null)
            pstmt.close();
      }
   }

   /**
   * Updates the problem record in the database
   * @param problem the problem object
   * @exception SQLException if a database error occurs
   */
   public void updateProblem(Problem problem)
      throws SQLException
   {
      // Verify that a connection exists

      if (!isConnected())
         throw new SQLException("No connection");

      PreparedStatement pstmt = null;
      try {

         // Prepare the query SQL

         pstmt = con.prepareStatement
         ( " update problems"
         + "    set"
         + "       description = ?,"
         + "       severity = ?,"
         + "       dateResolved = ?"
         + "    where problemID = ?"
         );
         pstmt.setString(1, problem.getDescription());
         pstmt.setInt(2, problem.getSeverity());
         if (problem.getDateResolved() != null)
            pstmt.setTimestamp(3,
               Util.toTimestamp(problem.getDateResolved()));
```

```
      pstmt.setString(4, problem.getProblemID());

      // Execute the update

      pstmt.executeUpdate();
   }
   finally {
      if (pstmt != null)
         pstmt.close();
   }
}

/**
* Returns the problem object corresponding to
* the current problem ID
* @exception SQLException if a database error occurs
*/
public Problem getProblem()
   throws SQLException
{
   // Verify that a connection exists

   if (!isConnected())
      throw new SQLException("No connection");

   // Verify that a current problem ID exists

   if (problemID == null)
      throw new SQLException("No problem ID");

   PreparedStatement pstmt = null;
   ResultSet rs = null;
   Problem problem = null;

   try {

      // Prepare the query SQL

      pstmt = con.prepareStatement
      ("select * from problems where problemID = ?");
      pstmt.setString(1, problemID);
```

```
         // Execute the query

         rs = pstmt.executeQuery();
         if (rs.next())
            problem = Problem.load(rs);
      }
      finally {
         if (rs != null)
            rs.close();
         if (pstmt != null)
            pstmt.close();
      }

      // Return the problem

      return problem;
   }

   /**
   * Returns the current problem search results
   */
   public List getProblems()
   {
      return problems;
   }

   /**
   * Uses the specified customer ID to query
   * the database for problems for that customer.
   * Creates a list of problem objects.
   * @exception SQLException if a database error occurs
   */
   public void customerProblemsSearch(String customerID)
      throws SQLException
   {
      // Verify that a connection exists

      if (!isConnected())
         throw new SQLException("No connection");

      PreparedStatement pstmt = null;
      ResultSet rs = null;
```

```
      problems = null;

      try {

         // Prepare the query SQL

         pstmt = con.prepareStatement
         ("select * from problems where customerID = ?");
         pstmt.setString(1, customerID);

         // Execute the query and copy the results
         // to a List

         rs = pstmt.executeQuery();
         problems = new LinkedList();
         while (rs.next())
            problems.add(Problem.load(rs));
      }
      finally {
         if (rs != null)
            rs.close();
         if (pstmt != null)
            pstmt.close();
      }
   }

   /**
   * Uses the specified product ID to query
   * the database for problems for that product.
   * Creates a list of problem objects.
   * @exception SQLException if a database error occurs
   */
   public void productProblemsSearch(String productID)
      throws SQLException
   {
      // Verify that a connection exists

      if (!isConnected())
         throw new SQLException("No connection");

      PreparedStatement pstmt = null;
      ResultSet rs = null;
```

```
      problems = null;

      try {

         // Prepare the query SQL

         pstmt = con.prepareStatement
         ("select * from problems where productID = ?");
         pstmt.setString(1, productID);

         // Execute the query and copy the results
         // to a List

         rs = pstmt.executeQuery();
         problems = new LinkedList();
         while (rs.next())
            problems.add(Problem.load(rs));
      }
      finally {
         if (rs != null)
            rs.close();
         if (pstmt != null)
            pstmt.close();
      }
   }

   /**
   * Returns the problemID.
   */
   public String getProblemID()
   {
      return problemID;
   }

   /**
   * Sets the problemID.
   * @param problemID the problemID.
   */
   public void setProblemID(String problemID)
   {
      this.problemID = problemID;
   }
```

A newProblem() method creates a new problem record for the current customer and product, initializes it, and adds it to the database, and an updateProblem() method modifies it. Methods exist for retrieving problems by customer and product, which store their results in a java.util.List that can be retrieved with getProblems().

```
// ============================================
//    ProblemLog methods
// ============================================

/**
* Adds a new problem log entry
* @param log a problem log object
* @exception SQLException if a database error occurs
*/
public void addProblemLog(ProblemLog log)
   throws SQLException
{
   // Verify that a connection exists

   if (!isConnected())
      throw new SQLException("No connection");

   PreparedStatement pstmt = null;

   try {

      // Prepare the insert SQL

      pstmt = con.prepareStatement
      ("insert into problog values(?, ?, ?, ?)");
      pstmt.setString(1, log.getProblemID());
      pstmt.setTimestamp(2, Util.toTimestamp(log.getLogTime()));
      pstmt.setString(3, log.getEventID());
      pstmt.setString(4, log.getComments());

      // Execute the statement

      pstmt.executeUpdate();
   }
   finally {
      if (pstmt != null)
         pstmt.close();
```

```
      }
   }

   /**
   * Uses the specified problem ID to query
   * the database for problem log entries for
   * that problem.
   * Creates a list of problem log objects.
   * @exception SQLException if a database error occurs
   */
   public void problemLogSearch(String problemID)
      throws SQLException
   {
      // Verify that a connection exists

      if (!isConnected())
         throw new SQLException("No connection");

      PreparedStatement pstmt = null;
      ResultSet rs = null;
      problemLogs = null;

      try {

         // Prepare the query SQL

         pstmt = con.prepareStatement
         ("select * from problog where problemID = ?");
         pstmt.setString(1, problemID);

         // Execute the query and copy the results
         // to a List

         rs = pstmt.executeQuery();
         problemLogs = new LinkedList();
         while (rs.next())
            problemLogs.add(ProblemLog.load(rs));
      }
      finally {
         if (rs != null)
            rs.close();
         if (pstmt != null)
            pstmt.close();
      }
```

```
    }

    /**
    * Returns the problemLogs.
    */
    public List getProblemLogs()
    {
       return problemLogs;
    }
}
```

Finally, the model has methods to add a log entry for a problem, to search for the log entries for an existing problem, and to retrieve the search results.

**WebModel Class** If you read the Model class carefully, you'll note it contains no Web-aware methods. This is deliberate. For testing purposes, you want to be able to run the model using a simple command-line view, so you don't want to have javax.servlet or javax.servlet.http classes used anywhere in the model. When it 's run from the Web, however, you want the model to take advantage of a little more knowledge about its environment. For this reason, you use a subclass of Model that has this awareness.

WebModel implements three methods:

- `void init(ServletContext context)` extracts application parameters from the web.xml deployment descriptor. These include the JDBC driver name, the database URL, and the name of the file containing the next available product ID. Using web.xml to specify these values makes configuring the product support application easy for different environments.
- `void valueBound(HttpSessionBindingEvent event)` is one of two methods that comprise the HttpSessionBindingListener interface. In this case, there's nothing to do in this method, but it must be implemented to satisfy the compiler.
- `void valueUnbound(HttpSessionBindingEvent event)` is the other of the two HttpSessionBindingListener methods. This is where you perform the important function of closing the database connection when the session times out or is invalidated.

The WebModel class is shown here:

```
package com.lyricnote.support.model;

import javax.servlet.*;
import javax.servlet.http.*;
```

```
import java.sql.SQLException;

/**
* HTTP-specific subclass of Model. Implements session
* binding and unbinding. Allows the database connection
* to be disconnected when the session times out or is
* invalidated.
*/
public class WebModel
   extends Model
   implements HttpSessionBindingListener
{
   /**
   * Initializes the database connection
   */
   public void init(ServletContext context)
      throws ServletException
   {
      // Set the model's JDBC driver property
      // from an application-scoped value
      // in web.xml

      String jdbcDriver =
         context.getInitParameter("jdbcDriver");
      if (jdbcDriver == null)
         throw new ServletException
         ("No jdbcDriver property specified");
      setJdbcDriver(jdbcDriver);

      // Do likewise for the database URL

      String databaseURL =
         context.getInitParameter("databaseURL");
      if (databaseURL == null)
         throw new ServletException
         ("No databaseURL property specified");
      setDatabaseURL(databaseURL);

      // and the problem ID assignment file

      String problemIDFile =
         context.getInitParameter("problemIDFile");
      if (problemIDFile == null)
         throw new ServletException
```

```
            ("No problemIDFile property specified");
         setProblemIDFile(problemIDFile);

         // Connect to the database

         try {
            connect();
         }
         catch (SQLException e) {
            throw new ServletException(e.getMessage());
         }
      }

      /**
      * Called when the model is bound to a session
      */
      public void valueBound(HttpSessionBindingEvent event)
      {
      }

      /**
      * Called when the model is removed from a session
      */
      public void valueUnbound(HttpSessionBindingEvent event)
      {
         disconnect();
      }
   }
```

**Util Class** The last of the application object classes is `Util`, a utility class providing miscellaneous supporting methods. These methods include the following:

- `dateFormat()` converts a `Date` object to a formatted date string
- `dateTimeFormat()` converts a `Date` object to a formatted date and time string
- `toTimestamp()` converts a `Date` object to a `java.sql.Timestamp` so it can be used in a `PreparedStatement.setTimestamp()` method.
- `quote()` surrounds a string with quotation marks if it contains any embedded commas. This is used by the `toString()` methods ini `Customer`, `Product`, and other business object classes to make values safe for the comma-separated-values format.
- `isClosingEvent()` returns `true` if the specified event ID is one that means the problem is closed.

The following is a listing of the `Util` class:

```
package com.lyricnote.support.model;

import java.text.*;
import java.sql.Timestamp;
import java.util.*;

/**
* Utility methods used in the model package
*/
public class Util
{
   private static final SimpleDateFormat DATE_FORMAT =
      new SimpleDateFormat("yyyy-MM-dd");

   private static final SimpleDateFormat DATE_TIME_FORMAT =
      new SimpleDateFormat("yyyy-MM-dd HH:mm:ss");

   /**
   * Formats a date using the default JDBC format
   */
   public static String dateFormat(Date d)
   {
      return d == null ? "" : DATE_FORMAT.format(d);
   }

   /**
   * Formats a timestamp using the default JDBC format
   */
   public static String dateTimeFormat(Date d)
   {
      return d == null ? "" : DATE_TIME_FORMAT.format(d);
   }

   /**
   * Converts a java.util.Date to a java.sql.Timestamp
   */
   public static Timestamp toTimestamp(Date d)
   {
      return (d == null)
         ? null
```

```
            : new Timestamp(d.getTime());
    }

    /**
    * Encloses a string in quotation marks
    * if it contains a comma.
    * @param s the string
    */
    public static String quote(String s)
    {
        if (s != null) {
            if (s.indexOf(",") > -1) {
                StringBuffer sb = new StringBuffer();
                sb.append('"');
                sb.append(s);
                sb.append('"');
                s = sb.toString();
            }
        }
        return s;
    }

    /**
    * Returns true if the specified event ID
    * represents a "close" action
    * @param eventID the event ID
    */
    public static final boolean isClosingEvent(String eventID)
    {
        return (
            eventID.equals("CNB") ||
            eventID.equals("CCP") ||
            eventID.equals("CFX"));
    }
}
```



## Testing Framework

One of the great benefits of the MVC architecture is that each component can be tested in isolation. During development, being able to unit test the model is particularly useful, and its API as methods are added and modified. In this section, you see a command-line shell that fills this role.

**Shell Class** The `test.Shell` class is a standalone Java application that acts as the controller and view for a `com.lyricnote.support.model.Model`. Like a Unix shell or a Windows command prompt, the `Shell` class prompts for commands, executes them, and displays the results. The syntax for these commands is simply the corresponding Java syntax that calls methods on the model, as well as a few commands for listing the available methods, showing help text, and similar control functions. `Shell` provides a simple means for exercising each part of the model without the added complexity of a GUI in the Web environment.

Like the `Model` class, `Shell` is fairly lengthy, so let's discuss it a section at a time.

```
package test;

import com.lyricnote.support.model.*;
import java.beans.*;
import java.io.*;
import java.lang.reflect.*;
import java.sql.*;
import java.util.*;

/**
* An interactive shell for testing the product support
* application model.
*/
public class Shell
{
   private static String PROMPT = "SHELL> ";
   private Model model;
   private InputStream stream;
   private boolean interactive;

   // ==============================================
   //    Class methods
   // ==============================================

   /**
   * Mainline
   */
   public static void main(String[] args)
      throws Exception
   {
      Shell shell = new Shell(new Model());
      shell.run();
```

```
}

/**
* Displays help text for this shell
*/
protected static void help()
{
   String[] text = {
      "",
      "Invoke a method by name,"
      + " or any of the following commands:",
      "",
      "quit       -  exits from the shell",
      "help       -  displays this help text",
      "methods    -  displays a list of model methods",
      "include <filename> - executes an included file",
      "",
   };
   for (int i = 0; i < text.length; i++)
      System.out.println(text[i]);
}

/**
* Extracts a quoted string argument value
* from a method call
*/
protected static String getArgument(String line)
{
   String arg = null;
   int p = line.indexOf("(\"");
   if (p != -1) {
      p += 2;
      int q = line.indexOf("\")", p);
      if (q != -1) {
         arg = line.substring(p, q);
      }
   }
   return arg;
}

// ==========================================
//    Constructors
```

```
// ============================================

/**
* Creates a new Shell with input from System.in
* @param model the model to be used
*/
public Shell(Model model)
{
   this(model, System.in);
}

/**
* Creates a new Shell with input from
* the specified input stream
* @param model the model to be used
* @param stream the input stream
*/
public Shell(Model model, InputStream stream)
{
   this.model = model;
   this.stream = stream;
   this.interactive = (stream == System.in);
}
```

`Shell` uses a simple `main()` method to create instances of the model and the shell, and then invokes that shell's `run()` method. The source for command input is initially `System.in` but, as you see, it can also be a set of commands stored in a file and processed with an `include` command.

```
// ============================================
//    Main read/execute loop
// ============================================

/**
* Runs the shell
*/
public void run() throws Exception
{
   // Open a line reader over the input stream

   BufferedReader in =
```

```
      new BufferedReader(
      new InputStreamReader(stream));

   // Read and execute each line

   while (true) {

      if (interactive)
         System.out.print(PROMPT);

      String line = in.readLine();
      if (line == null)
         break;

      // Parse and execute the command

      try {
         if (line.equals("quit"))
            break;
         else if (line.startsWith("get"))
            doGet(line);
         else if (line.startsWith("set"))
            doSet(line);
         else if (line.startsWith("customerSearch"))
            customerSearch(line);
         else if (line.startsWith("productSearch"))
            productSearch(line);
         else if (line.startsWith("productProblemsSearch"))
            productProblemsSearch(line);
         else if (line.startsWith("customerProblemsSearch"))
            customerProblemsSearch(line);
         else if (line.startsWith("problemLogSearch"))
            problemLogSearch(line);
         else if (line.startsWith("help"))
            help();
         else if (line.startsWith("methods"))
            methods();
         else if (line.startsWith("inc"))
            include(line);
         else if (line.startsWith("is"))
            doGet(line);
         else if (line.startsWith("connect"))
```

```
                doConnect();
            else if (line.startsWith("disconnect"))
                doDisconnect();
            else if (line.startsWith("newProblem"))
                doNewProblem();

            // none of the above

            else
                System.out.println
                    ("Unrecognized command [" + line + "]");
        }
        catch (Exception e) {
            e.printStackTrace();
        }
    }
    in.close();
    if (interactive)
        doDisconnect();
}
```

The `run()` method opens a character line reader over the input stream and starts prompting for and executing commands. The parser is a simple list of `if` statements that check for specific method names and call wrapper methods that execute them. For commands beginning with `get`, `is`, or `set` `Shell` uses reflection to find the corresponding getter or setter methods in the model and invokes them. If any errors are encountered, they're written to `System.out`.

Here's the rest of the class, consisting of the methods that can be called from the main loop (listed alphabetically):

```
/**
* Invokes the customer problems search method
*/
protected void customerProblemsSearch(String line)
    throws Exception
{
    String arg = getArgument(line);
    model.customerProblemsSearch(arg);
}

/**
```

```
* Invokes the customer search method
*/
protected void customerSearch(String line)
   throws SQLException
{
   String arg = getArgument(line);
   model.customerSearch(arg);
}

/**
* Invokes the connect command
*/
protected void doConnect()
{
   try {
      System.out.println("Connecting...");
      model.connect();
      System.out.println("Connected");
   }
   catch (SQLException e) {
      System.out.println(e.getMessage());
   }
}

/**
* Invokes the disconnect command
*/
protected void doDisconnect()
{
   System.out.println("Disconnecting...");
   model.disconnect();
   System.out.println("Disconnected");
}

/**
* Executes a "get" method
*/
protected void doGet(String line) throws Exception
{
   if (!interactive)
      System.out.println(line);
```

```
      // Get the read method name

      int p = line.indexOf("(");
      if (p == -1)
         p = line.length();
      String readMethodName = line.substring(0, p).trim();

      // Lookup the read methods to see
      // if this one is found

      BeanInfo bi =
         Introspector.getBeanInfo(model.getClass());

      PropertyDescriptor[] pds =
         bi.getPropertyDescriptors();

      for (int i = 0; i < pds.length; i++) {
         PropertyDescriptor pd = pds[i];
         Method method = pd.getReadMethod();
         if (method != null) {
            String name = method.getName();
            if (name.equals(readMethodName)) {

               // This method is the read method
               // for this property.
               // Invoke it and print the result

               Object[] args = {};
               Object result = method.invoke(model, args);
               System.out.println(result);
               return;
            }
         }
      }
      throw new IllegalArgumentException
      ("No " + readMethodName + " method found");
   }

   /**
   * Invokes the newProblem method
   */
   protected void doNewProblem() throws Exception
   {
```

```
      model.newProblem();
      System.out.println(model.getProblemID());
   }

   /**
   * Executes a "set" method
   */
   protected void doSet(String line) throws Exception
   {
      if (!interactive)
         System.out.println(line);

      // Line should look like this:
      //
      //    setSearchArgument("value")

      int p = line.indexOf("(");
      if (p == -1)
         throw new IllegalArgumentException
         ("No open parenthesis found");

      int q = line.indexOf(")", p);
      if (q == -1)
         throw new IllegalArgumentException
         ("No close parenthesis found");

      String writeMethodName = line.substring(0, p);
      String argument = line.substring(p+1, q).trim();

      // Argument must be a quoted string

      if (!(argument.startsWith("\"") &&
            argument.endsWith("\"")))
         throw new IllegalArgumentException
         ("Argument must be a quoted string");

      // Strip off the quotes

      argument = argument.substring(1, argument.length()-1);

      // Find the set method and execute it

      BeanInfo bi = Introspector.getBeanInfo(model.getClass());
```

```
      PropertyDescriptor[] pds = bi.getPropertyDescriptors();

      for (int i = 0; i < pds.length; i++) {
         PropertyDescriptor pd = pds[i];
         Method method = pd.getWriteMethod();
         if (method != null) {
            String name = method.getName();
            if (name.equals(writeMethodName)) {

               // This method is the write method
               // for this property

               Object[] args = { argument };
               Object result = method.invoke(model, args);
               return;
            }
         }
      }

      throw new IllegalArgumentException
      ("No " + writeMethodName + " method found");
   }

   /**
   * Runs a subshell for the file specified in
   * the include statement.
   * @param line an "include <path>/file" statement
   */
   protected void include(String line) throws Exception
   {
      if (!interactive)
         System.out.println(line);

      try {

         // Get the name of the file to be included

         StringTokenizer st = new StringTokenizer(line);
         st.nextToken();
         if (!st.hasMoreTokens())
            throw new IllegalArgumentException
            ("No file name specified for include");
         String fileName = st.nextToken();
```

```
         // Verify that file exists

         File file = new File(fileName);
         if (!file.exists())
            throw new IllegalArgumentException
            (fileName + " not found");

         // Run the subshell

         System.out.println("Including " + fileName);
         new Shell(this.model, new FileInputStream(file)).run();
         System.out.println("Done including " + fileName);
      }
      catch (IllegalArgumentException e) {
         System.out.println(e.getMessage());
      }
      catch (IOException e) {
         System.out.println(e.getMessage());
      }
   }

   /**
   * Shows the public methods available in the model
   */
   protected void methods()
   {
      // Get the list of declared methods

      Class cls = Model.class;
      Method[] methods = cls.getDeclaredMethods();
      System.out.println(methods.length + " methods:");

      // Print the list

      for (int i = 0; i < methods.length; i++) {
         Method method = methods[i];
         String name = method.getName();
         Class[] parameterTypes = method.getParameterTypes();
         StringBuffer sb = new StringBuffer();
         sb.append(name);
         sb.append("(");
         for (int j = 0; j < parameterTypes.length; j++) {
            Class parmClass = parameterTypes[j];
```

```
            if (j > 0)
               sb.append(",");
            sb.append(parmClass.getName());
         }
         sb.append(")");
         String s = sb.toString();
         System.out.println("    " + s);
      }
   }

   /**
   * Invokes the problemLogSearch method
   */
   protected void problemLogSearch(String line)
      throws Exception
   {
      String id = getArgument(line);
      model.problemLogSearch(id);
   }
   /**
   * Invokes the productProblemsSearch method
   */
   protected void productProblemsSearch(String line)
      throws Exception
   {
      String id = getArgument(line);
      model.productProblemsSearch(id);
   }

   /**
   * Invokes the productSearch method
   */
   protected void productSearch(String line) throws Exception
   {
      String arg = getArgument(line);
      model.productSearch(arg);
   }
}
```

To get an idea of how useful the shell can be, let's see it in action. When you invoke the `Shell` class, its `main()` method creates an instance of `Shell` and passes it a new instance of `Model`. If you type the `help` command, you see the following help text:

```
P:\classes\test>java -classpath .. test.Shell
SHELL> help

Invoke a method by name, or any of the following commands:

quit       - exits from the shell
help       - displays this help text
methods    - displays a list of model methods
include <filename> - executes an included file

SHELL>
```

To begin with, let's see what `Model` methods are available to call. Type the `methods` command to see this:

```
SHELL> methods
33 methods:
   connect()
   customerProblemsSearch(java.lang.String)
   customerSearch(java.lang.String)
   disconnect()
   getProblemID()
   newProblem()
   productProblemsSearch(java.lang.String)
   productSearch(java.lang.String)
   addProblemLog(com.lyricnote.support.model.ProblemLog)
   assignProblemID(java.lang.String)
   getCustomer()
   getCustomerID()
   getCustomerProducts()
   getCustomers()
   getDatabaseURL()
   getEmployee(java.lang.String)
   getJdbcDriver()
   getProblem()
   getProblemIDFile()
   getProblemLogs()
   getProblems()
   getProduct()
   getProductID()
   getProducts()
   isConnected()
```

```
    problemLogSearch(java.lang.String)
    setCustomerID(java.lang.String)
    setDatabaseURL(java.lang.String)
    setJdbcDriver(java.lang.String)
    setProblemID(java.lang.String)
    setProblemIDFile(java.lang.String)
    setProductID(java.lang.String)
    updateProblem(com.lyricnote.support.model.Problem)
SHELL>
```

How did this information get there? Looking at the `Shell` method that implements the `methods` command, you see it calls the `getDeclaredMethods()` method on the `Model` class, and then prints the resulting array. This shows a list of every method you can call from within the shell.

During development, as you add new methods to the model, you see them automatically added to this list. In the `Shell` class, all you need to add is an `if` statement in the `run()` method and a subroutine that simply invokes the model method and prints the results. As you see shortly, you don't even need to do this for the property getter and setter methods.

Back to the shell session. You know you can't do much without a database connection, so let's call the model method that reports whether a connection is established

```
SHELL> isConnected();
false
SHELL>
```

When the shell sees a command that starts with `is` or `get`, it interprets that as a call to one of the model's property accessor methods. The shell handles all such interpretation in its `doGet()` method. `doGet()` uses JavaBeans introspection to get a list of getter methods from the `Model` class. It then compares the method name from the command line to the names of the getter methods for a match. When the shell finds a matching method, it invokes the method and returns the result.

A similar approach is used for setter methods. Any command beginning with `set` is dispatched to the `doSet(String line)` method, which extracts the argument from the command line, goes through the same introspection to find the appropriate `set` method, and invokes the method with the command line argument.

This makes for a natural way of getting and setting model properties. When you called the shell's `isConnected()` method, it passed the call on to the model's `isConnected()` method, which reported no connection occurred.

To create a connection, you know the model needs a JDBC driver name and a database URL. Set these properties, and then call the `connect()` method:

```
SHELL> setJdbcDriver("org.enhydra.instantdb.jdbc.idbDriver");
SHELL> setDatabaseURL("jdbc:idb:D:/jspcr/Chap19/database/db.prp");
SHELL> connect();
Connecting...
Connected
SHELL> isConnected();
true
SHELL>
```

This time, the `isConnected()` method indicates the connection is available. If all you're testing for now is the database routines, you should call `disconnect()`, and then the `quit` command:

```
SHELL> disconnect();
Disconnecting...
Disconnected
SHELL> quit
```

Testing happens over and over, and typing long sequences of commands can be tedious. For this reason, the shell provides an `include` command. This allows shell commands to be read from a file and executed in a subshell. This facility is recursive, so included modules can, themselves, include other modules.

An immediately useful included module is one that performs the database connection because this is used with virtually all testing. This module contains the three commands you just typed to perform the connection:

```
setJdbcDriver("org.enhydra.instantdb.jdbc.idbDriver");
setDatabaseURL("jdbc:idb:D:/jspcr/Chap19/database/db.prp");
connect();
```

Now you can start a shell and simply invoke the external set of commands:

```
P:\classes\test>java -classpath .. test.Shell
SHELL> include connect.inc
setJdbcDriver("org.enhydra.instantdb.jdbc.idbDriver");
setDatabaseURL("jdbc:idb:D:/jspcr/Chap19/database/db.prp");
Connecting...
Connected
SHELL> isConnected();
true
```

Note, the contents of the included module are echoed to the console as they are read.

With a connection established, you can proceed to test any part of the model, duplicating the series of steps the GUI application will take and seeing if the results are what you expect. Let's try searching for the ScoreWriter product and drilling down through its problem reports:

```
SHELL> productSearch("Score");
SHELL> getProducts();
[023500,ScoreWriter,0040,0140,0070]
SHELL> productProblemsSearch("023500");
SHELL> getProblems();
[G0000179,Can't get triplets to work,3,2001-01-14 18:40:39,
2001-01-14 18:42:53,WAGNER01,023500]
SHELL> problemLogSearch("G0000179");
SHELL> getProblemLogs();
[
G0000179,2001-01-14 18:41:09,RPS,They just don't work!,
G0000179,2001-01-14 18:42:20,COM,Told customer to try F5,
G0000179,2001-01-14 18:42:53,CCP,That did it]

SHELL> quit
Disconnecting...
Disconnected

P:\classes\test>
```

Invoking the `productSearch()` method, and then `getProducts()`, you see the list of products matching the search argument (in this case, a list of one element). The object is represented by a comma-separated-values string listing the product ID, its name, and the employee IDs of the product support person, lead developer, and lead tester. The `productProblemsSearch()` method then finds the list of problems reported for ScoreWriter (in this case, also a list of only one element). Finally, the `problemLogSearch()` and `getProblemLogs()` methods get the log entries for the selected problem.[3]

## Using the Model

This completes the development of the model component. In the early stages of development, you want to write the `Model` and `Shell` classes in tandem, so each part of the model can be tested in isolation. When bugs are discovered, you can return to the shell to reproduce them without having to start and stop a Web server or search through debugging entries in the servlet logs. This results in a more reliable base for the rest of the application.

---

3 The listed results have been reformatted slightly to accommodate the line width.

There is, of course, more than one way to design the model. You needn't use an application container like the `Model` class; you could work with the business objects directly as JavaBeans in an `HttpSession`. What you saw in this section, however, is a workable design that accommodates a variety of application requirements without creating undue complexity in the view and controller.

## View Classes

The model could be attached to a standalone Java application. However, the product support system is accessed by users in at least four roles: call center agents, product support specialists, developers, and testers. In addition, management may want to measure quality statistics, such as the average length of time a problem waits in a queue, the average number of customer callbacks needed to resolve a problem, and the number of defects outstanding for a particular product. For this reason, the best system operating environment is probably the company's intranet, and the presentation layer consists of JSP pages. In this section, you see how JSP pages can be used as the view to which the model is attached.

Three general entry points exist into the system:

- **By customer** Call center agents on the phone with a customer first look up the customer ID by means of an alpha search of the `customer` table by customer name. After selecting a customer from the list of matches, the agent sees details about the customer, including the products this customer has purchased and the history of problems reported by the customer. From there, the call center agent can enter a new problem report or provide status about an existing one.
- **By product** Product support personnel, developers, and testers are all assigned to particular products rather than customers. Their initial view of the system, therefore, is by product. They can use an alpha search of the `product` table to find products by name and, from there, they can view the list of outstanding problems.
- **By problem** Any users of the system may already know the problem ID assigned to a particular defect. If they need to update the problem record, they can use a form that prompts for the specific problem ID.

In all three cases, the application eventually ends up showing a detailed view of a particular problem. From there, the user can update the problem description and severity, route the problem to another department, or close the problem. The last JSP view is then a confirmation screen showing what action was applied.

Figure 19-3 diagrams this application flow. Each of the rectangular boxes represents a particular JSP page. The circles represent controller actions, which you learn about shortly. For now, remember that controller actions are what cause changes in the model and cause the next view to be displayed. The arrows from the JSP view to the controller actions are labeled with the type of action the user takes with respect to the view: selecting from a list, entering a search argument, or clicking a submit button.

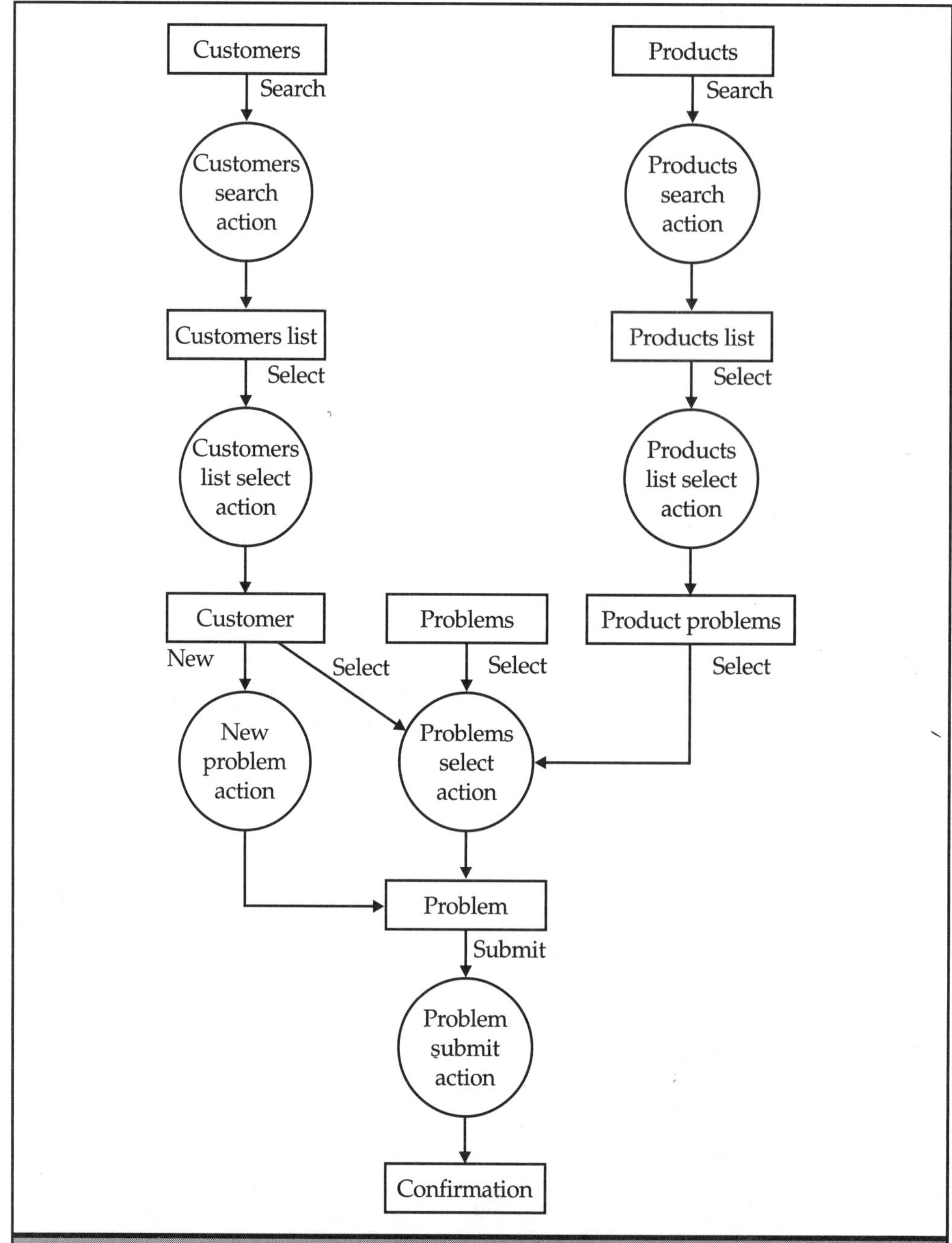


**Figure 19-3.** *View/controller interaction diagram*

You examine each of the JSP view pages in more detail shortly. First, however, you need to look at some supporting classes.

## Support Pages

Two sections of code are common to all the JSP view pages. Rather than duplicate them in every JSP file, you store them in separate text files and include them with the `<%@ include %>` directive[4].

**InitModel.jsp** Every JSP view page needs to declare the model as a session bean and ensure a database connection is available. This common function is accomplished by having the view pages include the following code:

```
<%-- Define and initialize the model --%>

<jsp:useBean
   id="model"
   scope="session"
   class="com.lyricnote.support.model.WebModel">
<% model.init(application); %>
</jsp:useBean>

<%-- Provide an alias for the controller servlet --%>

<%
   String BASEURL = request.getContextPath();
   String CONTROLLER = BASEURL + "/servlet/controller";
%>
```

This code in `initModel.jsp` does three things:

- Declares a JavaBean named `model` having session scope and initialized with a `com.lyricnote.support.model.WebModel` object.
- Invokes the model's `init()` method to extract application variables from `web.xml` and establish a session-aware database connection. This method is called only once, when the model is first bound to the session.
- Initializes constants specifying the base URL for the application and the name of the controller servlet. These constants are used in URLs and form action attributes elsewhere in the view.

4 Why the include directive rather than <jsp:include>? Because the included sections define and use constants that need to be common to both the included module and the including module.

**Banner.jsp** For a common look and feel in all the JSP view pages, a standard header is used. This header, stored in a file named `Banner.jsp`, contains an HTML table that includes the company logo and standard navigation links.

```
<TABLE BORDER=0 CELLSPACING=3 CELLPADDING=3 WIDTH=500>
<TR>
   <TD><IMG SRC="<%= BASEURL %>/images/logo.jpg"></TD>
</TR>
<TR>
<TD CLASS="menucell" ALIGN="RIGHT">
   <A CLASS="menuitem"
      HREF="<%= BASEURL %>/Problems.jsp">Problems</A>

   <SPAN CLASS="menuitem">|</SPAN>

   <A CLASS="menuitem"
      HREF="<%= BASEURL %>/Products.jsp">Products</A>

   <SPAN CLASS="menuitem">|</SPAN>

   <A CLASS="menuitem"
      HREF="<%= BASEURL %>/Customers.jsp">Customers</A>
</TR>
</TABLE>
```

Neither `InitModel.jsp` nor `Banner.jsp` is designed to be called directly by a user. To prevent this, they are stored in the `/WEB-INF` folder. This makes them visible to the application itself, but not to users on the Web.

**ErrorPage.jsp** A final supporting module is the error page, listed in the following:

```
<%@ page session="false" %>
<%@ page import="java.io.PrintWriter" %>
<%@ page isErrorPage="true" %>

<HTML>
<HEAD>
<TITLE>Error Page</TITLE>
<LINK REL="stylesheet" HREF="style.css">
</HEAD>
<BODY>
<H3>Error</H3>
The following error occurred:
```

```
<PRE>
<%
   exception.printStackTrace(new PrintWriter(out));
%>
</PRE>
</BODY>
</HTML>
```

`ErrorPage.jsp` does little more than display a stack trace for any uncaught exception. This is useful during system development, but should probably be replaced by something more user-friendly in production.

## JSP View Pages

Using Figure 19-3 as our road map, let's look at the nine individual JSP view pages:

- `Customers.jsp` Prompts for customer search argument
- `CustomersList.jsp` Selection list of customer search results
- `Customer.jsp` Detail view of a single customer record
- `Problem.jsp` Detail view of a single problem record
- `Confirm.jsp` Confirmation screen shown after problem update
- `Products.jsp` Prompts for product search argument
- `ProductsList.jsp` Selection list of product search results
- `ProductProblems.jsp` Selection list of problems for a product
- `Problems.jsp` Prompts for a product ID

**Customers.jsp** The initial entry point of call center agents is typically the customer search view, listed in the following:

```
<%@ page session="true" %>
<%@ page errorPage="/ErrorPage.jsp" %>
<%@ page import="com.lyricnote.support.model.*" %>

<%@ include file="/WEB-INF/InitModel.jsp" %>

<HTML>
<HEAD>
<TITLE>Customer Search</TITLE>
<LINK REL="stylesheet" HREF="<%= BASEURL %>/style.css">
</HEAD>
<BODY>
```

```
<%@ include file="/WEB-INF/Banner.jsp" %>

<H3>Customer Search</H3>
<FORM
   METHOD="POST"
   ACTION="<%= CONTROLLER %>/Customers/Search">
<B>Customer name</B>:
<INPUT TYPE="TEXT" NAME="customerSearchArgument" SIZE="20">
<INPUT TYPE="SUBMIT" VALUE="Search">
</FORM>

</BODY>
</HTML>
```

After including the model initialization and banner code, this JSP page uses an HTML form to prompt for a customer name search string. If the call center agent is talking to a customer named Eleanor Wagner, for example, the agent may search for names containing the letter `W`, as shown in Figure 19-4. When the agent clicks the search button, the form is then submitted to a servlet that performs the search (which is discussed later in this chapter in the Controller Classes section).

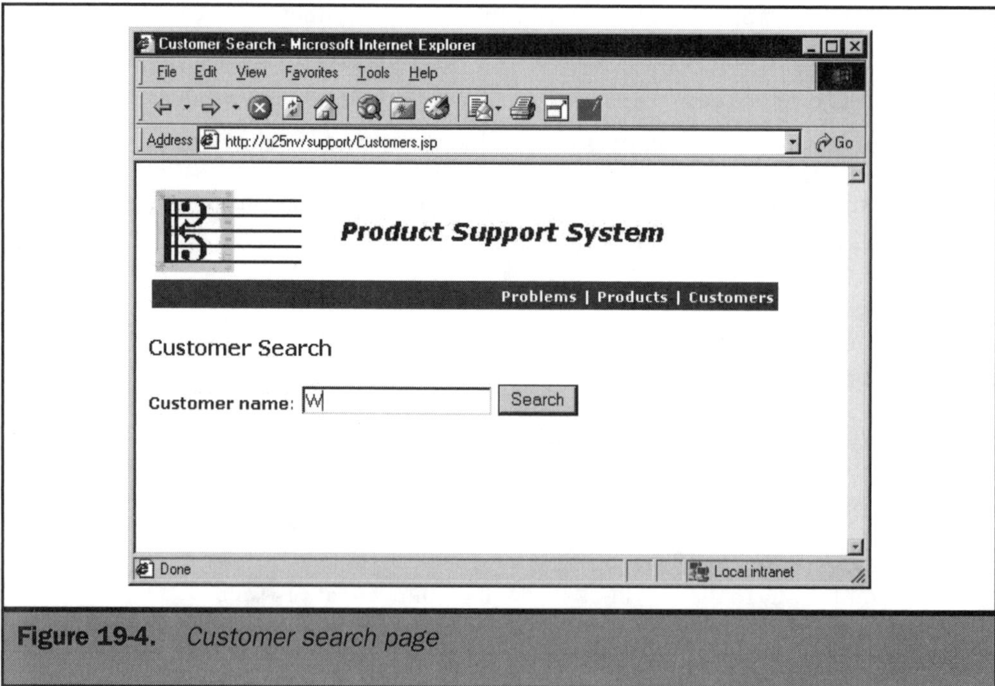


**Figure 19-4.** *Customer search page*

**CustomersList.jsp** The results of searching by customer name are stored in a `java.util.List` in the model. The `CustomerList.jsp` page extracts the list and displays it with the customer ID column as hyperlinks. The JSP source code is listed here:

```
<%@ page session="true" %>
<%@ page errorPage="/ErrorPage.jsp" %>
<%@ page import="java.util.*" %>
<%@ page import="com.lyricnote.support.model.*" %>

<%@ include file="/WEB-INF/InitModel.jsp" %>

<HTML>
<HEAD>
<TITLE>Customers List</TITLE>
<LINK REL="stylesheet" HREF="<%= BASEURL %>/style.css">
</HEAD>
<BODY>

<%@ include file="/WEB-INF/Banner.jsp" %>

<H3>Customers List</H3>
<TABLE BORDER=0 CELLSPACING=5 CELLPADDING=0>
   <TR>
      <TH ALIGN=LEFT>Customer ID</TH>
      <TH ALIGN=LEFT>Customer Name</TH>
   </TR>

<%
   List list = model.getCustomers();
   if (list != null) {
      Iterator it = list.iterator();
      while (it.hasNext()) {
         Customer customer = (Customer) it.next();

         // Get the customer select URL

         String customerID = customer.getCustomerID();
         String selectURL = CONTROLLER +
            "/CustomersList/Select?customerID="
            + customerID;
%>
   <TR>
```

```
        <TD><A HREF="<%= selectURL %>"><%= customerID %></A></TD>
        <TD><%= customer.getName() %></TD>
    </TR>
<%
        }
    }
%>
</TABLE>

</BODY>
</HTML>
```

The Web page with the list of customer whose names contain the letter `W` is shown in Figure 19-5.

**Customer.jsp** After selecting Eleanor Wagner from the list, the call center agent sees the customer detail page, as illustrated in Figure 19-6. This page has three sections:

- **Top left** contains the customer ID, name, and phone number.
- **Top right** has a list of products the customer has purchased. The list is in descending date of purchase order, and the product name is a hyperlink used to report a new problem.

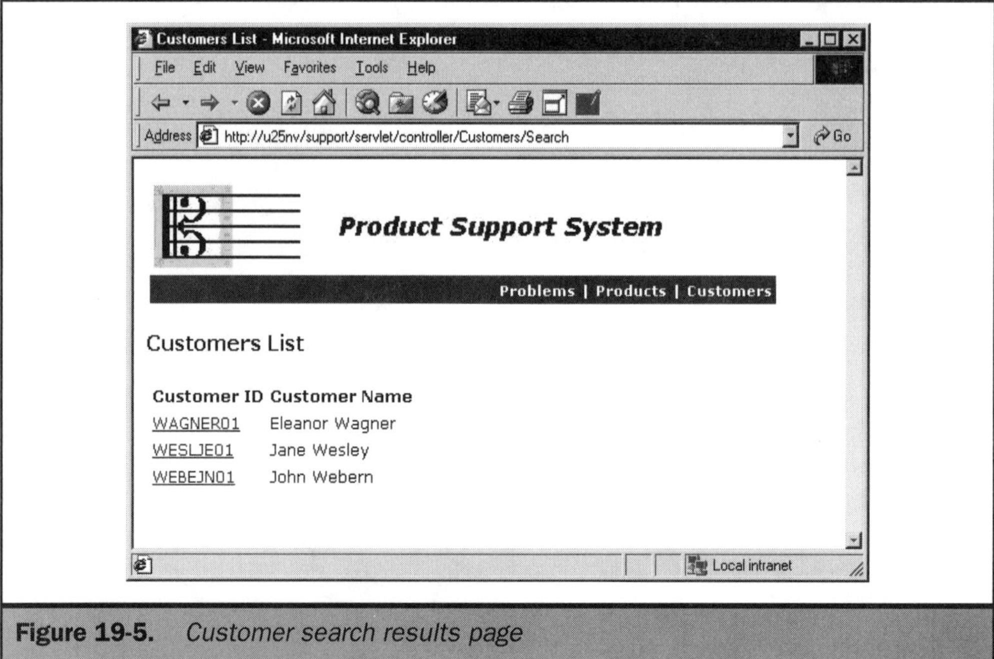


**Figure 19-5.** *Customer search results page*

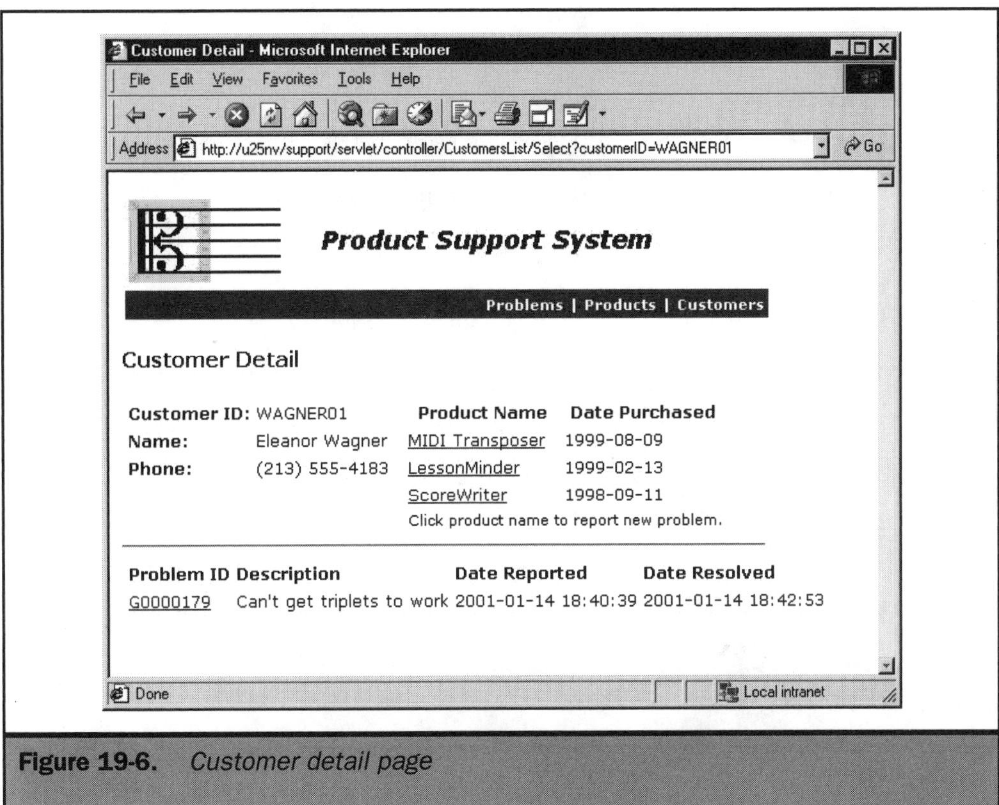


**Figure 19-6.** *Customer detail page*



- **Bottom** is a history of problems reported by the customer. In this case, you see one problem, one that has already been resolved.

The list of products enables the call center agent to determine the products for which Ms. Wagner is entitled to support.

The source code for `Customer.jsp` is shown here:

```
<%@ page session="true" %>
<%@ page errorPage="/ErrorPage.jsp" %>
<%@ page import="java.util.*" %>
<%@ page import="com.lyricnote.support.model.*" %>

<%@ include file="/WEB-INF/InitModel.jsp" %>

<HTML>
<HEAD>
<TITLE>Customer Detail</TITLE>
<LINK REL="stylesheet" HREF="<%= BASEURL %>/style.css">
```

```
</HEAD>
<BODY>

<%@ include file="/WEB-INF/Banner.jsp" %>

<% Customer customer = model.getCustomer(); %>

<H3>Customer Detail</H3>

<%-- Customer information and products purchased --%>

<TABLE BORDER=0 CELLSPACING=0 CELLPADDING=0>
<TR>

   <%-- Left side --%>

   <TD VALIGN=TOP>
   <TABLE BORDER=0 CELLSPACING=5 CELLPADDING=0>
   <TR>
      <TD><B>Customer ID:</B></TD>
      <TD><%= customer.getCustomerID() %></TD>
      <TD ROWSPAN=3>
      </TD>
   </TR>
   <TR>
      <TD><B>Name:</B></TD>
      <TD><%= customer.getName() %></TD>
   </TR>
   <TR>
      <TD><B>Phone:</B></TD>
      <TD><%= customer.getPhone() %></TD>
   </TR>
   </TABLE>
   </TD>

   <%-- Right side --%>

   <TD VALIGN=TOP>
   <TABLE BORDER=0 CELLSPACING=5 CELLPADDING=0>
      <TR>
         <TH>Product Name</TH>
         <TH>Date Purchased</TH>
      </TR>
```

```
<%
   List products = model.getCustomerProducts();
   if ((products != null) && (products.size() > 0)) {
      Iterator it = products.iterator();
      while (it.hasNext()) {
         CustomerProduct custprod =
            (CustomerProduct) it.next();
         model.setProductID(custprod.getProductID());
         Product product = model.getProduct();
         String productName = product.getName();
         String datePurchased =
            Util.dateFormat(custprod.getDatePurchased());
         String NEW_URL =
            CONTROLLER + "/Customer/NewProblem"
            + "?customerID=" + custprod.getCustomerID()
            + "&productID=" + custprod.getProductID() ;
%>
      <TR>
         <TD>
         <A HREF="<%= NEW_URL %>"><%= productName %></A>
         </TD>
         <TD><%= datePurchased %></TD>
      </TR>
<%
      }
%>
      <TR>
         <TD CLASS="fineprint" COLSPAN=2>
            Click product name to report new problem.
         </TD>
      </TR>
<%
   }
%>
   </TABLE>
   </TD>
</TR>
</TABLE>

<HR WIDTH=506 ALIGN=LEFT>

<%-- Problems Reported --%>
```

```
<TABLE BORDER=0 CELLSPACING=5 CELLPADDING=0>
   <TR>
      <TH ALIGN=LEFT>Problem ID</TH>
      <TH ALIGN=LEFT>Description</TH>
      <TH ALIGN=LEFT>Date Reported</TH>
      <TH ALIGN=LEFT>Date Resolved</TH>
   </TR>
<%
   List list = model.getProblems();
   if (list != null) {
      Iterator it = list.iterator();
      while (it.hasNext()) {
         Problem problem = (Problem) it.next();

         // Create the problem select URL

         String problemID = problem.getProblemID();
         String selectURL = CONTROLLER +
            "/Problems/Select?problemID="
            + problemID;

         String problemDescription = problem.getDescription();

         // Get the reported and resolution dates

         String dateReported =
            Util.dateTimeFormat(problem.getDateReported());
         String dateResolved =
            Util.dateTimeFormat(problem.getDateResolved());
%>
   <TR>
      <TD><A HREF="<%= selectURL %>"><%= problemID %></A></TD>
      <TD><%= problemDescription %></TD>
      <TD><%= dateReported %></TD>
      <TD><%= dateResolved %></TD>
   </TR>
<%
      }
   }
%>
</TABLE>

</BODY>
</HTML>
```

The JSP source is primarily composed of HTML, with a small amount of Java in scriptlets and expressions for interacting with the model. The current `Customer` object is retrieved from the model with the model's `getCustomer()` method. This allows JSP expressions to populate the customer ID, name, and telephone fields. For the list of products on the right-hand side, the JSP calls the model's `getCustomerProducts()` method, which returns a list of `CustomerProduct` objects. The model is used to get each product name and purchase date in turn. A similar technique is used to get the list of prior customer problems displayed at the bottom of the page.

**Problem.jsp** Ms. Wagner reports she's having a problem with the ScoreWriter product. When she tries to enter a *Db*, the software substitutes *C#* instead. The call center agent clicks the ScoreWriter hyperlink, which brings up the JSP view page shown in Figure 19-7.

After entering the description, the problem severity, and comments from the customer, the agent clicks the submit button to create the problem record.

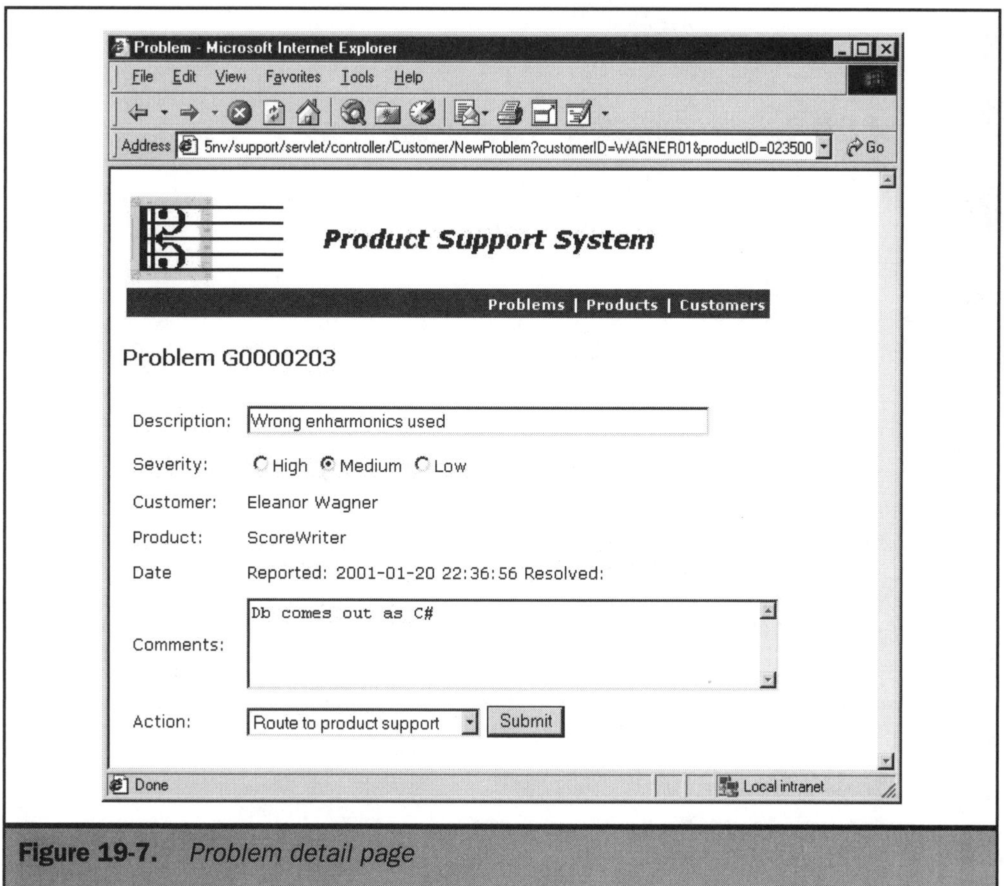


Figure 19-7. *Problem detail page*

Listed here is the source code for `Problem.jsp`:

```
<%@ page session="true" %>
<%@ page errorPage="/ErrorPage.jsp" %>
<%@ page import="java.util.*" %>
<%@ page import="com.lyricnote.support.model.*" %>

<%@ include file="/WEB-INF/InitModel.jsp" %>

<HTML>
<HEAD>
<TITLE>Problem</TITLE>
<LINK REL="stylesheet" HREF="<%= BASEURL %>/style.css">
</HEAD>
<BODY>

<%@ include file="/WEB-INF/Banner.jsp" %>

<%
   // Retrieve the problem from the model

   Problem problem = model.getProblem();

   // Get the customer

   model.setCustomerID(problem.getCustomerID());
   Customer customer = model.getCustomer();

   // Get the product

   model.setProductID(problem.getProductID());
   Product product = model.getProduct();

   // Determine the severity

   int severity = problem.getSeverity();
   String checked1 = (severity == 1) ? "CHECKED" : "";
   String checked2 = (severity == 2) ? "CHECKED" : "";
   String checked3 = (severity == 3) ? "CHECKED" : "";
%>

<H3>Problem <%= problem.getProblemID() %></H3>
```

```
<FORM METHOD="POST" ACTION="<%= CONTROLLER %>/Problem/Submit">
<INPUT TYPE="HIDDEN" NAME="problemID"
   VALUE="<%= problem.getProblemID() %>">
<TABLE BORDER=0 CELLSPACING=5 CELLPADDING=3>
<TR>
   <TD>Description:</TD>
   <TD>
      <INPUT
         NAME="description"
         TYPE="text"
         VALUE="<%= problem.getDescription() %>"
         SIZE="50"
         >
   </TD>
</TR>
<TR>
   <TD>Severity:</TD>
   <TD>
      <INPUT
         NAME="severity"
         TYPE="radio"
         VALUE="1"
         <%= checked1 %>
         >High
      <INPUT
         NAME="severity"
         TYPE="radio"
         VALUE="2"
         <%= checked2 %>
         >Medium
      <INPUT
         NAME="severity"
         TYPE="radio"
         VALUE="3"
         <%= checked3 %>
         >Low
   </TD>
</TR>
<TR>
   <TD>Customer:</TD>
   <TD><%= customer.getName() %></TD>
</TR>
```

```
<TR>
   <TD>Product:</TD>
   <TD><%= product.getName() %></TD>
</TR>
<TR>
   <TD>Date</TD>
   <TD>
      Reported:
      <%= Util.dateTimeFormat(problem.getDateReported()) %>
      Resolved:
      <%= Util.dateTimeFormat(problem.getDateResolved()) %>
   </TD>
</TR>
<TR>
   <TD>Comments:</TD>
   <TD>
<TEXTAREA NAME="comments" COLS="50" ROWS="4">
</TEXTAREA>
   </TD>
</TR>
<TR>
   <TD>Action:</TD>
   <TD>
   <SELECT NAME="eventID">
      <OPTION VALUE="COM">Comment
      <OPTION VALUE="RPS">Route to product support
      <OPTION VALUE="RPD">Route to development
      <OPTION VALUE="RQA">Route to test
      <OPTION VALUE="CNB">Closed - not a bug
      <OPTION VALUE="CCP">Closed - customer problem
      <OPTION VALUE="CFX">Closed - fixed
   </SELECT>
   <INPUT TYPE="SUBMIT" VALUE="Submit">
   </TD>
</TR>
</TABLE>
</FORM>

<%
   // Get log entries for this problem

   model.problemLogSearch(problem.getProblemID());
   List problemLogs = model.getProblemLogs();
   if (problemLogs.size() > 0) {
```

```
%>
<H4>Problem History</H4><P>
<TABLE BORDER="1" CELLPADDING="3" CELLSPACING="0">
<TR>
   <TH>Time</TH>
   <TH>Event Code</TH>
   <TH>Comments</TH>
</TR>
<%
      Iterator it = problemLogs.iterator();
      while (it.hasNext()) {
         ProblemLog log = (ProblemLog) it.next();
%>
<TR>
   <TD><%= Util.dateTimeFormat(log.getLogTime()) %></TD>
   <TD><%= log.getEventID() %></TD>
   <TD><%= log.getComments() %></TD>
</TR>
<%
      }
%>
</TABLE>
<%
   }
%>

</BODY>
</HTML>
```



Again, the JSP is composed primarily of HTML with some Java to access `Problem` object, its customer ID, product ID, description, and severity. The list of log entries for the problem comes from the model's `problemLogSearch()` method.

**Confirm.jsp** After the agent submits the problem record, a confirmation page (see Figure 19-8) is produced, listing the problem ID assigned, the description, the severity, the customer comments, and problem routing. The agent gives the problem ID to the customer on the phone and informs her that ScoreWriter product support will call her back. The confirmation source code is listed here:

```
<%@ page session="true" %>
<%@ page errorPage="/ErrorPage.jsp" %>
<%@ page import="com.lyricnote.support.model.*" %>
```

```
<%@ include file="/WEB-INF/InitModel.jsp" %>

<HTML>
<HEAD>
<TITLE>Confirmation</TITLE>
<LINK REL="stylesheet" HREF="<%= BASEURL %>/style.css">
</HEAD>
<BODY>

<%@ include file="/WEB-INF/Banner.jsp" %>

<H3>Confirmation</H3>
<TABLE BORDER=0 CELLPADDING=3 CELLSPACING=0>
<TR>
   <TD>Problem ID:</TD>
   <TD><%= request.getParameter("problemID") %></TD>
</TR>
<TR>
   <TD>Description:</TD>
   <TD><%= request.getParameter("description") %></TD>
</TR>
<TR>
   <TD>Severity:</TD>
   <TD><%= request.getParameter("severity") %></TD>
</TR>
<TR>
   <TD>Comments:</TD>
   <TD><%= request.getParameter("comments") %></TD>
</TR>
<TR>
   <TD>EventID:</TD>
   <TD><%= request.getParameter("eventID") %></TD>
</TR>
</TABLE>

</BODY>
</HTML>
```

**Note** *A useful addition to the system would be e-mail notification of the employee to which the problem is being routed. Chapter 21 explores ways to do this.*

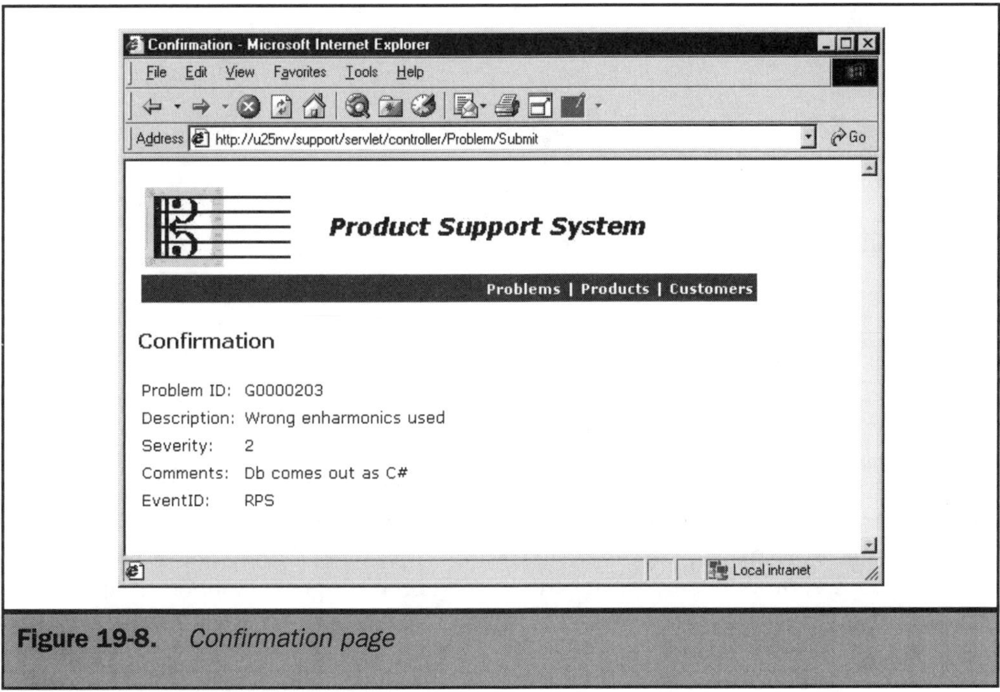


**Figure 19-8.** *Confirmation page*



**Products.jsp** Other users, such as product support personnel, developers, or testers, may start the application by looking for a particular product. Like the customer search page, there's a JSP view page for product search, listed here:

```
<%@ page session="true" %>
<%@ page errorPage="/ErrorPage.jsp" %>
<%@ page import="com.lyricnote.support.model.*" %>

<%@ include file="/WEB-INF/InitModel.jsp" %>

<HTML>
<HEAD>
<TITLE>Product Search</TITLE>
<LINK REL="stylesheet" HREF="<%= BASEURL %>/style.css">
</HEAD>
<BODY>

<%@ include file="/WEB-INF/Banner.jsp" %>
```

```
<H3>Product Search</H3>
<FORM
   METHOD="POST"
   ACTION="<%= CONTROLLER %>/Products/Search">
<B>Product name</B>:
<INPUT TYPE="TEXT" NAME="productSearchArgument" SIZE="20">
<INPUT TYPE="SUBMIT" VALUE="Search">
</FORM>

</BODY>
</HTML>
```

Like the customer search page, `Products.jsp` uses an HTML form to prompt for a search string. Figure 19-9 illustrates a search for products whose name contains the letter `S`.

**ProductsList.jsp** As Figure 19-10 shows, two product names contain the letter `S`: Music Teacher Studio and ScoreWriter. The `ProductsList.jsp` page shows the two product IDs, product names, and the names of the support personnel assigned. `ProductsList.jsp` is listed next.

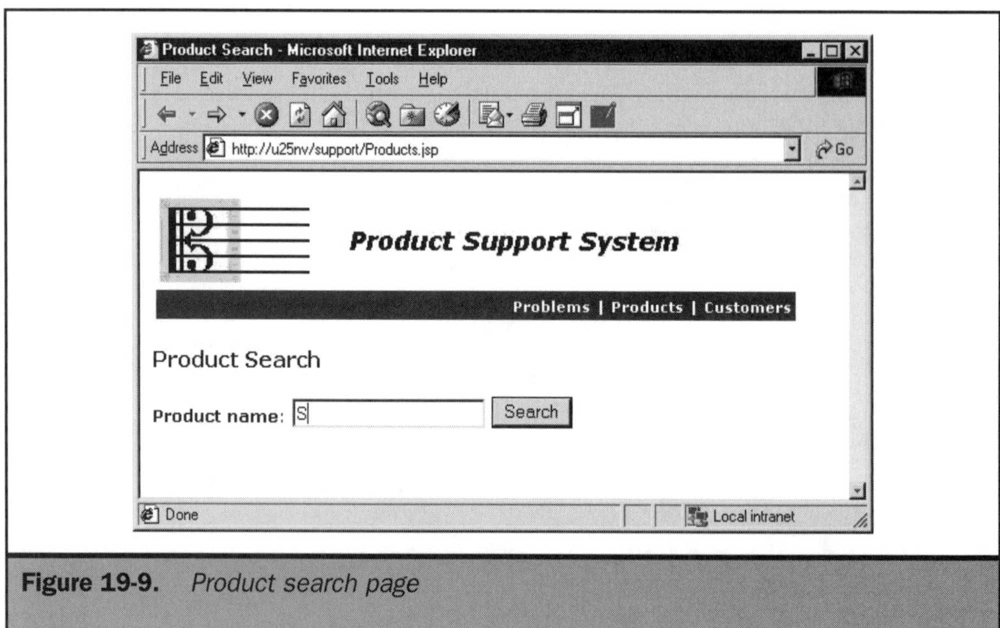


**Figure 19-9.** *Product search page*

```
<%@ page session="true" %>
<%@ page errorPage="/ErrorPage.jsp" %>
<%@ page import="java.util.*" %>
<%@ page import="com.lyricnote.support.model.*" %>

<%@ include file="/WEB-INF/InitModel.jsp" %>

<HTML>
<HEAD>
<TITLE>Products List</TITLE>
<LINK REL="stylesheet" HREF="<%= BASEURL %>/style.css">
</HEAD>
<BODY>

<%@ include file="/WEB-INF/Banner.jsp" %>

<H3>Products List</H3>
<TABLE BORDER=0 CELLSPACING=5 CELLPADDING=0>
   <TR>
      <TH ALIGN=LEFT>Product ID</TH>
      <TH ALIGN=LEFT>Product Name</TH>
      <TH ALIGN=LEFT>Support</TH>
      <TH ALIGN=LEFT>Developer</TH>
      <TH ALIGN=LEFT>Tester</TH>
   </TR>

<%
   List list = model.getProducts();
   if (list != null) {
      Iterator it = list.iterator();
      while (it.hasNext()) {
         Product product = (Product) it.next();

         // Get the product select URL

         String productID = product.getProductID();
         String selectURL = CONTROLLER +
            "/ProductsList/Select?productID="
            + productID;

         String productName = product.getName();

         // Get the names of the product support,
```

```
            // developer, and tester employees

            String productSupport = product.getProductSupport();
            String productSupportName =
               model.getEmployee(productSupport).getName();

            String developer = product.getDeveloper();
            String developerName =
               model.getEmployee(developer).getName();

            String tester = product.getTester();
            String testerName =
               model.getEmployee(tester).getName();
%>
   <TR>
      <TD><A HREF="<%= selectURL %>"><%= productID %></A></TD>
      <TD><%= productName %></TD>
      <TD><%= productSupportName %></TD>
      <TD><%= developerName %></TD>
      <TD><%= testerName %></TD>
   </TR>
<%
      }
   }
%>
</TABLE>

</BODY>
</HTML>
```

For each of the three employee IDs in the `Product` object, the JSP shows the corresponding employee name. It gets the `Employee` objects from the model's `getEmployee()` method, and then invokes the `Employee.getName()` method to get the name.

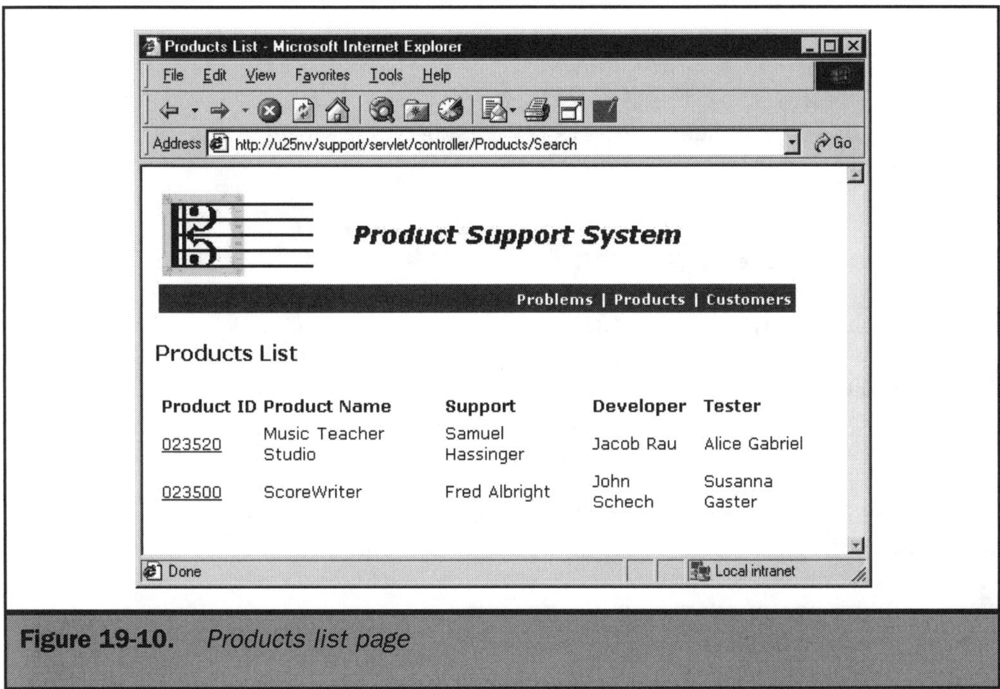


**Figure 19-10.** *Products list page*



**ProductProblems.jsp** If the ScoreWriter link is selected, the list of problems for that product is displayed, as shown in Figure 19-11.

```
<%@ page session="true" %>
<%@ page errorPage="/ErrorPage.jsp" %>
<%@ page import="java.util.*" %>
<%@ page import="com.lyricnote.support.model.*" %>

<%@ include file="/WEB-INF/InitModel.jsp" %>
```

```
<HTML>
<HEAD>
<TITLE>Problems by Product</TITLE>
<LINK REL="stylesheet" HREF="<%= BASEURL %>/style.css">
</HEAD>
<BODY>

<%@ include file="/WEB-INF/Banner.jsp" %>

<H3>Problems by Product</H3>
<%
   Product product = model.getProduct();
   String productID = product.getProductID();
   String productName = product.getName();
%>
<B>Product:<B> <%= productID %> - <%= productName %>
<TABLE BORDER=0 CELLSPACING=5 CELLPADDING=0>
   <TR>
      <TH ALIGN=LEFT>Problem ID</TH>
      <TH ALIGN=LEFT>Description</TH>
      <TH ALIGN=LEFT>Date Reported</TH>
      <TH ALIGN=LEFT>Date Resolved</TH>
   </TR>
<%
   List list = model.getProblems();
   if (list != null) {
      Iterator it = list.iterator();
      while (it.hasNext()) {
         Problem problem = (Problem) it.next();

         // Create the problem select URL

         String problemID = problem.getProblemID();
         String selectURL = CONTROLLER +
            "/Problems/Select?problemID="
            + problemID;

         String problemDescription = problem.getDescription();

         // Get the reported and resolution dates

         String dateReported =
```

```
            Util.dateFormat(problem.getDateReported());
         String dateResolved =
            Util.dateFormat(problem.getDateResolved());
%>
   <TR>
      <TD><A HREF="<%= selectURL %>"><%= problemID %></A></TD>
      <TD><%= problemDescription %></TD>
      <TD><%= dateReported %></TD>
      <TD><%= dateResolved %></TD>
   </TR>
<%
      }
   }
%>
</TABLE>

</BODY>
</HTML>
```



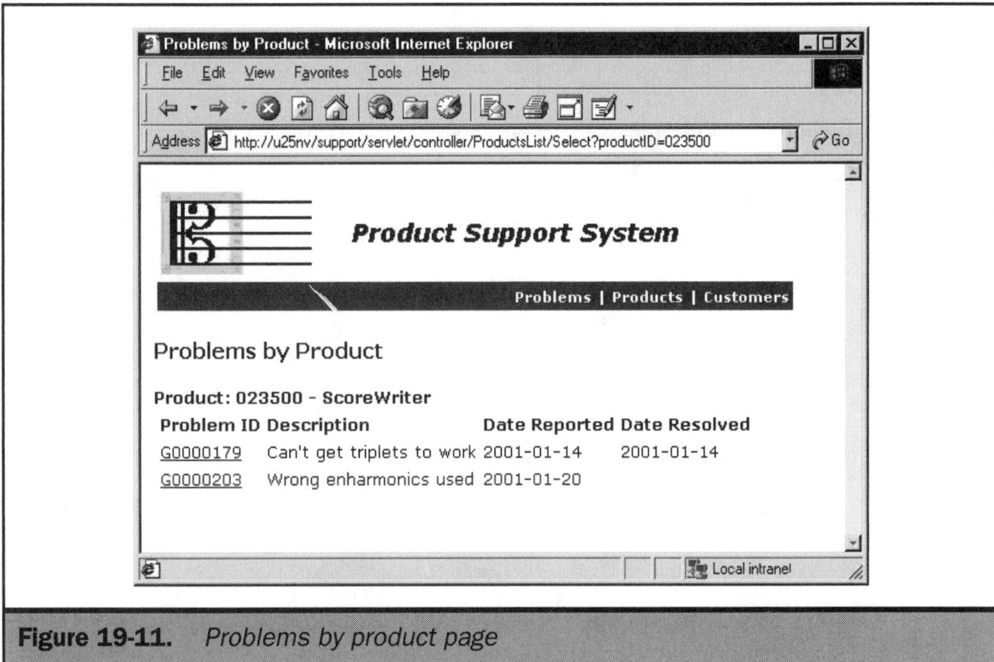


**Figure 19-11.** *Problems by product page*

As the listing of `ProductProblems.jsp` shows, the current `Product` object can be obtained from the model, as well as the list of problems for this product.

When Fred Albright, the product support person for ScoreWriter calls the customer to get more details about the problem, he selects the problem number from the list by clicking the hyperlink. He then sees an updated version of the problem (see Figure 19-12). He enters the results of the customer interview in the comments section and submits the problem update. The new confirmation is shown in Figure 19-13.

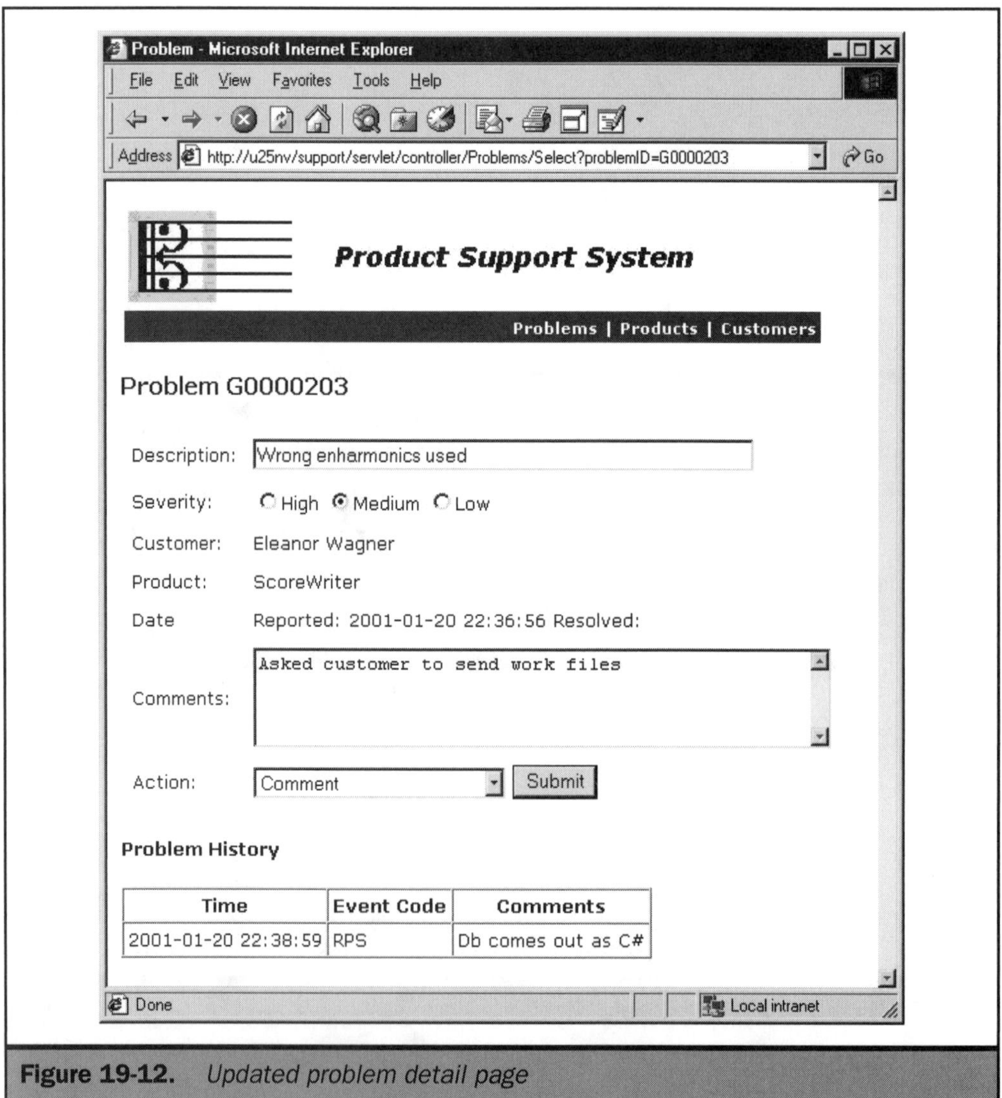


**Figure 19-12.** *Updated problem detail page*

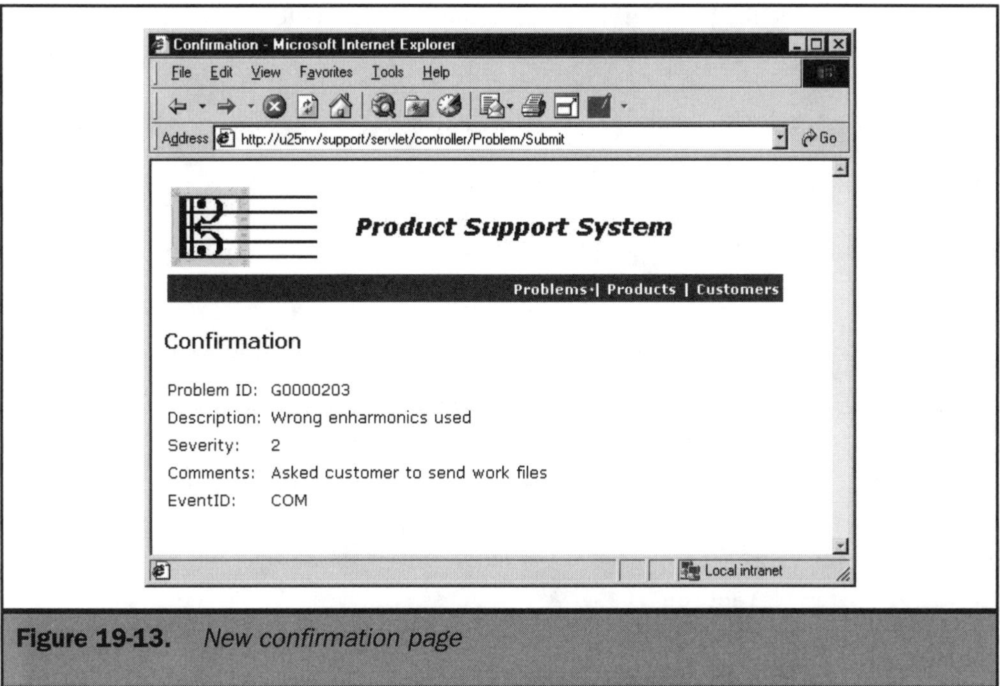


**Figure 19-13.** *New confirmation page*



**Problems.jsp** If the problem ID is already known, a user can select the problem directly, using the JSP view shown in Figure 19-14.

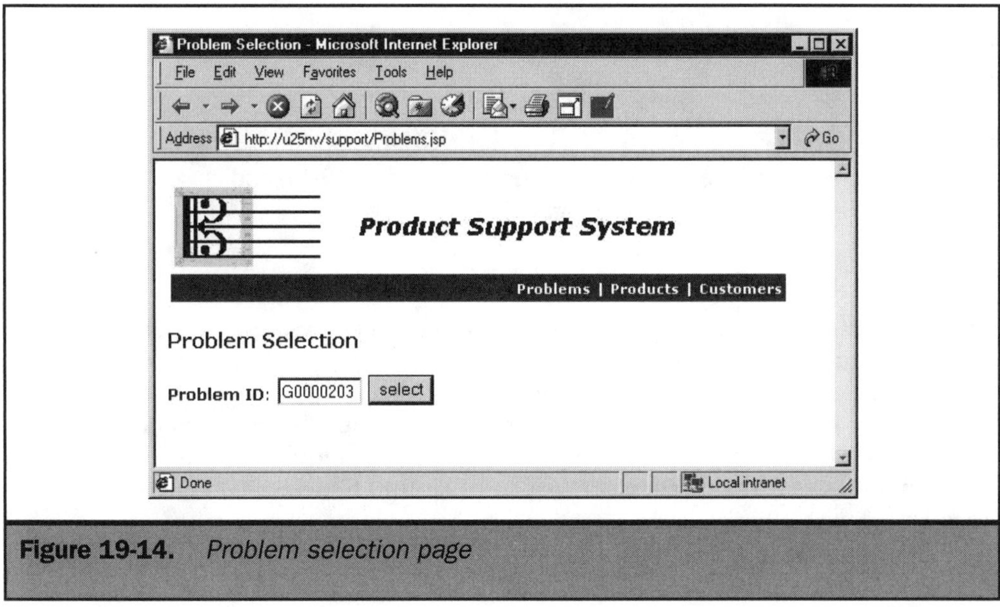


**Figure 19-14.** *Problem selection page*

The source code for Problems.jsp is similar to the customer and product search pages:

```
<%@ page session="true" %>
<%@ page errorPage="/ErrorPage.jsp" %>
<%@ page import="com.lyricnote.support.model.*" %>

<%@ include file="/WEB-INF/InitModel.jsp" %>

<HTML>
<HEAD>
<TITLE>Problem Selection</TITLE>
<LINK REL="stylesheet" HREF="<%= BASEURL %>/style.css">
</HEAD>
<BODY>

<%@ include file="/WEB-INF/Banner.jsp" %>

<H3>Problem Selection</H3>
<FORM
   METHOD="POST"
   ACTION="<%= CONTROLLER %>/Problems/Select">
<B>Problem ID</B>:
<INPUT TYPE="TEXT" NAME="problemID" SIZE="8">
<INPUT TYPE="SUBMIT" VALUE="select">
</FORM>

</BODY>
</HTML>
```

On further exploration of the problem, Fred Albright determines it was due to a user input error. He enters a comment to that effect (see Figure 19-15) and closes the problem. The confirmation screen is shown in Figure 19-16.

## Controller Classes

The last component to develop is the controller, the part of the system that operates on the model according to user input and selects the next view. In the product support system, this function is performed by a single servlet, appropriately named ControllerServlet.

The controller functionality can be built a piece at a time by using small, customized action classes to handle each state transition, rather than hard-coding each action in the servlet. The mechanism the controller uses to delegate to the action classes is explained next.

Each time the controller servlet is invoked, it needs to know two things:

- What is the current view?
- What action has the user selected from this view?

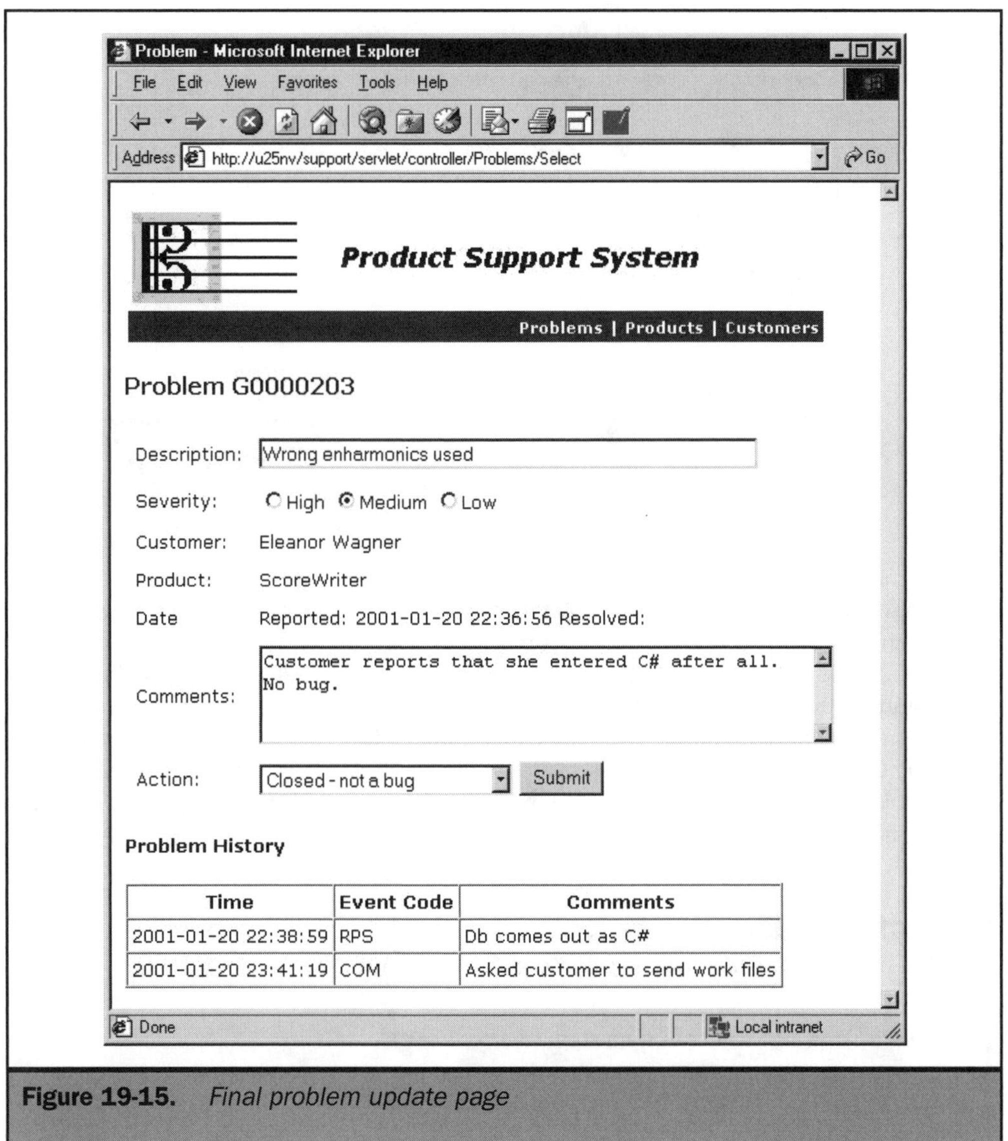


**Figure 19-15.** *Final problem update page*

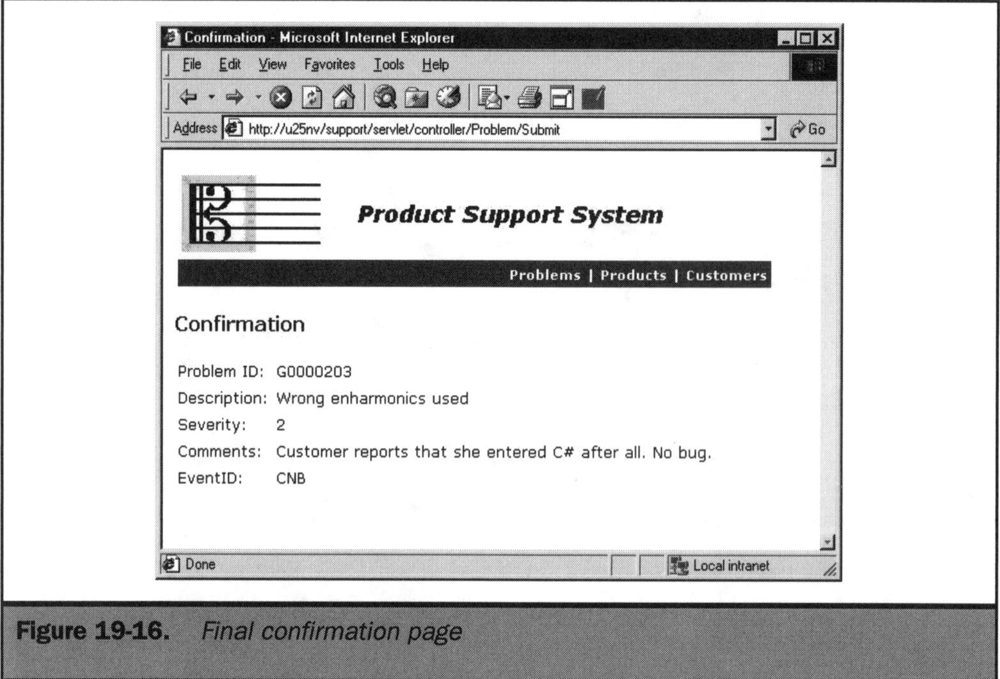


**Figure 19-16.** *Final confirmation page*

You may have noticed all the JSP view pages invoke the controller servlet with additional path information in the URL. This path information contains the name of the current view and a keyword describing the action the user selected. For example, from the `Customers.jsp` page, when the user enters a search string and clicks the search button, the form is submitted to the controller servlet with the path information `/Customers/Search`. Some view pages have more than one possible user action. From the `Customer.jsp` page, the user can either click a product name to report a new problem or select an existing problem for update. In any event, the controller takes the view name and action keyword, concatenates them, and appends the word `Action`. The result is the name of the class that can handle the state transition.

## The Action Base Class

Here is a listing of the abstract `Action` class:

```
package com.lyricnote.support.controller;

import com.lyricnote.support.model.*;
import java.io.*;
import javax.servlet.*;
```

```
import javax.servlet.http.*;

/**
* The base class for all state transitions
*/
public abstract class Action
{
   protected HttpServletRequest request;
   protected HttpServletResponse response;
   protected ServletContext application;
   protected Model model;

   /**
   * Executes the action. Subclasses should override
   * this method and have it forward the request to the
   * next view component when it completes processing.
   */
   public abstract void run()
      throws ServletException, IOException;

   /**
   * Sets the request.
   * @param request the request.
   */
   public void setRequest(HttpServletRequest request)
   {
      this.request = request;
   }

   /**
   * Sets the response
   * @param response the response
   */
   public void setResponse(HttpServletResponse response)
   {
      this.response = response;
   }

   /**
   * Sets the servlet context.
   * @param application the application.
   */
```

```
    public void setApplication(ServletContext application)
    {
       this.application = application;
    }

    /**
    * Sets the model.
    * @param model the model.
    */
    public void setModel(Model model)
    {
       this.model = model;
    }
}
```

Action contains instance variables for the servlet request and response, the servlet context, and the model itself. In addition to the getter and setter methods for these variables, there's an abstract method named run(). This method is the only one that must be implemented by the individual action handlers. The run() method calls model methods to effect the transition, and then creates a request dispatcher and forwards the request to the next view.

## The Controller Servlet

The controller servlet is the driver for all the state transitions. It maintains a cache in each session of action classes that have been invoked. When a request is made, the servlet checks the session action map to see if an instance of the class has already been loaded. If not, it extracts the view name and action keyword from the path information, concatenates them, and appends Action to the result to get the action class name. It then loads the class and creates an instance, storing this in the session action map. After ensuring a model already exists, the servlet then sets the request, response, application, and model properties in the action object and invokes its run() method.

ControllerServlet is listed here:

```
package com.lyricnote.support.controller;

import com.lyricnote.support.model.*;
import java.io.*;
import java.sql.*;
import java.util.*;
import javax.servlet.*;
import javax.servlet.http.*;
```

```
/**
* The controller component of the Model-View-Controller
* architecture for the LyricNote problem reporting system
*/
public class ControllerServlet extends HttpServlet
{
   /**
   * Handles an HTTP GET request
   */
   public void doGet(
         HttpServletRequest request,
         HttpServletResponse response)
      throws ServletException, IOException
   {
      doPost(request, response);
   }

   /**
   * Handles an HTTP POST request
   */
   public void doPost(
         HttpServletRequest request,
         HttpServletResponse response)
      throws ServletException, IOException
   {
      HttpSession session = request.getSession();
      Map actionMap = (Map) session.getAttribute("actionMap");
      if (actionMap == null) {
         actionMap = new HashMap();
         session.setAttribute("actionMap", actionMap);
      }
      ServletContext context = getServletContext();
      try {

         // Get the state and event from the path info

         String pathInfo = request.getPathInfo();
         if (pathInfo == null)
            throw new ServletException
            ("Invalid internal state - no path info");

         // Load the action object that handles
```

```
         // this state and event

         Action action = (Action) actionMap.get(pathInfo);
         if (action == null) {

            // This is the first time the servlet has seen
            // this action. Get the state and event name
            // from pathInfo.

            StringTokenizer st =
               new StringTokenizer(pathInfo, "/");

            if (st.countTokens() != 2)
               throw new ServletException
               ("Invalid internal state - invalid path info ["
               + pathInfo + "]");

            String state = st.nextToken();
            String event = st.nextToken();

            // Form the class name from the state and event

            String className =
               "com.lyricnote.support.controller."
               + state + event + "Action";

            // Load the class and create an instance

            try {
               Class actionClass = Class.forName(className);
               action = (Action) actionClass.newInstance();
            }
            catch (ClassNotFoundException e) {
               throw new ServletException
               ("Could not load class " + className
               + ": " + e.getMessage());
            }
            catch (InstantiationException e) {
               throw new ServletException
               ("Could not create an instance of "
               + className + ": " + e.getMessage());
            }
```

```
            catch (IllegalAccessException e) {
               throw new ServletException
               (className + ": " + e.getMessage());
            }

            // Cache the instance in the action map

            actionMap.put(pathInfo, action);
         }

         // Ensure that a model exists in the session.

         Model model = (Model) session.getAttribute("model");
         if (model == null)
            throw new ServletException
            ("No model found in session");

         // Now execute the action. The action should perform
         // a RequestDispatcher.forward() when it completes

         action.setRequest(request);
         action.setResponse(response);
         action.setApplication(context);
         action.setModel(model);
         action.run();
      }
      catch (ServletException e) {

         // Use the JSP error page for all servlet errors

         request.setAttribute("javax.servlet.jsp.jspException", e);
         RequestDispatcher rd =
            context.getRequestDispatcher("/ErrorPage.jsp");

         if (response.isCommitted())
            rd.include(request, response);
         else
            rd.forward(request, response);
      }
   }
}
```

The sections that follow describe each of the action classes used in the product support system.

## Action Classes

A review of Figure 19-3 shows seven state transitions occur from one view to another. These transitions correspond to the following action classes:

- CustomersSearchAction
- CustomersListSelectAction
- CustomersNewProblemAction
- ProductsSearchAction
- ProductsListSelectAction
- ProblemsSelectAction
- ProblemSubmitAction

**CustomersSearchAction Class** The `run()` method in this class is called to accept a customer search argument from the `Customers.jsp` view and invoke the `customerSearch()` method in the model. It then forwards the request to the JSP view page that displays the search results. A listing of `CustomersSearchAction` is shown here:

```
package com.lyricnote.support.controller;

import java.io.*;
import java.sql.SQLException;
import javax.servlet.*;
import javax.servlet.http.*;

/**
* Searches the database for customers matching the
* customer search argument
*/
public class CustomersSearchAction extends Action
{
   /**
   * Executes the action
   */
   public void run() throws ServletException, IOException
   {
      // Perform search
```

```
      String arg = request.getParameter("customerSearchArgument");
      if (arg != null) {
         arg = arg.trim();
         if (!arg.equals("")) {
            try {
               model.customerSearch(arg);
            }
            catch (SQLException e) {
               throw new ServletException(e.getMessage());
            }
         }
      }

      // Forward to customer list JSP

      final String next = "/CustomersList.jsp";
      RequestDispatcher rd =
         application.getRequestDispatcher(next);
      if (rd == null)
         throw new ServletException
         ("Could not find " + next);
      rd.forward(request, response);
   }
}
```



**CustomersListSelectAction Class** The user selects a customer from the list by clicking a hyperlink into the controller that carries the `CustomerList` view name and the `Select` action keyword. In addition, the hyperlink URL has the customer ID appended as a query string. From this information, the `CustomersListSelectAction` class does the following:

- Extracts the customer ID parameter from the URL and stores it in the model
- Invokes the model's customer problems search method
- Forwards the request to the customer detail JSP view

Here's a listing of the action class:

```
package com.lyricnote.support.controller;

import java.io.*;
import java.sql.SQLException;
```

```
import javax.servlet.*;
import javax.servlet.http.*;

/**
* Gets detailed information for this customer
*/
public class CustomersListSelectAction extends Action
{
   /**
   * Executes the action
   */
   public void run() throws ServletException, IOException
   {
      // Get customer ID and store it in the model

      String customerID = request.getParameter("customerID");
      if (customerID == null)
         throw new ServletException
         ("No customer ID specified");
      model.setCustomerID(customerID);

      // Get the list of problems for this customer

      try {
         model.customerProblemsSearch(customerID);
      }
      catch (SQLException e) {
         throw new ServletException(e.getMessage());
      }

      // Forward to customer detail JSP

      final String next = "/Customer.jsp";
      RequestDispatcher rd =
         application.getRequestDispatcher(next);
      if (rd == null)
         throw new ServletException
         ("Could not find " + next);
      rd.forward(request, response);
   }
}
```

**CustomerNewProblemAction Class** As noted previously, the `Customer` view has two possible actions: creating a new problem or updating an existing one. The new problem action is handled by the following action class:

```
package com.lyricnote.support.controller;

import java.io.*;
import java.sql.SQLException;
import javax.servlet.*;
import javax.servlet.http.*;

public class CustomerNewProblemAction extends Action
{
   /**
   * Executes the action
   */
   public void run() throws ServletException, IOException
   {
      // Get the customer ID and product ID

      String customerID = request.getParameter("customerID");
      if (customerID == null)
         throw new ServletException
         ("No customer ID");

      String productID = request.getParameter("productID");
      if (productID == null)
         throw new ServletException
         ("No product ID");

      // Create a new problem

      try {
         model.setCustomerID(customerID);
         model.setProductID(productID);
         model.newProblem();
      }
      catch (SQLException e) {
         throw new ServletException(e.getMessage());
      }

      // Forward to problem detail JSP
```

```
        final String next = "/Problem.jsp";
        RequestDispatcher rd =
           application.getRequestDispatcher(next);
        if (rd == null)
           throw new ServletException
           ("Could not find " + next);
        rd.forward(request, response);
    }
}
```

This action class does the following:

- Retrieves the customerID and productID parameters from the request generated by the view.
- Creates and initializes a new `Problem` object. It does so by invoking the `newProblem()` factory method in the model, which assigns a unique problem ID and writes the initial record in the database.
- Forwards the request to the problem detail view.

**ProductsSearchAction Class** Like the customer search action, the product search action takes a search string from the request and calls a search method in the model, forwarding the request then to the `ProductsList.jsp` view.

```
package com.lyricnote.support.controller;

import java.io.*;
import java.sql.SQLException;
import javax.servlet.*;
import javax.servlet.http.*;

/**
* Searches the database for products matching the
* product search argument
*/
public class ProductsSearchAction extends Action
{
   /**
   * Executes the action
   */
   public void run() throws ServletException, IOException
   {
```

```
        // Perform search

        String arg = request.getParameter("productSearchArgument");
        if (arg != null) {
           arg = arg.trim();
           if (!arg.equals("")) {
              try {
                 model.productSearch(arg);
              }
              catch (SQLException e) {
                 throw new ServletException(e.getMessage());
              }
           }
        }

        // Forward to product list JSP

        final String next = "/ProductsList.jsp";
        RequestDispatcher rd =
           application.getRequestDispatcher(next);
        if (rd == null)
           throw new ServletException
           ("Could not find " + next);
        rd.forward(request, response);
     }
  }
```



**ProductsListSelectAction Class** When a product ID is selected, this action class stores it in the model and invokes the model's product problem search. The request is then forwarded to the `ProductProblems.jsp` view, which displays the results.

```
package com.lyricnote.support.controller;

import java.io.*;
import java.sql.SQLException;
import javax.servlet.*;
import javax.servlet.http.*;

/**
* Searches the database for products matching the
* product search argument
```

```
*/
public class ProductsListSelectAction extends Action
{
   /**
   * Executes the action
   */
   public void run() throws ServletException, IOException
   {
      // Get product ID and store it in the model

      String productID = request.getParameter("productID");
      if (productID == null)
         throw new ServletException
         ("No product ID specified");
      model.setProductID(productID);

      // Get the list of problems for this product

      try {
         model.productProblemsSearch(productID);
      }
      catch (SQLException e) {
         throw new ServletException(e.getMessage());
      }

      // Forward to product problems JSP

      final String next = "/ProductProblems.jsp";
      RequestDispatcher rd =
         application.getRequestDispatcher(next);
      if (rd == null)
         throw new ServletException
         ("Could not find " + next);
      rd.forward(request, response);
   }
}
```

**ProblemsSelectAction Class** All three application entry points—customer, product, and problem—use a common problem select action, which the following lists:

```
package com.lyricnote.support.controller;

import java.io.*;
import java.sql.SQLException;
import javax.servlet.*;
import javax.servlet.http.*;

/**
* Sets the current problem ID
*/
public class ProblemsSelectAction extends Action
{
   /**
   * Executes the action
   */
   public void run() throws ServletException, IOException
   {
      String problemID = request.getParameter("problemID");
      if (problemID != null) {
         problemID = problemID.trim();
         if (!problemID.equals("")) {
            model.setProblemID(problemID);
         }
      }

      // Forward to problem JSP

      final String next = "/Problem.jsp";
      RequestDispatcher rd =
         application.getRequestDispatcher(next);
      if (rd == null)
         throw new ServletException
         ("Could not find " + next);
      rd.forward(request, response);
   }
}
```

The action class simply stores the problem ID in the model and forwards the request to the problem detail page.

**ProblemSubmitAction Class** The last action class needed is the one that accepts problem updates from the problem detail page. This class

- Retrieves the data entry fields from the requests.
- Retrieves the current `Problem` object from the model and updates its properties. If the event ID is one that indicates the problem should be closed, the `Problem` object's `close()` method is invoked.
- Updates the database record for the problem.
- Adds an entry to the problem log.
- Forwards the request to the next view—the confirmation.

```
package com.lyricnote.support.controller;

import com.lyricnote.support.model.*;
import java.io.*;
import java.sql.SQLException;
import javax.servlet.*;
import javax.servlet.http.*;

/**
* Submits a problem update
*/
public class ProblemSubmitAction extends Action
{
   /**
   * Executes the action
   */
   public void run() throws ServletException, IOException
   {
      // Get the parameters

      String problemID = request.getParameter("problemID");
      String description = request.getParameter("description");
      String severity = request.getParameter("severity");
      String comments = request.getParameter("comments");
      String eventID = request.getParameter("eventID");
```

```
        try {

            // Get the problem object from the model

            model.setProblemID(problemID);
            Problem problem = model.getProblem();

            // Update the problem object

            problem.setDescription(description);
            problem.setSeverity(Integer.parseInt(severity));
            if (Util.isClosingEvent(eventID))
                problem.close();
            model.updateProblem(problem);

            // Add a problem log record

            ProblemLog log = new ProblemLog();
            log.setProblemID(problemID);
            log.setLogTime(new java.util.Date());
            log.setEventID(eventID);
            log.setComments(comments);
            model.addProblemLog(log);
        }
        catch (SQLException e) {
            throw new ServletException(e.getMessage());
        }

        // Forward to confirmation JSP

        final String next = "/Confirm.jsp";
        RequestDispatcher rd =
            application.getRequestDispatcher(next);
        if (rd == null)
            throw new ServletException
            ("Could not find " + next);
        rd.forward(request, response);
    }
}
```

## Summary

This chapter brings together elements discussed throughout the book in a Web-based system for managing a product support center. The system supports the following process flow:

- A customer with a problem calls a toll-free number and speaks to a call center agent.
- The agent verifies the customer is entitled to support for the specified product, enters a problem report, gives the confirmation number to the customer, and routes the problem to product support.
- Product support calls the customer to determine whether it's a code problem or customer problem. If the problem turns out to be a code problem, for which no fix is currently available, it's routed to development.
- The responsible developer analyzes the problem. If the problem isn't a bug, the developer reroutes the problem to product support to inform the customer. If the problem is a bug, the developer codes and unit tests a fix and routes the problem to quality assurance.
- Quality assurance performs integration tests. If the fix needs more work, the problem is rerouted back to development. Otherwise, it's sent to product support, where the fix is forwarded to the customer and the problem is closed.

The data model required to support this system consists of relational database tables that represent customers, products, customer/product pairs, employees, problem reports, and problem log entries.

The system architecture employed is known as Model-View-Controller (MVC). This consists of three components:

- **Model** The internal workings of the application, including database access and business logic. Has no visual code—can be operated by a simple command-line driver.
- **View** The presentation layer that retrieves data from the model and displays it for the user's interaction.
- **Controller** The component that accepts user input and operates on the model to change its state and present the next view.

The resulting system keeps complexity to a minimum by partitioning code to provide components that can be tested in isolation. This yields a robust, full-featured, and easy to extend application.

The Complete Reference

# Part IV

## JSP and Other Web Components

JavaServer pages aren't only a presentation layer for Web applications; they can act as the client or server for other applications. The next two chapters deal with the larger context in which JavaServer pages are used—how they can communicate with Java applications, applets, Perl scripts, mail servers, and other server-side agents.

# Chapter 20

## Communicating with Other Clients

Web browsers are the most common JSP clients, but they aren't the only ones. As more applications become Web-enabled, network resources become important components in all types of systems. The Internet can serve as the communications link over which raw data can be delivered, without dictating how it's presented. For example, up-to-the-minute currency exchange rates can be made available for use in batch computations. Interactive travel booking can be part of an executive information system. Current weather conditions, news headlines, and stock prices can be embedded in small information windows in other applications—maybe even in consumer electronic products.

This is possible because any program that can use the HTTP protocol can act as a JSP client. Using basic classes in the `java.net` package, applications can make HTTP requests and read the results as if they were simply the contents of a file. What's more, the file content is dynamic and can be controlled by the parameters of the request.

In this chapter, you walk through the development of three types of nonbrowser JSP clients:

- A Java application
- A Java applet
- A Perl script

Each example consists of a JSP server and a client that can take advantage of it. But first, let's examine the basic technique.

# URL Connections

The key to being the server is appearing to be an input stream. The Java class libraries provide three classes that make this possible:

- `java.net.URL`
- `java.net.URLConnection`
- `java.net.HttpURLConnection`

## The URL Class

A *Uniform Resource Locator* (URL) is a unique address of an object available on a network, as well as an indication of the protocol that must be used to operate on that object.[1] These protocols include `ftp`, `http`, `gopher`, `mailto`, `news`, and others used in specialized applications. The URLs we consider in this chapter use the *Hypertext Transfer Protocol (HTTP)*.

1 The complete URL specification is in RFC 1738, which can be found at http://www.freesoft.org/CIE/RFC/1738/index.htm.

An HTTP URL consists of five parts:

*<scheme>://<host>[:<port>]/<path>[?<query string>]*

The scheme is either `http`, for unencrypted transmissions, or `https`, for transmissions that use an encryption technique such as *Secure Sockets Layer* (SSL). The host part is the fully qualified domain name of a network host, possibly represented as a dotted decimal IP address. The port number is optional and defaults to 80 if not specified. The path is an address within the host HTTP server's document space, which is usually structured as a directory tree. A URL can also contain request parameters encoded in the query string.

The `java.net.URL` class is an object-oriented wrapper for URLs. It provides methods to build URLs from strings and to access the previously described individual parts. In addition, the `java.net.URL` class has two important methods that allow the contents of the resource pointed to by the URL to be accessed and, in some cases, modified. These methods are listed in Table 20-1.

In many cases, reading from a remote network resource is as simple as this:

```
URL url = new URL("http://servername/path/filename");
InputStream in = url.openStream();
int c;
while ((c = in.read()) != -1) {
   // ... do something with this byte
}
```

| Method | Description |
|---|---|
| `public URLConnection openConnection()` | Makes a connection to the remote object represented by the URL. |
| `public final InputStream openStream()` | Opens a URLConnection and creates an InputStream for reading its contents. This is a convenience method that calls `openConnection().getInputStream()`. |

**Table 20-1.** *Some Useful Methods in java.net.URL*

## The URLConnection Class

The underlying class that makes this possible is `java.net.URLConnection`. This is an abstract class whose subclasses represent connections between a program and a remote network resource. Using a `URLConnection` involves four steps:

1. A `URLConnection` object is created by calling the `openConnection()` method of a URL.
2. The connection is configured for the specific task at hand. This may include indicating whether the connection should be used for input, output, or both, as well as setting request properties to indicate the content type, length, and other headers.
3. The connection is made, usually implicitly (although the `connect()` method can be used for this purpose).
4. The remote resource becomes accessible. The connection can supply the resource contents and any response headers sent with it.

A few of the methods you use most often are listed in Table 20-2.

| Method | Description |
|---|---|
| `public void setRequestProperty (String key, String value)` | Sets a general request property, such as an HTTP header, for the connection. An example might be a key of `Content-Length`, with an integer value representing the number of bytes in the data portion of the request. |
| `public OutputStream getOutputStream()` | Returns an output stream for writing data to the connection, such as form parameters in an HTTP POST request. |
| `public InputStream getInputStream()` | Returns an input stream for reading data from the connection. Programs that call this method typically wrap the result in a buffered stream of some kind for performance reasons. |

**Table 20-2.** *Some Useful Methods in java.net.URLConnection*

## The HttpURLConnection Class

URLConnection is an abstract, protocol-neutral class. For this reason, it doesn't have a public constructor. It can only be created by calling the openConnection() method of a URL. The actual object returned by this call is a protocol-specific subclass that handles the URL's protocol. For the examples in this chapter, this subclass is java.net.HttpURLConnection.

Well, almost. HttpURLConnection itself is abstract. The vendor of the Java virtual machine supplies an actual implementation class. You can see what that class is by calling the getClass() method of the object returned by openConnection():

```
import java.io.*;
import java.net.*;

public class ShowConnectionClass
{
   public static void main(String[] args)
      throws IOException
   {
      URL url = new URL("http://www.ibm.com");
      URLConnection con = url.openConnection();
      Class conClass = con.getClass();
      System.out.println
         ("Connection class is " + conClass.getName());
   }
}
```

With the Sun JVM, the output of this program is

```
Connection class is sun.net.www.protocol.http.HttpURLConnection
```

An HttpURLConnection provides three additional capabilities beyond what is supplied by URLConnection:

- A means of specifying the request method
- Direct access to the HTTP response code
- A set of constants that give mnemonic names to HTTP response codes

Table 20-3 describes several methods of interest.

In the following sections, you see how a URL connection makes it possible to view a JSP page as if it were a programmable file.

| Method | Description |
|---|---|
| `public int getResponseCode()` | Extracts the HTTP response code from the first line of the response. For example, if the response line is `HTTP/1.0 404 Not found`, this method returns 404. |
| `public String getResponseMessage()` | Returns the rest of the response line after the response code. For example, if the response line is `HTTP/1.0 404 Not found`, this method returns `Not found`. |
| `public static void setFollowRedirects(boolean set)` | If set to `true`, causes a response code of 301 (Moved Permanently) or 302 (Moved Temporarily) to result in another request to the forwarding address to be generated automatically. |
| `public void setRequestMethod(String method)` | Specifies the HTTP request method to be used: `GET`, `POST`, `HEAD`, `OPTIONS`, `PUT`, `DELETE`, or `TRACE`. |

**Table 20-3.** *Useful Methods in java.net.HttpURLConnection*

## Java Applications as Clients

Our hypothetical Internet music company, LyricNote.com, participates with other online retailers in a price quotation system managed by a discount product buying service. Customers can ask the buying service for a quote on a particular musical instrument, and the buying service then searches the Web sites of its participating suppliers for the best price. Each supplier returns a price quotation as an XML document in a standard format prescribed by the buying service.

### The JSP Price Quote Server

Because the price quote request is different every time, LyricNote.com cannot simply return a static XML document. Rather, it uses a JSP page to generate XML on the fly from the results of a database search. The JSP page (`PriceQuote.jsp`) is listed here:

```
<%@   page
      session="false"
      import="java.sql.*,java.text.*"
      contentType="text/xml"
%><%
   // Define constants for JDBC driver name and
   // database URL

   String DRIVER = "org.enhydra.instantdb.jdbc.idbDriver";
   String DB_URL = "jdbc:idb:"
      + "D:/lyricnote/WEB-INF/database/products/db.prp";

   // Get the product search argument and desired quantity

   String product = request.getParameter("product");
   if (product == null)
      throw new ServletException("No product specified");

   String qstring = request.getParameter("quantity");
   if (qstring == null)
      throw new ServletException("No quantity specified");

   int quantity = 0;
   try {
      quantity = Integer.parseInt(qstring);
   }
   catch (NumberFormatException e) {
      throw new ServletException("Quantity not numeric");
   }

   // Load the driver

   Class.forName(DRIVER);

   // Create a connection

   Connection con = null;
   try {
      con = DriverManager.getConnection(DB_URL);

      // Create a select statement

      PreparedStatement pstmt = con.prepareStatement
```

```
      (
        " select itemcode, price, description"
      + " from   products"
      + " where  prodtype = 'IN'"
      + " and    description like ?"
      + " and    onhand >= ?"
      );

      // Supply values for substitution parameters

      pstmt.setString(1, "%" + product + "%");
      pstmt.setInt(2, quantity);

      // Execute the query

      ResultSet rs = pstmt.executeQuery();

      // Create the XML

%><?xml version="1.0"?>
<price-quote>
   <supplier>LyricNote.com</supplier>
   <date><%=
      new SimpleDateFormat("yyyy-MM-dd")
      .format(new java.util.Date())
      %></date>
<%
      while (rs.next()) {
         String itemCode      = rs.getString(1);
         double price         = rs.getDouble(2) / 100;
         String description   = rs.getString(3);
%>    <item
      code="<%= itemCode %>"
      price="<%= new DecimalFormat("###.00").format(price) %>"
      description="<%= description %>"/>
<%
      }
%></price-quote><%
   }
   finally {
      if (con != null)
         con.close();
```

```
    }
%>
```

The JSP page extracts the product search argument and desired quantity from request parameters, and then opens a database connection to the LyricNote product database and searches for matching items. The results are written as XML.

The odd indentation scheme (with back-to-back delimiters in `%><%` and `%></price-quote>%<`) is used to prevent newline characters or other extraneous whitespace from being written to the output stream. A later example in this chapter shows another technique that can be used to accomplish this.

## The Price Quote Client Application

We consider only a simplified version of the client Java application—one that illustrates how to make the connection, not what to do with the data.

```
import java.io.*;
import java.net.*;

/**
* An example of a Java application that acts as a JSP client.
*/
public class PriceQuoteReader
{
   public static void main(String[] args)
   {
      // Define the supplier URL and the two search arguments.
      // These are hard-coded for the purposes of this example.

      String supplier =
         "http://www.lyricnote.com/PriceQuote.jsp";
      String product = "Clarinet";
      int quantity = 3;

      // Append the search arguments to the URL so that
      // they will be recognized as parameters to an
      // HTTP GET request

      StringBuffer sb = new StringBuffer();
      sb.append(supplier);
      sb.append("?product=");
```

```
        sb.append(URLEncoder.encode(product));
        sb.append("&quantity=");
        sb.append(URLEncoder.encode(String.valueOf(quantity)));
        String supplierURL = sb.toString();

        try {

           // Now create the URL instance

           URL url = new URL(supplierURL);

           // and open its input stream

           InputStream stream = url.openStream();

           // Read each line of the XML that is returned.
           // All this example does it print the results;
           // the real application would do something more
           // useful

           BufferedReader in =
              new BufferedReader(
              new InputStreamReader(stream));

           while (true) {
              String line = in.readLine();
              if (line == null)
                 break;
              System.out.println(line);
           }
           in.close();
        }
        catch (IOException e) {
           e.printStackTrace();
        }
     }
  }
```

`PriceQuoteReader` uses hard-coded values for the supplier URL, the product search string, and the requested quantity. It creates a URL that includes the search string and quantity as request parameters, and then calls `URL.openStream()` to initiate the connection. It then reads and prints the resulting XML document, shown here:

```
<?xml version="1.0"?>
<price-quote>
   <supplier>LyricNote.com</supplier>
   <date>2001-01-25</date>
   <item
      code="001130"
      price="369.00"
      description="Wendecker B Flat Clarinet"/>
   <item
      code="001140"
      price="522.00"
      description="Clemens-Altman B Flat Clarinet - Wood"/>
   <item
      code="001150"
      price="417.00"
      description="Gabriel E Flat Clarinet - Wood"/>
   <item
      code="001160"
      price="548.00"
      description="Wendecker B Flat Bass Clarinet"/>
   <item
      code="001170"
      price="307.00"
      description="Clemens-Altman E Flat Clarinet"/>
</price-quote>
```

The XML contains the supplier name and request date, followed by elements for each matching product—in this case, clarinet models with at least three available for purchase.



## A Java Applet Client

The buying service's main application has the capability to search specific sites in real-time. For this, it uses a Java applet.

A little background is necessary before proceeding. *Applets* were the first wave of Java technology, a means of embedding small interaction GUI applications in a Web page. They generated a great deal of attention quickly, before the technology was robust enough to justify the hype. Part of the problem was different browsers offered different levels of support, and the differences increased over time. Sun Microsystems came up with a workable solution to this problem, known as the Java plug-in.

## The Java Plug-In

The *Plug-in* is a browser-specific embedded object that manages its own Java virtual machine. This means it isn't dependent on the level of support provided by the browser, if any. Early versions of the Plug-in came with an HTML converter that transformed `<APPLET>` tags to their browser-specific counterparts `<OBJECT>` (for Microsoft Internet Explorer) and `<EMBED>` (for Netscape Navigator).

JSP introduced a simpler means of using the Plug-in in a Web page, namely, the `<jsp:plugin>` action. When `<jsp:plugin>` is used in a JSP page, it's replaced in the output HTML document by either the `<object>` or `<embed>` tags, depending on the browser. The rather formidable syntax of this tag is shown here:

```
<jsp:plugin
        type="bean|applet"
        code="<classname>"
        codebase="<codebase>"
        align="<alignment>"
        archive="<archiveList>"
        height="height>"
        hspace="hspace>"
        jreversion="<jreversion>"
        name="componentName>"
        vspace="vspace>"
        width="width>"
        nspluginurl="url>"
        iepluginurl="url>"
>
<jsp-params>
        <jsp:param name="name>" value="value>"/>
        ...
        <jsp:param name="name>" value="value>"
</jsp-params>
<jsp-fallback>Arbitrary text</jsp-fallback>
</jsp-plugin>
```

The JSP specification describes most of the attributes by saying they're "As defined by HTML spec," with the following exceptions:

- `type` This can be `bean` or `applet`.
- `jreversion` This indicates the level of the *Java Runtime Environment (JRE)* required, with the default being "1.1."

- `nspluginurl` The URL from which the Netscape version of the plug-in will be downloaded, if necessary
- `iepluginurl` The URL from which the Internet Explorer version of the plug-in will be downloaded, if necessary

The `<jsp-params>` section specifies the applet parameters to be used, and `<jsp-fallback>` contains text that will be displayed if the applet cannot be started.

Fortunately, only a few of the attributes are required, namely, `type`, `code`, `codebase`, `height`, and `width`.

The advantage of using the plug-in for applets is it makes having a stable, predictable JVM that supports Java 2 possible. In particular, it means applets can use the Java Foundation Classes (Swing) for their GUI.

## The PriceQuoteApplet

Listed here is the source code for the applet used to interrogate the price quote server:

```
import java.awt.*;
import java.awt.event.*;
import javax.swing.*;
import java.io.*;
import java.net.*;

public class PriceQuoteApplet extends JApplet
{
   private JTextField txtProduct;
   private JTextField txtQuantity;
   private JButton btnPost;
   private JTextArea txtOutput;

   /**
   * Creates the GUI components
   */
   public void init()
   {
      Container content = getContentPane();
      content.setLayout(new BorderLayout());
      JPanel pnl;

      // Top row
```

```
      pnl = new JPanel();
      pnl.add(new JLabel("Product:"));
      pnl.add(txtProduct = new JTextField(12));
      pnl.add(new JLabel("Quantity:"));
      pnl.add(txtQuantity = new JTextField(4));
      pnl.add(btnPost = new JButton("POST"));
      content.add(pnl, BorderLayout.NORTH);

      // Results panel

      pnl = new JPanel();
      pnl.add(txtOutput = new JTextArea(12, 40));
      content.add(pnl, BorderLayout.CENTER);

      // Start listening for button clicks

      btnPost.addActionListener(new ActionListener() {
         public void actionPerformed(ActionEvent event)
         {
            try {
               doPost();
            }
            catch (IOException e) {
               txtOutput.setText(e.getMessage());
            }
         }
      });
   }

   /**
   * Makes the request and writes the XML results
   * to the output text area
   */
   public void doPost() throws IOException
   {
      // Extract the parameters from the GUI

      String product = txtProduct.getText().trim();
      String quantity = txtQuantity.getText().trim();

      // Create POST data using the search arguments
      // as request parameters
```

```
StringBuffer sb = new StringBuffer();
sb.append("product=");
sb.append(URLEncoder.encode(product));
sb.append("&quantity=");
sb.append(URLEncoder.encode(String.valueOf(quantity)));
String postData = sb.toString();

// Create the URL from which the quote will be read

URL supplierURL = new URL(getCodeBase(), "PriceQuote.jsp");

// Open a URLConnection instance

HttpURLConnection con = (HttpURLConnection)
   supplierURL.openConnection();

// Set up for writing and reading

con.setDoOutput(true);
con.setDoInput(true);
con.setUseCaches(false);

// Tell the server that the input stream
// contains POST data and give it the length

con.setRequestProperty(
   "Content-type",
   "application/x-www-form-urlencoded");

con.setRequestProperty(
   "Content-length",
   String.valueOf(postData.length()));

// Open an output stream for the connection
// and write the POST data to it

OutputStream out = con.getOutputStream();
out.write(postData.getBytes());
out.flush();

// Open an input stream and copy the results
// into the output text area
```

```
            BufferedReader in =
               new BufferedReader(
               new InputStreamReader(
               con.getInputStream()));

            txtOutput.setText("");

            while (true) {
               String line = in.readLine();
               if (line == null)
                  break;
               txtOutput.append(line);
               txtOutput.append("\n");
            }

            // Close the output and input streams

            in.close();
            out.close();
         }
      }
```

The applet consists of two text fields for the product type and quantity, a button to initiate the search, and a text area to display the results. This isn't a book on Swing, so we won't go into the details of how the GUI is constructed. The method of interest is `doPost()`, for two reasons:

- It shows how an applet connects to a URL input stream
- It does so using the HTTP POST method

POST differs from GET because the request parameters are supplied through the request body, rather than appended to the URL. `doPost()` builds the request body as name/value pairs, using the URL encoding mechanism described in Chapter 12 (HTML Forms). It then opens a `URLConnection` to the JSP page, configures it with the content type and length, and then writes the request body. `doPost()` reads the results and shows them in the output text area.

The JSP page that contains the applet is listed in the following. Figure 20-1 shows the resulting output.

```
<%@ page session="false" %>
<jsp:plugin
   type="applet"
   code="PriceQuoteApplet.class"
   codebase="."
   width="500"
   height="300"
   jreversion="1.2"
   >
</jsp:plugin>
```

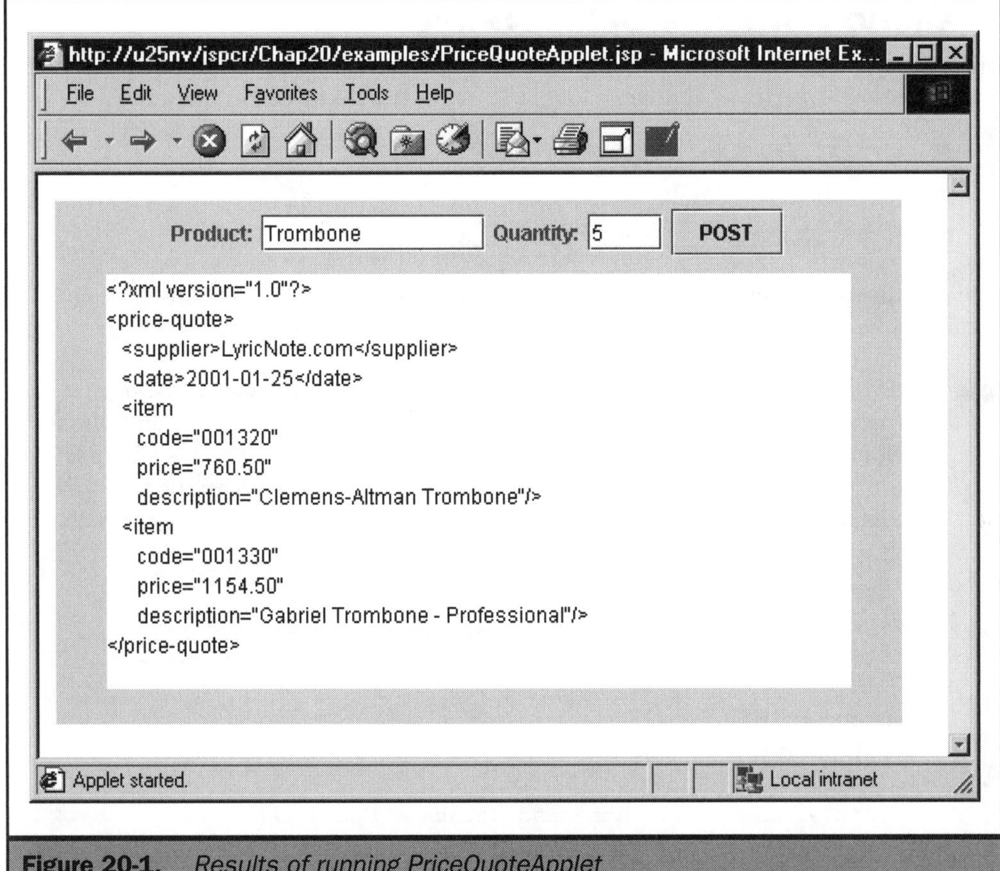


**Figure 20-1.** *Results of running PriceQuoteApplet*

# A Perl Client

Because communication between the JSP server and its clients uses HTTP, it isn't even necessary for the client to be written in Java. Perl, for example, is a widely used scripting language, particularly in CGI applications, text processing, and system administration. With excellent socket support, Perl can easily access server applications written in JSP.

An area in which JSP can extend Perl is by providing better database support. Because virtually all database systems are accessible through some form of JDBC driver, and because Perl can read from JSP URL connections, Perl applications can use JSP as middleware for database access.

## The Generic Database Select Server

The JSP page listed here provides a means for making SQL `SELECT` queries on any JDBC-accessible database. It accepts an HTTP request with three parameters:

- `DRIVER` The JDBC driver class name
- `URL` The JDBC database URL
- `QUERY` A `SELECT` statement to be executed

The results are written in tab-separated-values format, with the column names in the first row.

**Note** *This JSP page illustrates another technique for preventing extraneous whitespace introduced by JSP elements from interfering with the strict output format. This is done by calling response.reset() to clear the output buffer before it writes the first line of genuine text. Note, reset() also clears any headers that were written and the status code. For this reason, the Servlet 2.3 specification added a resetBuffer() method.*

```
<%@ page session="false" %>
<%@ page import="java.io.*" %>
<%@ page import="java.sql.*" %>
<%
   Connection con = null;
   try {

      // Get the driver name and database URL parameters

      String driver = request.getParameter("DRIVER");
      if (driver == null)
         throw new ServletException
```

```
   ("No driver class name specified");

String url = request.getParameter("URL");
if (url == null)
   throw new ServletException
   ("No url class name specified");

// Get the SELECT statement to be executed

String query = request.getParameter("QUERY");
if (query == null)
   throw new ServletException
   ("No QUERY parameter specified");

// Verify that it is a SELECT statement

query = query.trim();
if (!query.toUpperCase().startsWith("SELECT"))
   throw new ServletException
   ("Only SELECT statements are valid");

// Make sure the driver is loaded

Class.forName(driver);

// Open the connection

con = DriverManager.getConnection(url);

// Compile the query statement.  If it is invalid,
// a SQLException will be thrown.

PreparedStatement stmt = con.prepareStatement(query);

// Execute the query

ResultSet rs = stmt.executeQuery();

// Reset the response buffer to eliminate
// any nonsignificant whitespace

response.reset();
```

```
         // Write the column headings

         response.setContentType("text/tab-separated-values");

         ResultSetMetaData rmd = rs.getMetaData();
         int nColumns = rmd.getColumnCount();
         StringBuffer buffer = new StringBuffer();
         for (int i = 0; i < nColumns; i++) {
            int col = i+1;
            if (i > 0)
               buffer.append("\t");
            buffer.append(rmd.getColumnName(col));
         }
         out.println(buffer.toString());

         // Write the data from the result set

         while (rs.next()) {
            buffer = new StringBuffer();
            for (int i = 0; i < nColumns; i++) {
               int col = i+1;
               if (i > 0)
                  buffer.append("\t");
               buffer.append(rs.getString(col));
            }
            out.println(buffer.toString());
         }

         // Done

         rs.close();
         stmt.close();
      }
      finally {
         if (con != null) {
            try {
               con.close();
            }
            catch (SQLException ignore){}
         }
      }
%>
```

## The Perl Script

Perl's unofficial motto is "there is more than one way to do it." This being the case, any Perl script is only one of many possible implementations of the same task.

The script we use to access the JSP database server is `GetBooks.pl`. This opens a socket to the LyricNote Web server on port 80, and then makes an HTTP GET request with the three required parameters, including the SQL query to be executed.

```
#! perl -w

#  ==============================================
#  Program:        GetBooks
#
#  Description:
#
#     Sample Perl script that sends a database
#     query to the SQLSelect.jsp
#  ==============================================

use strict;
use IO::Socket;

my $hostName = "u25nv";
my $hostPort = "80";

#  Open a socket to the host

my $socket = new IO::Socket::INET(
      PeerAddr => $hostName,
      PeerPort => $hostPort,
      Proto    => "tcp"
      );

#  Set autoflush on

my $saveSelect = select $socket;
$| = 1;
select $saveSelect;

#  Create the command

my $cmd = "";
```

```
$cmd .= "DRIVER=" . encode("org.enhydra.instantdb.jdbc.idbDriver");
$cmd .= "&URL="   . encode("jdbc:idb:D:/lyricnote/WEB-
INF/database/products/db.prp");
$cmd .= "&QUERY=" . encode(<<EOF);
SELECT   itemCode, description
FROM     PRODUCTS
WHERE    PRODTYPE='BK'
EOF

my $cmdLength = length($cmd);

#  Send the HTTP request

print $socket (<<EOF);
POST /jspcr/Chap20/examples/SQLSelect.jsp HTTP/1.0
Content-Type: application/x-www-form-urlencoded
Content-Length: $cmdLength

$cmd
EOF

#  Read back the status code

my $line = <$socket>;
my ($httpVersion, $status) = split(/\s+/, $line);
if ($status != 200) {

   #  Handle the error ...

}
else {

   #  Skip the rest of the headers and display the results.
   #  End of headers is signaled by a blank line.

   my $inData = 0;
   while (<$socket>) {
      chomp;

      ($inData == 0) && do {
         $inData = 1 unless (/\S/);
         next;
```

```
      };

      ($inData == 1) && do {
         print "$_\n";
         next;
      };
   }
}

#  Done

$socket->close();

#  Subroutine to URL-encode a parameter string

sub encode {
   my $s = shift;
   $s =~ s/([^A-Za-z0-9 ])/"%" . sprintf("%02X", ord($1))/eg;
   $s =~ s/ /+/g;
   return $s;
}
```

In this case, GetBooks.pl requests the InstantDB database driver for use with the LyricNote product database, and requests the item code and description of every music-related book. The following shows the results:

```
itemcode    description
000030      Dorothy Wendecker: Bartok in New York
000040      Conrad Stock: Beethoven and the Weather
000120      Louis Krouse: The Bad Tsar
000150      Alice Gabriel: Did Salieri Do the Deed?
000160      John Glass: Stravinsky and the 20th Century Ballet
000170      Gray Raphael: Vox Humana
000200      Nicholas Thiers: Oh Boy! Oboe!
000220      Douglas Benton: Some Kind of Brass
000240      Theresa McDonald: The Lyric Viola
000270      Violet Barber: Who's Afraid of the Twelve Tone Row?
000280      Rita Fall: What's My Melodic Line
000290      Mary Wright: More Ballet Bloopers
000330      Anna Maria Pontius: Purcell Mania
```

## Summary

Although the most common JSP client is a Web browser, any program that can use the HTTP protocol can act as a client. This chapter illustrates three alternative clients:

- A standalone Java application that requests a dynamically created XML document
- A Java applet that uses HTTP POST to access the JSP server
- A Perl script that uses JSP as its database server

The flexibility offered by this HTTP communications link makes incorporating JSP-based components in applications of all kinds possible.

# Chapter 21

## Communicating with Other Servers

The preceding chapter demonstrated that clients other than Web browsers can access JSP pages. Using HTTP as the common technology, Java applications, applets, and programs written in other languages can use JSP pages as nonvisual components in systems of any kind.

The reverse is also true—JSP pages can act as clients to other servers. In this chapter, you examine two of these server environments and how JSP pages can interoperate with them.

# Server-Side Scripting Environments

JSP and servlets provide dynamic content over the Internet, but so do a number of other technologies:

- **CGI** The *Common Gateway Interface* drives thousands of interactive Web sites, usually with Perl scripts accessing databases and other system resources.
- **ASP** Microsoft's *Active Server Pages* is a widely used server environment that enables developers to intermingle HTML and scripting commands to provide dynamic content.
- **PHP** PHP is an open source cross-platform server scripting environment that uses embedded HTML and a Perl-like language.
- **Cold Fusion** Allaire's Cold Fusion is a server-side application environment that uses a tag-based server scripting language, called *CFML,* to perform database access and generate Web output.

Finding organizations that use more than one of these technologies or, perhaps all of them, isn't unusual. This is because enterprise computing resources are often widely distributed, with divisional or departmental needs dictating different solutions. Regardless of the merits of JSP or any of these technologies, it may be organizationally difficult to mandate a common application environment. Converting legacy applications is expensive. However, converting them may also be unnecessary because, in many cases, these applications can interoperate. The key infrastructure, once again, is the HTTP protocol, the common delivery mechanism used in all these environments.

## Interoperating with HTTP

A situation in which the need for interoperatability arises is joint activity of related companies. A group of companies may be owned by a parent company that uses a consolidated accounting system. The subsidiary companies may be required to submit budget figures, sales information, and payroll data. And they may need to download prices, discount rates, and corporate charges from the parent. These companies may not be using the same application systems, especially if they were combined in mergers or acquisitions.

Our hypothetical LyricNote.com is such a company. Its merchandise is priced in both U. S. and Canadian dollars, and its parent company guarantees the exchange rate. The rate to be used varies daily, and the parent company makes it available by means of a CGI program used by all its subsidiaries. The product catalog Web application at LyricNote.com needs to use this rate information. For the JSP pages, this means reading from URL connections.

## Reading from Remote Network Resources

You may recall from Chapter 20 that both `java.net.URL` and `java.net.URLConnection` provide methods for reading input streams generated by a remote network resource. The basic technique for a GET request is

```
URL url = new URL("http://servername/path?parm=value");
URLConnection con = url.openConnection();
InputStream in = con.getInputStream();
```

or, using a convenience method in `java.net.URL`:

```
URL url = new URL("http://servername/path?parm=value");
InputStream in = url.openStream();
```

The first method is preferable if you need to configure the connection further before opening the input stream. This can be the case if you need to send request headers or if you need to use the HTTP `POST` method, illustrated here:

```
import java.io.*;
import java.net.*;
import java.util.*;

public class PostRateRequest
{
   public static void main(String[] args)
      throws Exception
   {
      // Set up the two request parameters

      String postData = "c1=USD&c2=CAD";

      // Open the URL connection for reading and writing

      URL url = new URL(
         "http://u25nv/cgi-bin/currency/GetRate.cgi");
      URLConnection con = url.openConnection();
```

```
        con.setDoOutput(true);
        con.setDoInput(true);

        // Set request headers for content type and length

        con.setRequestProperty(
           "Content-type",
           "application/x-www-form-urlencoded");

        con.setRequestProperty(
           "Content-length",
           String.valueOf(postData.length()));

        // Issue the POST request

        OutputStream out = con.getOutputStream();
        out.write(postData.getBytes());
        out.flush();

        // Read the response

        InputStream in = con.getInputStream();
        while (true) {
           int c = in.read();
           if (c == -1)
              break;
           System.out.print((char) c);
        }
        System.out.flush();

        // Done

        in.close();
        out.close();
     }
  }
```

LyricNote.com uses this technique to read the U.S. to Canadian dollar exchange rate from its parent company's Web site. `CatalogSearch.jsp`, listed in the following, lists product prices in both U.S. and Canadian dollars. It gets the exchange rate from the currency CGI program used in the preceding example, this time embedded in its `jspInit()` method. Figure 21-1 shows the results.

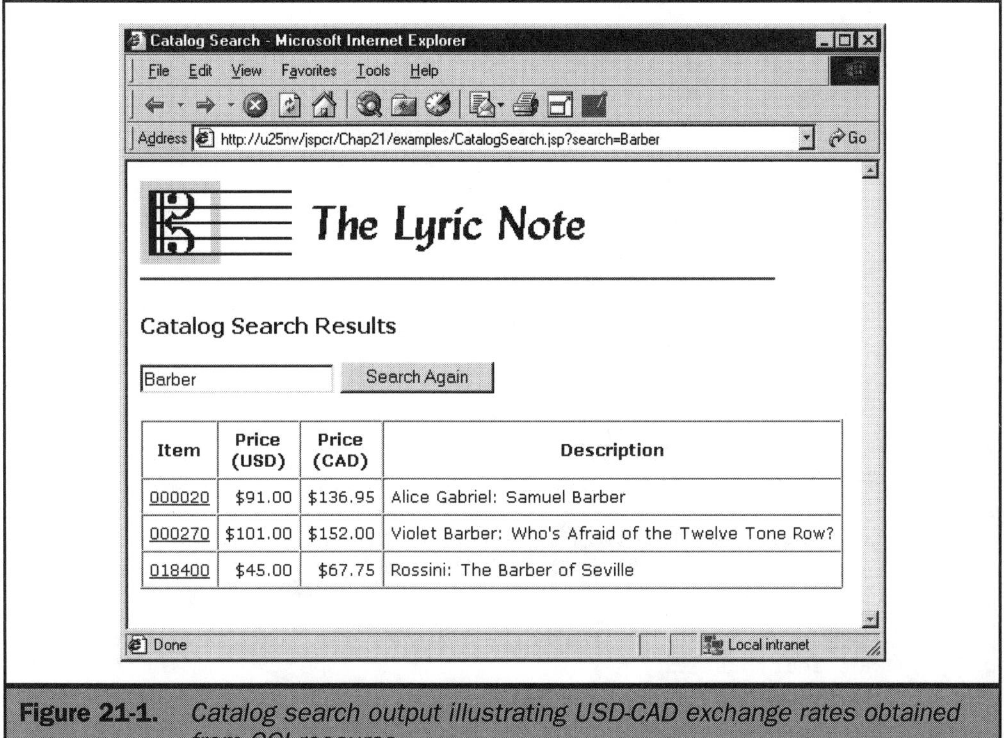


**Figure 21-1.** *Catalog search output illustrating USD-CAD exchange rates obtained from CGI resource*

In `jspInit()`, the JSP page uses an HTTP `GET` request for the USD-CAD exchange rate offered by the parent company. It reads the single line result and converts this into a double. Later on, prices (in whole cents) are read from the database and converted to dollars to two decimal places. The exchange rate is then applied to get the Canadian dollar equivalent, which is rounded to the nearest five cents.

```
<%@ page session="false" %>
<%@ page import="java.io.*" %>
<%@ page import="java.net.*" %>
<%@ page import="java.sql.*" %>
<%@ page import="java.text.*" %>
<%!
   private static double EXCHANGE_RATE;

   // Get the US to Canadian dollar exchange rate

   public void jspInit()
```

```
   {
      try {
         URL url = new URL(
            "http://u25nv/cgi-bin/currency/GetRate.cgi"
            + "?c1=USD"
            + "&c2=CAD");
         BufferedReader in =
            new BufferedReader(
            new InputStreamReader(
            url.openStream()));
         String line = in.readLine();
         in.close();
         EXCHANGE_RATE = Double.parseDouble(line);
      }
      catch (IOException e) {
         e.printStackTrace();
      }
   }
%>
<%
   // Get search string

   String search = request.getParameter("search");
   if (search == null)
      search = "";
   search = search.trim();

   // Connect to database

   String DRIVER = "org.enhydra.instantdb.jdbc.idbDriver";
   String DB_URL = "jdbc:idb:" +
      "D:/lyricnote/WEB-INF/database/products/db.prp";

   Class.forName(DRIVER);
   Connection con = null;
   try {
      con = DriverManager.getConnection(DB_URL);

      // Create a query using the search string

      PreparedStatement stmt = con.prepareStatement
         ("select itemcode, price, description"
```

```
            + " from products"
            + " where description like ?");
        stmt.setString(1, "%" + search + "%");

        // Run the query and display the results

        ResultSet rs = stmt.executeQuery();
%>
<HTML>
<HEAD>
<TITLE>Catalog Search</TITLE>
</HEAD>
<BODY>
<IMG SRC="images/lyric_note.png">
<HR WIDTH="500" ALIGN="LEFT" COLOR="#005A9C">
<H3>Catalog Search Results</H3>
<FORM>
<INPUT TYPE="TEXT" NAME="search" VALUE="<%= search %>">
<INPUT TYPE="SUBMIT" VALUE="Search Again">
</FORM>
<TABLE BORDER="1" CELLPADDING="5" CELLSPACING="0">
<TR>
   <TH>Item</TH>
   <TH>Price<BR>(USD)</TH>
   <TH>Price<BR>(CAD)</TH>
   <TH>Description</TH>
</TR>
<%
        NumberFormat fmt = NumberFormat.getCurrencyInstance();
        while (rs.next()) {
           String itemCode = rs.getString(1);
           double price = rs.getDouble(2) / 100;
           double price_c =
              ((long)(price * EXCHANGE_RATE * 20 + 0.5)) / 20.0;
           String description = rs.getString(3);
%>
<TR>
   <TD><A HREF="productDetail.jsp?itemCode=<%= itemCode %>"
         ><%= itemCode %></A></TD>
   <TD ALIGN="RIGHT"><%= fmt.format(price) %></TD>
   <TD ALIGN="RIGHT"><%= fmt.format(price_c) %></TD>
   <TD><%= description %></TD>
```

```
</TR>
<%
      }
%>
</TABLE>
</BODY>
</HTML>
<%
   }
   finally {
      if (con != null)
         con.close();
   }
%>
```

# Sending Mail from a JSP Page

The product support system case study in Chapter 19 glossed over a procedural difficulty. When a problem is routed to a support person, how does that person know? The developers and testers can read the current list of problems for products they support, but they don't know when a new one appears unless they happen to be looking for it. When a customer is waiting, having the appropriate support personnel notified by some active process is especially important. This situation is made to order for e-mail.

Notification by e-mail from within a program isn't always a good idea, especially if hard-coded addresses are used, which eventually become out-of-date. In this case, however, the identities of the support persons and their e-mail addresses are obtained from the product support database. Because e-mail is a familiar mechanism for which the infrastructure already exists, it's a good solution to this problem

## Approaches to Sending Mail

Several options exist for sending e-mail from within an application. This section considers three:

- SMTP using sockets
- The `sun.net.smtp.SmtpClient` class
- The JavaMail API

## SMTP

The simplest approach is to use the *Simple Mail Transfer Protocol* (*SMTP*) over TCP/IP sockets. Dating back to 1982, SMTP is one of the oldest Internet protocols. It employs a small set of text commands to supply the e-mail parameters:

| | |
|---|---|
| `HELO` | Identifies the sender domain. |
| `MAIL` | Identifies the sender. |
| `RCPT` | Identifies the recipient. More than one `RCPT` command may be used. |
| `DATA` | Indicates the beginning of the message body. Everything up to the next line with "." by itself is part of the body. |
| `QUIT` | Terminates the session. |

An example of an SMTP session is shown here (lines sent by the client are indicated by **boldface**):

```
220 pluto.lyricnote.com ESMTP Sendmail 8.9.3/8.9.3;
   Mon, 29 Jan 2001 06:58:24 -0500 (EST)
HELO lyricnote.com
250 pluto.lyricnote.com Hello dialup.rdu.lyricnote.com
   [209.170.132.190], pleased to meet you
MAIL FROM: phanna@lyricnote.com
250 phanna@lyricnote.com... Sender ok
RCPT TO: phanna@lyricnote.com
250 phanna@lyricnote.com... Recipient ok
DATA
354 Enter mail, end with "." on a line by itself
SUBJECT: Mail Test
This is a test of the mail system
This is only a test
Beeeeeeeeeeeeeeeeeeeeeeep
This concludes the test of the mail system
.
250 UAA07253 Message accepted for delivery
QUIT
221 pluto.lyricnote.com closing connection
```

The complete SMTP protocol specification is in RFC 821, which can be found at http://www.freesoft.org/CIE/RFC/821/index.htm.

SMTP mail can be sent simply by opening a `java.net.Socket` to the mail host, and using its input and output streams, as shown in the example. This socket-based approach has the advantage of being easy to implement, but it becomes more complex when things like attachments are added. For this reason, few applications use it directly.

## The sun.net.smtp.SmtpClient Class

Another option is to use the `sun.net.smtp.SmtpClient` supplied with the *Java Runtime Environment* (*JRE*) from Sun Microsystems. This class is a thin object-oriented wrapper around the raw SMTP socket protocol. The `SmtpClient` version of the preceding example is listed here:

```
import java.io.*;
import sun.net.*;
import sun.net.smtp.*;

public class MailTest
{
   public static void main(String[] args)
      throws Exception
   {
      SmtpClient client = new SmtpClient("mail.lyricnote.com");

      client.from("phanna@lyricnote.com");
      client.to("phanna@lyricnote.com");

      PrintStream out = client.startMessage();
      out.println("SUBJECT: Mail test");
      out.println("This is a test of the mail system");
      out.println("This is only a test");
      out.println("Beeeeeeeeeeeeeeeeeeeeeeeep");
      out.println("This concludes the test of the mail system");
      client.closeServer();
   }
}
```

While this approach is marginally simpler than using sockets, it suffers from one major drawback: the `sun.net.*` classes are undocumented and subject to change. Sun allows them to be used (indeed, the Sun JRE won't work without them), but warns they can be changed or dropped from future versions with no notice.

## The JavaMail API

The third option is the JavaMail API. *JavaMail* is a set of API's that model the components of a mail system in an abstract way—a pluggable architecture for POP, SMTP, IMAP, and other mail protocols. JavaMail is available for JDK 1.1.*x* and higher, and is a required component of the *Java 2 Enterprise Edition* (*J2EE*).

**Note** *JavaMail includes classes both for sending and receiving mail. Only the sending side is considered here. The JavaMail classes and complete documentation can be downloaded from http://java.sun.com/products/javamail.*

JavaMail's highlights are illustrated here, with the same example shown previously:

```
import java.util.*;
import javax.mail.*;
import javax.mail.internet.*;

public class JavaMailTest
{
   public static void main(String[] args)
      throws Exception
   {
      // Create a session with the LyricNote mail host

      Properties props = new Properties();
      props.put("mail.host", "mail.lyricnote.com");
      Session mailSession = Session.getInstance(props, null);

      // Create address objects for the sender and receiver

      Address fromUser =
         new InternetAddress("phanna@lyricnote.com");
      Address toUser =
         new InternetAddress("phanna@lyricnote.com");

      // Create the message body

      Message body = new MimeMessage(mailSession);
      body.setFrom(fromUser);
      body.setRecipient(Message.RecipientType.TO, toUser);
```

```
        body.setSubject("Mail Test");
        body.setContent(
           "This is a test of the mail system\n"
           + "This is only a test\n"
           + "Beeeeeeeeeeeeeeeeeeeeeeeeeeeep\n"
           + "This concludes the test of the mail system",
           "text/plain");

        // Send the message

        Transport.send(body);
    }
}
```

Typically, seven steps are involved in sending mail with JavaMail:

1. Create a session to the mail host using `Session.getInstance()`.
2. Create sender and recipient address objects with `new InternetAddress()`.
3. Create a message body with `new MimeMessage(Session session)`.
4. Specify the addresses with the `Message` object's `setFrom()` and `setRecipient()`.
5. Specify the subject with `setSubject()`.
6. Specify the message body and encoding type with `setContent()`.
7. Send the message with `Transport.send(message)`.

The first step creates a new `Session` object. `Session` acts as the connection to the mail host. A new instance of this object is obtained by calling the static method `Session.getInstance(Properties props, Authenticator auth)`. The properties supplied to this method must include, at a minimum, the mail host. The `auth` parameter can be null if no authentication is required.

Step two represents the sender and recipient(s) as `InternetAddress` objects. This class models addresses according to RFC 822, "Standard for the Format of ARPA Internet Text Messages," which can be obtained from http://www.freesoft.org/CIE/RFC.

Next, a message body object is created with `new MimeMessage()`. This class represents a multipart Internet mail message, including its content and headers. The constructor takes a reference to the `Session` object, so the message can be related to the mail host and other session parameters.

The fourth step sets the message body's from and recipient properties, using setFrom(Address fromUser) and setRecipient(Message.RecipientType type, Address toUser), respectively. The type parameter is used to distinguish among TO, CC, and BCC recipients.

Optional step five sets the subject of the mail message, using the message object's setSubject(String subject) method.

Step six creates the actual message text using the message object's setContent(Object body, String type) method. The body parameter specifies the text, and type indicates the MIME type (usually text/plain).

Finally, the mail is sent with the static Transport.send(Message message) method. Transport is an abstract class whose concrete implementation is supplied by the mail service provider, such as the Sun smtp.jar file.

## E-Mail Notification in the Product Support System

Back to the problem at hand. The product support system needs to notify the appropriate support person, developer, or tester when an problem is routed to that person. This routing occurs in the model component, in its addProblemLog() method (see the com.lyricnote.support.Model class listing in Chapter 19). The routing event IDs are as follows:

| | |
|---|---|
| RPS | Routed to product support |
| RPD | Routed to product development |
| RQA | Routed to test |

In addProblemLog(), you can determine if the event ID is one of these three. If so, call a new model method notifySupport(ProblemLog log), listed here:

```
/**
* Sends email to the appropriate support person
*/
public void notifySupport(ProblemLog log)
   throws SQLException, IOException
{
   // Get the problem object

   String problemID = log.getProblemID();
   setProblemID(problemID);
   Problem problem = getProblem();
```

```
// Create the subject line from the problem ID
// and problem description

StringBuffer sb = new StringBuffer();
sb.append("Problem ID: ");
sb.append(problemID);
sb.append(" ");
sb.append(problem.getDescription());
String subject = sb.toString();

// Get the product object. We need this to find out
// the support ID's and the corresponding e-mail
// addresses

String productID = problem.getProductID();
setProductID(productID);
Product product = getProduct();

// Determine the appropriate party to receive the mail

String employeeID = null;
String eventDescription = null;
String eventID = log.getEventID();
if (eventID.equals("RPS")) {
   employeeID = product.getProductSupport();
   eventDescription = "ROUTED TO PRODUCT SUPPORT";
}
else
if (eventID.equals("RPD")) {
   employeeID = product.getDeveloper();
   eventDescription = "ROUTED TO DEVELOPMENT";
}
else
if (eventID.equals("RQA")) {
   employeeID = product.getTester();
   eventDescription = "ROUTED TO TEST";
```

```
   }
   else
      return;

   eventDescription += "\r\n";
   eventDescription += log.getComments();

   // Lookup that person's email address

   Employee employee = getEmployee(employeeID);
   String email = employee.getEmail();

   // Send mail to the party

   Address fromUser = new InternetAddress
      ("support@lyricnote.com", "Product Support System");
   Address toUser = new InternetAddress
      (email, employee.getName());

   Properties props = new Properties();
   props.put("mail.host", "mail.lyricnote.com");
   Session mailSession = Session.getInstance(props, null);
   Message body = new MimeMessage(mailSession);

   try {
      body.setFrom(fromUser);
      body.setRecipient(Message.RecipientType.TO, toUser);
      body.setSubject(subject);
      body.setContent(eventDescription, "text/plain");
      Transport.send(body);
   }
   catch (MessagingException e) {
      throw new IOException(e.getMessage());
   }
}
```

Figure 21-2 shows this new feature in action. A problem is reported against the MIDI Transposer product. The call center agent fills out the problem report and selects "Route to product support" as the action. When the agent clicks the Submit button, the problem is added to the database and the model's `addProblemLog()` method is called. Because the event is RPS, the `notifySupport()` method is invoked, resulting in the message shown in Figure 21-3 being sent to the product support representative.

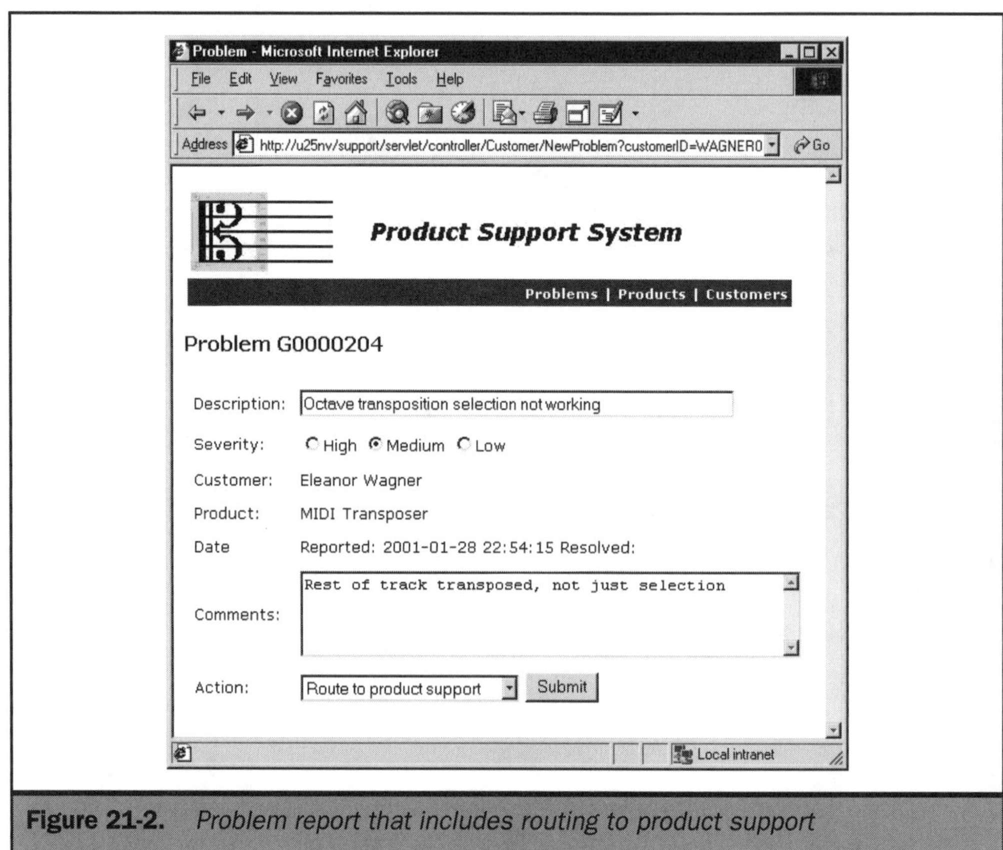


**Figure 21-2.** *Problem report that includes routing to product support*

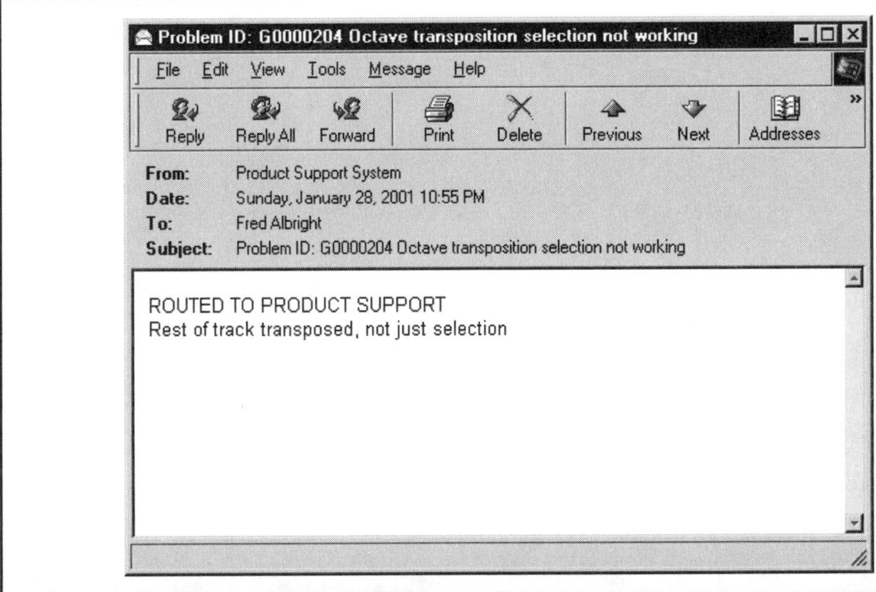


**Figure 21-3.** *E-mail message sent to the product support representative*

## Summary

Just as programs other than Web browsers can be JSP clients, so JSP pages can be clients to other servers. This chapter considers two such environments:

- Obtaining data from a CGI server
- Sending mail with the JavaMail API

JSP, servlets, CGI, PHP, and ASP, as well as other server-side scripting environments all use a common technology for delivering content to their clients: the HTTP protocol. The java.net package provides the `URL` and `URLConnection` classes, which have methods for accessing resources through HTTP.

The JavaMail API is a scalable and extensible architecture for modeling all parts of a mail system. Implementations of specific mail protocols such as POP, SMTP, and IMAP are freely available.

# Part V

## Appendixes

This section of the book contains reference material on the Servlet API, the JSP API, and the HTTP protocol.

The Complete Reference

# Appendix A

## Servlet API Version 2.3

This appendix describes each class in the two servlet packages:

- `javax.servlet` Servlet classes not specific to any protocol
- `javax.servlet.http` HTTP-specific servlet classes

For each class, the following sections are included:

- Class name
- Context (full name, type, superclass, interfaces implemented)
- Class description
- Details of each method in the class

*The classes and methods described here are based on the final public draft of the Servlet 2.3 specification. Although the final draft is likely to be very close to the official specification, there may be changes. Consult the latest version of the specification at http://java.sun.com/products/servlet/index.html if in doubt.*

A number of classes and methods are described as deprecated. This means that they are no longer recommended for use, and may be discontinued in future versions.

# Package javax.servlet

## Filter

**Full Name:** `javax.servlet.Filter`

**Type:** Interface

Classes that implement the `Filter` interface perform filtering tasks on a request, a response, or both. The classes implement `doFilter()` to do so.

### Methods

#### doFilter

```
public void doFilter(
     ServletRequest request,
     ServletResponse response,
     FilterChain chain)
  throws IOException, ServletException
```

This method is called by the servlet engine whenver a request is passed through the filter chain.

### getFilterConfig

```
public FilterConfig getFilterConfig()
```

Returns the `FilterConfig` for this `Filter`.

### setFilterConfig

```
public void setFilterConfig(FilterConfig filterConfig)
```

Sets the `FilterConfig` object. The servlet engine also calls this method with `null` when it is done with the `Filter`.

# FilterChain

| | |
|---|---|
| **Full Name:** | `javax.servlet.FilterChain` |
| **Type:** | Interface |
| **Superinterface:** | none |

Provides a view of the filter invocation chain. A `Filter` uses `FilterChain` to invoke the next filter in a chain.

## Methods

### doFilter

```
public void doFilter(
      ServletRequest request,
      ServletResponse response)
   throws IOException, ServletException
```

Invokes the next filter in the chain or the resource at the end of the chain.

# FilterConfig

| | |
|---|---|
| **Full Name:** | `javax.servlet.FilterConfig` |
| **Type:** | Interface |

Passes information to a filter during initialization.

## Methods

### getFilterName

```
public String getFilterName()
```

Returns the filter name.

### getInitParameter

```
public String getInitParameter(String name)
```

Returns the value of the specified parameter or `null`, if it does not exist.

### getInitParameterNames

```
public Enumeration getInitParameterNames()
```

Returns an enumeration of the servlet's initialization parameter names. If there are no initialization parameters, returns an empty enumeration.

### getServletContext

```
public ServletContext getServletContext()
```

Returns the ServletContext in which the caller is executing.

# GenericServlet

| | |
|---|---|
| **Full Name:** | `javax.servlet.GenericServlet` |
| **Type:** | Abstract class |
| **Implements:** | `javax.servlet.Servlet`<br>`javax.servlet.ServletConfig`<br>`java.io.Serializable` |

A base class for servlets that do not use HTTP protocol-specific features. `GenericServlet` implements the basic features of all servlets:

- Initialization
- Request handling
- Termination

The only method that must be overridden is `service()`, which actually handles requests.

`HttpServlet`, the base class for HTTP servlets, is more commonly used as the superclass for servlets.

## Constructors

### GenericServlet

```
public GenericServlet()
```

An empty constructor which performs no work. Any servlet initialization should be done in the `init()` method.

## Methods

### destroy

```
public void destroy()
```

Called by the servlet engine when the servlet is unloaded. Servlet authors can override this method to release any allocated resources.

In `GenericServlet`, this method simply logs the fact that it was executed.

### getInitParameter

```
public String getInitParameter(String name)
```

Given an initialization parameter name, returns the value of the parameter. If no such parameter exists, returns `null`.

### getInitParameterNames

```
public Enumeration getInitParameterNames()
```

Returns an `Enumeration` of the names of all the initialization parameter that exist for this servlet.

### getServletConfig

```
public ServletConfig getServletConfig()
```

Returns the `ServletConfig` object associated with this servlet.

### getServletContext

```
public ServletContext getServletContext()
```

Returns the `ServletContext` object associated with this servlet.

### getServletInfo

```
public String getServletInfo()
```

Returns identifying information about the servlet, such as author, version, and copyright.

### getServletName

```
public String getServletName()
```

Returns the name of this servlet instance.

### init

```
public void init() throws ServletException
```

A convenience method that calls `super.init(config)`.

### init

```
public void init(ServletConfig config)
   throws ServletException
```

Called by the servlet container to indicate that the servlet is being placed into service

### log

```
public void log(String msg)
```

Writes the specified message to the servlet log file.

### log

```
public void log(String message, Throwable t)
```

Writes the specified message to the servlet log file. The message in the `Throwable` is also written to the log.

### service

```
public abstract void service(
      ServletRequest req,
      ServletResponse res)
throws ServletException, IOException
```

Called by the servlet container to allow the servlet to handle a request.

# RequestDispatcher

**Full Name:** `javax.servlet.RequestDispatcher`

**Type:** Interface

An object used to pass requests from a client to any resource on the server.

## Methods

### forward

```
public void forward(
      ServletRequest request,
      ServletResponse response)
   throws ServletException, IOException
```

Passes a request from a servlet to another servlet, JSP page, or HTML document. `forward` can only be called before the response has been committed.

### include

```
public void include(
```

```
          ServletRequest request,
          ServletResponse response)
       throws ServletException, IOException
```

Includes the content of another servlet, JSP page, HTML document in current output buffer. The included resource may not set any response headers.

## Servlet

**Full Name:** `javax.servlet.Servlet`

**Type:** Interface

Defines the methods that all servlets must implement. The servlet API provides concrete implementations of this interface in the `GenericServlet` and `HttpServlet` classes.

### Methods

#### destroy

```
public void destroy()
```

Called by the servlet container when the servlet is being taken out of service.

#### getServletConfig

```
public ServletConfig getServletConfig()
```

Returns the `ServletConfig` object associated with this servlet.

#### getServletInfo

```
public String getServletInfo()
```

Returns identifying information about the servlet.

#### init

```
public void init(ServletConfig config) throws ServletException
```

Called by the servlet container when the servlet is being placed into service. The `init` method must complete normally before the servlet will receive any requests.

### service

```
public void service(
      ServletRequest req,
      ServletResponse res)
   throws ServletException, IOException
```

Called by the servlet container to handle a request.

## ServletConfig

**Full Name:** `javax.servlet.ServletConfig`

**Type:** Interface

Used by the servlet engine used to pass information to a servlet during initialization.

### Methods

#### getInitParameter

```
public String getInitParameter(String name)
```

Returns the value of the specified initialization parameter, or `null` if it does not exist.

#### getInitParameterNames

```
public Enumeration getInitParameterNames()
```

Returns an enumeration of the names of the servlet's initialization parameters, or an empty enumeration if none exist.

#### getServletContext

```
public ServletContext getServletContext()
```

Returns the `ServletContext` associated with the servlet.

### getServletName

```
public String getServletName()
```

Returns the name of the servlet instance as recorded in the `web.xml` deployment descriptor.

# ServletContext

**Full Name:** `javax.servlet.ServletContext`

**Type:** Interface

Defines the list of methods that are available to a servlet for communicating with its servlet container. The servlet context can store attributes that are available to all servlets in the application.

## Methods

### getAttribute

```
public Object getAttribute(String name)
```

Returns the application-level attribute with the specified name, or `null` if it does not exist. The object must be cast into the appropriate type.

### getAttributeNames

```
public Enumeration getAttributeNames()
```

Returns an enumeration of the attribute names in the servlet context.

### getContext

```
public ServletContext getContext(String uripath)
```

Returns the `ServletContext` object of another URL on the same server. The path must begin with "/" and will be interpreted as being relative to the Web server's document root.

### getInitParameter

```
public String getInitParameter(String name)
```

Returns the specified initialization parameter:

### getInitParameterNames

```
public Enumeration getInitParameterNames()
```

Returns an enumeration of the names of the servlet context's initialization parameters, or an empty enumeration if there are none.

### getMajorVersion

```
public int getMajorVersion()
```

Returns the integer to the left of the decimal point in the Servlet API version number.

### getMimeType

```
public String getMimeType(String file)
```

Returns the MIME type of the specified file, or `null` if the MIME type is not known.

### getMinorVersion

```
public int getMinorVersion()
```

Returns the number to the right of the decimal place in the Servlet API version number.

### getNamedDispatcher

```
public RequestDispatcher getNamedDispatcher(String name)
```

Returns a `RequestDispatcher` for the specified servlet, or `null` if the RequestDispatcher cannot be returned.

### getRealPath

```
public String getRealPath(String path)
```

Given a URI path in the current servlet context, converts the path into the absolute file name to which it refers.

### getRequestDispatcher

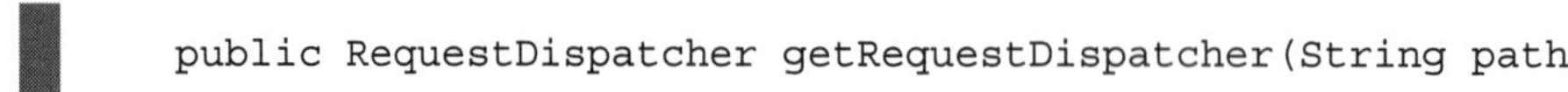

```
public RequestDispatcher getRequestDispatcher(String path)
```

Returns a `RequestDispatcher` for the specified resource, or `null` if it cannot be created. The path name must begin with "/" and is interpreted as being relative to the root of the servlet context.

### getResource

```
public URL getResource(String path) throws MalformedURLException
```

Returns a `URL` for the specified resource, or `null` if it cannot be created. The path name must begin with "/" and is interpreted as being relative to the root of the servlet context.

### getResourceAsStream

```
public InputStream getResourceAsStream(String path)
```

Returns an `InputStream` for the specified resource, or `null` if it cannot be created. The path name must begin with "/" and is interpreted as being relative to the root of the servlet context.

### getResourcePaths

```
public Set getResourcePaths()
```

Returns a `Set` of strings representing the paths to resources held in the web application. The paths begin with a leading /, and are relative to the root of the servlet context.

### getServerInfo

```
public String getServerInfo()
```

Returns the name and version of the servlet engine. The returned value is in the form *servername/version_number*.

### [deprecated] *getServlet*

```
public Servlet getServlet(String name) throws ServletException
```

No longer supported, for security reasons. See `HttpSessionListener` for an alternative approach.

### getServletContextName

```
public String getServletContextName()
```

Returns the name of the Web application, corresponding to the `display-name` element for this ServletContext in the `web.xml` deployment descriptor.

### [deprecated] *getServletNames*

```
public Enumeration getServletNames()
```

No longer supported, for security reasons. See `HttpSessionListener` for an alternative approach.

### [deprecated] *getServlets*

```
public Enumeration getServlets()
```

### [deprecated] *log*

```
public void log(Exception exception, String msg)
```

No longer supported. Use `log(String message, Throwable t)` instead.

### log

```
public void log(String msg)
```

Writes the specified message to the servlet log.

### log

```
public void log(String message, Throwable throwable)
```

Writes the specified message and a stack trace for a given `Throwable` to the servlet log.

#### removeAttribute

```
public void removeAttribute(String name)
```

Removes the attribute with the specified name from the servlet context.

#### setAttribute

```
public void setAttribute(String name, Object object)
```

Stores an object under the specified attribute name in this servlet context.

## ServletContextAttributeEvent

**Full Name:** `javax.servlet.ServletContextAttributeEvent`

**Type:** Class

**Extends:** `javax.servlet.ServletContextEvent`

Used for notifications about changes to the attributes of the servlet context of a web application.

### Constructors

#### ServletContextAttributeEvent

```
public ServletContextAttributeEvent(
   ServletContext source,
   String name,
   Object value)
```

Constructs a `ServletContextAttributeEvent` from the specified context for the specified name and value.

### Methods

#### getName

```
public String getName()
```

Returns the name of the attribute that changed.

### getValue

```
public Object getValue()
```

Returns the value of the attribute that was added removed or replaced. The value depends on whether the attribute was added, changed, or deleted. For changes or deletions, it is the value of the old attribute. For additions, it is the value of the new attribute.

## ServletContextAttributesListener

**Full Name:** `javax.servlet.ServletContextAttributesListener`

**Type:** Interface

**Superinterface:** `java.util.EventListener`

Classes implementing this interface will receive notification of changes to the servlet context's attribute list.

## Methods

### attributeAdded

```
public void attributeAdded(ServletContextAttributeEvent scab)
```

Called when a new attribute is added to the servlet context

### attributeRemoved

```
public void attributeRemoved
   (ServletContextAttributeEvent scab)
```

Called when an existing attribute is removed from the servlet context.

### attributeReplaced

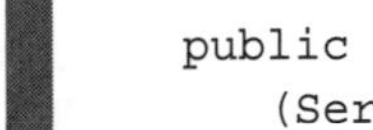

```
public void attributeReplaced
   (ServletContextAttributeEvent scab)
```

Called when an existing attribute is replaced in the servlet context.

# ServletContextEvent

**Full Name:** `javax.servlet.ServletContextEvent`

**Type:** Class

**Extends:** `java.util.EventObject`

Event class for notifications about changes to the servlet context.

## Constructors

### ServletContextEvent

```
public ServletContextEvent(ServletContext source)
```

Creates a `ServletContextEvent` from the given context.

## Methods

### getServletContext

```
public ServletContext getServletContext()
```

Returns the `ServletContext` that changed.

# ServletContextListener

**Full Name:** `javax.servlet.ServletContextListener`

**Type:** Interface

**Superinterface:** `java.util.EventListener`

Classes implementing this interface will receive notification about changes to the servlet context.

## Methods

### contextDestroyed

```
public void contextDestroyed(ServletContextEvent sce)
```

Called when the servlet context is about to be shut down.

### contextInitialized

```
public void contextInitialized(ServletContextEvent sce)
```

Called when the Web application is ready to process requests.

# ServletException

**Full Name:** `javax.servlet.ServletException`

**Type:** Class

**Extends:** `java.lang.Exception`

A generic servlet exception.

## Constructors

### ServletException

```
public ServletException()
```

Creates a new servlet exception.

### ServletException

```
public ServletException(String message)
```

Creates a new servlet exception with the specified message.

### ServletException

```
public ServletException(String message, Throwable rootCause)
```

Creates a new servlet exception that includes a message and the root cause exception.

### ServletException

```
public ServletException(Throwable rootCause)
```

Creates a new servlet exception that includes the root cause exception.

## Methods

### getRootCause

```
public Throwable getRootCause()
```

Returns the root cause exception for the current servlet exception.

# ServletInputStream

| | |
|---|---|
| **Full Name:** | `javax.servlet.ServletInputStream` |
| **Type:** | Abstract class |
| **Extends:** | `java.io.InputStream` |

An input stream a servlet can use for reading binary data from a client request Typically retrieved with the `ServletRequest.getInputStream()` method.

## Methods

### readLine

```
public int readLine(byte[] b, int off, int len)
   throws IOException
```

Reads one line at a time from the input stream, starting at the specified offset. Reads bytes into an array until it reads the specified number of bytes or a newline character (also read into the array). Returns -1 if end of file is reached before the maximum number of bytes is read.

# ServletOutputStream

| | |
|---|---|
| **Full Name:** | `javax.servlet.ServletOutputStream` |
| **Type:** | Abstract class |
| **Extends:** | `java.io.OutputStream` |

An output stream used to send binary data to a client. Typically retrieved with the `ServletResponse.getOutputStream()` method.

## Methods

### print

```
public void print(boolean b) throws IOException
```

Writes a `boolean` value to the client but no carriage return-line feed character at the end.

### print

```
public void print(char c) throws IOException
```

Writes a character to the client but no carriage return-line feed at the end.

### print

```
public void print(double d) throws IOException
```

Writes a `double` value to the client but no carriage return-line feed at the end.

### print

```
public void print(float f) throws IOException
```

Writes a `float` value to the client but no carriage return-line feed at the end.

### print

```
public void print(int i) throws IOException
```

Writes an int to the client but no carriage return-line feed at the end.

### print

```
public void print(long l) throws IOException
```

Writes a `long` value to the clientbut no carriage return-line feed at the end.

### print

```
public void print(String s) throws IOException
```

Writes a `String` to the client but no carriage return-line feed character at the end.

### println

```
public void println() throws IOException
```

Writes a carriage return-line feed to the client.

### println

```
public void println(boolean b) throws IOException
```

Writes a `boolean` value to the client, followed by a carriage return-line feed.

### println

```
public void println(char c) throws IOException
```

Writes a character to the client followed by a carriage return-line feed.

### println

```
public void println(double d) throws IOException
```

Writes a `double` value to the client followed by a carriage return-line feed.

### println

```
public void println(float f) throws IOException
```

Writes a `float` value to the client followed by a carriage return-line feed.

### println

```
public void println(int i) throws IOException
```

Writes an int to the client followed by a carriage return-line feed character.

### println

```
public void println(long l) throws IOException
```

Writes a `long` value to the client followed by a carriage return-line feed.

### println

```
public void println(String s) throws IOException
```

Writes a `String` to the client followed by a carriage return-line feed.

# ServletRequest

**Full Name:** `javax.servlet.ServletRequest`

**Type:** Interface

An interface that represents a client request to a servlet. The servlet engine creates a `ServletRequest` object and passes it as an argument to the servlet's `service` method. Has methods for retrieving parameter names and values, attributes, and the input stream.

## Methods

### getAttribute

```
public Object getAttribute(String name)
```

Returns the value of the specified attribute, or `null` if no attribute of the specified name exists.

### getAttributeNames

```
public Enumeration getAttributeNames()
```

Returns an `Enumeration` of the names of the attributes available to this request, or an empty `Enumeration` if the request has no attributes.

### getCharacterEncoding

```
public String getCharacterEncoding()
```

Returns the name of the character encoding used in the body of this request, or `null` if the request does not specify a character encoding

### getContentLength

```
public int getContentLength()
```

Returns the length of the request body or -1 if the length is not known. In HTTP servlets, this is the same as the value of the CGI variable `CONTENT_LENGTH`.

### getContentType

```
public String getContentType()
```

Returns the MIME type of the body of the request, or `null` if not known. In HTTP servlets, same as the value of the CGI variable `CONTENT_TYPE`.

### getInputStream

```
public ServletInputStream getInputStream() throws IOException
```

Retrieves the body of the request as binary data. Either `getInputStream()` or `getReader()` may be called to read the body, but not both.

### getLocale

```
public Locale getLocale()
```

Returns the preferred `Locale` in which the client will accept content, if specified. Otherwise, returns the default locale for the server.

### getLocales

```
public Enumeration getLocales()
```

Returns an `Enumeration` of `Locale` objects in order of user preference, or an `Enumeration` containing one `Locale`, the default locale for the server, if the client indicates no preferred locale.

### getParameter

```
public String getParameter(String name)
```

Returns the value of a request parameter as a `String`, or `null` if the parameter does not exist.

### getParameterMap

```
public Map getParameterMap()
```

Returns a `java.util.Map` of the parameters of this request.

### getParameterNames

```
public Enumeration getParameterNames()
```

Returns a `java.util.Enumeration` of the names of the parameters in this request, or an empty `Enumeration` if the request has no parameters.

### getParameterValues

```
public String[] getParameterValues(String name)
```

Returns an array of `String` objects containing all the values of the given request parameter, or `null` if the parameter does not exist.

### getProtocol

```
public String getProtocol()
```

Returns the name and version of the protocol the request uses. The value returned is in the form *protocol/majorVersion.minorVersion*. In HTTP servlets, this is the same as the CGI variable `SERVER_PROTOCOL`.

### getReader

```
public BufferedReader getReader() throws IOException
```

Retrieves the body of the request as character data. Either `getInputStream()` or `getReader()` may be called, but not both.

### [deprecated] *getRealPath*

```
public String getRealPath(String path)
```

No longer supported.

### getRemoteAddr

```
public String getRemoteAddr()
```

Returns the Internet Protocol (IP) address of the client that sent the request. For HTTP servlets, same as the CGI variable `REMOTE_ADDR`.

### getRemoteHost

```
public String getRemoteHost()
```

Returns the name of the client that sent the request, or the client's IP address if the name cannot be determined. For HTTP servlets, same as the CGI variable `REMOTE_HOST`.

### getRequestDispatcher

```
public RequestDispatcher getRequestDispatcher(String path)
```

Returns a `RequestDispatcher` object for the resource located at the specified path.The difference between this method and `ServletContext.getRequestDispatcher()` is that this method can take a relative path.

### getScheme

```
public String getScheme()
```

Returns the scheme used to make the request.

### getServerName

```
public String getServerName()
```

Returns the server host name for the server receiving the request. In HTTP servlets, this is the same as the CGI variable `SERVER_NAME`.

### getServerPort

```
public int getServerPort()
```

Returns the port number to which this request was sent. In HTTP servlets, this is the same as the CGI variable SERVER_PORT.

### isSecure

```
public boolean isSecure()
```

Returns true if this request was made using a secure channel, such as https.

### removeAttribute

```
public void removeAttribute(String name)
```

Removes the named attribute from this request.

### setAttribute

```
public void setAttribute(String name, Object o)
```

Binds an attribute to this request under the given name.

### setCharacterEncoding

```
public void setCharacterEncoding(String env)
   throws UnsupportedEncodingException
```

Specifies the character encoding used in the body of this request. Must be called before reading the request parameters or input data are read.

## ServletRequestWrapper

**Full Name:** javax.servlet.ServletRequestWrapper
**Type:** Class
**Implements:** javax.servlet.ServletRequest

An implementation of ServletRequest that can be subclassed to extend the servlet engine's implementation class.

## Constructors

### ServletRequestWrapper

```
public ServletRequestWrapper(ServletRequest request)
```

Creates a `ServletRequest` adapter for the given request object.

## Methods

### getAttribute

```
public Object getAttribute(String name)
```

Returns the value of the specified attribute, or `null` if no attribute of the specified name exists.

### getAttributeNames

```
public Enumeration getAttributeNames()
```

Returns an `Enumeration` of the names of the attributes available to this request, or an empty `Enumeration` if the request has no attributes.

### getCharacterEncoding

```
public String getCharacterEncoding()
```

Returns the name of the character encoding used in the body of this request, or `null` if the request does not specify a character encoding

### getContentLength

```
public int getContentLength()
```

Returns the length of the request body or -1 if the length is not known. In HTTP servlets, this is the same as the value of the CGI variable `CONTENT_LENGTH`.

### getContentType

```
public String getContentType()
```

Returns the MIME type of the body of the request, or `null` if not known. In HTTP servlets, same as the value of the CGI variable `CONTENT_TYPE`.

### getInputStream

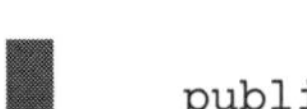

```
public ServletInputStream getInputStream() throws IOException
```

Retrieves the body of the request as binary data. Either `getInputStream()` or `getReader()` may be called to read the body, but not both.

### getLocale

```
public Locale getLocale()
```

Returns the preferred `Locale` in which the client will accept content, if specified. Otherwise, returns the default locale for the server.

### getLocales

```
public Enumeration getLocales()
```

Returns an `Enumeration` of `Locale` objects in order of user preference, or an `Enumeration` containing one `Locale`, the default locale for the server, if the client indicates no preferred locale.

### getParameter

```
public String getParameter(String name)
```

Returns the value of a request parameter as a `String`, or `null` if the parameter does not exist.

### getParameterMap

```
public Map getParameterMap()
```

Returns a `java.util.Map` of the parameters of this request.

### getParameterNames

```
public Enumeration getParameterNames()
```

Returns a `java.util.Enumeration` of the names of the parameters in this request, or an empty `Enumeration` if the request has no parameters.

### getParameterValues

```
public String getParameterValues(String name)
```

Returns an array of `String` objects containing all the values of the given request parameter, or `null` if the parameter does not exist.

### getProtocol

```
public String getProtocol()
```

Returns the name and version of the protocol the request uses. The value returned is in the form *protocol/majorVersion.minorVersion*. In HTTP servlets, this is the same as the CGI variable `SERVER_PROTOCOL`.

### getReader

```
public BufferedReader getReader() throws IOException
```

Retrieves the body of the request as character data. Either `getInputStream()` or `getReader()` may be called, but not both.

### getRealPath

```
public String getRealPath(String path)
```

Returns getRealPath(String path).

### getRemoteAddr

```
public String getRemoteAddr()
```

Returns the Internet Protocol (IP) address of the client that sent the request. For HTTP servlets, same as the CGI variable `REMOTE_ADDR`.

### getRemoteHost

```
public String getRemoteHost()
```

Returns the name of the client that sent the request, or the client's IP address if the name cannot be determined. For HTTP servlets, same as the CGI variable REMOTE_HOST.

### getRequest

```
public ServletRequest getRequest()
```

Returns the wrapped request object.

### getRequestDispatcher

```
public RequestDispatcher getRequestDispatcher(String path)
```

Returns a RequestDispatcher object for the resource located at the specified path. The difference between this method and ServletContext.getRequestDispatcher() is that this method can take a relative path.

### getScheme

```
public String getScheme()
```

Returns the scheme used to make the request.

### getServerName

```
public String getServerName()
```

Returns the server host name for the server receiving the request. In HTTP servlets, this is the same as the CGI variable SERVER_NAME.

### getServerPort

```
public int getServerPort()
```

Returns the port number to which this request was sent. In HTTP servlets, this is the same as the CGI variable SERVER_PORT.

### isSecure

```
public boolean isSecure()
```

Returns `true` if this request was made using a secure channel, such as `https`.

#### removeAttribute

```
public void removeAttribute(String name)
```

Removes the named attribute from this request.

#### setAttribute

```
public void setAttribute(String name, Object o)
```

Binds an attribute to this request under the given name.

#### setCharacterEncoding

```
public void setCharacterEncoding(String enc) throws
UnsupportedEncodingException
```

Specifies the character encoding used in the body of this request. Must be called before reading the request parameters or input data are read.

#### setRequest

```
public void setRequest(ServletRequest request)
```

Sets the request object.

## ServletResponse

**Full Name:** `javax.servlet.ServletResponse`

**Type:** Interface

Encapsulates all information about the response generated for a request, including response headers, the status code, and the output stream. `HttpServletResponse` extends this interface for HTTP-specific features.

### Methods

#### flushBuffer

```
public void flushBuffer() throws IOException
```

Causes the buffer to be written to the client, thus committing the response.

### getBufferSize

```
public int getBufferSize()
```

Returns the actual buffer size used in the response. If buffering is turned off, returns zero.

### getCharacterEncoding

```
public String getCharacterEncoding()
```

Returns the name of the character set encoding for this response.

### getLocale

```
public Locale getLocale()
```

Returns the locale used by the response.

### getOutputStream

```
public ServletOutputStream getOutputStream()
   throws IOException
```

Returns the `ServletOutputStream` for this response. Cannot be called if `getWriter()` has already been called for this response.

### getWrite r

```
public PrintWriter getWriter() throws IOException
```

Returns a `PrintWriter` for this response. Cannot be called if `getOutputStream()` has already been called for this response

### isCommitted

```
public boolean isCommitted()
```

Returns `true` if the response has already been committed, which implies that the response already had its status code and headers written.

### reset

```
public void reset()
```

Clears any existing data in the response buffer as well as the status code and headers. If the response has been committed, throws an `IllegalStateException`.

### resetBuffer

```
public void resetBuffer()
```

Clears any existing data in the response buffer. This method differs from `reset()` in that it does not clear the status code and headers. If the response has been committed, throws an `IllegalStateException`.

### setBufferSize

```
public void setBufferSize(int size)
```

Sets the preferred buffer size for the response body. The servlet engine will use a buffer at least as large as the size requested. The actual buffer size can be retrieved with `getBufferSize()`. Must be called before any body content is written, or it will throw an `IllegalStateException`.

### setContentLength

```
public void setContentLength(int len)
```

Indicates to the client the length of the content written to the response.

### setContentType

```
public void setContentType(String type)
```

Sets the content type.

### setLocale

```
public void setLocale(Locale loc)
```

Sets the locale of the response. Must be called before `getWriter()`. The default locale is the one used by the server.

## ServletResponseWrapper

**Full Name:** `javax.servlet.ServletResponseWrapper`

**Type:** Class

**Implements:** `javax.servlet.ServletResponse`

A base class for subclasses that implement `ServletResponse`. Its default behavior is to invoke corresponding methods in the servlet engine's `ServletResponse` implementation class.

### Constructors

#### ServletResponseWrapper

```
public ServletResponseWrapper(ServletResponse response)
```

Creates a `ServletResponseWrapper` for the specified response object.

### Methods

#### flushBuffer

```
public void flushBuffer() throws IOException
```

Causes the buffer to be written to the client, thus committing the response.

#### getBufferSize

```
public int getBufferSize()
```

Returns the actual buffer size used in the response. If buffering is turned off, returns zero.

#### getCharacterEncoding

```
public String getCharacterEncoding()
```

Returns the name of the character set encoding for this response.

### getLocale

```
public Locale getLocale()
```

Returns the locale used by the response.

### getOutputStream

```
public ServletOutputStream getOutputStream()
   throws IOException
```

Returns the `ServletOutputStream` for this response. Cannot be called if `getWriter()` has already been called for this response.

### getResponse

```
public ServletResponse getResponse()
```

Returns the wrapped `ServletResponse` object.

### getWriter

```
public PrintWriter getWriter() throws IOException
```

Returns a `PrintWriter` for this response. Cannot be called if `getOutputStream()` has already been called for this response

### isCommitted

```
public boolean isCommitted()
```

Returns `true` if the response has already been committed, which implies that the response already had its status code and headers written.

### reset

```
public void reset()
```

Clears any existing data in the response buffer as well as the status code and headers. If the response has been committed, throws an `IllegalStateException`.

### resetBuffer

```
public void resetBuffer()
```

Clears any existing data in the response buffer. This method differs from `reset()` in that it does not clear the status code and headers. If the response has been committed, throws an `IllegalStateException`.

### setBufferSize

```
public void setBufferSize(int size)
```

Sets the preferred buffer size for the response body. The servlet engine will use a buffer at least as large as the size requested. The actual buffer size can be retrieved with `getBufferSize()`. Must be called before any body content is written, or it will throw an `IllegalStateException`.

### setContentLength

```
public void setContentLength(int len)
```

Indicates to the client the length of the content written to the response.

### setContentType

```
public void setContentType(String type)
```

Sets the content type.

### setLocale

```
public void setLocale(Locale loc)
```

Sets the locale of the response. Must be called before `getWriter()`. The default locale is the one used by the server.

### setResponse

```
public void setResponse(ServletResponse response)
```

Saves a reference to the `Response` object being wrapped.

## SingleThreadModel

**Full Name:** `javax.servlet.SingleThreadModel`

**Type:** Interface

An interface that can be implemented by a servlet to indicate to the servlet engine that multiple threads cannot be used to access the `service()` method concurrently. This ensures that servlets will handle only one request at a time. There are no methods in this interface; it is simply a marker to indicate that it wants this behavior.

**Note** *Although this makes a single instance of the servlet thread-safe within its own* `service()` *method, it does not prevent multiple instances from accessing external resources at the same time.*

### Methods

`SingleThreadModel` does not define any methods; it is simply a marker interface.

## UnavailableException

**Full Name:** `javax.servlet.UnavailableException`

**Type:** Class

**Extends:** `javax.servlet.ServletException`

A subclass of `ServletException` thrown by a servlet when it can no longer handle requests, either temporarily or permanently.

### Constructors

#### [deprecated] *UnavailableException*

```
public UnavailableException(int seconds, Servlet servlet, String msg)
```

No longer supported.

#### [deprecated] *UnavailableException*

```
public UnavailableException(Servlet servlet, String msg)
```

No longer supported.

### UnavailableException

```
public UnavailableException(String msg)
```

Creates a new exception with a message specifying that the servlet is permanently unavailable.

### UnavailableException

```
public UnavailableException(String msg, int seconds)
```

Creates a new exception for the servlet with the specified error message indicating that the servlet is temporarily unavailable. Accepts an integer indicating the number of seconds the servlet is expected to be unavailable. If the number is zero or negative, no estimate is available.

## Methods

### [deprecated] *getServlet*

```
public Servlet getServlet()
```

No longer supported.

### getUnavailableSeconds

```
public int getUnavailableSeconds()
```

Returns the length of time in seconds the servlet expects to be unavailable, or a negative number if the unavailability is permanent or of indeterminate length.

### isPermanent

```
public boolean isPermanent()
```

Returns `true` if the servlet is permanently unavailable.

# Package javax.servlet.http

## Cookie

**Full Name:** `javax.servlet.http.Cookie`

**Type:** Class

**Implements:** `java.lang.Cloneable`

A cookie is a small collection of key/value pairs that a servlet sends to a requester. The requester (usually a Web browser) is asked to store the information locally and return it the next time it makes a request the same URL.

Servlet engines can use cookies to store session information that is unique to a particular client. This usage is transparent to the servlet author. You can also explicitly send and receive cookies with the `HttpServletResponse.addCookie()` and `HttpServletRequest.getCookies()` methods, respectively.

*Users can refuse to accept cookies, so your application should handle this case.*

### Constructors

#### Cookie

```
public Cookie(String name, String value)
```

Creates a new cookie with the specified name and value.

### Methods

#### clone

```
public Object clone()
```

Returns a copy of the cookie.

#### getComment

```
public String getComment()
```

Returns the cookie comment.

### getDomain

```
public String getDomain()
```

Returns the cookie domain name.

### getMaxAge

```
public int getMaxAge()
```

Returns the maximum number of seconds that the cookie should be stored before it is deleted. Note that this is relative to the time that `setMaxAge()` was called, not the current time.

### getName

```
public String getName()
```

Returns the cookie name. Note that there is no `setName` method; you must set the cookie's name in the constructor.

### getPath

```
public String getPath()
```

Returns the path under which the cookie is visible. A request for any URL in that path or any of its subdirectories will cause the cookie to be returned. See RFC 2109 for more information about cookie paths.

### getSecure

```
public boolean getSecure()
```

Returns `true` if the user agent (browser) will return cookies using a secure protocol.

### getValue

```
public String getValue()
```

Returns the cookie's value.

### getVersion

```
public int getVersion()
```

Returns the cookie protocol version:

0 Original Netscape specification
1 RFC 2109 specification

### setComment

```
public void setComment(String purpose)
```

Sets the cookie's comment field to the specified string.

### setDomain

```
public void setDomain(String pattern)
```

Sets the cookie's domain. A domain can be used to restrict the cookie's visibility to a subset of servers in a particular addressing scheme. The domain name is converted to lower case before it is stored. If no domain is specified, the cookie is returned only to the server that sent it. See RFC 2109 for details.

### setMaxAge

```
public void setMaxAge(int expiry)
```

Specifies the length of time in seconds that the cookie should persist. A positive or zero value requests the browser to delete the cookie after the specified interval. A negative value requests the browser to keep the cookie active only for the duration of the current browser instance.

### setPath

```
public void setPath(String uri)
```

Specifies a path in which the cookie should be visible. If a path of `/servlet/abc` is specified, for instance, then the cookie will be returned along with any requests for a URL containing that path, e.g., `/servlet/abc/def`. If no path is specified, / is assumed. The path must include the servlet that sets the cookie. See RFC 2109 for more details about cookie paths.

### setSecure

```
public void setSecure(boolean flag)
```

Tells the user agent (browser) whether to return the cookie using a secure protocol or not.

### setValue

```
public void setValue(String newValue)
```

Sets the cookie's value to the specified string.

### setVersion

```
public void setVersion(int v)
```

Sets the cookie protocol version:

0 Original Netscape specification
1 RFC 2109 specification

## HttpServlet

| | |
|---|---|
| **Full Name:** | `javax.servlet.http.HttpServlet` |
| **Type:** | Abstract class |
| **Extends:** | `javax.servlet.GenericServlet` |
| **Implements:** | `java.io.Serializable` |

An abstract base class for servlets that operate in an HTTP environment. `HttpServlet` is a thin extension of `GenericServlet` that provides specific methods for HTTP `GET`, `POST`, `PUT`, `DELETE`, `HEAD`, `OPTIONS`, and `TRACE` requests. The `service()` method determines the HTTP request type and invokes the appropriate method.

A typical `HttpServlet` subclass will override `doGet()`, `doPost()`, or both, but not `service()`.

## Constructors

### HttpServlet

```
public HttpServlet()
```

Default (empty) constructor. Performs no work. All servlet initialization should be performed in the `init()` method inherited from `GenericServlet`.

## Methods

### doDelete

```
protected void doDelete(
      HttpServletRequest req,
      HttpServletResponse resp)
   throws ServletException, IOException
```

Handles an HTTP `DELETE` request. As with `doPut()`, this type of request is not generally initiated directly by a Web browser.

### doGet

```
protected void doGet(
      HttpServletRequest req,
      HttpServletResponse resp)
   throws ServletException, IOException
```

Handles an HTTP `GET` request. By default, does nothing except return an error indicating that the servlet does not handle the `GET` method. Servlet authors that override `doGet()` will typically perform the following steps:

1. Read and handle `HttpServletRequest` parameters.
2. Get an output stream by calling either `getWriter()` or `getOutputStream()` in the `HttpServletResponse` object.
3. Set the `Content-Type` header in the response object.
4. Write the output HTML page.

### doHead

```
protected void doHead(
      HttpServletRequest req,
      HttpServletResponse resp)
   throws ServletException, IOException
```

Handles an HTTP `HEAD` request. This is functionally similar to the `GET` request, except that no response body is returned, only status and headers.

### doOptions

```
protected void doOptions(
      HttpServletRequest req,
      HttpServletResponse resp)
   throws ServletException, IOException
```

Handles an HTTP `OPTIONS` request and returns a list of methods that the HTTP server supports. This method is generally not overridden.

### doPost

```
protected void doPost(
      HttpServletRequest req,
      HttpServletResponse resp)
   throws ServletException, IOException
```

Handles an HTTP `POST` request. By default, does nothing except return an error indicating that the servlet does not handle the `POST` method. Servlet authors that override `doPost()` will typically perform the following steps:

1. Read and handle `HttpServletRequest` parameters.
2. Get an output stream by calling either `getWriter()` or `getOutputStream()` in the `HttpServletResponse` object.
3. Set the `Content-Type` header in the response object.
4. Write the output HTML page.

### doPut

```
protected void doPut(
      HttpServletRequest req,
      HttpServletResponse resp)
   throws ServletException, IOException
```

Handles an HTTP `PUT` request. The name of the resource to be written can be found by calling the request object's `getRequestURI()` method, and the resource data itself can be read from the request object's input stream. HTML forms do not support the `PUT` method; this type of request is not generally initiated directly by a Web browser.

### doTrace

```
protected void doTrace(
      HttpServletRequest req,
      HttpServletResponse resp)
   throws ServletException, IOException
```

Handles an HTTP `TRACE` request and echoes back the request headers. This method is generally not overridden.

### getLastModified

```
protected long getLastModified(HttpServletRequest req)
```

Returns the time (in milliseconds since January 1, 1970) that the request object was last modified, or -1 if the time is not known. The default implementation always returns -1.

### service

```
protected void service(
      HttpServletRequest req,
      HttpServletResponse resp)
  throws ServletException, IOException
```

The main entry point for HTTP requests. This method determines the request method (`GET`, `POST`, etc.) and dispatches the request to the appropriate handler method (`doGet()`, `doPost()`, etc.) In the case of the `GET` method, it tries to determine if the resource has been modified since it was last requested. If not, it returns just an HTTP `NOT_MODIFIED` status line. This method is generally not overridden.

### service

```
public void service(
      ServletRequest req,
      ServletResponse res)
   throws ServletException, IOException
```

A convenience method that converts a protocol-neutral request to an HTTP request, if possible, and then invokes the HTTP-specific `service()` method.

# HttpServletRequest

**Full Name:** `javax.servlet.http.HttpServletRequest`

**Type:** Interface

**Superinterface:** `javax.servlet.ServletRequest`

Encapsulates all information about an HTTP request: its parameters, attributes, headers, and input data.

## Methods

### getAuthType

```
public String getAuthType()
```

If the server uses an authentication scheme like `BASIC` or `SSL`, returns the name of this scheme, otherwise returns `null`.

### getContextPath

```
public String getContextPath()
```

Returns the portion of the request URI that specifies the servlet context (application). The path starts with but does not end with a "/" character.

### getCookies

```
public Cookie[] getCookies()
```

Returns an array containing all of the Cookie objects the client sent with this request. Returns null if no cookies were sent.

### getDateHeader

```
public long getDateHeader(String name)
```

Given a request header name, converts the corresponding header value into a Date object, which is returned as a long value (the number of milliseconds since January 1, 1970). If the specified request header does not exist, returns -1.

### getHeader

```
public String getHeader(String name)
```

Returns the string value of the specified request header, or null if the named header is not found in the request.

### getHeaderNames

```
public Enumeration getHeaderNames()
```

Returns an Enumeration of all the header names found in this request. If there are no headers, returns either null or an empty Enumeration, depending on the servlet engine.

### getHeaders

```
public Enumeration getHeaders(String name)
```

For headers that can occur multiple times in a request, this method will return an Enumeration of the header values.

### getIntHeade

```
public int getIntHeader(String name)
```

Given a request header name, converts the corresponding header value into an integer and returns the integer value. If the specified request header does not exist, returns -1.

### getMethod

```
public String getMethod()
```

Returns the HTTP method contained in the first line of the request, e.g., GET or POST.

### getPathInfo

```
public String getPathInfo()
```

Returns the substring of the request URL that follows the servlet name, or null if there is no additional path information. Same as the CGI variable PATH_INFO.

### getPathTranslated

```
public String getPathTranslated()
```

Returns the substring of the request URL that follows the servlet name converted to a real filesystem path, or null if there is no additional path information. Same as the CGI variable PATH_TRANSLATED.

### getQueryString

```
public String getQueryString()
```

Returns the substring of the request URL that follows the "?", or null if there is no query string. Usually found only in GET requests. Same as the CGI variable QUERY_STRING.

### getRemoteUser

```
public String getRemoteUser()
```

Returns the user name, if HTTP authentication is active and the user had logged in. Returns null otherwise. Same as the CGI variable REMOTE_USER.

### getRequestedSessionId

```
public String getRequestedSessionId()
```

Returns the value of the session ID returned by the client. Usually the same as the current session, but may refer to an old expired session. Returns `null` if the request does not specify a session ID.

### getRequestURI

```
public String getRequestURI()
```

Returns the substring of the request URL starting with the protocol name ( e.g., `http://` ) if present, and extending to but not including the query string (which starts with "?").

### getRequestURL

```
public StringBuffer getRequestURL()
```

Reconstructs the entire URL used for the request. Includes the protocol, server name, port number (if other than the default), and file name. Does not include the query string.

### getServletPath

```
public String getServletPath()
```

Returns the part of this request's URL that calls the servlet. This includes either the servlet name or a path to the servlet, but does not include any extra path information or a query string. Same as the value of the CGI variable SCRIPT_NAME.

### getSession

```
public HttpSession getSession()
```

A convenience method that returns the value of `HttpSession.getSession(true)`.

### getSession

```
public HttpSession getSession(boolean create)
```

Returns the current `HttpSession` object or creates a new one (if the `create` parameter is `true`). The returned value depends on whether the session already exists and whether the `create` parameter is `true` or `false`:

| Session Exists | `create` | Returned |
|---|---|---|
| false | `false` | `null` |
| false | `true` | new session |
| true | `false` | existing session |
| true | `true` | existing session |

### getUserPrincipal

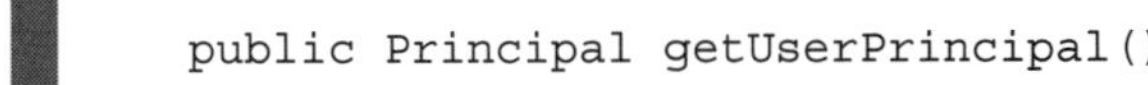

```
public Principal getUserPrincipal()
```

If the user has been authenticated, returns a `java.security.Principal` object for the user. Otherwise, the method returns `null`.

### isRequestedSessionIdFromCookie

```
public boolean isRequestedSessionIdFromCookie()
```

Returns `true` if the request session ID was received from a `Cookie` as opposed to being sent as part of the request URL.

### [deprecated] *isRequestedSessionIdFromUrl*

```
public boolean isRequestedSessionIdFromUrl()
```

No longer supported. Use `isRequestedSessionIdFromURL()` instead.

### isRequestedSessionIdFromURL

```
public boolean isRequestedSessionIdFromURL()
```

Returns `true` if the requested session ID came in as part of the request URL as opposed to being sent from a `Cookie`.

### isRequestedSessionIdValid

```
public boolean isRequestedSessionIdValid()
```

Returns `true` if the request specifies the ID of a valid, active session.

### isUserInRole

```
public boolean isUserInRole(String role)
```

Returns `true` if the authenticated user is included in the specified logical "role" in the deployment descriptor.

# HttpServletRequestWrapper

| | |
|---|---|
| **Full Name:** | `javax.servlet.http.HttpServletRequestWrapper` |
| **Type:** | Class |
| **Extends:** | `javax.servlet.ServletRequestWrapper` |
| **Implements:** | `javax.servlet.http.HttpServletRequest` |

This class is a concrete implementation of `HttpServletRequest` which can be overriden in servlet-engine-neutral way to provide additional functionality to the request object. By default, looks through to the corresponding servlet-engine-specific methods.

## Constructors

### HttpServletRequestWrapper

```
public HttpServletRequestWrapper(HttpServletRequest request)
```

Creates a request object wrapping the given request.

## Methods

### getAuthType

```
public String getAuthType()
```

If the server uses an authentication scheme like `BASIC` or `SSL`, returns the name of this scheme, otherwise returns `null`.

### getContextPath

```
public String getContextPath()
```

Returns the portion of the request URI that specifies the servlet context (application). The path starts with but does not end with a "/" character.

### getCookies

```
public Cookie getCookies()
```

Returns an array containing all of the `Cookie` objects the client sent with this request. Returns `null` if no cookies were sent.

### getDateHeader

```
public long getDateHeader(String name)
```

Given a request header name, converts the corresponding header value into a `Date` object, which is returned as a `long` value (the number of milliseconds since January 1, 1970). If the specified request header does not exist, returns -1.

### getHeader

```
public String getHeader(String name)
```

Returns the string value of the specified request header, or `null` if the named header is not found in the request.

### getHeaderNames

```
public Enumeration getHeaderNames()
```

Returns an `Enumeration` of all the header names found in this request. If there are no headers, returns either `null` or an empty `Enumeration`, depending on the servlet engine.

### getHeaders

```
public Enumeration getHeaders(String name)
```

For headers that can occur multiple times in a request, this method will return an `Enumeration` of the header values.

### getIntHeader

```
public int getIntHeader(String name)
```

Given a request header name, converts the corresponding header value into an integer and returns the integer value. If the specified request header does not exist, returns -1.

### getMethod

```
public String getMethod()
```

Returns the HTTP method contained in the first line of the request, e.g., `GET` or `POST`.

### getPathInfo

```
public String getPathInfo()
```

Returns the substring of the request URL that follows the servlet name, or `null` if there is no additional path information. Same as the CGI variable `PATH_INFO`.

### getPathTranslated

```
public String getPathTranslated()
```

Returns the substring of the request URL that follows the servlet name converted to a real filesystem path, or `null` if there is no additional path information. Same as the CGI variable `PATH_TRANSLATED`.

### getQueryString

```
public String getQueryString()
```

Returns the substring of the request URL that follows the "?", or `null` if there is no query string. Usually found only in `GET` requests. Same as the CGI variable `QUERY_STRING`.

### getRemoteUser

```
public String getRemoteUser()
```

Returns the user name, if HTTP authentication is active and the user had logged in. Returns `null` otherwise. Same as the CGI variable `REMOTE_USER`.

### getRequestedSessionId

```
public String getRequestedSessionId()
```

Returns the value of the session ID returned by the client. Usually the same as the current session, but may refer to an old expired session. Returns `null` if the request does not specify a session ID.

### getRequestURI

```
public String getRequestURI()
```

Returns the substring of the request URL starting with the protocol name ( e.g., `http://` ) if present, and extending to but not including the query string (which starts with "?").

### getRequestURL

```
public StringBuffer getRequestURL()
```

Reconstructs the entire URL used for the request. Includes the protocol, server name, port number (if other than the default), and file name. Does not include the query string.

### getServletPath

```
public String getServletPath()
```

Returns the part of this request's URL that calls the servlet. This includes either the servlet name or a path to the servlet, but does not include any extra path information or a query string. Same as the value of the CGI variable `SCRIPT_NAME`.

### getSession

```
public HttpSession getSession()
```

A convenience method that returns the value of `HttpSession.getSession(true)`.

### getSession

```
public HttpSession getSession(boolean create)
```

Returns the current `HttpSession` object or creates a new one (if the `create` parameter is `true`). The returned value depends on whether the session already exists and whether the `create` parameter is `true` or `false`:

### getUserPrincipal

```
public Principal getUserPrincipal()
```

If the user has been authenticated, returns a `java.security.Principal` object for the user. Otherwise, the method returns `null`.

### isRequestedSessionIdFromCookie

```
public boolean isRequestedSessionIdFromCookie()
```

Returns `true` if the request session ID was received from a `Cookie` as opposed to being sent as part of the request URL.

### isRequestedSessionIdFromUrl

```
public boolean isRequestedSessionIdFromUrl()
```

Returns the value of the deprecated `isRequestedSessionIdFromUrl()` method on the wrapped request object.

### isRequestedSessionIdFromURL

```
public boolean isRequestedSessionIdFromURL()
```

Returns `true` if the requested session ID came in as part of the request URL as opposed to being sent from a `Cookie`.

### isRequestedSessionIdValid

```
public boolean isRequestedSessionIdValid()
```

Returns `true` if the request specifies the ID of a valid, active session.

### isUserInRole

```
public boolean isUserInRole(String role
```

Returns `true` if the authenticated user is included in the specified logical "role" in the deployment descriptor.

# HttpServletResponse

**Full Name:** `javax.servlet.http.HttpServletResponse`

**Type:** Interface

**Superinterface:** `javax.servlet.ServletResponse`

Encapsulates all information about the response generated for an HTTP request, including response headers, the status code, and the output stream.

## Methods

### addCookie

```
public void addCookie(Cookie cookie)
```

Writes a `Set-Cookie` header for the specified `Cookie.`

### addDateHeader

```
public void addDateHeader(String name, long date)
```

Writes a date header for an HTTP header that can have multiple values.

### addHeader

```
public void addHeader(String name, String value)
```

Writes a general header for an HTTP header that can have multiple values.

### addIntHeader

```
public void addIntHeader(String name, int value)
```

Writes an integer header for an HTTP header that can have multiple values.

### containsHeader

```
public boolean containsHeader(String name)
```

Returns `true` if the response already contains a header with the specified name.

### [deprecated] *encodeRedirectUrl*

```
public String encodeRedirectUrl(String url)
```

No longer supported.

### encodeRedirectURL

```
public String encodeRedirectURL(String url)
```

Supports session tracking by optionally appending the encoded session ID as a parameter in a URL intended to be used with `sendRedirect()`. This is not necessary if the client supports cookies. The servlet engine makes this determination; it is always safe to filter URLs to be written through this method.

### [deprecated] *encodeUrl*

```
public String encodeUrl(String url)
```

No longer supported.

### encodeURL

```
public String encodeURL(String url)
```

Supports session tracking by appending the encoded session ID as a parameter in the specified URL if necessary. This is not necessary if the client supports cookies. The servlet engine makes this determination; it is always safe to filter URLs to be written through this method.

### sendError

```
public void sendError(int sc) throws IOException
```

Sets the HTTP status code to the specified value. The response object is committed after this method is called; any further writing to it has no effect.

### sendError

```
public void sendError(int sc, String msg) throws IOException
```

Sets the HTTP status code to the specified value and sets the status message. The response object is committed after this method is called; any further writing to it has no effect.

### sendRedirect

```
public void sendRedirect(String location) throws IOException
```

Sets the HTTP status code to 302 (moved temporarily) and writes a `Location` header with the specified value. The user agent (Web browser) will usually interpret this response and request the new URL automatically.

### setDateHeader

```
public void setDateHeader(String name, long date)
```

Writes a response header with the specified name and a correctly formatted date value.

### setHeader

```
public void setHeader(String name, String value)
```

Writes a response header with the specified name and value.

### setIntHeader

```
public void setIntHeader(String name, int value)
```

Writes a response header with the specified name and a string-formatted integer value.

### setStatus

```
public void setStatus(int sc)
```

Sets the status code for this response.

#### [deprecated] *setStatus*

```
public void setStatus(int sc, String sm)
```

No longer supported.

## HttpServletResponseWrapper

| | |
|---|---|
| **Full Name:** | `javax.servlet.http.HttpServletResponseWrapper` |
| **Type:** | Class |
| **Extends:** | `javax.servlet.ServletResponseWrapper` |
| **Implements:** | `javax.servlet.http.HttpServletResponse` |

A concrete implementation of `HttpServletResponse` which can be extended to allow customization of the response object. By default, methods in this class look through to their counterparts in the servlet engine's implementation class.

### Constructors

#### HttpServletResponseWrapper

```
public HttpServletResponseWrapper(HttpServletResponse response)
```

Creates a response adapter wrapping the specified response.

### Methods

#### addCookie

```
public void addCookie(Cookie cookie)
```

Writes a `Set-Cookie` header for the specified `Cookie`.

#### addDateHeader

```
public void addDateHeader(String name, long date)
```

Writes a date header for an HTTP header that can have multiple values.

### addHeader

```
public void addHeader(String name, String value)
```

Writes a general header for an HTTP header that can have multiple values.

### addIntHeader

```
public void addIntHeader(String name, int value)
```

Writes an integer header for an HTTP header that can have multiple values.

### containsHeade

```
public boolean containsHeader(String name)
```

Returns `true` if the response already contains a header with the specified name.

### encodeRedirectUrl

```
public String encodeRedirectUrl(String url)
```

Invokes the deprecated `encodeRedirectUrl()` method in the servlet-engine-specific class.

### encodeRedirectURL

```
public String encodeRedirectURL(String url)
```

Supports session tracking by optionally appending the encoded session ID as a parameter in a URL intended to be used with `sendRedirect()`. This is not necessary if the client supports cookies. The servlet engine makes this determination; it is always safe to filter URLs to be written through this method.

### encodeUrl

```
public String encodeUrl(String url)
```

Invokes deprecated `encodeUrl(String url)` method in the servlet-engine-specific class.

### encodeURL

```
public String encodeURL(String url)
```

Supports session tracking by appending the encoded session ID as a parameter in the specified URL if necessary. This is not necessary if the client supports cookies. The servlet engine makes this determination; it is always safe to filter URLs to be written through this method.

### sendError

```
public void sendError(int sc) throws IOException
```

Sets the HTTP status code to the specified value. The response object is committed after this method is called; any further writing to it has no effect.

### sendError

```
public void sendError(int sc, String msg) throws IOException
```

Sets the HTTP status code to the specified value and sets the status message. The response object is committed after this method is called; any further writing to it has no effect.

### sendRedirect

```
public void sendRedirect(String location) throws IOException
```

Sets the HTTP status code to 302 (moved temporarily) and writes a `Location` header with the specified value. The user agent (Web browser) will usually interpret this response and request the new URL automatically.

### setDateHeader

```
public void setDateHeader(String name, long date)
```

Writes a response header with the specified name and a correctly formatted date value.

### setHeader

```
public void setHeader(String name, String value)
```

Writes a response header with the specified name and value.

### setIntHeader

```
public void setIntHeader(String name, int value)
```

Writes a response header with the specified name and a string-formatted integer value.

### setStatus

```
public void setStatus(int sc)
```

Sets the status code for this response.

### setStatus

```
public void setStatus(int sc, String sm)
```

Invokes the deprecated `setStatus(int sc, String sm)` method in the servlet-engine-specific class.

## HttpSession

**Full Name:** `javax.servlet.http.HttpSession`

**Type:** Interface

An `HttpSession` is a repository of named references to objects belonging to a user's browser session. This repository remains active in the server between user requests. A session has a unique session ID assigned by the server that the client keeps track of and passes back with each subsequent request.

A session is created by calling the `HttpServletRequest.getSession(true)` or `HttpServletRequest.getSession()` method. The session ID is then passed to the client either by a cookie or as a parameter in a generated URL. The session is considered "new" until the client joins it, that is, until the client passes back the session ID in a subsequent request. The `isNew()` method can be used to determine this.

Objects are stored in the session using the `setAttribute()` method, and can be retrieved with the `getAttribute()` method. If an object in a session implements the `HttpSessionBindingListener` interface, it will be notified whenever it is bound to or unbound from a session.

## Methods

### getAttribute

```
public Object getAttribute(String name)
```

Returns the object with the specified name if it exists in the session, or `null` if it does not.

### getAttributeNames

```
public Enumeration getAttributeNames()
```

Returns an `Enumeration` of the names of all the objects bound to this session.

### getCreationTime

```
public long getCreationTime()
```

Returns the time the session was created in milliseconds from January 1, 1970.

### getId

```
public String getId()
```

Returns the session identifier.

### getLastAccessedTime

```
public long getLastAccessedTime()
```

Returns the time the session was last accessed in milliseconds from January 1, 1970.

### getMaxInactiveInterval

```
public int getMaxInactiveInterval()
```

Returns the maximum number of seconds this session can remain active between requests. If the time interval is exceeded, the servlet engine is permitted to terminate it.

*Some servlet engines erroneously treat this value as milliseconds or minutes. You should verify this method's operation if you depend on it being correct.*

### [deprecated] *getSessionContext*

```
public HttpSessionContext getSessionContext()
```

No longer supported.

### [deprecated] *getValue*

```
public Object getValue(String name)
```

No longer supported. Use `getAttribute(String name)` instead.

### [deprecated] *getValueNames*

```
public String getValueNames()
```

No longer supported. Use `getAttributeNames()` instead.

### invalidate

```
public void invalidate()
```

Closes the session, calling `valueUnbound()` for any `HttpSessionBindingListener` objects bound to the session.

### isNew

```
public boolean isNew()
```

Returns `true` if a session has been created but the client has not yet issued a request with that session ID.

### [deprecated] *putValue*

```
public void putValue(String name, Object value)
```

No longer supported. Use `setAttribute(String name, Object value)` instead.

### removeAttribute

```
public void removeAttribute(String name)
```

Removes a reference to an object in the session with the specified name. If the object implements the `HttpSessionBindingListener` interface, the servlet engine calls its `valueUnbound()` method. Ignored if the specified value does not exist in the session.

### [deprecated] *removeValue*

```
public void removeValue(String name)
```

No longer supported. Use `removeAttribute(String name)` instead.

### setAttribute

```
public void setAttribute(String name, Object value)
```

Stores a reference to an object in the session under the specified name. If the object implements the `HttpSessionBindingListener` interface, the servlet engine calls its `valueBound()` method.

### setMaxInactiveInterval

```
public void setMaxInactiveInterval(int interval)
```

Specifies the maximum number of seconds this session can remain active between requests. If the time interval is exceeded, the servlet engine is permitted to terminate it.

*Some servlet engines erroneously treat this value as milliseconds or minutes. You should verify this method's operation if you depend on it being correct.*

## HttpSessionActivationListener

**Full Name:** `javax.servlet.http.HttpSessionActivationListener`

**Type:** Interface

Objects can register to receive notification of session activation and passivation events by implementing this interface.

### Methods

#### sessionDidActivate

```
public void sessionDidActivate(HttpSessionEvent se)
```

Will be called when the session has just been activated.

#### sessionWillPassivate

```
public void sessionWillPassivate(HttpSessionEvent se)
```

Will be called when the session is about to be passivated.

## HttpSessionAttributesListener

**Full Name:** `javax.servlet.http.HttpSessionAttributesListener`

**Type:** Interface

**Superinterface:** `java.util.EventListener`

Objects can register to receive notification of attribute add/remove events by implementing this interface.

### Methods

#### attributeAdded

```
public void attributeAdded(HttpSessionBindingEvent se)
```

Will be called when an attribute has been added to a session.

#### attributeRemoved

```
public void attributeRemoved(HttpSessionBindingEvent se)
```

Will be called when an attribute has been removed from a session.

### attributeReplaced

```
public void attributeReplaced(HttpSessionBindingEvent se)
```

Will be called when an attribute has been replaced in a session.

# HttpSessionBindingEvent

**Full Name:** `javax.servlet.http.HttpSessionBindingEvent`

**Type:** Class

**Extends:** `javax.servlet.http.HttpSessionEvent`

An event object that is passed as a parameter to the `valueBound()` and `valueUnbound()` methods of an `HttpSessionBindingListener`. Using methods in the event object, the `HttpSessionBindingListener` can get the name by which it was bound and a reference to the `HttpSession` itself.

## Constructors

### HttpSessionBindingEvent

```
public HttpSessionBindingEvent
   (HttpSession session, String name)
```

Creates a new `HttpSessionBindingEvent` object for the specified session. The name parameter indicates the name by which the listening object was bound to the session.

### HttpSessionBindingEvent

```
public HttpSessionBindingEvent
   (HttpSession session, String name, Object value)
```

Creates a new `HttpSessionBindingEvent` object for the specified session. The name parameter indicates the name by which the listening object was bound to the session, and the value parameter contains its value.

## Methods

### getName

```
public String getName()
```

Returns the name by which the object is known to the session.

### getSession

```
public HttpSession getSession()
```

Returns the session to which the listener object was bound or unbound.

### getValue

```
public Object getValue()
```

Returns the value of the attribute being added, changed, or deleted.

# HttpSessionBindingListener

**Full Name:** `javax.servlet.http.HttpSessionBindingListener`

**Type:** Interface

**Superinterface:** `java.util.EventListener`

Objects that implement this interface are notified when they are bound to or unbound from an `HttpSession`. The object must provide `valueBound()` and `valueUnbound()` methods, each of which have a `HttpSessionBindingEvent` parameter that allows the object to determine its name and the session to which it belongs.

## Methods

### valueBound

```
public void valueBound(HttpSessionBindingEvent event)
```

Called when an object is bound to a session.

### valueUnbound

```
public void valueUnbound(HttpSessionBindingEvent event)
```

Called when an object is unbound from a session.

# HttpSessionContext

**Full Name:** `javax.servlet.http.HttpSessionContext`

**Type:** Interface

Formerly used to allow direct interservlet communication, this class is now deprecated.

## Methods

### [deprecated] *getIds*

```
public Enumeration getIds()
```

No longer supported.

### [deprecated] *getSession*

```
public HttpSession getSession(String sessionId)
```

No longer supported.

# HttpSessionEvent

**Full Name:** `javax.servlet.http.HttpSessionEvent`

**Type:** Class

**Extends:** `java.util.EventObject`

Represents an event notification for changes to sessions in a web application.

## Constructors

### HttpSessionEvent

```
public HttpSessionEvent(HttpSession source)
```

Creates a new session event from the specified source.

### Methods

#### getSession

```
public HttpSession getSession()
```

Returns a reference to the session that changed.

## HttpSessionListener

**Full Name:** `javax.servlet.http.HttpSessionListener`

**Type:** Interface

Classes that implement HttpSessionListener receive notification when sessions are created or invalidated.

### Methods

#### sessionCreated

```
public void sessionCreated(HttpSessionEvent se)
```

Called when a new session is created.

#### sessionDestroyed

```
public void sessionDestroyed(HttpSessionEvent se)
```

Called when a session is invalidated.

## HttpUtils

**Full Name:** `javax.servlet.http.HttpUtils`

**Type:** Class

A utility class providing methods useful in HTTP servlets.

## Constructors

### HttpUtils

```
public HttpUtils()
```

Creates a new `HttpUtils` object.

## Methods

### getRequestURL

```
public static StringBuffer getRequestURL
   (HttpServletRequest req)
```

Returns the entire URL used for the specified request. Includes the protocol, server name, port number (if other than the default), and file name. Does not include the query string.

### parsePostData

```
public static Hashtable parsePostData
   (int len, ServletInputStream in)
```

Reads the servlet request input stream for the specified length and parses it into key/value pairs by calling `parseQueryString()`.

### parseQueryString

```
public static Hashtable parseQueryString(String s)
```

Given a query string containing URLEncoded parameters and values, returns a `Hashtable` containing the parsed names and values. In the hashtable, the parameter name is the key and the corresponding value is an array of strings. If the parameter occurs only once, the array length is one; otherwise, there are multiple entries in the array. See `java.net.URLEncoder` for specifics of how the decoding is done.

The Complete Reference

# Appendix B

## JSP API Version 1.2

This appendix describes each class in the two JSP packages:

- `javax.servlet.jsp` Base JavaServer Page classes
- `javax.servlet.jsp.tagext` JSP custom tags

For each class, the following sections are included:

- Class name
- Context (full name, type, superclass, interfaces implemented)
- Class description
- Details of each method in the class

**Note** *The classes and methods described here are based on the proposed final draft of the JSP 1.2 specification. Although the final draft is likely to be very close to the official specification, there may be changes. Consult the latest version of the specification at http://java.sun.com/products/jsp if in doubt.*

# Package javax.servlet.jsp

## HttpJspPage

**Full Name:** `javax.servlet.jsp.HttpJspPage`

**Type:** Interface

**Superinterface:** `javax.servlet.jsp.JspPage`

A subinterface of `JspPage` that is implemented by HTTP-specific classes generated by a JSP engine. The JSP engine will automatically create a `_jspService()` method that contains all the scriptlet code defined in the page. The JSP author should not override this method.

### Methods

#### _jspService

L B-1

```
public void _jspService(
      HttpServletRequest request,
      HttpServletResponse response)
   throws ServletException, IOException
```

The body of the JSP page. The JSP author must *not* define this method, since it will be defined by the servlet code generated by the JSP container. `_jspService()` is where scriptlets are executed and where HTML template output is produced.

# JspEngineInfo

**Full Name:** `javax.servlet.jsp.JspEngineInfo`

**Type:** Abstract class

A class that provides information about the JSP engine. An instance of this class is returned by the `JspFactory.getEngineInfo()` method.

**Note** *This class is designed primarily for use by JSP engine developers.*

## Constructors

### JspEngineInfo

2

```
public JspEngineInfo()
```

Creates a new `JspEngineInfo` object.

## Methods

### getSpecificationVersion

3

```
public abstract String getSpecificationVersion()
```

Returns the JSP specification version supported by the JSP engine.

# JspException

**Full Name:** `javax.servlet.jsp.JspException`

**Type:** Class

**Extends:** `java.lang.Exception`

The generic base class for JSP exceptions. A number of methods in the custom tags classes throw this exception.

## Constructors

### JspException

L B-4

```
public JspException()
```

Creates a new `JspException` with no associated error message.

### JspException

L B-5

```
public JspException(String msg)
```

Creates a new `JspException` with the specified message.

### JspException

L B-6

```
public JspException(String message, Throwable rootCause)
```

Creates a new `JspException` with the specified message and associates the specified root cause exception with it.

### JspException

L B-7

```
public JspException(Throwable rootCause)
```

Creates a new `JspException` associated with the specified root cause exception.

## Methods

### getRootCause

L B-8

```
public Throwable getRootCause()
```

Returns the exception that caused this `JspException`.

# JspFactory

**Full Name:** `javax.servlet.jsp.JspFactory`

**Type:** Abstract class

A class that provides factory methods for creating the objects necessary to support the JSP environment. Includes a static method for assigning the default `JspFactory`.

*This class is designed primarily for use by JSP engine developers.*

## Constructors

### JspFactory

```
9   public JspFactory()
```

Creates a new `JspFactory` object.

## Methods

### getDefaultFactory

```
10   public static synchronized JspFactory getDefaultFactory()
```

Returns the currently registered `JspFactory` object.

### getEngineInfo

```
11   public abstract JspEngineInfo getEngineInfo()
```

Returns the `JspEngineInfo` object for this JSP implementation.

### getPageContext

```
12   public abstract PageContext getPageContext(
        Servlet servlet,
        ServletRequest request,
        ServletResponse response,
        String errorPageURL,
        boolean needsSession,
        int buffer,
        boolean autoflush)
```

Returns the `PageContext` object. Calling this method causes the `PageContext.initialize()` method to be invoked and causes the following attributes to be set:

- The requesting servlet
- The `ServletConfig` for the requesting servlet
- The `ServletRequest` object
- The `ServletResponse` object
- The URL of the JSP's error page, if one was specified
- Whether the JSP needs an HTTP session
- The buffer size
- Whether the buffer should be autoflushed on overflow.

These resources are released when the `releasePageContext()` method is called.

*A call to this method is automatically generated by the JSP engine and should not be coded by the JSP author.*

#### releasePageContext

L B-13 

```
public abstract void releasePageContext(PageContext pc)
```

Releases the `PageContext`, including any resources obtained when `getPageContext()` was invoked.

*A call to this method is automatically generated by the JSP engine and should not be coded by the JSP author.*

#### setDefaultFactory

L B-14 

```
public static synchronized void setDefaultFactory(JspFactory factory)
```

Sets the default `JspFactory` object. Should only be called by the JSP engine itself.

## JspPage

**Full Name:** `javax.servlet.jsp.JspPage`

**Type:** Interface

**Superinterface:** `javax.servlet.Servlet`

A subinterface of `Servlet` that is implemented by classes generated by a JSP engine. The `jspInit()` and `jspDestroy()` methods can be overridded by the JSP author to perform what the `Servlet init()` and `destroy()` methods do.

## Methods

### jspDestroy

```
public void jspDestroy()
```

A method invoked when the generated JSP servlet is destroyed. If used, it must be defined within a JSP declaration.This method should be overridden instead of `destroy()`.

### jspInit

```
public void jspInit()
```

A method invoked when the generated JSP servlet is initialized. If used, it must be defined within a JSP declaration.This method should be overridden instead of `init()`.

# JspTagException

| | |
|---|---|
| **Full Name:** | `javax.servlet.jsp.JspTagException` |
| **Type:** | Class |
| **Extends:** | `javax.servlet.jsp.JspException` |

A subinterface of `JspException` used in tag handlers to indicate a fatal error.

## Constructors

### JspTagException

```
public JspTagException()
```

Creates a new `JspTagException` with no associated message.

### JspTagException

```
public JspTagException(String msg)
```

Creates a new `JspTagException` with the specified message.

APPENDIXES

## Methods

# JspWriter

**Full Name:** `javax.servlet.jsp.JspWriter`

**Type:** Abstract class

**Extends:** `java.io.Writer`

A subclass of `java.io.Writer` that is used to write JSP output. Its role is primarily the same as `java.io.PrintWriter`. This class is instantiated by the generated `_jspService()` by calling the underlying servlet's `getWriter()` method, which makes it illegal later to call `getOutputStream()`.

The `out` implicit variable is an instance of this class.

## Methods

### clear

L B-19

```
public abstract void clear() throws IOException
```

Clears the page buffer. Throws an `IOException` if the buffer has already been cleared (i.e., if a full buffer of data has already been written to the output stream).

### clearBuffer

L B-20 

```
public abstract void clearBuffer() throws IOException
```

Clears the page buffer. Does not throw an IOException.

### close

L B-21 

```
public abstract void close() throws IOException
```

Flushes and closes the stream.

### flush

L B-22 

```
public abstract void flush() throws IOException
```

Flushes the output stream.

### getBufferSize

23
```
public int getBufferSize()
```

Returns the actual buffer size used.

### getRemaining

24
```
public abstract int getRemaining()
```

Returns the number of unused bytes remaining in the buffer.

### isAutoFlush

25
```
public boolean isAutoFlush()
```

Returns an indication of whether the JSP `autoFlush` flag is set.

### newLine

26
```
public abstract void newLine() throws IOException
```

Writes the system `line.separator` string.

### print

27
```
public abstract void print(boolean b) throws IOException
```

Prints a boolean value.

### print

28
```
public abstract void print(char c) throws IOException
```

Prints a character value.

### print

29
```
public abstract void print(char[] s) throws IOException
```

Prints an array of characters.

### print

L B-30

```
public abstract void print(double d) throws IOException
```

Prints a double-precision floating-point number.

### print

L B-31

```
public abstract void print(float f) throws IOException
```

Prints a single-precision floating-point number.

### print

L B-32

```
public abstract void print(int i) throws IOException
```

Prints an integer value.

### print

L B-33

```
public abstract void print(long l) throws IOException
```

Prints a long integer value.

### print

L B-34

```
public abstract void print(Object obj) throws IOException
```

Prints an object using its `toString()` method.

### print

L B-35

```
public abstract void print(String s) throws IOException
```

Prints a string.

### println

L B-36

```
public abstract void println() throws IOException
```

Prints the system `line.separator` character(s).

### println

37 `public abstract void println(boolean x) throws IOException`

Prints a boolean value followed by a newline.

### println

38 `public abstract void println(char x) throws IOException`

Prints a character value followed by a newline.

### println

39 `public abstract void println(char[] x) throws IOException`

Prints an array of characters followed by a newline.

### println

40 `public abstract void println(double x) throws IOException`

Prints a double-precision floating-point number followed by a newline.

### println

41 `public abstract void println(float x) throws IOException`

Prints a single-precision floating-point number followed by a newline.

### println

42 `public abstract void println(int x) throws IOException`

Prints an integer followed by a newline.

### println

43 `public abstract void println(long x) throws IOException`

Prints a long integer followed by a newline.

### println

L B-44
```
public abstract void println(Object x) throws IOException
```

Prints an object followed by a newline.

### println

L B-45
```
public abstract void println(String x) throws IOException
```

Prints a string followed by a newline

# PageContext

**Full Name:** `javax.servlet.jsp.PageContext`

**Type:** Abstract class

`PageContext` is a wrapper object that encapsulates all the details of a single invocation of a JSP to handle a request. It contains methods to initialize and release the session, writer, request, and response objects. It also provides methods to set and retrieve attributes in the various namespaces accessible to the JSP.

A `PageContext` object is created and initialized by the `JSPFactory` when its `getPageContext()` method is called and released when its `releasePageContext()` is called. These two method calls are automatically performed by code generated by the JSP engine.

## Constructors

### PageContext

L B-46
```
public PageContext()
```

Creates a new `PageContext` object.

## Methods

### findAttribute

L B-47
```
public abstract Object findAttribute(String name)
```

Searches the page, request, session, and application scopes (in that order) for the specified attribute, returning the value of the first match. If the attribute does not exist in any scope, returns `null`.

### forward

48
```
public abstract void forward(String relativeUrlPath)
   throws ServletException, IOException
```

Calls the `forward()` method associated with a `RequestDispatcher` for this servlet. See `javax.servlet.RequestDispatcher` for details.

### getAttribute

49
```
public abstract Object getAttribute(String name)
```

Returns the specified attribute in page scope, or `null` if the attribute does not exist.

### getAttribute

50
```
public abstract Object getAttribute(String name, int scope)
```

Returns the specified attribute in the indicated scope, or `null` if the attribute does not exist. Scope choices are indicated with the following constants:

```
PageContext.PAGE_SCOPE
PageContext.REQUEST_SCOPE
PageContext.SESSION_SCOPE
PageContext.APPLICATION_SCOPE
```

### getAttributeNamesInScope

51
```
public abstract Enumeration
   getAttributeNamesInScope(int scope)
```

Returns an `Enumeration` of attribute names in the specified scope. See `getAttribute(String name, int scope)` for a list of scope values.

### getAttributesScope

52
```
public abstract int getAttributesScope(String name)
```

Returns the scope of the first attribute of the specified name. See `getAttribute(String name, int scope)` for a list of scope values.

### getException

```
L B-53    public abstract Exception getException()
```

Returns the `Exception` object passed to an `ErrorPage`.

### getOut

```
L B-54    public abstract JspWriter getOut()
```

Returns the `JspWriter` for this response.

### getPage

```
L B-55    public abstract Object getPage()
```

Returns the servlet associated with this `PageContext`.

### getRequest

```
L B-56    public abstract ServletRequest getRequest()
```

Returns the `ServletRequest` associated with this `PageContext`.

### getResponse

```
L B-57    public abstract ServletResponse getResponse()
```

Returns the `ServletResponse` associated with this `PageContext`.

### getServletConfig

```
L B-58    public abstract ServletConfig getServletConfig()
```

Returns the `ServletConfig` associated with this `PageContext`.

### getServletContext

```
59    public abstract ServletContext getServletContext()
```

Returns the ServletContext associated with this PageContext.

### getSession

```
60    public abstract HttpSession getSession()
```

Returns the HttpSession for this request or null, if no session exists.

### handlePageException

```
61    public abstract void handlePageException(Exception e)
         throws ServletException, IOException;
```

Used to process an unhandled exceptions thrown by the current page. Calls the ErrorPage if one is active.

*Although this method is not deprecated, handlePageException(Throwable t) is more general and should be used instead of this method.*

### handlePageException

```
62    public abstract void handlePageException(Throwable t)
         throws ServletException, IOException
```

Used to process an unhandled exceptions thrown by the current page. Calls the ErrorPage if one is active.

### include

```
63    public abstract void include(String relativeUrlPath)
         throws ServletException, IOException
```

Calls the include() method associated with a RequestDispatcher for this servlet. See javax.servlet.RequestDispatcher for details.

### initialize

L B-64

```
public abstract void initialize(
   Servlet servlet,
   ServletRequest request,
   ServletResponse response,
   String errorPageURL,
   boolean needsSession,
   int bufferSize,
   boolean autoFlush)
throws IOException, IllegalStateException,
   IllegalArgumentException
```

Stores the `servlet`, `request`, `response`, `errorPageURL`, `needsSession`, `bufferSize`, and `autoFlush` attributes and makes the appropriate implicit variables available to the JSP. This method is called by the `getPageContext()` method and should not be called directly by the JSP author.

### popBody

L B-65 

```
public JspWriter popBody()
```

Restores the `JspWriter` saved by the previous `pushBody()`, and updates the `out` implicit variable and the value of the `PageContext` "out" attribute.

### pushBody

L B-66 

```
public BodyContent pushBody()
```

Saves the current `JspWriter` and creates a new `BodyContent` object, making it the value of the `PageContext` "out" attribute and the `out` implicit variable.

### release

L B-67 

```
public abstract void release()
```

Performs the opposite of `initialize`, releasing the `PageContext` and the resources it acquired. This method is called by the `releasePageContext()` method and should not be called directly by the JSP author.

### removeAttribute

```
public abstract void removeAttribute(String name)
```

Searches the page, request, session, and application scopes (in that order) for the specified attribute and removes the first matching attribute.

### removeAttribute

```
public abstract void removeAttribute(String name, int scope)
```

Removes the attribute associated with the specified name and scope. Scope choices are indicated with the following constants:

```
PageContext.PAGE_SCOPE
PageContext.REQUEST_SCOPE
PageContext.SESSION_SCOPE
PageContext.APPLICATION_SCOPE
```

### setAttribute

```
public abstract void setAttribute
   (String name, Object attribute)
```

Sets the specified attribute with page scope. `setAttribute(String name, Object o, int scope)` can be used to set attributes in other scopes.

### setAttribute

```
public abstract void setAttribute
   (String name, Object o, int scope)
```

Sets the attribute associated with the specified name and scope. Scope choices are indicated with the following constants:

```
PageContext.PAGE_SCOPE
PageContext.REQUEST_SCOPE
PageContext.SESSION_SCOPE
PageContext.APPLICATION_SCOPE
```

# Package javax.servlet.jsp.tagext

## BodyContent

**Full Name:** `javax.servlet.jsp.tagext.BodyContent`

**Type:** Abstract class

**Extends:** `javax.servlet.jsp.JspWriter`

`BodyContent` is a subclass of `javax.servlet.jsp.JspWriter`, but differs from its superclass, in that its contents aren't automatically written to the servlet output stream. Instead, they're accumulated in what amounts to a string buffer. After the tag body is completed, the original `JspWriter` is restored, but the `BodyContent` object is still available in `doEndTag()` in the `bodyContent` variable. Its contents can be retrieved with its `getString()` or `getReader()` methods, modified as necessary, and written to the restored `JspWriter` output stream to be merged with the page output.

### Methods

#### clearBody

L B-72

```
public void clearBody()
```

Resets the `BodyContent` buffer to empty. This can be useful if the body is being written to the enclosing writer in `doAfterBody()`.

#### flush

L B-73

```
public void flush() throws IOException
```

Overrides the `JspWriter.flush()` method so it always throws an exception. Flushing a `BodyContent` writer isn't valid because it isn't connected to an actual output stream to which it could be written.

#### getEnclosingWriter

L B-74

```
public JspWriter getEnclosingWriter()
```

Returns the writer object (possibly another `BodyContent`) next higher in the stack.

### getReader

```
public abstract Reader getReader()
```

Returns a reader for the body content after it has been evaluated. This reader can be passed to other classes that can process a `java.io.Reader`, such as `StreamTokenizer`, `FilterReader`, or an XML parser.

### getString

```
public abstract String getString()
```

Returns a string containing the body content after it has been evaluated.

### writeOut

```
public abstract void writeOut(Writer out) throws IOException
```

Writes the body content to the specified output writer.

# BodyTag

**Full Name:** `javax.servlet.jsp.tagext.BodyTag`

**Type:** Interface

**Superinterface:** `javax.servlet.jsp.tagext.IterationTag`

An extension of the `IterationTag` interface which adds new methods having to do with body handling.

## Methods

### doInitBody

```
public void doInitBody() throws JspException
```

A lifecycle method called after `setBodyContent()`, but just before the body is evaluated. If the body is evaluated multiple times, this method is called only once.

### setBodyContent

L B-79 

```
public void setBodyContent(BodyContent b)
```

Invoked by the JSP servlet after the current JspWriter has been pushed and a new BodyContent writer has been created. This occurs just after doStartTag().

## BodyTagSupport

| | |
|---|---|
| **Full Name:** | javax.servlet.jsp.tagext.BodyTagSupport |
| **Type:** | Class |
| **Extends:** | javax.servlet.jsp.tagext.TagSupport |
| **Implements:** | javax.servlet.jsp.tagext.BodyTag |

A useful base class that implements all the methods of BodyTag. Tag handlers can extend BodyTagSupport and override only those methods that need to be changed.

### Constructors

#### BodyTagSupport

L B-80 

```
public BodyTagSupport()
```

Creates a new BodyTagSupport object.

### Methods

#### doAfterBody

L B-81 

```
public int doAfterBody() throws JspException
```

Invoked at the end of each evaluation of the body. Returns Tag.SKIP_BODY by default. If you override this method, you should return either Tag.SKIP_BODY or IterationTag.EVAL_BODY_AGAIN.

#### doEndTag

L B-82 

```
public int doEndTag() throws JspException
```

Invoked at the end of the scope of a custom tag. Returns EVAL_PAGE by default but can be overridden by an implementation that returns SKIP_PAGE.

### doInitBody

```
33    public void doInitBody() throws JspException
```

A lifecycle method called after setBodyContent(), but just before the body is evaluated. If the body is evaluated multiple times, this method is called only once. By default, this implementation does nothing.

### doStartTag

```
34    public int doStartTag() throws JspException
```

See doStartTag() in the Tag interface. This implementation returns EVAL_BODY_BUFFERED.

### getBodyContent

```
35    public BodyContent getBodyContent()
```

Returns the current BodyContent.

### getPreviousOut

```
36    public JspWriter getPreviousOut()
```

Returns the surrounding JspWriter.

### release

```
37    public void release()
```

Releases the tag handler state.

### setBodyContent

```
38    public void setBodyContent(BodyContent b)
```

Stores a reference to the BodyContent object.

# IterationTag

**Full Name:** javax.servlet.jsp.tagext.IterationTag

**Type:** Interface

**Superinterface:** javax.servlet.jsp.tagext.Tag

An extension of the Tag interface that defines semantics for repeated evaluation of the tag body.

## Methods

### doAfterBody

L B-89 

```
public int doAfterBody() throws JspException
```

A lifecycle method called after the body has been evaluated, but while the BodyContent writer is still active. This method must return either EVAL_BODY_AGAIN or SKIP_BODY. If the return code is EVAL_BODY_AGAIN, the body is evaluated again and doAfterBody() is called again.

# PageData

**Full Name:** javax.servlet.jsp.tagext.PageData

**Type:** Abstract class

A class that can be listed in the TLD as a validator for a JSP page. Provides a method for reading the XML document that corresponds to the JSP page.

## Constructors

### PageData

L B-90 

```
public PageData()
```

Creates a new PageData object.

## Methods

### getInputStream

1

```
public abstract InputStream getInputStream()
```

Returns the JSP page as an XML document.

# Tag

**Full Name:** `javax.servlet.jsp.tagext.Tag`

**Type:** Interface

A set of lifecycle methods that must be implemented by custom tag handlers.

## Methods

### doEndTag

2

```
public int doEndTag() throws JspException
```

Called when the end tag has been encountered. The return code indicates whether the JSP implementation servlet should continue with the rest of the page (`EVAL_PAGE`) or not (`SKIP_PAGE`). The method can throw a `JspException` to indicate a fatal error.

### doStartTag

3

```
public int doStartTag() throws JspException
```

Called after the page context, parent, and any attributes coded on the start tag have been set. The return code indicates whether the JSP implementation servlet should evaluate the tag body (`EVAL_BODY_INCLUDE` or `BodyTag.EVAL_BODY_BUFFERED`) or not (`SKIP_BODY`). The method can throw a `JspException` to indicate a fatal error. `BodyTag.EVAL_BODY_BUFFERED` is valid only if the tag handler implements `BodyTag`.

### getParent

L B-94

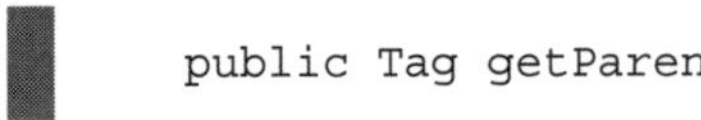

```
public Tag getParent()
```

Returns the parent tag (the closest enclosing tag handler), or `null` if there is no parent tag.

### release

L B-95

```
public void release()
```

Guaranteed to be called before page exit. Allows the tag handler to release any resources it holds and reset its state so it can be reused, if necessary.

### setPageContext

L B-96

```
public void setPageContext(PageContext pc)
```

The generated servlet calls this method first before requiring the handler to do anything else. The implementing class should save the context variable so it's available at any point in the tag lifecycle. From the page context, the tag handler can access all the JSP implicit objects and can get and set attributes in any scope.

### setParent

L B-97

```
public void setParent(Tag t)
```

Sets the parent tag. Enables a tag handler to find the tag above it in the evaluation stack. Called immediately after `setPageContext`.

## TagAttributeInfo

**Full Name:** `javax.servlet.jsp.tagext.TagAttributeInfo`

**Type:** Class

A class describing information on the attributes of a tag, available at translation time.

## Constructors

### TagAttributeInfo

```
98 public TagAttributeInfo(
      String name,
      boolean required,
      String type,
      boolean reqTime)
```

Creates a new `TagAttributeInfo`. Intended to be called only from code in the `TagLibrary` object.

## Methods

### canBeRequestTime

```
99 public boolean canBeRequestTime()
```

True if this attribute can hold a request-time value.

### getIdAttribute

```
100 public static TagAttributeInfo getIdAttribute
       (TagAttributeInfo[] a)
```

Utility method that searches an array of `TagAttributeInfo` objects for the attribute that is named "`id`".

### getName

```
101 public String getName()
```

Returns the attribute name.

### getTypeName

```
102 public String getTypeName()
```

Returns the attribute type as a string.

### isRequired

L B-103 

```
public boolean isRequired()
```

Returns `true` if the attribute is required.

### toString

L B-104

```
public String toString()
```

Returns the object formatted as a string.

# TagData

**Full Name:** `javax.servlet.jsp.tagext.TagData`

**Type:** Class

**Implements:** `java.lang.Cloneable`

Contains translation-time information about the attributes of a tag. Intended for use by JSP containers only.

## Constructors

### TagData

L B-105 

```
public TagData(Hashtable attrs)
```

Creates a new `TagData` object from a hashtable.

### TagData

L B-106 

```
public TagData(Object[][] atts)
```

Creates a new `TagData` object from a two-dimensional array of attribute/value pairs.

## Methods

### getAttribute

107
```
public Object getAttribute(String attName)
```

Returns the attribute having the specified name. Can also return `REQUEST_TIME_VALUE` if the value must be specified at request time, or `null` if the attribute was not specified in the tag.

### getAttributes

108
```
public Enumeration getAttributes()
```

Returns an `Enumeration` of the attributes.

### getAttributeString

109
```
public String getAttributeString(String attName)
```

Returns the attribute's value object in string form.

### getId

110
```
public String getId()
```

Returns the value of the `id` attribute, if it was specified.

### setAttribute

111
```
public void setAttribute(String attName, Object value)
```

Sets an attribute to the specified value.

# TagExtraInfo

**Full Name:** javax.servlet.jsp.tagext.TagExtraInfo

**Type:** Abstract class

A tag that needs to define variables or perform validation on its attributes must define a class that extends the `TagExtraInfo` class. This subclass is associated with the custom tag in the tag library descriptor.

## Constructors

### TagExtraInfo

```
L B-112    public TagExtraInfo()
```

Creates a new `TagExtraInfo` object.

## Methods

### getTagInfo

```
L B-113    public final TagInfo getTagInfo()
```

Returns the `TagInfo` for this class.

### getVariableInfo

```
L B-114    public VariableInfo getVariableInfo(TagData data)
```

Based on the list of attribute names and values in the `data` parameter, constructs an array of `VariableInfo` objects that describe the name, type, existence, and scope of each scripting variable to create.

### isValid

```
L B-115    public boolean isValid(TagData data)
```

Returns `true` if the attributes referred to in the `TagData` parameter are valid.

### setTagInfo

```
16 public final void setTagInfo(TagInfo tagInfo)
```

Sets the `TagInfo` for this class.

## TagInfo

**Full Name:** `javax.servlet.jsp.tagext.TagInfo`

**Type:** Class

An object representation of a `Tag` element in the tag library descriptor.

### Constructors

#### TagInfo

```
17 public TagInfo(
      String tagName,
      String tagClassName,
      String bodycontent,
      String infoString,
      TagLibraryInfo taglib,
      TagExtraInfo tagExtraInfo,
      TagAttributeInfo attributeInfo)
```

Creates a new `TagInfo` object from a tag library descriptor in JSP 1.1 format.

#### TagInfo

```
18 public TagInfo(
      String tagName,
      String tagClassName,
      String bodycontent,
      String infoString,
      TagLibraryInfo taglib,
      TagExtraInfo tagExtraInfo,
      TagAttributeInfo attributeInfo,
```

```
        String displayName,
        String smallIcon,
        String largeIcon,
        TagVariableInfo tvi)
```

Creates a new TagInfo object from a tag library descriptor in JSP 1.2 format.

## Methods

### getAttributes

L B-119

```
public TagAttributeInfo[] getAttributes()
```

Returns an array describing the attributes of this tag, or null if there are no attributes.

### getBodyContent

L B-120

```
public String getBodyContent()
```

Returns the bodycontent attribute of this tag as specified in the tag library descriptor.

### getDisplayName

L B-121

```
public String getDisplayName()
```

Returns the displayName attribute of this tag as specified in the tag library descriptor.

### getInfoString

L B-122

```
public String getInfoString()
```

Returns the info element for this tag as specified in the tag library descriptor.

### getLargeIcon

L B-123

```
public String getLargeIcon()
```

Returns the path to the large icon for this tag as specified in the tag library descriptor.

### getSmallIcon

124
```
public String getSmallIcon()
```

Returns the path to the small icon for this tag as specified in the tag library descriptor.

### getTagClassName

125
```
public String getTagClassName()
```

Returns the name of the tag handler class.

### getTagExtraInfo

126
```
public TagExtraInfo getTagExtraInfo()
```

Returns the name of the tag extra information class.

### getTagLibrary

127
```
public TagLibraryInfo getTagLibrary()
```

Returns a reference to the `TagLibraryInfo` object for this tag.

### getTagName

128
```
public String getTagName()
```

Returns the tag name.

### getTagVariableInfos

129
```
public TagVariableInfo getTagVariableInfos()
```

Returns the `TagVariableInfo` objects associated with this `TagInfo`.

### getVariableInfo

130
```
public VariableInfo getVariableInfo(TagData data)
```

Returns a reference to the `VariableInfo` object for this tag.

#### isValid

L B-131 

```
public boolean isValid(TagData data)
```

Returns the results of evaluating the `isValid()` method of the associated `TagExtraInfo` class.

#### setTagExtraInfo

L B-132 

```
public void setTagExtraInfo(TagExtraInfo tei)
```

Stores a reference to the `TagExtraInfo` for this tag.

#### setTagLibrary

L B-133 

```
public void setTagLibrary(TagLibraryInfo tl)
```

Sets the `TagLibraryInfo` property.

#### toString

L B-134 

```
public String toString()
```

Returns the object as a string for debugging purposes.

## TagLibraryInfo

| | |
|---|---|
| **Full Name:** | `javax.servlet.jsp.tagext.TagLibraryInfo` |
| **Type:** | Abstract class |

A class that encapsulates information associated with a taglib directive and its underlying tag library descriptor (TLD).

### Methods

#### getInfoString

L B-135 

```
public String getInfoString()
```

Returns the `info` property from the TLD.

### getPrefixString

36

```
public String getPrefixString()
```

Returns the prefix assigned in the taglib directive.

### getReliableURN

37

```
public String getReliableURN()
```

Returns the reliableURL property from the TLD.

### getRequiredVersion

138

```
public String getRequiredVersion()
```

Returns the required version of the JSP container.

### getShortName

139

```
public String getShortName()
```

Returns the short name property from the TLD.

### getTag

140

```
public TagInfo getTag(String shortname)
```

Returns the `TagInfo` object associated with a given tag name.

### getTags

141

```
public TagInfo[] getTags()
```

Returns an array of `TagInfo` objects for all tags defined in this tag library.

### getURI

142

```
public String getURI()
```

Returns the value of the `uri` attribute from the taglib directive.

# TagLibraryValidator

**Full Name:** `javax.servlet.jsp.tagext.TagLibraryValidator`

**Type:** Abstract class

A validator class that can be associated with a JSP page in the TLD. The validator operates on the XML document representation of the JSP page.

## Constructors

### TagLibraryValidator

L B-143

```
public TagLibraryValidator()
```

Creates a new `TagLibraryValidator`.

## Methods

### getInitParameters

L B-144

```
public Map getInitParameters()
```

Returns the initialization parameters.

### release

L B-145

```
public void release()
```

Releases validation data used by this validator.

### setInitParameters

L B-146

```
public void setInitParameters(Map map)
```

Provides initialization key/value parameters to the validator.

### validate

L B-147

```
public String validate
    (String prefix, String uri, PageData page)
```

Validates the JSP page. Returns `null` if the page is valid.

# TagSupport

**Full Name:** `javax.servlet.jsp.tagext.TagSupport`

**Type:** Class

**Implements:** `javax.servlet.jsp.tagext.IterationTag`
`java.io.Serializable`

A concrete implementation of the `Tag` interface. Tag handlers can extend this class and implement only those methods that need to be changed.

## Constructors

### TagSupport

48
```
public TagSupport()
```

Creates a new `TagSupport` object.

## Methods

### doAfterBody

49
```
public int doAfterBody() throws JspException
```

Invoked after the tag body is evaluated.

### doEndTag

.50
```
public int doEndTag() throws JspException
```

Called when the end tag has been encountered. The return code indicates whether the JSP implementation servlet should continue with the rest of the page (`EVAL_PAGE`) or not (`SKIP_PAGE`). The method can throw a `JspException` to indicate a fatal error. The `TagSupport` implementation returns `EVAL_PAGE`.

### doStartTag

```
public int doStartTag() throws JspException
```

Called after the page context, parent, and any attributes coded on the start tag have been set. The return code indicates whether the JSP implementation servlet should evaluate the tag body (`EVAL_BODY_INCLUDE` or `BodyTag.EVAL_BODY_BUFFERED`) or not (`SKIP_BODY`). The method can throw a `JspException` to indicate a fatal error.

APPENDIXES

BodyTag.EVAL_BODY_BUFFERED is valid only if the tag handler implements BodyTag. The TagSupport implementation returns SKIP_BODY.

### findAncestorWithClass

L B-151

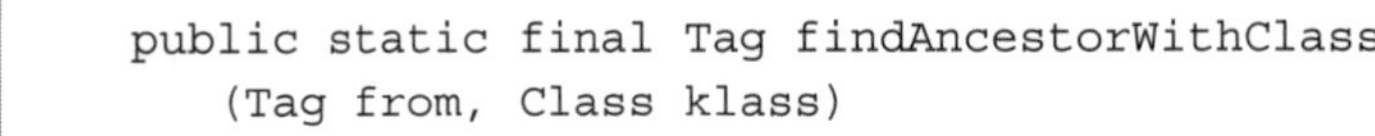

```
public static final Tag findAncestorWithClass
   (Tag from, Class klass)
```

Searches the stack of parent tags for the nearest tag handler of the specified class. This enables an "inner" tag to access information in its enclosing tags.

### getId

L B-152

```
public String getId()
```

Returns the value of the id attribute of this tag.

### getParent

L B-153

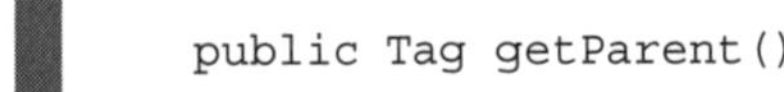

```
public Tag getParent()
```

Returns the immediate parent tag of this tag handler instance.

### getValue

L B-154

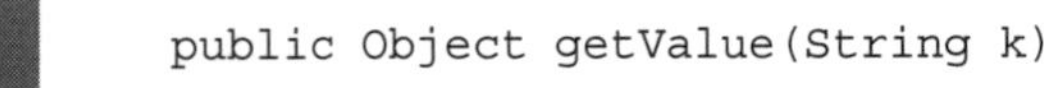

```
public Object getValue(String k)
```

Returns the object stored in this tag handler under the given name.

### getValues

L B-155

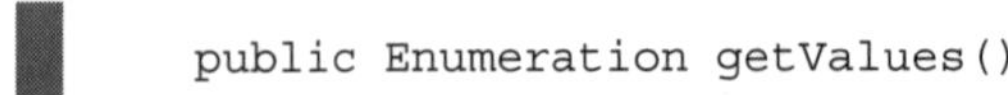

```
public Enumeration getValues()
```

Returns an enumeration of the names of the values stored in this tag handler.

### release

L B-156

```
public void release()
```

Guaranteed to be called before page exit. Enables the tag handler to release any resources it holds and reset its state so it can be reused, if necessary.

### removeValue

57
```
public void removeValue(String k)
```

Removes the value stored in this tag handler under the specified name, if any.

### setId

58
```
public void setId(String id)
```

Sets the id attribute for this tag.

### setPageContext

59
```
public void setPageContext(PageContext pageContext)
```

The generated servlet calls this method first before requiring the handler to do anything else. The implementing class should save the context variable so it's available at any point in the tag lifecycle. From the page context, the tag handler can access all the JSP implicit objects and can get and set attributes in any scope.

### setParent

60
```
public void setParent(Tag t)
```

Sets the parent tag. Enables a tag handler to find the tag above it in the evaluation stack. Called immediately after setPageContext.

### setValue

161
```
public void setValue(String k, Object o)
```

Stores the object under the specified name in the tag handler.

## TagVariableInfo

**Full Name:** javax.servlet.jsp.tagext.TagVariableInfo

**Type:** Class

A class that encapsulates tag variable information extracted from a tag library.

## Constructors

### TagVariableInfo

L B-162

```
public TagVariableInfo(
   String nameGiven,
   String nameFromAttribute,
   String className,
   boolean declare,
   int scope)
```

Creates a new TagVariableInfo object.

## Methods

### getClassName

L B-163

```
public String getClassName()
```

Returns the value of the <variable-class> element in the TLD.

### getDeclare

L B-164

```
public boolean getDeclare()
```

Returns the value of the <declare> element in the TLD.

### getNameFromAttribute

L B-165

```
public String getNameFromAttribute()
```

Returns the value of the <name-from-attribute> element in the TLD.

### getNameGiven

L B-166

```
public String getNameGiven()
```

Returns the value of the <name-given> element in the TLD.

### getScope

167 `public int getScope()`

Returns the value of the <scope> element in the TLD.

## TryCatchFinally

**Full Name:** `javax.servlet.jsp.tagext.TryCatchFinally`

**Type:** Interface

An additional interface that can be implemented by tag handlers to enable them to be called in the `catch` and `finally` blocks of the tag invocation.

### Methods

#### doCatch

168 `public void doCatch(Throwable t) throws Throwable`

This method is invoked in the `catch` block if an exception occurs while evaluating the body of a tag.

#### doFinally

169 `public void doFinally()`

This method is invoked in the `finally` block if an exception occurs while evaluating the body of a tag.

## VariableInfo

**Full Name:** `javax.servlet.jsp.tagext.VariableInfo`

**Type:** Class

A data structure that provides configuration information about scripting variables created by a custom tag. Use primarily in the `getVariableInfo()` method of a `TagExtraInfo` subclass.

## Constructors

### VariableInfo

L B-170

```
public VariableInfo(
   String varName,
   String className,
   boolean declare,
   int scope)
```

Creates a new `VariableInfo` object. The parameters are as follows:

- `varName` The name of the variable to be created
- `className` The fully qualified name of the variable class
- `declare` A boolean value that is `true` if the generated servlet should contain a declaration for the variable
- `scope` An integer representing the scope of the variable. May be `AT_BEGIN`, `AT_END`, or `NESTED`.

## Methods

### getClassName

L B-171

```
public String getClassName()
```

Returns the class name.

### getDeclare

L B-172

```
public boolean getDeclare()
```

Returns the boolean attribute representing whether the variable should be declared or not.

### getScope

L B-173

```
public int getScope()
```

Returns the integer representing the variable scope.

### getVarName

L B-174

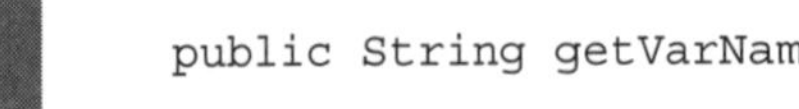

```
public String getVarName()
```

Returns the variable name.

# Appendix C

## HTTP Reference

This appendix consists of two tables, one describing Hypertext Transfer Protocol (HTTP) response codes and another describing HTTP headers. For more details about HTTP, refer to the specification, RFC 2616.

## HTTP Response Codes

Response codes are three-digit numeric codes that appear on the first line of the response sent by an HTTP server. There are five categories of response codes, indicated by their first digit:

- **1xx: Informational** Request received, continuing process
- **2xx: Success** The action was successfully received, understood, and accepted
- **3xx: Redirection** Further action must be taken in order to complete the request
- **4xx: Client Error** The request contains bad syntax or cannot be fulfilled
- **5xx: Server Error** The server failed to fulfill an apparently valid request

The following table lists the individual code and their meanings:

| Response Code | Meaning |
|---|---|
| 100 | Continue |
| 101 | Switching Protocols |
| 200 | OK |
| 201 | Created |
| 202 | Accepted |
| 203 | Non-Authoritative Information |
| 204 | No Content |
| 205 | Reset Content |
| 206 | Partial Content |
| 300 | Multiple Choices |
| 301 | Moved Permanently |
| 302 | Found |
| 303 | See Other |

| Response Code | Meaning |
|---|---|
| 304 | Not Modified |
| 305 | Use Proxy |
| 307 | Temporary Redirect |
| 400 | Bad Request |
| 401 | Unauthorized |
| 402 | Payment Required |
| 403 | Forbidden |
| 404 | Not Found |
| 405 | Method Not Allowed |
| 406 | Not Acceptable |
| 407 | Proxy Authentication Required |
| 408 | Request Time-out |
| 409 | Conflict |
| 410 | Gone |
| 411 | Length Required |
| 412 | Precondition Failed |
| 413 | Request Entity Too Large |
| 414 | Request-URI Too Large |
| 415 | Unsupported Media Type |
| 416 | Requested range not satisfiable |
| 417 | Expectation Failed |
| 500 | Internal Server Error |
| 501 | Not Implemented |
| 502 | Bad Gateway |
| 503 | Service Unavailable |
| 504 | Gateway Time-out |
| 505 | HTTP Version not supported |

# HTTP Headers

Headers are key/value pairs that describe attributes of the client or server, the resources to be transmitted, and how the connection should operate. There are four different types of headers:

- **General headers** Can be used either in a request or a response, and relate to the transaction as a whole rather than specific resources.
- **Request headers** Allow a client to pass information about itself and the form of response it is expecting.
- **Response headers** Used by a server to pass information about itself and the response.
- **Entity headers** Define information about the resource being transferred. Can be used either in a request or a response.

Headers are sent as individual lines of text in the form

*<name>: <value><CRLF>*

where

*name* is the header name, which is case insensitive;
*value* is the header value; and
*CRLF* is a carriage return/line feed.

Note that there is a colon and one or more spaces separating the name from the value.

A JSP page can read HTTP headers using the `getHeader()` method of its `request` object, and can write them with `response.setHeader()`. java.net.URLConnection provides similar methods for accessing headers in a URL stream.

The following table describes the headers available in HTTP/1.1:

| Header | Description |
|---|---|
| `Accept` | Specifies media types that the client is able to handle, in order of preference. Multiple types may be specified in a comma-separated list. Wildcards are acceptable. Example:<br>`Accept: image/jpeg, image/pjpeg, image/png, */*` |

| Header | Description |
|---|---|
| `Accept-Charset` | Specifies character sets that the client is able to handle, in order of preference. Multiple types may be specified in a comma-separated list. Wildcards are acceptable. Example:<br><br>`Accept-Charset: iso-8859-1,*,utf-8` |
| `Accept-Encoding` | Specifies the encoding mechanisms that the client understands. Example:<br><br>`Accept-Encoding: gzip,compress` |
| `Accept-Language` | Specifies the list of natural languages that the client prefers. Example:<br><br>`Accept-Language: en,de` |
| `Accept-Ranges` | A response header that allow the server to indicate that it will accept requests for parts of a resource at a given offset and length. The value of the header is the unit of measure in which range requests are understood. Examples:<br><br>`Accept-Ranges: bytes`<br>`Accept-Ranges: none` |
| `Age` | Allows the server to specify the length of time in seconds that has elapsed since the response was generated on the server. This header is primarily used with cached responses. Example:<br><br>`Age: 30` |
| `Allow` | A response header that specifies a list of HTTP methods supported by the resource in the request URI. Example:<br><br>`Allow: GET, HEAD, PUT` |
| `Authorization` | A request header used to specify the credentials (the realm and encoded user ID and password) necessary to access a resource. Example:<br><br>`Authorization: Basic YXV0aG9yOnBoaWw=` |

| Header | Description |
|---|---|
| `Cache-Control` | A general header used to specify caching directives. Example:<br>`Cache-Control: max-age=30` |
| `Connection` | A general header used to indicate whether or not to keep the socket connection open. Examples:<br>`Connection: close`<br>`Connection: keep-alive` |
| `Content-Base` | An entity header that specifies the base URI for resolving relative URLs within the entity. If the Content-Base header<br><br>is not specified, then relative URLs are resolved using either the Content-Location URI (if it is present and absolute) or using the request URI. Example:<br>`Content-Base: http://www.lyricnote.com` |
| `Content-Encoding` | A modifier to the media type that indicates how an entity has been encoded (zipped, compressed, and so on.) Example:<br>`Content-Encoding: gzip` |
| `Content-Language` | Used to specify the natural language of the data in the input stream. Example:<br>`Content-Language: en` |
| `Content-Length` | Specifies the length in bytes of the data contained in the request or response. Example:<br>`Content-Length: 382` |
| `Content-Location` | Specifies the location (URI) of the resource contained in the request or response. If this is an absolute URL, it also functions as the base from which relative URLs in the entity are resolved. Example:<br>`Content-Location:`<br>`http://www.lyricnote.com/newsletter` |

| Header | Description |
|---|---|
| `Content-MD5` | An MD5 digest of the entity body, used as a checksum. The sender and receiver both compute the MD5 digest. The receiver compares its computed value against the value transmitted in this header. Example:<br>`Content-MD5: <base64 of 128 bit MD5 digest>`<br>MD5 is described in RFC 1321. |
| `Content-Range` | Sent with a partial entity body; indicates the low and high byte offset of the section to be inserted. Also indicates the total length of the entity body. Example:<br>`Content-Range: 1001-2000/5000` |
| `Content-Type` | Indicates the MIME type of an entity body sent or received. Example:<br>`Content-Type: text/html` |
| `Date` | The date at which the HTTP message was sent. Example:<br>`Date: Mon, 06 Mar 2000 18:42:51 GMT` |
| `ETag` | An entity header which assigns a unique identifier to the resource being sent. For resources that can be requested using more than one URL, the ETag can be used to determine whether the same resource is actually sent. Example:<br>`ETag: "208f-419e-30f8dc99"` |
| `Expires` | Specifies a date after which the entity should be considered stale. Example:<br>`Expires: Mon, 05 Dec 2008 12:00:00 GMT` |
| `From` | A request header giving the e-mail address of the human user who controls the user agent. Example:<br>`From: webmaster@lyricnote.com` |

| Header | Description |
|---|---|
| `Host` | The host name (and, optionally, port number) of the resource being requested. This field is mandatory for requests made using HTTP/1.1. Example:<br><br>`Host: www.lyricnote.com` |
| `If-Modified-Since` | If included with a GET request, makes the request conditional upon the last modification date of the resource. If this header is present and the resource has not been modified since the specified date, a 304 (not modified) response should be returned. Example:<br><br>`If-Modified-Since: Wed, 01 Mar 2000 12:00:00 GMT` |
| `If-Match` | If included in a request, specifies one or more entity tags (see ETag). The resource is only sent if its ETag matches one in the list. Example:<br><br>`If-Match: "208f-419e-30f8dc99"` |
| `If-None-Match` | If included in a request, specifies one or more entity tags (see ETag). The operation is only performed if the resource's ETag matches none of the entries in the list. Example:<br><br>`If-None-Match: "208f-419e-30f8dc99"` |
| `If-Range` | Specifies an entity tag (see ETag) for a resource that the client already has a copy of. Must be used together with a Range header. If the entity has not been modified since the last time it was retrieved by the client, the server will send only the range specified, otherwise, it will send the entire resource. Example:<br><br>`Range: bytes=0-499`<br>`If-Range: "208f-419e-30f8dc99"` |
| `If-Unmodified-Since` | Similar to but opposite in sense from If-Modified-Since. The requested entity is only returned if it has not been modified since the specified date. Example:<br><br>`If-Unmodified-Since: Wed, 01 Mar 2000 12:00:00 GMT` |

| Header | Description |
|---|---|
| Last-Modified | Specifies the date and time the requested resource was last modified. Example:<br><br>`Last-Modified: Wed, 08 Mar 2000 12:00:00 GMT` |
| Location | Used to redirect the requester to another location for a resource that has moved. Used in conjunction with a 302 (moved temporarily) or 301 (moved permanently) status code. Example:<br><br>`Location:`<br>`http://www2.lyricnote.com/index.jsp` |
| Max-Forwards | A request header used with the TRACE method to specify the maximum number of proxies or gateways through which the request can be routed. Proxies or gateways should decrement the number before passing on the request. Example:<br><br>`Max-Forwards: 3` |
| Pragma | A general header that sends implementation-specific information. Example:<br><br>`Pragma: no-cache` |
| Proxy-Authenticate | Similar to WWW-Authenticate, but designed to request authentication only from the next server in the request chain (a proxy). Example:<br><br>`Proxy-Authenticate: Basic realm=Admin` |
| Proxy-Authorization | Similar to Authorization, but not intended to pass any further than a proxy server in the immediate server chain. Example:<br><br>`Proxy-Authorization: Basic YXV0aG9yOnBoaWw=` |
| Public | Lists the set of methods supported by the server. Example:<br><br>`Public: OPTIONS, MGET, MHEAD, GET, HEAD` |

| Header | Description |
|---|---|
| `Range` | Specifies a unit of measure and a range of offsets from which a partial resource is requested. Example:<br><br>`Range: bytes=206-5513` |
| `Referer` | A (misspelled) request header field that indicates the original resource from which a request was made. For HTML forms, this is the address of the Web page containing the form. Example:<br><br>`Referer: http://www.lyricnote.com/product/search.html` |
| `Retry-After` | A response header field sent by a server in conjuction with a 503 (Service Unavailable) status to indicate how long to wait before requesting the resource again. The time can either be a date or a number of seconds. Examples:<br><br>`Retry-After: 18`<br>`Retry-After: Thu, 09 Mar 2014 16:45:15 GMT` |
| `Server` | A response header that indicates the identity and version number of the Web server software. Example:<br><br>`Server: Apache/1.3.12 (Win32)` |
| `Transfer-Encoding` | A general header that indicates the type of transformation that has been performed on the message body that should be reversed by the receiver. Example:<br><br>`Transfer-Encoding: chunked` |
| `Upgrade` | Allows a server to specify a new protocol or protocol version. Used in conjunction with the 101 (Switching Protocols) response code. Example:<br><br>`Upgrade: HTTP/2.0` |

| Header | Description |
|---|---|
| `User-Agent` | Specifies the type of software used to make the request (typically, a Web browser). Examples:<br><br>`User-Agent: Mozilla/4.0 (compatible; MSIE 5.5; Windows NT; DigExt)`<br>`User-Agent: Mozilla/4.7 [en] (WinNT; I)` |
| `Vary` | A response header field used to signal that the response entity was selected from the available representations of the response using server-driven negotiation. Example:<br><br>`Vary: *` |
| `Via` | A general header containing a list of all intermediate hosts and protocols use to satisfy the request. Example:<br><br>`Via: 1.0 fred.com, 1.1 wilma.com` |
| `Warning` | A response header used to supply additional information about the status of a response. Example:<br><br>`Warning: 99 www.lyricnote.com Piano needs tuning` |
| `WWW-Authenticate` | A response header challenging the user agent to supply a user ID and password. Used in conjunction with the 401 (Not authorized) status code. Expects an Authorization header in reply. Example:<br><br>`WWW-Authenticate: Basic realm=lyricnote_mgmt` |

# Index

## Symbols



## A

## C

## D

## E

## F

## H

## I

## N

## Q



## R

## S

## U



## V

## X

## INTERNATIONAL CONTACT INFORMATION


**AUSTRALIA**
McGraw-Hill Book Company Australia Pty. Ltd.
TEL +61-2-9417-9899
FAX +61-2-9417-5687
http://www.mcgraw-hill.com.au
books-it_sydney@mcgraw-hill.com

**CANADA**
McGraw-Hill Ryerson Ltd.
TEL +905-430-5000
FAX +905-430-5020
http://www.mcgrawhill.ca

**GREECE, MIDDLE EAST, NORTHERN AFRICA**
McGraw-Hill Hellas
TEL +30-1-656-0990-3-4
FAX +30-1-654-5525

**MEXICO (Also serving Latin America)**
McGraw-Hill Interamericana Editores S.A. de C.V.
TEL +525-117-1583
FAX +525-117-1589
http://www.mcgraw-hill.com.mx
fernando_castellanos@mcgraw-hill.com

**SINGAPORE (Serving Asia)**
McGraw-Hill Book Company
TEL +65-863-1580
FAX +65-862-3354
http://www.mcgraw-hill.com.sg
mghasia@mcgraw-hill.com

**SOUTH AFRICA**
McGraw-Hill South Africa
TEL +27-11-622-7512
FAX +27-11-622-9045
robyn_swanepoel@mcgraw-hill.com

**UNITED KINGDOM & EUROPE (Excluding Southern Europe)**
McGraw-Hill Education Europe
TEL +44-1-628-502500
FAX +44-1-628-770224
http://www.mcgraw-hill.co.uk
computing_neurope@mcgraw-hill.com

**ALL OTHER INQUIRIES Contact:**
Osborne/McGraw-Hill
TEL +1-510-549-6600
FAX +1-510-883-7600
http://www.osborne.com
omg_international@mcgraw-hill.com